STEPHEN F. AUSTIN
Empresario of Texas

GREGG CANTRELL

STEPHEN F. AUSTIN
Empresario of Texas

Published in cooperation with the William P. Clements
Center for Southwest Studies, Southern Methodist University

YALE UNIVERSITY PRESS + NEW HAVEN AND LONDON

Designed by Sonia Scanlon.
Set in Bulmer type by
Tseng Information Systems, Inc.,
Durham, North Carolina.
Printed in the United States of America by
R. R. Donnelley & Sons Company,
Harrisonburg, Virginia.

Library of Congress Cataloging-in-Publication Data
Cantrell, Gregg, 1958–
Stephen F. Austin, empresario of Texas / Gregg Cantrell.
p. cm.
Includes bibliographical references and index.
ISBN 0-300-07683-5 (cloth)
ISBN 0-300-09093-5 (pbk.)
1. Austin, Stephen F. (Stephen Fuller), 1793–1836.   2. Texas—
History—To 1846.   3. Pioneers—Texas—Biography.
I. Title.
F389.A942C36   1999
976.4'03'092'DC21
[B]   98-51176

A catalogue record for this book is available from
the British Library.

The paper in this book meets the guidelines for permanence
and durability of the Committee on Production Guidelines for
Book Longevity of the Council on Library Resources.

10   9   8   7   6   5   4   3

Frontispiece: Stephen F. Austin, 1836. Austin had this portrait
painted in New Orleans in 1836 for his sister, Emily. Her
grandson, Guy M. Bryan, Jr., donated it to the state of Texas in
1919. It hangs in the state senate chamber. *Courtesy, Texas State
Library and Archives Commission.*

To *el jefe*, David J. Weber

✛ Contents ✛

+ Acknowledgments +

O f the many friends and colleagues who made this book possible, my first word of thanks must go to Professor Robert A. Calvert of Texas A&M University, who persuaded me to undertake this project when I myself doubted my capacity to do it. I received similar encouragement early on from my other mentor in Texas history, Professor Walter L. Buenger of Texas A&M, and from my doctoral adviser, Dale T. Knobel of Denison University, who, despite his busy schedule as a college president, still finds time for a bothersome ex-student.

I am likewise indebted to my former colleagues at Sam Houston State University, especially the world's greatest department chair, James S. Olson; deans Richard Cording and Christopher Baldwin; and former president Martin Anisman, who lightened teaching loads, granted leaves of absence, and supported me in numerous ways during this book's long gestation. Everyone in the SHSU history department deserves thanks for their friendship and assistance, but I particularly wish to thank Rosanne Barker, Mitchel Roth, and Thomas Camfield for being my sounding boards as I tried to solve the many riddles posed by Stephen Austin's life. It has also been my good fortune to have as a colleague Ana Carolina Castillo Crimm, who knew far more about Stephen F. Austin than I did in the beginning, and who has been a valuable source of information on Mexico and Texas, as well as a rigorous critic.

Many others have given generously of their time and expertise over the years. Adán Benavides of the University of Texas shared his notes and archival knowledge at an early stage of my research. Jesús F. de la

Teja of Southwest Texas State University fielded hundreds of questions over the years and kept me in the archives (and perhaps out of jail) during a two-week research trip to Mexico. Jack Jackson of Austin and Galen Greaser of the Texas General Land Office both shared little-known Mexican documents with me and spent many hours of their time helping me understand them. Margaret Swett Henson sent me notes and unpublished papers, fielded my many questions, and gave much moral support. So did David N. Gracy II of the University of Texas, James Crisp of North Carolina State University, and Paul Lack of McMurry University. Donald Frazier of McMurry expertly prepared the maps. These scholars, and many more like them, have taught me to wear the title "Texas historian" as a badge of pride rather than a mark of provincialism. I also wish to thank Tom Appleton, Art Bachrach, Scott Barton, Gervais Bell, Bill Bradshaw, Joan Coffey, Stephen Cook, J. C. Martin, Ron Davis, David Farmer, Robert Handy, Ricki Janicek, David LaVere, Charlann Morris, Joseph McKnight, Victoria Noll, Billy Price, Tom Primrose, Janice Sabec, Skipper Steely, and Bill Wright for favors large and small.

I will not attempt to list the many librarians and archivists who, in performing their jobs competently, contributed to the making of this book. But special mention must go to the staffs of the Beinecke Library at Yale University, the DeGolyer Library at SMU, and the Center for American History at the University of Texas. In Coahuila, Lic. Alfonso Vásquez Sotelo, Director del Instituto Estatal de Documentación, was a gracious host as well as a true professional.

During my research-related travels, a number of my friends and relatives opened their homes to me, including Ihor Bemko, Nelda Bravo, Mike and Diana Connor, Bob and Wanda Johnson, Karla Lacey, Carl and Pat Moneyhon, Shannon Smith, and Matthew Waters. As always, my parents, Jimmie and Mary Lynn Cantrell, have been my biggest boosters. Near the end of this project I also met my lovely bride, Brenda, and in the bargain acquired a terrific stepson, Drew. Their unexpected entry into my life probably delayed the completion of this book, but it has been well worth it. I thank them for helping me get my priorities straight. I also wish to thank the newest member of our family, Calvin Jefferson Cantrell, for having the good sense to wait until the week the book went into production to make his appearance in the world.

Finally, I must gratefully acknowledge the assistance of several institutions. The Sam Houston State University Research Council twice awarded summer grants that helped move the research forward. The National Endowment for the Humanities provided a generous fellowship that allowed me to spend the 1994–95 academic year in the city named for Stephen F. Austin, where I conducted the bulk of the research and wrote the early chapters. Ron Tyler and the Texas State Historical Association placed the resources of the University of Texas at my disposal during that year. The Dodge Jones Foundation of Abilene helped to underwrite the cost of illustrations. Lanny Hall, Craig Turner, Lawrence Clayton, and Paul Madden of Hardin-Simmons University have been supportive in many ways as the project neared completion.

My greatest debt of gratitude, however, must go to the William P. Clements Center for Southwest Studies at Southern Methodist University and the Summerlee Foundation, which together provided the fellowship that enabled me to finish the manuscript. The Summerlee Fellowship not only gave me a year of uninterrupted work in Dallas at the Clements Center, but it provided funding for research expenses and a subvention to underwrite publication costs. During that year the center's associate director, Jane Lenz Elder, and Clements Research Fellow Nancy Beck Young provided much moral support and helpful criticism, even though it took them away from their own important work. Everyone in the SMU history department was supportive, but I must say a special word of thanks to Professor William B. Taylor, who graciously spent untold hours helping me decipher nineteenth-century Mexican documents and understand Mexico's complex history. The Clements Center also brought together a panel of distinguished specialists who read the initial draft of the manuscript and then spent an extraordinary day with me exposing its shortcomings. Randolph Campbell, John Chávez, Donald Chipman, John Mack Faragher, Sam Haynes, Paul Lack, Sam Ratcliffe, and Andrés Reséndez are not responsible for the many flaws that remain, but whatever virtues the book may possess are largely due to their hard work as critics.

There is one person, however, without whom this book would not exist. Professor David J. Weber of SMU encouraged the project at a very early stage and then took an unwarranted gamble in committing the resources of the Clements Center to its completion, all the while serving as teacher, editor, critic, and friend. This book's dedication is my inadequate way of saying thanks.

A Note on Spelling, Punctuation, and Usage

The student of Mexican-era Texas faces multiple dilemmas in rendering the original nineteenth-century written sources intelligible to the modern reader. Among speakers of both English and Spanish, spelling, punctuation, and usage had few rules, and those rules were frequently ignored. Stephen F. Austin, for example, often used a dash or no punctuation at all to end a sentence, and the first word of the next sentence often was not capitalized. Spelling was an inexact art at best. These practices are further complicated by the various liberties that editors have taken over the years when transcribing and publishing original letters and documents. I have chosen to leave as much of the original spelling, punctuation, and usage as possible, but at times I have felt the need to make minor additions (such as the insertion of a period or the capitalization of the first word of a sentence) in order to avoid confusion. When possible I have indicated such changes by placing them in brackets. I have forgone the use of "*sic*" in all but a handful of instances where it seemed absolutely necessary. Readers may assume that misspelled or oddly spelled words were that way in the original.

The rendering of the many Spanish words and names in this book poses additional problems. Hispanic surnames usually include the names of the individual's father and mother, with the father's name preceding the mother's. For example, Lorenzo de Zavala's full name was Manuel Lorenzo Justiniano de Zavala y Sáenz (Sáenz was his mother's name). Zavala followed standard usage and normally called himself Lorenzo de

Zavala (he apparently chose to omit the additional given names Manuel and Justiniano). However, there are many exceptions to such practices. José Manuel Rafael Simeón de Mier y Terán usually signed formal documents as "Manuel de Mier y Terán," but on the occasions when he shortened it he used Terán (rather than the expected Mier). Hispanics and Anglos alike usually referred to him simply as Terán, so in cases such as this I have chosen to follow custom and the preference of the individual.

English speakers in Austin's day rarely bothered with the diacritical markings that are an integral part of the spelling of many Spanish words and names. Accordingly, when using quotations I have rendered the letters as they appear in the documents, with or without the accents. English speakers likewise normally omitted the accents from place names, such as México, Anáhuac, or Río Grande. Where these names have subsequently been incorporated into modern English usage without the accents, I have also omitted them. To avoid confusion, I have referred to the town known properly as San Fernando de Béxar by its common name, San Antonio.

STEPHEN F. AUSTIN

Empresario of Texas

+ Introduction +

My ambition has been to succeed in redeeming Texas
from its wilderness state by means of the plough alone,
in spreading over it North American population enterprise and intelligence. In doing this I hoped to make the
fortune of thousands and my own amongst the rest. My
success so far has fully equalled my expectation, and I
think that I derived more satisfaction from the view of
flourishing farms springing up in this wilderness than
military or political chieftains do from the retrospect of
their victorious campai[g]ns.
　　　　　　　　　　—Stephen F. Austin, 1829

Early on a July morning in 1821, sixteen men on horseback
paused at the east bank of the Sabine River. Behind them
lay Louisiana, the southwesternmost state of the United
States. One by one they urged their reluctant mounts into
the sluggish brown waters. When the horses scrambled up
the muddy bank on the opposite side of the river, they stood on the soil
of the Spanish Empire, in the frontier province of Texas.

Among the riders was a twenty-seven-year-old Missourian named
Stephen Fuller Austin. Slender and handsome, with curly auburn hair
and large, penetrating brown eyes, he carried in his saddlebag a document
that held the key to his future. Written in ornate Spanish and bearing the
signature of the commandant general of the Eastern Interior Provinces,

the document authorized Austin's father, who had died a month earlier, to settle three hundred American families in Texas.

Over the next fifteen years Stephen F. Austin would carry out his father's plan of populating Texas with American emigrants. His technical Mexican title would be *empresario,* or colonization agent, but the more generic English term "impresario" — defined as a "manager, producer, or sponsor" of some extravagant production — seems equally appropriate. With effort and cunning, diplomacy and deception, idealism and pragmatism, he would play a central role in shaping the events that led to the Texas Revolution and the establishment of the Lone Star republic. Within a generation, as a result largely of forces that he helped set in motion, Mexico would endure the humiliating loss of nearly half its national territory, and the United States would complete its drive for mastery over the North American continent.

Despite his historical importance, Austin remains an enigmatic figure. He has been the subject of only one full-length biography, published more than seventy years ago. As a result of Eugene C. Barker's 1925 classic *The Life of Stephen F. Austin,* generations of Texans have come to revere Austin as the Father of Texas, a modest, altruistic, self-sacrificing, peace-loving, tireless advocate of the nation-state he founded. Beyond this uncritical rendering, Barker had little to say about Austin's personality, motives, or character. "He was an unobtrusive, unassuming man," wrote Barker, arguing that Austin's public works were more important than the man himself. Accordingly, Barker wrote a book that, in his own words, was "primarily factual and direct rather than interpretative. It is in what he did and the manner of doing it that the admirable character and winning personality of the man must appear." By all measures Barker achieved his goal; his work was a model of scholarly research in its presentation of the facts of Austin's public career. But in his portrayal of Austin the man, Barker essentially embraced the persona that Austin himself carefully constructed. It is no great wonder, then, that the portrait of Austin bequeathed by Barker is a sort of cardboard cutout, without a real life or personality of his own.[1]

The Stephen F. Austin who emerges here contrasts sharply with the figure drawn by Barker. It would be impossible to subject any human being to biographical scrutiny and not conclude that he was "complex," but in Austin's case this truism applies with special force.

Austin grew up in the Missouri Territory, with its polyglot population of Indians, Frenchmen, Spaniards, Anglo-Americans, and African-Americans—a fascinating cultural milieu that would provide invaluable training for dealing with the diverse society he would encounter in Mexican Texas. Austin received a formal education in New England and Kentucky. As a young adult he lived for extended periods on the Arkansas frontier and in cosmopolitan New Orleans. At various times he operated a lead mine, a store, and a farm; served in the military and the legislature; engaged in large-scale land speculation; worked on a newspaper and studied law. He would thus enter into his great life's work, Texas colonization, with a background composed of a complicated mix of North and South, East and West, city and frontier.

Austin's intelligence, experience, and broad worldview prepared him to meet his challenges. But when he splashed into Texas that day in 1821 he also carried with him psychological and emotional burdens unusual for a man in his twenties. His life had already been marked by conflict and contradiction. He was the eldest son of an ambitious, egotistical, domineering father, and he had been raised since birth to achieve, at his father's insistence, "greatness in life." Moses Austin had made a fortune and achieved social prestige in the early American republic, and he expected his son to carry on that tradition. Yet Stephen had witnessed the humiliating collapse of Moses's business empire and the resulting disgrace of the family name. Although he loved and even revered his father, Stephen also held him responsible for the family's ruin and longed to escape his suffocating influence.[2]

Taking over his father's Texas colonization project gave the younger Austin the means of escaping his father's shadow while honoring that father's dying wish. It also offered a golden opportunity to recover the family's lost fortune, pay his own massive debts, and restore the house of Austin to its former status. Moreover, because the enterprise was in a foreign land, it presented a chance for Austin to leave behind the chaos of the depression-torn Mississippi Valley and his own chaotic private life, and seek order in Spanish Texas. Austin frequently spoke of his self-defined mission as being to "redeem Texas from its wilderness state," but what Texas really promised him was the chance for personal redemption. Texas colonization gave a disillusioned young man a cause worthy of his considerable talents. It gave him something he desperately needed—a calling in life. What better way to prove his worthiness as an Austin, to restore the family's name, and to establish his greatness in life than to become the Father of Texas?

Austin applied himself to that calling with the same zeal and single-mindedness that had characterized his father's business ventures years earlier. He became the consummate manager and exhorter, politician and diplomat, statesman and manipulator. He earned the respect of many and the enmity of some. The most important man in Anglo-Texas, he had few close friends. Persuasive and often eloquent in his public statements and political correspondence, he had difficulty communicating his feelings to those for whom he cared. A lover of literature, music, dancing, and the social graces, he spent most of his time on a crude, isolated frontier. Devoted to his family members, he allowed years to pass without seeing them. Charmed by the company of women, he never married.

The portrait that emerges of Stephen F. Austin is that of an ambitious, almost obsessively driven man, who constantly fought an internal battle between his own personal interests and his feelings of obligation toward others. He longed for peace and order in his private life, but his public affairs forced him to endure constant conflict and disorder. It is little wonder, then, that although he took pride in his accomplishments, he was rarely happy and frequently depressed. His reserve and dignity often barely concealed an unflattering tendency to indulge in self-pity.

Yet there remains an essential humanity about him that few of his contemporaries ever witnessed. His sister Emily and her family saw it, as did his cousins Henry Austin and Mary Austin Holley. Austin's long-suffering mother, Maria Brown Austin, thought him "such a Son as every fond parent might be proud of," and his younger brother, James Elijah Brown Austin, idolized him. Austin took his family obligations seriously and provided small empires of land for his siblings, cousins, nephews, and other relations. He could show true kindness, which often passed unnoticed and unrewarded, toward the often-exasperating colonists whom he viewed as "one great family who are under my care." He possessed a remarkable capacity to forgive a wrong. His dedication to Texas — whatever material or psychological benefits he may have derived from it — was absolute. In all these ways Austin commands our sympathy and even, at times, our admiration. To miss this side of Austin and focus only on his failings and foibles would be to render him less than human. Such a biography would be no more complete than one like Barker's.[3]

This book, then, is an attempt at biography in its most basic sense, which is to say that it is primarily the story of one man's life. It is not a history of Texas, the United States, or Mexico, nor is it the history of the American frontier, westward movement, or the Spanish Borderlands. Austin's life has much to tell us about all of these histories, but the focus remains on Austin — especially on his character, motives, and personality.

Nonetheless, my view of Austin has been influenced by a considerable body of historical literature. When Eugene C. Barker wrote his masterpiece in the 1920s, he was greatly influenced by historian Frederick Jackson Turner, who in 1893 proclaimed the famous "Frontier Thesis" of American history. Turner argued that the existence of a frontier and the constant westward movement of Americans had forced them to shake off the habits and attitudes of their European ancestors and develop such uniquely American traits as strength, energy, practicality, and self-reliance. The frontier served as a laboratory for democracy and a safety valve for the growing population of the east. The closing of the frontier, which Turner detected in the 1890 Census returns, signaled the end of "the first period of American history."[4]

For evidence of the influence that Turner exercised on Barker, one need look no further than the full title of Barker's book: *The Life of Stephen F. Austin, Founder of Texas, 1793–1836: A Chapter in the Westward Movement of the Anglo-American People*. Barker saw Austin's career in Texas as a case study affirming the validity of the Frontier Thesis. Austin and his colonists exemplified the democracy-loving rugged individualists who tamed the frontier and brought American values and institutions to it. The Turner thesis held sway among historians of the West until relatively recent times; Texas historians have been even more reluctant to question it. In an influential 1991 historiographical essay on the Texas revolutionary era, historian Paul Lack complained that Texas historians were still laboring "In the Long Shadow of Eugene C. Barker." Most historians of early Texas have been unwilling or unable to move beyond the Turnerian view of the frontier.[5]

While Texas historians (with some notable exceptions) continued to labor in Barker's shadow, in the 1980s a new generation of revisionist western historians began to advocate a "New Western History," questioning virtually every aspect of the Turner thesis. What Turner saw as *settlement*, the New Western Historians view as *conquest*. Instead of an essentially empty wilderness waiting to be tamed, they see a land already occupied by indigenous peoples with cultures of their own and long-established ties to the land. Where the Turnerians see self-reliant pioneers, the New Western Historians find profit-driven entrepreneurs closely connected to the capitalist economy of the east. Where the Turnerians find a disdain for big government, the revisionists discover cozy partnerships between government and business. Instead of viewing western history as an unbroken chain of successes (the Alamo and the Little Bighorn notwithstanding), the New Western Historians point toward the devastation of native cultures, the theft of Mexican territory, the degradation of the environment, and the oppression of the wage-earning majority by callous tycoons, all of it accompanied by large doses of racism and sexism on the part of arrogant Anglo-American male elites. Revisionists even take issue with the very notion of the *frontier,* arguing that Turner's concept of the frontier as a *process* ending in 1890 denies the reality of the West as a unique *place* with an ongoing history shaped by multiple cultures, classes, and genders. In short, the actual West, according to the New Western History, bears little resemblance to the romanticized Frontier of Turner and his disciples.[6]

The New Western History has much to offer the student of Stephen F. Austin and his times. To portray Austin and his colonists in triumphalist, Turnerian terms obscures the reality of the man and his region's history. We must escape the "long shadow" of Turner's Texas disciple, Eugene C.

Barker, who, as Paul Lack writes, "shared the fundamental view that Texas history in the period from 1821 to 1836 represented the march of Anglo-American democracy westward in triumph over inferior races."[7]

Indeed, the New Western History's revisionist model provides important balance to our understanding of Austin's life and career. His family made and lost its fortune in mining, an extractive industry exploitative both environmentally and in human terms. Austin came to Texas in 1821 with the straightforward goal of making a fortune so he could pay the huge debts from his failed mining business and from bad land speculation deals in Arkansas. He displaced Indians from their native lands through a combination of warfare and negotiation, aided by the spread of European diseases. He helped to bring slavery to Texas and struggled to preserve it. He speculated in land and maintained important business ties to the East. Before and after coming to Texas, he established close relationships with state and national politicians and manipulated those relationships to his own benefit. He knew that money could be used effectively to grease political wheels, and he was not above using it. Given his often-good relations with Mexican monarchists and centralists, it is clear that his devotion to democracy was not absolute. Moreover, his loyalty to Mexico was always conditional, depending on Mexico's treatment of Texas, and ultimately he did help lead the Texan rebellion against the Mexicans. He was well-educated, articulate, clever, and possessed of polished manners. In all of these ways, and many others, Stephen F. Austin defies the Turnerian image of the rugged, self-reliant, innocent, democratically inclined frontier leader. He was neither Davy Crockett nor John Wayne.

Yet Austin's story also presents some difficulties for those who would attempt to reinterpret it through the lens of the New Western History. Austin came to Texas legally, with the approval of the Mexican government. He learned Spanish, became a Mexican citizen, and pledged loyalty to his adopted country—a pledge he took seriously. He developed not only close professional relationships but also a few true friendships with Mexican elites in Texas and with leaders in the uppermost echelons of the Mexican government and military. Despite periodic conflict with Indians, he generally sought peaceful coexistence, albeit on his own terms. Austin was a constructive leader in Mexican society for fifteen years—arguably more constructive than many native Mexicans — rebelling only when confronted by an authoritarian government that dissolved the liberal Mexican constitution and drastically limited local self-government. These facts made it easy for Barker and subsequent historians to view Austin and his Texas career in Turnerian terms as a logical chapter in the march of enlightened Anglo-American civilization across the North American continent. The same facts seem to make it problematic to portray Austin in the harsher light of the New Western History paradigm. If he is no hero in the Turnerian sense, neither is he the grasping villain that the New Western History might suggest.

Texas itself has presented some difficulties for the New Western Historians. Most of these difficulties spring from the complexity and diversity of the state's geography and history. For Turnerians like Barker, who defined the frontier as the *process* of westward expansion, the colonization and eventual independence of Texas were natural steps in that process. But for many revisionists who see the West as a specific *place* defined largely by its aridity, roughly half of Texas does not even belong in their scheme. Austin's Colony lay between the ninety-fifth and ninety-eighth meridians, just east of the hundredth meridian, which New Western Historians generally accept as the starting point for the West. Rainfall in Austin's Colony ranges from more than sixty inches annually on its eastern edge to about thirty on the western edge. The types of crops cultivated, the manner of dress and housing, and the settlers themselves had their roots in the Old South, not in the arid West. In much of the New Western historiography, therefore, treatments of Texas — if they appear at all — deal only with such West Texas phenomena as the range cattle industry or the problems of water in the Panhandle. The most influential of these works, Patricia Nelson Limerick's *Legacy of Conquest,* typifies this tendency; she considers Texas a western state but barely mentions it in the book.[8]

These problems underscore the difficulty in applying one western history model or the other to the story of Stephen F. Austin; the story is not even entirely *western.* Austin was a product of the American South, with its distinguishing characteristics: plantation agriculture and racial slavery. Born in Virginia and raised in Missouri in a slaveholding household, he could not have been insulated from the effects of the South's

Peculiar Institution. He used hired slave labor on a large scale in the family mining business, and he himself owned one or two slaves during most of his years in Texas. More important, he peopled his Texas colony largely with proslavery southerners, and he worked to ensure that slavery would be protected and perpetuated there. His plans for the development of Texas hinged on the growth of a commercial cotton economy. The revolution he helped to lead in 1835–36 produced independence, which in turn brought annexation, the Mexican War, the resulting sectional conflict over slavery in the new territories, and ultimately the American Civil War. As a southerner, Austin adhered to most of the complex precepts of the southern gentleman's code of honor, once avoiding a duel only through the timely intervention of his Masonic lodge. To consider him only a "western" or "frontier" figure would be to ignore the impact of his southern background and attitudes.[9]

Yet just as Austin defies attempts to classify him as one or another type of western figure, the same must be said for his complexity as a southerner. Austin grew up in slaveholding areas, but he was not a product of the Deep South or of plantation society. His parents were raised in the northeast, and he spent several of his formative years attending prep school in New England when that section was first awakening to the evils of slavery. Coming from this background, he carried with him into adulthood conflicting attitudes toward slavery. Although he owned slaves, he accepted a handful of free blacks as colonists and granted them land in his colony on the same basis as whites. In 1831 he could describe slavery as "that curse of curses, and worst of reproaches, on civilized man; that unanswered, and unanswerable, inconsistency of *free* and liberal republicans." Then, two years later, he could state flatly that for economic reasons "Texas *must be* a slave country." Although he could be critical of Mexico's backwardness and on rare occasions employed crude stereotypes in describing that backwardness, he maintained cordial relations with many Mexican elites; indeed, he probably had a closer personal friendship with Tejano Erasmo Seguín than he did with any of his Anglo associates. And there can be little doubt that he made sincere, sustained efforts to understand and accept the language, customs, and culture of his adopted country. Thus we find a man who in his racial views was neither typically southern nor northern, neither liberal nor reactionary. In the end, we can only acknowledge his many shortcomings and inconsistencies while concluding that in the context of his times he was far less ethnocentric than the typical white southerner (or the typical white westerner, for that matter).[10]

If a modern biography of Austin must partake of both western and southern history, it must also be cast in the light of the history of Mexico and the Spanish Borderlands. Texas, after all, was part of Mexico for almost all of Stephen F. Austin's fifteen years there, and his oft-repeated personal motto during most of that time was "Fidelity to Mexico."[11] He held an officer's commission in the Mexican national militia, served in the state legislature of Coahuila y Texas, and had personal dealings with high-ranking Mexican leaders from Iturbide in 1822 to Santa Anna in 1836. The "wilderness" he colonized in the early 1820s had been an organized part of the Spanish empire for more than a century. It is with some justification that historians of Hispanic Texas scoff at the notion of Austin as the "father" of Texas.[12]

Scholars from Mexico have paid surprisingly little attention to the early decades of their nation's history. They have shown even less interest in the history of the far northern frontier, an omission not altogether surprising given the painful memories of the Texas Revolution and the subsequent war with the United States. As a result there is comparatively little Spanish-language research on Texas in the 1820s and 1830s, and much of what does exist was written by non-Mexicans. This dearth of scholarship has led at least one prominent Mexican scholar to label the entire era *"los años olvidados"*—the forgotten years. Although still quite useful, the standard Mexican work on Texas during Austin's time, Vito Alessio Robles's *Coahuila y Texas* (1945), is dated and relies heavily on Eugene C. Barker, noting Barker's devotion to "truth" and praising him for the "justice" he shows Mexico. Mexican historians are renewing their interest in the early decades of the nineteenth century, but even these recent works give short shrift to Austin and the era of Anglo colonization in Texas.[13]

More promising has been the recent trend to consider Texas as a region in the context of the Borderlands. The best of these works are David J. Weber's *The Mexican Frontier, 1821–1846: The American Southwest Under Mexico* (1982) and *The Spanish Frontier in North America*

(1992). Weber places Texas and the other northern Mexican frontier provinces in the broader sweep of Mexican and North American history by analyzing a wide range of social, economic, and political forces affecting the Borderlands. Frontiers, as Weber so aptly phrases it, "seem best understood as zones of interaction between two different cultures." Historian Gregory H. Nobles has recently elaborated on this idea, defining a frontier as "a region in which no culture, group, or government can claim effective control or hegemony over others." Nobles would agree with Weber's observation that "frontiers represent both place and process, linked inextricably." Seen from this angle, rather than simply from the perspective of westward-marching Anglo-Americans, Austin and his colonists emerge as actors in Mexico's unsuccessful attempt to integrate its frontier provinces into the national economy and polity. An interpretation such as this—embracing both the Turnerian and the revisionist definitions of the frontier—seems particularly useful in understanding the history of Stephen F. Austin's Texas.[14]

The numerous perspectives from which Austin and his era can be viewed underscore the value of a fresh look at his life. Although this book is a biography of one man and not a formal history of his times, the story of Stephen F. Austin nonetheless can shed some light on those times. Austin's life, like the history of Texas itself during this era, might best be thought of as a bridge connecting the history of the South with that of the West, Mexico with the United States, the Spanish Borderlands with the American frontier. To the extent that this biography constitutes history, its value lies in revealing those connections rather than in celebrating Austin's contributions to Texas or American history.

In pursuing this bridge metaphor, it can also be argued that Austin's life spans two very different eras in American history, thus highlighting both of those eras. He came of age in a transitional period in American history—the transition from the eighteenth century to the nineteenth, from the Jeffersonian era to the Jacksonian, from the Age of Enlightenment to the Romantic period. Even in the United States the eighteenth century was a hierarchical, elitist age in which men of substance adhered to well-defined norms of moral rectitude and noblesse oblige. The early nineteenth century, with its rapid economic change and emerging egalitarianism, embraced a new, individualistic, entrepreneurial ethos that frequently clashed with the older values.[15]

Austin embodied the conflicts and contradictions of his day. He was what modern Americans would term a workaholic, driven by his quest for success and fortune. Yet he also felt a Jeffersonian sense of duty and obligation to his fellow man, an urge that forced him to deny, both to himself and others, that he was just another self-interested Jacksonian "man on the make." Indeed, so strong was that inner tension between self-interest and moral rectitude that after committing himself to his Texas venture he did sometimes sacrifice his material interests for "higher" aims, even if those aims served important personal psychological needs. For years he claimed that his fondest desire was to quit public affairs and settle down to a quiet life as a landed gentleman; it comes as no surprise that he never could actually bring himself to do it.

Austin professed a love of democracy much in keeping with the spirit of the Jacksonian age, but he was driven almost to distraction by his difficulties in dealing with "many 'backwoods men' and 'rough fellows,'" as he described the colonists. "I do say that the North Americans are the most obstinate and difficult people to manage that live on the earth," wrote an exasperated Austin in 1830. This sort of elitism often set him apart from the frontiersmen who settled in his colony, and his self-avowed paternalism toward them frequently betrayed a disdain for the common man more typical of the eighteenth century than of the nineteenth.[16]

Austin's life also exemplifies the transitional nature of nationalism in the early nineteenth century. In the first years of the republic Americans generally had viewed their nation in legalistic terms. The Constitution was a political compact with the pragmatic purposes of ensuring individual rights and promoting economic interests. By the Jacksonian period Americans were just beginning to develop a romantic, emotional, almost sacred attachment to country and flag — what Lincoln would call "mystic chords of memory." Austin personifies this tension between the older and newer conceptions of American nationalism. On one hand he considered himself a patriotic American, lauding "the Patriots of '76," the "GENIUS OF LIBERTY," and the "SPIRIT OF INDEPENDENCE" in a rousing Fourth of July address in 1818. But only three years later he, along with numerous other Anglo-Texan colonists, would turn his back on that same United States and move into what was then a colonial outpost of a European monarchy, with no noticeable reservations about leaving behind his native land. "I expect to spend my Life in this Nation," he informed the Mexican government when obtaining his new citizenship papers. Even years later, when life for him under Mexican rule grew difficult, annexation of Texas by the United States remained a distasteful last resort.[17]

These examples illustrate Austin's usefulness in helping us understand the mindset of Americans in the early decades of the nineteenth century. Though he was in many ways an exceptional man, a close reading of his life reveals much that was quintessentially American. If his was a complex and often conflicted personality, his story reminds us that many of those very complexities and conflicts typified his generation.

In a 1990 essay in *The New Republic*, the Texas-born Larry McMurtry, author of several novels set in the American West, criticized revisionist historians for depicting "a West where people had only jobs, and crappy, environmentally destructive jobs at that." McMurtry agreed with much of the debunking done by the New Western historians, but he argued that "the winning of the West was an act based on a dream of empire dreamed by people with very different mentalities and ambitions from those historians or Westerners who may now direct a critical eye, quite fairly, at the legacy of that same dream and that same act." Such historians, wrote McMurtry, "in their effort to have the truth finally told, often fail themselves because they so rarely do justice to the quality of imagination that constitutes part of the truth. They may be accurate about the experience, but they simplify or ignore the emotions and imaginings that impelled the Western settlers despite their experience. Explorers and pioneers of all stamps needed imagination, much as athletes need carbohydrates. Fantasy provided part of the fiber that helped them survive the severity that the land put them to."[18]

McMurtry's observations regarding the emotions and imaginings of the men and women who settled the West apply with special force to the case of Stephen F. Austin. For all his materialistic motives, and whatever personal shortcomings or idiosyncrasies he may have possessed, Austin remains a man of vision. The path that led him to Texas and to fame may make him seem typical of the grasping, hypocritical frontier opportunists that revisionist historians rail against, but along the way something exceptional happened to Austin. At a point early in his Texas venture he began to realize that the work he had embarked upon meant more than just the restoration of his family's lost fortune. In a supreme act of imagination — imagination of the McMurtrian sort — Austin came to identify his very life with the settlement and prosperity of Texas. Although revisionists may, perhaps rightfully, see Austin as the self-pitying "injured innocent" who protests too much about his fate,[19] those who find *only* that miss the larger reality of Austin's vision. Austin articulated that vision eloquently and often, as in this example from an 1830 letter:

> Instead of roaming about in other countries to speculate I have devoted my life to the arduous task of trying to redeem this country from the wilderness and I have succeeded greatly beyond what was supposed possible, for I was ridiculed by some for attempting such a thing. I had no capital, and have supplied its defect by personal labor and attention, and by putting my shoulder to the wheel in earnest and in good faith. I have not made a fortune for my self (except in lands which now have no value) and probably shall not live to derive much personal benifit, but I have greatly benifited many others, hundreds of them, and made them and their families rich who were worth nothing before, and I have opened and enlarged a fine field for human enterprise and human happiness. This has always been the main object of my ambition and not a mere avaricious view to personal speculation.[20]

Austin's idealistic-sounding dream may indeed have concealed more pedestrian material and psychological motives. Perhaps, as McMurtry theorized, it was little more than a "fantasy" that enabled him to carry on in the face of adversity. If so, it was a fantasy that gave a very real direction to his life and helped shape the destiny of a vast land, three republics, and thousands of men and women.

A Foundation for Greatness
1793–1810

The eleven-year-old boy awoke to the gray chill of another New England winter morning. As he looked out at the dreary, snow-covered ground, home must have seemed very far away. Seven months had passed since that June afternoon in 1804 when his father had put him on the boat at Ste. Genevieve, a thousand miles away on the Mississippi River. He had written home in September but received no reply. Autumn came and went, followed by the Christmas holidays, and still nothing. He knew that the mail service was unreliable between Connecticut and Missouri, but that did little to ease the homesickness that he must have felt after such a long separation from family and friends.[1]

Soon he was off to school and another busy day of reciting lessons, practicing penmanship, and trying to avoid the wrath of Mr. Adams, the much-feared headmaster of Bacon Academy. That evening, back home at the Pennimans', where he was boarding, the long school day and his homesickness were momentarily forgotten. Lying on the table was an envelope bearing his father's unmistakable handwriting, addressed to "M^r. Stephen Fuller Austin, Colchester, Connecticut."

Stephen eagerly opened the letter. What was the news from Durham

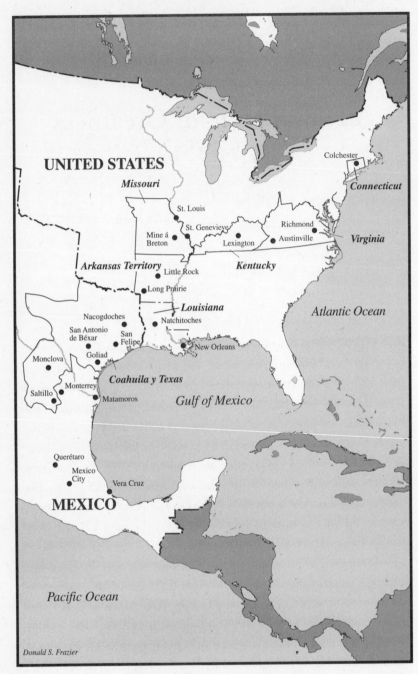

Map 1. Stephen F. Austin's World.

Hall, the family's rambling mansion at the Mine à Breton? Had there been any more Indian attacks? How were his younger sister, Emily, and his baby brother, Brown? Did his mother miss him? Such questions would not be answered in his father's letter. Moses Austin, the wealthy mining baron, patriarch of Durham Hall and idol of young Stephen, had more important things to say. "I hope and pray you will improve Every moment of time to the utmost advantage and I shall have the sattisfaction of seeing that my expectations are not Disappointed," wrote Moses. "Remember my Dear Son that the present is the moment to lay the foundation for your future greatness in life and that much money must be expended before your Education is finished and that time lost can never be recalled. Therefore be studious and attentive to obtain full information of all matters given to you to learn." [2]

Moses's letter provides an intriguing glimpse into the childhood world of Stephen F. Austin. He was barely eleven years old, but according to his father, Stephen was already engaged in a very serious undertaking. He had been sent to Connecticut not merely to get an education; he was there, as Moses had phrased it, to prepare for greatness in life. For the eldest son of Moses Austin, nothing less would be acceptable.

This admonition to strive for greatness was surely nothing new to young Stephen. Already he knew that he would someday succeed his father as patriarch of the Austin clan. Lest Stephen forget his duty, however, Moses reminded him once again near the close of his letter. "I hope to God I shall be spared until I see you arrive at an age to give protection to your Dear Mother and Sister and little Brother Elijah Brown," he wrote. "Remember that to you they will look for protection should it so happen that my life should be shortene d. Keep in minde that this may happen."

Moses also stressed smaller things. He lectured Stephen on the proper handling of money: "I do not expect you will expend money unwisely. Yet I do not wish you to render yourself Disagreeable to your young friends to avoid expending a few Dollars. When it appears necessary for you to form company pay readely your part of all expenses that may arise but Never lett yourself be impose d on by an improper Demand and if you finde a Disposition in any of your young friends to do such an Act, I charge you, have nothing more to Do with them, Keep not there

Company and promptly tell them the Cause." These were matters, Moses explained, that "many suppose of Small moment, but I do not. Its small things that stamp the disposition and temper of a man and many times, Boys lessen there greatness in life by small things which at the moment they think of little or no Consequence." This was a lesson Stephen would learn well. Throughout his adult life he would pay meticulous attention to details that others might have overlooked. As his father predicted, this habit would often pay dividends in important ways.

The only news of home that Stephen received in the letter was Moses's account of his own recent illness. Of the rest of the family, there was not a word except that his mother and sister sent their blessing. Other family members surely wrote their own letters to Stephen, but it is significant that of all the letters he must have received during his three years in Connecticut, this was the only one he apparently saved. That the letter was so carefully preserved suggests something of the importance that Stephen, first as a child and later as an adult, attached to his father's advice. There can be little doubt that he treasured this letter, saving it for posterity. The sentiments it contained—Moses's exhortations to strive for greatness as the anointed leader of the Austin family—would serve as a touchstone for Stephen F. Austin in his adult life.

For young Stephen, the sojourn to Connecticut was a return to his family's roots. The first Austin to set foot on the rocky soil of New England had been Stephen's great-great-great-grandfather Richard Austin, who arrived in 1638 from Hampshire County, in the south of England. Richard, a moderately prosperous tailor, was part of the great migration that filled Massachusetts with hardworking, pious Puritans seeking economic opportunities and religious freedom in America. Over the next century Richard Austin's descendants would carve out their niche in New England society as artisans, merchants, farmers, and community leaders. His great-grandson, Elias, moved to Durham, Connecticut, in the 1740s. Elias and his wife, Eunice Phelps, eventually had nine children. The youngest, Stephen's father, Moses, was born on October 4, 1761.[3]

In Durham, only twenty miles from where Stephen was now in school, Elias Austin had practiced the tavern-keeper's trade, an occupation on which his more orthodox Puritan forebears would have frowned. By this time, however, New England was well along in its journey from a subsistence agrarian society to a more diversified commercial economy. Religious orthodoxy was on the decline. In the Austin family, two of Elias's sons—Moses and Stephen (for whom Moses would name his own son)—would complete this Puritan-to-Yankee transformation by abandoning the family's traditional farming and craftshop professions to become entrepreneurs on an international scale. It was the Puritan sense of obligation to family and community, combined with the Yankee zeal for daring enterprise, that Moses Austin would transmit to his own son.

By the time Stephen F. Austin arrived in Connecticut to begin his schooling in 1804, he probably could recite the story of his father's rise from humble beginnings to wealth and prominence. Elias Austin had died when Moses was just fifteen. Fortunately, Moses's brother Stephen, fourteen years his senior, had already established himself as a tailor and merchant in Hartford. The older Austin brother prospered during the Revolution and moved, at the end of the war, to Philadelphia, where he became a successful importer of English goods. When young Moses reached majority he followed Stephen to Philadelphia and established his own store with his brother's cooperation. Moses's entire business life would be spent in partnerships with various relatives, eventually including his own son. With the strong family bonds inherited from their Puritan ancestors, the Austins took it as a given that business affairs would be family affairs.

In 1784 the two brothers had agreed that Moses would move south to Richmond, the new capital of Virginia, to open a branch office. Despite the beckoning opportunity, leaving Philadelphia must have been difficult for Moses, for he had fallen in love with a local woman. Mary Brown—more often called Maria by friends and family—had been raised since age thirteen by Benjamin Fuller, a wealthy great-uncle. Moses courted Maria by letter from Richmond, and in September 1785 he returned to Philadelphia to take her hand in marriage. The day after they said their vows the newlyweds departed for Virginia. As an adult, Stephen F. Austin would one day understand how difficult his mother's life had been as the wife of Moses Austin. But for Maria in 1785, at the very beginning of married life, it must have seemed very exciting.

Moses Austin. This portrait is of disputed
authenticity, but it is the only reputed likeness of
Stephen F. Austin's father. *Courtesy, Texas State
Library and Archives Commission.*

Stephen F. Austin never saw his parents' home in Richmond. Observers in the 1780s would have seen a rough, unappealing hamlet, but one
with great promise for men with vision and ambition. The Austin mercantile business thrived. Moses and Maria's first child, a daughter named
Anna Maria, arrived in 1787 but lived only a month. The following year
Moses's brother Stephen closed his business in Philadelphia and moved
to Richmond himself, bringing with him $25,000 in capital to invest in the
brothers' joint enterprise. The timing was good, for Moses had recently
become aware of a new opportunity. A remote lead mine, some 250 miles
southwest of Richmond, had become available for lease. Located in wild,

nearly inaccessible Wythe County, Virginia, the mine had been worked sporadically and without much success since its discovery in the 1750s. In 1789 Moses and Stephen signed a ten-year lease on the mine and plunged into the new business with typical Austin enthusiasm.

Taking over the mine, the Austin brothers rapidly expanded production. From the beginning they exhibited a willingness to use the government to promote their own private interests, a practice that would be repeated by Austins, including Stephen F., many times in the future. The brothers obtained a lucrative contract to install a lead roof on the new state capital and successfully petitioned Congress to enact a protective tariff on the mineral. In a new nation, protected by a new Constitution and led by a government eager to promote private enterprise, lead mining seemed to offer limitless potential.

In 1792 the Austins purchased the mines, and Moses and Maria prepared to move there from Richmond. The village that soon sprang up around the mines was named Austinville. This expansion of the family business took every dime the brothers had, and they borrowed heavily. The roofing contract for the state capitol turned out to be a disaster; the lead roof could not be made waterproof and had to be replaced, costing Moses and Stephen dearly. They decided to sell the mines. While Stephen traveled to England in an unsuccessful attempt to arrange a sale, Moses continued the day-to-day management of business at the mines, seemingly undaunted.

Although Moses's business affairs offered challenges, his personal life provided satisfaction. In his mid-thirties, he was not only the director of the Austinville mines but also the acknowledged leader of the new frontier community. He served as a justice on the local court and as an officer of the militia. More important, his marriage had proved a good one. Maria was well-educated, pious, and utterly devoted to Moses. The only cloud on the domestic horizon was the matter of children. After the death of their infant daughter, Maria had soon become pregnant again. A second daughter, Eliza, was born in 1790 but lived only seven months. So when Maria became pregnant for a third time, the news must have been both joyful and sobering. The couple had lived at the mines for less than a year, and as dangerous as life was for an infant in Philadelphia or Richmond, it might be even more so in the raw village of Austinville. These realities notwithstanding, November 3, 1793, was an important day in the Austin household. The boy born that day was named Stephen Fuller Austin in honor of his father's brother and his mother's great-uncle. Moses Austin had his heir.

Relatively little is known of the domestic environment in which Stephen F. Austin lived for the first few years of his life, but much can be surmised. Moses's business affairs made enormous demands on his time, so a large share of the child-rearing responsibilities probably fell to Maria. She seems to have lavished love and attention on young Stephen, perhaps in an effort to compensate for the pressures that her husband placed on the boy. Not surprisingly, Stephen would form an exceptionally close bond with his mother.

This is not to say that Moses Austin neglected his family. Austinville provided few outlets for socializing outside the home, so Moses probably spent most evenings in the company of his wife and child. Moreover, despite his volatile temper and exceedingly high expectations of his first-born son, Moses likely was an indulgent father. The detailed advice and instructions that he would give his children throughout his life indicate great concern for their welfare. Moses may have been demanding, but he was involved in his children's lives — at times perhaps overly involved. Nevertheless, judged by all the collective evidence from Stephen F. Austin's later life, his early childhood appears to have been happy. "The early part of my life," he wrote as an adult, "was spent happily in the quiet enjoyments of home. . . . My angel *Mother,* and my nobleminded and kind hearted father were my first standards of human nature."[4]

Stephen grew up in an era when organized religion had reached a low point in American history, and at any rate Austinville was probably too new a settlement to have a church. Moses apparently was raised a Congregationalist and Maria an Anglican, but religion seems not to have played a major role in in their adult lives or in Stephen's upbringing. Maria Austin was a pious woman personally, if later evidence applies to this time in her life, but neither she nor Moses ever seemed particularly concerned about the lack of a local church for their growing family. Indeed, given

Moses Austin's stated disapproval of bigotry, he may have welcomed the necessity of parental religious instruction over that of any church or denomination. The best clue about the religious environment of Stephen's early childhood comes from a letter he wrote to his mother many years later, after he had moved to Texas. Since the Mexican government required foreign emigrants to be nominal Roman Catholics, Austin wrote to his mother in Missouri to ask if he had been baptized into the Catholic Church when he moved at age five with his family to Missouri, then a part of the Spanish-owned Louisiana Territory. His mother responded, "No my Son, you and your Sister was baptised at Austin Vill by a protestant Clerjyman." The fact that she failed to mention a denomination, and that Stephen, then twenty-nine years old, apparently did not even know if he had been baptized at all, suggests something of the scant importance that the Austins placed on organized religion. Throughout his life Stephen Austin would generally disapprove of religious sectarianism, preferring a deistic belief in a creator and supreme being. What religious instruction he received as a child most likely came at the hands of his mother, perhaps reinforced by an occasional itinerant minister, such as the one who baptized him.[5]

Before Stephen reached his second birthday, he was joined by a sister, Emily. His relationship with Emily, though sometimes contentious, would be one of the most significant of his life. As an adult he would form important partnerships with each of her two husbands, and he would treat her children almost as if they were his own.[6]

Stephen had barely reached the age of three when momentous changes came to the Austin household. Struggling under obligations that were becoming increasingly difficult to meet, Moses Austin learned of a new opportunity. The greatest known lead deposits in North America lay hundreds of miles away in the Spanish province of Upper Louisiana (later the state of Missouri). In December 1796 Moses and a traveling companion left Austinville to investigate the Spanish mines. They rode down the Wilderness Road and through the Cumberland Gap into Kentucky, stopped in the frontier hamlets of Frankfort and Louisville, crossed the frozen Kentucky and Ohio Rivers, and eventually approached the village of St. Louis. A Spanish possession since 1763, Louisiana originated as a

French colony, and most of the non-Indian inhabitants, including officials of the government, were still ethnic Frenchmen.

Arriving on the outskirts of St. Louis, Moses employed a tactic that became a classic Austin maneuver, one that his son would emulate many times in his dealings with Mexican officials. The journey had been made through a bitter winter storm, and the travelers had endured severe hardships; but Moses realized that a ragged American stranger would be viewed suspiciously by the king's representatives. As the story goes, he dressed himself "in a long blue mantle, lined with scarlet and embroidered with lace," mounted the best horse available from among those in the small entourage he had accumulated along the way, and led a small "cavalcade" into the town. The chief Spanish official, Lt. Gov. Zenon Trudeau, was impressed. He gave Austin a letter of introduction to François Valle, the commandant of Ste. Genevieve, the nearest settlement to the mines, and instructed Valle to provide a guide for Austin.[7]

Valle and Austin got along well, and Valle permitted Austin to explore the tract known as the Mine à Breton (after the Frenchman François Azor Breton, who had discovered the lead deposits twenty-five years earlier). There he found lead ore, near the surface and barely touched, in amounts that dwarfed anything in Virginia. As soon as he could, he wrote to the Baron de Carondelet, governor general of Louisiana in New Orleans, and applied for a sixteen-league grant (about seventy thousand acres) centered on the mines. Austin made a strong case for his proposal, arguing that development of the mines would benefit Spain and that he was the only man on the continent capable of the project. This may have been true, but two other circumstances operated in Austin's favor. A recent change in Spanish policy favored American emigration into Louisiana to provide a buffer against the English, so Austin's proposal, which officials earlier would have scorned, received a respectful hearing. And Austin had hedged his bets by offering an interest in the enterprise to several of the local Spanish officials, including Valle.[8]

Stephen F. Austin grew up hearing the story of how his father won approval for his scheme from the Spanish government. Maintaining proper appearances, going through official channels, courting influential officials (with money if necessary), appealing to the national interests of a foreign government—these tactics would serve the younger Austin well someday. Upon his return to Austinville in the spring of 1797, Moses wrote a thirty-eight-page "Memorandum" of the trip "for the Use of my son." Moses's language speaks volumes about his expectations for Stephen. Moses explicitly prepared his memoir of the journey for Stephen's *use,* not just as family memorabilia. He viewed it as being of particular instructive value. It was an extraordinary thing for a father to do for a boy who was not yet four years old.[9]

That summer Moses and his brother Stephen met in Philadelphia to reorganize their tangled business affairs. Then, in the midst of the reorganization, they had a bitter falling-out, almost certainly over financial matters. After a month of argument the brothers not only failed to resolve their differences, but they could not even agree on how to dissolve their partnership.[10]

Moses returned to Virginia to await word from Louisiana. If he had had any doubts about pursuing the Spanish venture, the events of that summer had erased them. The increasingly untenable state of his finances and the estrangement from his brother had soured Moses's prospects in Virginia. If this were not enough, that same summer Congress had rescinded the tariff on imported lead. Prices plunged. In September 1797, Moses learned that Spanish authorities had approved his application, although they granted him only one league of land (4,428 acres) at the mines instead of the sixteen he wanted. He had a year to make the move. On June 8, 1798, Moses and Maria Austin, along with five-year-old Stephen, three-year-old Emily, and some forty other relatives, workers, and slaves, left Austinville forever.[11]

The journey may have been exciting for an eager five-year-old boy, but it was traumatic for those old enough to realize what happened along the way. The party traveled by land to the Kanawha River, where they boarded a flatboat for the Ohio. During the long float down the Ohio to the Mississippi, nearly everyone grew ill. Moses's sister and nephew died en route, and another nephew drowned in the falls of the Ohio. Various others either died or became separated from the main group. By the time they landed at Kaskaskia, Illinois, only seventeen of the original forty remained. Of these, Moses later reported, only two had the strength to walk ashore unassisted. If western Virginia had once seemed like the end of the earth to the cultured Maria Austin, this newest frontier must have been truly frightening.[12]

The Mine à Breton lay in a picturesque valley forty miles west of the Mississippi, amid a vast region of hills and forests almost untouched by Europeans. Earlier in the year Moses had sent a small group to begin work at the site, which possessed only a handful of crude structures, built by French miners. There would be no place to house the family at the mines for almost another year. The nearest town was the old French village of Ste. Genevieve, on the Mississippi. Here Moses bought a cabin for his family and Maria set up housekeeping.[13]

It was a foreign environment for the Austins, in more ways than one. The few hundred inhabitants, mostly Frenchmen but with a smattering of Spaniards, Anglos, and black slaves, lived a slow-paced life. Most earned their living as small farmers, supplementing their income by trading in pelts with the local Indians. The social life of the community revolved around the local Catholic church, whose ceremonies and processions provided the main sources of diversion. At the village school, classes were conducted entirely in French, but there is no record that Stephen attended. Boys his age found ample opportunities to play with friendly Indian children from a Kickapoo village a quarter of a mile away. Each day, following the afternoon Mass, children attended the public ball, which, as one inhabitant described it, "was by no means a place of frivolity, but rather a school of manners." Parents enforced the "strictest decorum and propriety" at these gatherings. They instructed their children in dancing the "minuette" and taught them the "secret of true politeness." It was perhaps at these balls that young Stephen first gained his appreciation of dancing and polite social interaction.[14]

Moses spent most of that year establishing his operation at the mines. His highest priority was to develop an efficient smelting process, a task at which he succeeded brilliantly. He spent part of his time engaging in legal and political squabbles over his title and the boundaries of his claim. Dealings with the local officials, including those whom he had taken on as partners, also proved difficult. But also on the list of priorities was the completion of his permanent home at Mine à Breton. Here, as in so many

Durham Hall, 1824. The Austin family mansion as it appeared around the time
Stephen Austin commenced Texas colonization. Note the additions that had
been made over the years to the rear of the house. *Courtesy, Musée d'Histoire
Naturelle, Le Havre (Charles Alexandre Lesueur Drawings #42052).*

other things he did, Moses Austin thought big. On a site on the clear-
running Breton Creek, not far from the cluster of huts that housed the
French miners, he erected an elegant two-and-a-half-story frame mansion.
With its graceful lines, sash windows, and circular window in the front
gable, it would not have been out of place on one of the plantations of
Tidewater Virginia. A year to the month after leaving Austinville, Moses
brought Maria and the children to their grand new house on the frontier.
He called it Durham Hall, in honor of the Connecticut town of Moses's
youth. Young Stephen Austin might grow up on the frontier, but it would
be an upbringing marked by luxury and refinement. The house stands as
an ideal metaphor for the complex influences that would shape Austin's
personality: a southern mansion, bearing a Yankee name, situated on a
very western frontier.[15]

Life went well over the next several years for Moses and Maria Austin.
Another son, James Elijah Brown Austin (called Brown by the family),
was born in 1803. Despite setbacks and difficulties, the mining business

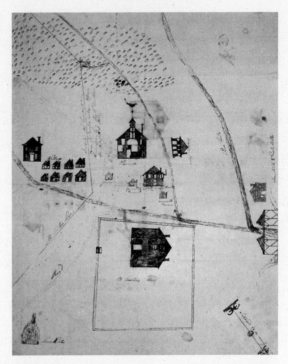

Mine à Breton, 1799. The layout of the Moses Austin's
frontier settlement, with Durham Hall at the bottom,
the various outbuildings associated with the mining
enterprise at center, and the small village that housed
the French laborers on the left. *Courtesy, Archivo
General de Indias, Sevilla (Mapas y Planos #198).*

proved spectacularly successful. By 1810, Moses estimated his assets at
$190,000, which, even allowing for probable exaggeration, was a magnifi-
cent fortune. Moses Austin's intense pride brought him into conflict with
those who envied his wealth, resented his power, or ran afoul of his volatile temper. But a child growing up in this environment would have taken
little notice of such adult concerns. Besides the large house, Mine à Breton
offered endless attractions for a curious and energetic boy to explore. The
first structure constructed at the site had been a furnace house that, in its
own way, was as impressive as Durham Hall. Workers manufactured lead
shot in the Austin shot factory. Saw and grist mills, a blacksmith shop,

and a distillery could provide entertainment as well as practical instruction. If these got boring, there was always the barn, stable, henhouse, and smokehouse. The dry goods store that Moses opened stocked an impressive variety of merchandise. If an inquisitive Stephen occasionally got in the way of the laborers, craftsmen, or clerks of Mine à Breton's various enterprises, the employees would have had little choice but to endure it with good humor. To correct Stephen would be to risk crossing Moses, and few would be foolish enough to make that mistake.[16]

Indeed, it was the people — the incessant activity — that would have made Mine à Breton a wondrous place for a boy. The environment of the eastern Missouri frontier played a crucial role in shaping Stephen Austin's character and personality. Much of the local population was still French, including the miners who brought their ore to Moses for smelting. A few Spaniards had drifted in since the cession of Louisiana to Spain. After the United States acquired Louisiana in 1803, the flow of Anglo-American traders, trappers, and adventurers increased. Moses had acquired his first slaves while in Virginia, and the number had grown since the family moved to Missouri. Given the scarcity of white women and children at the mines, it is likely that Stephen's first playmates were the children of his father's slaves.

And then there were the Indians. The local commandant had licensed Moses to trade with the tribes that inhabited the area, and the trade proved brisk. Many years later, when Stephen Austin was negotiating with Indians in Texas, he recalled that his father had sometimes entertained "hundreds" of the Shawnees and Delawares at the mines, and that as a boy he had "often played with the Shawnee children." In short, Mine à Breton was a crossroads for Frenchmen, Spaniards, Anglo-Americans, African Americans, and Native Americans. Stephen F. Austin spent his most impressionable years with unusual opportunities to interact with all of them. It is unrealistic to expect that this experience would enable him to overcome all prejudices as an adult, but it no doubt helped him to put aside those prejudices at times and at least to recognize that those different from himself were not automatically inferior. Survival in the milieu of eastern Missouri at the beginning of the nineteenth century required constant accommodation, negotiation, and compromise with people of different cultural backgrounds and conflicting interests. The result was a surprising degree of social and cultural tolerance, and even intermixture. The extent to which Austin learned these lessons during his Missouri childhood explains much of his later success in Texas colonization.[17]

This is not to imply that life at Mine à Breton was always harmonious. For one thing, not all the Indians were as accommodating as the Shawnees and Delawares that Stephen Austin so fondly recalled from his boyhood. The Osages deeply resented the incursion of the white men into their hunting grounds, and they periodically raided Austin's settlement, taking horses and harassing the settlers. By far the most serious occurrence came in May 1802, when a band of thirty Osages assaulted Durham Hall. It is not known whether Stephen, Emily, or Maria were home during the attack, but presumably they were. Moses and nine of his men repulsed the Indians, but it had been a frightening experience. What made it all the worse was that the local French miners, believing that Moses had displaced them from their land, deliberately rendered no assistance in the fight. Moses, who rarely forgot a slight, never forgave them.[18]

But even had there not been hostile Indians to deal with—even if the Austins had not lived on the frontier at all—the mere presence of Moses Austin would have guaranteed conflict. For all his charm and polish, Stephen's father seemed to attract enemies. Numbered among these was the territorial governor, Gen. James Wilkinson. Austin became closely identified with the anti-Wilkinson political faction in Upper Louisiana, and party strife raged. More than once, violent confrontations between the Austin and Wilkinson forces were narrowly avoided. Wilkinson was eventually implicated in the treasonous Burr conspiracy and replaced by a pro-Austin governor, but Moses would always have powerful enemies.[19]

In 1804, Moses and Maria decided to send Stephen east for an education. Since the only school Stephen could ever have attended was the French-language school in Ste. Genevieve, he probably had been taught the rudiments of a grammar-school education at home, enough to qualify him to enter a good New England academy.

Neither Moses nor Maria had spent much time in the northeast in many years, and they had no idea where to place Stephen. But Moses had relatives in Connecticut whom he trusted, and one of them, a cousin

Stephen F. Austin, age 12. *Courtesy, Texas Memorial Museum (Item 750-4).*

named Daniel Phelps, had recently visited Missouri. Moses arranged for Stephen to travel home with Phelps, to whom he gave detailed instructions about what was to be done once they arrived in New England. Moses requested that Stephen "be placed at the best school in your Country and that great Care may be taken that he formes no Improper Connections that may have A tendency to Corrupt his Ideas of propriety." It was important to Moses and Maria that Stephen be placed in an environment that would be appropriate for a "Young Gentl^n in his Situation." Always concerned about appearances, Moses instructed Phelps to make sure that Stephen was "furnished with such Clothing proper to appear as becomes a Gentl[ema]n." Phelps was also entrusted with reporting on Stephen's conduct. In short, Stephen was to be groomed to play the part of an upper-class gentleman—a son of Moses Austin could be nothing less. A small silhouette portrait made soon after Stephen reached Connecticut reveals a handsome, bright-eyed twelve-year-old with erect posture, sporting a stylish suit coat with wide lapels, shiny buttons, and a cravat.[20]

The long journey to New England did not go smoothly. The nature of the problem was not revealed, but if Stephen expected sympathy he was disappointed. Instead, Moses used the difficulties to impart one of his frequent pieces of fatherly advice to Stephen. "Your troubles on your Journey," wrote Moses, "will learn you a little of what you are to expect to meet with in life." It was a lesson that the younger Austin would indeed learn, at times too well for his own good. He would reach adulthood with an outlook that was an incongruous mix of near-jubilant optimism and pessimism so dire that it could lead to fits of deep depression. Always supremely confident of their abilities, the Austin men could approach any new enterprise with the expectation that they would succeed. But when things went wrong it was because a hostile world had conspired against them. The message to Stephen, even at age eleven, was clear: rely on yourself and place little trust in others.[21]

It took some time for Stephen's situation to become settled. The Phelps family apparently suffered financial reverses, making it impossible for them to care for Stephen themselves. So they placed him with the Pennimans, family friends. The Pennimans, probably conferring with Austin relatives, decided that Stephen should attend Bacon Academy, a new but well-recommended school in Colchester, Connecticut.[22]

Predictably, Moses Austin had strong views about the sort of education he wished Stephen to receive. In true Enlightenment fashion, he wanted his son to study "the Classicks in short I wish to make him a scholar," but he confessed that he disapproved of the boy spending excessive time on Greek and Hebrew. Such subjects seemed useful only if one were preparing for the "devinity," a career that he plainly did not wish his son to pursue. Moses issued a progressive prescription for Stephen's education: "If his talents will justify I wish him for the Barr but I have so many times in my life blamed Fathers for pressing on their sons a profession nature never intended them for that I shall make of him what Nature has best calculated him to be." The best education would be both scholarly and practical. Anticipating values that would become more prevalent in the Jacksonian era, Moses ordered that Stephen be trained as a "man of business." To this end he stressed the importance of learning to "write well." But the most important thing Stephen could learn was "a Correct mode of thinking both Religious and Political." Moses was emphatic on one significant point: "I do not wish my son a Bigot." [23]

Given these requirements, Bacon Academy proved an excellent choice. Academies were a fairly new institution in America, the first ones having been founded in the late 1700s. Their purpose was to provide secondary education, a bridge between the common school and the college. Before the academies came along, Latin grammar schools had provided secondary schooling, with the heavy emphasis on the classical languages that Moses Austin had hoped Stephen would be spared. The academies, of which Bacon was one of New England's earliest and best, were more attuned to the needs of nineteenth-century America and to the wants of practical-minded fathers like Moses Austin. [24]

Two hundred students enrolled at Bacon when it opened in 1803, just a year before Stephen's arrival. The school's founders designed the curriculum to provide students with a well-rounded education. Courses included English grammar and writing, logic, rhetoric, belles-lettres, mathematics, natural philosophy, astronomy, moral philosophy, geometry, geography, and at least a taste of Latin and Greek. The trustees hired John Adams as the school's first headmaster; he was a graduate of Yale who later went on to a distinguished career as the head of Phillips Academy in Andover, Massachusetts. [25]

The regimented life at the academy must have been a shock for Stephen after his unstructured boyhood at Durham Hall. The school prescribed strict discipline; the educators were required "to suffer no law or rule to be violated without due reprehension or punishment." Behaviors such as "loud talking, whistling, jumping or any boisterous noise," or appearing in either "slovenly" or "extravagant dress" were prohibited. The school day began early — 7 A.M. in the winter and 5:30 in the summer. Prayer was offered in the main hall, and the headmaster sometimes delivered a short lecture on the "studies, morals and deportment of the scholars." Each day, two or more of the scholars were chosen to deliver public declamations before the student body. At the end of each term the school held a "public examination," and periodic "public performances in speaking" gave students the chance to display their accomplishments to parents, teachers, and townspeople.[26]

A look at one of these public performances reveals much about the sort of education Stephen Austin received at the academy. Twelve-year-old Stephen was not among the performers in this particular 1806 exercise, but no doubt his chance came in due time, and the results were probably comparable. At the end of the May term a student group fancying itself the Adelphian Society performed literary and dramatic works written entirely by the students. By modern standards, the works seem terribly serious. In one declamation, for example, a young speaker wrestled with the question "What is man?" and urged that his listeners follow the dictum, "Know thyself." Mastering the "difficult science" of self-knowledge, the speaker argued, "will guard us from vice, and lead us in the paths of virtue."

This philosophical "Declamation" was followed by a three-act "Drama." Set in Barbary, the play revolved around the friendship between a rich boy and a slave with an inhumane master, with the rich boy attempting to take his enslaved friend's place. Other poems and essays exalted nature, truthfulness, and the Boston Tea Party. Taken as a whole, the students' literary productions give clear evidence of an education comprised of roughly equal parts Enlightenment rationalism and New England Congregationalist morality. Putting content aside, they also indicate that the young scholars received an education of rigor and high quality. No less an authority than Noah Webster in 1806 pronounced the academy an institution "of the first reputation."[27]

For unknown reasons, Stephen's living arrangement with the Penniman family did not last long. Rather than move into the academy's students' quarters, however, he instead was sent to board with the family of the school preceptor, John Adams. If Moses Austin had ever been concerned about lax discipline, his worries were over. Adams was described as a "large, dark man and stern in his government, sometimes called in by mothers of headstrong boys to chasten them for their disregard of maternal authority." One of his students left this vivid reminiscence of the Connecticut schoolmaster: "I remember well the instruction, and, to us little fellows, terrible presence of John Adams, whom I feared more than all other men—whose instructions were stamped so deep I can call them all up now. I remember almost everything I heard him say or saw him do. He made a scholar of me."[28] Indeed, as a disciplinarian Adams went beyond even what the academy's stodgy Congregationalist trustees thought proper. Shortly after Stephen completed his studies, Adams resigned rather than allow the trustees to place restraints on discipline. Given this record, it was no small accomplishment when, after Stephen's three years at Bacon, Adams commended him as an "obedient and studious" scholar and "as a boarder, unexceptionable."[29]

Life for Stephen in Connecticut, however, could not have been all discipline and crack-of-dawn recitations. There were schoolboy pranks to be played, such as the time the headmaster arrived at school one morning to find his chair occupied by a coffin that the boys had pilfered from the nearby cemetery. The numerous Austin relatives in the area entertained their young kinsman on school holidays. And Colchester itself was quite cosmopolitan, compared with the frontier hamlets in which he had grown up. The population of about 2,600 supported a variety of small-scale craftshop industries and mercantile establishments. Baptists and Methodists settled and built churches among the Congregationalists. Cities like Hartford and New Haven were only a day's journey away. Colchester became something of a magnet for African Americans, for the Bacon Academy trustees had established a "colored school" adjacent to the academy. With an initial enrollment of thirty or forty students, it was the only one of its kind in Connecticut. Association on a daily basis with the Yankee farmers, ministers, merchants, and manufacturers of Colchester; with sailors from the nearby seaport towns of Groton or New Haven or New London; and with black children from the colored school exposed young Austin to a world far removed from the one he had known in the far-off Missouri frontier. His experiences in New England would take their place alongside those of Virginia and Missouri in shaping the multifaceted character of Stephen F. Austin.[30]

At the end of 1807, having attended Bacon Academy for three full years, Stephen "passed acceptably the public examinations" and was ready for the next stage of his formal education. Originally his father had hoped that he would attend Yale and pursue legal training, but Moses instead decided that Stephen would attend college at Transylvania University in Lexington, Kentucky. The decision clearly went against the desires of Maria Austin, who had wanted her son to be a Yale man.[31]

First he traveled back to Missouri to visit his parents, sister, and brother, whom he had not seen in three and a half years.[32] Not yet eleven when he had left home for Connecticut, he was now fourteen. Most likely, it was during this visit that the decision was made for him to go to college in Kentucky. In many ways it made sense, for there seems never to have been any doubt that Stephen's future, like that of his father, lay in the West. At Transylvania he could receive a well-rounded education in the company of many of the present and future leaders of the region. Lexington was also much closer to Missouri, making it cheaper and simpler than sending Stephen to Yale. With Emily and Brown soon to be sent away for their own schooling, and with the Austin family business undergoing some difficult times, cost was something to consider. Moses Austin had strong reasons to place Stephen at Transylvania; Maria would have had no choice but to acquiesce.

When Stephen arrived at Transylvania in late 1808 or early 1809, Lexington was one of the most important towns west of the Allegheny Mountains. For several years it had served as the place where hemp, grain, and tobacco were exchanged for goods brought down the nearby Ohio River or brought overland from Maysville. Now the professions, mercantile trades, and some manufacturing enterprises were gaining footholds. Austin could stroll the streets of Lexington and see the stately brick homes that were replacing the log cabins of an earlier day. Lexington was also developing into a cultural center, and there were numerous diversions for a well-heeled young man like Stephen Austin. He could spend an evening at the theater or concert hall, or, for less highbrow entertainment, the saloon or the gambling house. It comes as no surprise that such a city would become a center of higher education as well.[33]

The intellectual environment of Lexington had been molded by the Virginians who founded the town in the late eighteenth century. Strongly influenced by the Enlightenment beliefs of Thomas Jefferson and James Madison, Lexington's founders were committed to education and religious freedom. Indeed, for Jeffersonians, one depended on the other; the mind could best search for truth when unfettered by religious dogma. It logically followed that any educational institution promoting a particular sectarian agenda would impede freedom of thought. Moreover, if such an institution were state-owned, sectarian influence or indoctrination would violate the central tenet of religious liberty: the separation of church and state.[34]

This brand of religious and educational liberalism dominated the thoughts and actions of Kentucky's leaders when they established Transylvania University at the end of the eighteenth century. Although the first two important administrators of the state-supported college were in fact clergymen, both held liberal views. By the early years of the nineteenth century, though, Protestant orthodoxy, in the form of the Presbyterian church, had begun to grow in Kentucky. Presbyterian trustees at Transylvania feared that students were being indoctrinated with religious and political liberalism — or, as they termed it, "infidelity," a catchword for deism, Unitarianism, Jeffersonian politics, and other radical notions. Four years before Austin came to the university the Presbyterians gained control of the institution's board and appointed a Presbyterian minister president. Students protested, and the faculty was divided. Transylvania had become a high-profile battleground between nonsectarian liberalism and Protestant orthodoxy. Despite the apparent ascendancy of the Presbyterians in those years, liberalism continued to flourish. Its impact on Austin revealed itself many times in the years to come. With his son in Lexington, Moses Austin would have little cause to worry that Stephen might become a bigot.[35]

When Austin enrolled at Transylvania, the student body numbered fewer than a hundred and occupied a small campus just north of Lexington's main street. In the years just before his arrival, the college had purchased a respectable quantity of scientific apparatus and enlarged the library to some 1,300 volumes. A brilliant young attorney, Henry Clay, had served as the law professor for two years, but he resigned before Austin's arrival. Clay remained a university trustee, however, thus ensuring a liberal presence on the board.[36]

For students like Austin, with adequate preparatory training, the bachelor's program normally took two years to complete. Austin, now fif-

Transylvania University's main building, as it would have appeared when Austin attended the college in 1809–10. *Courtesy, Transylvania University Library.*

teen, was about the average age for beginning students. Only the barest sketch of his life in Lexington can be constructed from the meager sources that survive. Academically, he continued the rigorous education he had begun at Bacon Academy. During his two and a half sessions at Transylvania he took courses in the "various branches of the Mathematics — Geography — Astronomy — Natural & Moral Philosophy — [and] read some History." Outside the classroom and laboratory he might have participated in the student Philosophical Society or one of the informal debating clubs. It is impossible to say whether he involved himself in the controversies over Presbyterian control of the university or in the partisan political battles of the day, but he certainly was exposed to them.[37]

Apart from his academic coursework, only one aspect of Austin's college life can be clearly documented. The surviving correspondence between Stephen and his male collegiate comrades demonstrates only a mild interest in the political disputes of campus or state. Intellectual or philosophical discussions were even rarer. Instead, one burning topic dominated all others: girls.

Teenagers love gossip and intrigue, especially when affairs of the heart are involved, and the correspondence between Stephen and his Lexington friends contains plenty of both. One of Stephen's classmates, Robert Todd, reported to Stephen about one "Eliza P.," "the little girl you are so fond of." Stephen instructed another classmate, Isaac Baker, that Baker's letters to him should "begin and finish" with news of Eliza. This Eliza apparently was Eliza Parker, a year younger than Stephen and daughter of one of Lexington's first families. Eliza would be only fifteen, however, when Stephen left Transylvania to return home, leaving his friend Robert Todd free to court her. Robert and Eliza were married in 1812; their daughter Mary would one day marry an Illinois lawyer named Abraham Lincoln.[38]

Eliza was just one of Stephen's favorites among the local belles. Writing soon after Austin's departure from Lexington, Baker told him he was forced "to lump [the news of] your other sweethearts [together] for I cannot notice them all singly." Baker believed it necessary to reassure his absent friend that he had not been "making at two or three of them" himself. A year later Austin's friend John Bowman also felt obliged to update Stephen on his "Amaretto near Lexington," reassuring the absent Stephen that "she is not yet mar[r]ied and have no doubt but she anticipates with pleasure the happy hour when you are to meet again." At about the same time, however, Baker told Stephen, "I am glad you have fallen in love in U[pper] Louisiana." Apparently nothing came of this relationship, for there was no further mention of it.[39]

The year and a half that Austin spent at Transylvania no doubt helped to instill in him a taste for refined society, an irony considering how rarely his subsequent career on the frontier allowed him to indulge such tastes. But while university policy dictated that "no student shall frequent Taverns, nor places of licentious or unprofitable amusement," and forbade gambling and the possession of liquor, there were still plenty of opportunities for young gentlemen to mix with young ladies at parties, dances, concerts, and theaters. As one of Austin's female contemporaries remarked, "Lexington has some charms; particularly its Gayety." She in

fact reported that one student party "was too large to be agreeable," with
sixty-seven "elegantly" dressed ladies in attendance. From such events
Austin gained his lifelong love of dancing, which of all social activities
seems to have given him the most pleasure.[40]

Though he appears to have made friends, performed well academically, and enjoyed the social life of Lexington, Austin was not able to
remain in Kentucky to finish his degree. In April 1810, at age sixteen-and-
a-half, he secured a certificate from Transylvania's administration stating
that he had "conducted himself in an exemplary & praiseworthy manner" during his sessions at the school. With that, he returned home to
Missouri.[41]

The circumstances surrounding his departure reveal something of the
dynamics of the Austin family. Stephen apparently did not make the decision on his own, for his mother later mentioned that he was "taken from
school." Maria could not hide her disappointment. She pointed out to
Moses that Stephen "could have finish'd his Education in [L]exington,"
but what she really had wanted was for him to attend Yale. Now neither
was going to happen. As always, Moses had made the decision unilaterally.
Business had taken a sharp downturn at about the time Stephen had gone
to college. Although Moses was far from insolvent, he did have trouble
meeting some of his financial obligations in 1809. Moreover, Moses himself was preparing to take a business trip to the East Coast; he needed
Stephen to look after the mines. Moses always believed that he knew what
was best for his family, and he would brook little in the way of argument
from Maria, Stephen, or anyone else.[42]

Stephen F. Austin completed his education and entered early adulthood at a critical time in the history of the North American frontier. The
Louisiana Purchase seven years earlier had opened the door to large-
scale westward expansion of the United States. America and Great Britain
were on a collision course for war—a high-stakes conflict in which the
Mississippi Valley would be a major battleground. The U.S. population
had grown dramatically in the decades since Independence, and much
of that restless population looked longingly toward the rich lands of the

Mississippi and beyond. If the British threat in the West could be eliminated, there would remain only two obstacles to westward expansion. One would be the Indians, who could not sustain themselves indefinitely against the Anglo-Americans. The other was the resource-rich but politically and militarily weak Spanish provinces to the southwest.

The West, then, presented unparalleled opportunities for Austin's generation of Americans; the risks were also daunting. But Stephen seemed well prepared to seize the opportunities and meet the risks. He had grown up in the vanguard of the republic's first westward movement. He was well acquainted with the diverse population of the West, be they Indians or blacks, Frenchmen or Spaniards, rough frontiersmen or elite gentlemen. He understood the need for patience and tolerance when dealing with such a mix. His nonsectarian upbringing and his education also had helped equip him for the career ahead. At Bacon Academy and Transylvania University he had drunk deeply of Enlightenment rationalism, with its secular emphasis on individual liberties, freedom of thought, and pursuit of self-interest. As a consequence, Austin matured into an inquisitive and open-minded young man. As his father had directed, Stephen F. Austin was no bigot. He had been trained to look and act the part of the gentleman, to feel comfortable in the company of diplomats, presidents, or emperors.

In terms of his personality, the younger Austin grew to adulthood in many ways the reverse of his father. Moses was outspoken, Stephen soft-spoken. Moses was prone to brash action, Stephen introspective and deliberative. Moses was incurably cheerful and optimistic, and Stephen — at least as an adult — was prone to severe spells of despondency and self-pity. Surely some of these differences were the result of Maria Austin's influence on her son. As a child Stephen idolized Moses and desperately wanted to please him, but he always seemed closer to Maria, who undoubtedly was a protective and loving mother to her first-born son. The striking personality differences between Stephen and his father also may have been caused in part by the long periods when Stephen was separated from his family. He learned at an early age to become emotionally self-sufficient, a characteristic he carried into adulthood. He felt his father's influence during these periods mainly through stern letters reminding him of his heavy obligations to the family. He must have grown up in awe — and perhaps even in fear — of such a father as Moses Austin.

Still, in some ways Stephen was his father's son. Both were highly intelligent, and they shared a proud, ambitious, acquisitive nature. Moses instilled an exceptional measure of self-confidence in Stephen, although it manifested itself more as quiet self-assurance than as audacity and bluster. Both men were distrustful of the intentions of others and tended to imagine conspiracies on the part of their enemies. Moses Austin had taught his son to think big. This willingness to undertake daring ventures would someday propel both men toward Texas.

Above all, though, Moses had imbued Stephen with strict notions of family pride and responsibility. To be an Austin, especially a first-born son, was to stand at the head of one of the republic's great families. As long as Moses Austin lived, he would be that head. But Stephen was raised knowing that he would inherit his father's mantle of leadership. The family name and reputation must never be sullied. Austins must always lead, never follow. When Moses Austin had exhorted eleven-year-old Stephen "to lay the foundation for your future greatness in life," he had defined the role that the entire family expected Stephen to play. Throughout his life Stephen F. Austin would chafe under this burden, which at times seemed impossibly heavy. It would often bring him hardship and frustration, and he could never escape it.

TWO

Successes and Failures
1810–1818

At an age when most young men begin thinking of leaving their parents and making their own way in the world, Stephen F. Austin returned to his family and the scenes of his childhood. Moses needed him in Missouri. As would be the case so often in his life, Stephen found weighty responsibilities thrust on him, perhaps before he was really ready for them.

No sooner had Stephen arrived at Mine à Breton in the spring of 1810 than Moses prepared to depart for New York City, where he hoped to purchase British goods to stock in his store. Moses left Stephen in charge, at least to the extent that a sixteen-year-old could oversee such a complex enterprise. In practice, this probably meant clerking in the store and keeping an eye on the various mining, smelting, and manufacturing operations. Whatever regret he may have felt at leaving college was offset by his pleasure at spending time with his mother and siblings, whom he had seen so little in six years.[1]

The younger Austin soon became aware of the precarious state of his father's business affairs. Lead had not sold well since 1808, and Moses had spent large sums trying to establish a claim to a mining tract not far from Mine à Breton. A yearlong attempt in 1811–12 to incorporate his operations proved an expensive failure. While the family's assets still looked formidable on paper, cash was in short supply.[2]

Moses had weathered the tumultuous years of the Louisiana Purchase and the treacherous Wilkinson administration, but he still had bitter enemies. One day early in 1811 that reality struck home. Back from his East Coast trip, Moses had been called away to Herculaneum, the town on the Mississippi River that he and a partner had founded as a shipping point for lead.[3] The day after Moses's departure for Herculaneum, Maria, her children, and some friends were enjoying a quiet evening at Durham Hall when several shots rang out. Bullets shattered the window glass, narrowly missing the room's occupants. An outraged Moses offered a $500 reward for the arrest and conviction of the "secret assassin or assassins," but the perpetrators were never apprehended.[4]

This episode, and many others over the years, convinced all the Austins that powerful, envious enemies were constantly plotting the family's ruin. When combined with his indisputable success, Moses Austin's temperament—which included generous measures of ambition, self-confidence, pride, and arrogance—bred genuine jealousy and animosity among many of his contemporaries. But enemies, real and imagined, also provided the family with a convenient explanation for virtually all their setbacks. Moses's wife and children, even more than Moses himself, developed something of a siege mentality—Austins alone against the hostile world. This conviction would grow as the family's fortunes declined further. Maria Austin frequently commented on "the Villinny, deception and perfidy" of those who pretended to be her husband's friends. She warned Moses of the "Duplissity & fals[e]hood of mankind," which should make one "suspi[ci]ous of every human being." The safest policy was "to place Confidence in no one, but on the Contrary to view every man . . . as men who would take every Advantage." Even after her husband's death Maria remained convinced that his troubles had stemmed from his "placeing Confidence in men that deceived and defrauded him," and she concluded that "the more I See of the world, the more reason I have to dislike its Inhabitants."[5]

The Austin children imbibed this conspiratorial view of the family's enemies and carried it with them into adulthood. Years later Brown Austin would comment on the "great and heartfelt satisfaction afforded to the Enemies of our house by its downfall" and look forward to the day when it would "be our turn to triumph." Emily and Stephen also felt that a hostile world was arrayed against the House of Austin. As individuals and as a family, this often isolated them psychologically and led them to ascribe their achievements entirely to their single-handed perseverance against that world. As a result, the contributions of others frequently went unacknowledged. However, the Austins' persecution complex could also serve a useful purpose; it drew the family members together and steeled them against hardship. Eventually Stephen even learned to be philosophical about it. When Emily in 1833 complained about her brother's enemies, Stephen calmed her by saying, "A man who has no enemies is a contemptable being, for he is not of sufficient consequence to excite envy or jealousy so that you may set your mind at rest as to that matter."[6]

Stephen turned seventeen in the fall of 1810, and Moses gradually added to his responsibilities. By early 1811 he seems to have been handling an increasing amount of the family mercantile business. He played a prominent role in the mines' public ceremonies commemorating the Fourth of July. At some point he either purchased, or Moses gave him, a sawmill valued at $13,000. But these responsibilities paled in comparison with the assignment his father planned for him in late 1811.[7]

In June of that year Maria Austin had traveled to the northeast to visit old friends and relatives and to place her two youngest children in school. Moses was unable to provide her with much cash for the trip, but he did send along a shipment of lead and other merchandise to be sold in New York, with part of the proceeds intended to defray his wife's expenses. For reasons now unclear, the arrangement netted Maria little or no money, and by late fall her funds were running low. She had found good schools for Emily and Brown, but they were expensive. Business at the mines had been depressed for some time, so Moses decided to send Stephen with a major shipment of lead down the Mississippi River to New Orleans. After conducting some business there for his father, he would then book passage for New York, where he was to sell his cargo, settle some of Moses's long-outstanding business accounts, and relieve his mother's financial plight. In the year he had worked at the mines, Stephen clearly had won his father's confidence. Now, at age eighteen, he was ready for a very adult responsibility.[8]

Unfortunately, there were delays. Stephen fell ill with "the ague and fever"—probably malaria—the first recorded episode of an ailment that would plague him for the rest of his life. Then word came that yellow fever was raging on the lower Mississippi, and neither Maria nor Moses would consider allowing Stephen to commence his journey before cool weather ended the epidemic. Between the depressed state of business and the absence of his mother, sister, and brother, life at the mines that fall was dull. Stephen tried to persuade his father's business associate James Bryan to come for a visit, remarking that "a little company would be very acceptable at this time for I never saw this place half so dismal as it appears now." But if Stephen longed to begin his exciting journey, he was destined for disappointment. One delay followed another. A massive earthquake, centered just south of the mines at New Madrid, struck in December. Aftershocks rocked the region in January and February, and river traffic was disrupted for weeks. Winter turned to spring, and still he could not leave for New Orleans.[9]

Only one incident during these months alleviated the boredom at Mine à Breton, and it may have accounted for at least part of the delay in leaving. The particulars are unknown, but Stephen became involved in a serious dispute with one of his father's many enemies. Identified by Maria Austin only as "that Unprincipeled W. S.," this individual seems to have insulted or otherwise wronged Moses, and the younger Austin apparently vowed revenge. A duel may have been imminent. Maria, learning of this dispute after the fact, expressed concern that if Stephen had met "the Wretch" one more time he might have killed him. Though she believed "it would be a happy Circumstance for mankind" if W. S. were "put out of the world," and while she thought that Stephen would have been justified in killing the "Villian" who had wronged Moses, Maria feared that the family's political foes would prosecute her son if this came to pass. "The thought is two dreadfull to dwell upon," she shuddered. But somehow the dispute was resolved, leading the pious Maria to detect "the Hand of providence" in the avoidance of violence.[10]

On April 28, 1812, Stephen rode out of Mine à Breton on the short overland trip to the Mississippi. Arriving at Herculaneum, he busied himself with last-minute preparations for the journey. Finally, around the second week in May, he boarded a barge loaded with lead and other trade goods and shoved off into the swirling waters.[11]

It was a dangerous voyage, hundreds of miles down the treacherous river. Moses provided Stephen with written instructions for the complicated transactions that were to be conducted in New Orleans and New York. He had intended to give his son much more advice—how to navigate the river, what hotels to stay in during his travels, and a dozen other important matters—but the emotion of the parting, he confessed, "drove all most Every thing from my thoughts." For all his swagger and self-confidence, Moses Austin knew that the months ahead would be lonely and uncertain. His wife and two youngest children had already been gone for almost a year, and now Stephen, on whom he had come to rely more than any other person, was leaving for at least several months. Collecting himself after his son's farewell, Moses sat down and wrote a long and thoughtful letter to Stephen containing all of the advice and instructions that the "fullness of my heart and mind" had prevented him from saying before Stephen's departure.[12]

Moses understood that his son was inexperienced in the cosmopolitan ways of large cities, so he took pains to ensure that Stephen would know how to conduct himself. As always, appearances were vastly important. "[A] word to you about your own Deportment a Young man must always remember that his apperance is greatly Noticed by Strangers," Moses advised. "You will therefore immedeately on your arrival obtain in Orleans such a Suite of Clothes as will be agreeably to the place." A black coat would be "in tast[e] in Orleans but also in Philadelphia," but other articles which would be appropriate for New Orleans would "be out of the Order of Dress" in northeastern cities. "You have been so long in the woods," Moses explained, "that you will finde an Attention to your Dress indispensable." He gave similar advice as to lodging—Stephen was to stay "in a Genteel part of the City"—and at dinner he was to "always informe yourself of the rules of the table and conform to them." Attention to these details was "absolutely Necessary," Moses said, for "with out them you will be Deficient in breeding." Such a deficiency would be unthinkable for a son of Moses Austin.[13]

The voyage went smoothly at first. Stephen tried to follow his father's detailed instructions concerning river navigation: never run after dark, avoid landing under a high bank, turn the stern downstream before landing, never let the boat float freely down the river without posting a lookout, secure the barge properly at night, put to shore in high winds, beware of the points of islands. By May 17 he had reached Cape Girardeau, and the next day he passed the mouth of the Ohio. Twenty miles above New Madrid the effects of the devastating earthquake became apparent, and Stephen could see the wisdom of delaying the trip until the aftershocks had subsided. The quake may have been the most severe in the history of North America; it was felt as far away as the East Coast. Virtually every house in the area was ruined. Uprooted trees clogged the river, and its banks were shattered. During the February aftershocks the bed of the river had risen and formed a falls that had rendered navigation dangerous until the spring floods washed it away. Stephen took a short trip into the interior to inspect for himself. Farmland had turned to swamp, lakes were created overnight, creeks were diverted or drained, huge fissures had opened in the ground and spewed out large quantities of sand and lignite. "As I view d the present situation of this place and reflected on the cause which desolated it," he wrote in his diary, "I could not refrain from heaving a sigh at its departed prosperity and at the same time from regarding with fearfull astonishment the Force of a Power sufficient thus to agitate the earth." With the "Philanthropic emotions" of his "soul" thus so "powerfully exercised," Stephen could only attribute the quake to "the wise Dispensations of Providence." Awed and fascinated, he boarded the barge and continued downriver.[14]

Sixty miles above New Orleans the journey abruptly ended. Stephen's barge struck a sandbar and sank in ten feet of water. Unable to do anything about the cargo until the river dropped, he went on to New Orleans. While he was there, grim news arrived from the nation's capital. "WAR!!!" screamed the July 10, 1812, issue of the *Louisiana Gazette*.[15]

"Business is almost anihilated," reported Stephen to his father following the declaration of war against Great Britain. Cotton prices collapsed. Prices for imported goods such as coffee skyrocketed. But in the midst of upheaval came opportunity. War could stimulate demand for lead, and prices for shot and sheet lead rose. Rather than wait for the river to fall, Stephen decided to raise the cargo as quickly as possible. In fact, he soon realized that the sinking had been *"truly fortunate."* Had he sailed with his load from New Orleans for New York according to schedule, he "should have undoubtedly been captured" on the high seas by British privateers.[16]

He returned to the accident site in early August and soon managed to recover the lead "with but little loss." Again it seemed that luck was on his side, for just as he was raising the last of the cargo, a hurricane hit New Orleans, damaging almost every ship in the harbor. Sixty miles up the river, Stephen was spared its fury. But if the sinking had let him avoid privateers and a hurricane, his luck was about to run out. By the time he made it back to New Orleans, the war had made shipping impossible. He could neither sell his lead for an acceptable price there nor take it to the East Coast, where prices were still decent. He lingered in New Orleans all that fall and into the winter, conducting sundry business errands for Moses and trying in vain to sell his cargo.[17]

In the meantime, Maria's financial situation grew more desperate. When she learned of Stephen's plight, she immediately took Emily out of school in order to cut expenses. With Stephen stuck in New Orleans, Moses accepted the offer of his friend and partner James Bryan to travel east and bring Maria and the children home. Bryan's motives were not entirely altruistic, for he had fallen in love with Emily and saw this as a golden opportunity to press his suit. It worked, and in June 1813 the Austin family was reunited in Missouri, and the thirty-seven-year-old Bryan had a promise of marriage from eighteen-year-old Emily.[18]

Stephen apparently had remained in New Orleans until January, finally returning to Missouri overland. In Mississippi he encountered American troops, who had been posted there to guard against hostile Indians and invading British. Since the beginning of the war American settlers along the frontier had lived in dread of a British-sponsored Indian uprising. It had been the first thing that Maria, far away in Philadelphia, had thought of when she first heard of the declaration of war. As she warned

Moses, "It will be in the Interrest of the British Government to give every Encouragement to the Indians to Joine them and the powerful Influence theay have over the different tribes, is two well known, for me to say any thing on that head." Still, Moses thought that the area around Mine à Breton was safe for the present. But if there was no imminent danger, Moses also believed—correctly, as it turned out—"that the Militia will be called on in the spring unless the *U S* government sends us troops."[19]

On May 24, 1813, Stephen was commissioned an ensign in the Missouri militia. The non-Indian residents of Missouri numbered only about 20,000, and they were almost all clustered in a thin strip of land running along the west bank of the Mississippi. In mid-1813, however, the greatest danger to the white settlements came from the East. Across the Mississippi River in Illinois, British agents had been active among portions of the Sac and Fox tribes, much as Maria Austin had warned the year before. If these Indians united with their fellow tribesmen in Missouri, and if the Osages and other tribes were enlisted in the British cause, many of the American settlements could be wiped out.[20]

Actual Indian attacks since the commencement of the war had been limited to hit-and-run raids, but these were frequent enough to instill terror in the settlers. Governors Benjamin Howard of Missouri and Ninian Edwards of Illinois, realizing that federal troops would not be made available for their territories' defense, successfully lobbied Congress to allow them to raise and equip militia forces sufficient to meet the threat. In the summer of 1813, General Howard, having resigned the governorship to take a field command, devised a plan. He would raise an army consisting of volunteer mounted militia and riflemen, and a smaller number of federal rangers and regular infantrymen, to ascend the Mississippi and Illinois Rivers, sweep the countryside of all hostile Indians, and construct a fort at Peoria. The militia companies were not the regularly constituted units that Austin had joined back in May, but rather companies made up of men who volunteered especially for this campaign. Enlisting as a private in the First Regiment of Mounted Militia under the command of Colonel Alexander McNair, Austin left Mine à Breton on September 1 for his regiment's rendezvous near St. Louis.[21]

It was a bittersweet time at Durham Hall. The family only recently had been reunited after the long absences of Maria and all three children, and Emily's marriage date had been moved up so that it could take place before Stephen's departure. Emily and James Bryan said their vows on August 31, and Stephen left the next day. "You can have some idea of my feelings upon this Solemn Occation," Maria wrote to her sister in Philadelphia, "when I tell you that the day after I received a Son in law, in my famaly, fate diprived me of the other & such a Son as every fond parent might be proud of." The campaign, as Maria understood it, was "a Hazardous & Dangerous Expedition, seven Hundred Miles up the river & though the force is great, at least 3000 strong [the actual number was 1,300] & every prospect of Subduing the Savages & bringing them to terms, this is but little consolation to my mind, when I reflect [upon the] many dangers he will have to Encounter through the Willderness." Maria no doubt spoke for the entire family when she resolved "to hope for the best & place my confidence in a kind providence, who has, heretofore protected us from every danger." [22]

No sooner had Austin joined his regiment at Portage des Sioux, just north of St. Louis, than he received a promotion. The First Regiment was "much in want of company officers," and Colonel McNair appointed the nineteen-year-old Austin quartermaster sergeant for the regiment. McNair's motives are not hard to comprehend. The Austins were one of the most prominent families in Missouri, and Stephen knew the mercantile business. Putting him in charge of supplies for his regiment made sense. [23]

General Howard's plan was daring but well thought out. Sending the small body of infantry regulars up the Illinois River on gunboats, he divided his remaining volunteers and federal ranger forces, sending one group a hundred miles up the east side of the Mississippi and personally leading the remaining troops, including Austin's regiment, up the west side. Here the men on Austin's side of the river stripped and swam their horses "with difficulty and danger" across the river. Their clothes and gear were placed on an improvised platform and rafted across. As quartermaster, Austin probably helped oversee this part of the operation. The newly reunited army then moved overland through the dangerous region between the Mississippi and Illinois Rivers, ranging as far north and east as the modern sites of Peoria and Chillicothe. They found few live Indians but burned numerous deserted villages. At Peoria the army camped for several weeks as the men labored hard to build a fort. On October 21, after seven weeks in the field, the volunteers were discharged. Despite the lack of actual fighting, the campaign was a success. There had been no casualties, the Indians' bases of operations had been dealt a hard blow, and the massive show of force discouraged further aggression.[24]

Given the absence of a real engagement, Austin probably saw more action as quartermaster than if he had been a line officer or a soldier in the ranks. The campaign had been gotten up quickly, and the soldiers were meagerly equipped. They had traveled light and quickly, sometimes covering thirty miles a day. Under such conditions, keeping several hundred men fed, clothed, equipped, and on fresh mounts, traversing rivers, swamps, and heavy woods, was no small accomplishment. To read the officers' accounts of the campaign, one would think that it had been a pleasant outing. Speaking of General Howard after the campaign, the *Missouri Gazette* claimed that "it may be truly said no general ever discharged troops who felt more pride and pleasure in being commanded by him." The enlisted men, however, complained bitterly of the hard labor and harsh conditions of the campaign, with one private claiming that General Howard was "universally detested."[25]

There is no way to know whether Austin's performance as quartermaster had contributed more to the disgruntlement of the men or to the strategic success of the campaign. But the experience he gained was significant. He learned the importance of a well-laid tactical plan. He witnessed the advantages of conducting an Indian campaign with various types of light cavalry, including his own mounted militia regiment, mounted riflemen, mounted spies, and, especially significant in light of his later career in Texas, elite ranger companies. Conversely, he now understood the difficulties inherent in imposing discipline on individualistic frontiersmen. The campaign had taught him that a show of force could be as effective as a pitched battle, and that burning villages and supplies could badly damage Indians' war-making abilities. All of these lessons would later be seen in his struggles to control the Indians who contested his presence in Texas.

Austin returned to Mine à Breton in October 1813 a much worldlier young man than the college boy who had arrived home from Kentucky three years earlier. Of the previous fifteen months, eight had been spent on the New Orleans trip and two on military campaign. He had seen more of the world before his twentieth birthday than many nineteenth-century Americans saw in their lifetimes. Now, though, there could be no avoiding the responsibilities at home. The war had devastated the depressed family businesses. Moses was terribly overextended, and meeting even small financial obligations had become increasingly difficult. It would take all the energies of both Moses and Stephen Austin to restore the family's damaged fortune.

Not only had the war disrupted shipping, it had also drained the frontier of two essentials: money and able-bodied laborers. With his usual exuberance and optimism, Moses—with Stephen as a willing participant—attacked both problems simultaneously. In January 1814 Stephen himself confessed to his new brother-in-law James Bryan that he had "not one Cent of money." He was not alone; throughout the frontier the shortage of money was acute. Missourians had to rely on private sources for credit, for there was not a single bank in the territory. To remedy this situation, Moses joined a group of St. Louis businessmen who sought to establish the Bank of St. Louis. The territorial legislature granted them a charter in August 1813, but the organizers were unable to raise enough capital to open the bank. Undaunted by their initial failure, they kept trying. On his frequent business trips to St. Louis, the younger Austin monitored the progress of the bank proposal. However, it was late 1816 before the bank finally opened its doors. Moses won a seat on the board of directors, and he and Stephen hoped that this new source of money, along with the end of the war, would usher in an era of prosperity for Missouri and the Austin enterprises.[26]

As Moses and his associates wrestled with the problems of chartering and capitalizing their bank, Moses and Stephen plotted a new course for the mines. Labor had been hard to find even in good times; the war had exacerbated the problem. It was the same challenge that Stephen Austin would face several years later in Texas: On the frontier land was fairly cheap. Why would anyone perform backbreaking work for someone else when he could acquire his own piece of land? The solution seemed obvious. If the labor of free men was unavailable, use slaves. In the absence of moral objections—and neither of the Austins expressed any hesitation on that account—the only barrier was cost.

For the Austins in 1814, cost was a high barrier indeed. Purchasing slaves was out of the question. So that fall, as diplomats worked in Europe to negotiate an end to the war, Moses dispatched Stephen to Russellville, Kentucky, to do some negotiating of his own. His mission was to lease some twenty-five slaves from Col. Anthony Butler, a wealthy slaveholder and political crony of Andrew Jackson's. How the Austins knew Butler is unclear, but in February 1815, the month after the smashing American victory at the Battle of New Orleans, Stephen and Butler sealed the deal. With the end of the war, the lead market showed signs of improving, so instead of the original twenty-five slaves, the agreement was for sixty. Some of these may have gone to work for James Bryan and two other Austin associates, but at least half of them went to Mine à Breton. Shortly after the new hands arrived, the ever-optimistic Moses voiced the belief that he would be able to "sett all things right again in a few months." [27]

When met with financial setbacks, Moses Austin had always preferred expansion over retrenchment. Sometimes his boldness had paid off; this time it brought disaster. Just feeding the slaves was an enormous burden. Although economic conditions were improving in 1815 and 1816, they did not improve enough for Moses to satisfy his many creditors and meet his expenses. The creditors began to sue, and one unfavorable court judgment followed another. Even nephew Henry Austin, who had so generously supported Maria and the children when they were stranded in the East five years earlier, obtained a $2,000 judgment for the money Moses owed him. [28]

Moses continued to regard the situation as temporary. After all, the family still owned the sprawling Mine à Breton tract, with its rich mineral deposits and handsome improvements, and many other valuable properties scattered about eastern Missouri. In 1813, Moses had successfully lobbied the territorial legislature to create the county of Washington and to locate the new county seat, which he named Potosi, on Austin land adjacent to the Mine à Breton. Settlers were pouring into the territory; statehood could not be far off. Surely things would turn around.

The Austins struggled through most of 1816, their situation growing worse. That fall Moses reached a momentous decision: he would retire from the lead business. This astonished all who knew him, including his family. "Their is strange revulitions taking place at Durham Hall," Emily observed. Not only did Moses intend to get out of the lead business, he planned to leave Mine à Breton altogether and move to Herculaneum.[29]

Stephen probably understood his father's actions better than most. For one thing, Moses had been so ill that fall that he could scarcely leave the house. Relief from the daily grind of managing the mines and a change of atmosphere might help. Moreover, Moses may have wanted the freedom to explore other ventures. As early as 1813 he had been eyeing Spanish Mexico in the "belief that an adventure to that Country would be both safe and advantageous." At that particular time he was probably referring to trade possibilities, not colonization, but given his later actions this much was clear: Moses Austin had no intention of retiring to his rocking chair. Whatever he did next would be limited only by his imagination. He just needed to reorganize his affairs and regain his health in preparation for the next daring move.[30]

Not surprisingly, Stephen figured prominently in Moses's plans. Rather than sell Mine à Breton, Moses decided to lease the entire operation to Stephen for five years, beginning in January 1817. The rent was to be 20 percent of the lead produced. What made Moses think that this would enable him to begin meeting his obligations? And more important, what made the younger Austin think he could begin making profits sufficient to keep the entire family afloat? The key lay in making the operation more efficient. The first crucial step was to bring labor costs under control. It had been nearly two years since the Austins had leased Anthony Butler's slaves. While the precise terms of the lease are not known, the agreement, together with the upkeep of the slaves, had placed an unbearable strain on the Austins. So Stephen traveled back to Kentucky with a new proposal for Butler: the leasing agreement would be nullified, and the two men would become partners. Butler's contribution would be the slaves — thirty "working hands" — and Stephen's would be the property, plus his services as manager. Butler's specified share of the profits is not known. "I have taken possession of the Mines and the whole establishment here and Commenced business under the Stile of S. F. Austin and Co.," Stephen announced to his brother-in-law in February 1817, "and am flattering myself with the pleasing hope of being able by the end of this year to free the Family from every embarrassment."[31]

He knew it would not be easy, but the twenty-three-year-old possessed enormous energy and determination. He enthusiastically plunged into his new enterprise. "I shall literally bury myself this Spring and Summer in the Mines," he wrote, sounding much like his father, "and if attention and industry will affect anything I shall do much." Soon he was sinking new mine shafts and smelting as much lead as possible. There would be few distractions, because Moses and Maria were about to leave Durham Hall for their new home on the Mississippi River in Herculaneum. Brown was in school back East. Emily and James Bryan and their one-year-old son, William Joel, lived twenty miles away at Hazel Run. As the nearest members of his immediate family, Stephen hoped that they would visit often. Joel's "prattle would be music to me," he remarked rather melodramatically, "compared to the *dull* cheerless, chil[l]ing Silence which will pervade the Hall when deserted by all but a Solatary Batchelor!!!"[32]

But life for Austin was not all toil and solitary bachelorhood. His father had groomed him to be a man of public affairs as well as a businessman. Moses had always been deeply involved in politics. Whether seeking a state roofing contract, lobbying Congress for a protective tariff or incorporation, applying for a Spanish government land grant, or securing a territorial bank charter, he had understood that a successful large-scale business enterprise needed the patronage, protection, and good will of the government. The image of the frontier as a place where rugged individualists pursued their dreams unfettered and unassisted by governmental institutions was romantic nonsense, and both Moses and Stephen Austin knew it. It was no accident that when called upon to offer a toast at a Fourth of July celebration several years earlier, Moses had chosen to salute Alexander Hamilton, the early republic's greatest proponent of government economic activism.[33]

Stephen had carefully laid the groundwork for a political career that would complement his business activities. His militia service provided important connections and the military credentials so often deemed necessary for politicians. He had even gotten a promotion. A year after the campaign against the Indians, Governor William Clark (of Lewis and Clark fame), citing "special trust and confidence in the patriotism, valour, fidelity and abilities of Stephen F. Austin," appointed him adjutant of the sixth regiment of the territorial militia. A few months later, in June 1815, he had been initiated into the Ste. Genevieve Masonic Lodge, the first chapter of that order west of the Mississippi. His membership in the Masons, like his militia experience, would be a valuable asset in the years ahead.[34]

Two months after becoming a Mason, Austin ran for a seat in the territorial legislature, winning the four-man race with 200 votes to 177 for his nearest competitor. In December 1815, barely twenty-two years old, he took his seat in the lower house. This was only the second legislature in Missouri since its creation as a territory apart from Louisiana, so there were no veteran legislators. The members, who met only a few weeks a year and received a modest per diem salary, were not professional politicians. So in spite of his youth and inexperience, Austin was about as well poised as anyone to play a constructive role in the legislature.[35]

He soon demonstrated that he understood the game. The first responsibility of any elected representative is to help the home district. Representing Washington County, which was then still largely an undeveloped frontier region, Austin worked successfully for bills establishing public roads and post offices.[36]

Other measures that he advocated were as vital to the territory overall as they were to his constituents in particular. This was especially the case with legislation concerning the "final adjustment and settlement of land claims in this territory," by far the most important political issue facing the territory. Because of Missouri's long and irregular history under the rule of three different nations, land titles were a tangle of overlapping and conflicting claims. The Austin family had endured its share of such title disputes. So bad was the situation that, as of 1816, not a single acre of

Missouri's public lands had been offered for sale, even though the United States had owned the territory since 1803. Squatters proliferated. During the legislative session, both Governor Clark and President James Madison issued proclamations evicting squatters from the public lands, evoking a huge outcry among the settlers. Austin's old regimental commander from the War of 1812, Col. Alexander McNair, said the militia would refuse to march against the squatters. The legislature wisely passed resolutions delaying the enforcement of the eviction proclamations, and it appears that Austin supported this popular measure. Indeed, the protracted brouhaha over land titles must have made a deep impression on him; later, when issuing thousands of land titles in Texas, he vividly remembered the "difficulties and confusion which arose" over titles in Missouri and thus worked zealously to obtain precise surveys and to issue sound titles.[37]

The voters apparently approved of their young representative's work in St. Louis, for in the summer of 1816 he won reelection. Austin served three more one-year terms in the legislature, rapidly gaining a reputation as one of the territory's ablest lawmakers. He continued to champion measures that served his constituents' interests as well as his own. In the 1816–1817 session, for example, he introduced a bill to send a memorial to Congress requesting a higher tariff on imported lead. Lead mining was not only his own business, it was the principal business in his district. Virtually everyone in his county depended either directly or indirectly on the prosperity of the lead industry. Significantly, Austin coupled his memorial with another cause: a portion of the revenue from government-owned lead mines would go to support an academy. He supplemented this provision with another bill that would establish a public lottery for the benefit of an academy in Potosi. Who could argue with legislation that promoted education, especially if local taxes did not have to be raised to pay for it?[38]

These pieces of legislation reveal a great deal about the young representative. Even more than his work to clear up the confusion over land titles, they demonstrate Austin's belief that using official influence to promote private interests was legitimate, so long as those interests were consistent with the public good. His legislative record also shows consistent support for an activist government. Transportation, finance, education, and industrial development should not be left strictly in private hands, he

The Pierre Chouteau, Sr., residence, St. Louis, where
the Missouri Territorial Legislature met during
Austin's time as representative.
Courtesy, Missouri Historical Society.

believed. Austin's views on the proper role of government stemmed from his family background and education in Federalist New England, the example of his pro-government father, and his exposure to the progressive nationalism of Henry Clay's Kentucky. Had his career path kept him in American politics for another decade, he would have found himself in agreement on many issues with Clay's Whig Party.

But whenever business and government become bedfellows, the line between constructive public policy and conflict of interest can be terribly thin. For example, Austin could argue with some justification that the lead tariff would benefit Missouri as a whole, not just himself. In his pursuit of banking legislation, however, the case for the greater public good is not so clear cut. When Austin first entered the legislature his father's pet project, the Bank of St. Louis, still existed only on paper. The legislature had granted the institution's charter two years earlier, but the wartime money shortage had made it impossible to raise the capital required to open for business. The directors decided to seek a restructuring of their charter. Among the changes would be reducing the price of the stock to make it affordable to more investors and bringing in the territorial government as a partner in the bank, giving the institution a quasi-public status roughly analogous to that of the Bank of the United States. As the directors formulated these ideas, a rival group laid plans to open a competing bank, the Bank of Missouri.[39]

Moses drew up a long document to guide Stephen in his quest to secure the desired changes in the bank charter and to defeat the competitors' request. When Stephen took the floor in December 1816 he realized that his motives were suspect. "I most sensibly feel the disadvantages under which I labor," he explained, "in consequence of my connection with and Interest in the Bank of St Louis as a Stockholder." The "Supposition" that he was acting "from Motives of Self interest" was "already fixed in some of your Minds," he told his fellow representatives. "I should spurn those traitorous motives and recoil with horror from those incentives of individual Interest which would lead me to adopt a course in the slightest degree incompatible with the interest of my Constituents or . . . of my Country. . . . [W]ere I as disconnected with the Bank of St L[ouis] as I am with that of M[issouri] . . . the course I have adopted would have been the same." Believing the best defense to be a good offense, he proceeded to denounce any "implication" of impure motives as being "most infamous and malicious," "unfounded and uncharitable and base." He went on like this for some time, arguing that those who condemned his conduct were themselves guilty of "Self-Interest prejudice and hatred," deserving only of "contempt."[40]

Clearly the youthful representative protested too much. He *was* the Bank of St. Louis's inside man in the legislature, and the Austin family stood much to gain by the success of the bank—especially if it could secure a monopoly on banking in the territory. This is not to say that the reasoning behind his arguments was all fallacious. The rapidly growing, cash- and credit-strapped territory did need a strong financial institution. Very likely the bank would be able neither to attract the capital nor hold the confidence of the populace without the active participation of the territorial government. And Missouri quite probably could not support two banks at this point in time. In the immediate wake of his speech his proposals passed, but before the end of the session they had been overturned. The Bank of St. Louis did not receive the special patronage of the government, and the rival bank received its charter and opened a few months later.[41]

THREE

New Beginnings
1819–1820

L and. In the years after the War of 1812, the word rang in the ears of Missourians. With the British threat ended and Indians a decreasing problem, immense quantities of public land lay to the west. Poor men looked to the valleys of the Missouri, Arkansas, or Red Rivers for fertile, affordable farms. Rich men, or those who would be rich, looked at these regions and saw golden visions of quick profits through speculation.

At the beginning of 1819, Stephen F. Austin was immersed in his failing mining business, his legislative career, and the affairs of the embattled Bank of St. Louis. Yet he, too, heard the call of western lands. Despite his precarious financial condition—or perhaps because of it—he could not resist. He seems not to have considered that the call of easy riches might actually be a siren song, luring the unwary toward disaster.

It had begun innocently enough. Some time in 1818, Austin acquired an interest in a tract on the Red River called Long Prairie, in the southwestern corner of what is today Arkansas. It was common practice for American settlers to squat on public land in the expectation that their presence on the property and physical improvement of it would give them a right to the land by preemption once the government officially made lands in that area available. The year before, a Methodist preacher named William Stevenson had led a group of settlers from Washington County, Missouri—Austin's home county—and established a settlement in the vicinity of the Red River site. This must have been the source of Austin's initial connection with the place. He could not yet get legal title to the land, but by January 1819 his letters were mentioning his "improvement in the Long Prairie." There is no way to know the nature of this improvement, how it got there, or how Austin could claim it as his. Preemption claims, though, rarely required an elaborate improvement; something as modest as the construction of a shack sometimes sufficed. Since Austin apparently had never been to the site, he probably had paid one of the Stevenson settlers a nominal amount for work they had done there.[1]

Austin understood that his claim might not hold up, especially since nobody knew precisely when, or by what rules, the public lands would become available. But he also knew that when the federal government officially opened the public lands and organized the territorial government, those who had already located the best sites and established some sort of claim to them would be in a prime position to profit from speculation. Austin needed to strengthen his claim at Long Prairie.[2]

The best way to do this was through the use of New Madrid certificates. When Austin had taken his ill-fated trip down the Mississippi with his father's lead barge in 1812, he had witnessed the devastation of the massive New Madrid earthquake. The quake had rendered an extensive region unusable for farming. In 1815, Congress issued certificates allowing farmers impoverished by the quake to claim public lands farther west. These certificates soon fell into the hands of speculators, and over the next few years the certificates circulated freely in Missouri, rising and falling in value with the speculative environment. In Arkansas, New Madrid certificates offered speculators their surest way to establish titles to the most valuable tracts of land in the new territory.[3]

In January 1819, Austin heard that surveying would soon commence in the Red River country, the first step toward opening the public lands to settlement. In partnership with James Bryan, he bought a New Madrid certificate to help secure his claim to the Long Prairie site. He furthermore advised Bryan "to return as quick as possible with all the Money you [can] and buy Madrid Claims."[4]

Austin was buoyant about the opportunities in Arkansas. He estimated his "improvement in the Long Prairie" to be worth the astronomical figure of $100 an acre, although there is no way to know how many acres he was referring to or how he could have sold the land without having clear title to it. He was certain, though, that "choice Land will sell for not less than 50$ at the publick sales on Red River." The land boom would also mean a market for merchandise, and he urged Bryan to send goods to Long Prairie in the belief that "a small Store will do very well there." He also accepted Bryan's offer to provide him with "four yoke of oxen, or two yoke of oxen and four Horses Ten Cows and one or two Bulls." At the very least Austin intended to raise livestock on the place, and he left it up to Bryan "whether you will enter into the Cotton business or not."[5]

Austin's plans for developing the Long Prairie property were just the beginning of his interest in Arkansas. He had caught the speculation fever and caught it badly. But before he could leave for Arkansas he had to attend the December legislative session in St. Louis. It was during this trip that he made his vow never to marry until he could free the family from debt. A day or two later he traveled back down the river to Herculaneum, where he was "endeavoring to arra[n]ge my Father's business and my own so as to leave this country." With those arrangements finally finished in late January, he hurried back to St. Louis to negotiate the purchase of as many New Madrid certificates as possible. By the end of February he had bought more than $9,000 worth of the claims, all on credit, with plans to locate them on multiple sites across Arkansas. It was an immense gamble. If it succeeded, he might realize his dream of freeing the family from debt. If it failed, he was ruined.[6]

Austin itched to get his enterprise at Long Prairie under way and to locate and survey the other Arkansas sites that he hoped to claim. Delays could allow competing speculators to claim the choicest tracts. But he could not simply drop everything in Missouri and depart for Arkansas; his business affairs were too much in disarray. At great cost he had already terminated the ill-conceived slave-leasing arrangement with Anthony Butler, essentially shutting down the mines, but that was not his only large obligation. In November 1818, Austin and Bryan had terminated one of their joint mercantile ventures, leaving Austin owing $3,000 to his brother-in-law. Numerous other creditors continued to press him. And as bad as his own affairs were, his father's were worse. "My Fathers business is all in confusion," Stephen wrote from Herculaneum in January, as he and Moses plotted to keep their creditors at bay. That was no mean task. In February, as Stephen was borrowing $9,000 from individuals to buy New Madrid claims, the Bank of St. Louis filed suit to recover the more than $9,000 he already owed the bank. An agreement was worked out whereby Moses assumed responsibility for the debt, but no sooner had that occurred than the struggling bank called on Moses to repay $15,000 that he had borrowed earlier against the Mine à Breton property. Both Austins were outraged that the bank would make this sudden demand from one of its founders and strongest supporters, but they thought that everything probably could be worked out. Still, it could not have come at a worse time. "I am very much embarrased, as every cent I owe in the Country must be paid before I can start [for Arkansas]," Stephen wrote in April.[7]

Of course he did not mean that he would actually *pay* all of those debts at once; the best he could do was pay the most urgent ones, refinancing and deferring the rest. Some, like the notes that the bank held, were shifted onto his father. To cover others he took out new loans. In April he was able to state that he had "nearly settled" his affairs in Missouri. "My bank debt will be arranged by my father who has assured the payment of it, and when I start I shall be able to go nearly *quite free.*" How long that "freedom" would last depended mightily on his success in Arkansas.[8]

In April 1819 Stephen left Missouri for Arkansas. He floated down the Mississippi to the Red River, which he then ascended to Long Prairie. From there he could travel to the Arkansas and Ouachita rivers to scout out the specific sites where he and his partners hoped to establish claims. The goal of the speculation was town-building. In a scheme repeated countless times during the settlement of the American West, Austin and his associates hoped to identify sites along future trade routes, establish title, lay out towns, and then profit handsomely from the sale of lots as the towns began to flourish. The general locations had been determined that spring in St. Louis. One was to be at Long Prairie, another near the juncture of the Ouachita and Caddo Rivers, and a third at a place on the Arkansas River known as the Little Rock. The latter held the most potential for quick profit, because it was thought to be a leading candidate for the future seat of the territorial government. In addition to James Bryan, Austin's partners in the speculation were Missouri businessmen George Tennille, William M. O'Hara, and Robert Andrews. Of these, Austin's involvement with Tennille was the most significant; Austin had bought half of four different New Madrid claims from Tennille for $7,400.[9]

At this juncture, Austin did a rather puzzling thing. Shortly after arriving in Arkansas he sold all his interest in the three claims to Bryan, who assumed the debts that Austin had incurred in acquiring them. The exact purpose of this move is not clear, but it would be a mistake to assume that Austin had lost all interest in Arkansas land speculation. Upon his marriage to Emily Austin, James Bryan had become as much a member of the Austin family as if he been born an Austin. In nineteenth-century fashion, Stephen always addressed him as "brother," and Moses considered him a third "son." Just as Moses's and Stephen's business affairs had always been inextricably conjoined, so now were Stephen's and Bryan's. Most likely the transfer from Stephen to his brother-in-law was done for accounting purposes, better to allow the Austins to manage their increasingly heavy burden of debt. Stephen continued to work to ensure the success of the speculation, labor that he would not have expended had he been disconnected from the venture. Above all, Stephen knew that if the speculation failed and the promissory notes went unpaid, the creditors would come to him.[10]

Austin remained hopeful through the summer of 1819. "The locations we have made are considered by every one to be the best that could have been made in the country," he reported to William O'Hara, "and will certainly yeild a handsome profit the moment they can be brought into market." He believed that the Arkansas properties would soon be worth $200,000, which would solve all the family's problems. In August, Moses reported to Brown Austin the news that Stephen "was well and in good health and that his prospects were great and that he was in high spirits." Apparently as a part of the deal with Bryan, Stephen had received Bryan's interest in all of the livestock, implements, improvements, and the crop growing at the Long Prairie farm.[11]

As summer turned to fall, Austin's optimism began to fade. It is impossible to know much about the nature of the farming operation, but neither the farm nor the store at Long Prairie brought much profit. Austin appears to have taken three or four of the family slaves to Arkansas to do the menial labor—raising hogs, cattle, and horses, and growing corn and perhaps some peas and beans. For twenty dollars a month he employed a white man named Leroy Ferguson, probably as an overseer. By October Austin's disillusionment was apparent. "[I] am not as well satisfied as I expected," he explained. Navigation of the Red River, on which his business depended, had proved "much more difficult" than he had anticipated. Even worse, the country turned out to be *"very sickly."* Austin had been ill "nearly the whole summer as indeed has almost every person around me." His farmhands were frequently unable to work. "These reasons," he explained, "induce me to wish for a *change* of situation." Austin wrote these lines in a letter to an old friend, Jacob Pettit, with whom he had served in the Missouri militia. Pettit owned a cotton plantation on the lower Mississippi near Baton Rouge, and Austin was impressed with the country. He asked Pettit if he knew "of any *Small Estate* that could be purchased on a liberal credit." Austin told Pettit that he could "put on four or five negros of my own the first season & as many the 2d season." If such a plantation could not be purchased, Austin would consider renting. However, he thought he could raise between $1,000 and $1,500 for a down payment, if necessary.[12]

It is difficult to imagine Stephen F. Austin as a Louisiana cotton planter, but his inquiry to Pettit demonstrates his determination to pursue other options. Over the next six months Austin would make several false starts toward such a change. In none of them did he act vigorously and decisively. His indecision makes sense only when viewed in the context of developments within his extended family and with the economy of the frontier.

The Panic of 1819, which struck the eastern United States early in the year, had finally reached the Southwest. Money had been tight at least since the War of 1812, but the brisk traffic in land and strong immigration from the East had somewhat insulated the frontier from the depression. That all came to a halt at about the time Austin moved to Long Prairie. Back home, Austin's creditors began to sue. His father and James Bryan had assumed his largest debts, but in November two smaller creditors won civil judgments in Missouri courts. This time he could not turn to his father or brother-in-law for relief, for both of them were themselves the targets of lawsuits, and both began to lose property to foreclosure. In the meantime, Moses was desperately trying to sell Mine à Breton, which he had mortgaged to the now-insolvent Bank of St. Louis. Moses's debt to the bank stood at $25,000, and frantic, last-minute negotiations failed to produce an agreement to postpone the disaster. On March 11, 1820, the Austin family suffered its most humiliating defeat. The sheriff of Jefferson County, Missouri, appeared at Moses Austin's doorstep and arrested him for nonpayment of his debts. Following a short stay in jail, Moses was forced to watch as the entire Mine à Breton estate was sold at auction.[13]

As these traumatic proceedings unfolded in Missouri, Stephen muddled along in Arkansas. The territorial government was being organized, and in November elections were scheduled to choose Arkansas's delegate to Congress. Five men announced their candidacy, but Austin was not among them. Then, less than two weeks before the election, he announced for the office. It was too late to do much campaigning; indeed, his candidacy apparently was not even known north of the Arkansas River. Yet he ran surprisingly well, finishing a close second. A contemporary observer remarked that it was "undoubtedly true that he was the most popular man among the candidates," and it seems almost certain that a more serious campaign would have brought him victory. Austin himself left no explanation of his candidacy, but clearly his heart was not in it. Most likely he was drafted to run by his inner circle of business and political associates, who needed an influential voice in territorial politics.[14]

In spite of the failed congressional race and his inquiries into planting opportunities in Louisiana, Austin stayed at Long Prairie into early 1820. Why did he linger when he clearly yearned for a change? There was, of course, a crop of some sort to harvest and hands to provide for at the farm. Returning to Missouri was not an option. He had relinquished his seat in the Missouri legislature, the Panic had killed all business opportunities there, and Moses's creditors were about to seize Mine à Breton. Stephen himself might risk imprisonment for debt were he to return. Long Prairie had proved unhealthy and unprofitable as a farm, and a town site that Bryan and his partners laid out there failed to attract much interest. The partners' speculation on the Ouachita apparently met a similar fate. The financial salvation of the Austin family came down to one hope: their claim on the Arkansas River at the site known as the Little Rock.[15]

It did in fact appear that the territorial capital would be placed at Little Rock. Unfortunately, a competing group of speculators led by William Russell claimed title to the same site based on preemption rights.[16] Both sides laid out towns, one on top of the other, and hired lawyers to press their claims. The stakes were high, for if the legislature indeed chose the site for the new capital, land values would skyrocket.[17]

In the spring of 1820, as the dispute escalated and the legislature deliberated on the location of the capital, Austin left Long Prairie to lobby for his group's interests at the temporary capital, Arkansas Post. He believed that he could sell part of Bryan's share in the speculation "in a way that will secure the seat of Government if any thing will do it." Plainly put, Austin would bribe key members of the legislature by offering them a part of Bryan's share in the Little Rock claim.[18]

As it happened, their partner, William O'Hara, had anticipated this tactic and had already brought Governor James Miller into the group by selling him a one-twelfth interest in the claim (no doubt at a bargain price), thus assuring the partners a degree of political influence in the territorial government. The problem was that the preemption claimholders were playing the same game; William Russell had brought the territorial secretary, the receiver of public monies, and the speaker of the house into *their* group in the same manner. None of this was illegal; it was all highly unethical. But that was the norm on the frontier. The rush to turn a quick profit seemingly blinded otherwise honorable men.[19]

Stephen took the preemptioners' tactics personally. He entertained no doubt that his own group's claim was the strongest and would be confirmed. The actions of the opposition could be explained only by greed and dishonesty—never mind that both groups were playing the same game. Russell appears to have been a long-standing enemy of the Austins.

"Were it not for this man Russell," Austin complained, "our unfortunate family might yet be enabled to secure a small, but decent competence for if his opposition was removed I believe there would be no difficulty in getting the seat of government removed to the L. Rock, which might be the means of saving a worthy and respectabl[e] family from total ruin and want whereas he gains nothing by his opposition, *but the pleasure* of gratifying his enmity and passions." It was the old conspiratorial view of the family's enemies that Austin had learned from his parents. Convinced of his own rectitude, he could ascribe only sinister motives to those who opposed him. This conviction that the family's enemies were out to ruin him fed Austin's growing cynicism. "I have *now* learnt to be surprised at nothing I see in man, unless it is when I find him honest," he wrote. "My opinion of mankind has, unfortunately perhaps, been as bad as it could be for some years, but the longer I live the worse it grows." [20]

Ultimately the warring groups of speculators compromised and shared the claims to the Little Rock site, but the delays caused by the dispute robbed Bryan and the Austins of their chance to share in the profits. Before the final settlement Bryan signed over his share to Henry Elliott, a kinsman of the Austins, apparently to shield it from foreclosure. Elliott died before the family could realize any profit from the claim, which fell into the hands of his creditors.[21] In the meantime, Austin left Arkansas Post in May to try to salvage what he could from his and Bryan's neglected stores. Both men needed to sell all their assets and collect on all outstanding accounts in order to pay their debts. "If my father should come to Little Rock," Austin instructed Bryan dully, "you may tell him that I wish to go to the Mouth of White River to live if I can take any thing there to begin with and if that cannot be done I shall go down the Mississippi and seek employ." It was hardly an inspired plan.[22]

But Austin was not destined to leave Arkansas yet. On July 10, 1820, barely a month after Austin told Bryan of his plan to seek employment elsewhere, Gov. James Miller appointed Austin judge of Arkansas's First Circuit Court. Austin may have actively sought the appointment, for it paid the decent salary of $1,200 a year. Or his friends, knowing the state of his finances, may have urged the governor to consider him for the post. The appointment, however, may also have involved a little political back-scratching: Miller may have been repaying the favor of receiving an interest in the Austin group's Little Rock speculation.[23]

All in all, it was a promising opportunity for a young man who had suffered such overwhelming setbacks. The workload was light, and although the salary could not begin to cover the family's debts, at least it was steady income. Judges served three-year terms unless removed by the governor. His creditors might show some forbearance in prosecution of the debts owed by a judge. But if Austin made such calculations in accepting the position, he had not bargained on the capricious actions of territorial legislature. Three months after his appointment the legislature abolished the circuit court system and transferred its cases to other courts. Austin was out of a job almost before he had started it. Indeed, only slender evidence survives to suggest that he actually presided at court. One remark from his cousin Elias Elliott in a July 28 letter seems to confirm that Austin actually did hear some cases: "Stephen is at Lawrence [County] Court," Elliott told James Bryan. The only other indication of Austin's tenure on the bench is the fact that later he was occasionally addressed as Judge Austin.[24]

His stint with the circuit court probably did little to lift the overall sense of gloom that had settled over Austin, and the poor health that he had suffered at Long Prairie cannot have helped matters. Earlier in the spring he had retreated to "the springs" in search of a cure for "Fever and vomiting and purging Blood." But his low spirits, evident in several of his letters of 1820, must have been largely caused by helplessness. To be an Austin was to be master of one's fate, and Stephen nor Moses nor James Bryan could pretend to possess such mastery. The news of Moses's brief imprisonment, followed by the loss of Mine à Breton, must truly have come as a blow to Stephen. His own affairs were nearly as bad. Although he had sold his interest in the New Madrid speculations to Bryan, the creditors still held Austin's promissory notes. If Bryan could not pay — which he manifestly could not — the creditors would come after Austin. The largest of them, George Tennille, did exactly that in June 1820, hiring a lawyer to sue Austin for $1,526. And that was only the first of five installments that would eventually fall due on this particular debt. Unlike his father, Stephen Austin had no grand estate that could be foreclosed upon.

In the absence of anything resembling modern bankruptcy laws, debtors could expect little relief from the courts. Debts such as those to Tennille and to Anthony Butler would hang over his head for years to come.[25]

Given these realities, there can be little wonder at the severity of Austin's depression. "I shall remain here this summer," he told Bryan in the spring of 1820, "and after that it is uncertain where I shall go. If my Father saves enough to support him and you get through your dificulties so as to support Emily in the stile she aught to live, I shall be satisfied. As for myself I believe I am nearly indifferent what becomes of me, or whether I live or die." Moses Austin, bent but not broken by his own misfortune, would have been horrified to hear such defeatist words from his oldest son. But Stephen placed an important qualifier onto the end of this dreary statement: "unless I am to be of use to my Family by living, and then I should be as anxious to live as any one." He could not surrender to apathy and depression, even if he wanted to. There had to be a way out.[26]

Moses Austin believed he knew the way. Ordinary men might have been broken—or at least humbled—by what he had recently gone through, but Moses Austin was no ordinary man. While Stephen brooded in Arkansas his father had been formulating a plan to redeem the family's shattered fortune and tarnished reputation. As had been the case twice before in Moses's life, redemption lay in the West.

He had been eyeing Mexico at least since 1813, when he had ventured the opinion that "an adventure to that Country would be both safe and advantageous." He had probably been referring to trade with Santa Fe, but Moses understood the opportunities that might await an enterprising American in the resource-rich but underdeveloped Spanish colony. After all, he had seized just such an opportunity back in 1797 when he journeyed into Spanish Louisiana and persuaded the authorities there to grant him the Mine à Breton.[27]

Moses had not been alone in following the more recent events taking place in Mexico. Since the beginning of the Mexican independence movement in 1810, Americans on the southwestern frontier had been fascinated by the struggle unfolding to the south and west. Indeed, some Americans' interest in Mexico had gone beyond mere fascination; there had been several well-publicized armed expeditions by American adventurers seeking to advance the cause of Mexican independence or, more deviously, to detach Texas from Spain. A private army commanded by former U.S. Army officer Augustus Magee joined what had evolved into an independence movement by 1812–13 and briefly controlled Texas. After Magee's death his successor was defeated by royalist forces in a bloody battle. In 1819 another expedition, under the command of Natchez merchant James Long, had invaded and controlled parts of Texas, with mixed success. The outcome of his expedition was still undecided when Moses began seriously studying his Texas options.[28]

These events took place against the backdrop of important international developments. Spain, long in decline as a world power and buffeted by the Napoleonic Wars, had enacted a liberal constitution in 1812. This had helped to convince Americans like Moses Austin that Spain would open its borders to international trade. However, the repeated military incursions along the U.S.-Texas frontier, along with continuing instability in Spain, had prevented this dream from coming true. Another source of instability was the indefinite boundary between the United States and Spanish Texas. Many Americans believed that the Louisiana Purchase had included much of present-day Texas, and they noisily demanded that the American government assert that claim.

The turmoil and uncertainty in the northernmost provinces of New Spain, together with America's rapid westward expansion, convinced many Americans that the region must inevitably capitulate to American-style republicanism, if not to actual control by the United States. Stephen F. Austin's attitude was typical. In an Independence Day speech at Potosi in 1818, he had extolled the virtues of American civilization and the Founding Fathers. Near the end of the oration he alluded to Mexico's struggle for independence:

> *the same spirit that unsheathed the sword of Washington* and sacrificed servitude and slavery in the flames of the Revolution, will also flash across the Gulph of Mexico and over the western wilderness that separates independent America from the enslaved colonies of Spain, and darting the beams of intelligence

into the benighted souls of their inhabitants awake them from the stupor of slaves to the energy of freemen, from the degradation of vassals to the dignity of sovereigns. Already is this great work commenced, already are the banners of freedom unfurled in the south. Despotism totters, liberty expands her pinions, and in a few years more will rescue Spanish America from the dominion of tyranny.[29]

Predictions notwithstanding, Spain still controlled Mexico, and in 1819, Spain and the United States signed the Transcontinental (or Adams-Onís) Treaty, which designated the Sabine River as the boundary between the U.S. and Spanish Texas. Disgust over the treaty had led to the James Long expedition, but this very confirmation of Spain's ownership of Texas spurred Moses Austin to a different kind of action. The treaty meant, among other things, that the Spanish government would be able to issue valid land titles in Texas.

Precisely when Moses first began considering the possibility of Texas colonization remains uncertain. The Transcontinental Treaty was signed in February 1819, and news of it soon reached Missouri. Years later, long after Moses's death and his own successful colonization of Texas, Stephen Austin gave this account: "In 1819, he [Moses] proposed to me the idea of forming a colony in Texas. The treaty of De Onis had been brought to a conclusion, and the right of Spain to Texas appeared unquestionable, and grants from the Spanish authorities would therefore be valid. The project was discussed by us in Durham Hall at 'Mine A. Burton' for several days, and adopted." [30]

It is possible that the Austins did indeed discuss Texas opportunities before Stephen's departure for Arkansas in April 1819, just as Stephen's account suggests. Maybe their discussions even touched on a colonization venture. But it is unlikely that such a definite course of action was actually "adopted" by both men at that early date. Stephen's activities in Arkansas over the following sixteen months gave little, if any, indication that he was preparing to colonize Texas. It was convenient, several years later, for him to act as though the move to Arkansas had been simply the first step in a well-laid plan. (Taking credit for the good things that happened to him was an Austin trademark.) As Austin told it to his brother, following his conference with his father he had commenced the Long Prairie farm specifically "to facilitate us in our Texas colonization project." The available evidence suggests otherwise.[31]

The earliest recorded discussion of Texas in the Austin correspondence dates to the summer of 1819, after Stephen had left for Arkansas. Stephen reported to Moses that "two grand expeditions are now underway for the spanish country. 300 families are making ready to take possession of that part of Red River with in the *spanish lines which* comes within 10 miles of his plantation. An Other is now making up — to take possession of *St. Antone* [San Antonio] under the command of a General Long." More Texas news, most of it exaggerating the success of the Long expedition, followed in subsequent letters. Moses relayed this information to his friend, the renowned naturalist Henry Schoolcraft, and told Schoolcraft that he wished to visit Texas with Schoolcraft if Schoolcraft was going. By September, Moses's plans were a bit more definite. "I shall as soon as my business is Closed in this Country visit St. Antonia, which place I have but little doubt is now in the hands of the Americans," he informed Schoolcraft.[32]

These letters shed light on the Austins' position regarding Texas in mid-1819, when Stephen first went to Long Prairie. From the beginning of the Arkansas venture the younger Austin had touted Long Prairie as a profitable location for agriculture, merchandising, and town building. There was always the *possibility* that the development of the region would spill over into Texas — if Spain allowed emigration, if the United States acquired Texas, or if Texas gained independence via James Long or someone else. No matter which of these happened, Stephen would be in a good position to profit. It is a far cry from these calculations, however, to the conclusion that he had established the Long Prairie farm as a jumping-off point to a planned Austin colony in the interior of Texas. In mid-1819 both Austins believed that Long might succeed, so it is unlikely that they would have launched a "colonization project" in the midst of such upheaval. Given the uncertainty of the situation, Moses could not have had a very definite plan in mind when he began talking of visiting San Antonio.[33]

In February 1820, nearly a year after the conference in which Moses and Stephen allegedly "adopted" their colonization project, Moses wrote Brown Austin that he intended to "go down the Country in the spring to see your brother [in Arkansas] and determine what I shall then do." This vague plan was hardly a step toward executing a master design for the colonization of Texas. At this point Stephen was fighting off severe illness, operating the Long Prairie farm, struggling with his and Bryan's stores, and lobbying for the success of his group's Little Rock speculation. Stephen knew that his father might be coming to see him in Arkansas, but he did not seem particularly eager for the visit. As noted, he had told James Bryan that if Moses showed up in Little Rock, Bryan was to tell him that Stephen wanted to go to the White River or down the Mississippi to find work. Getting involved in whatever new scheme Moses might be hatching was the last thing Stephen needed.[34]

Moses did travel to Little Rock that spring, whether or not Stephen was ready to see him. Before he left Missouri, though, he had taken one step that indicated his seriousness about visiting Texas. He wrote to Washington, D.C., for a copy of the passport that the Spanish authorities had issued him back in 1797. It came in time, and with Spanish passport in hand he arrived in Little Rock, only to fall desperately ill with fever. Moses remained there through the summer and into the fall of 1820, recovering from his illness, observing the battle over the ownership of the capital site, and following events in Texas. Finally, in the second or third week of November, he was ready to leave Arkansas.[35] He borrowed fifty dollars and a gray horse from Stephen, a mule from James Bryan, and he secured Stephen's slave, Richmond, as a traveling companion. With a shotgun strapped to his saddle and a pistol at his side, the fifty-eight-year-old Moses Austin set out for Texas.[36]

And what of Stephen? Had Moses convinced him that the family's salvation lay in Texas? The answer, unequivocally, is no. Almost immediately after Moses's departure for Texas, Stephen made good on his threat to leave Arkansas and move south, to Louisiana. His object, though, was not farming, although he would have taken almost any position with decent pay. Instead, he floated down the Red and Mississippi Rivers to New Orleans, arriving in November 1820. He was desperate for almost any sort of fresh start.[37]

In his 1829 telling of the story, Stephen depicted the move to New Orleans as another carefully orchestrated step in his and Moses's grand scheme for the colonization of Texas. "In the fall of 1820," he recalled, "my father came on from Missouri, and proceeded to visit the Spanish authorities of Texas . . . and I went to New Orleans to make such arrangements as circumstances might require or permit." This explanation, like his account of the move to Long Prairie, was self-serving and simply untrue. In reality, he had no definite design regarding Texas when he moved to New Orleans. His most concrete purpose in making the move was to escape the legal and financial quagmire into which he and his family had fallen. Stephen revealed his plans, such as they were, to his mother shortly after his arrival. "I came here," he wrote, "with a hope of getting employ; I offered to hire myself out as clerk, as an overseer, or anything else." He also pointedly told Maria that "I know nothing as to my father's objects or prospects."[38]

This disclaimer may have been something of an exaggeration, for he and Moses had been together in Arkansas right up until the time Moses left for Texas. Stephen surely knew *something* about his father's objects — probably more than he wanted to know. But Maria must have been at least as leery of Moses's visionary schemes as Stephen was, and Stephen may have wanted to assure her of his own intentions to get reasonable work and provide for the family's immediate needs. Nevertheless, had Stephen known very much about what his father was doing, he surely would have given a terribly worried Maria at least some encouraging news of Moses's prospects. On balance, his explanation of why he went to New Orleans was candid: he was ruined in Missouri and Arkansas, the family needed some means of support, and he could see little chance of his father's Texas gambit succeeding. If by some stroke of fate Moses did succeed in Texas, Stephen might be of some assistance in New Orleans. But this seemed so unlikely that he did not even bother to mention it to Maria. The more distance he could put between himself and his father's quixotic adventures, the more peace of mind there would be for both himself and his mother.[39]

Stephen arrived in New Orleans at an inauspicious time. The recession that had devastated the economy in the rest of the nation had not spared the most important city in the Deep South. Normally a bustling center of trade and finance, the city's economy had slowed to a crawl. "[B]usiness is too dull here to get into business," Austin reported to his mother in January 1821. "There are hundreds of young men who are glad to work for their board." The prospects of being able to support himself were grim enough, but Stephen had to think about more than just himself. Back in Missouri, Maria was nearly destitute. "As to Bryan and Sister," Stephen told her, "my heart bleeds for their troubles—if I can be of any servise to you or them let me know it, and I will go home; I will do anything that is right." But he clearly did not relish the thought of going home.[40]

It was all too depressing. "My reputation is *all* I have on earth," Stephen frankly wrote to Maria. But with his creditors growing impatient in Missouri and Arkansas, even his reputation and the honor that accompanied it were at risk. "If *that* is destroyed I can be of no use to you or any one else," he stated grimly, "and there will no longer [be] a necessity of remaining either in this Country or any other." If there is any truth in the saying that the darkest hour comes just before dawn, Stephen F. Austin's darkest hour had arrived. Then, at the very moment of defeat and disillusionment, the first light broke. Into Austin's life stepped Joseph Hawkins.[41]

Texas
1820–1821

When Stephen F. Austin stepped onto the river landing in New Orleans in November 1820, he had just turned twenty-seven years old. He was broke, and the depressed economy offered little promise of gainful employment. His spirits had reached a low ebb. "There are hundreds of young men who are glad to work for their board," he told his mother as he reported on conditions in the Crescent City.[1]

Only one thing was certain: Stephen wanted nothing to do with his father's Texas scheme. He was worried about his father, but his concern was not that Moses would fail in his mission to San Antonio, but that he might succeed and summon him to participate in it. "If I am left alone a few years," Stephen wrote, "I may get up and pay all [of my debts] off." But would Moses leave him alone? To defy his father would be unthinkable. Stephen probably knew, deep down, that if Moses issued such a summons, he could not refuse. But he was hoping it would not come.[2]

Stephen hit the chilly, drizzly New Orleans streets in search of employment. He could not afford to be particular. Fortunately, his father had connections, one of whom was William Kenner, a prominent merchant who had handled Moses's business affairs in New Orleans for many years. Stephen sought out Kenner, who promised help, but weeks passed with no contact. Stephen bitterly resented the slight. "In this state of things," he informed his mother in January 1821, "it was my good fortune to get acquainted with Joseph H. Hawkins."[3]

Austin did not know Hawkins, but he surely knew *of* him. Hawkins's younger brother Littleberry had attended Transylvania University with Austin. Joseph Hawkins represented Lexington in the Kentucky legislature and briefly in the U.S. House of Representatives. By 1820 he had moved to New Orleans.[4]

Whether Austin sought out Hawkins or they met by chance is not known. But shortly after Austin's arrival in New Orleans, Hawkins came to his rescue. Hawkins not only gave Austin "employ in an office," but he also took him into his household and advanced him money to purchase groceries to send to his mother and sister—an indication of how desperate things were back home. Austin told his mother of his arrangement with Hawkins: "If I will remain with him he will board me, permit me the use of his books, and money for clothes, give me all the instruction in his power until I am well fitted to commence the practice of law in this country. For my board and the use of his books he will charge *nothing,* and for the money he advances he will wait until I make enough by my profession to repay him." So moved was Austin by these acts of kindness that it "almost made me change my opinion of the human race." It would take eighteen months to learn Louisiana civil law and enough French to practice there; "I then shall have the means of fortune within my reach," he concluded. In the meantime—probably through Hawkins's influence—he also got a part-time job helping to edit a New Orleans newspaper, the *Louisiana Advertiser.*[5]

The arrangement with Hawkins reinforces the conjecture that Stephen had no intention of participating in Moses's enterprise. He would not have embarked on an eighteen-month course of legal study, including French language studies, if he had any intention of joining his father in Texas. But Hawkins's offer promised more than a mere business agreement and a way to distance himself from his father's reach. In Hawkins, Austin had discovered a kindred spirit and a true friend.

He was grateful for Hawkins's kindness, but it rested on a shaky financial foundation. "Mr. Hawkins is a lawyer of the [highest] standing in this place—he is not rich—but he has a generous heart," Austin discovered. Two years later Austin would describe Hawkins as "my *adopted brother*" and declare that "a better or truer friend never existed." Perhaps it was because Austin reminded him so much of himself that Hawkins formed such a close bond with his new friend and protégé. However, it takes no great leap of imagination to understand why Hawkins would be attracted to Austin; in his own quiet way the young Missourian could exert considerable charm.[6]

The best description of Austin as an adult comes from the pen of his nephew, Moses Austin Bryan. Bryan, who knew his uncle intimately, depicted him as "slender, sinewy, of graceful figure and easy, elastic movements, with small hands and feet, dark hair inclined to curl when damp, with large, hazel eyes, fair skin when not sun-burned, about five feet eight or nine inches in height." Austin had learned well from his father the importance of dressing in a manner befitting his station in life, and he always took great pains to appear dignified yet stylishly attired. He made a good first impression. A prospective Texas immigrant who met Austin in 1821 described him as "one of the most retiring, quiet gentlemen one would meet in a month, a small, quite handsome gentleman." The portraits of Austin painted from life confirm this image of a handsome, even elegant, man.[7]

Austin's personality and cultivated manners also served him well in new situations. "His face," Moses Austin Bryan sentimentally recalled, "was grave and thoughtful when not in the social circle—then it was animated and lit up by the gentle soul within; his voice was manly and soft, his colloquial powers fluent, persuasive and attractive, without his being conscious of it himself; his magnetic power over others gave him the great influence he possessed." Naturalist Henry R. Schoolcraft, who met Austin in Missouri in 1818, described him as a "gentleman of an acute and cultivated mind, and great suavity of manners. . . . He possessed a cautious, penetrating mind, and was a man of elevated views." Austin

Stephen F. Austin, c. 1823. Probably painted in Mexico City, this portrait shows Austin in his prime at age thirty, before illness and hardship had taken their toll. *Courtesy, Dale Glenn and Dan Morris, Corsicana, Texas.*

described his own temperament as "naturally hasty and impetuous and sensitive to a fault," a description seemingly more appropriate to Moses than to Stephen Austin. But if this self-description was accurate, Austin's nephew observed, "no one would suppose so from intercourse with him, for with others he had such ways as to make every one like and be easy

Joseph H. and George Anne Hawkins. Hawkins, a New Orleans lawyer and former Kentucky congressman, befriended Austin in 1821 and provided vital financial assistance when Austin commenced his Texas venture. Austin later deeded more than forty thousand acres of Texas lands to the couple's five children in repayment of his obligation. *Courtesy, Kentucky Museum, Western Kentucky University, Bowling Green.*

with him."[8] These flattering portrayals of Austin by friends and family should be accepted with appropriate allowances for bias; however, even unsympathetic observers often described him in terms such as "diplomatic," "diligent," "enterprising," "wily," "talented," and "cunning."[9]

Austin moved in with the Hawkins family at their home on Poydras Street, four blocks west of the French Quarter. Here he spent the next six months, making the short walk each day to the Hawkins law office on Royal Street in the Quarter and to his job with the newspaper. Evenings were lively in the Hawkins household, for Joseph and his wife, George Anne, had six young children—five boys and a girl. After the children were put to bed, Austin, an avid reader, could enjoy his host's fine library.[10]

For a man of Austin's tastes—and one who had just spent eighteen months living in primitive cabins on the raw Arkansas frontier—

New Orleans must have been a stimulating environment. The city supported several bookshops and newspapers. On one typical evening, the entertainment bill at the Orleans Theatre featured such productions as *Jocrisse's Despair* ("a comedy in two acts"), *The Married Batchelors* ("an opera in one act"), and *I Don't Care, I Am in a Frolick* ("a vaudeville in one act"). Other nights the offerings were a bit more highbrow: a full symphony, a piano concert, and a scene from *Romeo and Juliet,* followed by a formal ball. Ailing citizens could patronize Dr. Depuy's establishment on St. Peter street, where the doctor would administer "sulphureous fumigations" to treat such ailments as "the Itch," "the scurf," "atomic Gout," and "Leprosy in its early stages." Every week ships arrived from such far-off places as Boston, Bremen, Liverpool, Bordeaux, or Málaga. Sailors in New Orleans that year invented the game of poker. And then there were the dozens of restaurants, coffeehouses, and saloons—of both the respectable and not-so-respectable variety—where gentlemen gathered to conduct business, talk politics, or discuss the news from abroad. In the spring of 1821 such discussions invariably turned to the stirring developments from Mexico, where the War of Independence against Spain was reaching its climax.[11]

Austin could not have heard news of Mexico without pondering his father's fate. In January 1821—two months after parting ways with his father—Stephen wrote Maria that he had no news whatsoever of Moses. Had the younger Austin known what was happening on his father's mission to Texas, his worst fears would have been realized: Moses was on the verge of success.

Accompanied by Stephen's slave Richmond, Moses had crossed the Sabine River into East Texas at the end of November 1820. For three weeks the men journeyed, crossing four hundred miles of nearly deserted wilderness. Reaching San Antonio de Béxar two days before Christmas, Moses sought an audience with the provincial governor, Antonio Martínez. Nervous over the renewed filibustering campaign of James Long, and acting under orders of his superiors, Martínez summarily ordered Austin to leave Texas and not return. As a dejected Moses Austin retraced his steps across the dusty plaza of the century-old capital, his eyes fell upon a vaguely familiar face. It belonged to Philip Hendrik Nering Bögel, better known as the Baron de Bastrop. The two had met almost twenty years earlier, when both were in New Orleans on business. They struck up a conversation. Bastrop sympathized with Austin's plight and offered to speak to the governor on his behalf.[12]

Bastrop was the ideal ally. Born of a prominent family in Dutch Guiana but raised mostly in the Netherlands, he had served in the Dutch army and later was a provincial tax collector. Accused of embezzlement in 1793, he fled the Netherlands to Spanish Louisiana, where, after inventing his baronial title, he secured a contract to colonize European immigrants on a land grant in the Ouachita Valley. The Louisiana Purchase ended this project, and he moved to San Antonio in 1805. Although poor, he became a respected community leader there.[13]

Bastrop took Moses back to Martínez's office and persuaded the governor to allow the American to remain a while. For the next two days Bastrop and Austin plotted their strategy in the Baron's one-room adobe house. On the day after Christmas they presented a proposal to Martínez. With Bastrop interpreting, Moses asked permission to settle three hundred American Catholic families in Texas and to establish a town at the mouth of the Colorado River. Again, luck was on Moses's side. Since Martínez's arrival in Texas three years earlier, he had labored unsuccessfully to develop the economy of the frontier province. Native Mexicans showed little interest in moving there, and an unsettled Texas could offer little defense against American invasions or hostile Indians. Martínez concluded that Austin was "a man of some honesty and formality, and that the proposal he is making is, in my opinion, the only one which is bound to provide for the increase and prosperity of this province." Martínez forwarded Austin's application, along with a positive recommendation, to his superiors in Monterrey.[14]

Three days later Moses Austin rode out of San Antonio for the United States. Serious trouble occurred along the way. He and Richmond had acquired a traveling companion named Jacob Kirkham, who turned out to be a trafficker in stolen mules. This worried Moses considerably, for association with such a man could scuttle all his plans. The men traveled uneasily together for several days. Then one night as they camped on the Trinity River, Kirkham took all of the party's mounts and gear and slipped away, leaving Moses and Richmond alone and afoot. Over the next eight days they braved cold weather, swollen rivers, and a frightening panther attack, living on roots and berries. They arrived at McGuffin's cabin west of Natchitoches in mid-January, barely alive.[15]

Moses fought his illness—variously described as "flux" and "fever" —from his sickbed at McGuffin's for the next three weeks. He exerted himself only enough to write letters reporting the Kirkham incident to the Spanish officials and updating the Baron de Bastrop on his plans. Unfortunately, bad news awaited him in Louisiana. The Bank of St. Louis, which had briefly reorganized, had finally collapsed altogether, leaving Moses liable for massive new debts in the amount of some $30,000. Instead of proceeding to New Orleans to recruit settlers, he would have to return to Missouri to "settle and save the balance of my property." Still very sick, Moses finally departed for home, arriving in Herculaneum in late March, haggard and exhausted. Word shortly arrived that his petition had been confirmed by the provincial officials in Monterrey.[16]

Pushing himself hard, Moses began organizing his affairs so that he might return to Texas. He needed to accomplish two things as quickly as possible. First, he needed to negotiate a settlement with the Bank of St. Louis; he regarded the bank's latest demands as entirely unreasonable. Then he had to persuade Stephen to join him in the Texas venture. Neither task proved easy. Negotiations with the bank took several weeks, but finally the defunct institution agreed to settle for $280. Persuading Stephen proved even more difficult.[17]

During the four months since Moses had reached his agreement with Antonio Martínez, the younger Austin had settled comfortably into his new life in New Orleans. His arrangement with Hawkins brought order to his chaotic life for the first time in many years. The daily trip to the post office was now his most regular occasion for anxiety. Any day the mail might bring the news that some awful fate had met his father on the hazardous journey to San Antonio. Or, almost equally dreadful from Stephen's perspective, it might bring a summons for him to join in the venture. When the letter finally came, it was the latter. In announcing to his family the news of his success, Moses undoubtedly assumed that they would see the incontestable logic of his plans. "I have made a visit to St.

Antonio and obtained liberty to settle in that country," he wrote, "*as I am, ruined, in this* [country], I found nothing I could do would bring back my property again and to remain in a Country where I had enjoyed *welth* in a state of *poverty* I could not submit to."[18]

Stephen's resistance can be inferred from the letter Moses wrote him in May. "I hope and pray you will Discharge your Doubts, as to the Enterprise," implored Moses. Realizing that mere pleading might not sway the reluctant Stephen, he closed his letter with a classic dose of breathless Moses Austin optimism: "Raise your Spirits times are changing a new chance presents itself nothing is now wanting but Concert and firmness I am aff[ectionately] Your Father." Could Stephen possibly refuse?[19]

With or without Stephen, Moses was finally on the verge of settling his affairs and leaving Missouri. But weeks of relentless work and travel, coming so soon after his debilitating illness, had further weakened his health. In the first week of June he suffered a relapse. He took to his sickbed at the Bryan home at Hazel Run, suffering from a "Violent attack of Inflamation on the brest and lungs, attended with a high fever." On June 8, Maria Austin notified Stephen that his father might not live. The doctor had bled and blistered him, but his condition had only worsened. A distraught Maria described the scene that day to Stephen: "He called me to his bed side and with much distress and difficulty of speech, beged me to tell you to take his place and if god in his wisdom thought best to disappoint him in the accomplishment of his wishes and plans formed for the benefit of his family, he prayed him to extend his goodness to you and eneable you to go on with the business in the same way he would have done had not sickness and oh dreadful to think of perhaps death, prevented him from accomplishing." Two days later, Moses Austin died.[20]

It was not his father's deathbed request that finally persuaded Stephen to enlist in the Texas project. On June 18, 1821, nine days before word of Moses's death reached New Orleans, Stephen had departed for Natchitoches, on the western edge of Louisiana, aboard the steamboat *Beaver*. There he intended to meet a party of Spanish officials headed by Erasmo Seguín and travel overland to Texas. Moses was to have proceeded to New Orleans and then taken a ship with settlers and supplies to the mouth of the Colorado. Moses's urgings had been forceful, but those urgings alone had not persuaded Stephen. With or without Stephen's knowledge, Moses had written to Joseph Hawkins, offering him a "joint interest in the grant and settlement." Hawkins was immediately enthusiastic about the plan. Next, at the instigation of Moses, James Bryan wrote to Stephen strongly urging him to heed his father's request. Stephen could not withstand the combined pressure from Hawkins and Bryan. The influence of Hawkins was probably decisive. Stephen Austin not only valued the advice of his friend and mentor, but Hawkins's willingness to underwrite the financing of the venture suddenly made it seem less visionary. As Hawkins explained to Maria on June 27, "Stephen and myself both concluded it was best for him to set out immediately and meet the Spanish officers waiting at Natchitoches to conduct him to the grant." [21]

In Natchitoches, Erasmo Seguín had been on the verge of giving up on Moses. But he had recently heard that Moses had a son in New Orleans, and he had just written to Stephen to ask whether Moses was alive or dead when Stephen arrived in Natchitoches on June 26. After meeting with Seguín and learning the details of the concession, the younger Austin immediately began making preparations for the trip to Texas. His highest priority was to publicize the colonization plan in hopes of attracting immigrants. On July 1, still unaware of his father's death, Austin wrote a letter intended for widespread publication in American newspapers. In it he informed prospective settlers of Moses's grant to settle three hundred families in Texas. The families, he wrote, would be given land, and with the Spanish Constitution of 1812 "in full operation," they would be assured of "the most liberal privileges . . . both in regard to commercial intercourse and civil rights." Those interested in immigrating were to write Moses in Herculaneum for details. Only those who came "well recommended" would be considered. Newspapers as far away as Frankfort, Kentucky, carried Austin's letter.[22]

Austin took time in Natchitoches to inform friends of his undertaking and to encourage those who might consider joining him. Here, for the first time, he gave evidence of excitement about his prospects. To his old militia comrade Jacob Pettit, whom Austin had asked for help in finding employment two years earlier, Austin now wrote, "If you do not consider yourself settled for life, you could not do better than to join us. The prospects are much better than they ever were in upper Louisiana for the Country is much better, and will settle faster than that ever was." Austin even seemed to be looking forward to the overland journey. "I have a party of 10 fine companions," he told Pettit, "and think shall have a pleasant trip." [23]

The trip got off to a slow start. On July 3, Austin sent most of his party ahead toward the Sabine, staying behind with the Spaniards and one other American in order to complete last-minute arrangements, including the sale of the slave Richmond. On the sixth he started west and soon caught up with his party, which had been detained by straying mules. At last, on July 9, the men arrived at the Sabine. At dawn the next morning a rider overtook them and told Austin of his father's death. Sending his party on to the East Texas village of Nacogdoches with instructions to wait for him, Stephen immediately returned to Natchitoches. He consulted with the Spanish agent there, who offered the opinion that Stephen would probably be allowed to proceed with the plan in place of his father. On July 13, Austin set out again for the Sabine. [24]

Before leaving, he took time to write his mother a letter of condolence, and also to inform her of his decision to proceed without Moses. Never a religious man in the conventional sense, he could only tell her that "we must resign ourselves to the dispensations of Providence, death must finally terminate the career of us all." Then, in a statement that reveals much about his feelings toward Moses, Stephen explained, "This news has effected me very much, he was one of the most feeling and affectionate Fathers that ever lived. His faults I now say, and always have, were not of the heart." [25]

That Stephen would allude to those faults at such a time underscores his conflicted feelings toward Moses. That there had been love, respect, and admiration cannot be doubted, but psychologically, Moses's death liberated Stephen. He understood that Moses's volatile personality had often brought disaster to the family. As long as Moses lived, Stephen would never be free to manage the family's affairs, or his own, in a more prudent manner. No one knew these things better than Maria Austin; she commented only a few months after her husband's death about "his Sanguine temper and will," which caused him to "Anticipate a thou-

Austin's pistols and tomahawk. Moses Austin carried
this tomahawk with him on his initial journey to Texas
in 1820 and later passed it down to his son. Stephen
Austin probably carried these pistols during his stint
as commander of the Texas army in 1835. *Courtesy,
Center for American History, University of Texas at
Austin (Prints and Photographs Collection #CN03195).*

sand pleasing projects which he [could] never realize." Stephen would
take command of his father's enterprise armed not only with the memory of Moses Austin and the knowledge that he was fulfilling his father's
dying wish, but also with an invaluable understanding of the personal
shortcomings that had so often frustrated the elder Austin's plans. Alive,
Moses almost certainly would have proved a liability in the difficult times
to come. In death, he freed Stephen to manage the Texas venture in ways
that otherwise would have been impossible.[26]

Early on Monday, July 16, 1821, Austin, Seguín, and fourteen others
—mostly Spaniards who had accompanied Seguín—forded the Sabine
River into Texas. Crossing the river where Toledo Bend reservoir now
stands, they camped the first night in the piney woods on Boregas Creek
just north of modern-day Hemphill. The following day took them as far
as the cabin of Josiah H. Bell, an old Missouri friend who had been squat-
ting in the area for a year or two. After two more days of travel through
the tall pines and red clay hills the party rode into the old Spanish town
of Nacogdoches.[27]

There Austin got his first notion of why the Spanish authorities had been receptive to his father's proposal to sponsor immigration into Texas. The old village, which once had boasted a polyglot population of more than six hundred, was virtually deserted, a victim of the turmoil resulting from the decade-long struggle for independence from Spain. Austin counted only a church and seven houses standing among the ruins. Word of the Austin grant had reached the area at least as early as June, however, and a few of the families in the Nacogdoches area already planned to relocate to Austin's proposed colony. The government officials in San Antonio ordered Erasmo Seguín to inform the remaining residents that the government wished them to remove either to the San Antonio area or to Austin's colony. If Anglo-Americans were to be living in Texas, the authorities much preferred that they live in the interior, under the watchful eyes of loyal officials, rather than scattered along the Texas-Louisiana border, where they might give aid and comfort to future American invaders. Seguín was able to muster only thirty-six inhabitants to tell them of the government's wish, but apparently most of them were amenable to the idea. A goodly number of Austin's early colonists would be attracted from the Nacogdoches area with offers of better land and valid titles to it.[28]

After two days in Nacogdoches, Austin and his companions began the three-hundred-mile trek across eastern and central Texas to San Antonio de Béxar. Austin kept a detailed journal of the trip, a first and necessary step in familiarizing himself with the vast wilderness in which he would establish his colony and spend most of the remainder of his life. Reading Austin's journal, one is struck by the richness and variety of the land, and its utter wildness. The old royal "road" from Nacogdoches to San Antonio—*el camino real*—was no road at all, and barely even a trail in most places. More than once members of Austin's entourage who straggled or left to hunt game got separated and lost, necessitating lengthy searches. For most of the trip the travelers found abundant game, dining frequently on fresh venison, turkey, and honey. On two occasions even Austin—a more accomplished woodsman than some in the party but never a great hunter—killed bucks upon which the travelers dined.

The party maintained a leisurely pace, and the journey into San Antonio took three weeks. Austin quickly recognized the good fortune of his father not to be granted land in far eastern Texas. Seguín and several others fell ill with fever soon after departing Nacogdoches. Passage through the swampy bottoms of the Neches and Trinity Rivers proved difficult. Austin remarked in his journal that much of the East Texas country reminded him of the pine barrens of Kentucky, although in places the land supported a lush growth of native grasses. The travelers kept an eye out for Indians, and one night the man appointed to the watch sounded the alarm; daylight revealed the Indian to be an uprooted tree stump. Not a single Indian was sighted between the Louisiana border and San Antonio. For Austin, who had seen firsthand the terror that hostile Indians instilled in the settlers of the Missouri frontier, this must have been a relief.

As the men neared the Brazos River, the character of the landscape gradually changed. Pine trees gave way to oaks, hickories, cedars, and pecans, with frequent natural openings where lush native grasses grew. Rich soil—black in some places, sandy in others—became more common. Reaching the Brazos on August 1, Austin noted that the land reminded him of the fertile Red River country at Natchitoches, though the Texas river water was of better quality. Deer and black bears were plentiful. The river bottoms supported abundant wild grapevines. Crossing the river, the men struck the first of the large prairies that dot the region and saw their first buffalo. On August 7 they reached the Colorado, which with its clear water and clean gravel bottom reminded Austin of the Cumberland River, only bigger. He had now crossed what would become the northern width of his colony. Any doubts as to the desirability of the country were gone.

On August 10 the party reached the swift-running Guadalupe River north of San Antonio. Austin thought this "country the most beautiful I ever saw." The weather had turned unpleasantly hot, and some nights the travelers rode until ten o'clock to take advantage of the cooler evening temperatures. Seguín sent some of his men ahead to San Antonio to prepare for their arrival, and on August 12 these men met the incoming party on the outskirts of the provincial capital with news of the independence of Mexico. "The Spaniards," Austin noted, "hailed this news with acclamations of 'viva Independencia' and every other demonstration of joy." The wives of Seguín and his men sent out "various Spanish dishes," and the travelers enjoyed their first civilized meal in three weeks. In "high spirits," Austin and his party rode into San Antonio at eleven o'clock in the morning. There they found that under the deft leadership of Governor Martínez an orderly transition from Spanish to Mexican rule had taken place three weeks earlier.[29]

Martínez and other dignitaries treated him with respect and went to great lengths to facilitate his plans. As he had done eight months earlier for Moses Austin, the Baron de Bastrop offered his services as an adviser and translator. Austin at this point knew little if any Spanish. Although the Baron probably understood some English, the two men apparently discovered that they could communicate best in French. Austin readily accepted Bastrop's offer, and for the immediate future the language barrier was conquered.[30]

Moses Austin's agreement with the Spanish government had been very general; it specified only the number of families who would be allowed into the new colony—three hundred—and that they be Roman Catholics of good character and industrious habits. Soon after Stephen's arrival the governor asked him to submit a plan for distributing land to the settlers. Several days later Austin submitted his proposal: Each family should receive 320 acres of farm land fronting a river and 640 acres of grazing land farther back. The head of each family would also receive two hundred acres for his wife, one hundred for each child, and fifty for each slave, with these lands to be divided equally between farming and grazing land. Martínez approved this recommendation and gave Austin permission to promise land in these amounts to the colonists, contingent on approval of the superior authorities. Martínez also reminded Austin that until the colonists were placed under civil authority, "they must be governed by and be subordinate to you."[31]

Austin remained in San Antonio for nine days, conducting his business with the governor, discussing trade opportunities with Bastrop and Seguín, and buying horses, apparently with permission to take them back to the United States for sale. On August 21, Austin and his party rode out of San Antonio past the dilapidated Spanish missions strung along the San Antonio River south of town. The travelers had several contacts with Tonkawa Indians, who proved peaceable and whose chief even professed to be "pleased" when Austin told them of his proposed settlement. After six days' travel they arrived at the only other actual town in Texas, La Bahía, later renamed Goliad.[32]

Here Austin was delayed for another week, owing to bureaucratic confusion over who was to serve as his guide for the upcoming reconnaissance. During his wait he met the local priest, José Valdés, a "great friend of the Americans" who voiced a desire to be appointed curate of the new colony. Austin also decided to dispatch six of his men to Louisiana to sell sixty of the horses he had bought in San Antonio. Taking advantage of this means of communicating with the United States, Austin wrote several letters. One went to John Sibley, a prominent citizen of Natchitoches who had long followed Texas affairs. Austin enthusiastically reported that Mexican independence had not affected his plans in the least, and that "the country is the most beautiful & desirable to live in I ever saw. . . . The most liberal Encouragments will be afforded to settlers and families of fair character." Sibley could be counted on to spread the word.[33]

At last one of Goliad's *regidores* (town councilmen), Manuel Becerra, was appointed as Austin's guide, along with three Aranama Indians from the local mission. For the next week the men explored the lower San Antonio and Guadalupe Rivers and the vicinities of Lavaca and Matagorda Bays. Austin hoped to find the site of the original La Bahía mission and presidio, which was located near the head of Lavaca Bay before being moved to the current Goliad site, but he was frustrated by poor communication with his guides. Becerra thought that Austin wanted to be taken to the site of the old mission Nuestra Señora del Refugio, thirty miles to the southwest. Going there would violate his orders, which were to take Austin to the Colorado. After several days of aimless wandering, Austin finally concluded that his guides knew nothing about the country, so he sent them home, resuming explorations on his own.[34]

Becerra returned to Goliad and reported to his superior, *Alcalde* (chief magistrate) Tomás Buentello, who in turn reported to Governor Martínez that Austin had not explored the Colorado at all. Equally troubling was the fact that during the entire trip "no religious act was observed." Moreover, none of Austin's men "appeared to be the legitimate families who were suposed to come." They spoke nothing but English the entire time, and Buentello concluded that "they will be more harmful than beneficial." Given the history of American intervention in Texas's affairs, the Goliad officials may have suspected Austin of being a spy. At the very least, they seemed concerned that he might attempt to establish his colony too close to Goliad, encroaching on the lands of the region's Tejano ranchers.[35]

These fears proved groundless. After shedding their guides, Austin and his men struck a northeasterly course and on September 15 arrived at the Colorado, north of present-day Wharton. For the next three days the party followed the river southward. Austin was impressed by the rich river-bottom land, broad prairies, good water, and excellent timber. On the seventeenth Austin was startled by what he thought was an "Indian war whoop," and he looked up to see a chief followed by fourteen warriors advancing toward the Americans. The Indians made "signs of Friendship," so Austin approached them after instructing his men to be prepared for a fight. The chief identified his band as belonging to the Cocos, a subsidiary branch of the Karankawas.[36]

Even though the Mexican government officially considered the Cocos a friendly tribe, Austin had been told that they "lived with the Karankawas." Given the Karankawas' violent reputation, he took no chances. He declined their invitation to join them at their camp, but he decided that they did not have warlike intentions when one of the chiefs came unarmed to Austin's camp, along with five women and a boy. Austin distributed gifts, and the encounter ended peacefully. Much like Thomas Jefferson, Austin was a keen student of things foreign and exotic, and he recorded with fascination his observations of the natives. "These Indians," he wrote, "were well formed and apparently very active and athletic men, their Bows were about 5 1/2 to 6 ft long, their arrows 2 to 3 well pointed with Iron or Steel. [Some] of the squaws were handsome & one of them quite pretty—they had Panther skins around their waist painted, which extended down to the knee & calf of the leg—above the waist tho. they were naked—their breasts were marked or tatooed in circles of black beginning with a small circle at the nipple and enlarging as the breast swelled."

Fascination aside, Austin had already formed an opinion of the Indians. The Tejanos feared and distrusted the Karankawan tribes, believing them to be savage cannibals, but they had never sought to exterminate them. Austin's reaction revealed the influence of the Tejanos' beliefs, along with his own Anglo-American conception of what must inevitably occur when "civilized" people encounter those whom they consider "savages": "These Indians and the Karanquas may be called universal enemies to man," he noted in his journal, "they killed of[f] all nations that came in their power, and frequently feast on the bodies of their victims — the [approach of] an American population will be the signal of their extermination for there will be no way of subduing them but extermination." Austin might be willing to coexist with Indians if they would agree to be "subdued" on the white man's terms — whatever those terms might encompass — but like most other Anglo-Americans of his time and place, he never questioned the right of the white man to settle and control Indian-occupied lands. He would, however, try to locate his colony and conduct its affairs in such a way as to avoid armed conflict with the Indians whenever possible. Such a course need not imply benevolence; it simply was expedient.[37]

The Cocos told Austin that a large body of their Karankawan cousins were camped at the mouth of the Colorado, so after moving another ten miles downriver, the Americans prudently turned northeastward and traversed the country between the Colorado and the Brazos. On September 19 they struck the Brazos near the Atascosito crossing. "The Prairie comes bluff to the river just below the Tuscasite road, and affords a most beautifull situation for a Town or settlement," Austin recorded in his journal. "The bluff is about 60 feet high — The country back of this place and below for about 15 miles (as far as we went) is as good in every respect as man could wish for, Land all first rate, plenty of timber, fine water — beautifully rolling." Three years later the spot would become the site of San Felipe de Austin, the headquarters of Austin's Colony.[38]

At the Brazos, Austin divided his party into two groups, and for two days each moved northward on opposite sides of the river, exploring as much territory as possible. Austin remarked on the number of bears and wild cattle they saw. Continuing north, the party struck the San Antonio Road and began retracing the route to Louisiana. By October 6 they had reached Nacogdoches, and a few days later they were back in Louisiana.[39]

At Natchitoches, Austin paused for a few days to recuperate from a month of hard riding and sleeping on the ground, and to conduct some necessary business. One of his first tasks was to make a full report to Governor Martínez. Austin wrote that he had chosen the boundaries of his colony as follows: a line between the Brazos and the San Jacinto rivers on the northeast, the Lavaca on the southwest, the Gulf coast on the southeast, and a line just above the San Antonio Road on the northwest. This vast region encompassed essentially all of the watersheds of the lower Brazos and Colorado rivers, the finest agricultural lands in Texas.[40]

Austin soon realized the magnitude of the public response to his enterprise. At Natchitoches he found nearly a hundred letters from Missouri, Kentucky, and other states requesting information about the colony. Many more undoubtedly awaited him in New Orleans or Missouri. And this did not include the fifty or more families already in the Natchitoches-Nacogdoches region who were planning to immigrate in the next two months, even before Austin would be back in Texas. "I am convinced," he told Martínez, "that I could take on fifteen hundred families as easy as three hundred if permitted to do so." He apparently had assumed that settlers would have to apply to the authorities of Texas personally for permission to immigrate. Austin now proposed that it would be much better "if the whole superintendence of the Emigration from the U.S. was intrusted to one agent whose general knowledge of the American character, and particularly of the people of the western country and also of the situation of the lands of the Province of Texas would enable him to conduct the formation of the settlement." Austin stopped short of saying that he was the most logical choice to fill this position of "general Commissioner or Agent for the Province," but the implication was unmistakable. Such a commissioner should "have pretty extensive discretionary powers as to the distributing of lands" and would work closely with the surveyor general of the province to put the settlers in possession of their land. Austin also asked that the boundaries of the grant be extended to the Guadalupe River in the west and the Trinity in the east, an even larger area than he had proposed just the day before. Nobody could accuse him of timidity.[41]

As the plans for the colony progressed, one glaring question remained unaddressed, at least in the official proceedings. What was Austin to gain from his grandiose scheme? The purpose of the entire enterprise, after all, was to rescue the family from debt and restore the Austins to their former wealth and prominence. Yet there had been no mention of any sort of compensation, either in money, land, a trade monopoly, or anything else. Certainly both Moses and Stephen had calculated how they would profit from Texas colonization. In March 1821, shortly after learning that his petition had been confirmed by the provincial authorities, Moses Austin had written one of his typically optimistic letters to Brown Austin in Kentucky. "I have already offers to fill up the families which will bring me about 18,000 dollars," he said, "but of this I will write you more fully." How he arrived at this figure is unclear, but Moses apparently believed he would be able to charge emigrants a fee for their lands, although there is no guarantee that three hundred families could have produced the necessary cash in those hard times. Moses also must have envisioned opportunities in trade and in town development, from which he had profited in Missouri.[42]

Stephen's calculations of potential profits are elusive, for in his correspondence of the period he never discussed the matter. But in the letter he wrote to Martínez suggesting the appointment of a general commissioner to oversee emigration, Austin suggested "that the commissioner be authorized to exact from each settler a sufficient per cent on the land grant[d] to compensate him for his trouble and expense in attending to the business." Since Austin had strongly hinted that he should be appointed to the position, he obviously was placing himself in a position to collect those fees. He had already settled on the figure of twelve and a half cents per acre as the amount of the fee. Here his calculations come into sharper focus. Using the land formula that he had recommended to Martínez, a family composed of a husband, wife, and two children would receive 1,280 acres—two square miles of land. At twelve and a half cents an acre, a family of this size would pay $160. Multiplying this figure by three hundred families would mean a gross revenue of $48,000. Those with slaves or larger families would of course receive more land and pay more in fees. The costs of surveying, issuing titles, and all other expenses associated with the enterprise would have to be paid from these funds, but Austin must have believed that he would still net a handsome profit. On top of this would be any personal land grants he might receive and the trade opportunities that might unfold, although there is no evidence that the authorities discussed such compensation with Austin. If Austin had known the difficulties he would encounter in realizing the sort of profits that he anticipated, he probably would have made greater efforts to secure a more formal arrangement with the Mexican government up front. But that lay in the future, and things had gone so smoothly to this point that he could see no cause for concern. The future looked bright.[43]

By early November Austin had completed his business in Natchitoches and departed for New Orleans, where Joseph Hawkins eagerly awaited his arrival. Hawkins had not been idle during Austin's absence. He had been seeing to all manner of business relating to the Texas venture, particularly handling correspondence and publicity. He had made sure that announcements of Austin's grant were published in western newspapers, and consequently word of the enterprise was spreading. Before the end of the year the publicity appeared in papers as far away as Baltimore. "Just then Stephen Austin and Joe Hawkins were crying up Texas—beautiful country[,] land for nothing etc.," recalled one of the settlers who had shortly thereafter sailed from New Orleans for Texas.[44]

Financing the project remained one of Austin's greatest problems. He simply had no money of his own, and old Missouri debts continued to dog him. Moreover, appearances mattered now more than ever. He would need to set up headquarters at a respectable New Orleans hotel during the weeks of preparation for launching the colony. There would be significant expenses associated with outfitting and transporting the initial immigrants. Austin knew firsthand how wild and dangerous Texas was; he could not afford to send colonists unprepared for the challenges they would meet there. The money for all this would have to be borrowed.[45]

Hawkins had already helped Austin considerably, and he continued to contribute what he could to the undertaking. Austin soon formalized the agreement that Hawkins and Moses Austin had made before Moses's death. The new written contract, signed on November 14, 1821, specified that Stephen F. Austin, as heir and agent of his father, was now bound by the same provisions as the earlier informal agreement. Austin acknowledged to have received $4,000 from Hawkins. In return, Austin promised his friend "one equal half part of the monies, effects, property and profits arising from the sale of lands, lotts, or from any other sources growing out of the grant of lands" in Texas. Their agreement was to be a "joint and equal copartnery . . . in all matters and concerns touching the lands to be granted to them or either of them, or touching the emoluments or profits claimable from said Grant of lands or to the sale or settlement thereof, and all other purposes and objects in which they may embark in said province of Texas." Austin later denied having received the entire $4,000, which is probably true in terms of actual cash paid. But it appears that Hawkins's actual out-of-pocket expenditures eventually exceeded even this amount, although Austin probably never knew about all of them. In any case, Austin did ultimately uphold his end of the contract and sign over half of the land he received for the first colony to the Hawkins family.[46]

Hawkins, however, was not in a position to finance the entire endeavor, so Austin had to turn to elsewhere. Edward Lovelace was a Louisiana planter who had accompanied Austin on the previous summer's expedition to Texas. On their return to Louisiana in November, Lovelace made three loans to Austin totaling $700. Using $400 of this money and $200 provided by Hawkins, Austin purchased a small thirty-ton schooner, the *Lively,* which was to take the first settlers to the colony. Austin and Hawkins hired a crew of men to overhaul the boat, and in three weeks it was ready to sail.[47]

Austin understood the critical importance of the first settlers. Their success or failure would influence the decisions of others, and they would form the nucleus of the colony. Accordingly, Austin chose fourteen sturdy men to sail on the *Lively* and signed special contracts with them. They would embark as soon as the ship was ready and take soundings of the coast from Galveston Island to the mouth of the Guadalupe. After landing at the Colorado, they were to build cabins and a stockade, and clear and cultivate at least five acres of corn apiece. Austin promised to furnish the ship, tools, seed, draft animals, and other provisions, and to give each man 640 acres and a town lot free of all expenses. Austin would proceed by land and rendezvous with them on the Colorado.[48]

One issue continued to weigh heavily on Austin's mind. Since his father's death, his family's circumstances had grown steadily grimmer. A grieving Maria had borne herself with dignity and fortitude, but times were hard in Missouri. It was not easy for her to encourage her oldest son to proceed with the risky Texas venture, which had in large part cost her husband's life and which would deprive her of a united family for an indefinite time. Yet, knowing it was Moses's dying request, she resigned herself to it.[49]

More immediately troubling was Brown Austin's situation. Brown was in school in Nicholasville, Kentucky, where he had fallen into debt. By early 1820 his position had become untenable. With the help of his niece's husband, Horace Holley, now president of Transylvania University, Moses persuaded Henry Clay to recommend Brown to the secretary of the Navy for a midshipman's commission. The effort failed, and Brown's situation grew more urgent. For reasons unclear, the seventeen-year-old Brown could not simply come home. He may have been under some sort of legal constraint not to leave Kentucky without paying his debts; it is possible that he had been thrown in jail. Shortly after Moses's death, Maria expressed to Brown "the anxiety and many painfull felings I experience in Consequence of your detention in Kentuckey and not haveing it in my power to relieve you." Neither she nor Stephen nor James Bryan had a dime to send him.[50]

With Moses dead and Stephen far away, the entire family looked to Bryan for support. Unfortunately, Bryan's fortunes had come crashing down along with Stephen's in Arkansas, and he was as broke as anyone. The lingering effects of the Panic of 1819 continued to paralyze the economy of the Mississippi Valley. By August 1821, Bryan had decided to settle his affairs and join Stephen in the Texas project. With the tangled state of his finances, though, it would take time. About this time a dispute arose between Bryan and Austin. As complex and ruinous as their interconnected business affairs had been over the past few years, it is understandable that the two men could have quarreled over any number of perceived wrongs. However, the trouble seems to have revolved around Brown's plight. Stephen apparently believed that Bryan shirked his responsibility to secure Brown's return from Kentucky. Maria played the peacemaker. "You may be assured your Brother would not have been this long in K^y if he [Bryan] could have raised the money by selling flower or whisky at half price," she insisted, telling Stephen that when he and Bryan meet again "everything will be explained and you will find J B not the man his Enimys paint him to be and that he is still worthy of your confidence and friendship." To Maria, Bryan was "an affectionate kind son and tender husband and father" who would never intentionally disregard the family's needs.[51]

This explanation must have satisfied Stephen. When he returned to New Orleans in November to make final arrangements for launching the Texas colony, he wrote to Bryan, "I have thought that I had cause to be dissatisfied with you, perhaps I may have been wrong, and perhaps not — be that as it may, let the past be *forgotten for ever*. Your family shall participate fully in whatever advantage I may be enabled to Secure in Texas." In extending this olive branch, Austin was again displaying the concern for family that would be a hallmark of his life. But he was also showing signs of a new characteristic, one which no other member of the Austin clan, including the women, shared: the ability simply to walk away from a perceived injury and, as he said, let the past be forgotten. This extraordinary trait is rare in ambitious public men with robust egos; it was virtually nonexistent in Moses Austin. For Stephen Austin it would prove invaluable in the coming years, when so much would depend on harmony and diplomacy.[52]

By the time Austin was ready to leave for Texas at the end of November, everything seemed to be falling into place. The *Lively* was ready to sail. The tiff between Austin and James Bryan was mended, and Bryan told his brother-in-law, "I hope to God you may enjoy good health and succeed in the Grand object." Best of all, from Austin's perspective, Brown had somehow managed to pay enough of his bills to escape Kentucky; by late January the high-spirited youth, of whom his brother was intensely fond, would be camped on the Colorado River. Maria Austin sent Stephen on his mission with these words: "Farewell my dearest son, may guardien angels watch and protect you by day and by night and hasten the period that will restore you to the anxious arms of your affectionate mother." Sometime during the second week of December 1821 — almost exactly a year since his father had first made the same journey — Stephen F. Austin once again splashed across the Sabine River into Texas. It would be nearly fourteen years before he would see his native country again.[53]

Mexico
1821–1823

Austin's crossing the international boundary into the Mexican province of Texas in December 1821 marked the beginning of a new era in the history of two profoundly different nations and cultures. The population of newly independent Mexico stood at something over 6 million, about two-thirds that of the United States. The racial composition and social structure, however, differed dramatically from those of the United States; some 60 percent of Mexicans were Indians, 22 percent of mixed race, and 18 percent white. The country was rigidly stratified along racial and economic lines, with the bulk of the large nonwhite majority leading hard lives as laborers in the haciendas and mines. Slavery, although legal, had almost died out, for it was cheaper to exploit free labor. The mixed-race Mexicans, known as *mestizos* or *castas,* sometimes rose above the condition of laborer, but they seldom achieved the status reserved for the white minority. Even among whites, inequality was the rule. Much of the wealth and power rested in the hands of a relatively small number of the ultra-rich, whose extended families usually included individuals of Spanish birth as well as Mexicans of pure Spanish ancestry.[1]

Though rich in natural resources, Mexico in 1821 was an economic shambles. Living standards in New Spain had been declining for several decades prior to independence, and then the devastating ten-year independence struggle cut the country's output in half. Historically the Mexican economy had been mercantilist, producing raw materials for the Spanish empire and leading to great inequalities of wealth. In Mexico City, the richest families rivaled the European aristocracy in their opulent lifestyles. In the countryside, *hacendados* boasted landholding empires measured in the hundreds of thousands of acres.[2]

Along with the upper class, two institutions exercised enormous power in Mexico. Roman Catholicism was the only religion permitted, and priests enjoyed special legal privileges known as *fueros*. The church was the nation's greatest property holder and moneylender. Although it would decline in wealth and influence during the tumultuous years of the struggle for independence, it would remain a powerful and pervasive force in Mexican life. Liberal politicians who criticized it did so at considerable risk. During his first sojourn into the interior of Mexico, Austin would complain that religious "fanaticism reigns with a power that equally astonishes and grieves a man of common sense," a typical observation coming from one raised in a Protestant country with religious toleration.[3]

The military was the other powerful institution in Mexico. Like the clergy, army officers enjoyed special legal privileges. In the period of severe political instability during and after the wars of independence, generals who could field troops and command their loyalty were a force to be reckoned with, often independent of their civilian superiors.[4]

The Mexican independence movement had begun in 1810 as a series of local insurrections. It continued for a decade, mostly in the form of guerrilla warfare. Events in Spain finally turned the tide, though not in a direction that would benefit the masses. With the ascendance of a liberal government in Spain, the conservative ruling classes of Mexico grew fearful that Spanish liberalism might threaten their privileged position. In late 1820, as Moses Austin had been making his way into Texas, the principal royalist general, Agustín de Iturbide, turned against the Spanish government. In 1821, after a decade of sporadic warfare, Mexico achieved independence with relative ease.[5]

Iturbide succeeded in uniting Spanish royalists, conservative Mexi-

Stephen F. Austin, date unknown. *Courtesy, San Jacinto Museum of History, Houston.*

can monarchists, and republicans of various stripes in favor of independence. He became a national idol nearly overnight, and in the euphoria over independence most Mexicans could overlook their nation's deep political, ideological, and economic disagreements. Iturbide's blueprint for independence, the Plan de Iguala, called for the establishment of a constitutional monarchy to be presided over by a member of the Spanish royal family, subject to the will of an elected congress. In the meantime the country would be ruled by a provisional government with Iturbide as its key figure. All this was taking place during 1821, as Stephen Austin was exploring the site of his grant, returning to New Orleans to make final arrangements, and then hurrying back to meet the first colonists. Considering the turmoil in Mexico City, it comes as no surprise that he found conditions in Texas in a transitional state as well.[6]

Since the late 1700s, Texas had been part of an administrative entity called the Eastern Interior Provinces, which also comprised Coahuila, Nuevo León, and Nuevo Santander (later Tamaulipas). Although each province had its own governor, the provinces were really ruled by a commandant general in Monterrey who answered directly to the king. Texas historically had served mainly as a buffer against hostile neighboring powers. The principal Hispanic institutions of the frontier were the missions, which sought to Christianize and "civilize" the natives, and the *presidios,* or forts, manned by permanent military garrisons. Over a century's time a small civilian population had taken root in the vicinities of the missions and presidios.[7]

Frequently threatened by hostile Indians, the Mexican Texans, or Tejanos, clustered in San Antonio and Goliad, with a handful living on ranches scattered in the outlying areas. The third major outpost of Hispanic settlement, Nacogdoches, was all but abandoned, as Austin had recently discovered. Of all the northern provinces, Texas had experienced the worst ravages of the wars of independence. In a major battle fought in 1813 on the Medina River near San Antonio, royalist forces killed a thousand insurgent soldiers and their Anglo allies. Then, in a reign of terror across Texas, they slaughtered several hundred more Tejano civilians suspected of sympathizing with the rebels. Texas had never fully recovered from this carnage, and its population had dropped from a high of about 4,000 in 1800 to a mere 2,500 when Austin arrived in the province.[8]

Though few in number and living under trying circumstances, the Tejanos found ways to survive. They served in the military, farmed, raised horses and cattle on their *ranchos* (often selling them illicitly in Louisiana), and worked as artisans and laborers. The *ayuntamientos* (town councils) enforced laws, refereed disputes, and provided basic community services. Religious and patriotic holidays provided diversion, as did cockfights, horse races, weddings, and dances. One early Anglo immigrant, not entirely approving of the Tejano lifestyle, observed that "on Sunday Evening [they] will make what they call a Vandango & will play the violin & Dance the whole night." *Norteamericanos* such as Austin described Texas as a "wilderness"—and certainly vast areas were virtually untouched by European hands—but they erred when they overlooked the long history of the Tejano settlements or discounted the importance of the Hispanic culture that had evolved in Texas over a century's time. And Hispanic and Anglo alike tended to place the indigenous peoples of Texas beyond the pale of civilization, the most common term for them used by the Tejanos being *indios bárbaros,* literally "barbaric Indians." [9]

Mexican independence strained the already-weak bonds between the northern provinces and the national core. Long in decline, the missions were on the verge of collapse. The presidial garrisons were underpaid and undermanned. It often took weeks for news from the capital to reach the Tejano settlements. As Governor Martínez reported to his superior officer in February 1822, Texas required better ports, foreign trade, and a strong military presence to prevent trade in contraband, defend against Indians, and stop the entrance of American "vagabonds." Admitting foreigners would be the best method of achieving and paying for all this. The governor was staking much on Austin's success. [10]

Austin's movements during the two months following his return to Texas are not well documented. Unlike his initial trip the previous year, he kept no journal and had no means of mailing letters. It was a critical time, for the first colonists were arriving. For the colony to succeed, crops had to be planted and the settlements made secure against the Indians.

Austin counted heavily on the arrival of the *Lively,* with its cargo of men, tools, seed, and supplies. Sailing from New Orleans at the same time Austin left by land, the schooner should have arrived at the mouth of the Colorado ahead of him. But the *Lively* had encountered trouble. On entering the Gulf of Mexico it was blown far off course to the east, and it took most of a month to reach the Texas coast. Then for some reason the captain landed the colonists at the mouth of the Brazos. Eager to meet the *Lively,* Austin had headed straight to the Colorado, where he spent the first weeks of 1822 searching for the missing party. This marked the beginning of a series of setbacks that threatened all his well-laid plans.[11]

Interest in the colony had spread throughout the American Southwest. Before Austin had even made it back to Texas, John Sibley in Natchitoches wrote of the "prodigious moving of family and settlers" into Texas. "I should not be surprised if in 18 months 50,000 Americans should migrate thither," he speculated. From Missouri, Austin's old friend Daniel Dunklin informed him that Texas "has become a subject of considerable interest in this section of Missouri." James Bryan reported in January that "it appears to be the General rage in every quarter to Move to Texas," and he had "no doubt the Colony will be filled up immediately." That same week, writing from East Texas, Josiah Bell told Austin that "all things are Going on well and people Crowding on their way to the brassos and Collorado and are all coming for your Claim." By March, Sibley could report that "the Road by Nackitosh is full" of Texas-bound settlers.[12]

The reasons for this intense interest in Texas are not hard to understand. Before 1820, the United States sold its public lands on credit with generous repayment terms, but in 1820 Congress began requiring full cash payment up front. At $1.25 an acre, few frontiersmen could come up with the $100 needed to buy an eighty-acre farm, the smallest size available. This change came at a bad time, because the Panic of 1819 had drained the country of cash and depressed business everywhere. With these conditions prevailing, Austin's offer of thousands of acres, with minimal costs and easy terms, was almost irresistible.[13]

Austin failed to locate the *Lively*'s men and supplies, but he did find a handful of settlers already on the Colorado. More arrived during January and February. Reporting to the Mexican congress in May, he claimed that when he had left the colony at the beginning of March there were a hundred men on the Colorado and fifty on the Brazos. Only eight had thus far brought their families, but they planned to send for them in the fall. Among the January arrivals—to Austin's great joy—was Brown Austin. Austin had not seen his eighteen-year-old brother in nearly three years. Their relationship would be extremely close over the difficult years to come. Stephen assumed a paternalistic role in his brother's life, and Brown became his trusted lieutenant.[14]

In early March, with the settlers clearing land and planting corn, Austin rode to San Antonio with Brown to report to the governor. Martínez passed along troubling news. Mexican independence and the resulting change in governments had thrown everything into confusion. Martínez had forwarded to his superiors in Monterrey Austin's earlier recommendations regarding the boundaries of the colony, the amounts of land the colonists should receive, and the appointment of a commissioner to distribute the lands. They replied that Austin had no authority to distribute land, appoint judges, or do anything else without securing the permission of the supreme government. Meanwhile, the immigrants could be settled only provisionally, on lands designated by the nearest ayuntamiento and approved by the governor. There may even have been doubt about the validity of Austin's permission to establish a colony in Texas. Martínez himself was operating on uncertain ground; he was Spanish-born, and he might be removed from office at any time. What was Austin to do? "I applied to the Governor for advice," he later recalled, "informing him that I would rather die than not effect what I had promised to the Settlers." Martínez urged Austin to take his case personally to the new government in Mexico City. Although the idea of leaving the fledgling colony at such a critical time mortified him, Austin realized that he had no choice. "One nights deliberation" was all it took for him to decide.[15]

Austin spent two weeks preparing for the journey. Brown was to remain with the Seguíns in San Antonio, where he would study Spanish and act as his brother's unofficial representative. The previous fall Austin had named his old Missouri friend Josiah H. Bell justice of the peace for the colony. Now settled on the Brazos, Bell would exercise authority over the colonists for the duration of Austin's absence. In mid-March, Austin and two American traveling companions set out on horseback for the Rio Grande.[16]

Riding southwest out of San Antonio, they crossed the Medina River and made their way into the most desolate country Austin had ever seen. "It is generally nothing but Sand, entirely void of Timber, covered with

Central plaza, Mexico City, as it appeared when Austin first visited there in 1822. The equestrian statue of Spanish King Charles II had been removed by the time of Austin's second trip in 1833. *Courtesy, Texas State Library and Archives Division.*

scrubby thorn bushes and Prickly Pear," he noted. Early in the trip the travelers camped near the Nueces River and Austin received a bad scare. It was just before sunrise, and his companions were away from camp tending to the horses. Suddenly fifty Comanche Indians charged out of the brush, surrounding the surprised Austin. "Resistance was useless," he later wrote. Soon the Indians brought the other two Americans back into camp. Austin had heard that the Comanches hated the Mexicans but harbored no animosity toward Americans, who had occasionally been their trading partners. "I then expostulated with them for treating their Friends the Americans in such a manner," Austin related, and "when they found there was no Spaniards with me, they gave us back our Saddle bags, saddles, and everything else except 4 blankets, a bridle, my Grammar and Several other little things and all our provisions." One can only speculate as to why the Comanches wanted a Spanish grammar book, but Austin was convinced that only the fact of their being Americans had saved their lives. His firm "expostulation" in the face of hopeless odds may have also gained him the Comanches' respect. The Indians subsequently kept the travelers under surveillance but left them alone. The small party rode into the Rio Grande village of Laredo on March 21.[17]

Austin was undoubtedly thankful to reach Laredo, although, as he observed, the area was "as poor as sand banks, and drought, and indolence can make it." He remained there several days, replacing the provisions lost to the Indians and waiting for a larger traveling party to gather. The next leg of the journey was reputed to be bandit-infested, and he wished to take no chances by going with too small a group. Soon a comfortably large party had assembled, and by April 10 he had arrived safely in Monterrey. Austin was forced to make the rest of the journey with only one companion. To discourage bandits, the two men disguised themselves in ragged clothes and blankets. They reached San Luis Potosí on April 20, and on the 29th they descended into the central valley of Mexico. "After a long and tedious journey," Austin reported to Joseph Hawkins, "I am at length at the fountain head of the *new born nation*." [18]

Mexico City had long been one of the world's greatest capitals. "This city is truly a magnificent one," Austin marveled, "as regards the external appearance of the buildings, and altho I at first thought it not larger than New York, I now think after a better examination of it that it is much larger than any city in the U.S. and much more populous." Home to some 150,000 in 1822, it was in fact more populous than New York, and the domes and spires of its Spanish colonial architecture were dazzling. It boasted more than a hundred churches, nearly forty monasteries and convents, twelve hospitals, a botanical garden, an art academy, the world's best mining college, and a superb university. The boulevards were wide and well lighted, and the public buildings impressive. The wealthy lived in luxury, while an estimated 20,000 inhabitants were beggars. Austin would have ample time to become well acquainted with the ancient capital and its people—far more time, as it would turn out, than he wanted.[19]

He found lodging in a hotel that catered to foreign visitors. Here he met Robert Leftwich and Andrew Erwin, Tennesseans who had arrived ten days earlier. Leftwich and Erwin represented a group of some seventy investors known as the Texas Association, whose membership included Sam Houston and many of Nashville's leading men. Like Austin, they were seeking a grant to colonize Texas. Glad for the company and eager to minimize living expenses, Austin and the two Tennesseans took a room together.[20]

Austin was acutely aware that every day he spent away from Texas increased the chances of trouble in the colony. He naively believed that ten or twelve days would allow him to conclude his business and set out for home. However, it took that long merely to prepare his petition and have it translated into Spanish. When completed, it gave a detailed history of the Austin enterprise and essentially asked that the terms of his previous agreement be confirmed. He included a request for the "quantity of land that the Government might consider as just compensation for his labor and for all the hardships that he had experienced" in establishing the colony. Significantly, he also asked to be granted full Mexican citizenship. He laid the memorial before the Mexican congress on May 13.[21]

His timing was poor. Political events, which had been unsettled since the winning of independence a year earlier, reached a turning point just days after Austin presented his petition. For the previous several months, Mexico had been ruled by a provisional government dominated by Iturbide. The terms of the treaty that secured independence had called for a constitutional monarchy with a Bourbon monarch at its head, but no European prince had stepped forward to accept the invitation. All attention focused on Iturbide.

Austin noted "the existence of two parties, Imperial and Republican," but in reality there was little open support for a republic in the spring of 1822. Even men who would later be counted as leading republicans, such as Valentín Gómez Farías and Lorenzo de Zavala, kept their inclinations largely to themselves and endorsed the idea of an Iturbide-led monarchy. As the young general from Veracruz, Antonio López de Santa Anna, put it in April, "The most sensible and enlightened part of the people adopts the constitutional monarchical government. The Republican system has few adherents." [22]

Austin agreed with this assessment. In his first letter from Mexico, he wrote that "Gen. Iturbide seems to have the happiness of his country much at heart, and I have no doubt he will act as a great and good man ought to do." On the night of May 18, less than three weeks after Austin's arrival, a demonstration led by Iturbide's own regiment paraded through the streets, firing their guns in the air and noisily calling for the general's coronation as emperor. The next morning congress met and overwhelmingly proclaimed him Emperor Agustín I. Witnessing these stirring events, Austin felt optimistic that at last Mexico would have a government that was stable and sympathetic to his cause. "I hope this event will be a fortunate one for the Country," he wrote to Brown on May 22. "I shall return as soon as I can, but it is uncertain when that will be, everything is now at a stand, my prospect[s] are very good and I think everything will be right." [23]

Three days later Austin paid his respects to the new monarch. In a deferential letter, he congratulated "the hero of Iguala, the Liberator of his Country" and briefly told Iturbide of his own situation. "I make a tender of my services, my loyalty, and my fidelity to the Constitutional Emperor of Mexico; a tender which I am ready to verify by an oath of allegiance to the Empire," he wrote with great earnestness. "This solemn act cuts me off from all protection or dependence on my former government — my property, my prospects, my future hopes of happiness, for myself and family, and for the families I have brought with me, are centered here. This is our adopted Nation." [24]

Congress had been working on a general colonization law even before Austin's arrival in Mexico, and now Austin could do nothing but wait for the deliberations to resume. [25] The interlude gave him the chance to learn more about the city and its inhabitants and to work on his Spanish.

Like other first-time visitors to Mexico City, he was impressed by the capital's broad avenues, fine mansions, bustling markets, splendid churches and governmental palaces. On clear days the great snow-covered volcanoes, Popocatépetl and Iztaccíhuatl, loomed in the distance. But Austin could not help but note the stark contrasts between the grandeur of the city and the grinding poverty and ignorance of the masses. "The population however is very much mixed," he noted, "and a great proportion of them are most miserably poor and wretched, beggars are more numerous than I ever saw in any place in my life — robberies and assassinations are frequent in the Streets — the people are biggoted and superstitious to an extreem, and indolence appears to be the general order of the day—in fact the City Magnificent as it is in appearance is at least one century behind many other places in point of intelligence and improvement 'in the arts' and the nation generally is in the same situation." [26]

Austin's nonsectarian upbringing and his liberal education created in him an almost unavoidable distaste for the influence of the Catholic Church on the Mexican people. As he told his brother at the end of the Mexico trip, "to be candid the majority of the people of the whole nation as far as I have seen them want nothing but tails to be more brutes than the Apes. The Clergy have enslaved them to the last degree of oppression." Despite these strong words, it is worth noting that Austin laid the blame for Mexicans' benighted state on the clergy, not on their racial makeup or any inherent defect of character. Some Mexican intellectuals of the day voiced nearly identical criticisms of the church and clergy. Indeed, with political enlightenment seemingly on the horizon, Austin soon optimistically predicted that the Mexican nation would "assume her rights in full, and bursting the chains of superstition declare that *man has a right to think for himself*." But until that happy day, he understood that he had cast his lot with a Roman Catholic nation and that he could not allow his personal disapproval of Mexican Catholicism to affect his plans. After complaining about Mexican religious "fanaticism," he warned Brown to "keep this to yourself," for it "wont do" to let such opinions be known in Texas.[27]

Austin played his cards wisely in vowing his loyalty to the government, seeking Mexican citizenship, and working through the official channels with great formality and deference to authority. Few American frontiersmen could have navigated these strange waters so skillfully, but for the well-bred son of Moses Austin it seemed to come easily.

Nothing illustrates this better than his approach to surmounting the language barrier. Austin spoke virtually no Spanish when he first came to Texas in July 1821. He left no written account of his efforts to learn, but apparently he dedicated himself to the task in a single-minded, almost fanatical, fashion. His campaign to get his brother to learn Spanish reveals much about his own experience. Before Brown even arrived in Texas, Austin was practically demanding that he study Spanish. On his way to Mexico City, Austin had made a point of writing to Brown to make sure he was applying himself "closely to Study." He instructed Brown to get a Spanish grammar book "and Study the familiar phrases and lessons, and *write them,* also repeat your verbs as you learn them to Francisco or some other who can correct your pronunciation. A bad pronunciation at the start will be difficult to correct. Therefore take no lessions from any but those who are capable of giving them — Remember that it is all important to learn to *write* the language." He lectured Brown through the mail on rules of spelling and usage that even well-educated native speakers often violated. From Mexico City, Austin forcefully reminded his younger brother that he must "remember that all your hopes of rising in this country depend on lear[n]ing to speak and write the language correctly. Without that, you will do nothing." He insisted that Brown "rise at day light and be at your studies and continue at them all day, only taking exercise and amusement enough to keep you in health and to relax the mind." Siestas were out of the question.[28]

This sort of regimen is undoubtedly how Stephen learned Spanish so quickly. After only a few weeks in Mexico City he was writing long letters in simple but grammatical Spanish. Soon his fellow Americans in the capital had grown dependent on him because of his facility with the language. Aside from the practical need for communicating, Austin must have known that the Mexican officials would be more receptive to the needs of a foreigner who had so dedicated himself to learning his new country's ways. The strategy paid handsome dividends in the close relationships that he formed with well-placed Mexicans over the coming months and years.[29]

The presence of other foreigners in the capital seeking favors from the new government complicated Austin's situation. Some of them were pursuing the same object as Austin — permission to colonize Texas. Philip O'Reilly, James Barry, and their Mexican partner, Tadeo Ortiz de Ayala, were asking for a large grant to introduce 10,000 emigrants from Ireland and the Canary Islands. Robert Leftwich and Andrew Irwin, as previously mentioned, were seeking a grant on behalf of the Texas Association of Nashville. Haden Edwards, Lucius Woodbury, William Parrott, and Anthony Wolfe also laid their requests before the government at about the same time.[30]

The O'Reilly-Barry-Ortiz group pressed its claim — and undermined

Austin's—by arguing that colonizing Anglo-Americans in Texas threatened Mexico's security. The Nashville group, on the other hand, made common cause with Austin from the start. As Leftwich noted in his diary, Austin was "pleased with our views as forming other settlements with emigrants from the United States would enhance the value of his own." The Americans tried without success to impress this logic on their rivals. "If they [O'Reilly-Barry-Ortiz] had pursued the plan which had been strongly urged on them to let Judge Austins business (who had higher claims than any other) be first acted on," complained Leftwich, it would have established a precedent for the granting of other colonization contracts. "In doing this each wou[l]d have succeeded previous to a general law on the subject," he believed. By late July, congress was still debating the colonization issue. "Judge Austin's business is yet pending," Leftwich wrote, "but no doubt [is] entertained of his success." [31]

The most famous American in Mexico City during those months was retired U.S. Army general James Wilkinson, Moses Austin's old adversary from the early Missouri days. Wilkinson had been connected with Texas schemes for the past twenty-five years, from the plots of Philip Nolan and Aaron Burr to the more recent campaigns of James Long, who was married to Wilkinson's niece Jane. Wilkinson had long maintained close ties to Spain, and now he had important connections with the Mexican government. He was the houseguest of the provincial commandant general, and Iturbide himself had even paid him a visit. Austin could not have grown up in the Moses Austin household without hearing how Wilkinson, as governor of the Louisiana Territory, had tried to ruin Moses. Likewise, Wilkinson certainly knew Stephen Austin was Moses's son. But this was no time to harbor old grudges. Austin sought out Wilkinson (as did Leftwich and Erwin) to enlist his aid. The general obliged by writing a warm letter of recommendation, saying that Austin's service as legislator and judge in the United States had been conducted in a manner that was "beyond reproach and with the utmost integrity." The following year Wilkinson sought reciprocal assistance from Austin in securing his own colonization contract for Texas. While Austin was obviously happy to have Wilkinson's support, there is no record that he felt obliged to return the favor. By that point Austin probably realized that Wilkinson, as an empresario, could only cause trouble for him in Texas. The welfare of his own enterprise came first.[32]

Continuing his campaign to befriend influential men, Austin met Gen. Arthur W. Wavell, an Englishman who had compiled a distinguished military record in the service of Great Britain, Spain, Chile, and finally Mexico. He had held the rank of major general in the armies of the latter two countries and, like Wilkinson, enjoyed many high-level connections in the Mexican government. Wavell was immediately impressed by the young American, describing Austin as "a man of intellect, and energy." Many years later Wavell claimed to have helped Austin prepare his documents in Spanish, lent him money, furnished him a room, and introduced him to influential Mexicans at a time when Austin desperately needed all of those things.[33]

Wavell may have exaggerated the extent of his help, but there was some truth to his claims. In late June and early July 1822, he and Austin signed a set of agreements forming a partnership, subject to the fulfillment of certain terms. Any grants of land received or other Texas-related business ventures that either of them entered into were to be for the mutual advantage of both men. Wavell's main obligation was to travel to London to raise the sum of $50,000 or more from British capitalists in order to "form a Company . . . to carry on the business of settling lands, farming, Mining or Commerce." The same day the two men signed their final agreement, Wavell applied to the emperor for his own empresario grant in Texas, to be located to the east of Austin's, between the San Jacinto and Trinity rivers.[34]

Wavell quite likely did introduce Austin to some of the high-ranking officials of the government, and he did lend Austin money, although the amount is unknown. However, Austin seems not to have accepted the general's offer of a room; he appears to have roomed with Leftwich the entire time. Furthermore, Wavell left for England on a diplomatic mission in August, just a month after he and Austin signed their partnership agreement, so he could have done little to influence the subsequent course of Austin's business in Mexico City. Wavell's later claim that without his assistance Austin's grant "would *never have been obtained*" must be viewed with skepticism.[35]

There is no question, though, that Wavell took the potential partnership seriously. Over the next year he bombarded Austin with letters from England, describing his efforts to fulfill his end of the agreement. In May of the following year, Wavell wrote from London to inform Austin that he had received "a proposal made me by one of the largest and richest houses in this City to furnish 20,000 £ (say 100,000 Dollars) for one half the concern on the conditions proposed in the contract you gave me." All he needed was written confirmation of Austin's grant, and the funds would be released.[36]

Austin ignored Wavell's letters. During most of that year the grant was still unconfirmed by the government, so he could not have given Wavell the go-ahead in any case. Moreover, when the grant was finally confirmed and a general colonization law passed, it did not give the empresario any land outright, but rather entitled him to receive premium lands as payment for his services only after two hundred families had immigrated. This probably would have discouraged potential investors who would require collateral for their investment. Given the tortuous course of Austin's business in Mexico City, and the final form of the law, it is unlikely that the sort of company envisioned in the 1822 Wavell-Austin agreement actually could have been created. Nevertheless, Austin's handling of the situation does not reflect well on him. Wavell was almost frantic to hear from him — "Do not for Heavens sake delay ONE SINGLE MOMENT," he wrote from England — but Austin remained silent. Finally, two full years after the two had parted, Austin jotted a short note to Wavell, who had finally returned to Mexico. Austin claimed to have written him "often," which even with bad mail service could not have been true. Then he essentially dismissed Wavell with the following not-entirely-accurate report: "You ask how I am getting on to which I answer not very well — and I assure you I am heartily sick of the whole business and shall gain nothing by it but losses and fatigue, and if you wish to keep out of trouble let Colonization matters alone. . . . If I had encouraged you to bring out goods to a large amt. perhaps you would have blamed me more. I have spent more in this dammed affair than it will ever be worth. . . . I can return you the money you let me have, and will secure a piece of land here for you."[37]

Wavell gave up on Austin and eventually did secure his own empresario contract from the state government of Coahuila y Texas. But he never really forgave his would-be partner for reneging on their agreement and for leaving him incommunicado so long in England, while he worked so hard to uphold his end of the deal. He also claimed that Austin never repaid him the money he had borrowed, although Austin, who usually if slowly repaid old debts, probably would have settled with him without much fuss. In the end, Austin must have simply decided that a partnership with Arthur Wavell would not be in the best interests of his colony or himself. Knowing he could simply turn his back on the agreement, he did exactly that.

Enlisting the aid of influential foreigners like Wavell and Wilkinson and making allies of fellow applicants like Leftwich and Irwin may have been useful to Austin, but his fate ultimately rested with Mexican leaders. As he waited for his petition to be acted on and for the general colonization law to wind its way through congress, he began the essential task of winning friends in the central government. After the emperor, the most important connection to be made in the executive branch was with the minister of domestic and foreign relations, José Manuel de Herrera. Herrera had spent some time in New Orleans several years earlier raising funds for the insurgent cause, and this may have created some common ground between him and the young American. It appears that the two men developed a cordial relationship, and that Herrera helped put the colonization issue high on the government's agenda.[38]

Among the military, Austin courted the favor of Gen. Anastacio Bustamante, whom Iturbide had recently named commandant general of the Interior Provinces. His handling of Bustamante, who wielded considerable influence with Iturbide, displays Austin's skill at making a good impression through the indirect approach. Soon after arriving in Mexico City, Austin addressed a long letter to Bustamante giving a detailed account of the complex Indian situation in Texas. Without specifically asking the general to intervene with the Iturbide government on his behalf, he built a strong case for the importance of his colony in solving the Indian problem. Austin succeeded in winning Bustamante's confidence and forging a relationship that would prove helpful in the near term, and even more important a decade later, when the general would occupy the presidential chair at a critical period in Texas affairs.[39]

The highest immediate priority was to get some favorable action from congress, and here Austin put forth his best diplomatic effort. Early in his trip he made the acquaintance of Juan Bautista Arizpe, a scholar and politician from Monterrey and a member of one of northern Mexico's most prominent families. It was Arizpe who in June 1822 first brought Austin's case to the attention of congress, at a time when it appeared that he might be overlooked. Arizpe also was instrumental in helping Austin obtain his formal Mexican citizenship papers, something that Austin wanted very badly. At the end of his Mexico City sojourn, a circumstance arose in which Austin needed to obtain some papers from a procrastinating cabinet minister. Again Arizpe intervened on behalf of his American friend. After leaving the city, Austin left a rare glimpse into his operating methods in a letter to Robert Leftwich, in which he explained how to secure such influential allies as Arizpe:

> Enclosed is a letter recommending you to Don Juan Arizpe. I employed him to get my papers from the Minister for which I gave him two Doubloons. I advise you to give him about five or six Doubloons and if your business can be done at all he will do it immediately. He is a great friend of the Ministers and his family connections give him great weight. He is a relative of Ramos Arizpe a brother in law to General Garza, a relation [of] Padre Mier &c. You had better do this for you will spend ten times that much in expences waiting if you do not and the friendship of Arizpe's family is a matter of great importance to any person who intends to settle in the internal provinces.[40]

Austin also needed to win the confidence of members of the congressional colonization committee, which would play a large role in crafting Mexico's immigration policies. A key committee member was the thirty-three-year-old Lorenzo de Zavala of Yucatán. Enthusiastic and energetic, Zavala met with the American applicants and became a staunch supporter of a liberal colonization policy. Ten years later he remembered Austin as an "active and industrious foreigner," and five years after that, when the Texas Revolution briefly brought the two men together as housemates in Texas, Austin declared that there was never a better man than Zavala.[41]

Another member of the colonization committee whom Austin cultivated was Valentín Gómez Farías. Like Bustamante, Gómez Farías would eventually occupy the presidential chair. Austin's long-term relationship with him would be troubled, but in 1822 Gómez Farías, like Zavala, supported a liberal colonization policy and apparently viewed Austin favorably. After returning to Texas, Austin considered both Zavala and Gómez Farías his "amigos."[42]

Austin wisely befriended men of all ideological persuasions. Arizpe, Zavala, and Gómez Farías were among those who could be called liberals, as was Father Servando Teresa de Mier, who in August 1822 would be arrested by Iturbide for plotting against the monarch. Austin would pay a sympathetic visit to Mier in prison at the very time that he was lobbying Iturbide's government for approval of his colonization scheme. Simultaneously currying favor with both sides in Mexico's political struggles became one of Austin's standard tactics.[43]

Indeed, Austin was at least as comfortable in the company of conservatives. Former royalists and army officers such as Herrera and Bustamante figured prominently in this group. But in 1822 Austin also met Manuel de Mier y Terán, the brilliant young engineer, scholar, and soldier.[44] Terán was probably the most conservative member of the colonization committee on the issue of foreign immigration. As Leftwich put it, "We had reason to believe [he was] opposed to settling Texas with emigrants from the United States." Austin left no record of his initial impression of Terán, and it is unlikely that Terán relented in his opposition to a pro-American colonization law. But several years later, when Terán became a central figure in the affairs of Texas, the two men forged a remarkable relationship. Though they often disagreed on policy, Austin came to respect and even admire Terán.[45]

Austin probably played one additional card in his campaign to meet and befriend highly placed Mexicans—his membership in the Masonic fraternal order. Just as his Masonic connections had conferred political benefits in the United States, so they would have helped in Mexico. Two of his influential contacts, Lorenzo de Zavala and Servando Teresa de Mier, definitely held Masonic membership when Austin met them. Minister of Relations Herrera, who had spent time in the United States, was probably already a Mason, and Bustamante and Terán may have been. By 1826, competing Masonic orders would become the organizing vehicle for Mexican politics, and Masonic affiliation would take on a much different meaning. For now, though, Austin could use freemasonry as a means of establishing common ground with men whose influence he needed, regardless of their ideological or political orientations.[46]

If Austin exhibited political acuity in his cultivation of influential Mexicans, he also displayed another important quality: patience. Even with economic stability and political unity, the very newness of the imperial government would have slowed its deliberations. But the economy was a shambles, the treasury empty. The country still had no constitution, and Iturbide soon faced stiff opposition in congress. Governing Mexico would prove far more difficult than winning independence. The empire's inherent instability would create one frustrating delay after another for Austin.

Austin and the other American expatriates met at the U.S. consul's house and together attended Iturbide's coronation in late July 1822. Afterward Austin wrote, "The Government is I think now established on a much more solid basis than it heretofore has been, the legislative powers are all vested in the congress, and the Emperor has sworn to support the Constitution which that body may form, so that there is every reason to believe that the Govn.ᵗ will be as free and liberal as any man could wish." He predicted he would soon be on the road home. To Josiah Bell back in Texas, he sent these words of good cheer: "Tell them (the settlers) not to be discouraged at the gloomy prospect which wild woods present to them on their first arrival, a short time will change the scene, and we shall enjoy many a merry dance and wedding frolick together."[47]

There were really two distinct issues that directly concerned Austin: a general colonization bill that was already being drawn up in committee, and his own individual application to have his grant confirmed. In August, a month after Iturbide's coronation, the colonization committee sent its first bill to congress. This bill stipulated that Mexican or foreign colonists, who must be Roman Catholics, could receive a square league, or *sitio* of land (4,428 acres), and a *labor* (177 acres) if they intended to farm and raise livestock; that they must improve the land within six years; that they would pay no taxes for six years; and that they could bring tools and implements duty-free. They could bring their slaves, but the slave trade was to be outlawed and children born of slaves freed at age fourteen. As compensation for their work, empresarios would receive fifteen square leagues and two *labores* of land, a total of 66,774 acres for each two hundred immigrants introduced. Details would change before such a bill became law, but this was the basic blueprint for the nation's colonization policy over the next decade. Significantly, it granted individuals more than double the amount of land that Austin had called for in his previous agreements with officials in San Antonio and Monterrey.[48]

Congress debated the bill for a few days and then sent it back to the committee for revisions. No sooner had this happened than Iturbide arrested nineteen members of congress on charges of treason, throwing the entire government into an uproar for two weeks. Robert Leftwich, probably echoing Austin's fears, expressed "serious doubts whether the Emperor wou'd in the event of the passage of the Colonisation law feel disposed to distribute any lands to the applicants from the United States as part of the members imprisoned were among our greatest friends." At any rate, the emperor made it known that he would take no action on applications for grants until the general colonization bill had been passed. A petition from Austin asking provisional authority to fix the boundaries of the colony and assign lands to settlers fell on deaf ears.[49]

Throughout September and October the colonization bill made slow progress, as did the rest of the congress's business. On October 31 the emperor dissolved congress, again throwing into uncertainty all matters relating to Texas colonization. After six months in the capital, a frustrated Austin seemed no closer to achieving his mission than when he had arrived. "These people will not do for a Republic," he concluded a few weeks later, "nothing but a Monarchy can save them from Anarchy."[50]

Austin again turned to the emperor, diplomatically renewing his request for provisional authority to move forward with his colonization plans. But Iturbide was already in the process of appointing a scaled-down version of congress called the *junta nacional instituyente* to legislate until a new congress could be elected. The junta created its own colonization committee, with most of the same members as the old congressional committee, and set about drawing up a new bill. At the urging of Minister of Relations Herrera, the legislation moved fairly quickly this time, and on November 26 the junta passed the bill to the emperor for his signature. On the eve of the bill's passage, Austin predicted that within ten days he would be "dispatched with everything freely arranged."[51]

It was not to be. In early December, before Iturbide got around to signing the junta's bill, armed rebellion broke out in the province of Veracruz. On Christmas Day, Austin addressed a letter to his "dear and beloved Brother" Brown, who would no doubt be "astonished" to learn that he was still in Mexico City. "A Gen[l.] Santana has proclaimed a *Republic*," Austin explained, though he thought that the revolt would probably be put down. Matters soon grew more serious. First, the old insurgent general Guadalupe Victoria united with Santa Anna, and in early January two of Iturbide's other generals, Vicente Guerrero and Nicolás Bravo, joined the rebellion. " 'Blessed is he that holdeth out to the end,' " wrote Austin to his brother, "and I am determined to persevere." Finally, on January 4, 1823, the emperor found time to sign the colonization bill. It did not, of course, specifically confirm Austin's grant, but the way was now cleared for such approval.[52]

On January 8, Austin reported that Herrera had assured him that confirmation of his grant was imminent. But still nothing happened, and at the beginning of February, Austin and Leftwich decided to sit outside Herrera's office until they got a personal interview. When they were the only two people left in the waiting room, Herrera finally emerged and, as Leftwich described it, "received us in an unusual pleasant manner." As it turned out, Austin's grant had been confirmed by Iturbide's council of state in mid-January; it awaited only the emperor's signature. By February 19, after still further delays, the signed papers were in Austin's hands.[53]

But still he could not set out for Texas. The decree confirming his grant had ratified certain details contained in Austin's original petition without actually listing those details. The decree would not be complete unless it was accompanied by a certified copy of Austin's petition of the previous May. It was a simple matter of getting the bureaucracy to issue such a copy, but once again events interposed themselves between Austin and his plans. The revolt against Iturbide was reaching its climax, and before Austin could get the document, the entire cabinet was forced to resign. The newly appointed minister of relations, José de Valle, was a stranger to Austin.[54]

Faced with this most recent setback, Austin sought help from a powerful friend. On February 25, he and Leftwich boldly rode twenty-four miles out to the headquarters of Gen. Anastacio Bustamante, who was on campaign with the imperial army. "[We] were received in the most friendly manner and partook of a sumptuous dinner in his quarters," Leftwich noted in his diary. Bustamante graciously issued letters of introduction and recommendation for the two Americans, as well as their passports for the return home. By March 11, Austin had all his papers signed and certified.[55]

But again the fast-changing course of Mexican politics had caught up with Austin. As he had waited for his final papers, Iturbide, under intense pressure, convened a new congress. Austin concluded that it would be best to obtain this latest congress's approval for his project. The new body convened on March 5, but it came too late to save Iturbide; he abdicated on March 19. Congress appointed a three-man Supreme Executive Power to serve as the nation's interim executive. It was the end of March before congress obtained a quorum, and on April 5, Austin asked the new body for confirmation of his grant. It turned out to be a necessary move, for congress annulled all acts passed under the Iturbide regime. Had he not stayed in the capital and continued pressing his case, the many months in Mexico City would have been for naught. The contacts that Austin had established in the congress and the executive branch now paid off, and by April 14 his petition had cleared congress and had been approved by the executive department. With the colonization law now repealed and Austin's the only individual grant approved, all the other foreign applicants for empresario contracts in Texas, including Leftwich and several others, were left out in the cold. On April 18, 1823, Austin rode out of Mexico City, having been there just ten days short of a year.[56]

Austin's return to Texas took him through Querétaro (April 23), Saltillo (May 8), and Monterrey (about May 14).[57] At Saltillo he visited Miguel Ramos Arizpe, the leading statesman of Coahuila and a kinsman of Juan Bautista Arizpe, who had helped Austin so much over the past year. Ramos Arizpe had recently returned from Europe, where he had represented Mexico in the liberal Spanish parliament. Greatly influenced by Enlightenment doctrines, he returned an ardent republican and became an outspoken opponent of the Iturbide regime.[58]

Ramos Arizpe and Austin became friends, perhaps in part because both men were Masons. They discussed the political affairs of Mexico City and Texas, and shortly thereafter Austin went on to Monterrey, the military and political nerve center of northern Mexico. There Austin met with Ramos Arizpe's brother-in-law, Gen. Felipe de la Garza, the new commandant general of the Eastern Interior Provinces. Again Austin had played his cards well, for he had met Garza in Mexico City and considered him a "particular friend of mine." With both Ramos Arizpe and Garza on his side, Austin was able to report that the authorities in Monterrey "have the best disposition in my favor, and will render me all the support and aid necessary to carry into speedy execution" the plans for establishing the colony on a solid basis.[59]

Austin needed the provincial government in Monterrey to clarify several details of his grant, including the extent of his judicial powers over the colonists, organization of the colony's militia, and the designation of a port for the colony. Again there were delays. Garza did not appear until May 28, two weeks after Austin's arrival. Then the provincial deputation had to be consulted. Understandably there were other items on the government's agenda more pressing than Austin's business.[60]

Austin again sought constructive ways to fill his time while he waited. He had always been fascinated by constitutional theory, and he clearly considered himself an expert on the topic. Three times during the year in Mexico City he had drawn up working plans for the organization (or reorganization) of the Mexican government. The first, written in August 1822, gave a detailed proposal for organizing congress into a bicameral legislature with American-style checks and balances. The second, addressed to Iturbide's Junta Instituyente in January 1823, urged the calling of a fairly elected congress and the writing of a constitution, and it expostulated on matters such as natural rights and popular sovereignty. The third, dated shortly before his departure from the capital, was a full-blown draft of a national constitution. There is no evidence that any of these documents were actually laid before the government, although the 1822 plan for organizing congress bore some similarities to a proposal put forward subsequently by Lorenzo de Zavala. As a foreigner seeking favors from the government, Austin would not have jeopardized his delicate position by publicly casting himself into the middle of the rancorous national debate over what form of government the nation should adopt. However, if he thought he had earned the confidence of an influential Mexican statesman, he would not have hesitated to share his ideas with that statesman with the hope that in this indirect and anonymous way he could play an active part in shaping public affairs.[61]

This is precisely what Austin now did. He drew up "A Plan of Federal Government" and shared it with Ramos Arizpe, who apparently came on to Monterrey from Saltillo in early June. The plan combined elements of the Spanish Constitution of 1812 and the U.S. Constitution and was similar to the draft constitution Austin had written in Mexico City. He showed it to Ramos Arizpe, who wrote comments in the margins and suggested that it be published. Six months later, as a member of the newly convened national congress, Ramos Arizpe wrote the *acta constitucional,* which became the blueprint for the Mexican Constitution of 1824 and earned its author fame as the "father of Mexican federalism." Austin's draft constitution and Ramos Arizpe's were similar in broad terms, leading Austin as well as some latter-day scholars to conclude that Ramos Arizpe used Austin's constitution as a guide when writing the acta constitucional. "I believe that this plan had much influence in giving unity of intention and direction to the Federal party," Austin later said of his document, "Arispe was the chairman of the Committee who drew up the 'Acta Constitutiva'

Miguel Ramos Arizpe, the Father of Mexican
Federalism. Austin shared his theories on
constitutional law with this northern
Mexican statesman.

and a comparison of that act with this plan will shew a very striking simi-
larity." [62]

In reality, Austin's plan probably had relatively little influence on the
Mexican statesman, for Ramos Arizpe was already intimately familiar with
the American Constitution and while in Spain had been instrumental in
writing the Spanish Constitution of 1812. Moreover, the similarities are
not really as "striking" as Austin stated.[63] But this episode shows that he
intended to play an active role in guiding the destiny of his adopted country. As a newcomer, he knew that he had to work quietly to avoid controversy. Austin's advice to the colonists in Texas, written to his brother from
Saltillo, sounds almost hypocritical, coming from a man who himself had
been so deeply involved in Mexican politics for the past year:

I wrote to the settlers on the Colorado and Brazos that they ought not to meddle with politics, and to have nothing to do with any revolutionary schemes, I hope they have followed my advise — they are as yet too recently established in the country to take an active part in its political affairs — if any questions are asked them as to their opinion of the Gov ͭ etc. they ought to answer that they moved here to live under the government which the nation may establish. They can do themselves no good by meddling in politics and at such a time as this when the Gov ͭ is not yet settled and the nation in a state of political fermentation it is embarking on a doubtfull voyage to embrace any party — as foreigners we have a good excuse for remaining neutral without being lyable to suspicions and this is the safe course.[64]

This was wise advice, although convincing the colonists to follow it would be a constant struggle. But for himself, Austin adopted it only for the sake of appearance. He would never stop trying to influence Mexican politics — often at the very highest levels of government — in every way that he deemed necessary. Reflecting on his experiences many years later, he penned a revealing explanation of his pragmatic political approach toward the Mexicans:

> They are a strange people, and must be studied to be managed.
> They have high ideas of National dignity should it be openly attacked, but will sacrifice national dignity, and national interest too if it can be done in a *still* way, or so as not to arrest public attention. "Dios Castiga el escandolo mas que el crimen," (God punishes the exposure more than the crime) is their motto. This maxim influences their morals and their politics. I learned it when I was there in 1822, and I now believe that if I had not always kept it in view, and know the power which *appearances* have on them, even when they know they are deceived, I should never have succeeded, to the extent I have done.[65]

Austin had clearly gained an education in the political culture of Mexico, and his unguarded moments reveal that it had bred in him a certain cynicism. But key Mexican leaders believed that they had found in

Austin the possible beginning of a constructive solution to one of their nation's most pressing problems. Whatever their political persuasion— monarchist or republican, liberal or conservative, federalist or central- ist, or some combination thereof—most Mexican politicians understood that preserving the territorial integrity of Mexico required the expeditious peopling of the northern frontier. The United States was quickly popu- lating its own frontier regions because its rapidly growing population and expanding capitalist economy provided incentives for settlers to move west. But Mexico was a precapitalist economy, impoverished by a decade of warfare and hindered by the semi-feudal remnants of three centuries of colonial domination. In the social, political, and economic context of the western world, the northern Mexican frontier was a peripheral region of a peripheral nation. To leave the northern provinces populated only by a handful of tiny settlements, crumbling missions, and understaffed military garrisons would be to surely lose those provinces to the aggres- sive, land-hungry *norteamericanos*. As the astute cabinet secretary Lucas Alamán noted in May 1823, Mexico had to populate the provinces of the north in order "to impede a quiet occupation invited by their present abandonment."[66]

Austin's sincere professions of loyalty to his adopted country, his punctilious deportment, and his seemingly inexhaustible patience had won him the confidence of Mexicans in places of power. The terms of his contract seemed to offer reasonable safeguards against the introduction of unruly or disloyal settlers. It is important also to remember that he was asking to bring only three hundred families, scarcely a threat to a republic of more than 6 million, no matter how poor or weak the republic might be.

Felipe de la Garza and the provincial deputation were as convinced of this logic as the powers in Mexico City had been, and after a month in Monterrey Austin had received all the information he had requested and had been given all the authority he needed to begin administering his colony effectively. He left Monterrey around June 17 and headed north toward Texas. Three hundred miles later, weary from his long journey but immensely satisfied with all he had accomplished over the past year, the empresario of Austin's Colony reined his horse into the dusty streets of San Antonio.[67]

Empresario Estevan F. Austin
1823–1825

Newspaper subscribers in such western cities as Nashville, St. Louis, and Little Rock opened their morning
papers in the summer of 1822 to read the sad news that
Stephen F. Austin had drowned in the Colorado River.
"The death of judge Austin is considered a great pub-
lic loss—he possessed enterprize, was of a conciliating disposition, and
having talents of no ordinary kind, would have been a considerable man
in the country had he lived," wrote the *Nashville Clarion.* Other stories
had him shot, lost at sea, or killed by Indians. Reports contradicting these
rumors soon filtered back to the United States, but the realities of circumstances in the colony were grim enough. While Austin was in Mexico
City, drought had gripped Texas, resulting in a near-total crop failure.
Disease had taken its toll, and Indians posed a serious threat. Colonists
were forced to subsist on venison, but the deer were in such poor condition that some settlers opted for the flesh of wild mustangs.[1]

The press in the western states did its part to publicize such reports,
for those states had no desire to compete with Mexican Texas for immigrants. The *Arkansas Gazette,* in a widely copied series of stories, warned
settlers that they had "better wait" two or three years rather than "run the

risk they now do of suffering vastly from the total destitution of every thing like comfort in the country, and even of such things as are essentially necessary to those accustomed to privations." Remarking on the "wretchedness and poverty" of the settlers in Texas, the *Gazette* expressed the hope that their experiences would "operate as a serious warning to others; and teach them to limit their emigrations to their own country." If natural hardships were not reason enough to avoid Texas, the western press also noted the preponderance of "murderers, horse-theives, counterfeiters, and fugitives from justice" in Texas. Of course, the *Gazette* maintained that "we intend no injury to Mr. Austin." Brown Austin summed up the situation in a letter to his brother written shortly before Stephen's return to Texas: "The Enemies to the *Austin* Grant have been *busy, very busy* during your absence to discourage anything like emigration to the Country." Brown's description of these "enemies" cannot be written off entirely as another manifestation of the Austin family's persecution complex; the public-relations battle was real, and the Austins were losing it in 1822 and 1823.[2]

It is impossible to say how many emigrants were deterred by these gloomy reports, and how many came despite them. From the Louisiana border, Hugh McGuffin reported in September 1822 that "the emigration is considerably stop[p]ed . . . for the present in consiquence of the badness of the crops on the Brazos and Colorado Rivers [but] still there appears to be a considerable number who wishes to go on." The most immediate problem was the condition of the emigrants already in the colony. As Brown informed Stephen the following May, "The settlers have been much discouraged at your long stay and the dread of the Indians . . . [but] they have concluded to wait untill fall and if Crops are not good they will all move back." Thus matters stood upon Austin's return to Texas in June 1823.[3]

Though eager to return to the colony, Austin spent most or all of July in San Antonio. He certainly would have found plenty to occupy him there. First would be the happy reunion with his brother, who had lived with the Seguíns for more than a year. There would be much personal business demanding his attention. Piles of unanswered correspondence awaited him. He would have to establish a good working relationship with yet another governor, Luciano García. Austin also must have spent many hours meeting with the Baron de Bastrop, who now was ready to enter into his duties as land commissioner for the colony.[4]

At the beginning of August, Austin and Bastrop left San Antonio for the colony. They established headquarters at the farm of Sylvanus Castleman, on the upper Colorado near present-day La Grange. Austin's priorities were to establish his authority over the colonists and reassure them that the worst was over. Accordingly, he and Bastrop immediately issued proclamations to the colonists. Bastrop informed the settlers that Austin had been named lieutenant colonel in the national militia and had been given "full powers to administer justice and preserve good order in the colony untill it can be regularly organized agreeably to the constitution and laws of the nation."[5]

Austin's proclamation set forth rules for obtaining land. Farming families were guaranteed a minimum of 177 acres, but that could be increased to any size that Austin and Bastrop deemed appropriate. In practice, most families ended up receiving a full league (4,428 acres), the amount guaranteed to ranching families. Land titles, when issued, would be "perfect and complete for ever, and each settler may sell his land the same as he could do in the United States." He explained that the costs of surveying the land and issuing titles must come out of his own pocket and that therefore "those who have the means must pay me a little money on receipt of their titles." If a settler had no money, Austin would accept livestock, furs, beeswax, cloth, deerskins, or any other goods of value, and he would give them three years to pay. Austin also urged the colonists "to remember that the Roman Catholic is the religion of this nation," and he instructed them to "respect the Catholic religion with all that attention due to its sacredness and to the laws of the land." Except for the larger quantity of land allowed, none of this differed significantly from the terms that Austin had originally published in American newspapers in 1821 and 1822. If anything, the terms were more generous.[6]

Austin also sought to explain his personal motives to the settlers. From the beginning he had downplayed his own financial incentives in undertaking the Texas venture. Like the politician that he was, he portrayed himself as acting primarily out of a sense of obligation to the settlers. "I was animated by the gratifying hope of providing a home for a number of meritorious citizens and of placing them and their families in a situation to make themselves happy the balance of their lives," he announced. "One of the greatest pleasures a virtuous mind can receive in this world is the consciousness of having benefited others. This pleasure I now have in prospect."[7]

This sense of noblesse oblige surely came naturally to the son of Moses Austin. But as time went by, Stephen's paternalism endowed his difficult undertaking with an importance that transcended his private goal of restoring the Austin family to wealth and respectability. It helped to transform him from a mere businessman and speculator to a statesman, a father-figure, and a visionary leader. The success of the colony, he told the settlers, "depends on me . . . ; but to enable me to benefit them to the full extent that I wish, it is necessary that the settlers should have confidence in me, and be directed by me. I have a better opportunity of knowing what will be advantageous to them as regards their conduct and intercourse with the Government than any of them could have had, and I feel almost the same interest for their prosperity that I do for my own family — in fact I look upon them as one great family who are under my care." With such obligations to others, he could never turn back, no matter how difficult his path might become.[8]

Austin closed his proclamation with an exhortation for unity and perseverance among the colonists — and also with a stern paternal reminder. "The settlers have now nothing to fear, there is no longer any cause for uneasiness," he assured them.

They must not be discouraged at any little depradations of Indians, they must remember that *American blood* flows in their veins, and that they must not dishonor that noble blood by yielding to trifling difficulties. . . . *Let every man do his duty, and we have nothing to fear — Let us be united as one man — discord must be banished from amongst us, or those who cause it will meet with most severe treatment.*

Hoping to meet you soon in peace and happiness, I am Resp[ec]t[fu]lly your friend and fellow citizen

Stephen F. Austin

With its paternalistic tone, its disclaimer of self-interest, and its emphasis on unity and harmony, Austin's proclamation set the tone for his style of leadership. He would adhere to that style for years to come, and for the most part it would serve him well.[9]

No one knows how many settlers were actually in the colony when Austin returned in August 1823. In a report written two months later, Gov. Luciano García stated that there were only fifty Anglo-American families living on the Colorado and Brazos. This figure seems low, however, because by the following September, Bastrop and Austin had issued land titles to 272 families. Most likely the fifty-family figure did not include the considerable number of men who had come in advance of their wives and children. If there had been only fifty men in the fall of 1823, divided between the Brazos and the Colorado settlements, Austin would scarcely have been able to muster the manpower needed to address the colony's most immediate problem—Indian depredations.[10]

Up to this point Austin's only real encounters with Indians had been with a small band of Cocos near Goliad in 1821 and with the Comanches on the road to Laredo in March 1822. Neither episode had taken place in the area that would become Austin's Colony, and both had ended peacefully. Indians certainly ventured into the region of the colony periodically, but it was not the home of any permanent villages, nor did any tribes make it their exclusive hunting grounds. The Karankawas came closest to being full-time residents of the colony, but they also ranged the coastal regions of Texas, far above and below the limits of Austin's grant.[11]

The absence of permanent Indian settlements within the colony did not, however, prevent conflict between colonists and natives. The Karankawas caused the most trouble in the early days. Other tribes that occasionally clashed with the settlers included the Tonkawas, Wacos, and Tawakonis. These tribes' home territories were north of the colony, although hunting, raiding, and war-making expeditions sometimes took them into Austin's Colony. None of these tribes numbered more than a few hundred individuals, and some were much smaller than that. Moreover, they often were enemies of one another, which enabled the Anglo-Americans to play one tribe against the other.

Poor relations with the Karankawas already existed by the time Austin returned from Mexico City. Relatively few colonists ever died at their hands, but these few cases were enough to strike fear into the hearts of the settlers. Karankawan warriors often stood six feet tall and shot three-foot arrows from six-foot cedar bows. "They might . . . be termed a race of giants," settler W. B. Dewees noted. They went about naked but painted their faces, tattooed and pierced their bodies, and smeared alligator grease on themselves to ward off mosquitoes. The settlers believed that the Indians practiced cannibalism. Most of Austin's colonists shared the Tejanos' view of the Karankawas as barbarians who should be killed or driven from the colony as soon as possible.[12]

One of the first ships to bring colonists to Texas, the schooner *Only Son,* arrived at the Colorado in June 1822. When the immigrants moved inland, leaving their provisions at the river's mouth with four guards, the Karankawas killed the guards and took the supplies. This became a general pattern; the Karankawas attacked when they found whites alone or in small groups, and when there were valuables to be taken. The settlers almost always retaliated, either in ad hoc posses or as an organized militia. When the offenders could be located, they were no match for American guns.[13]

Austin preferred peace, but between Karankawas and colonists it proved nearly impossible. In late 1823 he ordered the militia on the lower Colorado to make war on any Karankawas who might appear on the coast or the river. Clashes continued, and the following spring Austin ordered the "Chief of the Karankawases" to withdraw "his whole nation" from the colony and go to the mission at Refugio until peace could be established. Austin failed to realize that there was no individual "chief" with authority over all the Karankawas, because they lived in small, roving bands and had no real tribal structure. Austin's order thus had little effect, and four months later, in August 1824, the empresario took the field to drive the Karankawas from the colony.[14]

Taking a chapter from his War of 1812 experience, Austin divided his force of sixty-two men and descended both sides of the Colorado, sending spies ahead to scout for Indians. The only sign of the Karankawas was an abandoned camp on a creek where Austin found the "bones of two men which had been cut up and boiled." Austin's men buried the bones, christened the stream Cannibal Creek, and concluded that the Indians had retreated westward, toward the San Antonio River. The September weather was oppressively hot, and after a week or so Austin decided to rest, resupply, and reinforce his company. Jared Groce, the only large slaveholder in the colony, contributed thirty armed and mounted slaves to the force, and with other additions the number of men now approached ninety. Austin led them to the outskirts of Goliad, where the Indians had taken refuge in the mission. A messenger from the town met Austin and his men on the outskirts of the village, asking that they not enter, a request that Austin honored. The Americans made camp and soon received a delegation of Goliad's civil and ecclesiastical leaders. They explained that the Karankawas had pledged to remain west of the San Antonio River for a year in return for a cessation of hostilities. Austin agreed and later told the Goliad officials, "It is not our wish to deprive the Indians of their hunting or fishing grounds. . . . I sincerely hope with all my heart that . . . confidence will be mutually established between us and the Indians so that we may mix with each other without suspicion on either part." The expedition returned to the colony. Trouble with the Karankawas eased for a while, but the Indians continued to appear in the colony from time to time, and a year later Austin again gave the militia orders to pursue and kill Karankawas wherever they might be found, with the exception of one peaceful band that was staying west of Buffalo Bayou. Hostilities would erupt several more times over the ensuing years.[15]

Relations with the other tribes who occasionally ranged into the colony were more complex, for the Tonkawas, Wacos, and Tawakonis usually professed peaceful intentions. Unlike the Karankawas, however, these tribes valued horses, and most of their conflicts with the colonists involved horse stealing. The settlers particularly viewed the Tonkawas, a small tribe of hunters who normally ranged north of the colony, as inveterate thieves and beggars. Austin's handling of them vividly illustrates his overall outlook and strategy for dealing with Indians.[16]

When Austin arrived on the Colorado in the summer of 1823, the settlers were losing livestock to the Tonkawas, who lived in two distinct bands under different chiefs. In late August, Austin sent ten men, including Brown, to search for the culprits and reclaim the horses. This apparently failed, and several weeks later, after the Tonkawas raided settlements on the Brazos, Austin himself took command of a force of colonists to punish the thieves. With about thirty men, Austin headed down the Brazos. Surprising the Tonkawas in their camp, Austin demanded that their chief, Carita, bring forward the guilty parties. Carita named five young braves, and Austin dictated the punishment: Each man was to receive fifty lashes and have his head shaved. Half the lashes were to be inflicted by Carita himself. The sentence was carried out, although Carita was said to have applied the whip "very lightly," frequently pausing to ask Austin *"cuantos"*—how many lashes—had been inflicted. Austin left the Tonkawas with a warning to leave the colony at once and never to molest the settlers again, or face being shot the next time.[17]

This episode reveals much about the Indian situation in the colony's early days and about the strengths and limitations of Austin's understanding of the problem. On one hand, it is clear that the empresario preferred peace over war—peace was cheaper and safer. Austin's tactic of making the chief sanction the punishment helped give it much more authority than if the whites had unilaterally inflicted it. But Austin was blind to the underlying dynamics of the situation. In cultures such as the Tonkawan, capturing an enemy's horses was a coming-of-age tradition for young men. Carita surely lost credibility among his own people by acceding to Austin's demand that he participate in the punishment. As with the Karankawas, Austin seems not to have understood that all Tonkawas would not be bound by any pledges that Carita might make. In fact, bands under the other Tonkawa chief, Sandia, continued to conduct occasional raids on the settlements. Conversely, one settler reported in December 1823 that if friendly Tonkawas had not supplied the colonists with dressed deerskins, many of the Americans would have been "entirely destitute of clothes." Whatever the intentions of the Tonkawas, Carita's agreement to participate in the whipping of his own men demonstrates the weak position that the small tribe must have found itself in. Described by one colonist as a "very shrewd Indian," Carita must have known that he had little choice in the matter. Annihilation was the likely alternative, as Austin had made clear.[18]

But there were limits to how far even Carita would go to placate the settlers. Later on, Austin naively presented the chief with seed corn and farming implements and secured his promise that his people would clear land in the Colorado bottom and abandon their hunting (and stealing) ways. Not surprisingly, the Tonkawas simply ate the seed corn. When Austin subsequently visited the tribe, Carita informed him that the Great Spirit had instructed him to keep to the tribe's traditional ways. Austin told the chief that the Indians would starve if they did not become farmers, but the Tonkawas never adopted the sedentary habits of the white men. In the context of the American frontier, Austin's repeated attempts to find a peaceful accommodation with the Indians could be viewed as enlightened; he did not believe that the only good Indian was a dead Indian. He essentially took the Jeffersonian approach to the Indian problem: if Indians would adopt the white man's ways and become "civilized," there might be a place for them in society. But if the Jeffersonian approach failed, there was always the Jacksonian solution of removal or destruction.[19]

In his dealings with the other two principal tribes that sometimes ventured into the colony, Austin followed a similar policy. The Wacos and Tawakonis were closely related Wichita-speaking peoples who lived in prosperous, permanent agricultural villages far north of the colony in the vicinity of present-day Waco. Because they could field several hundred warriors, and because they were sometimes allied with the Comanches to the west, they potentially posed a greater threat to Austin's people than did the Karankawas or Tonkawas. The most notorious incident in the early days of the colony came just after Austin had returned to Texas in 1823. John Tumlinson, who had been chosen as the provisional *alcalde* (presiding municipal officer) of the Colorado settlement in Austin's absence, was attacked and killed by Indians believed to be Wacos, or perhaps

Tawakonis. Austin took the cautious approach. "We must be vigilent," he told Josiah Bell. "I [wish] if possible to avoid an open rupture with them for six months longer at least, by that time we shall have more strength, but if they commit any more depradations the only alternative will be an expedition to distroy their village, but this I wish to avoid until next year if possible." Austin instructed the settlers to "treat them friendly but tell them firmly the consequences of a war. I wish for peace, but am ready for war if it cannot be avoided."[20]

As usual, pragmatism governed his thinking. A year later, with Tumlinson's killers still at large, Austin sent a negotiating party to the Wacos' village on the upper Brazos. The Indians received the commissioners warmly and denied having had any connection with the murder or with horse-stealing. In a message to the Wacos, Austin demanded the punishment of the guilty individuals, expressed his desire for peace, and threatened war. The commissioners apparently were satisfied that the Wacos were not guilty, and the Indians "smoked the pipe of peace with the embassy and pledged themselves to peace and amity with the colonists."[21]

This, however, did not end problems with the Wacos, and subsequent developments put Austin's diplomatic abilities to the test. In 1825 the empresario found himself pressured from two sides to make war on the Wacos and Tawakonis. On one hand, colonists who continued to lose horses clamored for "open war with said tribes." On the other hand, the Mexican military commandant in San Antonio ordered Austin to attack the Waco village because the Wacos were now allied with the Comanches, with whom the Mexicans were at war. Austin wrote the commandant, pleading the inability of the colonists to conduct such a war. The commandant allowed Austin to postpone the attack until a body of Comanches had left the Waco village. This gave the empresario time to write again, pleading once more that the colonists be allowed to remain neutral. Austin simultaneously wrote to all of his militia commanders, offering strong arguments against an offensive. "In this state of feeling is there not some danger that all the Indians in the Province may be induced to unite against the American settlements?" he asked. "If we destroy the Waco Villages will not the other tribes consider it warning of the fate that must in the end befal[l] them if the american settlements progress. And is there no danger that they may become alarmed and united to cut us off in our infancy?" History, Austin argued, "presents numerous and hor[r]ible examples of such combinations, which in most instances might have been avoided by a greater degree of prudence and forbearance on the part of the settlers in the first years of their establishment."[22]

Austin's pacific arguments carried the day, both with the colonists and with the Mexican authorities. The Mexicans were reportedly displeased with him, but colonist John P. Coles summed up what must have been Austin's own feelings in the matter. It would be better, Coles wrote, for the colonists to "be driven out of the country by the Government than by the Indians." Coles deemed it preferable to "put up with some abuse" from the Indians than to disrupt the peace that now existed. The Mexican government would provide no assistance in the event of a war, he accurately observed, "and we are unable . . . to contend with them and my oppinion is that the only policy for us is to let those Indians alone[,] say nothing to them and If the Government will force us into a war with them we must make the best of It."[23]

And so it went for many years. Austin pursued his pragmatic policy of negotiation and appeasement, backed with threats of dire consequences and occasionally enforced with military action. He tried to involve the various Indian chiefs as much as possible in executing his policies, and he treated them with more dignity than many Anglo-Americans would have. But in Indian affairs, as in all other matters, his colony came first. The protection of Indian "rights" — or, for that matter, the wishes or needs of the Mexican government — were always secondary considerations.[24]

As Austin struggled with the Indian problem in the last half of 1823, he also worked to establish a system of government for the colony. His empresario contract provided little guidance. He was simply instructed to govern and take responsibility for the colonists until civil law was established, subject to the direction and approval of provincial officials whose own powers were not clearly defined. Consequently, Austin had enormous latitude to administer the colony as he saw fit.

Before leaving for Mexico City, Austin had appointed Josiah Bell provisional justice of the peace for the colony, but the governor subsequently ordered the Baron de Bastrop to organize a more formal temporary government. Bastrop traveled to the Colorado settlement in November 1822 and oversaw an election in which the settlers chose the ill-fated John Tumlinson as alcalde. The settlers also elected militia officers and a constable. Settlers on the Brazos elected Bell alcalde of their settlement. Since the colony's most important business — the issuance of land titles — could not proceed until Austin returned, the main function of this skeleton government was to protect the colonists from Indians.[25]

Two principles guided Austin in establishing a system of government for the colony. First, he tried to conform with Mexican law and practice as much as possible. Second, he sought to extend as much American-style democracy to the colonists as he could. As usual, pragmatism guided his thinking. He knew that Mexican officials would be watching him; adopting Mexican models and nomenclature would be a sign of loyalty to his new country. But Austin also knew Americans. Although he was vested with near-dictatorial powers over the colonists, he realized that exercising such powers could arouse the resentment of the proud, egalitarian frontiersmen. He had to give them a voice in their own affairs.

Implementing this strategy proved difficult. As the first empresario, Austin had no written rules to follow beyond the vague terms of his colonization contract and the bare-bones guidelines he had secured from Monterrey. These said nothing about laws for the colony. The transitional state of government in Mexico compounded his difficulties. Not only was there still no national constitution, but nobody knew whether Texas would become a separate state in a future federal system or whether it would be joined with other northern provinces into some other administrative entity. Austin faced the task of devising nearly from scratch a system of local government — one that would please the Mexicans and satisfy the colonists, and, above all, one that would work.

The colony stumbled along during the last half of 1823, with Austin too busy with land matters and Indian problems to take much action in regard to government. As the population grew, legal and administrative problems multiplied, and by the end of the year the empresario knew that he had to take steps to establish laws to guide the colony. In January 1824 he issued a set of Civil and Criminal Regulations, which with periodic alterations served as the governing charter of the colony for the next four years.[26]

The basic political unit of the colony was the district. Initially there were only two—the Colorado and the Brazos—but Austin subdivided the Brazos district to create a third in December 1823, and eventually the number grew to seven. The Civil Regulations gave the alcalde of each district jurisdiction in small lawsuits; larger suits could be appealed directly to the empresario. When conflicts arose, the alcalde was instructed to attempt to negotiate an "amicable compromise" between the two parties. If that failed, either party could request the appointment of two arbitrators. Although the code, in keeping with Hispanic custom, did not provide for trial by jury in civil cases, it soon became the practice for extralegal juries to be seated at the request of either party. The presiding officer (one of the alcaldes or Austin himself) then pronounced a verdict based on the jury's verdict. This system perfectly illustrates Austin's approach to governing the colony—catering to Mexican law and custom while seeking to satisfy the American colonists. Indeed, it epitomizes much of Austin's Texas career; scratch what appears to be a thoroughly Mexican surface, and you often find something very American underneath.[27]

The Criminal Regulations similarly mixed Hispanic and Anglo legal principles, pragmatically tailoring them to meet the colony's unique needs. Laws dealing with Indians came first. Militia captains were to investigate wrongdoing by Indians, and on finding such wrongdoing the captains could order the guilty parties whipped, expelled from the colony, or delivered to their chiefs. Whippings could not exceed twenty-five lashes. However, colonists who should "ill treat, or in any manner abuse any indian or indians, without just cause," faced the stiff fine of $100 for the first offense and $200 for the second. In requiring that the settlers treat the natives "at all times and in all places in a friendly, humane and civil manner," Austin established a relatively enlightened Indian policy, at least on paper. Nonetheless, the rules left no doubt that the Indians were to follow Austin's standards of conduct, regardless of the Indians' customs or beliefs.[28]

Subsequent portions of the criminal code prescribed penalties for theft, assault, and other common crimes. Alcaldes presided over trials, but in the Anglo tradition, findings of fact were made by a six-man jury. The rest of the process followed Hispanic procedure: the defendant's declaration, the facts of the case, and the alcalde's ruling were transmitted in writing to a superior judge for final judgment. Here Austin encountered a new obstacle; the provincial authorities in Monterrey had instructed that criminals "of the higest grade" should be put to hard labor on the public works until the superior government could decide their cases. This hampered Austin's efforts to maintain law and order in the colony. The nearest jail was in San Antonio, the superior courts were in Monterrey or Saltillo, and the colony could not afford to maintain its own prison or guards. This concerned Austin so much that he wrote to Mexican secretary of relations Lucas Alamán seeking relief. The government's decree, Austin explained, makes a criminal "laugh at the laws and civil Authorities," for the authorities are forced to "turn him loose on Society to Commit new depredations." This situation could be solved "by vesting authority in some tribunal here to punish by Corporal punishment" and, in the case of foreigners, to banish them from the province. Such a tribunal was never established, and over time the inadequacy of the criminal justice system became one of the colonists' major grievances against the Mexican government.[29]

If these sections of the Criminal Regulations constituted a mixing of Anglo and Hispanic legal concepts, one group of articles was thoroughly American. These were the articles regulating the institution of racial slavery. The code prescribed whippings for slaves caught stealing or running away. This violated Mexican law, under which slaves were treated the same as free men who broke the law. The code also dictated strict punishments for whites who stole slaves, harbored runaways, or traded with slaves without their masters' permission. In these respects, Austin's slave code embodied all the usual features of the codes of the southern United States. Despite its very un-Mexican character, the chief government official in San Antonio approved it, along with the rest of the Criminal and Civil Regulations, without comment.[30]

The problems surrounding the Indians and the government were incidental to the most important business at hand. That business, of course, was land. Settlers came for the land Austin promised, and he intended to make his fortune by becoming the bestower of that land. The entire enterprise depended on the immigrants getting settled on land that satisfied them, obtaining titles, and then raising crops. For Austin, everything else had to be subordinated to achieving these ends.

His empresario grant empowered him, "in union with the Governor of Texas, or a commissioner appointed by the latter, to proceed to divide, and designate land, and put each of the new colonists in possession of the quantity above indicated [a league and a labor for those who raised stock and farmed], and issue to them the titles in the name of the government." To Austin's satisfaction, the Baron de Bastrop was appointed commissioner. The prospects for completing the land business seemed auspicious when the two men arrived at the Colorado in the summer of 1823. After the drought of the preceding year, expectations ran high for a prosperous agricultural season. "The settlers are perfectly satisfied and determined to stick," observed Joseph Hawkins's brother Littleberry in April. "Many of them have butter cheese and milk and fat cattle in abundance and fine prospects for good crops on Both rivers." A month later, Brown Austin reported, "The settlers are in high spirits at the thoughts of getting lands soon, the season has been remarkably fine so far and if it continues (which it bids fair to do) they will all raise more corn than they will know what to do with." Such promising reports, plus the return of Austin to Texas, spurred "quite a tide of emigration."[31]

Austin hired surveyors to begin the laborious and often dangerous process of establishing the boundaries of settlers' lands. Almost all of the 4,428-acre tracts fronted the Brazos, the Colorado, or their tributaries. Most of the 177-acre tracts were laid off in a cluster at the mouth of the Brazos, or higher up the river in the immediate vicinity of the colony's soon-to-be-founded capital, San Felipe de Austin. The leagues were normally rectangular, with river frontage equal to one-fourth of the tract's length. Austin understood the importance of obtaining precise surveys, and he chose his early surveyors with care. He also frequently accompanied the surveyors on their expeditions. This gave him a detailed knowledge of the colony's geography as well as a personal acquaintance with many of the settlers. Such attention to the details of the land business became one of the keys to Austin's success as an empresario, in marked contrast to most of the empresarios who followed.[32]

The weather again turned dry in the fall of 1823, and hardship returned. Crops were poor, and wild game was no longer as plentiful as it had been in the first two years of settlement.[33] But with the colony now on surer legal footing and with land being distributed, immigration picked up. By late summer 1824 most of the three hundred families had arrived and selected their land. Bastrop began issuing land titles in July, and by the end of August, 272 titles had been issued. Unfortunately, Bastrop was called away to serve in the newly created state legislature at Saltillo, and the rest of the titles could not be issued until another commissioner came in 1827–28. Nevertheless, Austin had essentially fulfilled the terms of his contract by late 1824.[34]

Austin's empresario contract—and necessity—required the establishment of a town to serve as the capital of the colony and headquarters for the all-important land business. He had scouted potential locations on his first trip to Texas in 1821 and had identified a site on the Brazos as a "most beautifull situation for a Town or settlement." After briefly considering an alternate site on the Colorado, Austin in the late summer of 1823 chose the Brazos location. It lay almost exactly at the geographic center of the colony, about sixty miles below the San Antonio–Nacogdoches road and an equal distance from the coast. Situated where the Atascosito Road (an ancient trail used by Indians and livestock smugglers) crossed the Brazos, it sat atop a sixty-foot bluff on the west bank of the river. Good timber and drinking water abounded, and the surrounding soil was quite fertile. Two brothers, Achilles and John McFarland, were already operating a ferry at the crossing. Gov. Luciano García ordered that the town be named San Felipe de Austin.[35]

Austin had a large number of one-labor tracts laid off above, below, and opposite the river from San Felipe. Apparently concerned about secu-

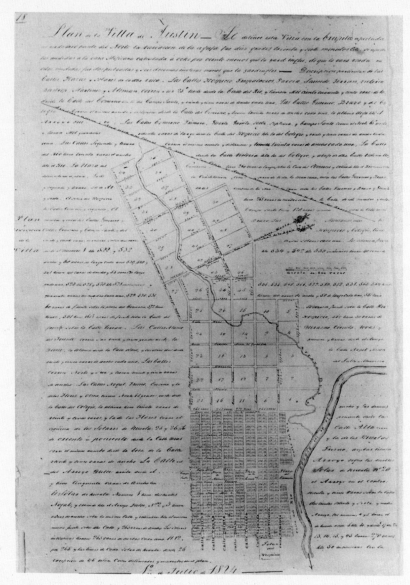

Plan of San Felipe de Austin, 1824. *Courtesy, General Land Office, Austin, Texas.*

rity, he wanted the settlers whose farms were scattered for miles along the Brazos to move to these compact tracts; there would be time enough for improving the one-league tracts later. Austin knew that his hopes were probably futile, for he had already tried to encourage the same thing on the Colorado and failed. The colonists, he was finding out, could be a stubborn lot. On the Brazos, as on the Colorado, most settlers preferred to live on their vast new estates, even though they could not possibly cultivate more than a tiny fraction of the land.[36]

By the end of the summer of 1824, surveyor Seth Ingram had laid out the town in traditional Mexican fashion according to Austin's instructions. Seven streets paralleled the river, combined with ten perpendicular avenues to form a grid. Three public squares were named for their primary functions: Commercial Plaza was nearest the ferry landing and would become the central business district; two blocks back lay Constitutional Plaza, which would house the civil government and a proposed Catholic church; two blocks beyond that would be Military Plaza, to be used for militia musters. Ever aware of the need to cultivate the goodwill of Mexican officialdom, Austin named the principal streets for prominent national statesmen and Texas officials.[37]

The earliest structures were rough log cabins typical of the American frontier, and tree stumps dotted the streets for many years. The grids of the town were never entirely filled in with structures, so even a decade after its founding San Felipe looked more like a random collection of cabins, stores, inns, and taverns than the orderly Mexican city that Austin had so carefully planned. As the town began to take shape in early 1824, Austin built a log cabin to serve as his home and another one to house the land office on a lot just north of the planned Commercial Plaza.[38]

One piece of exceedingly good fortune befell Austin as he worked to establish the colony in late 1823. While staying at Sylvanus Castleman's farm on the Colorado in August, he learned of a man named "E. Eccleston," who was said to be a schoolmaster and clerk fluent in Spanish and French. Austin told Josiah Bell that if Eccleston were reliable, he wished to employ him as a secretary to help with land titles, correspondence, and other business of the colony. Eccleston had come to the colony with his wife on the *Good Intent* a year earlier and had already made him-

Samuel May Williams, c. 1836. As Austin's secretary
and partner, Williams played a vital role in Austin's
success as empresario, but his land speculation
activities caused a painful estrangement between
the two men near the end of Austin's life.
Courtesy, Rosenberg Library, Galveston, Texas.

self useful to various settlers as an interpreter, tutor, and clerk. Austin met
him personally that fall, and by November the new colonial secretary had
moved to the fledgling settlement of San Felipe and was handling much
of Austin's correspondence.

The empresario soon learned that "E. Eccleston" was an alias. The
man's real name was Samuel May Williams. The Rhode Island native was
two years younger than Austin and had worked for a wealthy uncle in the
mercantile, banking, and insurance business. Williams later spent time in
Buenos Aires, where he learned Spanish and made international mercantile connections, and subsequently he worked as a clerk in New Orleans

during the time Austin lived there. He came to Texas under an assumed
name, probably because he owed his employer over $700 that he could
not repay. Austin could hardly reproach a man for having fled old debts,
and he soon discovered in Williams a kindred spirit. The new secretary
was smart, loyal, and tremendously hard working. Like Austin, he was
slight of build, and he tended to be introspective and moody. His education and New England background gave him an air of elitism that did
not always endear him to the colonists. The value that Austin placed on
his new secretary is evident from his promised annual salary: he would
receive $1,000, which would have to be paid out of the empresario's own
pocket. As clerk and translator Williams played a pivotal role in enabling
Austin and Bastrop to issue land titles to the bulk of the Old Three Hundred in the summer of 1824.[39]

By mid-1824 Austin was making real progress toward his goals, but
his biggest problem was coming from an unexpected quarter—the colonists themselves.

Austin knew that frontiersmen were proud and fiercely independent.
Therefore he had gone to considerable lengths to ensure that the people
coming to Texas understood the rules and realities of their new situation.
This was not the United States, he emphasized. In Austin's Colony, all
men were not created equal. The empresario and the Mexican government were prepared to offer exceptional benefits to the settlers, but the
settlers had to submit unquestioningly to their superiors. Necessity required it, as did the law. Discord could threaten the colony as much as
could hostile Indians or a capricious Mexican government. From his initial recruiting announcements in American newspapers to his letters and
proclamations in the colony itself, Austin constantly reminded the colonists of their obligations to him, to the colony, and to Mexico. But as he
learned in 1824, all of the public and private announcements, letters, or
proclamations in the world would not change the character of the people
he sought to lead. A minority of them, at least, began openly to challenge
the empresario's leadership and loudly demand their "rights." By June
1824 affairs were reaching a state of crisis.

The complaints revolved around land policy. Most of the settlers had come to Texas after reading Austin's announcements in U.S. newspapers. Operating on the provisional guidelines set forth by provincial officials in 1821, Austin had promised the earliest colonists a minimum of one square mile of land (640 acres). With the additional amounts that were to be granted for dependents, a family composed of a husband, a wife, and two children came to Texas expecting to receive about two square miles of land. But when the Mexican government confirmed Austin's grant in the spring of 1823, it allowed families who raised livestock to receive a square league (4,428 acres). Only those families who immigrated after mid-1823 came to Texas knowing that they would be receiving these larger amounts of land. Most colonists embraced the chance to own seven square miles of land instead of two. But this change brought with it far-reaching and largely unexpected consequences.[40]

The key fact was this: Austin's plans for making a fortune relied on the twelve-and-a-half cents per acre fee that he intended to charge the colonists. After bearing the expenses of surveying and issuing titles, the remainder of the money would be Austin's to keep. He had clearly explained this fee in his announcements, and in the act of immigrating, each colonist became contractually bound to Austin to pay the fee. Since no land title could be secured without Austin's approval, he held the power to enforce those terms. Arithmetic becomes significant here. For a hypothetical colonist with a wife and two children and who thus qualified for 1,280 acres, the fee under the original land-distribution plan would have been $160. Under the new arrangement, wherein a colonist received a full league of land, that colonist now found himself owing Austin $553. Although twelve-and-a-half cents per acre was still a great bargain in per-acre terms, in absolute terms $553 was a huge sum to the settlers.

Austin granted relatively easy terms. He allowed the earliest immigrants three years to pay, and he would accept all manner of valuable goods in payment. From those coming later he required half the money down with the other half payable in a year; he would accept only livestock or slaves in lieu of cash.[41] Of course, the costs of surveying increased with the added amounts of land. But other expenses, such as the cost of issuing official land titles, remained essentially fixed. Austin's out-of-pocket cost for surveying a league averaged about $70, plus about $38 for the expenses of producing a legal title. So even after deducting these costs Austin stood to realize a profit of $445 from from the colonist who received one league of land. Multiplied by three hundred, Austin's profit from the land fees would be the princely sum of $133,500. In dramatically expanding the amount of land that each family could be granted, the Mexican government unintentionally had laid the groundwork for Stephen Austin to become very wealthy. The cash-strapped colonists may not have realized exactly how much Austin stood to make on his enterprise, but they could certainly look at how much they had to pay and conclude that it was too much. Their resentment grew accordingly.

Of course there were many other expenses that Austin had already borne, not the least of which was the year he spent in Mexico City. And in his willingness to accept in-kind payment in multi-year installments, he was not going to realize his newfound wealth immediately. Austin seemed surprised when the colonists began grumbling about the twelve-and-a-half-cent fee. Surely, though, he knew that the change in the planned amount of land for the colonists dramatically altered the finances of the entire project. He desperately hoped that he would still be able to collect the per-acre fee, but he soon learned that those hopes were not realistic.

Most of the direct evidence of the settlers' dissatisfaction comes from men who for various reasons left the colony. One William Gibbons, who fled following a theft conviction, spread the rumor "that the people are much dissatisfied with Austin[,] think he has no right to sell the lands[,] that [he] compels every man to take a league at $700 [and to pay] half down[,] that many would leave the settlement and that Austin will about abandon the settlement." A friend in San Antonio reported to Austin on an American who had recently arrived there from the colony, where he had been telling the colonists that Austin was "dece[i]ving and swin[d]ling the people" and that they should not be paying more than $30 per league.[42]

The actions of the highest-ranking Mexican official in Texas, political chief José Antonio Saucedo, reveal the growing seriousness of the issue. In April 1824, Saucedo instructed the colonists to "listen with attention and confidence to your immediate Chief (Col. Austin)" and to "disregard and dispise all those idle slanders and vague stories which are put in circulation by the enemies of good order for the sole purpose of creating

confusion and discontent." A month later, as Saucedo prepared to visit
the colony, he felt it necessary to deny publicly any intention to remove
Austin as empresario. But the damage had been done. When Saucedo arrived at San Felipe he annulled Austin's twelve-and-a-half-cent charge and
established a fee bill that required colonists to pay only $192 for a league.
Of this amount, $127 went to the land commissioner (Bastrop), $27 to the
surveyor, $8 to pay for the titles, and $30 to the state. The empresario got
nothing.[43]

Austin tried not to panic. There is no indication that he sought to
have the decision reversed. But Saucedo's move shattered the empresario's plans for a quick restoration of the Austin family fortune. Unless
Bastrop could be persuaded to commit his share of the new fees to de-
fraying the expenses of the land business, Austin faced the prospect of
losing money on each colonist's land business, for the $35 that Saucedo
allowed for surveys and titles would not come close to meeting the actual
expenses. Fortunately, Bastrop agreed to give Austin one-third of the
commissioner's fee, or about $42 per league. This allowed him to meet
expenses, but just barely. There would be little or no profit.[44]

On June 5, 1824, Austin issued a long address to the colonists. He
reviewed the history of the colonization project and explained all of the direct and indirect expenses that he had incurred. He reminded the settlers
that they had accepted his terms and that they were about to get clear titles
to their land. It was true, he admitted, that he would receive twenty-two
and a half leagues of premium land from the government as compensation for his labors, but half of this would go to Joseph Hawkins, and the
remainder would have little or no cash value for years to come. The financial burden of entertaining prospective settlers, fighting Indians, dealing
with the Mexican government, paying a secretary, and administering the
justice system all fell on him alone. "And then ask yourselves," he stated,
"whether you would not rather take your Single League of Land in peace
than to receive what I am entitled to together with the 12 1/2 cts an acre
And be involved in the Labyrinth of trouble and Vexation and responsibility that I am—As regards the equivalent which you were to receive for
this 12 1/2 cts an Acre, *was it not worth it?* And if you could not have obtained it any other way would you have been unwilling to pay that Sum

for it? And could you or would you ever have obtained it unless through my exertions?" [45]

Two motivations lay behind the address. Austin presumably still held out hope that the colonists would view their obligations to him as morally binding—even if the government had made them legally void—and pay him anyway. But he knew human nature well enough to know that that was unlikely. More important to Austin was restoring the colonists' faith in his integrity, a faith that the fee controversy had badly shaken. Whatever the settlers might decide in regard to paying the fees, he wrote, "I hope they will do me the justice to take a full and impartial view of the whole subject and not be too ready to condemn me as a speculator on the poor, a charge which I am told a few discontented Men have made against me And One which I think is unmeritted." [46]

If the fee controversy had been the only source of disgruntlement, Austin's appeal might have been more effective. But even as the issue of the fee was unfolding, other land-related complaints began to surface. These proved even more damaging to Austin's public image, and they persisted long after the fee controversy was laid to rest.

Austin's empresario contract gave him great latitude in the amounts of land that he could grant to individuals. Although a majority of the Old Three Hundred willingly settled for either a single league or the slightly larger amount of a league and a labor, Austin granted certain individuals greater amounts if they brought assets such as slaves, sawmills, or cotton gins. Others received extra land as compensation for special service to the colony. In all, some forty-eight of the Old Three Hundred were granted these larger amounts of land. John P. Coles, for example, brought a large family and several slaves to Texas, served as alcalde of the Brazos district, and built a mill, for which he was granted eight and a half leagues. Seth Ingram, the surveyor who laid out the town of San Felipe, received two leagues and a labor. Samuel May Williams, Austin's valuable secretary, was granted two leagues and three labors. Jared Groce, who came from Georgia with nearly a hundred slaves, received the largest grant of all, ten leagues. [47]

To many of the colonists, this smacked of favoritism, and understandably so. Even with all his slaves, Jared Groce could hardly put 44,000 acres to productive use. As employees of the colony, Seth Ingram and Sam Williams were paid salaries; why should they also get extra land? Worse still, what justified Austin in granting his own brother—a single man not yet twenty-one years old—three leagues and two labors? Such perceived inequalities were compounded by the inevitable complaints over the location and relative quality of land. Even Josiah Bell, one of Austin's oldest friends and most valued lieutenants, apparently grumbled when Austin reserved for himself a quarter-league that Bell coveted. Austin responded petulantly, stating that if Bell felt that way, then he [Austin] would "not take an inch at that place if I have to drink river water." If someone as close to Austin as Bell could complain about the empresario's land policies, it is easy to predict the response of others.[48]

Other practices exacerbated the settlers' complaints. Single men were not happy about receiving less land than married men did. Occasionally, when a colonist had no ability to pay his land fees, Austin agreed to pay the fees in exchange for half of the colonist's land. Although this left the colonist with more than two thousand acres absolutely free, it appeared to some that Austin was taking unfair advantage. James Gaines, a longtime resident of the Texas-Louisiana border who had fought in the Mexican Wars for Independence, advised Austin in November 1824 "to wind up your Colony Business as soon as you can" or face the "Curses and Abuse" of dissatisfied colonists. "[T]hey accuse you of Every thing bad and threaten Continually Revenge," Gaines wrote. "They say . . . you Slight them By Reserving to yourself all the good Land they say you are never govern[d.] Two days by the same Rule nor Law. [Y]ou give some young men 1/4 League of Land and others one and more Leagues. Some men of wealth and Respectability you wont give but one League[,] Others of Less wealth get Two three or four Leagues." When such settlers finally get their titles, warned Gaines, all it will take is whiskey for them to "Look for the Revenge so Long threatened."[49]

Gaines had his own private gripes against Austin, and he was writing from the vantage point of an outsider, but his observations were still perceptive. Some of the unpopular policies came from government decree and were beyond Austin's control.[50] But hindsight suggests that he would have avoided much of the discord and criticism if he had adhered scrupulously to a policy of granting all settlers equal amounts of land on exactly the same terms.

In the spring of 1825 the complaints forced Austin to take a stand. Aylett C. "Strap" Buckner, like Gaines, was a veteran of the independence movement and had predated Austin in Texas. He had been one of the very first settlers on the Colorado, and as such he believed that he merited special consideration from the empresario. While Austin was in Mexico City, Buckner had selected a league and a half that he thought Austin would confirm. Austin refused to let him have part of the land, apparently because another settler had a stronger claim to it. The crusty, quick-tempered old man believed himself the victim of discrimination. "Now Sir," he wrote to Austin,

> I will appeal to your-self or any candid man whither other men ought to have more land or has a better right to request more than Myself or Not. I know no other reasons of their getting better treated except that they have more Money—I have viewed everything in as fair a light as I could; from report I know that sum men get half a league and dont pay a cent because the other half is transferred to You or Your Brother. I know that lands are unequilly divided. I do not considder Myself a perfect simpleton[;] neither am I blind. My Eyes are open and I look and watch with vigilence: My demands are small compared to what the demands of others are. . . . [I]f You refuse granting that which I think the Government will generously bestow on me I shall apply to that authority which governs us both for so much as I think in justice I am lacking— [51]

Buckner took his case to the court of public opinion. He and a supporter posted notices calling for a public meeting to protest Austin's land policies as well as the government-imposed fee bill. Buckner should have known that, under Mexican law, public meetings could be called only with government permission. This was all Austin needed. He immediately ordered Buckner's arrest on charges of sedition and disorderly conduct. In informing Saucedo of his action, Austin also asked for an official examination of his own conduct and requested that the political chief make it clear to the colonists that he was acting according to government orders. The empresario then issued another address to the colonists, in which he "regretted to see that a Spirit of discontent and contention has manifested itself in a few individuals of this colony since its first commencement." It was his "painful duty, to change the mild course" that he had heretofore followed, but now he had no choice. If any of the settlers had complaints, he would help them present their grievances to the government in a legal manner. "I call on all the Inhabitants . . . to unite in the support of the laws and protection of the constituted authorities of the Government, and I command them to hold themselves in readiness at all times to suppress any acts of insubordination," Austin concluded.[52]

Buckner feigned amazement that Austin would arrest him "for undertaking one of the most just causes in my opinion imaginable." He feebly suggested that Austin call a general meeting of the colony, and if a majority endorsed his grievances, those grievances could be forwarded to the government. Austin would have none of this. Witnesses were subpoenaed, and the date set for a hearing.[53]

Buckner's support withered away. A number of prominent colonists publicly spoke out against him and prepared to offer damaging testimony. Jared Groce, whose own relations with the empresario were not always the best, told Austin, "I think you are takeing a stand now that will releave you of Much difficulty."[54]

What followed was a classic example of Austin's leadership style. Rather than push through a guilty verdict and send Buckner in chains to Saltillo, where the Mexican authorities undoubtedly would have backed his decison, Austin tried conciliation. Exactly how he went about it is not recorded, but Austin reported that an investigation of the facts "has satisfied me that the acts of said Buckner which were deemed exceptional proceeded from misconception" and that Buckner now "manifested a submission to the Laws and authorities of the Goverment." To avoid further "excitement," Austin recommended that the episode "be totally forgotten and consigned to oblivion." Although Buckner could still be irascible in his relations with other colonists, he became one of Austin's staunchest supporters. Two months later he addressed the empresario as "my friend" and humbly asked whether he could "purchase or make arrangements for one thousand acres of Land." He closed his request: "Yours with the highest Esteem and Respect." He went on to command the militia in two separate Indian campaigns and backed Austin in the tense days of the Fredonian Rebellion. Austin's ability to conciliate his enemies and his capacity to forgive and forget once again proved valuable management tools.[55]

In these early years Austin rarely had contact with anyone in the Mexican government higher than the provincial authorities in San Antonio. When José Antonio Saucedo replaced interim governor Luciano García in September 1823, his new title was political chief (*jefe político*), but his duties remained those of governor. At the same time, Texas got its own representative body, an eleven-member provincial deputation. Fortunately for Austin's Colony, the Baron de Bastrop won election to the body. He returned to San Antonio to take his seat in January 1824, and he safeguarded the colony's interests there until he returned to San Felipe in June to begin issuing land titles. When dissent mounted over land policy, Bastrop urged Austin to keep the faith. He knew Austin well enough by then to understand the empresario's moodiness and susceptibility to depression. "[Y]ou must ignore all this," wrote the Baron in reference to the growing criticism over land policy. "You may be certain that in the deputation you have two friends, Saucedo and me, and I believe the others do not wish you harm."[56]

Bastrop might also have mentioned another of Austin's Tejano friends, Erasmo Seguín, but Seguín was absent from Texas. In late 1823 he had been sent to Mexico City to represent Texas in the Constituent Congress that was convened after the overthrow of Iturbide. The courtly, well-read Seguín was Austin's oldest and staunchest ally among the Mexican Texans. Most contemporaries regarded him as the ablest Tejano statesman of the era, and he was uncompromisingly liberal in his political and economic philosophies. Seguín faced the task of representing the interests of Texas in this crucial phase of nation-building. Congress's job was to write Mexico's first constitution, a tremendous challenge in a republic as diverse as Mexico and with so little experience in self-government. Austin had already expressed his ideas about what sort of government the young republic needed when he presented Miguel Ramos Arizpe with his

draft of a constitution in the spring of 1823. He hoped to see a federal republic, incorporating elements of the U.S. Constitution and the Spanish
Constitution of 1812. Back in Austin's Colony, meanwhile, the empresario
tactfully reported to the authorities that the colonists "have manifested a
unanimous disposition to submit to any form of government adopted by a
majority, inclining however, in favor of a federal republic." Such a constitution is precisely what the delegates in Mexico City eventually produced.[57]

Privately, Austin felt some concern over the issues being debated in
the Constituent Congress, but he could do little except trust Seguín to
do the right thing. Austin did mention two issues to Seguín: he feared
that congress might interfere with slavery, and he hoped for a greater degree of religious toleration. His concern was not so much over the effects
of these matters on the colonists who were already there; relatively few
of them owned slaves, and even fewer seemed particularly bothered by
the lack of religious freedom. But Austin knew that in the long run an
antislavery, Catholics-only Texas would attract fewer emigrants from the
United States. Even at this early date he clearly was staking much of his
own future on the continuing Americanization of Texas.[58]

Curiously, Austin seems to have been relatively unconcerned with
one crucial issue being debated in Mexico City. For all Texans, Anglo
or Tejano, the most important matter to be decided in the congress was
Texas's status within the emerging Mexican federation. There were three
options: Texas could become a state or a federal territory, or it could be
joined with one or more of the other Eastern Interior Provinces to make
a new state. In a perfect world, all Texans would have preferred to have
their own state, but practical considerations rendered this impossible.
With only a few thousand Tejanos and a few hundred Americans, most of
them poor, Texas had neither the population nor the financial resources
to support its own state government. This left Texas on the horns of a di-
lemma. Territorial status meant turning over the vast public domain and
most decision-making to a distant central government in Mexico City. But
attaching Texas to one or more of her sister states of the north would
shift the locus of power from San Antonio to the capital of Coahuila or
Tamaulipas or Nuevo León. Either way, Texans faced a loss of local control over their affairs, and particularly over their valuable public lands.

Arriving in Mexico City, Erasmo Seguín soon recognized the impossibility of separate statehood for Texas. He first advocated the territorial option; this brought him into conflict with the influential Miguel Ramos Arizpe, who wanted Texas joined with his own home state of Coahuila, thus giving control of Texas lands to the state government at Saltillo. Seguín resisted at first, but Ramos Arizpe persuaded him to change his mind. In April 1824 the state of *Coahuila y Texas* was born. Seguín did secure one concession that would become important later: the law provided that when Texas had sufficient resources to support its own state government the Texans could apply for separate statehood. Ironically, the act produced no significant response from Austin or the colonists. But before another decade would pass, the Anglo-Texans had joined their Tejano neighbors in bitterly resenting it.[59]

On the issues of slavery and religion, there was cause for neither joy nor panic. Congress passed a vaguely worded decree prohibiting the slave trade, but Austin and most Mexican officials interpreted it as not banning the importation of slaves by their owners. In fact, emigrants would be allowed to bring their slaves to Texas for many years. Similarly, Catholicism remained the established religion in Mexico, but neither Seguín nor Austin could see any problem with Protestantism, as long as it was practiced discreetly.[60]

News that congress had adopted federalism reached Austin quickly, and on May 1, 1824, he issued a proclamation to the colonists grandiloquently announcing the event. "I am convinced that there is not a breast amongst you that will not palpitate with exultation and delight that the prospects of Freedom, Happiness, and Prosperity which the *Federal Republican System of Government* presents to your View," Austin wrote. By late October he had received a copy of the finished document, which he promptly translated and published. The following spring the "greater part of the inhabitants" of the colony gathered at San Felipe to celebrate the new system of government. The militia fired a twenty-three-gun salute to honor the states and territories of the Mexican union, and the settlers then sat down to an elaborate banquet. On March 12, 1825, with the Mexican flag flying, Austin read the constitution and administered the oath of allegiance to the assembled colonists. Order prevailed the entire day, and the people expressed "general enthusiasm in favor of the Government of our adopted Country."[61]

To the thirty-one-year-old empresario it now seemed as if many of the highest obstacles had been overcome. The first three hundred families had arrived and chosen their land. Austin had selected the twenty-two and a half leagues of premium land that would constitute his pay as empresario. A legal system was operating, albeit imperfectly, in the colony. The new state of Coahuila y Texas would soon have a state constitution, and Austin could foresee the day when his settlement would come under regular civil control and he would be relieved of the extraordinary burdens of administering the colony. Bastrop was called away to represent Texas in the legislature at Saltillo, but as soon as he could return to the colony the last of the Old Three Hundred could receive their land titles. There were still problems — raiding Indians, complaining settlers, unpredictable weather, insufficient cash flow, and an overwhelming daily workload, to name a few — but Austin was becoming adept at meeting such challenges.

By the end of 1824 he had decided to apply for a second empresario contract. Other than his premium lands, the first colony had produced little in the way of tangible rewards. There was still a large amount of unoccupied land in the colony, although the choicest tracts on the Brazos and Colorado were taken. Austin initially applied to the federal government for the new contract, but in August congress had passed a national colonization law that largely delegated immigration policy to the states. Austin therefore resubmitted his application to the governor and the state legislature. The state enacted its own colonization law in March 1825, with Bastrop playing a key role in securing its passage. The law established the empresario system along lines very similar to Austin's original contract. The most significant addition was a six-year time limit; if an empresario failed to settle at least a hundred families in this time, the contract would be canceled. Austin's new contract to introduce three hundred families was granted in April and enlarged to five hundred in May. The families were to be settled on the remaining lands of the first colony, excluding the land within ten leagues of the coast, which the national colonization law closed to further foreign settlement (see map 3). A month later, after receiving an additional request from Austin, the state increased the number

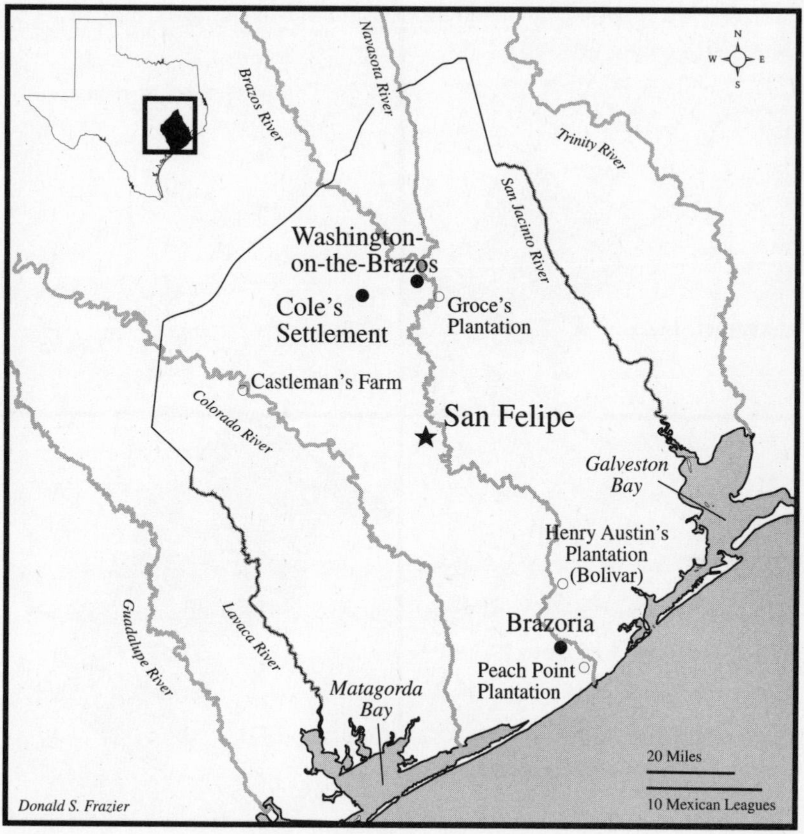

Map 2. Austin's First Colony.

of settlers to five hundred. He also gained permission to open a port of entry at Galveston.[62]

Financially this colony would be more lucrative, for Austin obtained Saucedo's permission to collect a $60 fee from each colonist above and beyond the established charges for titles, surveying, and other costs. This would bring in $30,000, which would help to relieve the empresario's chronic cash shortage. Austin would also receive about 115,000 acres in premium lands under this contract. Despite these more favorable terms, Austin now understood that it would take years, if not a lifetime, to make his fortune. The hard-to-collect fees would be consumed largely by the costs of administering the colony, and the premium lands would have little cash value for the foreseeable future. To his sister in Missouri Austin

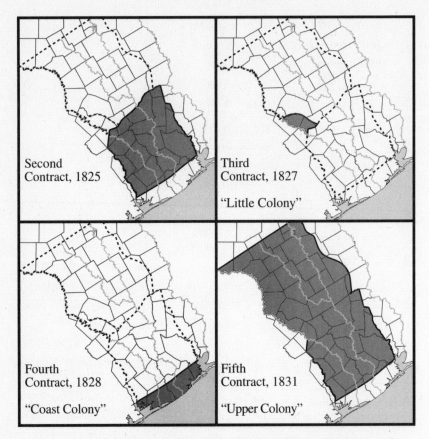

Map 3. Austin's Subsequent Empresario Contracts. Notice that the second, fourth, and fifth contracts overlap partially with the territory of Austin's first contract, thus allowing settlers to acquire land that was still available after the fulfillment of previous contracts. Outlines of modern Texas counties are indicated.

explained, "My labors in this country altho arduous and in every way perplexing will not yield me anything for some years and then not the fortune which some have supposed. I shall benefit others much more than myself in proportion." Such statements underestimating the potential for profit and exaggerating his sacrifices had already become standard fare for Austin, and they would remain so for the rest of his life. The bitterness of past defeats and his own pessimistic nature would rarely allow him to

revel in his present successes or to predict a grander future. Low expectations protected against disappointment.[63]

But by now it mattered little. The status and respect that he derived
from being the symbolic father of his colony offered fulfillment enough
for the present, even if that fulfillment was mostly psychological. Riches
could wait. "I make no more calculations except to spend my life here,"
he told Emily at the end of 1824; "wheither rich or poor, here (that is in
this colony) I expect to remain permanently."[64]

With the first colony founded and populated, and with another contract being consummated, Austin could devote some attention to his personal concerns. Affairs in Missouri had taken a distressing turn in the past
three years. He had left his family under the care of his brother-in-law and
former business partner, James Bryan. Bryan, whose fortunes had come
crashing down along with Moses and Stephen Austin's after the Panic of
1819, intended to bring his own family and Stephen's mother to Texas
as soon as he could settle his tangled financial affairs. But in September
1822, two days after Emily gave birth to their fourth child, Bryan died in
a fever epidemic. Emily, her children, and the aging Maria were left to
fend for themselves. Reduced to poverty, the resourceful Emily held the
remnants of the once-proud family together during Stephen's long year
in Mexico City by teaching school and taking in boarders. Maria took increasing solace in reading the Bible and writing her eldest son letters that
often went months without an answer.[65]

Stephen had been back from Mexico City only six months when he
began making plans to bring Maria, Emily, and the children to Texas.
That he would even consider subjecting his relatives, including an aging
woman and four young children, to the hazardous journey and the even
more hazardous life in Texas is a measure of how desperate things were in
Missouri. But as he later explained to Emily, "The thoughts of your destitute situation sometimes almost ran me mad." First he had to raise travel
money, which he apparently did by selling some powder, deerskins, and
beeswax that he had received in lieu of land fees. Five months later he
was ready to send Brown to Missouri to fetch the family. Brown left Texas

in May 1824, armed with detailed instructions regarding the route to take and a long list of items to bring back with him. Stephen also directed him to reunite and bring to Texas a family of former Austin slaves that had been separated by the recent years' turmoil, if the scattered family members could be purchased "without paying too much money." Stephen carefully explained to Emily and Maria what to expect from life in the colony. The family was to wear nothing but homespun for several years. Cost was one factor, but more important, "it will set an example to the rest of the Settlers that will have a very good effect." Their new house in Texas likewise was to be "plain and pritty much like the rest of my neighbors." This was coming at the height of the furor over Austin's land fees, and the empresario understood his precarious position with the colonists. "The situation I am placed in here will cause all the acts of any of my family to be observed," he explained, "and it will require a uniform affible deportment to all, without regarding their appearance or poverty to prevent giving offences. The only distinction that must be shown here is between the *good* and the *bad* and that must be very marked and decisive." [66]

When Brown arrived in Louisiana he learned that Maria Austin had died four months earlier. She was buried beside her husband. Brown continued on to Missouri, where he found the late James Bryan's financial affairs hopelessly confused, just as Moses's and Stephen's outstanding concerns there continued to be. Never one to mince words, Brown confided to Stephen that "the *wisest* plan *I* can pursue, is to *leave* the *dam* [d] country as soon as possible—with Emily and her family—and leave the rest for *you* to finish should you *ever* visit Mo." [67]

As he prepared to leave, Brown met with yet another shock. Emily announced her intention to marry James Franklin Perry, a local merchant. Brown and Stephen both knew Perry, and although there are some hints that they may have questioned her choice initially, they both acknowledged that Perry was respectable and that Emily was old enough to make her own decisions. What really troubled her brothers was that Emily and her new husband would stay in Missouri. Brown would return alone. Emily assured Stephen by letter that she would "make use of every means to perswaid" Perry to immigrate to Texas as soon as possible. But Stephen stated emphatically that Perry would have to visit Texas first to make up his own mind. Still, Stephen could not hide his disappointment. "I want to free my self from debt and then to sit quietly down on a farm in this Country for the balance of my life," he told Emily, "and [I] hope to see Brother married and settled on one side of me, and if it could be[,] Mr Perry and you on the other[,] but all my plans have been broken in upon."[68]

With his mother and James Bryan dead, Emily remarried, and Brown still in Missouri, Austin found himself very alone. He tried to maintain his spirits, telling Emily that "things are going on well" and that he had "every confidence that the Colony will flourish rapidly." But at the same time, he could not keep from indulging in a little self-pity. "Adieu my Dear sister," he wrote to Emily a week before Christmas, 1824:

> my lot is cast in the wilderness but I am content. [T]rouble and fatigue have become so very familiar to me that they begin to appear like bosom friends. . . . I am still very poor and live poor — corn coffee — corn bread — milk and Butter and a Bachelors household, which is confusion, dirt, and torment, are small items of my living — your marriage will force either Brother or me to marry for I must have somebody to keep house. . . . I am fast loosing the desire I once had to make a fortune, which encourages me to hope that I am yet to enjoy much happiness, for a gready man can never be happy, the loss of a cent makes him miserable.[69]

Austin's loneliness was made worse by the news that his close friend and financial backer Joseph Hawkins had died in Louisiana. Between 1821 and his premature death in October 1823, Hawkins had invested more than $7,000 in Austin's venture. He had served as the empresario's agent in New Orleans, handling correspondence and publicity for the colonization project and dispatching several shiploads of emigrants and supplies to the colony. "Joseph H. Hawkins is my *adopted brother,* a better or truer friend never existed," Austin had remarked to Brown just four months earlier. An able attorney but a poor businessman, Hawkins had gambled his last dime on Austin's project and played a crucial role in its survival while Austin was in Mexico City. "I am bent down almost to the very ground," he wrote to Austin in February 1822, referring to his debt burden. "In fact my dear Sir I turn my mind towards you as the wrecked mariner does towards the glimerings of the light house which promises a Haven of safety—Were it not for you my path would now be cheerless if not hopeless." Hawkins's pleadings sounded much like those of Austin during this period: "If I could obtain through your efforts the means to pay my debts I would join you immediately and spend my life in plowing the soil—and teaching my children the ways of virtue." As his health worsened, Hawkins began to realize that he probably would not live to enjoy the fruits of his and Austin's enterprise. "To die a slave would be insupportable—To leave as the only legacy to my children *hungry creditors* would be to have lived in vain and die miserable," he observed. In the event of his death, Hawkins instructed his wife, George Anne, to rely on Austin "as the firmest pillar in our *building*." [70]

When Hawkins died, he left a grieving wife, five young children, and a mountain of unpayable debts. "My good friend J. H. Hawkins is dead," Austin wrote to Josiah Bell when he heard the sad news. "I have met with some things to vex me and fear my best friends will sometimes think my temper a little unruly—but they must bear with me and in the end they will find that my heart is right." When he sat down to write a letter of condolence to Hawkins's widow, Austin was almost at a loss for words. "I have so long esteemed Mr Hawkins as a brother, as a bosom friend that indeed I feel too much in need of consolation myself for his loss to be able to offer it to others," he wrote. "[W]e must console ourselves with the hope that he has passed from a world of trouble and care to one of peace and happiness. The friendship I had for Mr Hawkins was of a nature that cannot be easily or soon forgotten, while living I viewed him as a brother, and as such lament him." For a man like Austin, who had many acquaintances but few close friends, the loss was severe. [71]

Austin offered to make the same arrangements in Texas for George Anne Hawkins and her children that he was then making for his own mother and sister, but George Anne's relatives would not hear of it. Austin tried to comfort the widow by telling her that Hawkins's share of the grant should provide a "handsome fortune for his family at no very distant period." By the terms of their 1821 partnership agreement, Austin owed Hawkins half of the twenty two and a half leagues of premium land that he was to receive for the first colony. But at the time of Hawkins's death, Austin had not yet received title to the land, and he would not for some time. Even if he had, all parties involved in administering the insolvent Hawkins estate agreed that Austin should keep all the land in his own name, lest Hawkins's half fall into the hands of his creditors. Austin faithfully abided by this plan until the children were old enough to claim their legacy, which they finally did in 1833.[72]

Brown was gone for nine months, and Stephen missed his brother badly. He needed frequent doses of Brown's abundant optimism. With each passing year the younger Austin must have reminded Stephen more of their father. One can almost hear the echo of Moses Austin's voice when, after returning to Texas, Brown would proclaim,

> we can . . . congratulate ourselves that not withstanding the many vississitudes and difficulties we have encountered (and the great and heartfelt satisfaction afforded to the Enemies of our house by its downfall) *we have proved to the world* that *regardless* of them all—We *have* accomplished an enterprize that will perpetuate our name and place it with honor on the page of history. It will then be our turn to triumph. . . . Our old Enemies will in a few years more dwindle into insignificance and would lick the dust from our shoes to gain a favor—It will then be a satisfaction a 'heavenly satisfaction['] for me to assist them—That is the revenge which will be sweet to me.[73]

When he could put aside his gloom, Stephen perhaps felt similar emotions. But after the successful establishment of the first colony he seems to have spent little time dwelling on the family's traumatic past in the United States. He had so completely identified his personal interests—indeed, his very existence—with his colony that its welfare became almost the only thing that mattered. If it survived and prospered, so would he. When its survival and prosperity seemed doubtful, his spirits sank. In mid-1825, as the settlers poured into Texas in fulfillment of his second empresario contract, the closest he could come to a boast was this characteristic statement: "I have had an unpleasant and unhappy life time of it but I look forward to better days and a better population and have the consolation to reflect that I have done my duty to the Settlers and to the Gov^t as far as my situation would permit and I think in the end they will all acknowledge it." [74]

Austin might occasionally have romanticized about settling down on a farm, marrying, and living quietly, but to do so would have been highly uncharacteristic. He still craved that "acknowledgement" by the people, a craving that could be fulfilled only by occupying a position of leadership. Some people are content to have a job; others need a calling. Austin had found his in Texas. Becoming the great empresario had given him more than simply the opportunity to restore the family fortune; it had given a discouraged young man languishing in the shadow of a domineering father a grand cause in which to pour all his energies. It had made Stephen Austin the central, indispensable figure in what he viewed as a great drama. In 1825 that drama was only beginning to unfold on its frontier stage.

Staying the Course
1825–1827

The mid-1820s were heady days for the young Mexican nation. After the downfall of Iturbide's empire, Mexico established a federal republic. The Constitution of 1824 deemed all men equal and guaranteed individual rights. In the first national elections, one of the most admired heroes of the Wars for Independence, Guadalupe Victoria, won the presidency. The young intellectual from Yucatán, Lorenzo de Zavala, was elected president of the national congress. Liberalism and federalism seemed triumphant.[1]

Yet Mexico was not destined to follow the pattern set by the United States and become a stable federal republic. Dire economic conditions lay at the heart of the country's troubles. Spanish imperial policies had drained wealth from New Spain for decades prior to 1810, and then ten years of internal warfare made the flight of capital much worse. Mexico emerged from its independence struggle facing a devastated infrastructure, a decimated merchant class, a crippling debt burden, and an inability to attract new capital. These severe economic problems account for much of the political instability that the country would experience in its early decades.

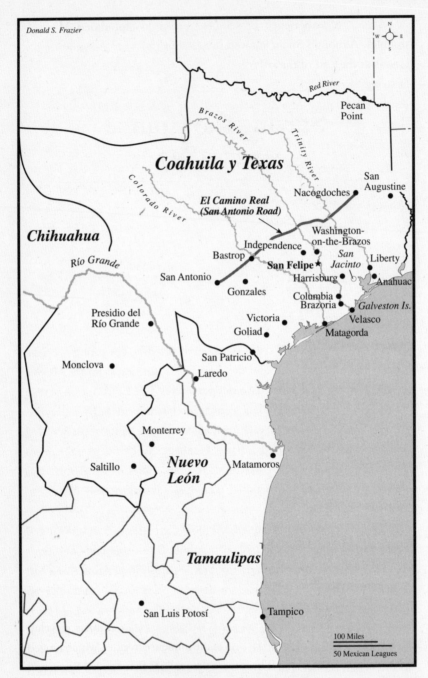

Map 4. Coahuila y Texas, 1836.

A lack of experience in self-government compounded Mexico's troubles. Although Spain allowed the establishment of provincial deputations at the end of the colonial period and a significant measure of de facto regional autonomy had existed even before then,[2] Mexico had never possessed a degree of self-government comparable to that of the British North American colonies. The early Mexican republic thus found itself on the periphery of the world capitalist system, lacking the capital, the trade connections, and the political institutions to modernize. Creating an American-style political system on paper in 1824 could not compensate for these inadequacies.[3]

Some Mexicans knew that the federalist Constitution of 1824 would not remake Mexico in the image of the United States. The country was rife with internal divisions, including clashing regional interests and an aspiring middle class at odds with conservative elites who enjoyed the support of the army and the church. Cautious statesmen like Lucas Alamán and Manuel de Mier y Terán — and the old monied classes they represented — believed that their country first had to achieve unity and stability if it were to modernize and prosper. That could not happen under a weak, fragmented, decentralized political and economic system. With all its advantages, even the United States had been forced to abandon decentralized government in the 1780s in favor of a more centralized Constitution in order to achieve prosperity and economic modernization. But Mexican federalists, who equated economic liberalism with political decentralization, gained the ascendancy in 1824 and carved Mexico into semiautonomous states based on the old colonial provinces. The result was a political system not unlike that of the United States under the Articles of Confederation, but with even greater obstacles to overcome.

Even under Spain the sparsely settled northern frontier provinces had never been well integrated into the national core. The Wars for Independence and the creation of a decentralized republic made the situation worse. Mexico lacked the resources to suppress hostile Indians, develop the economy, and guard the borders of the immense frontier, which ranged from Texas to California.[4] These were the realities that had led Spain and then Mexico to grant the initial requests of Moses and Stephen Austin to introduce American settlers into Texas.

In keeping with the spirit of federalism, the national congress gave the states most of the power over colonization matters. By November 1824 the Baron de Bastrop had arrived in the capital of Coahuila y Texas, Saltillo, and taken his seat as Texas's sole representative in the legislature. Outnumbered ten to one by the members from Coahuila, Bastrop worked tirelessly and effectively for passage of a state colonization law. Some of the Coahuilan legislators opposed allowing the immigration of Americans, but Bastrop and his liberal allies triumphed. The law was passed in March 1825, establishing the empresario system as an official state policy. Austin could now apply for new colonization contracts, as could other foreigners and native Mexicans. By opening the door to foreign immigration and controlling that immigration from Saltillo, this law would have a profound impact on the history of Texas.[5]

Austin had his own ideas about how the state should handle colonization. As the law was being debated, he had suggested to Erasmo Seguín that "the Government appoint two Individuals with complete authority to settle as many good families as may be needed to give strength and wealth to the Province." One should be a North American and the other a native Mexican, both "worthy of public confidence, and having a permanent interest in this Province." Their powers should be "very broad for surveying lands, putting colonists in possession of them, and issuing their titles of ownership to them in conformity with the Laws and the instructions of the Government in the matter." For the Mexican appointee, Austin suggested the highly respected Seguín. For the North American he recommended himself, citing his many services and sacrifices for Texas, and listing his unique qualifications. In short, Austin was proposing that he and Seguín be named joint empresarios and land commissioners for all of Texas. If enacted, such an arrangement would give Austin and Seguín a monopoly on Texas colonization. It also would leave all other applicants for empresario contracts empty-handed.[6]

A Tejano official in San Antonio forwarded Austin's plan to Bastrop, who would have to shepherd it through the legislature. When three of those aspiring empresarios—Robert Leftwich, Haden Edwards, and Frost Thorn—accidentally learned of Austin's proposal, "they were all shocked at this and could not reconcile it with his past professions." Leftwich, however, remembered all the favors that Austin had done him in Mexico City and reassured the others that they had nothing to fear from Austin and the Baron. In fact, Austin's plan arrived in Saltillo too late to be considered; he would have to share the colonizing of Texas.[7]

Edwards later would consider this scheme an indication of Austin's potential for treachery and selfishness. But of course Austin saw it differently. He considered himself the only truly qualified person to administer the colonization of Texas. Nobody had suffered as he had. Nobody possessed his understanding of how to handle unruly colonists and inscrutable Mexican officials. While there was considerable truth in this, Austin's ego would not allow him to believe that others might also prove competent at the arcane vocation of empresario. Of course, the pecuniary and psychological rewards that he would reap from a monopoly on the colonizing business undoubtedly reinforced his conviction that he (along with Seguín) should be granted that monopoly. Austin had so thoroughly identified his own interests with those of Texas that in his mind the pursuit of one almost invariably involved the pursuit of the other. What was good for Stephen Austin was good for Texas, and vice-versa.[8]

Yet when his plan came to naught, Austin, as was also frequently his way, seems to have given it no further thought. He welcomed the passage of the actual colonization law and frequently rendered support, advice, and encouragement to his fellow empresarios, especially the ones in whom he had some measure of confidence. He realized that the introduction of ever-greater numbers of Americans into Texas, even if they were coming under the sponsorship of other empresarios, lent security to his own colony and enhanced the prospects that Texas—and Stephen F. Austin along with her—would rise to prominence and prosperity.[9]

Three weeks after the passage of the state colonization law, four American applicants received empresario contracts. Robert Leftwich and Haden Edwards each contracted to introduce eight hundred families, while Green DeWitt and Frost Thorn each gained permission to settle four hundred. Leftwich's colony would be located to the northwest of Austin's; Edwards's and Thorn's to the northeast; and DeWitt's to the southwest. If successful, these new colonies would provide a ring of civilized settlement around Austin's Colony, enhancing the value of Austin

Colony lands and insulating the colonists from Indian attack. Austin's second contract for five hundred families to be located on unclaimed land within the first colony was approved shortly thereafter.[10]

As the new empresarios struggled to launch their enterprises, immigration into Austin's Colony continued steadily, although it was slower than Austin would have liked. A census of the colony taken in the fall of 1825 counted 1,800 inhabitants, including 443 slaves. Louisiana appears to have contributed the most settlers, followed by Missouri, Arkansas, and Mississippi in roughly equal numbers. Not surprisingly, given the hardships to be expected, immigrating to Texas was an act undertaken disproportionately by the young; about 80 percent of the heads of households were under forty. A majority of the settlers were, of course, married, and the typical family consisted of a husband, wife, and between three and four dependents (children, servants, or both). Large extended families were rare.[11]

Identifying who immigrated to Austin's Colony is one matter; explaining *why* they came is much more difficult. Single men sometimes came for the adventure of life on a wild frontier, and among them were a fair number of rowdies and the occasional criminal or fugitive from American justice. "It was the regular thing to ask a stranger what he had done [in the United States]," recalled settler Noah Smithwick, "and if he disclaimed having been guilty of any offense he was regarded with suspicion." It was reportedly a standing joke to ask a newcomer what his name had been before coming to Texas. A ditty sung in the colony in the 1820s included the following verse: "The United States, as we understand, / Took sick and did vomit the dregs of the land. / Her murderers, bankrupts and rogues you may see, / All congregated in San Felipe."[12]

Texas's reputation as a haven for adventurers, scoundrels, and fugitives was too widely known to have been entirely without foundation. But most immigrants were family people, and their motivations were rarely frivolous or criminal. As one would expect, there were both "push" and "pull" factors contributing to their decisions to emigrate. For most, the allure of cheap, fertile Texas land exerted the main pull. Hard times in the United States usually produced the push. But what, exactly, had made times hard enough back home to cause a man to uproot his family and subject it to the hardships and uncertainties of colonizing a foreign frontier? And how are the conflicting images of the colonists as lawless scoundrels and family-oriented pioneers to be reconciled?

Perhaps the images are not as contradictory as they seem. True criminals, of course, were rare. The government required that immigrants show proof of good character, a rule that Austin enforced "with the utmost rigour" by demanding written testimonials from local authorities from the immigrant's place of origin. More than once in the early days he summarily expelled newcomers from the colony when they proved, in Austin's words, to be "men of infamous character and bad conduct." But while most colonists were not criminals, many were fleeing circumstances that had become unbearable back home. The Panic of 1819 and the restrictive land policy of the U.S. government have already been noted as causes of general financial distress. Caught in the crunch of these events, many Texas-bound emigrants left behind debts that they had no means — and often no intention — of paying. Faced with the prospect of total ruin, imprisonment, or perhaps even violence at the hands of angry creditors, a fresh start in a foreign country held great appeal.[13]

This description clearly applies to many of Austin's colonists, especially the more prominent ones. At the top of the list was the empresario himself. Five years after leaving the United States, he still owed well over $10,000 to creditors in Missouri. Before her death in 1823, Austin's mother had felt compelled to warn him that he "would meet with Difficulty was you to come to Missouri," and later that year his sister wrote that if he returned to New Orleans he would "meat with some unpleasent things." Likewise, the second-most-important man in the colony, Austin's secretary Samuel May Williams, had left behind in New Orleans at least one unpaid debt in the amount of $700, compelling him to sail for Texas under an alias. Henry Smith, later an alcalde and Austin's future political rival, cryptically admitted in his memoirs that "misfortunes and reverses" had led to his decision to emigrate in 1826. And from the opposite side of the issue, a prominent citizen of Alexandria, Louisiana, wrote Austin in 1824 to complain of the "many persons having left this place who are indebt to me and having gone to your section of the c'try ... all of whom are slave holders."[14]

Jared Ellison Groce. A wealthy planter
who brought a hundred slaves to Austin's
Colony, the contentious Groce did not
get along well with Austin, but Austin
needed men of substance in the colony
and thus tolerated him. *Courtesy, Center
for American History, University of Texas
at Austin (Prints and Photographs
Collection #CN01812).*

No colonist, however, personified the dual image of substantial citizen and fugitive debtor more than Jared Ellison Groce. Groce had lived in Virginia, Alabama, and Georgia before coming to Texas in early 1822 and settling on the Brazos with nearly a hundred slaves. Easily the wealthiest man in the colony, he eventually received ten leagues of land and built an impressive plantation. The large land grant incurred the resentment of many colonists, who viewed it as favoritism toward the rich, but Austin later claimed that the political chief in San Antonio had dictated the amount Groce should receive. Groce soon proved to be a contentious citizen, involving himself in petty legal disputes with fellow colonists and Mexican officials. As one of his adversaries noted, "his Excentricities and Exalted notions of himself is his worst foibles. He is . . . a warm friend or bitter Enemy Just as his Immidiate Interest is Effected."[15]

Groce also apparently irritated Austin by quarreling with prominent San Antonian Juan Veramendi and quibbling over surveys of his land. Remarking on the latter issue, alcalde John P. Coles told Austin, "You know Groce. If you were to give him Twenty Leagues he would want forty." It probably came as no surprise, then, when Austin began to hear disturbing reports about Groce's past. Groce, Austin learned, had been a business partner in Georgia to Andrew Erwin, who along with Robert Leftwich had been in Mexico City in 1822-23 seeking a colonization contract on behalf of the Texas Association. Erwin and his son James (who was also involved in the business) wrote to Austin claiming that Groce had fled the country owing them $10,000 when the business failed. Evidence later surfaced indicating that Groce may not have actually owned a substantial number of the slaves he brought to Texas. There seemed to be sufficient evidence to substantiate both charges, but Austin never took action against Groce. The empresario needed men of substance and ambition in the colony, and he learned that he could count on Groce's support when it mattered. Unlike many colonists, Groce paid his land fees promptly. He contributed slaves and horses for a campaign against the Karankawas. He occasionally sold Austin goods that the empresario needed, lent him small amounts of money, and leased slaves to him. He stood by Austin in the land-fee conflict with Buckner, and he would help supply the expedition against the Fredonian rebels in 1827. Austin had to ignore whatever misdeeds Groce might have committed in the United States and any small transgressions in Texas. For all his shortcomings, Groce was an asset to the colony, and as usual that was all that mattered to Austin.[16]

Considering the character of the settlers and the condition of the Mexican government, Austin's success in holding the colony together and placing it on a relatively secure footing is little short of remarkable. It would be too much to say that he had learned to control both elements of this volatile mix, but by 1826 he had at least become adept at managing them. The expansion of the empresario system, however, created problems over which he had less control. What went on in neighboring colonies inevitably affected Austin and his colony. Events unfolding in Haden Edwards's new grant brought this reality home to Austin in 1826 and 1827.[17]

Austin met Edwards in Mexico City when both were seeking empresario contracts. Although little is known about their relationship at that time, the men apparently became friends, and Austin presumably assisted Edwards, just as he had helped Robert Leftwich. All the aspiring empresarios except Austin, though, were eventually forced to seek their grants from the state government in Saltillo. Still, Edwards remained friendly with Austin; in Bastrop's letters to Austin written from Saltillo in 1825, the Baron repeatedly referred to Edwards as Austin's "amigo," along with Leftwich and Frost Thorn. When Edwards learned of Austin's proposal to make himself and Seguín empresarios for all of Texas, Edwards understandably questioned Austin's fidelity. But Leftwich apparently allayed his fears, and Edwards and Austin remained on good terms when Edwards returned to Texas from Saltillo to found his colony.[18]

The Edwards Colony covered a large region north and east of Austin's, including the village of Nacogdoches. Unlike Austin's grant, the region had long included a diverse assortment of Anglo-Americans, Frenchmen, and Spaniards, most of whom had drifted into the area from Louisiana. It was also home to a sizable number of Indians, most notably a band of Cherokees recently forced from their ancestral homes farther east. Whatever their race or nationality, few of the inhabitants of the area could produce titles to their land, and most titles that did exist were of dubious legality. The Cherokees had even sent a representative to Mexico City to petition the central government for land, an effort that had failed. The town of Nacogdoches already had a bare-bones municipal government when Edwards arrived to assume his commission as empresario. As hard as Austin's job had been, Edwards's would be harder, for he would have to deal with this diverse, suspicious population, many of whom would view him as an interloper.

Haden Edwards had a brother, Benjamin, who would act as an unofficial partner in the colonizing venture. Both brothers shared a blustery, impatient, prideful disposition, which would not serve them well in an enterprise requiring patience and tact. Benjamin Edwards visited Austin's Colony in the summer of 1825, shortly after Haden had secured his grant, and subsequently he and Austin opened a frank but cordial correspondence touching on all aspects of the colonization business.

Austin went to great lengths to explain the colonization laws to Edwards. He recited his litany of difficulties over the past several years, dwelling on the problems stemming from perceived inequities in the selection and distribution of land. Austin admitted making errors and candidly discussed his personal shortcomings. One of these, he explained, "is that my temper is naturally rather hasty and impetuous." He credited himself with generally controlling it, although he said it had been difficult. Perhaps the most valuable insight he shared with Edwards was his shrewd assessment of the colonists' character:

> It is innate in an American to suspect and abuse a public officer whether he deserves it or not—I have had a mixed multitude to deal with collected from all quarters. Strangers to each other, to me, and to the laws and language of the country, they come here with all the ideas of americans and expect to see and understand the laws they are governed by, and many very many of them have all the licentiousness and wild turbulence of frontiersmen. Added to this when they arrive here the worst of the human passions avarice is excited to the highest extent and it directs the vanguard in their attacks on me. Jealousy and envy direct the flanks and maliciousness lurks in the rear to operate as occasion may require.

In light of this, Austin told Edwards, he had tried to exercise as much patience and leniency as possible toward the colonists. His friends, he noted, "blamed me for being too mild," but he "deem d it the safe side to err on and I still think so considering the temper and dispositions of the people with whom I had to deal." He concluded this exposition with a penetrating summation of the American frontier character and the implications it held for an empresario: "Among the ignorant part of the Americans indipendence means resistance and obstinacy[,] right or wrong—this is particularly the case with frontiersmen—a violent course with such dispositions might have kindled a flame that would have destroyed them and the settlement entirely." The Edwards brothers, as events would soon demonstrate, would have done well to listen to Austin's analysis.[19]

In what would later stand out as an ironic twist, Benjamin Edwards replied with his own advice to Austin—advice that sounds as if it had come from Austin himself. Edwards urged Austin to "expect censure and abuse," "suppress you feelings," and "humor the prejudices of the people you have to deal with." He recommended that Austin exercise a "proper degree of *forebearance* and perseverance" and told him to direct all his energies "to the preserving of a good understanding" with the Mexican authorities. Austin should let all of the "little bickering and commotions" of the colonists "pass unregarded and occupy but little of your time." "Your greatest misfortune Austin," wrote Edwards, "has been the want of a proper knowledge of human nature." That Edwards could proffer such counsel to Austin is nothing short of astonishing, considering what was about to transpire.[20]

Haden Edwards arrived in Nacogdoches in September 1825 and immediately proceeded to ignore this sound advice. He posted a notice ordering all the inhabitants of his colony to produce valid titles to their lands, which most could not do. He also announced his intention to collect a land fee considerably higher than Austin's. When this inflamed the old settlers, Edwards issued an ultimatum. "[I] sounded the trump all around bidding defiance to all their threats and bidding them to leave the lands or come forward and make arrangements to pay for them," he arrogantly informed Austin, as if Austin would approve of such a course. In December, the pro-Edwards candidate for alcalde of Nacogdoches claimed victory over the old settlers' candidate on the strength of votes from recently arrived squatters. This fueled the raging fire over land titles and fees. In San Antonio, protests began to land on the desk of Political Chief Saucedo, who overturned the election and set in motion an investigation of Edwards's conduct.[21]

Austin viewed the developing crisis with alarm. In March 1826 he sent a blunt warning to Haden Edwards. "I will here, with perfect candor and in friendship remark that your observations generally are in the highest degree imprudent and improper, and such as are calculated to ruin yourself and materially to injure all the American settlements," Austin wrote. "One moment's sober reflection" would surely show Edwards the error of his ways. But neither Haden nor Benjamin Edwards would hear the voice of reason. In reality, it was already too late, for word of the controversy had reached federal authorities. In June, President Guadalupe

Victoria issued an executive order annulling Haden Edwards's contract and expelling him from Mexico.[22]

It took weeks for the order to filter down to Saucedo in San Antonio, and even then he had to pocket it while he raised a sufficient military force. Not until December would the Mexican authorities be ready to march on Nacogdoches. In the meantime, the next act in the drama was unfolding. On November 22, thirty-six armed men sympathetic to Edwards galloped into Nacogdoches and arrested the anti-Edwards alcalde, Samuel Norris, and a handful of other local officials. Next they went to the ranch of José Antonio Sepúlveda, commander of Nacogdoches's tiny Mexican military garrison, and took him into custody. The leader of the rebels was Martin Parmer, a rowdy Missourian nicknamed the Ringtailed Panther. It is unclear how much advance knowledge the Edwards brothers had of Parmer's uprising, but if they were taken by surprise, they certainly played along with him. Parmer even arrested Haden Edwards along with the other officials, but when the men were tried in a kangaroo court, all were convicted but Edwards, whose charges were dropped.[23]

When word of these proceedings reached Austin in San Felipe, he quickly moved to limit the damage. He calmly wrote to Saucedo and tried to put the best possible face on events, explaining that the uprising resulted from local problems "and not any ill feeling against the Government." All that was needed at Nacogdoches was "an intelligent and impartial man to administer justice" and everything would be fine. "There are, however, some bad and rebellious men, who must be expelled from the Country," he admitted.[24]

In his communications to the rebels, though, Austin sounded a very different note. "I have heard with the deepest regret and astonishment of the late proceedings against the Authorities of Nacogdoches," he wrote on December 14. "It appears as tho. the people in your quarter have run mad or worse—they are distroying themselves, building up the credit of their enemies with the Gov' and jeopardising the prospects of hundreds of innocent families who wish to live in peace and quietness in the country." Austin strongly urged them to present themselves in person to the political chief "and acknowledge at once and without any reserve or stiff and foolish republican obstinacy that wrong steps were taken. . . . You may deem the course I have pointed out an unpleasant one or make a thousand imaginary object[ion]s *but you may rely on it that it is the only one that can save you.* You *must* humble yourselves before the Government and that *immediately.*"[25]

Ten days later Austin again wrote to B. J. Thompson, an acquaintance implicated in the revolt, and told him that "you are deluding yourselves" in the belief that the government would not use force to put down the up-rising, "and this delusion will ruin you." He also assured Thompson that Austin's Colony would not support the rebels. "I am unwilling to believe that you have all run mad," Austin wrote incredulously.[26]

By all appearances, they had. On December 16, 1826, the rebels again rode into Nacogdoches, this time raising the flag of independence in the public plaza. Now Benjamin Edwards rode alongside Martin Parmer. Five days later the two Edwards brothers, Parmer, and several others signed a document declaring the independence of the Republic of Fredonia, which, astonishingly, was to include all of Texas from the Sabine to the Rio Grande. Realizing the improbability of succeeding with only a small band of Anglo-American supporters, the rebels negotiated an alliance with a representative of the local Cherokees, Richard Fields. Texas — or more properly, Fredonia — was to be divided along an east-west line. After independence was secured the Indians would receive the northern half and the Anglos the southern half.[27]

Government troops commanded by Col. Mateo Ahumada and ac-companied by political chief Saucedo finally departed San Antonio on December 13. After making a stop in Goliad and suffering delays caused by heavy rains, they arrived at San Felipe on January 3, 1827. Austin had been busy in the meantime. Indeed, his actions during this period did more to ensure the ultimate suppression of the rebellion than did the actual military campaign that followed. His first priority was to counter the campaign of propaganda that the Edwardses were waging. Benjamin Edwards had written to prominent settlers in Austin's Colony and else-where, urging them to support the "standard of Liberty and Indepen-dence" against the "corrupt and despotick Government" of Mexico.[28]

Austin fought fire with fire. On New Year's Day he addressed his colo-nists, stating that a "small party of infatuated madmen at Nacogdoches have declared Independence" and reminding the settlers of their duty "as men of honor, as Mexicans, and as Americans." In this war of words, he was helped considerably by the Fredonians' alliance with the Cherokees. It might have been difficult to persuade his colonists to take the side of Mexico against fellow Anglo-Americans, but Austin could now inform his people that the Fredonians had "invited the Indians from Sabine to Rio Grande to join them and wage a war of Murder, plunder, and desolation on the innocent inhabitants of the frontier." The rebels, he said, had forfeited their right to be called Americans "by their unnatural and bloody alliance with Indians." [29]

Resolutions of loyalty poured in from every corner of the colony. In his letters to the colonists, Austin had also called for volunteers to accompany the Mexican troops on their march to Nacogdoches. He could have officially called the colony's militia to active duty, but relying on volunteers was a part of his overall strategy for turning the rebellion into a positive public relations stroke for his colony. He explained the strategy clearly in his New Year's Day address:

> This is a mark of respect we owe these [Mexican] officers and at this particular time it will have a decissive influence on the future prospects of this colony — it will also have a very great influence in quieting and settling the difficulties in that part of the country, for the men who go on from here, by their presence under the banners of the gov[t] will at once dissipate the errors which those people have been induced to believe by a few artfull men as regards the part this colony would take. It will have a much better effect for the people to voluntier on this service, than to be called on officially and in order to give them a full opportunity of shewing their patriotism and their love of good order virtue and justice, I have made no official call. [30]

Not content to rely on letters and proclamations while he waited for the troops to assemble, Austin also began devising a diplomatic strategy. [31] When Saucedo and Ahumada arrived from San Antonio, they approved his plans. The strategy consisted of several parts. First, letters were written to the Cherokees in an attempt to dissuade them from their alliance with the Fredonians. Next, Austin persuaded Saucedo to offer amnesty to the Fredonians if they would lay down their arms. Finally, an open letter to the people of East Texas informed them of the approach of troops and sought their help in reestablishing order. These communications also carried reminders of the severe consequences of continued resistance.

Austin appointed three reliable colonists, Richard Ellis, James Cummins, and James Kerr, to deliver these messages. When they returned on January 22 they reported that they had been rebuffed by the Edwardses and the Cherokee diplomats. Still, the effort had not been a waste. The commissioners had learned that the settlers of the region—especially those in areas away from Nacogdoches—were not united behind the revolution. This also appeared to be the case with the Cherokees; decision-making in the tribe was decentralized, and several dissident chiefs disapproved of the Fredonian alliance. Moreover, the inhabitants now knew that troops were prepared to put down the rebellion. Support for the Fredonian cause began to crumble.

Delayed by bad weather and waiting for reinforcements, the Mexican troops lingered at San Felipe for nearly three weeks. But on January 22, Colonel Ahumada and one battalion marched for Nacogdoches. More Mexicans departed the following day, followed a few days later by Austin and his mounted volunteers. A small detachment of Austin's militia, under the command of colonist Lawrence Richard Kenny, was sent to pacify the settlers on Ayish Bayou in far East Texas, and another under the command of Abner Kuykendall received orders to patrol the San Antonio road at the northern boundary of Austin's Colony. Austin also sent a second peace commission to negotiate directly with the dissident Cherokee chiefs. Overestimating rebel strength, Saucedo finally ordered Austin to call additional militiamen to active duty. Rendezvous points for these reinforcements were specified along the line of march. The government forces were to meet at the Trinity River for the final approach to Nacogdoches. Everyone was taking the affair very seriously.

In the meantime, the Fredonians were experiencing internal troubles. The Edwards brothers and Parmer had never succeeded in uniting all the Anglo-American settlers of the area, much less the non-Anglos. At least two groups of these loyalists had already taken up arms against the

Fredonians, and the only real fight of the rebellion had taken place in Nacogdoches on January 4 between rebels in the town's Old Stone Fort and loyalists under the command of ousted alcalde Samuel Norris. The Fredonians won that skirmish, but it marked the beginning of the end for the rebels. As word spread of the approach of the Mexican and Anglo troops, internal divisions among the Fredonians worsened and opposition to their cause grew stronger. On January 28 the rebellion collapsed, and most of the rebels fled to Louisiana.

The main body of Austin's militia was ordered home before reaching the Trinity. Stephen and Brown Austin agreed to remain with the Mexican troops as interpreters and advisers. The small army marched into Nacogdoches on February 8 to find that the town was already in loyalist hands. The Edwards brothers and Parmer escaped, but the Cherokee leaders who had conspired with them were condemned by a tribal council, hunted down, and executed by their own people. The Fredonian Rebellion was over.[32]

Austin remained in Nacogdoches for a month to help the Mexican officials restore order. At his urging, Saucedo and Ahumada adopted a lenient and conciliatory course toward all but the ringleaders of the revolt. After nearly a month in Nacogdoches, Colonel Ahumada decided to tour the area between the Atoyac and the Sabine, which had become home to 168 families of squatters during the years that the region was a neutral ground between the United States and Mexico. Since most of the squatters were Americans and the country unfamiliar, the Mexican officer insisted that Austin accompany him. "I go with great reluctance for my thoughts and feelings are all in the Colony and I am heartily tired of this country," Austin wrote to Samuel May Williams back in San Felipe. "It is perhaps a fortunate thing for me that I have learned patience in the hard School of an Empresario for I assure you that in this place I have had full use for all I possessed."[33]

Austin's sojourn with the Mexican troops did have its benefits. The clemency that Austin recommended undoubtedly helped win the confidence of many Anglo-Americans in Texas who had viewed the Mexican government as arbitrary and cruel. As Brown Austin put it, the insurgents were "treated with a degree of lenity by the Mexicans they had no right to expect from the nature of their crimes—and which I vouchsafe would not have been shewn them in their native country for similar offences." [34]

The benefits for Austin's Colony were obvious. The colonists' actions seemed to demonstrate that the Americans under Austin's leadership were serious about their oath of loyalty to Mexico. After the rebellion ended, the War Department sent an official communique acknowledging the "important service" that the colonists had rendered to the nation. The episode further enhanced Austin's stature with Mexican leaders. Anastacio Bustamante, commandant general of the Interior Provinces and soon to be acting president of the republic, wrote Austin from Goliad to say that he wished he could see Austin personally and give him *"un Extrechisimo abrazo"*—a very strong embrace—for the "happy result of the Expedition to Nacogdoches." [35]

Even if Austin had supported the Fredonian Rebellion and it had succeeded, he stood to lose much and gain little by the achievement. All he had to show for his years in Texas were the titles to his premium lands for the first colony—half of which belonged to Joseph Hawkins's heirs—and he feared that those titles were imperfect. An independent Texas could not have sustained itself in 1827, and annexation by the United States was highly uncertain. Even in the event of annexation, the empresario system would have been disrupted or abolished, robbing Austin of the rewards that he hoped to receive from his recently granted second colonization contract. He took his oath of loyalty to Mexico seriously, but his personal interests made it easy for him to do so.

Although Austin managed to turn the Fredonian Rebellion to his advantage by demonstrating his loyalty and that of his colonists, the revolt was, in Austin's words, "dreadfully illtimed." Not only was he trying to complete the first colony, pacify Indians, soothe unruly settlers, establish a functioning legal system, and begin fulfilling his second empresario contract, but political developments in Saltillo were requiring his attention. The legislature of the new state of Coahuila y Texas was ponderously working to draft a state constitution and laws that would have an enormous impact on the long-term prospects of Austin and his colony. He could not allow the disturbances at Nacogdoches to interfere with his efforts to ensure that the emerging state government would create an environment favorable to his interests.[36]

After the passage of the state colonization law, the most important issue was slavery. The federal Constitution of 1824 contained an anti-slavery clause, but its vague wording made it almost meaningless. Texas was the only place in the republic where slavery was growing in economic importance, so the state legislature in Saltillo was the logical forum to decide the future of slavery in Texas. With Mexican sentiment generally opposed to slavery, and with Texas having only one representative in the legislature compared with Coahuila's ten, Austin knew that he would be fighting an uphill battle if he wished to protect the interests of slaveholders in his colony.

On no topic was Austin more quintessentially American than in his attitudes toward the institution of slavery. Like Thomas Jefferson, Austin thought slavery an evil in the abstract. He knew it contradicted the principles of liberty on which the United States was founded. In private correspondence he strongly condemned slavery as "that curse of curses, and worst of reproaches, on civilized man; that unanswered, and unanswerable, inconsistency of *free* and liberal republicans." But Austin's great moral shortcoming — like that of America itself — was the failure to act on his convictions. He knew that slavery was wrong, but he capitulated to the nearly irresistible social, economic, and political pressures to preserve and defend the institution.[37]

It would be a mistake to characterize Austin as tortured over slavery. He owned a handful of slaves at various periods of his life and had employed a sizable force of them in his ill-fated lead-mining partnership with Anthony Butler in Missouri. The aspect of slavery that seemed to concern him the most was not the denial of freedom to enslaved individuals but rather the long-term effects of slavery on white society. Reflecting on the bloodiest slave revolt in history, Austin wrote, "I sometimes shudder at the consequences and think that a large part [of] America will be Santo Domingonized in 100, or 200 years." That such a fate might someday befall his beloved Texas disturbed him. "The idea of seeing such a country as this overrun by a slave population almost makes me weep," he told a northern cousin in 1830. "It is in vain to tell a North American that the white population will be destroyed some fifty or eighty years hence by the negros, and that his daughters will be violated and Butch[er]ed by them. 'It is too far off to think of'—'they can do as I have, take care of themselves'—'something will turn up to keep of the evil' etc, etc. Such are the silly answers of the slave holder. To say any thing to them as to the justice of slavery, or its demoralizing effects on society, is only to draw down ridicule upon the person who attempts it." [38]

Austin was not about to subject himself to such ridicule, so he kept these sentiments to himself or shared them only with sympathetic listeners, usually northerners. Despite the occasional written statement expressing hope that Texas would not permanently allow slavery,[39] he worked repeatedly from the time of his first journey to Mexico City until the Texas Revolution to ensure that immigrants would be allowed to bring their slaves to Texas and keep them once they were there. His reasoning was straightforward and pragmatic: in the short term, the populating of his colony depended on emigration from the slave states; in the longer term, the economic development of Texas depended on commercial agriculture, primarily cotton. Southerners would not emigrate without their slaves, and plantations could not function without laborers.[40]

Austin sometimes seemed to favor a labor system in which nominally free blacks would be placed under a form of servitude milder than American-style slavery. Once, when slavery appeared politically threatened by the Mexican government, he mused over what he saw as the realities and possibilities inherent in the situation. "Color," he wrote, "forms a line of demarkation between [blacks] and the whites. The law must assign their station, fix their rights and their disabilities and obligations—something between slavery and freedom, but neither the one nor the other. Either this, or slavery in full *must* take place. Which is best? Quien Sabe? It is a difficult and *dark* question." This was hardly a ringing endorsement of freedom and equality.[41]

Firm in his conviction that Texas must preserve slavery or something akin to it, Austin determined to do all he could to see that the new state constitution would not threaten slavery in Texas, at least not any time soon. His first comprehensive proposal came in August 1825, when he drew up a lengthy memorial to the state government recommending that immigrants be allowed to bring their slaves to Texas until 1840. These bondsmen and their children would be slaves for life, but their grand-children were to become free—at age fifteen for females and twenty-five for males.[42]

This memorial apparently had little effect, and another year passed before the legislature actually turned to the issue. In the summer of 1826 the committee working on the constitution reported an article that would have abolished slavery outright, with some sort of financial compensation for the owners. The proposed article alarmed the slaveholders of Texas, and some began preparing to leave the state in the event of its passage. A concerned Austin responded with another memorial to the legislature, re-iterating the necessity for slavery in Texas and arguing that at the very least the government was obligated to allow the Old Three Hundred to keep their slaves. In San Antonio, Saucedo and the ayuntamiento supported Austin's position and communicated their views to Saltillo. But as the empresario soon learned, even when the Anglos and Tejanos presented a united front on the issue, they still faced a seemingly impossible battle in a legislature dominated ten-to-one by Coahuilans. With slaveholders on the verge of panic over impending abolition and the Fredonians on the brink of open revolt, Austin fell into one of the deepest depressions of his life.[43]

Fortunately, Brown Austin was becoming an increasingly valuable as-set in both business and political affairs. When he returned to Texas from Missouri in 1825 he moved ahead enthusiastically with plans to establish a ranch, cotton gin, and "commercial business" on a large tract of land that Stephen had secured for him on the lower Brazos. In mid-1826 the younger Austin prepared to travel to Coahuila and Nuevo León to buy livestock. Brown had intended to stop in Saltillo to visit the Baron de Bas-trop and deliver a report that Stephen had prepared on the proposed port of Galveston, but his visit to the state capital now took on a new urgency. He and Bastrop were to persuade the hostile legislature to come around to the Texan position on slavery.[44]

Following a "fatigueing journey" Brown arrived in Saltillo on Sep-tember 22. He immediately visited Bastrop, who was pessimistic over securing concessions on the slavery issue. The best that could be hoped for, thought the baron, was a provision allowing the original three hundred colonists to keep their slaves. So Brown and Bastrop, armed with Stephen's memorial giving the practical arguments against immediate abolition, lobbied individual legislators and soon secured pledges from most of them that no slaves already in Texas would be freed. Brown and the baron then hoped to convince the lawmakers that the children of slaves should remain enslaved until they reached age twenty-one or twenty-five. After two weeks of intense lobbying, Brown thought he had succeeded and left the city. He would arrive back in Texas just in time for the campaign against the Fredonians. The legislature, however, did not draft the final slavery article for another three months. When it finally appeared at the end of January 1827, it recognized existing slavery and allowed the introduction of slaves until the end of November, but children of slaves were to be free at birth. The article would not prove immediately ruinous, but it fell far short of what Austin had desired. As Bastrop pointed out, a new legislature would be convened after the passage of the constitution, and perhaps it would enact more favorable slavery legislation. Subsequent events would prove him right.[45]

The final debates on the state constitution coincided with the termination of the Fredonian Rebellion. Back in San Felipe at the end of May 1827 the empresario called the colonists together and read the new constitution, praising it as "liberal," "Republican," "just," and "enlightened." Without mentioning specifics, Austin reminded the colonists that any "evils or embarassments in its details or operations" could be remedied by amendment. He closed with yet another flowery exhortation for loyalty and gratitude to the Mexican government.[46]

Actually, apart from passing the important state colonization law and giving limited sanction to slavery, the legislature that met between 1824 and 1827 had only modestly benefited Austin and his interests. The Baron de Bastrop had struggled mightily not only to secure the colonization and slavery laws but also to win political support for such measures as protecting the settlements from Indians, improving mail service, allowing the settlers to cultivate tobacco (a state monopoly), and opening a port at Galveston. Support for these causes did not always translate into action, but that was often as not because of the dismal financial condition of the fledgling state. Still, as Brown Austin remarked to his brother during the slavery debate, "The Old Baron has strove hard for us—I know not what would have been our fate if he had not been a member of the Legislature. Our situation would have been a deplorable one indeed."[47]

What the wily old baron had really accomplished transcended individual pieces of legislation. With the active connivance of the Austins he had helped to forge a nascent political coalition among three groups: the Anglo-American colonists in Texas, the Tejano elites in San Antonio, and most important, a group of powerful would-be capitalists based in the Coahuilan towns of Parras and Monclova. The latter group was led by the brothers José María and Agustín Viesca of Parras. Like Lorenzo de Zavala at the national level, the Viescas dreamed of a northern Mexico that would embrace economic liberalism. The production and export of cotton lay at the heart of their vision. This made Austin and the Anglo-American colonies a pivotal element in their design. In short, their plans for the development of Coahuila y Texas echoed those of Austin, Seguín, and other Texans.[48]

By 1828 this coalition was beginning to demonstrate its effectiveness. With José María Viesca and several of his allies uniting with Bastrop in the legislature, they had won passage of the state colonization law, which opened the door to cotton growers from the United States. The coalition had protected—at least partially—the slave labor force needed to produce cotton in large amounts. And most important, it had succeeded in placing men friendly to its agenda in key positions at all levels of the government. José María Viesca was elected governor in 1827, and Agustín Viesca represented the state in the national senate. Another member of the coalition, Victor Blanco of Monclova, served alternately as governor and vice-governor between 1826 and 1831. The important post of secretary of state during much of this period was held by Juan Antonio Padilla, also a member of the liberal faction. In Texas, the appointment of Saucedo as political chief from 1825 to 1827 was another critical link in the alliance (and he was succeeded in that position by another ally, Ramón Músquiz, in late 1827). The local power structure of San Antonio also was dominated by Tejanos sympathetic to these views, including Erasmo Seguín, Juan Martín Veramendi, and José Antonio Navarro, all of whom could usually be found serving on the town's ayuntamiento, which functioned as an important mouthpiece for Texas in its relations with the state government. It was Austin's good fortune that Bastrop shared his vision for Texas and could serve as a catalyst in bringing these disparate groups together in a common political cause.[49]

The baron had been in declining health at least since mid-1826, when he began to complain of "dropsy in the chest," probably a sign of heart disease. Though a close ally of Austin, he was his own man to the end. He never hesitated to scold the young empresario when he thought that Austin had let him down. For example, Bastrop chided Austin in 1825 for not keeping a promise to construct a house for him in San Felipe. "I have learned from experience that it is easier to make a promise to a friend when he is present than to fulfill it when he is absent," he lectured Austin. He then reminded Austin of all the baron had done for the colonies and suggested that if Austin wished for him to continue such service Austin would have to do better by him. "Sometimes it is appropriate to make small sacrifices in order to obtain large and lasting benefits," Bastrop said bluntly. "Think it over." Similarly, Austin had promised financial support during Bastrop's long stay in Saltillo, but often the funds were slow in coming. "I need at least 2,000 pesos more, which you will please send me as soon as possible," Bastrop pleaded in May 1825. "I am expecting a categorical answer so that I shall know what to do, because I counted on your promises, and, when these are not kept, it puts a fellow into a bog hole where it is very difficult to get out." Always pressed for cash, Austin procrastinated but finally sent funds.[50]

With the benefit of his age and experience in Mexican affairs, Bastrop could also see Austin's occasional mistakes. In one instance, he believed that Austin had raised the issue of slavery prematurely. "Austin had good intentions," Bastrop told Robert Leftwich, "but he acted very imprudently when he raised this question." Austin had also urged Bastrop to come home from Saltillo to finish issuing land titles to the Old Three Hundred. Bastrop wisely refused, knowing that the debate over slavery was about to reach a critical stage. Frustrated by what he viewed as excessive timidity on the empresario's part, he complained that Austin could have gone ahead with the issuance of the titles "without my presence, if he had had a little more nerve and resolution."[51]

These disagreements never truly affected the relationship between the men, for they were bound by six years' mutual labor in what both understood to be a grand undertaking. On January 3, 1827, Bastrop left the legislative hall for the last time. Two weeks later he drew up a will, naming Austin first administrator of his estate. On February 22 he died in Saltillo. The legislature had to pay for the funeral, but Austin later sent Secretary of State Juan Antonio Padilla 185 pesos to help cover the expenses.[52]

Through his astute politicking, Bastrop had built a foundation for others. When the state constitution went into effect soon after his death, Texas would have two representatives instead of one. Those two men, Miguel Arciniega and José Antonio Navarro of San Antonio, continued to nurture the coalition between Anglos, Tejanos, and the Viesca faction in the state government. They met with constant opposition from Saltillo-based conservatives who did not share their liberal vision of political and economic modernization.[53]

The spring of 1827 brought a rare period of quiet to Austin and his colony. Empresarios Green DeWitt and Martín de León united with him in negotiating a new treaty with the Karankawas. Likewise, the Mexican military authorities made peace with the Tawakonis, Wacos, and even the Comanches. The empresario set aside Mondays through Thursdays to work on concluding the business of the first colony. Other days he devoted to processing applications for land under the second contract. With the Fredonian troubles behind him and the state government showing signs of progress, Austin's gloomy outlook brightened. "Our prospects are very good as to crops, emigration, peace, government etc etc.," he wrote to his brother-in-law James Perry in May. "The state constitution is a very good one. You may set down every thing you see in the news papers unfavourable to Texas as false."[54]

As immigration to the colony continued, San Felipe began to look more like a town. By 1827, Austin's capital consisted of twenty or thirty log structures, including a handful of businesses. The population numbered between one hundred and two hundred. Austin's cabin and the adjacent land office were the scene of a constant flow of colonists and would-be colonists recording titles, paying fees, checking on the availability of land, and visiting with the empresario about numerous other matters. His house, he complained, was a "thoroughfare for the whole country." A saloon or two soon opened for business, and one of them even acquired a billiard table. Soon a school opened. Life at the center of the settlement gradually became too hectic for Austin, who made plans to have a new house built on the north edge of town. He also contracted with a local builder to have his old cabin disassembled, expanded into a two-story building with tongue-and-groove floors, siding, and shutters. This structure he then leased to James Whiteside to operate as an inn, no doubt hoping that visitors to San Felipe would stay there instead of at his own residence.[55]

Over the course of five years Austin had forged a close friendship with his secretary, Samuel May Williams. The hardworking, multitalented Williams shouldered an increasing share of the empresario's tedious land business. Williams's own life since coming to Texas had not been without trouble. Although little is known of the circumstances, his marriage was apparently an unhappy one. In mid-1826 his wife departed Texas never to return, leaving the couple's infant child with his father. As might be expected, this created a scandal, but Brown Austin expressed relief that Williams' "*devil*" was gone, and he hoped that Williams would find "more peace of mind than formerly." Local gossip held that he had banished her in order to marry a younger woman. The gossip may have been true, for within two years Williams took twenty-year-old Sarah Scott as his new bride. Their first child, born in 1830, was named Austin.[56]

Growth of the colony brought with it the occasional troublemaker, and one such individual threatened to disrupt the relative peace and quiet of 1827. Dr. Lewis Dayton was one of a group of Americans who had settled illegally at Pecan Point on the Red River. Dissatisfied with the treatment he had received from the Mexican government, Dayton came to Austin's Colony, presumably to obtain land there. The empresario probably had already identified Dayton as a malcontent and apparently denied his request. Dayton then began to criticize Austin and Williams and attempted, with some limited success, to organize the colonists against them. Matters came to a head in September on the streets of San Felipe.

Dayton modified the words to a barroom ballad and hired a strolling minstrel to sing the song, now titled "Mrs. Williams's Lament" in reference to the departed ex-wife of Austin's secretary. Two of the surviving verses illustrate the defamatory nature of the tune:

> The first of those villains who came to this State
> Was runaway Stephen F. Austin the great;
> He applied to the Mexicans as I understand
> And from them got permission to settle this land.
>
> The next was my husband, for you will now see
> How Austin coaxed him to San Felipe,
> To this great Sanhedrin, and not very mild,
> That I should be banished, then robbed of my child.[57]

Austin, who had tried to ignore Dayton, happened to be absent from San Felipe at the time. But Williams later confronted Dayton, who then threatened to burn the land office. Whatever public support Dayton may have enjoyed in the settlement evaporated at this point; torching the land office and its records would have been a disaster for all. A mob, which apparently included Williams and Brown Austin, gathered and proceeded to "arrest" Dayton. The "trial" convened in the local tavern. The sentence was tar and feathers, followed by immediate banishment from the colony. The precise role of Williams and the younger Austin in carrying out the sentence is not known, but one suspects that the proud, strong-willed Brown—free from the moderating influence of his brother—took special delight in punishing this malefactor of the Austin name.[58]

The longer Austin dealt with such problems, the more he was coming to understand the character of the colonists. While he could not openly applaud the action against Dayton, he knew that it was far better for a troublemaker to be condemned in the court of public opinion than for the government to prosecute him. Distrust of public officials—be they Anglo or Mexican—ran deep. The government, Austin subsequently wrote, should "let such firebrands alone, and the good sense of the sound and reflecting part of the colony, will put them down much sooner and more effectually than opposition or irons, by the authorities. If the civil authority had taken hold of Dayton, he would have become popular, altho he was a most perfect jack ass and a scoundrel." [59]

His analysis underscores the complexity of the relationship that had developed between Austin and the colonists by the late 1820s. The line between respect and resentment could be terribly thin, and he knew it. Many decades later an old-timer who had known the empresario told a revealing story that, while perhaps apocryphal, nonetheless rings true. It seems that one night a group of old settlers, having "participated in something more stimulating than water . . . went on to indulge their independence of spirit by a general denunciation and cursing of Steven F. Austin." A newcomer among them joined in the fun, at which point one of the old-timers "beckoned him outside and, having reached a retired spot, politely informed the new-comer that he was a going to whip him." The newcomer, "surprised and astonished," asked what he had done. "He was briefly informed that all those old colonists had been many years in Texas, that they had a right to curse Austin, though every one loved and would fight for him, that Austin could never possibly have given him any cause to curse him, and therefore he deserved it and he was a going to whip him." The fight was averted by a profuse apology, but as the storyteller noted, "it taught him a lesson not soon to be forgotten." [60]

Affairs in the colony had stabilized enough by August 1827 for Austin to leave Texas for a long-overdue business trip to Coahuila. After the usual extended stop in San Antonio, he set out through the three hundred miles of scorched sand and cactus for Saltillo, armed with a long list of important matters to lay before the state government. By the beginning of October, Austin had reached his destination, undoubtedly relieved to be in the cool, dry climate of the mile-high state capital. [61]

Austin spent two months in Saltillo, in part seeking clarification of details that the current state of political affairs had left vague. For a person with Austin's meticulous mind and cautious nature, it was maddening when the government failed to provide specific guidelines on how to execute its policies. A prime example was the matter of land fees. One of his greatest headaches had been the government's failure to establish a clear policy regarding how much he could charge the colonists for his services. As a result, he had instituted the ill-fated twelve-and-a-half-cent-per-acre fee. When he had applied for his second contract in 1825, the political chief allowed him to charge sixty dollars for each league granted in the new colony, but this had never been ratified by the higher authorities. Austin, no doubt remembering his earlier experience, now petitioned the state government to publish an official fee schedule that would ratify what he was already doing in practice.[62]

Regularizing the land fees was especially important because Austin was now ready to request a third empresario contract. This time he sought permission to settle one hundred new families and establish a town in a small area bordered by the San Antonio Road on the southeast and the Colorado River on the southwest, encompassing parts of modern-day Bastrop and Travis counties. Austin justified the request on the grounds that several citizens of San Antonio had asked him to establish the town "with a view not only to afford the necessary facilities to the travellers of that road, but also to penetrate with the new settlements, farther into the interior of the country, towards the Savage Tribes." The legislature granted Austin's petition. The new grant became known informally as the Little Colony, with Bastrop as its principal settlement (see map 3). Years later, at a site farther up the river in the Little Colony, the Republic of Texas would found the capital city that today bears Austin's name.[63]

While in Saltillo, Austin also performed a service for another Anglo-American colonization venture. In Mexico City five years earlier he had assisted Robert Leftwich and Andrew Erwin in their attempt to obtain an empresario contract on behalf of the Texas Association of Nashville. Leftwich had eventually succeeded in securing the contract after the passage of the state colonization law, but after that the company's efforts to introduce settlers stalled. Leftwich stepped down as the company's agent, and over the next two years the company authorized two other men to conduct its business in Texas. Neither brought any settlers, and by the summer of 1827 the company had appointed yet another agent, Hosea H. League, a young Nashville businessman who had settled in Austin's Colony the year before. The company authorized League to go to Saltillo and petition the government to recognize him as empresario in place of Leftwich, to extend the geographical limits of the colony, to give the company more time to settle the grant, and to expand the colony to eight hundred families.[64]

League had hoped to accompany Austin to Saltillo, but the Nashville stockholders failed to provide funds for the trip. Austin went alone. League later sent him a power of attorney and a copy of the company's petition, which Austin presented to the government, along with his own endorsement and recommendations for implementation. The legislature granted the request and issued a new contract to the company, granting all its requests with the exception of the time extension. For Austin and the Texas Association it was a win-win situation; the contract breathed new life into the association's moribund colonization project, and Austin gained a potential buffer between his colonies and the Indian tribes to the north and west.[65]

The timing of this trip to Saltillo had been no accident. The new state constitution was about to go into effect, and Austin needed to be certain that it would be implemented without disadvantage to his colony. For example, the legislature could place a strict or loose construction on the constitution's slavery clause. When Austin arrived in the capital, that issue was being debated. Legislator José Francisco Madero, although generally sympathetic to Austin's causes, spoke for progressive Coahuilans in these debates over slavery. Madero decried the "hard and cruel treatment with which the Anglo Americans handle the slaves," noting that most of the Anglos believed that blacks "are of a different species than whites." He had spent time in New Orleans, where he had heard Americans say that "blacks were the same as mules and should be treated as such." Confronting such attitudes from his *friends* in the legislature, Austin could lobby with only limited success this time for the loose interpretation of the slavery clause.[66]

There were also many technical issues concerning the civil government soon to be installed in Austin's Colony. The empresario requested information on the manner and timing of local elections, the means of paying minor civil officials, the functioning of the justice system, and the organization of the militia. In accordance with Mexican legal tradition, all such requests had to submitted via formal letters to the governor, who then transmitted them to the legislature for action. All of this took time, but Austin used the time wisely to become better acquainted with influential Coahuilans, including governors Ignacio de Arispe and José María Viesca. The success of these efforts is witnessed by the glowing letters of recommendation that he obtained from both men.[67]

By early December, Austin had concluded his business in Saltillo. He retraced his route through the rocky hills and across the bleak desert of northern Mexico, finally arriving in San Felipe at Christmastime. "I am happy to find myself once more amongst my large family after so long an absence," he wrote to his old friend Josiah Bell on New Year's Day 1828. That "family," of course, was made up of the colonists, for his brother remained his only blood kin in Texas. A month later elections were held in the colony, signaling the end of Austin's extraordinary governing powers and integrating the Anglo colonists into the Mexican body politic. He could now turn over the reins of the colony's government to regularly elected officials and concentrate on the completion of what he had always viewed as his real mission: developing the Texas frontier into a populated, prosperous, civilized country, with Stephen F. Austin as its leading citizen.[68]

Crises, Personal and Political
1828–1830

The early days of spring usher in the most beautiful season of the year in the Brazos River valley. Oaks and hickories begin to show new growth. Redbuds, dogwoods, and magnolias splash the woods with pink and white blossoms. The prairies grow lush and green, soon to be blanketed with gaudy wildflowers. For a few weeks, nights remain cool while days grow warm with bright sunshine and brilliant blue skies.

Back in San Felipe after his long trip to Saltillo, even the frequently despondent Stephen F. Austin found cause for optimism. "We move on here slowly, but quietly—this country will present a second Eden to posterity—wheither *we* shall find it such or not depends on the progress of emigration and improvements," he wrote in March 1828. Six months later he reported that the colony had enjoyed health that year and that "we are getting on pritty well in every respect." He even planned to visit Missouri "as soon as possible." These reports—downright cheerful by Austin standards—capture the empresario's generally sanguine outlook in 1828. And why not view the future with optimism? Relieved from the heaviest burdens of administering the colony's government, he could now concentrate on the land business and see to his long-neglected personal affairs.[1]

As Austin had noted, however, the fulfillment of his vision for Texas and his own future still hinged on the continuing flow of immigrants to his colony. He had now signed three empresario contracts permitting him to settle nine hundred families in Texas. A few months later he would be granted a fourth contract, for the settlement of three hundred more families along the coast between the Lavaca and San Jacinto rivers (see map 3).[2] Add to that figure the Anglos who had settled outside Austin's Colony, and it becomes clear that the Tejanos had become a minority in their native land. Any concerns that Austin had in 1828 about the "progress of emigration" would soon prove groundless, for during the next two years the population of the colony would more than double.[3]

Moreover, political developments seemed encouraging. When the state constitution went into effect, Texas gained a second seat in the legislature. Miguel Arciniega and José Antonio Navarro, Tejanos sympathetic to Austin's views, were elected. Their presence in Saltillo would prove important in securing favorable legislation on several subjects of concern to Austin and his colonists.

From Austin's viewpoint, the most important of these topics was the debate over slavery. The Baron de Bastrop had been lucky to secure any concessions at all regarding slavery; the state constitution had protected existing slavery and allowed the introduction of slaves until the end of November 1827, with children of slaves to be free at birth. Later the legislature passed a law prohibiting the slave trade and emancipating slaves of masters who died and left no direct heirs. On his recent trip to Saltillo, Austin had lobbied against all these antislavery laws, but he secured only two relatively minor changes.[4] The fact remained that if the existing slavery laws as of 1828 were enforced, no more southern slaveholders would be allowed to immigrate with their slaves, and existing slavery in Texas was to be phased out over time. These realities could greatly hinder Austin's plans for the economic development of his adopted land.[5]

But once again things were going his way. In February 1828 Austin held local elections as authorized by the state government, thus creating the ayuntamiento of San Felipe.[6] In one of its first official acts the new three-man council petitioned the legislature for a law guaranteeing the "Contracts made by emigrants to this state or Inhabitants of it with the servants or hirelings they introduce." Austin entrusted the bill to Texas representative José Antonio Navarro, who quietly secured its passage at a moment when the legislators were distracted by another matter. The law, of course, was a subterfuge. It allowed American slaveholders ostensibly to "free" their slaves before emigrating and then to sign "contracts" with them making them indentured servants for life. Austin and his allies in the legislature knew that the law might be repealed when its true intent became more widely understood, and Austin continued to lobby the government for more secure and comprehensive legislation protecting slavery. For the time being, though, the empresario could reassure prospective emigrants that they could still bring and hold their slaves. At about this time Austin himself again moved into the ranks of the slaveholders, buying a forty-year-old female domestic servant for $350.[7]

Another pro-immigration measure for which Austin successfully lobbied was a law protecting settlers from foreign creditors. Gov. José María Viesca agreed wholeheartedly with Austin's proposal and personally laid the bill before the legislature. When it passed in January 1829 the law granted colonists a twelve-year exemption from seizure of land or tools for nonpayment of debts that they had contracted in foreign countries before emigrating. Texas already enjoyed a reputation as a haven for debtors from the United States; this act—Texas's first homestead law—helped to justify that reputation.[8]

The homestead law undoubtedly came as a relief to many of Austin's colonists, although most of them probably knew little or nothing about his key role in securing its passage. It is tempting to see the strong hand of self-interest in Austin's actions, because he was among the largest debtors in Texas whom the law would protect. Certainly the law gave the empresario some breathing room, but in reality by 1828 he was already planning to pay off his pre-Texas debts.

This was possible because of two developments. First, the land fees he was allowed to charge under the second and third contracts now provided a regular cash flow. Second, he finally had finished the business of the first colony and perfected the titles to his initial twenty-two and a half leagues of premium lands. Austin had materially completed this contract three years earlier, but he apparently felt uneasy about the titles to his lands because Bastrop had died before issuing all the titles to the Old Three Hundred. But at last in March 1828 the new commissioner, Gaspar Flores, arrived to issue the remaining titles. He finished by the end of May, and Austin got Flores to draw up an official document declaring the contract fulfilled and confirming the empresario's titles to his premium lands. He could now sell these lands — when he could find a buyer.[9]

Austin still had three sizable debts outstanding. First was the large amount he owed his ex-partner Anthony Butler from the ill-fated Missouri lead-mining venture. Next came the equally large debt to George Tennille incurred in the disastrous Arkansas land speculation scheme of 1819. Finally there was his obligation to the heirs of Joseph Hawkins arising from the Hawkins-Austin partnership of 1821.

The Butler debt, more than $6,000, vexed Austin the most, for he believed that he owed Butler much less. "This has been a cruel affair and has harrassed me very much, more than any event of my life ever did," Austin wrote in early 1829. "I hope it is done with." In fact it was not done with, but Austin had taken a major step at that point by agreeing with Butler on the amount and a payment schedule. Austin made the first payment of $2,000 at that time, and the others followed on time over the next four years. A similar settlement of the $7,000 Tennille debt took place over the same period. Simultaneously, Austin initiated steps to settle the Hawkins obligation, although through no fault of his own the final land distribution would not take place until 1832. So determined was he to pay all the old debts tarnishing the family name that in 1829 he even took steps to satisfy a court judgment against his father and James Bryan still pending in Jefferson County. Paying such debts must have given great psychological comfort to Austin. If he had long struggled to escape the long shadow of his domineering father, what better way to make that escape than to pay the debts that in his own lifetime Moses had been unable to pay?[10]

Even family matters took on a brighter aspect in the spring of 1828. The occasion was the marriage of Brown Austin to Eliza Westall. "He has made a good choice and I think has secured his domestic happiness," the empresario noted with satisfaction. Austin had used his influence to secure large land grants for his younger brother, and now he was assisting Brown in establishing a mercantile business in the new town of Brazoria.

(Brown would be partners in this business with one John Austin, an Old Three Hundred colonist from Connecticut who may have been distantly related to Brown and Stephen.) Stephen even renewed talk of marriage himself, telling a Missouri friend that "a Small farm a moderate independence and a wife would render my life much happier than it is or has been lately," but as usual he said that he was still "too poor" to consider matrimony just yet. "Brother has denounced me as an old bachelor confirmed and hopeless and has undertaken to fit up a fruit garden for me to growl away old age in," explained Austin with a rare touch of humor, adding, however, that "I shall disappoint him I hope tho [I] am in favor of the fruit." But even if the elder Austin did not marry, he would at least have a namesake and potential heir, for less than a year after Brown's marriage, Eliza gave birth to a son. The proud parents named him Stephen F. Austin, Jr.[11]

While developments in the colony and the state seemed mostly positive, the larger picture of Mexican politics provided cause for concern, if not alarm. Mexico's deepening economic crisis was bringing long-standing political disagreements to a head. Federalists, led by such men as Lorenzo de Zavala, took a Jeffersonian position in favor of decentralized government, while centralists such as Lucas Alamán were more Hamiltonian, advocating a strong national state. Rather than establishing American-style political parties, however, the Mexican factions used rival Masonic lodges as their organizational vehicles—the York Rite (*Yorkino*) for the federalists and the Scottish Rite (*Escosés*) for the centralists. By 1827, Mexican politics had assumed a dangerously volatile character that made United States politics seem tame.[12]

That year centralists initiated an armed revolt against the Victoria government. The revolt failed, but it set a dangerous precedent. When the next presidential election was held in September 1828, centralist candidate Manuel Gómez Pedraza narrowly defeated federalist Vicente Guerrero.[13] Now the federalists, led by Zavala and Antonio López de Santa Anna, rebelled and placed the defeated Guerrero in the presidential chair; Zavala took the reins of the treasury department. Federalists, whose policies would presumably continue to favor Anglo immigration and local autonomy, remained in control of the national government, but their power now rested on an illegitimate foundation. Politics by force was becoming the rule in Mexico, and that spelled uncertainty for the small colony of Anglo settlers clustered along the Brazos and Colorado rivers in Texas.[14]

Austin seemed surprisingly unalarmed by the upheavals in Mexico City.[15] Perhaps he believed that the political turmoil would distract the attention of both political factions away from Texas. But no matter how distant and unimportant the far northern frontier might seem to some national leaders, others remained critically interested in Texas affairs. Two such leaders were key cabinet members from the early days of the Guadalupe Victoria administration. Secretary of War Manuel de Mier y Terán and Secretary of Relations Lucas Alamán, progressive-minded intellectuals with centralist tendencies, had long harbored suspicions about American intentions in Texas. Terán's opposition to American colonization in Texas dated as far back as 1822, when he had served on the imperial colonization committee.[16] Alamán had paid attention to the issue of Texas in 1825 by pressing the case for a boundary and trade treaty with the United Sates. But at that point centralists like Terán and Alamán had lost favor with the Victoria administration, and by September 1825 both men were out of the cabinet.[17]

Oddly enough, it had then fallen to an Englishman to serve as the chief anti-American voice in Mexico City. Henry G. Ward was the British chargé d'affaires in the Mexican capital. Ever concerned about the threat that American expansionism posed to British interests in Mexico, Ward repeatedly warned Guadalupe Victoria about American "backwoodsmen" in Texas and urged the Mexican president to send a commission to the northern frontier to report on conditions there. Ward also recommended the appointment of Terán to head the commission and likewise urged Terán to accept the appointment.[18]

The British diplomat succeeded in achieving both objectives. However, with pro-colonization federalists in the ascendancy in the government after 1825 and with the economy in increasingly dire straits, congress failed to appropriate funds for the investigative commission for two full years. It took the the Fredonian Rebellion to shake the government from its lethargy. On September 6, 1827, congress appropriated 15,000 pesos to finance the expedition. Although ostensibly the chief purpose of Terán's expedition was to survey the U.S.-Mexico boundary, his real task was to provide the central government with a realistic assessment of conditions in Texas and to make concrete recommendations about how the government could save Texas from Anglo-American encroachment and eventual takeover. Two months later Terán, riding in a massive, silver-inlaid coach, led his entourage out of Mexico City and headed north toward Texas.[19]

The commander of the Comisión de Límites (boundary commission) would play a central role in the affairs of Texas and of Stephen Austin over the next five years. José Manuel Rafael Simeón de Mier y Terán was among the finest intellects in Mexico during its early years of nationhood. Born in Mexico City in 1789, he graduated from the prestigious College of Mines, where he excelled in mathematics and engineering. He served with distinction in the Wars for Independence as an artillery commander under Morelos. In 1821 he joined Iturbide in the final phase of the independence struggle. Elected to the first constituent congress in 1822, he served on the colonization committee, where he probably met Austin for the first time. After Iturbide's overthrow he rose to the rank of brigadier general in the army and soon thereafter was named minister of war by Guadalupe Victoria. He returned to active army duty nine months later, apparently having lost favor because of his centralist political views. It is possible that Victoria's later act of naming Terán to head the boundary commission was a convenient way to ship a potential political rival off on a long mission to a far-flung frontier, but more likely the president appointed him because he realized that no one in Mexico was better qualified for the task. Whatever ideological differences the two men may have had, Victoria probably knew that Terán could be trusted to place the best interests of Mexico ahead of any partisan interests.[20]

Terán's expedition, which included a mineralogist, a biologist, and a cartographer, as well as a small military escort, arrived in San Antonio in March 1828. Although we know little about how Terán occupied his time during the six weeks the party lingered there, he undoubtedly had ample opportunity to visit with local Mexican officials and ordinary citizens. After a month in San Antonio, Terán drafted a twenty-three-page report to President Victoria in which he discussed Texas and made some policy

Gen. Manuel de Mier y Terán, soldier, scientist, and
Mexican patriot. Terán and Austin respected each
other, but their visions of Texas's future conflicted in
irreconcilable ways.

recommendations that he strongly urged the president to consider. The
report sheds important light on Mexican attitudes toward Austin and his
colonists, and it reveals some of the obstacles that Austin would have to
overcome if he were to succeed in his plans for Texas and for himself. It is
important to note that Terán composed this document before he actually
visited Austin's Colony, so it must have been influenced almost entirely
by sources in San Antonio.[21]

"The empresario Austin," wrote Terán, "who has some resources at
his disposal, takes the best land that exists in all the extent of Texas; his
dedication and economy have made it very productive." The general cited

the large Anglo-American population of Austin's Colony and discussed its expanding commercial agricultural economy. Commenting on slavery, Terán told the president that there was no way to know the true number of black slaves held by the colonists because the settlers conceal that figure from the authorities. But since Jared Groce alone owned 150 bondsmen, the total number in the colony must be "considerable." [22]

Terán also briefed Victoria on the Indian situation, noting that Austin had selected for his colony a site not "frequented by the most powerful of the barbarous tribes." But the general explained that the Anglo-Americans understood better than Mexicans how to deal with hostile Indians. In the early years of the colony, the settlers organized a militia to track down and kill ten Indians, "of any age or sex," in retaliation for each colonist the Indians killed. The result of this policy could be seen in the fate of the Karankawas, who, as Terán explained, had been reduced "to a result that is never spoken of, because it seems as if [the colonists] have exterminated them." [23]

Unlike his junior officer Lt. José María Sánchez, who would characterize the colonists as "lazy people of vicious character" who treated their slaves harshly, Terán was not particularly judgmental in his comments on the colony's rapid growth, the settlers' use of slave labor, or their methods of dealing with the Indians. He simply made the factual observation that the colonists' background and abilities made them more successful in settling the land than the Tejanos, whose population was composed disproportionately of military men. But Terán *was* critical of those foreigners who roamed the country stirring up trouble with talk of revolution. "The uproar is incessant and a week never passes," he wrote, "without the disturbing news that Nacogdoches is besieged, and that from such and such point there has entered an army of troublemakers, always with savage murdering Indians in its vanguard." The Mexican officer observed that the Tejanos of San Antonio expected a revolution to break out at any time, and that indeed some of the elements for such a revolt seemed already to be in place. All the evidence pointed toward the loss of "this beautiful part of the Mexican territory" if steps were not taken. [24]

Terán made several concrete proposals. First, he suggested, the president should send an additional cavalry company to San Antonio under the command of Commandant Gen. Anastacio Bustamante, a man whom the foreigners respected. Second, the colonization of North Americans in Texas should be suspended, although the established colonies should be protected. If slavery were to be permitted, it should be permitted to foreigners and native Mexicans alike; if abolished, it should abolished for all. Finally, East Texas—specifically, the region of the lower Trinity River—should be colonized by Mexicans. On this last matter Terán was adamant. The colonists should be farmers from Yucatán, the only Mexicans whose background and abilities would enable them to develop the plantation economy of East Texas. It was, in fact, the only thing that the government could do that would make his mission to Texas worthwhile. It would take six thousand Yucatecos "to counterbalance the proportion of foreigners" in Texas, Terán argued. The general even offered to oversee personally the emigration from Yucatán.[25]

Terán's March 28 report survives only in draft form in his personal letterbook, and there is no evidence that Guadalupe Victoria received it. What is important is that even before visiting Austin in San Felipe, Terán had already concluded that the linchpin of Austin's plans—the continuing Americanization of Texas—must be stopped, and that steps must be taken to counterbalance Anglo-American influence in Texas. Austin almost certainly did not realize it, but his dreams already were in jeopardy when Terán's expedition slogged into the muddy streets of San Felipe on April 27, 1828.

Austin was away from San Felipe when the boundary commission arrived, but Sam Williams met the Mexicans and escorted them to quarters that Austin had prepared. The empresario arrived home four days later. During the following week he played host to the dignitaries, and subsequent correspondence between him and Terán indicates that the two men developed a high degree of mutual respect, if not actually a close friendship. However, each had his own agenda. Austin was politician enough to know that Terán could wield tremendous influence over the fate of Texas, and the empresario deployed all of his charm and his considerable powers of persuasion to "educate" the general. Terán appears to have been circumspect in his discussions with Austin. Reserved and dignified, he probably listened more than he talked, and when he did talk the topics were likely to be of a scientific or geographical nature. Although they got along well, each man kept his own counsel and carefully sized up the other.

Terán left no direct account of his impressions of Austin after this visit, although he wrote much about the American colonists in general.[26] But two of the other officers on the boundary commission commented at length on the empresario. Lieutenant Sánchez was not fooled by Austin's ingratiating manner, explaining in his diary that the "diplomatic policy of this empresario, evident in all his actions, has, as one may say, lulled the authorities into a sense of security, while he works diligently for his own ends." The expedition's botanist-zoologist-physician, a Frenchman named Jean Louis Berlandier, recorded a similar impression, describing Austin as an "enterprising man endowed with a wily policy as well as a great deal of talent" who "always knew how to conduct himself to lull the authorities to sleep." If Sánchez and Berlandier were able to size up Austin so perceptively, there can be little doubt that Terán reached similar conclusions.[27]

The boundary commission remained in San Felipe for nearly two weeks, their departure delayed by spring rains that swelled the Brazos and turned the trails that passed for Texas roads into quagmires. When they finally departed, the members of the party spent three weeks making their way through bad weather, difficult terrain, and clouds of mosquitoes, finally arriving at Nacogdoches. There Terán established his base of operations for the rest of the year, exploring the region dividing Texas from the United States.[28]

During those months he and Austin corresponded frequently, sharing scientific and geographical observations and sometimes discussing the weightier matter of Mexican policy toward Texas. Austin used these communications to try to bring Terán around to his own pro-immigration positions, most of which contrasted sharply with the general's view that Anglo-American immigration must be halted. Regardless of Terán's opinions, Austin was taking no chances. He carefully explained to the general the policies that the government should adopt toward Texas. Immigrants should be allowed to bring slaves into Texas for another six or eight years. The ban on the settlement of foreigners along the Gulf coast and the

Louisiana border should be lifted. The government should extend the colonists' exemption from tariffs for another seven years (the initial seven-year exemption enjoyed by his original colony being about to expire). Finally, Texas should be separated from Coahuila and be made a federal territory with its own judges, governor, and legislature, with salaries paid by the federal government. As always, Austin argued forcefully that only through these pro-immigration and pro-American measures would Texas prosper. "The true interest of the Mexican Government," he wrote, "is to populate the coast and all the rest of Texas with a prosperous, enterprising and industrious population whose interest is to sustain good order and to defend the Government."[29]

Austin must have felt encouraged by the response he got from Terán, who seemed to come around to the empresario's position on many issues. "On the measures likely to contribute to the increase of the new population of Texas we are equally in agreement," the general wrote from Nacogdoches. He conceded that it would be difficult to request the slavery law that Austin desired, but he added that the same result might be achieved through some "deception" (*dicimulo*) — which, as it turns out, the Texas members of the state legislature were obtaining that very month. Regarding the issue of separating Texas from Coahuila, Terán replied somewhat disingenuously that such an act would never take place if it were promoted only by travelers or bureaucrats like himself, "without the inhabitants pronouncing in an energetic way their rationale and will." He obviously wished to downplay his own influence, which was considerable.[30]

Encouraged by Terán's seeming agreement on most of the major issues, Austin sent the general a lengthy history of Austin's Colony and the development of Texas over the previous seven years. This rather bombastic document, running close to five thousand words, presented the litany of hardships and obstacles that Austin and his colonists had overcome since 1821. The colonists' character, he wrote, "is agricultural, enterprising, industrious, peaceful and easy to govern." There had never been the need for a single soldier; there was no jail; there had never been a capital crime committed by a colonist. The settlers had freely spilled their blood fighting the Indians, and they had patriotically sustained the nation in the Fredonian Rebellion. "No other colonization enterprise has progressed in Texas, and the prosperity of this had resulted principally from the efforts of its founder," the empresario immodestly explained. "Austin dedicated the best years of his youth[,] his capital, risked his health, his life, his all, in this undertaking that already had cost the life and fortune of his father."[31] Such exercises in self-promotion may have sounded egotistical—and Austin knew that they did[32]—but he also knew that given the political uncertainties of his position, there might come a time when he would need to call in some favors; he wanted to ensure that everyone in the Mexican government fully realized the nation's obligation to him.

Offering Austin "a thousand thanks for the historical note on the colony," Terán continued with his inspection tour through the remainder of 1828.[33] Political disturbances and a Spanish invasion called him south of the Rio Grande in 1829, but he kept in contact with Austin, and their relationship remained cordial. However, Terán never wavered in his conviction that Texas would be lost to Mexico if radical steps were not taken to diminish Anglo-American influence and strengthen ties to the rest of Mexico. As an individual, Austin seemed to have gained the general's confidence; Terán clearly sympathized with his position, and he would try to manage affairs so that Austin's personal interests were not unduly damaged by government actions. But it was a difficult balancing act. In his numerous reports and letters to highly placed Mexicans over the next two years, Terán repeatedly recommended that Texas be saved from falling into the orbit of the United States.[34] Had Austin fully comprehended Terán's position—and had Terán fully comprehended Austin's—both men would have understood their fundamental incompatibility.

The summer of 1829 found Terán in Tampico, joining forces with Santa Anna to repel a Spanish invasion. In Texas, personal trauma, followed by political crisis, shattered the relative peace that Austin had enjoyed the previous year.

In early August, twenty-five-year-old Brown Austin sailed for New Orleans on business. He arrived in the midst of a yellow fever epidemic. Three days later he was dead. Stephen Austin had lost his only relative in Texas and his dearest friend in the world. The elder Austin had in many ways lived vicariously through his younger brother, drawing strength from

Brown's optimism, rejoicing in his happy marriage, and delighting in the birth of Stephen F. Austin, Jr., now eight months old. Stephen had taken great pride in Brown's business success, and Brown had proved a valuable ally in everything from political lobbying to Indian fighting.[35]

"I have never met with such a blow in my life," Stephen wrote without exaggeration when the news reached Texas. The impact on him was devastating. He was immediately stricken with a bout of the chronic malarial fever that had plagued him all his adult life. The fever, apparently induced by the stress of the news, confined him to his bed for nearly a month. During much of that time he was "insensible and at the point of death." Two weeks into the illness an official of the San Felipe ayuntamiento alerted the political chief in San Antonio about the "extremely critical state" of Austin's health, explaining that the empresario was "prostrate in bed, immobile and incapable of doing anything whatsoever." Brown's widow, Eliza, wrote that those around Austin thought that every moment might be his last. By September 22, Austin was well enough to prop himself up in bed and write a brief letter to his cousin Henry. But he would not pronounce himself recovered until October, and even then he reported that he was "not in a situation to write connectedly on any subject."[36] He expressed his grief most freely to his Tejano friend José Antonio Navarro:

> I have just returned (so to speak) from the brink of the grave and I have received a terrible blow in the death of my only brother, companion in so much hardship and privation that we passed through together in this wilderness.
>
> Only the hope of seeing this country flourish has enabled me to bear the life that I have spent, but my brother is no longer here to enjoy this pleasure. He was, like me, an enthusiast in favor of Texas and he had begun to live in some comfort. Now he is in peace far from the difficulties and frustrations of human life. Perhaps it is for the best.[37]

Austin never fully recovered from the loss of his brother. For the rest of 1829 and well into 1830 his health remained poor and his spirits low. As Austin lay near death, a new crisis came when the Guerrero administration issued a nationwide abolition law. Austin feared that if the government truly abolished slavery, the economic progress of Texas would be "doubtful." However, Political Chief Ramón Músquiz suspended the publication of the decree in Texas, and Austin's chief ally in the federal government, Minister of Relations Agustín Viesca, prevailed on Guerrero to exempt Texas from the law.[38]

Before his death Brown had commented that Stephen was "getting *old fast*" and that "the wrinkles are becomeing plainer daily." Now, four months after Brown's death, those closest to Austin expressed serious concern for the empresario's physical and mental health. Brown's widow worried that Stephen was "now nothing but a mere shadow, and if he does not quit his desk, ride about and take some more exercise, his life will be but short." She was unable to erase "that gloomy melancholy look" from his face. Brown's ex-business partner, John Austin, concurred, urging Austin "to go into the woods this winter." Austin himself admitted that his constitution was "much broken" and "failing rapidly." He spoke openly of his own death.[39]

His bouts of melancholy and preoccupation with death would become more pronounced over the next six years. These traits, along with his periodic reveries about retiring to a pastoral life, reveal Austin as a product of the early Romantic period, just as his political and religious beliefs mark him as a late Enlightenment figure. The Enlightenment side of Austin's character wanted badly to believe that man was the master of his world and that reason could overcome all obstacles. But when events seemed to demonstrate his own helplessness, then gloom and melancholy—or retirement to the picturesque remoteness of a rural retreat— offered irresistible psychological comfort. These two sides of Austin's personality would be always at war with each other.

With his brother gone, Austin longed more than ever for his sister Emily and her family to join him in Texas. Her husband's hesitation only deepened Austin's loneliness and depression. Eliza Austin wrote to Emily, saying that "if Stephen was sure that you would move in the spring, he would fatten up and be a different man." In late 1829 and early 1830 the empresario began to bombard James Perry with letters beseeching him to emigrate. As time passed with no concrete response from Perry, Austin grew increasingly insistent: *"You must remove and that immediately."*

Finally Austin was able to inform his brother-in-law that the governor of the state had agreed to grant Perry eleven leagues, or nearly fifty thousand acres, of prime land. "It is *what very few people can get*," implored Austin, "and it will be trifling with fortune not to accept it." Still, the first three months of 1830 passed with no definite word from Perry. "I have now done all that I can do," a frustrated Austin wrote to James and Emily at the end of March.[40]

As Austin battled illness and depression in Texas, events in Mexico City were about to deal him another heavy blow. In late 1829, a revolt deposed President Vicente Guerrero and replaced him with Vice-President Anastacio Bustamante. Far more conservative in his political views than Guerrero, Bustamante placed men with centralist leanings in key administration positions. Bustamante offered the war ministry to Terán, who declined it in favor of his close friend José Antonio Facio. Terán remained commandant general of the Eastern Interior Provinces, a position he had received during the Spanish invasion a few months earlier. The Bustamante government would not overthrow the federalist structure of the republic by replacing it with a centralist constitution, but it would attempt to bring more order and control to Mexico by weakening the states and strengthening the central government.[41]

The rise of an administration inclined toward centralism placed Austin in a paradoxical situation. On the positive side, a personal friend now occupied the presidency; Austin and Bustamante had enjoyed good relations since Austin's 1822 trip to Mexico City. Indeed, soon after taking office the new president wrote Austin a warm letter assuring him of the administration's continuing support. Moreover, with Terán more influential than ever, Austin had reason to believe that the new administration would pursue an enlightened policy toward Texas. But Coahuila y Texas lost its most powerful voice in the administration when Lucas Alamán replaced Agustín Viesca as minister of relations.[42]

Assessing the new government, Austin described Bustamante as a "very good man" who might have "ambitions" but "not to a criminal extent." Austin was not yet personally acquainted with Alamán, the administration's chief policy maker, but he knew that Alamán was talented

Anastacio Bustamante, friend of Austin,
commandant general of the Eastern
Interior Provinces, and acting
president of Mexico.

and there seemed to be no reason for excessive concern about him. "Genl. Teran is the best of the whole bunch," Austin wrote to a cousin back east. "As to his politics I think he is what would be called in the U.S. a rank federalist, as distinguished from a rank Democrat, & I like *that* system of politics the best. Some suspect him for being a centralist. I do not think he is — tho he is in favor of giving sufficient power to the Govt. to keep its members together." This was a sound view not only of Terán but also of Bustamante, Alamán, and the administration as a whole. With his elitist upbringing and his roots in Federalist New England, Austin no doubt could see the advantages of a strong and decisive central government, especially in a young republic as economically weak and socially fragmented as Mexico.[43]

The paradox lies in what course such a government would pursue toward Texas. While Bustamante, Alamán, and Terán seemed to promise enlightened leadership, the question was what would constitute a truly enlightened and progressive Texas policy. For Alamán and Terán, at least, the answer was clear. Both had given signals as early as 1822 that they opposed the liberal immigration policies that had led to the Anglo-American colonization of Texas.[44] Whatever personal esteem they might have for Stephen Austin would not change that reality. Even Bustamante, while commandant general over Texas, had been alarmed by the Fredonian Rebellion. All the leading lights of the new government agreed that the rapidly expanding *norteamericano* influence in Texas jeopardized Mexico's territorial integrity. The only real question in the spring of 1830 was what concrete steps the new government would take in order to check that influence. Action, as Terán had said back in 1828, was already overdue.

For two years Terán had been the government's eyes and ears on the northeastern frontier, and his superiors respected his opinion. In November 1829 he wrote his friend José Antonio Facio, saying, "If the colonization contracts in Texas by North Americans are not suspended, and if the conditions of the establishments are not watched, it is necessary to say that the province is already definitely delivered to the foreigners." Facio became minister of war a few weeks later and passed Terán's letter on to Alamán.[45]

On January 6, 1830, during the first week of the Bustamante administration, Terán drew up a formal set of recommendations and sent them to Facio. The report called for a vigorous program to colonize Texas with native Mexicans as well as Swiss and German emigrants, measures to encourage trade between Texas and the rest of Mexico, and the strengthening of the Mexican military presence in Texas. It also called for Austin's fourth empresario contract, the so-called Coast Colony, to be changed in order to return control of settlement in the ten-league-wide coastal reserve to the federal government. The government, in Terán's words, had acted "very imprudently" in granting Austin that contract in the first place. Curiously, nowhere in the report did he propose cutting off all Anglo-American immigration. Yet this was precisely what he had suggested as early as March 1828 and in his November 1829 letter to Facio. It is unlikely that a mere two months later Terán had changed his mind about

Lucas Alamán. A powerful cabinet
minister with centralist proclivities,
Alamán liked Austin personally, even
visiting him in prison. But it was Alamán
who drafted the legislation that became
the fateful Law of April 6, 1830,
disrupting the empresario system.

the desirability of this action; more likely, he had decided that to do it immediately would pose too great a risk of inflaming hostilities among the
North Americans.[46]

Minister of Relations Alamán was willing to run that risk. In early
February he put before the congress a proposed bill, or *iniciativa,* urging
that immediate steps be taken to save Texas. The document incorporated
Terán's January recommendations and added his earlier proposal that
the granting of empresario contracts be halted. Colonists already settled
could stay, but no more were to be allowed in, effectively freezing immigration. The introduction of any more slaves was to be prohibited. Over
the next few weeks congress met in secret session and drafted a law based
on Alamán's ideas. The congress toned down some of the harshness of
Alamán's proposals; neither Austin nor his controversial fourth contract
were mentioned specifically. But congress retained the articles prohibit-

ing further Anglo-American immigration and the introduction of slaves. The bill became law on April 6, 1830.[47]

Word of the law reached Austin simultaneously with Bustamante's friendly letter of March 20. Austin tried to appear gracious in acknowledging Bustamante's gesture, but he could not conceal his feelings about the measure, which, if strictly interpreted and fully implemented, would cripple his long-term plans. The object of the law, Austin frankly told Bustamante, "seems to be to destroy in one blow the happiness and prosperity of this colony which Your Excellency has always protected."[48]

Many times over the previous nine years Austin had confronted government actions that imperiled his great undertaking. The first of these had required a costly year spent in Mexico City having his grant confirmed. Another had come when Antonio Saucedo overturned the land fees he had intended to charge the colonists. Several times Austin had faced the prospect of the government abolishing slavery. Each time he deployed his considerable political abilities to surmount these obstacles or mitigate their worst features. Somehow, despite his pessimistic nature, he had maintained his faith that his dreams for himself and Texas could best be achieved under Mexican rule. "Fidelity to Mexico" had remained his motto.

The Law of April 6, 1830, however, marked a turning point. Whether or not it would actually result in a permanent prohibition on Anglo-American immigration into Texas, the law created a crisis of confidence in Austin and among his colonists. Coming as it did in the midst of such a difficult period in his private life, it might defeat him totally. By 1830, achieving his vision of a prosperous Texas had assumed, as Austin later phrased it, the "character of a religion." But the coming months and years would sorely test his devotion to that religion.[49]

We Will Be Happy
1830–1831

The passage of the Law of April 6, 1830, set in motion a chain of events that threatened the future of Anglo colonization and, with it, all of Stephen F. Austin's plans. It was rapidly becoming apparent how much Austin's vision of Texas's future differed from that of the Bustamante administration. One thing was certain: the Law of 1830 and the regime that enacted it would put Austin's political skills to their supreme test.

When he learned the particulars of the law, Austin wrote letters of protest to Acting President Bustamante and to Commandant General Terán, who now also bore the title of general commissioner in charge of colonization affairs for Texas. Over several years Austin had assiduously cultivated the friendship and respect of both men; now the time had come to reap what he had so carefully sown. Austin argued that the law was unwise because of its effects on the economy and on the morale of the people. Furthermore, it was unjust to Anglo immigrants who had done so much to civilize and bring prosperity to Texas. He hoped to secure the law's repeal, but this would take time. For the present, he sought to have his own enterprise exempted from the law's provisions as much as possible.[1]

He seized on the wording of two of the law's articles. Article 10 stated that there would be no change made to "colonies already established"; Article 11 suspended "contracts that have not been fulfilled." Here semantics—and translation—were crucial. Clearly Austin's Colony, in the generic sense of the overall settlement founded by Stephen F. Austin, was well "established." But "Austin's Colony" legally consisted, at this point, of four empresario *contracts*. Only the first of these actually had been fulfilled in the sense that all of the families specified in the contract had moved to Texas. None of Austin's other three contracts (for five hundred, one hundred, and three hundred families, respectively) was even close to being completed. The Spanish word *cumplimiento* could be translated as "complied with," "fulfilled," "carried out," or even "expired." Lucas Alamán almost certainly intended for the law to cut off all further immigration of Anglos to Texas. But in his appeals Austin creatively combined the notion of a *colony already established* (Article 10) with that of a *contract that had been fulfilled* (Article 11). In short, since Austin and Green DeWitt were the only two foreign empresarios who had actually brought any significant numbers of colonists to Texas, they should be allowed to continue their colonization enterprises as if the law had never been passed.[2]

Much to Austin's relief, Terán endorsed this ingenious interpretation of the law. Austin told Ben Milam that Terán "is not the enemy to Texas which some have supposed he is. . . . I have full confidence in him." Col. José de las Piedras of the Nacogdoches garrison concurred with Terán's position. Austin took advantage of Mexican officials' poor understanding of the actual immigration process. He always had led them to believe that he or his agents formally contracted with individual emigrants prior to their exit from the United States. But in reality most colonists simply heard of Austin's Colony and showed up unannounced in San Felipe, where they were welcomed by the empresario. In May 1830, Austin actually had made prior contact with only a minuscule number of would-be emigrants. Yet he told Bustamante that "all the families with whom I have contracted to introduce are already en route or have made preliminary preparations to move here." This blatant lie helped Austin build the case that the government would be committing a gross violation of good faith if it did not allow him to finish fulfilling his three outstanding contracts. If Terán knew the truth about how immigration worked—which he probably did—he gave no sign of it. He was either showing considerable faith in Austin's fidelity, or else he felt compelled to go along with Austin rather than risk a revolt.[3]

When Terán informed Alamán of his liberal interpretation of the law, the cabinet minister responded with a reasonable requirement: let Austin furnish the government a list of all those emigrants with whom he had contracted, and they would be admitted. This, of course, was impossible, since Austin had no idea who was actually emigrating or planning to emigrate. Again Terán came to the rescue, ordering that emigrants entering Texas only need show some evidence that they intended to settle in Austin's or DeWitt's colonies. When many could not produce such documentation, Austin resorted to a Machiavellian tactic—printing up blank certificates of admittance, signing them, and distributing them to trusted associates at strategic points along the U.S.-Texas border, to be filled in and given to emigrants as they entered Texas. Colonel de las Piedras at Nacogdoches apparently participated in this deception. In his deft handling of key officials, Austin again had demonstrated his political savvy.[4]

The April legislation ordered additional troops to Texas to enforce the ban on immigration and the law's other provisions. Accordingly, Terán authorized the establishment of a fort and town named Anahuac, at the mouth of the Trinity River on upper Galveston Bay. He appointed Col. Juan Davis Bradburn, a Kentuckian in the Mexican service, to command the post. By the spring of 1831 Bradburn had 170 soldiers at the fort, alongside a growing civilian population of some 300.[5]

A commitment to enforcing Mexican customs laws accompanied the military buildup. The exemption from customs duties that colonists had enjoyed since 1823 was to expire near the end of 1830. Austin's repeated efforts to win an extension of the privilege had failed, although the Law of April 6 did allow the duty-free importation of food and lumber through the ports of Galveston and Matagorda. Moreover, in a well-intentioned effort to strengthen ties between Texas and the rest of Mexico, the law for the first time allowed foreign ship captains to engage in trade between Mexican ports.[6]

The presence of the new troops and the attempts to enforce the customs laws soon caused trouble. On one hand were Mexican officials such as Terán and Bradburn, who answered to the new centralist-inclined national government in Mexico City. On the other hand were the Anglo-American settlers, who wanted local autonomy, and their federalist allies, who controlled the state government in Saltillo. Caught in the middle was Stephen F. Austin, whose unenviable task, as he saw it, was to preserve order and harmony while quietly promoting the development of Texas. This had always been his strategy, but as the Anglo population grew and the national government sought to bring Texas under tighter control in the early 1830s, the task grew ever more formidable.

Austin's influence with Terán had won him the exemption of his colony from the immigration ban, but pacifying the settlers was more difficult. The sheer size of the population made it harder for him to maintain as much personal contact with individual colonists as he had enjoyed in earlier times. Not knowing their empresario well, they were less likely to defer to his leadership. His task was complicated by the great increase in Anglo settlers outside Austin's Colony. In addition to the immigrants in the Nacogdoches area and the untold number of squatters in the region bordering Louisiana, hundreds of Anglo-Americans now had moved into the Atascosito neighborhood just east of Austin's Colony, where they had not been able to get land titles and where they increasingly came into conflict with Bradburn and his garrison at Anahuac.

One weapon Austin could use in his campaign to preserve the peace in Texas was the press. In the fall of 1829 an itinerant newspaperman named Godwin B. Cotten came to San Felipe and began publishing the *Texas Gazette*. Since Cotten could not make the press profitable though subscriptions and advertising, he had no choice but to rely on Austin's patronage. This allowed the paper to become Austin's mouthpiece. Austin used the press in late 1829 to print his *Translation of the Laws, Orders, and Contracts on Colonization,* the first book ever published in Texas. While the press was busy with this project, Guerrero's 1829 decree abolishing slavery reached Texas. Conveniently, Austin was able to delay informing the public of that decree until January 30, 1830, by which time he had received word that Texas had been excluded from the decree's provisions. He then could publish both the bad news and the good news in the same issue, accompanied by his own glowing explanation of how this demonstrated the government's benevolence.[7]

Austin dealt with the Law of April 6 in a similar manner. He waited five or six weeks to publish a complete translation of the law. Then he largely ignored the objectionable Article 11, which canceled unfulfilled empresario contracts. Instead, he emphasized the beneficial aspects of the law. The troops being sent to Texas would protect against Indians and provide consumers for Texas goods. Opening the coasting trade would be a boon to the economy. Not until September did he comment editorially on Article 11, and then he put the mildest possible interpretation on it, saying that it was intended to keep riffraff out of Texas. For good measure, he sent similar explanations back to the United States for publication in papers there.[8]

Only to his closest confidant, Samuel May Williams, did Austin share his true feelings and explain his artful tactics. "The law of 6 April was founded in error and unjust suspicions," wrote the empresario, "but to have said so, would have been very impolitic, and highly injurious, for it would have wounded *self love, pride,* etc. (dangerous things to touch among any people) and it would have strengthened the suspicions which produced the law." As a result it made sense to defend the law in the press instead of condemning it. As the empresario noted, his cagey policy "explains the reasons why so many more favors have been extended to that colony than to any other." The colonists did not realize it, Austin told Williams, "but *you* and *I* know that emigration to that colony could have been stopped, and that all the ports could have been closed." As usual, Austin felt that his efforts for the people had gone unnoticed or unappreciated: "It was my duty to steer my precious bark (the Colony) through all the shoals and quicks regardless of the curses and ridicule of the passengers. *I* knew what I was about—they did not." This time, at least, it is hard to dispute his assertion; without Austin's skillful maneuvering, the effects of the Law of April 6 on Texas would have been drastically different. For the present, the damage had been minimized, and Austin always believed that with time and patience the law could be repealed.[9]

With the crisis finally under some semblance of control, Austin could turn his attention to personal matters. He had long hoped that his sister's family would join him in Texas. Emily now had seven children, four by the late James Bryan and three by current husband James F. Perry, with another on the way. At last, after several years of resisting, Perry in March 1830 agreed to investigate Texas firsthand. He left Missouri before learning that Austin had secured the family an eleven-league land grant. When Perry arrived in late April 1830, Austin was out with a surveying crew on Galveston Bay. Perry struck out overland from the Brazos to find his brother-in-law.[10]

Austin was "most agreeably surprised" when the stranger who suddenly appeared on the deserted, windblown prairie adjacent to Galveston's West Bay turned out to be Perry. As it happened, Austin was actually surveying Perry's land. "It appears to be a singular coinsidence," he wrote to Emily back in Missouri, "that he found me on the very spot where I presume we shall spend a large portion of the balance of our lives." Perry was "delighted with the situation," and the empresario felt sure that Emily would be too. The men spent another ten days with the surveyors, laying off the nearly fifty thousand acres that the government had bestowed on the Perry family. It was the most encouraging thing that had happened to Austin in a long time. "I am really happy at the idea of your leaving that cold region," he told Emily. "I look forward to many days of peace and enjoyment in this country. I hope in a few years to free myself from all my debts and to close my affairs here so that I may live a quiet and retired life in the society of my sister and her family." [11]

Perry remained in Texas for several weeks before heading back to Missouri. He planned to settle his business affairs there, travel to New York City for supplies and mercantile goods to be shipped to Texas, and then emigrate with his family and slaves. Arriving home, Perry found a letter from Austin written four months earlier discussing Perry's land grant. Having just spent so much time in Texas, Perry was dismayed to discover that half of the grant was in his name and the other half in Emily's. He immediately wrote to Austin, saying that he was "mortifyed" to learn the truth about the grants. Perry's complaint and Austin's response to it reveal much about the empresario's lifelong difficulty in communicating with those who should have been closest to him.[12]

Perry explained that he was "mortifyed not because the grants ware different from what I understood but at your silence on that subject to me. What the object of your silence was I am at a loss to conceive." They had spent many days and nights together in Texas, yet Austin had apparently failed entirely to mention that the eleven leagues were divided between James and Emily. "When with you on the bay I thought you was verry reserved towards me," Perry told Austin, "but [I] did not expect you would have been reserved in anything that related to the sole object of my journey to that country." He then lectured Austin on the need for candor between relatives.[13]

Austin now realized he had not been very communicative.[14] "I was surprised that you thought me silent and reserved," he wrote,

> it was what I never dreamed of . . . however I hope it is enough for me to say that if I appear reserved exteriourly I was not so in heart, and I will here apprise you and Emily of a change which time[,] care and something like disgust towards the world and human affairs, has wrought upon my disposition. . . . I have for the last few years been gradually loosing my taste for society, or for conversation. I am getting tactiturn, or what may be called absent minded. Silence is more agreeable to me than talking or noise. This thing is becoming habitual and in spite of myself it is growing upon me very rapidly. I therefore apprise you both that if you move here, you must not expect to find me the cheerful companion I once was. If you wish to know any thing from me, you must ask the question direct. If I answer, *yes,* or *no,* and say no more, which may often be the case, you must not think that it proceeds from coolness on my part.

He was apologetic, but in a postscript to Perry penned four days later, Austin allowed his characteristic self-pity, along with a barb of temper, to show through. "I cannot request you to advise any of my relations to come here," he remarked. "They would all think as you have that I am silent reserved cold or some thing else — better live apart than in that way so for the future I never will say one word about any person who is in any degree related to me, removing to this country." Of course he did not really mean this; he would continue to talk of retiring from public life and surrounding himself with various Austin cousins and other members of his extended family.[15]

It was important not to alienate Perry, because Austin wanted Perry to manage his business affairs in Texas. Those affairs had almost always taken a back seat to his public duties. He had countless collections to make, both on official fees and private debts owed him by the colonists. Merely selecting and surveying his own premium lands was a monumental task. And there were a thousand other smaller personal matters that Austin's public obligations prevented him from fulfilling.[16]

As long as Brown was alive, Austin could rely on him to help with such business. He had also been able to count on Sam Williams to shoulder some of this burden, and Williams had never complained when Austin blurred the lines between Williams's official duties as the colony's secretary and his unofficial role as Austin's right hand. Increasingly, though, Williams wanted to pursue his own interests. Certainly Austin had done his best to see that his lieutenant was well compensated; he had helped Williams get a grant of seven leagues (thirty-one thousand acres) from the state for his services to the colony. Austin also turned over to Williams the responsibility for settling the one hundred families in the Little Colony in return for half of the premium lands that Austin would receive under that contract. But the truth was that the combined load of each man's private concerns, along with the colony's land business and governmental responsibilities, was more than Austin and Williams combined could handle. Austin needed Perry in Texas.[17]

That need became even more acute in August 1830, when Austin learned that he had been elected as one of Texas's two representatives to the state legislature. Austin was flattered at this, particularly because the movement to elect him had originated among the Tejanos of San Antonio and Goliad. Flattery notwithstanding, Austin truly did not want the position, and for good reasons. It would require a difficult and costly trip to Saltillo, with an absence from the colony for several months. There was relatively little in the way of productive legislation that one man could effect, and there was the added danger that the mere presence of an Anglo-American in the legislature would arouse the suspicions of certain legislators. In the meantime the six-year time limit for completing Austin's second empresario contract was to expire in June, and the colony was well short of the required five hundred families. Nevertheless, he agreed to be a candidate, and, once elected, he was required by law to attend the session. To his chagrin, the Perrys still had not arrived in Texas by the time Austin departed in mid-December 1830. More than ever the empresario would have to depend on Williams to manage both men's public and private affairs until his return.[18]

Political developments made early 1831 a particularly bad time to be gone. With the arrival of the troops at Anahuac, the government would soon enforce the new immigration restrictions and customs collection; friction between colonists and the Mexican authorities was likely. Moreover, during most of the prior year federalist rebels led by ex-president Guerrero had waged civil war in southern Mexico against the Bustamante regime. Guerrero's capture and execution at the beginning of 1831 further discredited a government that many Mexicans already viewed as repressive and illegitimate. Full-fledged civil war could not be far away.

Austin departed on December 19, 1830, for Saltillo. He left his will with Williams, saying that "all are liable to acc[iden]ts." Pausing in San Antonio, he wrote back to Williams with instructions—or more accurately, orders—for managing the colony in his absence. Austin realized how delicate his political position had become. He had to maintain good relations with the centralists in the Bustamante government. But neither could he afford to antagonize his federalist allies—the Viesca faction—who controlled the state government and supported Anglo colonization. "There can scarcely be a more difficult thing than to play a *double game,*" Austin told Williams. "It is dangerous, and it is at times, a nice point to draw the distinction between such a game and dishonor." Dangerous or not, the double game had to be played. "Silence, prudence, and vigilance, must all be called in requisition," he declared. "I shall have a dreadful task at Saltillo." If forced to take sides, though, he knew he would have to go with the federalists.[19]

The journey on horseback through the bleak deserts of northern Mexico went well. Ten days after leaving San Antonio, Austin arrived in Monclova, where the weather turned cool and wet and the surrounding mountains were white with snow. The cold made the final leg of the trip into Saltillo uncomfortable, but Austin enjoyed good health and found satisfactory lodgings with his fellow representative from Texas, Father Manuel Múzquiz, and another legislator. Taking his seat in the legislature, he found to his relief that "great harmony prevailed" and that "all appear pleased that I have come on."[20]

One of his top legislative priorities was to seek judicial reforms for Texas. There was no trial by jury, and all but the most minor civil and criminal cases had to be reviewed by the state supreme court in Saltillo, three hundred miles away from the settled parts of Texas. Early during the session Austin thought that reform might be forthcoming, but nothing happened. His earlier prediction that he would face a "dreadful task" in the legislature proved accurate, as he found considerable anti-foreign hostility among the legislators. He had to fight to defeat a bill that would have banned foreigners from engaging in the retail trade. In the midst of the session he contracted a bad cold, and his health remained poor for more than a month. By the time the session ended in late April, Austin could only "thank God" that it was over and breathe a sigh of relief that the legislature had at least done "no harm."[21]

The desultory pace of the legislature left plenty of time for Austin to pursue two personal business matters in the state capital. Both of these involved land, and they would eventually hurt his reputation, although he had no way of knowing it at the time.

In an effort to raise revenue, the legislature in 1828 had begun allowing native Mexicans to buy up to eleven leagues of public land in Texas at bargain prices. Predictably, speculators began to take advantage of a loophole that allowed the unrestricted resale of the lands. The procedure was simple. A Mexican would purchase eleven leagues from the government and turn a quick profit by selling the land to an Anglo-American, who would then select the land in Texas and hold it for speculative purposes.

One of the first to take advantage of this was James Bowie, who traveled to Saltillo in 1830 and purchased sixteen of the eleven-league grants, nearly 780,000 acres.[22]

Now Austin took advantage of the law to purchase three eleven-league grants, or about 146,000 acres. He made an initial payment of $1,000 to three Mexicans who had acquired the lands from the state, with more to be paid later. Austin's purpose in this transaction was not purely speculative. He intended to locate two of the three grants on the upper Colorado River for his personal use as a "mountain retreat." The site was "well watered with springs" and "very healthy," according to Austin, "with some rough mountain land, wild scenery etc." Eventually he hoped to establish a "large sheep farm" on the land and spend his summers there, away from the swampy coastal lands where he suffered so frequently from malarial fever. Although it would be a working farm, Austin's pet project was to be the establishment of an academy, "with which I can amuse myself and do good to others." Several years later, after Austin's death brought his plans for the site to an end, others would see the desirability of the location and choose it for Texas's new capital.[23] The educational institution founded there several decades later would undoubtedly have pleased the empresario in its location, its scale, and its name: the University of Texas at Austin.[24]

Austin's reputation would later suffer when his name became associated with unscrupulous speculation, but in comparison with what others such as Bowie were doing, the scale of his activities was comparatively small. More serious was the other land-related project that Austin embarked upon that winter in Saltillo. It concerned Austin's fifth and final empresario contract, and it eventually brought him much grief.

The problem involved the empresario contract of Robert Leftwich, with whom Austin had roomed in Mexico City in 1822 and to whom Austin had rendered so much assistance while there. Representing a group of Nashville investors known as the Texas Association (also called the Nashville Company), Leftwich finally obtained his contract from the state of Coahuila y Texas. He gained permission to settle a colony in a large area adjoining Austin's Colony to the northwest.[25]

Austin knew the subsequent story well. By law Leftwich's contract would expire in April 1831. Between 1825 and 1830 the company named a succession of agents to perform the duties of empresario, but none brought any settlers. Austin tried to help in 1827 when he carried a petition to Saltillo for the company and secured its requests for expansion of the colony and approval of a new man as empresario, Hosea H. League. However, instead of pursuing the interests of his Nashville sponsors, League settled in Austin's Colony and rose to respectability as a member of the San Felipe ayuntamiento. There, in September 1830, he was involved in a street shooting and was arrested as an accessory to murder. He was thrown in chains and left to languish while the interminable legal process got under way. There League remained, chained to a cabin wall in San Felipe, with the affairs of the Texas Association chained up with him.[26]

League's status would seem a moot point, for the Law of April 6 had now suspended all colonization contracts but Austin's and DeWitt's. But back in Tennessee there were finally signs of activity. One of the company's stockholders, Sterling C. Robertson, left Nashville in September 1830 with nine families. At Nacogdoches the Mexican authorities properly enforced the April 6 law and denied them permission to proceed. Nevertheless, Robertson rode on to San Felipe, where he found League imprisoned.[27] League signed a power of attorney allowing Robertson to conduct the business of the Texas Association; Robertson became, in effect, an agent of an agent. According to Robertson's later testimony, he then visited Austin and secured the empresario's "word of honor" that Austin would lobby the government to allow the company to proceed with its colony.[28] Shortly thereafter Austin departed for Saltillo.

It seems unlikely that Austin could have given Robertson much encouragement about his chances of success.[29] It had been a major feat just to persuade the government to count his own and DeWitt's colonies as "established" and thus to exempt them from cancellation under the 1830 law. The Texas Association had not established a single colonist in Texas as of April 6, 1830, nor had Robertson signed any agreements with prospective colonists. Only the *national* government could have allowed the Nashville company to proceed with its colony. That would have required the intervention of General Terán on Robertson's behalf—an impossibility if ever there was one. And even if Austin could have gotten the

Nashville contract exempted from suspension under the Law of April 6, the contract was about to reach the standard six-year limit within a few weeks of the time Austin arrived in Saltillo. There was no precedent for extending an empresario contract. In fact, Austin's own second contract was about to expire, and he never sought such an extension for himself. If Austin thought it pointless to seek extensions for his own contracts, he hardly could have expected to win one for Robertson.

In short, the Nashville colony was a dead letter, and Austin knew it. But here he made the first of several mistakes. He should have told Robertson outright that there was no chance of saving the contract. Instead, he apparently promised some sort of assistance, although its exact nature cannot be stated with certainty.[30]

Austin may have been less than frank with Robertson because Austin knew something else Robertson could not know: with the Nashville contract suspended and about to expire anyway, Austin and Samuel May Williams were planning to apply for an empresario grant encompassing the area of the Nashville colony. (It would, of course, have to be filled with Mexican and European colonists, as the Law of April 6 required.) Austin would use his influence in Saltillo to ensure that the application was approved.

With his scant knowledge of the Mexican political situation, Robertson must have been unable to understand the hopelessness of his situation. Therefore it was easy for him to interpret Austin's and Williams's plan as a conspiracy to "steal" the Nashville contract. Austin probably concluded that it would just be simpler to tell Robertson what he wanted to hear—even if it would be impossible to achieve—and deal with the consequences later. Perhaps he thought that Robertson would be gone and out of the way by the time he returned from Saltillo; maybe he simply failed to think through the entire question with his usual care. But whether by design or oversight, Austin set himself up for trouble. When Robertson discovered what had happened, he did draw all the wrong conclusions.

Austin might have handled Robertson with greater care if he had known more about him. Only two years earlier Robertson had killed a man on the streets of Nashville, apparently in an argument over a slave. He was convicted of manslaughter and sentenced to nine months in jail and a branding on the hand. His case was on appeal when he came to Texas. With this history, he undoubtedly would have failed the "good character" test required of immigrants. Austin was about to cross a quick-tempered man whose ambition was matched only by his arrogance.[31]

Arriving in Saltillo, Austin wasted little time in applying for the new empresario contract. He later claimed to have made inquiries on Robertson's behalf, only to be rebuffed by the secretary of the legislature, Santiago del Valle. Whether or not Austin actually made such inquiries, the answer would have been no.[32] On February 25, 1831, the legislature granted Austin and Williams a contract to settle eight hundred Mexican and foreign families in a region that included the territory formerly encompassed by the Nashville grant (see map 3). Austin seems to have known that his maneuvering might raise eyebrows in Texas. As he told Williams, "I am operating on a pritty large scale, for a taciturn and noisless man, but I have no other object in view [than] the gen[l] prosperity of *us all* and particularly of this nation and government." He warned Williams to keep quiet about it for now.[33]

Austin's statement deserves closer examination. He had been successful in large measure because of his ability to reconcile and harmonize his own personal interests with those of Texas, or at least with those of Anglo Texas. He no doubt thought that securing this latest empresario contract would be consistent with that approach. As long as the Nashville investors had possessed a valid contract to settle the Indian-dominated region north of the San Antonio Road, Austin had encouraged and assisted them. He and his colony stood to benefit from a buffer to the northwest, and he supported Anglo-American immigration in almost all cases. But the passage of five years and the suspension of the Texas Association's contract had ended any chance of that company settling the grant, despite whatever false hopes Austin may have allowed Sterling Robertson to harbor. Furthermore, Austin had recently learned that a French company was applying for the grant. If a group of Tennessee speculators had failed to bring a single settler in five years, what were the chances of French speculators doing any better? Even though it would require the difficult task of recruiting colonists from Mexico and Europe, Austin still had good reason to believe that he and Williams could do it better than anyone else.

Yet, as usual, there were more utilitarian elements in Austin's plans. When he referred to the "gen¹ prosperity of *us all*," he was also referring to the real profits that the new enterprise would generate. As with all colonization contracts, there would someday be premium lands awarded to the empresarios if they were successful in settling the grant. A general increase in the number of industrious settlers would result in expanding markets and rising land prices, which would benefit large landowners and entrepreneurs like Austin and Williams. But there were also more immediate profits to be reaped from the new contract. If granted, it would give Austin and Williams control over the disposition of a vast area of land. With the passage of the 1828 law allowing the sale (and resale) of eleven-league grants, the new empresarios could allow those tracts to be located within the boundaries of the new colony and collect handsome location fees from the speculators. If the restrictions on Anglo-American immigration were someday lifted — as Austin believed they must be — the new colony would be even more profitable to the empresarios.[34]

For the present, though, the colony would have to be settled by native Mexicans or Europeans. With this in mind, Austin had an idea that made sense in more ways than one. "I wish the [B]*oss,* to take a part in this," he told Williams. "If he will, all is safe." The "Boss" was General Terán. If the general joined Austin and Williams in the enterprise, he could directly pursue a cause he had long advocated. Nobody in Texas or Coahuila would have the nerve to interfere with it, including Sterling Robertson, the Texas Association, or capricious legislators in Saltillo. Furthermore, once Terán had a vested interest in Texas colonization and discovered how difficult it was to attract Mexican and foreign settlers, he might relent in his longstanding opposition to Anglo-American immigration and help to repeal the Law of April 6. Despite Terán's substantial role in framing the hated law, Austin's "faith in *Boss,*" as he explained to Williams, was "unimpaired." "Better break all the timber in Texas, than to break *Boss,*" he remarked on another occasion, "for the former is plenty and can be replaced, but the lat[t]er being a fine texture is not to be found everyday." Unfortunately, Terán was less than enthusiastic about the whole enterprise, telling Austin rather grimly that it would take "miracles" to complete such a contract. Time would prove just how astute the Boss was this time.[35]

Austin departed Saltillo on May 9, thankful to be heading home after five months away. He arrived in San Felipe in early June.[36] The summer of 1831 passed quietly as the empresario attended to the business of his colony. A top priority was to issue as many land titles as possible to settlers, some of whom had been in Texas for several years. In this matter Austin had been bedeviled by the failure of the government to appoint a land commissioner who would actually come to the colony and issue titles. Gaspar Flores, who had succeeded the Baron de Bastrop, had finished the titles for the Old Three Hundred but had found a variety of excuses for avoiding the performance of his duties for Austin's second contract. Flores was finally replaced by Juan Antonio Padilla in 1828, but Padilla barely arrived in Texas before being arrested for murder. The colonists continued without a commissioner until the appointment of Miguel Arciniega in late 1830. Arciniega finally arrived in Texas in the spring of 1831 and was busy working on titles when Austin returned from Saltillo. Over the next three years he would issue more than five hundred titles for settlers under Austin's second and third contracts.[37]

Apart from securing land titles, one of the colonists' most pressing needs was for a qualified clergyman. Like all Mexicans, they were required to be Roman Catholics, but this was a provision that the authorities never attempted to enforce and that many settlers apparently ignored. By most accounts Austin's colonists were not a particularly religious lot, but they did feel the need to have their marriages legally recognized and their children baptized. For a decade Austin had tried without success to have a priest sent to the colony. Now, with more than five thousand souls in the Austin municipality, the government finally sent a priest to serve as curate for the Anglo colonies.[38]

Michael Muldoon was a jovial fifty-year-old Irishman with a keen mind and wide-ranging interests. Austin met him in Saltillo in January 1831 and was immediately impressed. "I must believe," he wrote, "that if the general Govt. wished to harass us, they would not have sent a man . . . who is so liberal and so enlightened, on religious subjects." By "liberal" and "enlightened," Austin of course meant that the new clergyman would not cause trouble when he found the colonists to be such indifferent Catholics. But in Father Muldoon, Austin detected advantages that went

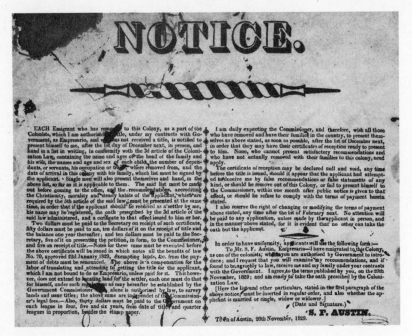

"Notice" to emigrants. Broadside issued by Austin in 1829, urging emigrants to present themselves to him to have their land titles issued. *Courtesy, Center for American History, University of Texas (Broadsides Collection #CN09587).*

beyond purely religious matters. The priest, it turned out, was the "warm and bosom friend" of both Terán and Alamán, as well as a "great favorite" with the powerful Viesca brothers. In short, Muldoon could be an important political ally. By the time Muldoon left Saltillo, he had obtained, in Austin's words, "a large *bite* of land" from the government and was planning to settle in Texas permanently. As Austin had so often done with important Mexicans, he tried to link Muldoon's personal interests with those of the Texas colonists. The empresario thus hinted to Muldoon that if recent restrictions on slavery and immigration could be repealed, "Texas might be made a Bishoprick in a few years." Austin paid him the ultimate compliment when he characterized the departing clergyman as a "true *Austinian.*"[39]

Muldoon soon became a favorite with the colonists, who found him a delightful change from the somber Methodists and Presbyterians they had known back home. He apparently spent little time preaching, but he loved the parties and feasts that accompanied weddings and christenings. He regaled the colonists with witty original poetry in the pages of the colony's newspaper and was no stranger to the barrooms of San Felipe and Brazoria. The colonists discovered that he could appreciate a good joke, even when he was the victim of a settler's prank. The nominal Catholicism that passed for orthodoxy in Austin's Colony seemed to suit priest and parishioners alike. Not long after his arrival in Texas, Muldoon publicly expressed his surprise "to find so much *order*—to receive so much personal respect—and to discover such a *general* and *voluntary adhesion* to the Catholic religion." In answer to the inevitable charge that the settlers' conversion stemmed strictly from self-interest, Muldoon replied that self-interest was the "principal ingredient among mortals" and that even religious martyrs "felt a deep interest in their martyrdom!! otherwise, they must have been *insipid* and *insensible fools.*" The settlers could voice a hearty "amen" to this logic, and with tongue somewhat in cheek they proudly called themselves "Muldoon Catholics." [40]

In the summer after Austin's return, the two men traveled through the colony together, with Muldoon baptizing children and officiating at multiple-couple weddings. Years earlier, necessity had led Austin to devise a sort of unofficial civil marriage, whereby a man and woman wishing to wed appeared before an alcalde and signed a bond promising to get legally married as soon as a priest was available. They could then set up housekeeping as husband and wife. Since some of the couples presenting themselves to Muldoon for marriage had been joined in this manner for some time, they were often "surrounded at the hymeneal altar," as one settler recalled, "by the prattling products of their civil marriage." Austin no doubt enjoyed these rare occasions when he could play the part of patriarch and promote a sense of community among the colonists. He also succeeded in building a strong relationship with Muldoon, who developed into precisely the sort of political ally for which Austin had hoped. [41]

The summer of 1831 was made even more pleasant for Austin by the long-awaited arrival of a number of his relatives. Except for a brief visit from his cousin Henry Austin, the only blood kin he had had in Texas since his brother's death two years earlier was Brown's two-year-old son Stephen. The first relative from back east to arrive was Emily's son Moses Austin Bryan. Why Emily sent the thirteen-year-old ahead of the rest of the family is unclear, but she may have thought that his energy and sunny disposition would provide some cheer for her often melancholy brother. The boy, called Austin by his family, landed in Brazoria in January 1831, while his uncle was in Saltillo. He stayed with various Austin friends until the empresario's return and seemed to enjoy the adventure of it all.[42]

The remainder of the large Perry family arrived in August. Emily, who was six months' pregnant, settled with the children temporarily in San Felipe while James studied the merits of his various tracts. Austin wanted the Perrys to set up housekeeping at the tract known as Peach Point, on the lower Brazos River. Perry, however, was leaning toward a picturesque but relatively isolated tract where Chocolate Bayou empties into Galveston Bay. Austin explained that the Peach Point property should appreciate greatly in value as the nearby town of Brazoria grew and prospered. He warned Perry that Emily "may complain that I sent you to Chocolate Bayou," but Perry did not heed and soon began construction of temporary quarters there.[43]

With the arrival of his sister's family, Austin began to think more seriously about retiring from public affairs and settling down to life as a landed gentleman. Later that fall he drew up elaborate plans for the Perry-Austin plantation headquarters. The house was to be a sprawling twelve-room brick structure with one wing earmarked for the empresario's bedroom and study. Expansive galleries would be built on the front and rear of the house. Austin laid out the grounds with the same care that he drafted the floor plan, including such features as a detached kitchen, smokehouse, carriage house, stables, hen and bee houses, and a large garden and orchard. At nearly three thousand square feet, the house might not be the largest in Texas, but there would be none more meticulously designed. Although Austin had preferred the Peach Point site near Brazoria as the family's permanent home, he deferred to Perry's choice of the Chocolate Bayou location. The site at least had the advantage of prettier scenery, and Austin situated the house so that it would afford a fine view of the bay.[44]

The dynamics of Austin's relationships with his sister and brother-in-law shed additional light on his personality. That he loved Emily and her family and cared about their welfare cannot be doubted, but the empresario could not resist the urge to control his sister's life. The unflinching self-confidence that had been a key factor in his success as empresario rendered Austin certain that he knew what was best for Emily and her family. He had virtually demanded that they emigrate in 1829 and had been greatly frustrated when Perry procrastinated. He did not hesitate to tell Emily, even from afar, how her sons should be educated and what professions they should follow.[45] Now that the Perrys were in Texas, he issued nonstop advice regarding James's and his own business affairs, both of which he expected James to manage.[46] And of course he took it upon himself to design their house and to include his own living quarters in the plan. It never occurred to him that his advice and assistance all too often sounded like peremptory orders. The fact that Austin's advice was usually sound probably did not make it any easier for Emily and James, for they were both proud and strong willed in their own right. It comes as no surprise, then, that Austin felt deeply wounded when James questioned him or when Emily complained, as both sometimes did.[47] For now, though, the Perrys seemed satisfied with their decision to emigrate. Emily expressed pleasure with her brother's house plans, although she wondered if they could afford such a grand home.[48] Perry would serve his brother-in-law in countless ways in the next five years. The intrepid Austin Bryan became a favorite of his uncle and would later serve as his secretary. Austin was gratified to have all of them in Texas.

Mid-1831 also saw the arrival of other relatives. First cousin Henry Austin was a sometime ship's captain and full-time dreamer. As a young sailor he had seen the Falkland Islands, China, and the Persian Gulf. Returning to his native New England, he failed at various commercial enterprises. Next he sailed for Mexico, where he failed in the ginning and commission business. Finally he bought a steamboat with the intention of navigating the Rio Grande. Failing yet again, he then brought his steamboat up the coast to Austin's Colony in 1830, where with Austin's encouragement he successfully applied for a ten-league grant from the government. In May 1831 he settled on the lower Brazos, established a plantation that he named Bolivar, and sent for his wife and five children, who arrived in December. Despite his cousin's business ineptitude, Austin had tremendous affection for Henry, who was eleven years his senior.[49]

As much as Austin welcomed the coming of these kinfolk, he awaited the arrival of yet another relative with special anticipation. A year earlier, Henry's sister Mary Austin Holley had inquired about opportunities in Texas. Stephen had not seen this cousin in twenty-five years, when she was a twenty-three-year-old newlywed and he a fourteen-year-old school-boy in Connecticut. Mary had studied music and languages in New Haven before marrying Horace Holley, a brilliant clergyman who went on to become president of Transylvania University. Holley died in 1827, leaving the forty-three-year-old widow to raise their twelve-year-old son. With her polished education and refined manners, Mary secured a well-paying position as governess for a wealthy Louisiana plantation family and published a biography of her late husband. "I am happily and use-fully situated where I am," she explained, "but I am *alone,* and think—I am sure—I should prefer a place of tolerable comfort, *entirely my own,*— *a permanent home,* to all this luxury."[50]

Time had not dimmed Austin's memory of his cousin. When she ar-rived later in the year he would find her still beautiful and vivacious, much younger looking than her forty-seven years. He instructed Williams to set aside a good league of land for her, explaining that she would be the "most valuable acquisition we have ever yet received in the female line, or probably will receive." There had long been a utopian undercurrent in Austin's long-range conception of his Texas enterprise. In unguarded mo-ments he could dream of the day when a flourishing Texas would support culture and education. If this were ever to happen, Texas needed women like Mary Holley. As Austin told her in a letter, "The idea of your removal here, and of the society which will of course spring up under the influence of your wand, gives me more real pleasure than anything which has oc-curred for some years." She would also fit neatly into his own personal, if highly idealized, retirement plans. "May we not form a little world of our own where neither the religious, political, or *money-making* fanaticism, which are throwing the good people of our native country into all sorts of convulsions, shall ever obtain admission?" he asked. "Let us unite a few choice families and make a *neighborhood* as we say in this country."[51]

By the time Mary sailed for Austin's Colony that autumn, she had decided to write a book about Texas. Austin approved, for there was very little accurate information available in print for prospective emigrants. The book would be particularly useful in encouraging English emigration, for by law the new Austin and Williams contract would have to be filled with emigrants from countries other than the United States.

Mary arrived from New Orleans in late October 1831. At the time, Terán was on his way to Anahuac to supervise the opening of the customs house and to assess the state of affairs along the coast. Throughout 1831 friction had grown between the Anglo settlers and Colonel Bradburn on Galveston Bay, and also between Bradburn and Francisco Madero, the state-appointed land commissioner for the area east of Austin's Colony. Austin planned to ride from San Felipe to Anahuac to confer with Terán and then go from there to Henry's plantation, but in October he again fell sick with fever. The empresario lay in bed forty-five days, and all his plans had to be placed on hold. By mid-November he was on the mend but still too sick to travel. Terán left for Matamoros before Austin was well enough to make the trip to Anahuac, so in early December Austin impetuously borrowed horses from Perry and rode directly from San Felipe down the river to Henry Austin's plantation. The weather was so cold that it made his face ache, and his pain was compounded by the mercury he had been given as treatment for his fever. Nonetheless, the prospect of seeing his cousins—and especially Mary—put him in a buoyant mood. "I am in better spirits than I have been for Six months," he wrote to Perry shortly before his trip, "all things are working around right."[52]

Bolivar House, as Henry called his three-room log cabin, was the scene of a boisterous reunion. Henry's wife arrived from the United States with the couple's five children and household goods about the same time as Austin. Since Mary was already gathering material for her book, she passed many hours plying her cousin for information on the history, geography, economy, and politics of Texas. Austin, who so rarely had the opportunity to tell the full story of his decade-long odyssey in the wilderness, found an eager and admiring listener in Mary. For perhaps the first time in his adult life he had found a woman whose intellect was every bit as keen as his own. They discovered a shared love of books and

Mary Austin Holley. Austin was captivated by the
charm and sophistication of his widowed cousin and
urged her to settle in Texas. *Courtesy, Center for
American History, University of Texas at Austin
(Prints and Photographs Collection #CN00165).*

music, and in the evenings Mary, Stephen, and the entire extended family
joined in singing "The Brazos Boat Song," Mary's romantic new composition about Texas. For once, Austin's many pressing business obligations
would have to wait. Could the empresario have been falling in love?[53]

There are, of course, many varieties of love, and Austin probably
would have denied that his seeming infatuation with Mary was anything
more than platonic affection of the cousinly sort. It would have been distinctly out of character for him to have admitted otherwise, given his long-
standing difficulty in communicating his inner feelings. But it is precisely
this reticence—or "taciturnity," as Austin himself often described it—
that sustains the conjecture that this was indeed the beginning of some-

thing like a love affair. His letters to Mary in the ensuing days and weeks reveal anything but reticence. The first one came on Christmas Day, only a few days after their parting. Five more letters followed in close succession, apparently one with each mail, ending only when Austin left Texas for the long journey to the next legislative session.[54]

These letters reveal an Austin rarely seen, even by those closest to him. In one very long narrative he recounted the history of his life and especially his years in Texas. The hardships he had endured, and the "selfishness, envy, jealousy, false pride[,] disappointed vanity, and vindictive, furious revenge" he had witnessed had "soured, disgusted, and sickened" him, Austin wrote. He reflected bitterly on the loss of his brother and the long separation from his sister. "I had become convinced that I could not find happiness in a general and extended intercourse with the world," he confessed. "And yet I was a social being. The life of a hermit is odious to me." He frankly acknowledged his need for a "social circle — a few friends of congenial tastes." The arrival of Emily's and Henry's families were now fulfilling that need. "[A]nd you — my friend, you, — how shall I ever thank you for venturing into this wilderness," he asked, "how express the happiness of the ten days visit at Henry's?" He provided his own answer: "Yes, we will be happy. Before you came I had begun to change the opinion that I was laboring here solely for others and posterity, and now I am convinced that I shall enjoy some of the fruits of my planting." He vowed to wash his hands of public affairs as soon as possible. "We will then arrange our cottages — rural — comfortable — and splendid — the splendor of nature's simplicity," he gushed. "Gardens, and rosy bowers, and ever verdant groves, and music, books, and intellectual amusements can all be ours; and that confidence and community of feeling and tastes which none but congenial minds can ever know; all these, without excessive wealth we can have."[55]

Nowhere in the thousands of surviving Austin letters can be found such an outpouring of romantic emotion. Austin surprised even himself. "On reviewing what I have written I fear you will laugh at my enthusiasm," he ruefully admitted, "and think I am suffering my fancy to wander in the *Elysian Fields* when every thing around ought to remind me that before I can enter them the *Styx* and *Infernus* are to be passed. It may be so; but even that can not prevent enjoyment by *anticipation.*" Subsequent letters were less effusive, but they carried romantic closings such as "Adios, amiga mia" and, in his final letter before leaving for Saltillo, "Farewell, a long farewell." Commenting on the ten days spent at Bolivar House in a letter to James Perry, Austin was more circumspect, merely remarking that "Mrs. H. is a *divine* woman—she will be a neighbor at peach point. . . . I mean to make a little world there of my own." [56]

Austin's dreams seemed to be materializing, but he also saw the obstacles that still lay ahead. The Law of April 6 had fostered a growing disaffection among the colonists, who feared that the restrictions on immigration would cut them off from loved ones back home and damage their economic prospects. As a result, friction was increasing between the Mexican authorities and the colonists. While Austin was in Brazoria shots had been fired between Mexican soldiers and Anglo settlers over the payment of customs duties. Terán would not be pleased, and Austin was naturally concerned.

Even more sobering was the crisis building in the heart of Mexico. In a matter of days Antonio López de Santa Anna would raise the banner of open revolt against the Bustamante regime, plunging the nation deeper into political turmoil. *"There must be a change of some kind,"* Austin wrote to Mary on December 29. "To remain as we are, is impossible." Yet despite his fears, as the new year dawned Austin could still express optimism. He had never been happier than in the past few weeks. As he told Mary, "I think the Government will yield, and give us what we ought to have." [57]

On January 2, 1832, Austin mounted his horse and made the long ride from Brazoria back to San Felipe. Reaching his destination, he found sister Emily dancing at a ball "in fine spirits." Remembering Mary's "injunction to 'laugh away care,' " Austin, in his own words, "caught the excitement" of the moment. The grueling forty-seven-mile ride was forgotten, and the empresario danced the night away.[58]

The Call of Duty
1832–1833

At his headquarters in Matamoros, Gen. Manuel de Mier y Terán fumed. Dispatches on his desk told the disturbing news of violent clashes between Anglo settlers and Mexican soldiers on the Brazos. A month earlier, in December 1831, three Anglo captains had sailed their ships past the Mexican fort at the river's mouth without paying customs duties. Shots were exchanged, wounding a soldier. John Austin and other settlers subsequently threatened open attack on the Mexican garrisons in Texas. Anglo colonists seemingly stood at the brink of the revolution that Terán had long dreaded.[1]

Two letters on Terán's desk from Stephen F. Austin particularly angered him. The first was addressed to Juan Davis Bradburn, the commander of the fort at Anahuac. In it Austin blamed the violence on George Fisher, whom Terán had named customs collector for the Port of Galveston.[2] Fisher had issued an order requiring all ships then in Texas ports to have their papers cleared at Anahuac before sailing. It was this order that provoked the December incidents, for Anahuac, at the far north end of Galveston Bay, lay more than a hundred miles from Brazoria. Captains in port at Brazoria would have to make that long and difficult round trip overland for their papers before they could leave the Brazos. Austin told Bradburn that the order was "impracticable"—which indeed it was— and urged its suspension. He went on to point out to Bradburn that "the people in Texas have just causes and very many of them to complain." Was it the government's purpose to have Texas "totally broken up and all commerce totally annihilated?" Austin asked. "Is that the object of the Government—if it is I wish to know it." Were the people of Austin's Colony "to be shut out from the whole world and have all their commerce destroyed[?] I think not," Austin flatly stated. "This is no time for ambiguity, for it will require all our management united to keep things quiet [until] a more Liberal System is adopted towards the people."[3]

Austin had not intended for Terán to see this letter, which was so critical of policies that Terán himself had helped shape. In fact, the empresario had written a much milder letter to Terán, admitting that there had been some minor disturbances but assuring him that everything was now straightened out. Austin planned to visit Terán in February or March, and then they could discuss everything fully, including Austin's proposal that the general become a partner in his and Williams's new eight-hundred— family colonization venture.[4]

It is easy to see why Terán was incensed. Bradburn and Fisher were only obeying government orders, yet the colonists, with Austin's apparent approval, had forcefully resisted those orders. And now Austin had the nerve to pretend that it was a small matter. "Do you dare to say, as in the letter of Señor Davis [Bradburn], that the view of the Government is to destroy the commerce of your Colony?" an incredulous Terán replied to Austin. He curtly reminded Austin of Mexico's generosity, adding that he had nearly compromised his own responsibility to the government by granting favors to the colonists. The people of Texas were justified in complaining? "This is news to me," Terán remarked sarcastically. "You want the government to adopt a more liberal policy. You should say what liberality you long for beyond that which you already receive." Every nation in the Americas collects customs duties at its ports, the general reasoned: "Only in Brazoria is it believed that there is a reason for rebellion. So they sail their ships clandestinely and fire like pirates, wounding a Mexican soldier, who, believing that those colonists are fellow citizens, is undefended and trusting. And is this the hospitality that a soldier in the Mexican service encounters among your colonists, Señor Austin?"[5]

Terán's ire soon subsided. He agreed that Fisher's order had been unreasonable and arranged to open a branch of the customs house at Brazoria to accommodate Brazos River traffic.[6] Terán and Austin remained on friendly terms, but as 1832 wore on both would be swept up in the politics buffeting Texas and all of Mexico. Austin was forced to keep playing his "double game": supporting federalists who championed local autonomy and at the same time coexisting with the centralist national government. Terán found himself pummeled by those same forces, but in a different way. He could not risk pushing Texas federalists into open revolt, but he was also convinced that Mexico could survive only by maintaining a strong central government. If federalists took control, the republic itself would soon fracture. Texas would be the first piece to fall.

Austin's own thinking about the future of Texas had undergone a gradual transformation. As the population had grown, he increasingly was willing to contemplate separation from Mexico. Austin always presented the issue as a contingency—a course that might have to be considered if life under Mexican rule became unbearable. "If the Gov' [of Mexico] stands and prospers Texas must prosper under it," he explained to William H. Wharton in 1829. "If the Gov' falls the bonds which bind Texas and Mexico will of course be severed by that fall, and in this event Texas can either unite herself to the North under the necessary guarantees from that Gov' or become an independent speck in the galaxy of nations." What Austin meant by the government "falling" is unclear; the key word in this statement is "prosper." If it ever became apparent that Texas would or could not prosper under Mexican rule, other alternatives would have to be pursued. Austin's loyalty to Mexico, then, was always conditional. He was resolute in his dedication to his adopted country, but only so long as union with Mexico furthered his version of Texas's interests. Into the early 1830s he continued to believe that such a union was still best for Texas and thus for himself.[7]

The Law of April 6 and its aftermath made Austin think more about separation. "I will die sooner than violate my duty to this government," he declared. But it was a reciprocal duty, contingent on Mexico doing its duty to him. If that government "would let me work I would make Texas the best state that belongs to this nation," he explained to his cousin Thomas Leaming, "but my dear sir the truth is that the Mexicans cannot sustain a republic." Austin knew that Texas was still too weak for independence unless it became some sort of protectorate of the United States, "and the protection which the strong affords to the *weak* is much to be feared," he astutely noted. "If we had population, our course would be a very plain one, but we have it not. Territory we have to form a snug republic." For the present, then, there was little choice. "I am in hopes the federal system may stand a few years longer and that by that time we shall get in some thousands of swiss, Germans, etc, and North Americans — the emigration is still uninter[r]upted to my colony and there will be a great accession of strength this fall." [8]

If remaining under Mexican rule indeed became impossible, and independence was not yet a viable option, what about the third alternative: annexation by the United States? This was Austin's least preferred option. Curiously — and always in letters to northern friends — he based his opposition on the grounds that annexation "would of course intail slavery on this fair region, which may be made the Eden of America. Satan," he argued, "entered the sacred garden in the shape of a serpent — if he is allowed to enter Texas in the shape of negros it will share the fate of Eden." This of course was disingenuous on Austin's part, for he had labored repeatedly to ensure the future of slavery in Texas. He probably hoped that as time passed, a Mexican or independent Texas would develop a diversified economy in which slavery would become less important. However, if Texas became a slaveholding state of the United States, it would probably follow the southern model and grow increasingly dependent on cotton and slavery.[9]

The issue of slavery actually was a convenient smokescreen for Austin's real motives. He still longed for the status, respect, and personal fulfillment that would come from being the acknowledged founder and leader of a prosperous Texas. He had once thought that he could attain these things under a constitutional monarchy or an enlightened central republic, but he now understood that his interests were best served by decentralized government. Only Mexican federalism would give himself and his colonists the personal freedom to enjoy the fruits of their massive land-holdings without fear of burdensome taxes, restrictive land laws, or ruin-ous monetary policies—the very things that had driven so many Ameri-cans out of the United States. For the present, then, he would work for the reforms that would bring autonomy to the Mexican federation: open immigration, free trade, and local control over such matters as slavery and the judiciary. Should Texas fail to secure these reforms, he ominously ex-plained to Mary Holley in December 1831, "we shall go for *Independence,* and put our trust in our selves, our riffles [rifles], and—our god." [10]

Matters remained tense between the colonists and Mexican authori-ties in Texas when Austin finally left to attend the legislative session in March 1832. The session had actually begun in January, and state law com-pelled members to attend, but Austin had been desperately ill in October and November. Although he recovered by mid-December, he used the sickness as an excuse for delay. Only after receiving an urgent summons from the government did he set out for Saltillo. [11]

Austin took along Moses Austin Bryan, who was to study Spanish and serve as his uncle's secretary. For the fourteen-year-old Bryan, the trip was a great adventure. Along the way they visited the Seguíns on their ranch near San Antonio and then made a quick side trip to Goliad, where they enjoyed the hospitality of the alcalde. After leaving San Antonio the empresario enjoyed showing the boy the site of the terrible Battle of Me-dina, where Royalist forces had slaughtered a thousand rebels in 1813. Two days later they stopped for a meal, and Austin regaled his nephew with the story of his brush with fifty-four Comanches on that very spot in 1822. South of the Rio Grande the desert grew bleaker, and Bryan wrote with amazement about the "pore miserable" ranches where they purchased meager fodder for their horses. [12]

In his saddlebags Austin carried petitions from the San Felipe and San Antonio ayuntamientos asking for free trade, the removal of Fisher as customs collector, and repeal of the ban on Anglo immigration. By the time he and his nephew arrived in Saltillo, only three weeks remained in the legislative session. The lawmakers had already passed the law that he had helped to defeat a year earlier, banning foreigners from engaging in the retail trade. He did arrive in time to participate in the creation of a separate ayuntamiento for Brazoria and the passage of a new colonization law. The legislature sent the Texans' reform petition to the acting president with a positive recommendation. The new colonization law, which Austin said was "as favorable as could be obtained or expected at present," had no immediate effect on Austin since it applied only to future colonies.[13]

When the legislature adjourned, Austin could only express his satisfaction that "this legislature have done no harm except the retail law, and some good." Its greatest accomplishment was inaction—refusing to take sides in Mexico's civil war. "Our *Congresito,* very wisely I think, have adopted the turtle sistem," he wrote. But he was thoroughly tired of elected office and made it clear that he would refuse reelection.[14]

Outside the legislative chamber, Austin worked to complete the purchase of three eleven-league grants he had initiated the year before. Moses Austin Bryan later recalled his uncle taking "from his baggage I think seven or eight hundred dollars mostly silver dollars" to pay for the land. These grants were to be the means by which the empresario hoped to secure his cherished tract on the upper Colorado for a summer estate.[15]

He also had not forgotten about the Upper Colony, as he commonly called the Austin and Williams empresario contract. Austin had never intended to conduct the business of settling that colony by himself. He was far too busy and weary of the grinding day-to-day labor of the colonizing business to pursue it alone. Since the contract presently could not be filled with Anglo-Americans, he was looking for help in attracting native Mexican emigrants. To this end he apparently discussed subcontracting all or part of the contract with Mexican friends in Saltillo. He reported to Williams that he had "rec ᵈ very favorable offers to settle our contract," but before agreeing to any of them he wanted to see "the GENERAL." All along he had intended to bring in Terán as a partner in that contract. Even though Terán had shown no interest, Austin still had not given up on the idea. So absolute was his confidence in his own persuasive powers that he believed he could bring anyone around to his position, even the iron-willed commandant general.[16]

Leaving Moses Austin Bryan to continue his Spanish studies, Austin decided to pay a visit to the general, who was locked in a bloody struggle with Santa Anna's forces in Tamaulipas. Bryan seems not to have minded being left behind; many years later he noted with some pride that he had "learned to speak Spanish and to smoke shuck cigarettes" in Saltillo, although Austin himself revealed the equally important news that his nephew had acquired a "Mexicanita sweetheart" there. Departing Saltillo on May 12, Austin rode east to Monterrey and then south toward Tampico, where another battle between Terán's government forces and the Santanistas was brewing near Tampico. "I shall go on tomorrow, and may see, a new sight, to me, a battle, or a city stormed," Austin reported to Williams on May 22.[17]

Austin did not get to see the anticipated battle, but he did finally get to see the "Boss." Terán had established his most recent headquarters at the hacienda de Buena Vista del Cojo, about sixty miles inland from Tampico. The civil war had reached a critical stage at that point. Word had just reached Terán that Alamán and the other embattled cabinet ministers had resigned. This was the ostensible object of the revolt, but Santa Anna's forces were not about to lay down their arms when military victory seemed so imminent. Presidential elections were scheduled for September, and to many observers Terán seemed the only leader capable of uniting the warring federalists and centralists and leading Mexico out of the morass. Indeed, a poll of the nineteen state legislatures taken that spring indicated that twelve favored his election. But Terán himself understood that it was too late for compromise. Santa Anna and his federalist forces were bent on ousting the remnants of the Bustamante regime, and Terán was that regime's supreme commander in the north. Daily the noose tightened around his neck.[18]

Austin found the general gloomy and in poor health. Commanding an outnumbered army in the midst of a desperate civil war, cut off from supplies and still smarting from a recent military defeat, Terán undoubtedly had more important things to do than chat with the Texas empresario. Despite their frequent policy differences and occasional suspicions of each other, the men were still kindred spirits in many ways, and they enjoyed a cordial visit. Austin reported that Terán expressed "great interest for the prosperity of the settlers" and was "in favor of repealing the 11 Article of the law of 6 April and of extending the commercial privileges." Like

Alamán, Terán may have simply found it easier at this point to tell Austin what he wanted to hear, for he must have known that he would probably never again be in a position to influence Texas policy. But Austin sensed something of Terán's desperate mood. "The Gen¹ was greatly perplexed, and overwhelmed with *affairs* when I saw him at the cojo," he told Williams after his visit.[19]

Austin rode back to Matamoros to find that the revolt had spread there as well. On June 28 he witnessed a curious scene. Rebels under the command of Col. José Antonio Mexía marched into one end of the town, and government forces marched out the other end, all in orderly fashion. Austin now became convinced that the revolution would succeed and the Bustamante government fall. If the Santanistas lived up to their federalist professions, the new government would reduce the power of the military and the church, shift power back to the states, and ultimately give Texas the autonomy Austin believed it needed to grow and prosper. For now, though, he hoped that the colonists would remain neutral in the conflict and keep the civil war out of Texas.[20]

At the front, Terán's depression deepened. On June 25 he wrote Austin in despair, saying, "The affairs of Texas are understood only by you and me, and the two of us are the only ones who can regulate them; but there is no time." It was the last letter he would write to Austin.[21]

Austin realized how untenable Terán's situation had become, and he dreaded the prospect of Terán's army attacking Mexía's forces in Matamoros. Two days after Terán wrote his gloomy letter to Austin, the empresario sent Terán a letter exceptional for its frankness. Austin almost pleaded with the general to give up his allegiance to the doomed government. Austin couched his appeal in the language of high-minded liberalism, a language he knew Terán understood. Until military power and privilege were reduced and religious toleration established, Mexico would never enjoy peace or stability, he argued. The statesman who could bring about these reforms would be justly called the Washington of Mexico. "Ah! my friend, what a crown of glory there will be for you, whose name already belongs to history as the defender of independence from the first epoch of the revolution. This will be a crown for which a republican can and must yearn." The party of Santa Anna was misnamed, Austin argued. It should be called the "democratic republican federal party," because the liberal principles behind the revolt were larger than any one person. Liberalism and federalism, Austin wrote, must inevitably triumph in Mexico as they had in the United States and in Europe. "This is the natural order of things. Water flows downhill, and man rises from a state of nature to civilization and the sciences, from slavery to freedom, advancing like stair steps. These are laws of nature, at times late and slow in their operation, but certain in their results." [22]

But Terán could not share Austin's professed faith in a democratic future for Mexico. On July 2, as Austin prepared to throw his support behind the revolution in Matamoros, Terán penned a long letter to Lucas Alamán. "A great and respectable Mexican nation, a nation of which we have dreamed and for which we have labored so long, can never emerge from the many disasters which have overtaken it," he wrote. "How could we expect to hold Texas when we do not even agree among ourselves? It is a gloomy state of affairs. If we could work together, we would advance. As it is, we are lost. . . . Texas is lost. . . . What will become of Texas? Whatever God wills." [23]

The next morning the general rose early, donned his finest dress uniform, buckled on his sword, and went for a walk. He had recently moved his headquarters to the ancient village of Padilla, and now he found himself standing on the exact spot where Iturbide, the first leader of independent Mexico, had been executed. Terán drew his sword, braced its handle against a stone, and plunged the blade through his heart. [24]

News of Terán's suicide erased any lingering doubts about the course Austin would follow. The double game he had played so adroitly was over. He must now throw his support behind Santa Anna's revolution. [25]

Developments in Texas added urgency to this decision. While Austin sojourned south of the Rio Grande, the long-simmering tension between the Anglo-American colonists and Mexican authorities on Galveston Bay had broken into open conflict. There was no single source of the difficulties; a variety of small grievances, some valid and others spurious, contributed to the growing hostilities between the colonists and the principal object of their ire, Colonel Bradburn at Anahuac. [26]

The trouble had been building for a year. In 1831 a state-appointed land commissioner, José Francisco Madero, had arrived on the Trinity River near Anahuac. He organized a new municipality named Liberty and began to issue land titles. Unfortunately, Liberty lay within the ten-league coastal reserve and fell under federal jurisdiction, and the undiplomatic Bradburn arrested Madero and attempted to dissolve the new Liberty ayuntamiento. He also took steps to inspect the titles that Madero had issued and to crack down on Anglo attorneys practicing law without Mexican licenses. These were legally proper actions, but the settlers resented such strict conduct, especially at the hands of one they regarded as a countryman.

Bradburn had further antagonized the colonists in his administration of Mexican antislavery laws. When he granted asylum to some runaway slaves from Louisiana, lawyers William B. Travis and Patrick C. Jack sought to scare Bradburn into releasing the slaves by falsely reporting that an armed force was marching from Louisiana to recover the fugitives. Jack was already in trouble for organizing an extralegal militia, and Bradburn arrested both men. Settlers from the lower Brazos then marched on Anahuac, and several days of alternating skirmishes and negotiation ensued.

As the Anahuac confrontation unfolded, another party of settlers commanded by John Austin brought a cannon down the Brazos for use against Bradburn. At Velasco, the post at the river's mouth, the Mexican commander Domingo de Ugartechea opposed their passage. In the battle that followed on June 26, a handful of men on both sides were killed, including Austin's erstwhile antagonist, the irrepressible Aylett "Strap" Buckner.

Meanwhile, the Anglo forces outside Anahuac withdrew to nearby Turtle Bayou. Hearing of Santa Anna's impending victory in Mexico's civil war, they now attempted to put their actions in the best possible light. They drew up resolutions stating that they were merely freedom-loving federalists supporting Santa Anna's crusade against centralism.[27] At this point Col. José de las Piedras, the Mexican commander at Nacogdoches, arrived at Anahuac. Piedras, who outranked Bradburn and had generally gotten along with Anglo-Americans, prudently sided with the settlers, relieved Bradburn of command, and restored a semblance of order to the region.[28] Bradburn's garrison soon declared in favor of Santa Anna and federalism. The unfortunate Bradburn fled to Louisiana.

In June and early July, news of these dramatic events began to reach Austin south of the Rio Grande. Throughout the spring his letters home had constantly urged Sam Williams to maintain a *"dead calm"* in the colony. Williams had striven to obey these orders at the cost of his own standing with the colonists, who increasingly viewed him as a tory. July 2, the day before Terán's suicide, marked the beginning of a change in Austin's neutrality policy. If "the state of things requires it," he now instructed Williams from Matamoros, the colonists should "approve of the principles of the democratic constitutional federal party, of which Genl. Santana is the active leader." [29]

The mail, however, moved slowly, and events caught up with Williams before Austin's letter. As the unsuspecting Williams continued his efforts to discourage agitation, Austin's staunchest allies threw their support behind the rebellion and joined in the opposition to Bradburn.[30] Sam Williams, clinging to his last instructions from the empresario, was soon the most hated man in Austin's Colony.

Events in Matamoros now dictated Austin's course. Word of the Anglo uprising had reached both the Santanista commander, José Antonio Mexía, and his loyalist counterpart, Juan Mariano Guerra. With the national territory at risk, the two colonels put aside their political differences and decided to sail together for Texas to suppress the settlers' revolt.

Once again, Austin's year in Mexico City paid dividends. While there in 1822-23 he had met Colonel Mexía, and the two apparently enjoyed friendly personal relations. Mexía had subsequently served as secretary of the Mexican legation in Washington, where he became interested in Texas colonization affairs. In fact, in 1830, Mexía's English wife, who was in New York, had assisted Austin's cousin Archibald in obtaining a military uniform for Austin befitting his rank as lieutenant colonel in the Mexican national militia. Now Austin, probably wearing that very navy blue uniform with its gold epaulets, sash, and scarlet vest, consulted with Mexía on how to handle the disturbances in Texas. As a result, Mexía and Guerra jointly asked him to accompany them on the expedition. Austin of course agreed to this—he probably would have insisted on it—and he reassured the Mexican officers that they would find a warm welcome from the loyal settlers. In reality, though, Austin could not have known what sort of reception to expect in Texas. Had he played the double game too long?[31]

Five ships carrying Mexía, Guerra, their troops, and Stephen Austin landed at the mouth of the Brazos on July 16. Austin leaped into action, writing key officials across Texas to persuade them to pronounce unequivocally for Santa Anna. These efforts met with instantaneous success everywhere but San Antonio, where the cautious political chief, Ramón Músquiz, delayed pronouncing until late August. When they arrived in Brazoria, Austin and Mexía were met with jubilation by the settlers. Assuring the Mexican officers that they harbored no rebellious intentions, the residents of Brazoria threw a dinner and "grand Ball" for Austin and for the officers of Mexía's self-styled Liberating Army.[32]

Poor Sam Williams did not fare so well. While Austin was in Brazoria, local rowdies burned Williams in effigy for having opposed the attacks on the Mexican garrisons. Austin sought to comfort his beleaguered secretary and partner, telling him, "Don't let these matters worry you, what you have done was for the best." Lest Williams persist in thinking that Austin had intentionally allowed him to suffer the consequences of the empresario's own failed policy, Austin put the blame on "that most consummate of all fools, Bradburn," who, as Austin bitterly phrased it, "was too much of a jack ass to be governed by reason or judgement, or anything else except brutal passion." Williams seems to have accepted this explanation, but in a subtle way it may have contributed to his growing determination to put his own interests ahead of Austin's. Significantly, despite the words of reassurance and explanation, there is no record of an actual apology from Austin for having placed his friend in such an untenable position. Explanations might be useful when things went awry, but apologies were not the Austin way.[33]

At San Felipe, Austin received a hero's welcome. His return to Texas with Mexía had surely saved his reputation among the colonists. The opprobrium of toryism was left on the shoulders of Williams. Austin, presumably still sporting his handsome colonel's uniform, was able to present himself as having played a key role in saving Texas from centralist tyranny by bringing Mexía's Liberating Army to the Brazos. He was met on the outskirts of the village by a delegation of citizens, led by Patrick Jack and his settlers' militia, who were now styling themselves the Santa Anna Volunteer Company. Jack made a short speech welcoming Austin home and concluding with the words, "Well done thou good and faithful servant; thou art welcome; thrice welcome, to thy home, and to thy friends; and may health and happiness always attend thee."[34]

Austin responded with a long and able speech, lauding Santa Anna as the savior of Mexican democracy. At the end of his speech he was saluted with twelve rounds of cannon and small arms fire and escorted to his house on the other end of town. Later in the day he was visited by the Mexican troops who had so recently been arrayed in pitched battle against Jack's militia at Velasco. Those troops had declared for Santa Anna since the battle, and now Austin embraced their officers. They all drank toasts to one another and to Santa Anna and the Constitution. The toast made to Austin by the ranking Mexican officer, Lieutenant Moret, is significant. "May the Supreme Being preserve the life of Colonel Austin to the citizens of Texas for twenty years and longer," Moret proposed, "so that they may have the benefit of his exertions to separate Texas from Coahuila, and form it into a state of the great Mexican Confederation, as the only means of securing its prosperity, and the true interests of the Mexican Republic."[35]

Austin's glowing tributes to Santa Anna concealed his concerns about the general's true intentions. In 1831, Austin had perceptively described Santa Anna as a "sort of Mad Cap difficult to class" politically. While in Saltillo the empresario found that many of the leading men there who supported federalism nonetheless opposed Santa Anna, believing that "*his* real object is *centralismo*." Terán had certainly never trusted the mercurial general. But the civil war in Mexico and the settlers' revolt against Bradburn had forced Austin to abandon his efforts to appease both sides in Mexico's political struggle. The die was now cast; Austin's Colony and most of the rest of Texas embraced Santa Anna, and expectations ran high that a Santa Anna–led government would produce the reforms that most Texans—Anglo and Hispanic—longed for. Chief among these reforms, as Lieutenant Moret had affirmed, was separation from Coahuila.

As Austin told Political Chief Músquiz in the aftermath of the revolt, "My own and the general wish is, to see Texas forming by itself a State of the Federation, and as long as it is not so, we can expect no peace, progress nor government, and in fact nothing."[36]

For the moment the storm had passed. Austin was home, and most of the colonists still viewed his leadership as indispensable. His unexpected return to Texas with Mexía at least had the happy consequence of providing a convenient excuse for not attending the fall 1832 session of the legislature. Citing the unrest lingering throughout eastern Texas, Austin informed the state government that his duties as militia colonel for the department required his presence at home. "My position is rather delicate," he explained, hoping that the authorities in Saltillo would not view his absence and the recent events in Texas as evidence of disloyalty.[37]

Restoring tranquility to Texas required a considerable amount of his attention that fall, but Austin also found time to attend to some long-neglected personal business. For more than a decade the debt to Joseph Hawkins had troubled him greatly. Austin owed the Hawkins estate half of the nearly one hundred thousand acres that he had received as premium lands for the first colony. Hawkins's widow, George Anne, died before any settlement could be made, leaving five minor children as heirs to the land. Austin did not receive a clear and final title to those lands until 1828. Since then he had maintained sporadic contact with several different representatives of Hawkins's heirs, but none had actually come to Texas prepared to execute a settlement.[38]

In the fall of 1832, both Austin and the heirs finally were ready to settle the debt. One of Hawkins's sons, Edmund St. John Hawkins, had immigrated to the colony and finally reached majority age, preconditions for receiving title to land under Mexican law. An agent for the heirs came to Texas to help oversee the division of the premium lands. Austin spent parts of September, October, and November on the lower Brazos, going out with surveyors, examining deeds and plats, and running the dividing lines. He split seventeen individual pieces of land exactly down the middle, making sure that neither party received inferior portions. For the few plots that Austin had already sold to third parties, he made a cash settlement based on the market value of the land. The five children of Joseph Hawkins received title to about forty-two thousand acres and $2,000 cash.[39]

In this case, as in others, Austin had scrupulously honored obligations that he probably could have dodged indefinitely. The largest of these pre-Texas debts, those to Anthony Butler and George Tennille, were paid off within a year. "I am fast getting through my business and before spring I will take leave of public matters for the balance of my life," he told James Perry in September. "I intend to live principally with you, or near you and go to farming." A month later news came that a new state-appointed land commissioner, Miguel Arciniega, was on his way to the colony. Between them, Austin, Williams, and Arciniega would have the power to issue all the remaining land titles for all of Austin's empresario contracts. Austin published a notice calling on "All persons who are included in any of my Colonies, whose land business is not completed . . . to come forward, in person, and take out their titles." Those who had not done so by mid-December would forfeit their right to receive land. At the same time Austin submitted his resignation as militia colonel. By all appearances he was dead serious about retiring from public life.[40]

But private matters could never come first. If Austin had expected that the removal of Bradburn, Fisher, and most of the Mexican military presence in Texas would pacify the settlers, he was mistaken. Moreover, it was now becoming clear that he could no longer control public opinion or public affairs, even in his own colony. The population had grown too large and diverse for that. As long as Austin held the same views and supported the same policies as most of the settlers, they would still defer to his leadership. But if he disagreed with them, they would seek other leaders. He was about to find himself in the same position as Sam Williams a few months earlier. He would have to play a new double game, but this time its goal would be to maintain his position of leadership amid an increasingly divided Anglo population within Texas.

The colonists' success in removing the Mexican troops from their midst emboldened them to push for more lasting reforms. They did not realize how lucky they had been during the past summer. Had their uprising against Bradburn not coincided with Santa Anna's success in the other northern states, and had Austin not so adeptly managed Colonel

Mexía and the overall situation, matters would have turned out drastically different, probably resulting in a crushed rebellion and disaster for
Anglo Texas.

The settlers soon displayed their new self-confidence. In August 1832
the San Felipe ayuntamiento called for a convention. Austin probably opposed the movement, but, unable to dissuade the instigators, he went
along with it. On October 1, fifty-eight delegates assembled at San Felipe
and elected Austin president of the body over William H. Wharton. All
the municipalities except San Antonio sent delegates. The convention
respectfully petitioned the state and national governments for reforms,
including liberal tariff privileges, repeal of the ban on immigration from
the United States, and most important, separate statehood. Wharton was
to carry the petitions to Mexico City. The convention also established
committees of correspondence for each municipality, as well as a seven-
member central committee empowered to call future conventions. Austin
was named to the central committee, but it was clear that he could not
control it.[41]

As he had so often done in controversial causes, the empresario tried
to get the Tejano communities to lead the reform movement. This time,
though, he probably could predict the reaction of Political Chief Ramón
Músquiz. Both men knew that the convention constituted an illegal assembly under Mexican law. Músquiz felt some sympathy for the causes
espoused at San Felipe, but he' could not sanction the actual gathering.
Furthermore, he was by nature and necessity a cautious leader. He knew
that no reforms could be expected as long Bustamante clung to power
in Mexico City and the republic remained embroiled in civil war. Músquiz had little choice but to annul the convention. Wharton's mission was
abandoned. Austin breathed a little sigh of relief and returned to Brazoria
to finish surveying the Hawkins lands.

He knew, however, that the Anglo Texans would not give up easily. In
November he traveled to San Antonio in an effort to place the Anglo and
Tejano portions of Texas on common political ground. He succeeded in
enlisting his allies there in the cause of reform. As a result, the ayuntamiento of San Antonio drafted a strong pro-reform petition, which the
ayuntamientos of Goliad, San Felipe, and Nacogdoches soon endorsed.

Reluctantly, Músquiz forwarded the petition to the governor, but he accompanied it with an apology, saying that he was forced to do so in order to avoid a revolution. Such an action obviously would displease the powers in Saltillo. However, four days after the San Antonio ayuntamiento's actions, Bustamante finally faced the inevitable and stepped down from the presidency. Santa Anna entered Mexico City in triumph on January 3, 1833. Perhaps the Texans' requests would finally be heard. In this state of affairs, Austin again stated his clear intent to Perry: "I mean to wash my hands of the politics of Texas and try to settle myself along side of you."[42]

On March 1, the Mexican states elected Santa Anna president. Valentín Gómez Farías, a doctrinaire federalist whom Austin had met in Mexico City in 1822, won the vice-presidency. But the Texans were not willing to wait for the ponderous wheels of the incoming government to turn their way. Austin had scarcely returned from his mission to San Antonio when the colonists' central committee issued a call for another convention. Elections for delegates were held in March, and the meeting convened in San Felipe on April 1. Among the delegates was the flamboyant, hard-drinking ex-governor of Tennessee, Sam Houston, representing Nacogdoches. This time the convention chose William Wharton to preside over the gathering, a sign that Austin's cautious policies had fallen from favor. Meeting for two weeks, those attending the convention called for the same reforms as the previous assembly. This time, however, it went a step further, drafting a provisional state constitution for implementation when the petition for statehood was granted. Ironically, though the delegates selected Wharton over Austin as convention president, they wisely chose Austin to carry the petition to Mexico City.[43]

Austin's attitude toward the convention was complicated. Whether or not he approved of its initial calling or of the particulars of its work, by the time it adjourned he had decided to support it. There would be no more waiting for San Antonio's Tejanos to take the lead. The passage of time probably had much to do with his change of heart. Since 1830 he had counseled patience and expressed optimism that the hated law of that year would be repealed. For even longer he had believed that separate statehood for Texas must inevitably be granted, as promised by congress in

1824. For three years he had seen the republic wracked by rebellions and instability, and it was by no means clear that Santa Anna's regime would end the cycle. If he had not gained full support of all the Tejano leaders, he at least had it partially. Thus it was a combination of factors that led him to agree to undertake the mission to Mexico City. The political environment in the capital should be favorable, and Texas now was approaching the critical population mass necessary to sustain a state government of its own. For Austin, the benefits of Texas's union with Coahuila no longer exceeded the costs. His patience was nearly exhausted.

One additional factor should not be underestimated. By 1833, Austin had reached a critical juncture in his relationship to the Anglo-American settlers of Texas. However sincere he was in his professed desire to retire from public affairs, he could not consider relinquishing his status as the beloved leader of his people. Even in retirement he wanted and needed their respect. The events of the past year had demonstrated how precarious that status had become. A letter written at this point by one of the oldest and most prominent colonists, John P. Coles, reveals Austin's predicament with crystal clarity. Commenting on Austin's impending mission to Mexico, Coles wrote: "Col. Austin's sincerity in this matter is much doubted by many people in Texas. I hope however that Austin will not forget himself and his Friends. He is closely watched and his future prospects depend greatly upon his Conduct in this matter. If he succeeds he will do well for himself and if for the want of proper Exertion on his part the application should fail Col. Austin will be a Ruined man in Texas." [44]

In short, he had no choice. To refuse the call of duty now would mean surrendering the thing that meant the most to him in life: his standing with the people of Texas.

Austin hurriedly prepared to leave for Mexico City. He left his colonization and land business in the hands of Sam Williams and John Austin. James Perry would manage his private business affairs. The empresario's attitude as he prepared for his journey was a curious mix of optimism and dread. "I go with considerable — I may say — strong hopes of success," he told his cousin Henry. "The course taken by the convention is the true one I think. . . . I can see no just reason why any offence should be taken [to] it by the Government, nor why it should be refused. . . . I approve fully of the application for admission as a state and I think it will succeed." [45]

But Austin also realized that the application might not be granted. If that happened, he would advise the Texans immediately to organize a state government on their own and then present a "second application for admission, *as organized.*" In the meantime, they should obey all laws and give the government no excuse for aggression. If the government still refused the application for statehood, Austin stated bluntly, "I am then ready for war or any thing. So soon as I am convinced that there is no hope of success I shall return as quick as possible by water. . . . The old settlers and all persons will suffer much by a revolution or a war, but if there is no other remedy, I am for going into it fully, and united, make a business of that at once." In his own mind, then, Austin had already crossed the Rubicon by April 1833. It would be statehood or revolution. There would "be no middle course left," he declared.[46]

Suddenly all the plans he had made for a quiet retirement seemed very distant. The mission to Mexico City would be long, costly, and possibly dangerous. As he bluntly told Henry, "The consequence of a failure will no doubt be war." There was, however, one more difficult letter to write before he set out on his journey. Two days before he left San Felipe, Austin penned the following words to Mary Austin Holley:

> I do not know that, in the whole course of my life I have so sensibly felt the extremes which ardent and sanguine temperaments are liable to, as during the last eighteen months. When you were here we permitted our imagination to ramble into futurity with untiring, and more than full grown wings. The result has been what calm and calculating judgment would have foreseen—an unnatural flight, and consequent disappointment. Well, so be it. I had rather at least be capable of being moved by bright visions, never realized, than to pass through the world without being touched by the recollection of the past, the events of the present, or the anticipations of the future.[47]

Austin never explained precisely where his and Mary's imaginations had rambled during their time together. Perhaps he referred merely to his utopian dream of having a refined circle of close friends and family gathered about him in his retirement, with Mary as a key member of that circle. Maybe it was something more; he had occasionally spoken of his desire to "hunt a jolly old widow" and get married once his life became more normal. In either case, Austin now seemed to realize that such a life was a foolish dream, an "unnatural flight." As he had told Wharton several years earlier, he was a "kind of slave," with Texas as his master. If that master called him to Mexico City or placed him at the head of a revolution, then he must heed the call without hesitation.[48]

Still, he could not quite relinquish the dream of a more settled life. "If I succeed in this mission I intend it shall terminate my participation in public matters," he told Mary. "I have contributed very much to the settling of the Country, and if I am now successful, I shall be contented, and think I have done my part." But he knew this was not likely. Returning to reality, he confessed that he was "done calculating on the future." Instead of enjoying the quiet pleasures of life on his farm, he noted forlornly, "I am on the *wing* for twelve hundred miles, on a mules back (not a pegasus) over plains and mountains, to the City of Montezuma, farther from all hopes of farm and home than I ever was."[49]

Prison
1833–1834

Austin mounted his mule on April 22, 1833, and rode west out of San Felipe for San Antonio. Springtime rains made travel difficult, and the 170-mile trip took a full week. Fortunately, the empresario could find a hot meal and a dry bed at almost any settler's cabin. As he slogged down the familiar trace, crossing the Colorado, Lavaca, and Guadalupe Rivers and finally emerging onto the plains surrounding San Antonio, he had ample time to reflect on the political course he was taking.[1]

By all appearances he had made up his mind. He would go to Mexico City to win statehood for Texas and repeal of the hated Law of April 6, 1830. He would do it by diplomacy if possible and by force if necessary. "This is my last effort to serve Texas," he had told cousin Henry Austin before departing. "If I succeed I shall be happy, and will try to enjoy some comfort in [the] future and have nothing to do with politics or public business. If however I fail, and war is the result, I will take a hand in that, and enter the ranks as a soldier of Texas." He sounded determined, but doubts remained. Caution and patience had always been his watchwords in dealing with the Mexican government. There were men in high places who would listen to him, men who could understand how greater autonomy for Texas would benefit the Mexican nation. It would be hard to force a confrontation over the statehood issue as long as they gave him hope for eventual reform.[2]

He would try the diplomatic approach first. An important step in this was to secure the backing of the key Tejanos. At Austin's request the "principal citizens" of San Antonio met to debate the statehood issue. After lengthy and heated discussions, none but Erasmo Seguín would endorse the San Felipe petition. Mexican law was clear on the matter. The convention had been illegal; only the state legislatures had the right to petition congress. The Tejanos were understandably concerned that revolution was brewing in the colonies and that they would be caught in the crossfire of an Anglo revolt and a vengeful central government. Even Don Erasmo, though agreeing with Austin's views, conveniently pleaded that personal business kept him from accompanying the empresario to Mexico City. A disappointed Austin would go alone.[3]

On May 10 he left for Goliad, where he found no more support for his mission than in San Antonio. After a long, monotonous ride across the rain-soaked, nearly treeless coastal plain south of the Nueces, Austin arrived at Matamoros. He immediately was stricken with what he believed to be cholera, which was plaguing the region. Although weak, he made a point of calling on the new commandant general, Vicente Filisola. Austin liked Filisola, describing him as a "blunt, honest, candid and prompt soldier" whose "principles are liberal and republican." Austin assured him that rumors of rebelliousness in the colonies were unfounded. A sympathetic Filisola replied that the colonists should obey the laws and be patient. Since Austin was too ill to make the trip to Mexico City overland, he decided to forward the petition for statehood through Filisola's office—still an extralegal maneuver, but at least it had an air of legitimacy.[4]

Just then an opportunity arose to travel by sea to Veracruz and from there take the short route overland to Mexico City. Austin disliked sailing, but the prospect of spending the summer in the hot, sickly climate of Matamoros persuaded him to seize the chance. He sailed in a small schooner called the *Comet*. Unfavorable winds apparently plagued the vessel, and the voyage, which should have taken a week, took an entire month. For ten days water was rationed and the passengers given nothing but salt provisions. Austin suffered from seasickness the entire time. "I had a wretched trip," he noted tersely in a letter home.[5]

The journey from Veracruz to Mexico City was almost as bad. The stagecoach route took Austin through a war zone—a revolt against the new Santa Anna–led government had already broken out—and it took several days to gain passage through the lines. Then at Jalapa a bureaucratic mixup involving the Texan's passport brought further delays. On July 18, after thirteen frustrating days of jolting, stop-and-start travel on the rocky roads of central Mexico, Austin entered the historic capital.[6]

He found Mexico City little changed since his first sojourn there ten years earlier. The ancient cathedral and imposing government palaces still stood watch over the expansive central plaza of the city. The ubiquitous beggars and street urchins still vied for space with vendors, teamsters, laborers, merchants, and the occasional aristocrat's carriage on the bustling streets. He took a room at the Washington Hotel, a preferred headquarters for well-heeled visitors, and the following day launched his political offensive.

Despite a decade of constitutional government, Mexicans still disagreed in fundamental ways about what sort of government and economy best suited their nation. Austin had approached each faction's rise to power with an open mind, cooperating first with monarchists, then federalists, and finally centralists. But now he had concluded that only the federalists were liberal enough to give Texans the freedom they needed to pursue their interests in land, agriculture, and commerce unhindered by government restrictions. Free trade, open immigration, a responsive judicial system, and toleration of slavery were the keys. With Santa Anna's victory placing liberal federalists in power again, perhaps these demands would be granted.

Austin had been patient. At his insistence, most of the old settlers had been patient. But everyone's patience was wearing thin, and newer arrivals to Texas from the United States possessed far less of it. Austin proceeded to force the issue.

The first few days' developments were encouraging. He called on Vice-President Valentín Gómez Farías, the arch-liberal who was serving as president while Santa Anna was on campaign against centralist rebels, and got a "kind and friendly" reception. He obtained similar results in interviews with the ministers of relations and justice. With the Texas petition for statehood before the executive branch, Austin then submitted to the government his other principal request, repeal of the objectionable portions of the Law of April 6—especially Article 11, which curtailed Anglo immigration. Writing to James Perry on July 30, he expressed "very strong and well founded hopes of complete success—I believe that Texas will be a state in a short time with the approbation of the Govt." But if the application were refused, he reiterated, "I am totally done with concilliatory measures."[7]

The events of August and September, however, took a bruising toll on Austin's hopeful state of mind. Cholera had reached Mexico City. On August 12, he felt the early symptoms of the disease. Absorbed in his work, he pushed himself beyond prudent limits of endurance. "This brought my simptons to a crisis," he later recounted, and soon he was stricken by "excessive purging of a whitish mucos character, great pain in bowels, cold feet, legs, hands, etc, pains over the body—no cramps—moderate vomiting." Fearing the rapid collapse that the disease usually brings, he applied an unspecified remedy. "In about 3/4 of an hour I was relieved by a fine perspiration which I think saved my life," he noted, "for others have died in less than one hour whose simptons were similar to mine." Although he recovered, the attack left him greatly weakened. With probable accuracy, he theorized that his frequent attacks of fever over the years and the large doses of mercury-based calomel he had taken for them had exacerbated his condition. "My stomach is so debilitated that I have to diet with great caution to avoid a relapse," he explained. It remains an open question whether that diet was aided or harmed by the six bottles of wine, two bottles of ale, thirty-six glasses of brandy, twenty-two miscellaneous toddies, slings, and cocktails, and nine cigars that appeared on his hotel bill.[8]

As he struggled with illness, political events presented frustratingly mixed signals. The epidemic caused congress to adjourn in early August without acting conclusively on Austin's petitions. But on September 5 he reported that his spirits were the highest they had been since his arrival. Article 11 of the Law of April 6 would be repealed, and customs duties would be suspended for at least a year. The statehood question, he believed, would have to be submitted to the states for ratification, but it would eventually be granted. With passage of the other reforms appearing imminent, Austin seemed to back down from his militant position on statehood in favor of continued patience.[9]

None of Austin's correspondence between September 11 and October 2 survives, but during that time his optimism faded. Congress did not meet again until late September, and then it did not immediately repeal Article 11. All around him people were dying. Austin estimated the casualties at eighteen thousand in Mexico City alone. "[I]t was horrible," he grimly reported. To make matters worse, in seven weeks he had received only a single letter from home, one from John Austin in June. As he dealt with the pestilence at his doorstep, word came that the epidemic was also raging in Texas. At the beginning of October devastating news arrived. Emily's young daughter Mary had died in the epidemic, as had John Austin and his wife and daughter. There were rumors that Sam Williams had perished. "I am much so much afflicted by accounts of the deaths by cholera in Texas that I can scarcely write anything," a distraught Austin wrote to Perry. "Good God what a blow. And whether it has taken you all off is uncertain. I am too wretched to write much on this subject or any other." It was all too easy to lapse into depression. He closed his October 2 letter to Perry on a note of self-pity: "You do not write to me [no one] writes to me."[10]

Later that day, in this dismal state of mind, Austin penned a fateful letter to the ayuntamiento of San Antonio: "The happenings of the civil war also have frustrated all the public business, so that until now nothing has been done, and . . . in my opinion nothing will be done. . . . Therefore I hope that you will not lose one moment in sending a communication to all the Ayuntamientos of Texas, urging them unite in a measure to organize a local government independent of Coahuila, even though the general government withholds its consent." Instead of ending the communiqué with the standard Mexican closing, *dios y libertad* (God and liberty), he signed it with a new and unmistakably pointed closing: "Dios y Tejas."[11]

Austin was counseling sedition, or nearly so. With his knowledge of Mexican law, he could not have been ignorant of that fact. He later tried to convince Mexican officials that he had only advised the ayuntamientos to organize a state government "in case the General Congress did nothing to remedy the evils of Texas." Thus, he reasoned, "my recommendation was entirely conditional, subject to the developments of the future, a precautionary measure and nothing more." As soon as he learned that Article 11 was in fact repealed, he explained, "I informed the ayuntamientos, and in so doing believed that I had revoked the recommendation made in my letter of October." He claimed that the letter to San Antonio had resulted from a "moment" when, "discouraged and irritated," he had lost "hope and patience."[12]

This explanation does not ring entirely true. In reality, he followed up the October 2 letter with another to the ayuntamiento on October 16, *after* he knew of the impending repeal of the objectionable article. He reported on the repeal but then closed by saying, "I consider doubtful the resolution of the statehood question and thus reiterate the opinion expressed in my last official communication, that all the ayuntamientos must place themselves in agreement to organize a local government under the article in the law of May 7, 1824, as soon as the resolution of congress on this matter is known." In other words, even after repeal of Article 11 was a fait accompli Austin was still urging the Texans to move unilaterally toward statehood. If he had made the recommendation in a moment of impatience, it was a moment that lasted two weeks.[13]

Events in Texas had influenced Austin's actions more than had those in Mexico City. In September, colonist John P. Coles had apparently reported to him that the Anglo-Texans were about to hold another extralegal convention to declare Texas independent from Coahuila. Under such circumstances, Austin concluded, it would be far better "that such organization be made by the local Authorities than by means of a popular tumult summoning another convention." He well knew that a third convention, held in his absence, might drag a divided Texas into disastrous armed revolt. It would be far better to have all the regularly constituted authorities of Texas — the ayuntamientos — conduct a separatist movement with the San Antonio Tejanos taking the lead than to have the Anglos undertake it alone.[14]

Austin's letters to San Antonio, therefore, were more the product of calculation than of a moment of rashness. If the Tejanos followed his

advice and began consulting with the other ayuntamientos on forming a
state government, they could arrest the Anglo convention movement for
a while and buy him time to get home. As Political Chief Ramón Músquiz later explained, Austin's October 2 letter was a "mere attempt to
quiet down the parties concerned." And if the Tejanos refused to follow
Austin's advice? Surely there would be no adverse consequences for him
personally; Austin must have believed that his friend Músquiz would use
his influence with the ayuntamiento to keep the letter quiet. What Austin
did not count on was Músquiz being absent from San Antonio at the time
and his replacement forwarding the letter to the state government.[15]

Congress did repeal Article 11 and send it to the president's desk.
Vice-President Gómez Farías was still acting as president in Santa Anna's
absence. Two weeks after sending his first letter to San Antonio, Austin
again visited Gómez Farías to press the statehood question. Austin had
reason to expect a sympathetic hearing. Along with Lorenzo de Zavala,
Gómez Farías was one of the most outspoken liberals in Mexican politics.
Austin had known him and counted him as an "amigo" since 1823, when
Gómez Farías sat on the congressional committee that wrote Mexico's
first colonization law. Surely his federalist beliefs would allow him to support Texas statehood now.[16]

These circumstances led Austin to believe that he could speak frankly
with the acting president. The Texan undoubtedly repeated what he had
earlier put in writing to the minister of relations, that *"Coahuila cannot
govern Texas; and the latter cannot remain, and will not remain in harmony or quietude united with the former."* Moreover, Austin emphasized,
"it is useless to try to subject or regulate Texas by military force. That
country has to be governed by moral force." Austin later summarized the
outcome of the meeting with Gómez Farías: "I told the vice President the
other day that Texas must be made a state by the Govt. or she would make
herself one. This he took as a threat and became very much enraged —
however when he understood that my object was only to state a positive
fact which it was my duty to state, he was reconciled." Austin probably
mistook the degree to which Gómez Farías was "reconciled" to his statements. But the Texan never would have employed such confrontational
tactics had he not believed that Texas was now strong enough to play

Valentín Gómez Farías. A liberal
champion of federalism who alternated
with Santa Anna in the Mexican
presidency, he ordered Austin's arrest
and imprisonment on sedition charges.

power politics on the national stage. His militant position was worth the risk.[17]

Several days after Austin's confrontation with Gómez Farías, Santa Anna returned to Mexico City and resumed the presidency. During the general's first few days back in power, Austin visited him twice. Victor Blanco, Coahuila's delegate to the national senate, left a detailed account of one of these meetings—probably the second one. Santa Anna called the meeting and invited Blanco, two other Coahuilan congressmen, four cabinet ministers, three generals, Lorenzo de Zavala, and Austin. Near the end of three hours' debate, Austin pressed hard for Texas statehood. On this issue, Blanco reported, Austin "was fought by my colleagues and even more by me," with Austin's opponents "triumphing victoriously." The inclusion of the three legislators from Coahuila practically guaranteed Austin's defeat; no Coahuilan politician would ever consent to surrendering control over Texas and its immense public lands.[18]

Nevertheless, Austin had achieved significant concessions, and he was pleased. Santa Anna approved the law repealing Article 11, although he delayed its implementation for six months. "He speaks very friendly about Texas," the empresario told Perry. "I am of [the] opinion that if you all keep quiet and obey the state laws that the *substance* of all Texas wants will be granted. The appearance of things is much better than it was a month or even two weeks ago." Austin continued to lobby for statehood, but his efforts suddenly had an unexpected and unwelcome effect: it was proposed that Texas might be separated from Coahuila and then be made a federal territory rather than a state. From the Texan point of view, this was worse than union with Coahuila, for then politicians in Mexico City would gain control of Texas's public lands and have an even greater voice in the territory's affairs. Austin made certain that Santa Anna understood the unacceptability of this option to both Texas and Coahuila, and he apparently succeeded in quashing the movement.[19]

By the end of November it had become clear that neither the president nor congress would act promptly on the statehood petition. But Austin had gotten a respectful hearing from Santa Anna and others, and the empresario described the "State question" as being merely "hung up." In truth, he was not totally displeased with the results of his four months in the capital; reestablishment of the empresario system was a significant accomplishment, and judicial reform and tariff relief appeared imminent. "Texas matters are all right," he wrote to Sam Williams on November 26, "nothing is wanted there but *quiet*. . . . It is now very important to harmonise with Bexar. Keep this in view. I shall be at home soon." He gave little thought to the letters he had written to San Antonio.[20]

Austin left Mexico City on December 10, sharing a carriage with liberal congressman Luis de la Rosa and two others. The winding, three-week trip took the travelers six hundred miles through the cities of Querétaro, Lagos de Moreno, and San Luis Potosí. It was Austin's most extensive journey through the interior of central Mexico since 1823, and the leisurely pace of the trip provided ample time for observation and reflection on conditions in the country.[21]

He was troubled by what he saw. After a decade of republican government, Mexico seemed poorer and more backward than ever. The nation possessed rich resources but showed few signs of developing them. Austin blamed the Catholic Church. His party toured many of the churches and convents along the route, and he was amazed at their number, size, and opulence in the midst of so much poverty. "One is astonished at seeing these monuments of the barbarity & ignorance of the tenth and twelfth centuries, preserved with so much care in the 19th century, & in a Republic." Convents particularly irked him. "Marry women with God," he wrote. "How ridiculous." Still the Enlightenment man in his religious views, Austin directed stinging sarcasm at the superstition he detected among Mexico's common people. But what really bothered him was that the money spent on religion could be used for the economic development of the republic. "What a pity," he wrote, "that Rome did not set down as a dogma, that the man who should leave his property to open roads, canals, to establish schools, foment agriculture & the arts, should go straight to heaven as soon as dead. . . . Rome could have made the Catholics the civilizers and patrons of the arts." He concluded his diarist's tirade with a revealing lament: "Rome! Rome! until the Mexican people shake off thy superstitions & wicked sects, they can neither be a republican, nor a moral people." Austin could defend Roman Catholicism as "a religion whose foundation is perfect harmony, a union of principles, & of action." But he condemned the brand of Catholicism then practiced in Mexico— a religion, as he put it, "in theory divine, in practice infernal." [22]

This trip through the heart of Mexico had made a profound impression on the Texan. Several weeks later, pondering the needs of Mexico, he prioritized them in this way:

1st Religious toleration
2nd Foreign emigration
3rd Protection of agriculture . . .
4th The improvement of the navigation of all the rivers, and the opening of carriage roads . . .
5th The establishment of manufactories.

A decade earlier he had naively thought that liberal political ideals would soon triumph and that religious enlightenment would naturally follow; now he realized that Mexico faced a much more difficult road to modernization. This realization contributed to his growing disillusionment with his adopted country.[23]

At Lagos de Moreno, Austin parted ways with his traveling companions and continued northward on horseback accompanied only by a hired servant. For several days he rode hard, trying to catch up with the new commandant general, Pedro Lemus, who was on his way to the northern provinces to replace Vicente Filisola in Terán's old post. Failing to overtake Lemus, a saddle-sore Austin reached San Luis Potosí on December 24, where he spent yet another Christmas among strangers. On January 2, 1834, he finally arrived in Saltillo. The following day, at 3 o'clock in the afternoon, he walked into the office of Lemus, who himself had just arrived from Mexico City. Austin knew and respected Lemus. The empresario was stunned, then, when Lemus placed him under arrest.[24]

The action was the result of Austin's October 2 letter. The San Antonio ayuntamiento had been greatly alarmed by the empresario's advice that Texans form their own state government without waiting for federal approval. The ayuntamiento expressed the "greatest regret and surprise" at Austin's "exceedingly rash" proposal. "It is certainly very regretable that you should breathe sentiments so contrary and opposed to those of every good Mexican, whose constitution and laws prohibit in a positive manner this class of proceedings." The ayuntamiento then forwarded Austin's letter to the state government (which had recently been moved to Monclova), where the letter caused an even greater stir.[25]

The American abolitionist Benjamin Lundy was visiting Monclova at the time, seeking a colonization contract. He recorded the reaction of authorities there. "It is rumored," Lundy wrote on November 27, "that the governor here is taking measures to apprehend Austin, on a charge of treason." The rumors multiplied, and two days later Lundy learned "that S. F. Austin has used very disrespectful language to the Vice President . . . and that it is feared that it will lead to something serious. Austin's recklessness astonishes our friends generally." The acting governor, Francisco Vidaurri y Villaseñor, told Lundy that the "purport of Austin's treasonable letters was, that the general government being weak and distracted, it was a favourable moment to establish, without its consent, a state government for Texas, separate from that of Coahuila." He predicted that the people of Texas would refuse to follow the empresario's lead, and when that happened, the "disgrace and the punishment will fall on him alone." Vidaurri apparently spoke for many Coahuilans in the conclusion he reached; the governor, according to Lundy, "thinks Austin must be partially insane."[26]

On December 11, Vidaurri issued confidential orders to officials throughout the state calling for Austin's arrest. Vidaurri noted that Austin's October 2 letter "contains certain statements capable of promoting . . . a scandalous revolution, especially if it succeeds in being presented in the *Villa* that bears his name [San Felipe de Austin] before the Superior Government of this State dictates the necessary measures to suffocate in the cradle such very dangerous principles." After issuing the arrest order, Vidaurri then informed the federal authorities of the situation and asked that the president take appropriate measures. Ten days later, acting on orders from Gómez Farías, the secretary of war issued his own orders for Austin to be arrested and returned to Mexico City.[27]

This placed Commandant General Lemus in a difficult position. Like so many Mexican officials, he liked Austin personally. Though admitting that the charges appeared to have some substance, he was loath to turn the Texan over to either the state or the federal authorities. Lemus therefore sought middle ground, obeying but not fully complying with his orders. Noting Austin's valid passport issued by the executive branch, and pleading that he lacked the resources to put down any uprising that might occur in Texas if Austin were sent back for trial, he informed the secretary of war that he would "detain" Austin but suspend the remainder of the arrest order until he received further instructions from Mexico City. Lemus politely informed the Coahuilan authorities that he could not deliver Austin to them because had received the federal arrest order first.[28]

The following day Lemus invited Austin to share a coach with himself and his family as they returned to his headquarters in Monterrey. "The Genl treated me with the greatest attention & delicacy for which I am, & will always be grateful," Austin wrote. He remained there for two weeks. "I was put in a very convenient & clean room, with a guard at the door," he recalled. "My servant went out & came in when he pleased, & thus everything was furnished me, nothing was wanted but liberty." Much later, Lemus received an order from Gómez Farías branding Austin a "state criminal of the greatest seriousness" and ordering that he be held in "absolute isolation without permitting him to write or speak with absolutely anyone."[29]

Thanks to the slow mail service, however, Austin was able to send lengthy letters to an extensive list of Mexican officials, including Tejano leaders in San Antonio, Governor Vidaurri in Monclova, the influential Coahuilan politician José María Viesca, and two friendly congressmen. He also notified friends and family in Texas. "I hope there will be no excitement about my arrest," he told Williams. "All I can be accused of is, that I have labored arduously, faithfully, and perhaps at particular moments, pationately, and with more impatience and irritation than I ought to have shewn, to have Texas made a State of the Mexican Confederation separate from Coahuila. This is all, and this is not crime." Self-pity, tinged with bitterness, crept into his letters. If his enemies should consider his actions criminal, he complained, "it will not take me by surprise." He remarked that ever since the calling of the first Texan convention a year earlier, he had been "suspended over the altar of sacrifice." The more radical colonists kept pushing rashly for unilateral action on statehood; liberal Coahuilan politicians and the colonists who benefited from their land-speculation partnerships with those politicians opposed rash action; concerned Tejanos were torn according to their varying interests and the intensity of their fears. "Party spirit and envy," Austin lamented, focused everyone's blame on him "because he was Austin — he, must be suspected and watched — *he,* who has labored so many years regardless of personal fatigue or responsability to build up Texas, settle it and make the fortunes of its inhabitants — bien, muy bien. Such is human nature and such it will always be — I am tired of it and for the future wish to have as little to do with mankind or their affairs as practicable."[30]

In a letter to the ayuntamiento of San Felipe, Austin repeated his request that Texas "keep quiet" and "discountenance all revolutionary measures or men." A few weeks earlier John Wharton, editor of the *Advocate of the People's Rights,* a stridently anti-Austin newspaper published at Brazoria, had printed an editorial expressing the "hope that the Mexicans will hold on to him until he undergoes a radical change." The Wharton brothers, it would seem, had suddenly become pacifists! But now Whar-

Stephen F. Austin with long rifle and dog. This small watercolor on ivory was painted by British artist William Howard at Austin's request when the empresario was in Mexico City in 1833. *Courtesy, Center for American History, University of Texas at Austin (Prints and Photographs Collection #CN01436).*

Santo Domingo Plaza, Mexico City. The building to the right of the church with
the large doorway facing the plaza is the Inquisition prison where Austin was
kept in solitary confinement for three months in 1834.

ton applauded the empresario's request for calm, saying, "The Col. will
find in me a firm supporter, so long as he continues a true friend to
Texas . . . but should he be actuated by an inordinate ambition for wealth
and power[;] should he be disposed to sacrifice the interest of thousands
to promote his own private views, he will find in me, — though there be

no Cassius to instigate, a Brutus with an arm uplifted against him." With such friends at home, Austin could do without enemies.[31]

Back in Monterrey, Commandant General Lemus finally concluded that he would have to obey orders and send his prisoner to the national capital. On January 20, Austin rode south out of Monterrey, accompanied by a seven-man armed guard. Three weeks later he arrived in Mexico City and was put in prison.[32]

When the Spanish conquistadors overthrew the Aztec empire in the sixteenth century and founded New Spain on its rubble, they brought with them the barbaric institution of the Inquisition. In the decades preceding independence, those unfortunate enough to be branded as heretics were incarcerated in a bleak stone building that had been a Dominican convent. After Spanish rule ended and the Inquisition was abolished, the state used the structure to house political prisoners, of which there was no shortage. Here Stephen F. Austin was placed while the government built its case against him.

Cell number 15, which he described as a sixteen-by-thirteen-foot "dungeon," had stone walls three feet thick and no windows. The high ceiling contained a small skylight that, Austin explained, "barely afforded light to read on very clear days when the sun was high, say from 10 to 3 o'clock." Ironically, he had actually been inside this very cell before. In 1822 he had paid a visit there to Father Servando Teresa de Mier, an iconoclastic congressman who had been imprisoned for opposing the Emperor Iturbide. Now Austin found himself in solitary confinement, staring— when light allowed—at "a number of figures of snakes, landscapes &c, drawn by a prisoner of the inquisition, more than 60 years ago." Given that he was a prisoner in a dungeon, things actually could have been worse. He was allowed to have decent meals delivered from outside, including wine and cheese, albeit at his own expense. The prison housed only political prisoners. The guards were humane.[33]

The worst part was the boredom. The guards strictly enforced the order that Austin be held incommunicado. They allowed him only brief periods in the prison yard for exercise, and even then he was segregated from other prisoners and constantly watched. Jailers delivered his meals

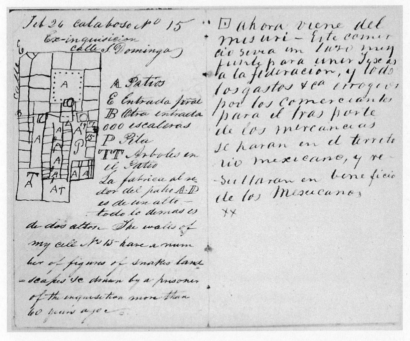

Austin's sketch of the Inquisition prison, February 1834. He was kept in cell 15.
Courtesy, Center for American History, University of Texas at Austin
(S. F. Austin Papers #CN07586).

in silence through a slit in the door of the cell. He began sharing a few crumbs with a mouse, which soon became tame enough to pet. His court-appointed attorney paid a short visit on February 15 to get Austin's signature on a form and then returned a week later to say the case had been assigned to someone else. The empresario's only other diversion was to write brief diary entries with a pencil and small notebook that he had hidden in his clothing when he was first jailed. His requests for books were refused. "What a horrible punishment is solitary confinement, shut up in a dungeon with scarcely light enough to distinguish anything," Austin lamented.[34]

Apart from the lawyer, the only visitor allowed in during the first few weeks was Father Muldoon, who obtained the privilege through, as he put it, the "use of Priestcraft." It is not clear why Muldoon was in Mexico City, but Austin was glad to see a friendly face. Unfortunately,

The interior courtyard of the Inquisition prison.

the men could converse only in the presence of the prison commandant and in Spanish, which considerably limited their discussions. The priest did help to arrange better meals for his friend and promised to secure books, but the books were not allowed. Muldoon, who apparently knew Santa Anna personally, reported that if Vice-President Gómez Farías had his way he "would have suffered [Austin] to rot there without once offering him the remotest hope of his enlargement." "Time drags on heavily," Austin noted forlornly.[35]

Gradually conditions improved, in part because he "loaned" thirty pesos to the prison commandant and ten more to his guard. On March 2 Austin finally obtained a book, which he identified only as "a tale called yes & no." "I prefer bread & water with books, to the best of eating without them," he declared. "In a dungeon, the mind & thoughts require aliment more than the body." Two weeks later he received more substantial reading material, a French-language history of Spain's King Philip II. This book may have provided some intellectual stimulation, but not of the sort that Austin really needed. The story of Philip, an autocratic champion of the Inquisition who was thought to have ordered his own son's execution, only seemed to darken the Texan's mood—an understandable effect, considering his current place of residence. His diary erupted in another diatribe against religious intolerance.[36]

Austin apparently obtained the books through Victor Blanco, the Monclova politician who represented Coahuila y Texas in the national senate. Blanco and his brother-in-law Ramón Músquiz, the longtime political chief in San Antonio, both made exertions in Austin's behalf to secure his release or at least to ease the conditions of confinement. They did so despite the fact that they, like almost all Coahuilans and some Tejanos, had opposed the cause of statehood for Texas. Austin considered it one of the few bright points during these grim weeks that Blanco, Músquiz, Muldoon, "and many others in Bexar" had been so "firm and unwavering in their friendship to me."[37]

Back in Texas, certain Anglo-Texans were not quite so unwavering. For three years Sterling Robertson had burned with resentment over losing the old Texas Association empresario contract to Austin and Williams. Now, as Austin brooded in his dungeon, Robertson rode to Monclova to lay his case before the state government. He had to prove that he had brought a hundred colonists to Texas prior to April 6, 1830. On April 2, 1834, he laid a petition and supporting documents before the legislature. In a preamble to his petition, the imperious Tennessean blasted Austin. In applying for the Upper Colony, he declared, Austin had used the "same Jesuitic and insidious policy with which he has always marked with black footprintes the crooked path along which he has traveled, under cover of darkness, in carrying out his nefarious and perfidious designs." After venting his spleen, Robertson asked that the legislature take the contract away from Austin and Williams and return it to him. Robertson blatantly lied, stating that "in the autumn of *1829*" [emphasis added] the Texas Association had sent him to Texas "with a considerable number of families." This had actually taken place in the autumn of *1830;* in the fall of 1829 Robertson had been busy in Nashville standing trial for murder. (Even then, a total of nine families constituted the "considerable number" to which Robertson referred.) Robertson continued his perjury: "I returned to the United States of the North in December of the same

Sterling Clack Robertson. The would-be
empresario of the colony to the north and
west of Austin's Colony, Robertson
bitterly resented Austin and Samuel May
Williams for gaining the contract to settle
the Upper Colony in 1831. *Courtesy,
Texas State Library and Archives
Commission.*

year of 1829 [again, actually 1830] with the object of introducing other
families. Early in the following year I introduced into the country, directly
or indirectly, more than three hundred families."[38]

Robertson "documented" his assertions with depositions from several settlers who had ended up in Austin's Colony. Curiously, these colonists did not confirm Robertson's assertions that he had introduced colonists prior to April 6, 1830, but instead only swore that a large number of
Robertson-sponsored immigrants had arrived in Texas *prior to April 15,
1831* — a crucial difference. There is no way to ascertain the numbers and
actual arrival dates of most of these alleged immigrants; the few that can
be verified came to Texas at the very end of 1830 or in the spring of 1831.
But the point is moot; for Robertson's case to have any validity, the immi-

grants would have had to arrive in Texas by April 6, 1830, not April 15, 1831. This clearly had not happened. Ultimately, Robertson's cause rested on the perjured testimony of one man: Sterling C. Robertson.[39]

Austin knew nothing of these latest developments, though he had known for some time that Robertson wanted the colony back.[40] But Sam Williams acted decisively, hiring San Felipe merchant Thomas W. McQueen to go to Monclova and present evidence to counter Robertson's claims. Unfortunately, Indians ambushed McQueen on the road, and he died several days later. Before Williams could secure another agent, the governor ruled in Robertson's favor.[41]

At first glance, Robertson's success in Monclova defies explanation. Surely the governor was capable of examining the settlers' affidavits and realizing that they were irrelevant, even if true, because they failed to prove that Robertson had introduced a single colonist before April 6, 1830. Having dismissed Robertson's documentation, he then would have been left only with Robertson's own perjured word as evidence. But two factors were operating in the Tennessean's favor. One was Austin's extreme unpopularity in the state capital. The official who decided the case was none other than Governor Francisco Vidaurri y Villaseñor, the man who had ordered Austin's arrest. The other factor was the likelihood that Robertson bribed Vidaurri. Writing from Coahuila in June, Oliver Jones, who represented Texas in the 1834 legislature and knew the Monclova political scene well, told James F. Perry the news of Robertson's achievement and stated matter-of-factly, "I believe it cost a bribe of about thirteen hundred dollars." Other Texans also believed the story. That the governor could be bought seems substantiated by a letter written by another American in Monclova at about the same time. John T. Mason, seeking to have a land commissioner appointed for East Texas, reported that he had to submit his request, as he delicately put it, "with an argument more potent than words. Nothing is done without a gratification as they call it." Sam Williams's attorney, Spencer Jack, also later stated that the "clink of gold" had influenced the governor. Although the bribery charge in Robertson's case was hearsay, it takes no great leap of imagination to believe that Robertson was capable of it.[42]

When Austin finally learned of Robertson's coup, he exhibited little concern. "I care nothing about the upper colony," he remarked, "except to show that all my conduct in regard to it has been correct, as it has been." From the standpoint of his financial interests, Austin spoke the truth; he did not care about the colony because he had already sold his interest in it to John Austin. Besides, the empresario now owned more than two hundred thousand acres of Texas land. If Texas could achieve political stability and be assured of continuing population growth, his fortune was secure. Whether his name remained on the empresario contract for the Upper Colony was a minor thing indeed.[43]

But Austin had been absent from Texas for a year now, and he did not fully comprehend the damage that Robertson was doing to his reputation. During that year Robertson and his attorney, Thomas Jefferson Chambers, spared no effort to vilify Austin throughout Texas. They circulated bitter public letters accusing Austin of betraying Robertson. One of these, signed by Robertson but probably written by Chambers, likened Austin to Iago in *Othello:* "He would smile, and smile again, and still play the villain." This accusation, according to Robertson, "does not need any special witness because everybody who knows him will certify to the exactness of the charge." Another of Robertson's denunciations referred to "St. Stephen & his trumpeter Sam" and spoke of the "foul representations" that Austin and Williams had used to obtain the colony. "[T]he day of that Judge Austin from whom there was no appeal, & of his successors even more corrupt & tyrannical than himself must cease when the people will it to be so," Robertson proclaimed with self-righteous indignation.[44]

Frank Johnson, a member of Austin's inner circle in San Felipe, described the effects of Robertson's actions in March 1834: "I find the Robinson [Robertson] fever raging in this peaceful land, and am informed that it is raging below [in Austin's Colony] in a way calculated to alarm the fears of every well wisher of peace and harmony. Is Texas like Mexico destined to *commotions* and *Civil Wars?* I hope not, but fear the result of this damnable contagious poisen emitted throughout the Land by Robinson and his sattelites." In July, Robertson published another broadside announcing the return of the colony to him and abusing Austin for his alleged "treachery" and "malice." It was easy enough for those who had

thought Austin too conservative on the statehood question or who resented Austin's land policies now to believe Robertson's propaganda.[45]

In April, Santa Anna returned to power and relaxed the conditions
of Austin's incarceration. After three months in solitary, he now could
mingle with other prisoners, receive writing materials, and entertain visitors. News from Texas began to trickle in. Understandably, the empresario
was troubled by the rumors that firebrands in Texas who had criticized
him for his earlier caution on the statehood issue were now trying to
prolong his imprisonment. With the Whartons principally in mind, he
wrote, "That *these same men* should now try to ruin me and perpetuate
my imprisonment, and should rejoice and exult at my sufferings, is what I
cannot understand. . . . This I cannot believe, altho such a thing was told
me—I cannot yet believe it."[46]

Austin's case bounced from court to court. Nobody in Mexico City
seemed to know who had jurisdiction over the matter. On June 15 the
military court to which the case initially had been assigned decided that it
lacked jurisdiction and sent the case to a local civil court. That court sat
on the case for two months before sending it to the Federal District court,
which in turn sent it to the Supreme Court. Eight months after his arrest
Austin still had not been indicted for a crime, and there seemed little sign
that anything would happen soon.[47]

In June the government moved its prisoner to the Acordada Prison,
on the outskirts of the city. Austin was confined in a room with a window
and a small balcony overlooking the street near the prison's main entrance.
An American businessman living in Mexico City, George Hammeken,
visited him frequently in the prison and devised an escape plan. On a
dark night, when the lone sentinel posted on the street below dozed or
could be disabled, Austin would be thrown a rope, which he would then
use to slide from the balcony to the street. A horse would be waiting to
take him to safety. According to Hammeken, the empresario approved the
plan in the event that his case turned out "unfavorably," but as long as he
had hope of eventual release he would remain in prison.[48]

Despite the frustrating delays, Austin managed to maintain a degree
of hope. "The President Santana is friendly to Texas and to me," he wrote

to James Perry in late August. "Of this I have no doubt. [H]e would have set me at liberty long since, and in fact issued an order to that effect in June, but some statements arrived about that time (as I am told for I have seen nothing) from the State government of Coahuila and Texas against me, which I understand have contributed mainly to keep me in prison so long." The state government allegedly based its hostility on anti-Austin informants—*Anglo* informants from Texas. Although he had been provided no names and professed not to believe the rumors, Austin nonetheless mentioned Chambers and William H. Wharton as two likely candidates. Near the end of the letter, without direct reference to any individuals, he blamed much of his troubles—and the troubles of Texas—on "inflamatory men, . . . political fanatics, political adventurers, would-be-great-men[,] vain talkers, and visionary fools." The letter eventually found its way into print in Texas, where it infuriated Wharton. A radical on the statehood issue, Wharton hotly denied perpetuating Austin's imprisonment. Castigating the empresario's "disgusting self conceit," "arrogant dictation," and "inconsistent stupidity," the quick-tempered Wharton vowed that "when this obeyer of instructions[,] this man of so many personal friends, this disinterested benefactor of Texas, this oracular weathercock, this political Proteas[,] this innocent victim, this maker of mottos, this organizer of parties, this presumptious dictator returns" he would "brand him on the forehead with a mark that shall outlast his epitaph." [49]

Actually a number of factors combined to prolong Austin's confinement. The overworked and underpaid judicial bureaucracy of Mexico probably would have moved with glacial speed in any case. The volatile condition of the executive branch kept its officers preoccupied with more pressing matters. State officials in Coahuila, terrified at the prospect of losing control over public lands in Texas, needed little prompting to do whatever they could to make things rough for Austin. And there *were* Texans who wanted nothing more than for him to be imprisoned indefinitely. One of the Old Three Hundred settlers, Alexander Calvit, wrote to Gen. José Antonio Mexía even before Austin's arrest to say that "we generally hope that you detain S. F. Austin for five years, because really he is very noxious to Texas as well as to the general government." Certainly Robertson and Chambers delighted in Austin's predicament and missed few opportunities to poison Mexican as well as Texan attitudes toward him.[50]

But not all the news from Texas was bad. Austin had not been mistaken in believing that Santa Anna would treat Texas kindly. Indeed, the hero from Veracruz recommended that the Coahuila y Texas legislature enact several important reforms, which it did in the spring of 1834, even as Austin languished in prison. These included a liberal land law, which allowed Anglos to purchase land from the state government on easy terms. Texas now was granted three representatives in the legislature, and Anglos were elected to two of the seats. Austin's nemesis Thomas Jefferson Chambers was appointed state attorney general, an important symbolic gesture to the growing Anglo population, even if Austin disliked Chambers personally. The law banning foreigners from the retail trade was repealed. The legislature made English an official language of the state, extended a number of empresario contracts, and established a system of trial by jury, something unique in all of Mexico. Local autonomy received a boost with the creation of four new municipalities — Matagorda, San Augustine, Bastrop, and San Patricio — with their own ayuntamientos. When Austin learned of the reforms in July, he felt tremendously gratified. "In short," he wrote, "every evil complained of has been remedied — this fully compensates me for all I have suffered." He now decided that statehood could wait. He recommended that the people of Texas, through their ayuntamientos, declare "their attachment and firm adhesion and union to the state of Coahuila and Texas and to the Mexican confederation." As a part of that declaration, he added, the people might also put in a good word for him.[51]

Ironically, this spate of liberal legislation and Austin's earlier admonitions against "excitement" over his arrest had tended to discourage efforts by Texans to secure his release. In April and May the ayuntamientos of San Felipe, Matagorda, and Liberty framed petitions calling for his release, but they were not forwarded to the government. Austin's supporters renewed their efforts only after the arrival of his despondent letters from the Inquisition prison asking if he had been forgotten. During the summer the ayuntamientos in the Anglo sections of Texas issued a new round of petitions. In August, two Anglo-Texan lawyers, Peter W. Grayson and Spencer H. Jack, agreed to carry the petitions to Mexico City.[52]

It was unlikely, though, that the government would act in any positive manner as long as Mexican leaders feared an impending revolt in Texas. The conventions of 1832 and 1833, followed by Austin's provocative letter to San Antonio, had created an atmosphere of great uncertainty and anxiety in Mexico City. In an effort to ascertain the true state of affairs in the far north, Gómez Farías commissioned Col. Juan Almonte to head a fact-finding mission to Texas. Publicly his mission was to determine the needs and document the resources of Texas; his private instructions called for him to "paralyze the movements of the colonists," report on their fighting capabilities, and report back to the government, presumably with recommendations on how Mexico could prevent the loss of Texas. "If the colonists wish to know anything about Sr. Austin," read Almonte's instructions, "Sr. Almonte will answer that he has only been arrested on account of having been accused of having instigated a revolution in the colonies against the supreme government, but that it is hoped that he will clear himself, proving his innocence." Almonte left Mexico City the same month — February 1834 — that Austin entered prison.[53]

Almonte, son of the revolutionary hero José María Morelos, was educated in the United States and spoke fluent English. Austin knew him personally and had confidence in him. Almonte first sailed to New Orleans, where Texas was always a topic of public discussion. While there he read an inflammatory letter from Texas in a local newspaper; the letter predicted that if Austin's blood were spilled, "five thousand swords will leap from their scabbards." Almonte forwarded the letter to Mexico but kept an open mind, for he had also heard reports — more accurate, as it turned out — that despite Austin's arrest, Texas remained quiet.[54]

When he arrived in Texas, Almonte found that indeed most of the colonists were peaceable and industrious. The most incendiary utterances concerning Austin's imprisonment had arrived, surprisingly, in letters from an anonymous American in Mexico City. Signing his letters "O. P. Q.," the writer accused Almonte of being a government spy sent to determine the "best mode or the safest point from which to attack" Texas. "O. P. Q." closed his second letter by urging the Texans to seize Almonte

Col. Juan Nepomuceno Almonte. Special
envoy sent by the Mexican government to
investigate conditions in Texas in 1834,
Almonte's influence contributed to
Austin's release from prison
the following year.

and hold him as a hostage until Austin was released. Almonte soon learned
the identity of "O. P. Q."—it was none other than Austin's bitter enemy
and former Missouri business partner Anthony Butler, now the U.S. consul to Mexico. Butler, who had meddled shamelessly in Mexican politics
since his appointment to the diplomatic post by Andrew Jackson, had no
interest in freeing Austin. Instead, he was doing everything in his power
to foment revolution in Texas, a fact of which an incredulous Almonte
soon became convinced. Austin's account of the affair a year later sounds
paranoid, but in fact it probably comes close to the truth. "At the time he
wrote the O P Q letters he was my enemy," Austin explained, "and yet he
wrote them as tho they came from a friend of mine, and consequently they
were well calculated to rouse the people of Texas into rebellion, and also
to throw suspicion on me and perpetuate my imprisonment, and *this imprisonment* was used by him as a lever to create and keep up excitements
in Texas, at the head of which he expected to be placed." To Almonte's
credit, he could see through the machinations of Butler. He urged the ad-

ministration to request Butler's recall, but his recommendation went unheeded. Almonte undoubtedly would have seconded Austin's assessment:
"I have never in all my life known so bad, and base a man as Butler." [55]

Austin believed that his fate depended on Almonte. Reporting from
Nacogdoches in May, the Mexican envoy did not dismiss the idea of liberating Austin, but he suggested that it should take place only after troops
had been placed in Texas and the territory firmly secured. To free Austin
sooner would be seen as a sign of the government's weakness. However,
by late July, after visiting with prominent friends of Austin in San Felipe
and Brazoria and finding the colonists peaceable, Almonte recommended
that Austin be released for political reasons. Before leaving Texas, he led
Austin's friends to believe that the empresario would soon be freed. [56]

With this encouraging news, Grayson and Jack nearly canceled their
mission to Mexico to seek Austin's release. But Almonte apparently encouraged them to proceed, and he even promised to assist them when he
returned to the capital. Grayson and Jack carried with them the petitions
from the Anglo ayuntamientos; a stop along the way to secure one from
the ayuntamiento in San Antonio apparently failed. In Monclova, though,
they encountered better luck. Francisco Vidaurri y Villaseñor, who nine
months earlier had ordered Austin's arrest, had just been removed as governor and replaced with Juan José Elguézabal. Grayson and Jack secured
a favorable letter from the new governor through the intercession of the
secretary of state, Austin's old friend Juan Antonio Padilla. Armed with
the Texan petitions and the governor's letter, the two Texans arrived in
Mexico City on October 15, 1834. [57]

While Grayson and Jack lobbied on Austin's behalf in Monclova, the
federal authorities moved Austin again, this time to the city prison, also
known as the Prison of the Deputation. His living conditions did not
change materially, but the prison itself was on the capital's main plaza. Its
central location would mean an increase in visitors and thus greater access
to news from the outside world. [58]

Austin's mood ebbed and flowed, depending on what news he heard
about his case. After three weeks in the new prison, he wrote that the
prospects for his freedom were no better than they were nine months ago.
He still believed Santa Anna to be friendly to him, but he was convinced

that the minister of relations, Francisco Lombardo, headed a "host of bitter enemies" determined to ruin him. The Mexican legal system, which allowed a man to remain in jail indefinitely while the government collected its evidence, further soured Austin's outlook toward his adopted country. His spirits reached a low point in early October, and he poured them out in a letter to Sam Williams: "My situation is desolate—almost destitute of friends and money, in a prison amidst foes who are active to destroy me and forgotten at home by those I have faithfully labored to serve. I have been true and faithful to this Gov^t and nation—have served them laboriously—have tried to do all the good I could to individuals and to the country—have been a philanthropist, and I am now meeting my reward. I expect to die in this prison." [59]

A week later the jailer announced that Austin had visitors. To his surprise, into the cell walked Peter Grayson and Spencer Jack. The gloom lifted when they showed him the petitions from the Texas ayuntamientos and the governor. The Texas lawyers also brought encouraging letters from friends and family. "You must have experienced the desolate situation of a long imprisonment far removed from your friends, with even a doubt that some of them had forgotten you or were indifferent as to your situation, to be sensible of the pleasure I have rec^d from hearing from you all in Texas, and knowing that I still occupy a place in your remembrance, and in your regard," he wrote. "I sincerely thank you all." Even more gratifying was the news that he had again been elected to the state legislature, something that he would have thought impossible a month earlier. The fact that he could not actually take his seat did nothing to diminish his pleasure at the honor.[60]

Austin soon dismissed the rumors he had heard about the plotting of his enemies to keep him in jail. He now became convinced that Minister of Relations Lombardo was not "personally hostile," and Almonte's report, it turned out, "was *favourable*." He was especially pleased to find that William H. Wharton had signed one of the petitions for his release, and he sent an offer of personal thanks to his erstwhile enemy, saying that "if we do not shake hands as friends in the future it will be his fault not mine." As for Robertson and Chambers, Austin tried to be philosophical:

"I view them as the captain of a noble ship does the worms who are eating into the sides of his vessel at a time when the waves are driving him upon a rocky shore. The greater danger absorbs the lesser." Still, he knew that if what he had heard about their activities was true, they had done much harm. "When I reach Monclova I can form an opinion as to these matters," he noted, "and until then I shall suspend it." [61]

The arrival of Grayson and Jack coincided with Almonte's return to Mexico City, whereupon Austin's case began to show signs of movement. On November 6 the empresario noted a "very favorable change in my favor" as a result of Almonte's influence. Lucas Alamán, Miguel Ramos Arizpe, Victor Blanco, and Almonte all paid him visits, and Austin believed that they "contributed very materially to my liberation." [62]

The latest court to be given jurisdiction finally delivered to the prison the documents that constituted the government's case against Austin. Nowhere in the huge bundle of papers could Austin or his lawyers find anything resembling an indictment, nor could anyone determine the statute under which he was charged. The Texans finally employed a Mexican advocate to draft Austin's official response to the charges, and soon the government made, in Austin's words, a "verry minute investigation of my case." Knowing that this could take some time, Grayson and Jack made efforts to seek their client's release on bail. "This could only be effected by the exertion of personal influence with the Judge," Grayson later recalled cryptically. "It is needless to detail here, the various efforts that were made to influence the Judge to grant bail to the prisoner." [63]

Whatever those efforts were, they worked. With the help of friends, Austin posted bond under the condition that he not leave the capital until his case was resolved. On Christmas Day 1834 the empresario walked out of the prison onto the immense cobblestone plaza and breathed the crisp, fresh air of the Mexico City winter. [64]

War Is Our Only Resource
1835

The year Austin spent in prison had at least one positive consequence: it gave him a new appreciation of freedom. Though he longed to return to his beloved Texas, the terms of his release required that he not leave Mexico City until the government resolved his case. Santa Anna had proposed a general amnesty for political prisoners, but until congress approved it, all Austin could do was wait.

Naturally he had no problem occupying his time. His private affairs in Texas demanded attention, which he could conduct only through correspondence with Perry, Williams, and others. There was also much lobbying to be done on behalf of Texas and himself. The empresario attacked these tasks with his usual energy, but he still found time for more social pursuits. Despite its troubles, Mexico City remained one of the world's great capitals. For once, Austin was determined to enjoy himself.

He resumed his residence at the Washington Hotel. There he frequently entertained such friends as Father Muldoon, with Austin invariably picking up the tab for the generous quantities of wine, ale, brandy, and gin consumed over dinner. He attended operas, masquerades, and an elegant ball hosted by the British minister. After three months he moved to a house rented by another American, Capt. Washington W. West. Austin's friend George Hammeken, who had earlier proposed to break the Texan out of prison, also lodged there. Austin, West, Hammeken, and U.S. consul James S. Wilcocks developed a warm friendship. Among Wilcocks's circle of Mexican friends was a "very sprightly young lady" whom Austin was said to be "particularly pleased with," and whose family allegedly used their influence with Santa Anna to help win the empresario's freedom. To show his gratitude, Austin purchased expensive box seats for the young lady and their mutual friends to view the premier entertainment event of the season — the first-ever ascent of an "aeronaut" in a balloon over the city. Austin's American friends joked with him that if centralism ever triumphed in Mexico, Austin would be named duke of Texas, and thereafter they referred to him as Duke. "I am in tolerable health and very good spirits — tho much older in both respects than when I left home two years ago," he reported in March.[1]

With his circle of congenial friends and the cultural attractions of Mexico City, Austin might well have sought to extend his stay there. As it happened, the amnesty law experienced repeated delays, so he had no choice. But no matter how much he might savor the diversions of the capital, he never lost sight of his priorities. The city's "extra amusements," he remarked, "cannot divert my thoughts from Texas, and home."[2]

The sporadic reports he received from home in the spring of 1835 left him ill informed about developments there. Since the disturbances of 1832, a loose faction of radicals in Texas, led by William and John Wharton, William Barret Travis, and others, had advocated force in order to secure greater autonomy for Texas. They were soon dubbed the War Party. More conservative men, including David Burnet and Josiah Bell, took their cues from Austin and earned the Peace Party label. Comparing the leaders of the two factions, War Party men tended to be younger, more often single, more recently arrived from the United States, and more likely to be native southerners and slaveholders. Austin considered them hotheads and adventurers, descriptions that had some basis in fact. In contrast, Peace Party leaders were older, usually married, had been in Texas for a longer time, and had more ties to Mexicans. A significant number of them, like Austin, had roots in the northeastern United States and owned few or no slaves. Both factions desired a greater degree of autonomy for Texas, but Peace Party men took their oaths of loyalty to Mexico more seriously and also questioned military resistance on practical grounds.[3]

What the empresario could not fully appreciate, given his long absence from Texas, was the extent to which these political divisions had been exacerbated by the growing size and complexity of Texas society. Following the repeal of the Law of April 6, 1830, emigration from the United States had reached flood proportions. In March 1835 Sam Williams reported to Austin that a thousand colonists had arrived at the mouth of the Brazos each of the previous two months. That same month Alcalde Asa Brigham of Columbia, Texas, described the recent immigration as "astonishing." Near the Louisiana border, colonist George W. Smyth likewise noted that the "tide of Emigration is pouring in from all parts of the United States bring[ing] with them wealth and talents." Although estimates vary considerably, it seems likely that during 1835 the Anglo population of Texas approached, and perhaps exceeded, thirty thousand. Anglo Texans now outnumbered Tejanos nearly ten to one. Had Mexican officials realized the true scope of this immigration, they would have been forced to recognize that for all practical purposes it constituted an Anglo-American invasion of Mexico's northern frontier.[4]

Many of these new settlers sought land in Austin's Colony, only to find that the most desirable locations were already taken and that prices on the open market were on the rise. Those who settled in other colonies often found themselves entangled in disputes between rival empresarios, with the result being confusion and difficulty in gaining clear titles. Would-be colonists who settled outside any empresario grant sometimes found it impossible to obtain their titles. A different problem arose in deep East Texas, where three empresarios—Lorenzo de Zavala, David G. Burnet, and Joseph Vehlein—illegally sold their contracts to the Galveston Bay and Texas Land Company of New York, which then sold worthless scrip to emigrants who were misled into believing they would get title to the land. The War Party found supporters among those settlers whose real experiences in Texas had not lived up to their expectations; the Mexican government, wracked by turmoil and instability, provided an easy target for the ire of the discontented.[5]

Austin also was inadequately informed of developments in the state government of Coahuila y Texas. As the empresario waited for his freedom, events at the state level had taken an alarming turn. Ever since 1833, when the liberal, federalist faction headed by the Viesca brothers had engineered the move of the state capital from Saltillo northward to Monclova, relations between the Viesca faction and their more conservative Coahuilan rivals had deteriorated. Conservatives who opposed the pro-immigrant, pro-Texan legislation emanating from the Monclova legislature looked to Mexico City and to centralists there to rein in the Monclova liberals and their Texan allies. With the state treasury empty and with opposition to the liberal federalism of Gómez Farías mounting in Mexico City, Agustín Viesca took office as the new governor in early 1835.[6]

Like so many Mexicans, Austin had been deceived by Santa Anna's liberal gestures and professions of friendship. It was Santa Anna, after all, who had supported repeal of the Law of April 6, 1830, along with other pro-Texas measures, as well as the empresario's release from prison. But Santa Anna had used his vice-president, Gómez Farías, as a stalking horse for his own ambitions. He allowed the arch-liberal Gómez Farías to push sweeping reforms through congress and then waited for the response. If the reforms proved successful, Santa Anna could take credit; if not, he could blame Gómez Farías. By the spring of 1835 it was clear that Gómez Farías had gone too far. He had alienated the two bastions of conservatism in Mexico, the church and the army. In April, Santa Anna returned to Mexico City and replaced Gómez Farías for the final time. He dissolved congress and had himself proclaimed the sole authority in the Mexican government. He then overturned the liberal laws of Gómez Farías, installed a new congress composed of centralists, dissolved the state legislatures, reduced the state militias to a token number, and abolished the states themselves, turning them into departments. The worst fears of Austin and of all Mexican federalists were about to be realized.[7]

As the legislative session got under way, a visitor arrived from Texas. It was Samuel May Williams. Austin's longtime lieutenant rode to Monclova in March 1835 with an ambitious agenda that mixed public and private business on a scale that even Austin had never attempted. First he laid the facts of the Upper Colony controversy before state officials. Embarrassed by what Sterling Robertson had accomplished the year before, they quietly promised Williams that the colony would be returned to him and Austin, which indeed was done near the end of the legislative session. Williams also received a charter to establish a bank in Texas and then sold some $85,000 in stock to his fellow legislators. Most important, however, he helped persuade the legislature to pass a bill authorizing the governor to sell four hundred leagues — 1.2 million acres — of Texas lands in order to finance armed resistance to Santa Anna in case of a centralist attack. Two days after Viesca signed the bill, Williams and two others bought the entire four hundred leagues before the land was offered to the public. A month later the increasingly desperate Viesca approved a petition from Williams and two others for an additional four hundred leagues, this time to be granted in exchange for the trio's promise to raise five hundred troops.[8]

Williams must have known what Austin's reaction to these schemes would be, for he conveniently failed to mention them in his correspondence with the empresario. Austin learned of the initial land bill's passage from other sources, and it horrified him. "The legislature at Monclova has involved matters in a beautiful tangle by the cursed law authorizing the Govr to dispose of 400 leagues of land as he pleases," he wrote to Williams a month after the law's passage. "I fear this law will [cre]ate much more discontent in Texas [tha]n anything which has happened. Nothing could have been more imprudent. . . . I hope they have had sense enough at Monclova to take no part in the civil war that seems to be commencing. Keep out of such things." Unable to believe that his trusted partner would participate in such a foolish transaction, Austin closed his letter by telling Williams, "I know nothing of what is going on at Monclova, nor of your opinions about these matters — but [I] feel confident they are similar to mine."[9]

The empresario's warnings about the imprudence of the land sale were as prophetic as they were late. In his gambit to corner the market on a vast area of the remaining public lands in Texas, Williams had not only failed to "keep out of such things," he had placed himself at their very center. The result was just as Austin predicted. As soon as word of the four-hundred-league sale became known in Texas, Williams and his

cronies were almost universally condemned as unprincipled land speculators. Never popular with the masses, Williams became perhaps the most
hated man in Texas. His reputation never recovered. For years afterward
Williams and the others involved in the "Mammouth Speculation at Monclova" would bear the stigma of this episode. Austin, though blameless,
would suffer by virtue of his long association with Williams, and he spent
his remaining days denying his involvement in it.[10]

The episode also underscores the crucial difference between Austin
and other men who found themselves in positions of power in Texas.
Although Austin certainly used his official influence for personal gain
on many occasions, he rarely let his own financial interests collide with
those of the colonists. His intelligence and his deep understanding of the
settlers' temperament never would have allowed him to commit a public-
relations blunder of the magnitude that Williams had just made. His grand
dream of seeing Texas flourish—under the benign guidance of Stephen F.
Austin, of course—meant far more to him than amassing more wealth
with grandiose land speculation schemes.

Unable to do much to shape the events unfolding in Texas or Coahuila, Austin turned his attention to the task of educating key Mexican
officials on the issues facing Texas and the nation. During his first weeks
out of prison he published a thirty-page pamphlet entitled "Explanation
to the Public Concerning the Affairs of Texas" (*Esposición al público sobre
los asuntos de Tejas*). In it he persuasively argued that the "true interests"
of both Texas and Mexico required separate statehood for Texas within
the Mexican federation. Then he offered a lengthy account of the circumstances surrounding his arrest and imprisonment, along with a spirited
defense of his actions. Despite his renewed call for statehood, he closed
by assuring readers that Texans were satisfied with the reforms of 1834
and that they were presently "quiet," attending to their domestic pursuits
"unmindful of insurrections, political upheavals, or revolution." After the
publication of the pamphlet, Austin reported that "I have more friends
here now than I ever had, and so has Texas—my exposition has had a
good effect."[11]

He also continued to curry favor with important government officials, especially Colonel Almonte, who was publishing his own statistical report based on his recent inspection tour of Texas. "Col Almonte is the true and active friend of Texas in all these matters," Austin remarked approvingly. "The present minister of relations, [José María] Gutierrez Estrada, is a very enlightened and good man." Lucas Alamán, Austin's friend and frequent visitor in prison, had returned to prominence as a member of the senate, where he numbered among the leading advocates of centralism.[12]

But the key to all Mexican political matters in 1835 was the unpredictable Antonio López de Santa Anna. From the start of his career the forty-one-year-old general had given no discernible evidence of being guided by any particular ideology or principle. Instead, he had invested his time and effort in building a cult of personality around his military exploits, cemented by a loyal following among certain army officers and sustained by the impressive personal fortune he had accumulated over the years. Politicians on all sides distrusted him, and with good reason. His usual strategy was to wait until he was certain which direction the political winds were blowing, then place himself at their head and reap the benefits. Throughout 1834, as Austin languished in prison, Santa Anna had watched the growing power of conservative elements in Mexican society and had carefully laid plans to capitalize on their discontent with the liberalism of Gómez Farías. But he concealed his intentions so well that even the most informed observers could not be sure what he would do.[13]

For his part, Austin seems to have grown a bit jaded in regard to the political turmoil in the capital. He recognized the probability that Santa Anna would move toward a centralization of power, but he seemed to believe that the president's friendship toward Texas and the reforms of the previous year would remain in place, and that Texas would be able to continue enjoying the rapid growth and prosperity that it had experienced in recent times. "The political character of this country, seems to partake of its geological features—all is volcanic," he wrote to Perry in March. "If there is sound judgment and common sense in Texas, the convulsions here will not affect that country. The prosperity of Texas should flow onward like the silent current of a river—nothing from this quarter

Antonio López de Santa Anna. Before
Santa Anna became president of Mexico,
Austin described him as a "sort of Mad
Cap difficult to class." Later, Santa Anna
allowed Austin's release from prison in
Mexico City, and Austin subsequently
helped arrange the plan for Santa Anna's
release from captivity in Texas.

can, or will, impede its progress. This has always been my view of the subject, and hence it is that I have uniformly adopted (when left to my own
judgment, or not controul d by circumstances) a silent, and concilliatory
course. That policy has settled Texas, and if pursued a few years longer
will secure its happiness and prosperity."14

In February and March a series of federalist revolts erupted in various parts of the republic, and in April Santa Anna took command of the
army and prepared to march northward to Zacatecas to put down the
most serious of them. "Genl· Santana leaves in three days for the interior
(Zacatecas)," Austin reported. "He informed me yesterday that he should
visit Texas and take me with him, after these other matters are settled. He
is very friendly to Texas and it would be an advantage to that country if he
would pay it a visit." Austin believed "that the federal system is in no dan-

ger at the present." There would be "some change," he speculated, "but not a radical one." But by the end of April he was forced to admit that "I do not understand [the politics] of the day—who does?" He could only advise the Texans to "Keep quiet and still" and wait to see what happens.[15]

As Santa Anna's troops suppressed the federalist revolt in Zacatecas, Austin turned his thoughts to his own immediate future. Congress finally passed the general amnesty on May 6, and although there would be many more bureaucratic delays before the empresario was cleared to leave, he began resurrecting his long-cherished dream of retirement from public life. He planned to return to Texas long enough to put his private affairs in order, and then, as he put it, "spend a year or two in a ramble" in the United States. The thought put him in an uncommonly good mood: "I am happier than I have been for 14 years, for during all that period my mind has been laboring and worrying for the benefit of others and for the common good. My thoughts are now confined, or I should say are beginning to confine themselves to a narrower space—myself, my family, my own individual affairs. It is a novelty, a new life to me, for heretofore I have thought more of other matters than of my own—but I shall soon get accustomed to it and be much happier. I want some money to travel next year. This at present is all my cuidado [care]."[16]

In June, Santa Anna returned from his Zacatecas campaign to a hero's welcome. Meanwhile, Austin waited for the courts to determine whether his case fell under the provisions of the May amnesty. The matter was once again passed from court to court, but by the end of June the necessary judges ruled in his favor. As he prepared to leave for home, he gave little indication of alarm over political matters. "Everything is tranquil in this part of the country," he wrote to Perry. "There seems to be no doubt that the system of Gov^t will be changed from federal to central, tho it probably will be some months before the new constitution can be framed and published." If he anticipated imminent revolution in Texas, his parting advice to his brother-in-law gave little indication of it: "Keep the children at school. They ought to learn Spanish. It will always be usefull to them."[17]

Austin received his passport on July 11 and departed by stagecoach a few days later, accompanied by his friend Washington West. On July 23 he sailed out of Veracruz on a brig named *Wanderer*. When the vessel docked at New Orleans, forty-one-year-old Stephen F. Austin set foot on American soil for the first time in almost fourteen years.[18]

In New Orleans, Texas seemed to be the chief topic of conversation. The Crescent City had always been a crossroads of travel and trade between the United States, Mexico, and Texas. Out-of-favor Mexican leaders spent their exiles there, plotting their next intrigues. American filibusters plotted and launched their invasions of Latin American countries from the city. A vigorous press kept the populace well informed about all of it.[19]

By the time Austin reached New Orleans in early August 1835, matters in Coahuila and Texas had grown increasingly complicated. Governor Viesca's disposal of millions of acres of Texas lands at fire-sale prices to Williams and his cohorts showed just how desperate the situation had become for the embattled federalists in Monclova. The new commandant general in Saltillo, Santa Anna's brother-in-law Martín Perfecto de Cos, ordered the arrest of the Monclova federalist legislators and land speculators. When Governor Viesca later attempted to escape to Texas, Cos arrested him. The state government now rested in centralist hands. Never fond of the distant state government, Anglo Texans ignored the governor's calls for volunteers to defend the state from Santa Anna's centralist troops. Williams and his cronies managed to escape to Texas, where they echoed the governor's call for armed resistance. A majority of the settlers dismissed these pleas as a cynical attempt by the Williams clique to secure their massive land grants. Whatever chances the Viesca government had for military support from the Anglo Texans had evaporated when the Monclova Speculations became known.[20]

At the end of June, a body of men led by William Barret Travis captured the Mexican garrison at Anahuac, where the collection of tariffs and the enforcement of trade restrictions had recently resumed. Travis found relatively little support for his actions, and throughout July and into August the advocates of peace, led by Henry Austin, James F. Perry, and others close to Austin, prevailed in the court of public opinion in Texas. Even War Party leader John Wharton counseled moderation. With no large-scale military invasion of Texas yet to materialize, and with Austin still absent, most Texans seemed content to tend their crops and bide their time.[21]

Austin lingered in New Orleans for about three weeks awaiting passage to Texas. His only surviving letters from the city were written at the very end of his stay there, but they make it clear that his attitudes had undergone a change in the five weeks since leaving Mexico. He expressed those attitudes in an extraordinary letter to Mary Austin Holley, the first known correspondence that had passed between them in two years. The lengthy letter focused solely on Texas and politics—not a word about personal matters or when they might see each other again. In a characteristic understatement, the empresario stated that the "situation of Texas is daily become more and more interesting." Neither the United States nor Mexico could much longer ignore it. In his *Esposición* and his many letters to Mexican officials, Austin had frequently argued that populating Texas with enterprising Americans benefited Mexico; now, writing to his American cousin, he made no mention of Mexico's interests. Instead, he expounded at length on the importance to the United States of "Americanizing" Texas. He apparently hoped that Mary would turn her talented pen to the cause of encouraging immigration to Texas. But Austin left no doubt where he stood in regard to the ultimate fate of Texas. "A gentle breeze," he wrote, "shakes off a ripe peach. Can it be supposed that the violent political convulsions of Mexico will not shake off Texas so soon as it is ripe enough to fall[?] All that is now wanting is a great immigration of good and efficient families, this fall and winter. Should we get such an emigration, especially from the western states—all is done—the peach will be ripe." Austin was not advocating armed revolution just yet. He still hoped that Mexico would realize the hopelessness of holding Texas and sell it to the United States. "The fact is, we must, and ought to become a part of the United States," he stated flatly. "Money should be no consideration."[22]

Political matters on all fronts were changeable, so it was impossible to predict what would actually happen. But one thing was clear—the empresario no longer placed much trust in Santa Anna. "Gen: Sant[a] Anna told me he should visit Texas next month—*as a friend,*" Austin explained to Mary. "His visit is uncertain—his friendship much more so. We must rely on ourselves, and prepare for the worst. A large immigration will prepare us, give us strength, resources, everything. . . . A great immigration from Kentucky, Tennessee etc, each man with his rifle or musket, would be of great use to us—very great indeed." In his urgent call for immigrants, Austin abandoned all pretense of following Mexican government protocol and cast caution aside: "I wish a great immigration this fall and winter from Kentucky, Tennessee, *every where,* passports, or no passports, *any how.* For fourteen years I have had a hard time of it, but nothing shall daunt my courage or abate my exertions to complete the main object of my labors—*to Americanize Texas.* This fall, and winter, will fix our fate—a great immigration will settle the question."[23]

As if to confirm the direction his thoughts were turning, he visited a bookseller and bought a number of books. Among them were J. C. de Sismondi's *A History of the Fall of the Roman Empire,* Washington Irving's *Chronicle of the Conquest of Grenada,* and James Mackintosh's *History of the Revolution in England in 1688.* He might still hope for a peaceful resolution of the situation in Texas, but war and revolution were on his mind.[24]

One other significant occurrence took place while Austin was in New Orleans. He encountered Sam Williams, who was traveling to the United States to sell stock in his proposed bank. Neither man left a direct account of their meeting, but it appears to have been friendly. Austin expressed his desire to invest in the bank, and he provided Williams with letters of introductions to important men back east. Surprisingly, it appears that the subject of the Monclova Speculations did not come up; in a letter that Austin wrote to Williams just after Williams's departure, he made no mention of the affair. Given the empresario's strong disapproval of those transactions and his warnings to Williams from Mexico City to keep away from such matters, it seems probable that Williams continued to keep Austin in the dark about his involvement in the deals. It would become a source of great tension and eventually a painful estrangement between the two longtime friends.[25]

On August 25, Austin boarded the schooner *San Felipe,* bound for Brazoria. The *San Felipe* belonged to Thomas F. McKinney, Sam Williams's partner in the mercantile business, and was carrying a load of munitions back to Texas. Nearing the mouth of the Brazos on September 1 after an uneventful voyage, the passengers heard gunfire. Looking ahead, they spied an armed Mexican naval schooner, the *Correo de México,* engaged with an American merchant brig. A small Texan steamboat, the *Laura,* had come to the brig's rescue. The commander of the *Correo,* an Englishman in the Mexican service named Thomas M. Thompson, had been seizing ships suspected of smuggling, which of course earned him the animosity of Anglo captains. During a lull in the action, the *Laura* approached Austin's ship. Aboard the *Laura* were Thomas McKinney and Austin's nephew William Joel Bryan. When McKinney recognized the empresario, he began "hurrahing the fact, whirling his hat above his head and throwing it as far as he could send it into the Gulf." The *Laura* intended to pursue the fleeing Mexican schooner, but McKinney and the others first insisted that Austin and the valuable cargo be put ashore. As Moses Austin Bryan later recalled, his uncle "was too valuable to Texas, and now he had just got back safe they intended to keep him in Texas." Once ashore, Austin was taken to McKinney's house at Velasco, where a number of old friends "greeted him with laughter and tears of joy." [26]

Later that evening Austin excused himself and walked the beach until late in the night, "hoping to hear or see something of the vessels." Hearing nothing but the warm Gulf breeze, the breaking waves, and the cries of seabirds, he had ample time to ponder the course he would pursue in the coming days and weeks. That course was still not clear in all its details; it depended on what he found in the interior and what moves the Mexicans made next. But in his own mind he had already reached the most critical conclusion: Texas must be free from Mexico. [27]

It was not a decision born of a day or a week or even a year. His long and arbitrary imprisonment, in which he was deprived of anything that an American would recognize as due process, played an important role in his determination. Santa Anna's movement toward centralism, now a certainty, also loomed large in his thinking. While in New Orleans, Austin had undoubtedly heard stories of the brutal suppression of the Zacatecas federalists, in which Santa Anna's troops had allegedly engaged in two days of rape and pillage, killing more than two thousand civilians. [28] Everything Austin had worked for in the past fourteen years could be wiped out by such a campaign in Texas. But as he walked the beach and contemplated all this, Austin's thoughts must have returned to the vision of the future that he had forged at the beginning of the Texas venture—a vision of a thriving Texas "redeemed" from the "wilderness," populated by industrious settlers, with the once-disgraced Austin family restored to wealth and prominence, all through the efforts of Stephen F. Austin, recognized patriarch of the Austin family and of all Texas. Events had finally convinced him that only independence from Mexico could make this vision a reality. The question was no longer one of ends, only of means.

The next day Austin learned that the *Laura* had captured the *Correo*. He knew that this incident, coming on the heels of Travis's attack on the garrison at Anahuac, would inflame the Mexicans further. After two months of uneasy quiet, the movement for a general convention or "Consultation" in Texas was gaining momentum daily. Word of the empresario's return had spread rapidly throughout the colonies, and he was immediately in high demand as the disunited and confused settlers sought to fashion a coherent response to events. A week after his arrival in Texas he accepted an invitation from the citizens of Brazoria to attend a meeting and welcome-home dinner in his behalf.[29]

Austin got to spend a few days at Peach Point plantation, home of his sister's large family. Emily received her long-absent brother "with a full heart, for she had often despaired of ever meeting him again," recalled Moses Austin Bryan. In her own way Emily had endured as much hardship as Stephen over the years, and the two surviving children of Moses and Maria Austin had sometimes quarreled, as might be expected of strong-willed siblings who shared so many traits. But Moses Austin Bryan surely did not exaggerate when he remarked that "words cannot express the feelings of these two, so dear to each other after so long an eventful and dangerous absence." Austin gathered Emily's younger children around him, holding the smallest ones on his lap, and regaled them with stories of his adventures in Mexico. Domestic moments like these, which Austin treasured but seldom got to enjoy, were about to become even rarer.[30]

On September 8 a large crowd gathered at Brazoria to welcome the empresario home. For Austin, who so often felt unappreciated, the reception was gratifying. "I take the liberty," intoned one speaker, "to welcome you once more to the soil, which, through your instrumentality you have procured for thousands of families, who otherwise could never have possessed a foot. . . . You have raised a monument as imperishable as time;— and babes yet unborn will lisp the name of Austin."[31]

Austin responded with one of his ablest speeches, recounting the events of his mission to Mexico. "I fully hoped to have found Texas at peace and in tranquility," he explained, "but regret to find it in commotion; all disorganized, all in anarchy, and threatened with immediate hostilities." He laid the blame for this state of affairs on the political instability of Mexico and told of Santa Anna's conversion to centralism. "Whether the people of Texas ought or ought not to agree to this change, and relinquish all or a part of their constitutional and vested rights under the constitution of 1824, is a question of the most vital importance," he stated. This question could be decided only by the people in a specially called convention. "Texas needs peace, and a local government," Austin declared. "Its inhabitants are farmers, and they need a calm and quiet life. But how can I, or any one, remain indifferent, when our rights, our all, appear to be in jeopardy? It is impossible." He closed his oration with a toast: *"The constitutional rights and the security and peace of Texas — they ought to be maintained; and jeopardized as they now are, they demand a general consultation of the people."*[32]

Following the speechmaking, the participants retired to a "grand dinner and Ball." Sixty men paid a steep seven-dollar cover charge, and the food and drink were plentiful. After dinner the "long room was filled to a Jam," and sixty or eighty ladies "danced the sun up." Even so, as Henry Austin reported, "the Oyster Creek girls would not have quit then had not the room been wanted for breakfast — you never saw such enthusiasm."[33]

Moses Austin Bryan captured the mood of the occasion. The colonists, he recalled, greeted Austin " 'as one risen from the dead.' No man ever received a warmer greeting and no one ever appreciated such greeting more." Henry Austin, who had ridden "all night through the swamp and rain" to meet his cousin, asserted that the empresario's arrival united both the War and Peace Parties. "Now we meet on middle grounds. Strict

Republican Principles." God, "who ever decides in favor of the rightious cause, will be our sword and our shield," Henry predicted, "and The Texians will be as safe as the Israelites in the land of the Philistines."[34]

Others joined in the accolades. Frank W. Johnson, longtime Austin insider and participant in the Monclova Speculations, wrote Austin "with feelings inexpressible" at the news of his return. "The God of Nature seems to have arranged all things better than even men could have desired," Johnson wrote. "Your coming would always have been hailed by the people as the coming of a father, but your coming at this time is doubly dear to the people of all Texas." Even William Barret Travis, a War Party man whose militant anti-Mexican acts had run counter to Austin's conciliatory policies, wrote Austin to say, "All eyes are turned towards you. . . . Texas can be wielded by you and *you alone;* and her destiny is now completely in your hands. I have every confidence that you will guide us safe through all our perils."[35]

The next day Austin rode up the valley to San Felipe. He moved into the empty house recently vacated by Sam Williams, probably because his own cabin was in disrepair or still unfinished. Although he had neither beds, sheets, nor basic provisions, he immediately turned his attention to pressing public business. On September 12, San Felipe's Committee of Correspondence and Vigilance held a meeting similar to the earlier one in Brazoria, with identical results. The committee promptly elected Austin its chairman, and soon he was coordinating the efforts of the various municipalities to agree on a time and place for the upcoming Consultation. When word arrived that General Cos was on his way to Texas with troops, the tone of Austin's communications turned more serious. Writing to the committee at Columbia on September 19, Austin stated that the "real object" of Cos's expedition was "to destroy and break up the foreign settlements in Texas." He called on each district to organize its militia and begin forming volunteer companies. "Conciliatory measures with Gen$^{l.}$ Cos and the military at Bexar are hopeless," he added. "WAR is our only resource."[36]

Cos intended to disarm the colonists and arrest certain enemies of the Santa Anna regime before they could foment revolt. These included the Texas delegates to the recent state legislature, other participants in the Monclova Speculations, and the leaders of the recent attack on Anahuac.

Sam Williams, Frank Johnson, Robert M. Williamson, José María Carba-
jal, and William Barret Travis headed the list, along with a recent arrival
to Texas, Lorenzo de Zavala. The great federalist statesman and intellectual moved in with Austin, and from their spartan quarters they worked to
keep Texas united in the face of the growing crisis. Emily and her female
friends tried to dissuade Austin from "keeping bachellors hall," as Austin
termed it. "It is a dog's life to say the least," he confessed, but he knew
that if he did not stay in San Felipe "to finish the land business and to try
and systematise our political affairs . . . we shall *all* go overboard." Austin
made it sound as if he were staying in San Felipe only out of necessity, but
he was clearly thrilled to be back in the town he had founded, at the center of events. Unpleasant as his living conditions might be, he was thriving
on the challenges facing him and stimulated by the presence of Zavala
and others who had gathered there. "There is much to do," he told James
Perry, "and it is of the greatest importance — circumstances have made me
a kind of center for public opinion." Whatever sacrifices his current situation demanded, he cheerily admitted that "I am compensated for it fully,
by the society of such men as Zavala and [Peter] Grayson — there never
were better men than they are." [37]

On the last day of September, Austin succinctly described the tasks
facing him: "The formation of a govt. (perhaps of a nation) is to be
sketched out. The dayly progress of events is to [be] watched over, and
public excitement kept from going too fast, or too slow." The Consultation
hopefully would begin the process of forming a workable government; in
the meantime, Austin cobbled together a temporary government by requesting the vigilance committee of each district to send a representative
to San Felipe to constitute a so-called Permanent Council.[38]

Austin understood that without unity the Texan revolt stood no
chance of success. The overwhelming reception he received on his return
to Texas and the numerous claims of both War and Peace Party men that
all were now united behind his leadership probably gave Austin a misleading view of how much unity really existed. Many old settlers — landed
conservatives who had always followed Austin's conciliatory leadership
and who stood to lose much by a bloody revolution — were privately dismayed to see the empresario essentially cast his lot with the War Party.

Lorenzo de Zavala. Liberal Mexican statesman who
cast his lot with the Texas revolutionaries in 1835 and
was named provisional vice president of the Texas
republic, he briefly shared living quarters with Austin.

Those who supported revolution were cut from the fiercely individualistic cloth of the American frontier, and they would be difficult to mold into
a disciplined force, either politically or militarily.

Zavala, who knew something about revolutions, played the useful
devil's advocate in reminding his new housemate of the daunting challenges ahead. Although he hoped that Austin could hold Texas together,
he worried about disunity among the Texans. "There is individual patriotism," he warned Austin on September 17, but "there is no unified patriotism. . . . They will defend their private rights until death; but still they
do not realize the necessity for cooperation." Zavala feared that the Consultation would either declare independence prematurely or, worse, do
nothing and leave Texas in its "present anarchy." The politician from
Yucatán possessed impeccable credentials as a liberal and a federalist,
but he understood the absolute necessity of creating a strong provisional

government, a near-impossible task "among a people where there are no public powers and where each citizen is a king like unto Adam." Events would show the wisdom of his warning, for no one would be able to unite Texans. Dissension, apathy, and near-anarchy would characterize the Texas rebellion for its duration. Not even the great empresario himself would be able to contain the Texans' self-destructive tendencies, as he would learn from bitter experience.[39]

As the Texans haltingly organized, military affairs moved closer to a flashpoint. On September 20, General Cos landed on the lower Texas coast with five hundred troops and marched toward San Antonio. Before he arrived there, however, Col. Domingo de Ugartechea, the commander of the small Mexican garrison already in San Antonio, brought matters to a head. Four years earlier Ugartechea's predecessor had lent a small cannon to the settlers in Gonzales, headquarters of Green DeWitt's Colony, for Indian defense. Now Ugartechea demanded that the colonists surrender the cannon. They refused, and when Ugartechea sent troops to take it by force, the settlers hung a banner on the gun reading "COME AND TAKE IT." In the ensuing skirmish, on October 2, two Mexican soldiers were killed before their comrades withdrew to San Antonio. Two days after the incident, Ugartechea wrote Austin asking him to "make use of your influence . . . to have the gun delivered up to me." This was followed by an ultimatum. If the colonists refused, the colonel told Austin, "I will act militarily and the consequence will be a war declared by the Colonists, which shall be maintained by the Government of the nation with corresponding dignity." [40]

Volunteers were soon pouring into Gonzales, joining the men who had defended the cannon from the Mexicans. On the sixth of October a group of the volunteers, including Peter Grayson, Patrick Jack, and James Fannin, sent an urgent message to Austin requesting him "earnestly to come on *immediately,* bringing all the aid you possibl[y] Can." They wanted Austin to bring powder and lead, but even more they needed his prestige and influence; the men had already fallen to bickering among themselves and their officers to vying for position.[41]

Austin needed time to rest because his return to the malarial Texas coast had adversely affected his always delicate health. Nevertheless, he answered the army's call, and on October 8 he set out from San Felipe, accompanied by Simon, the slave who served as his bodyservant, and his nephew Moses Austin Bryan, who was again acting as personal secretary to his uncle. Austin was so weak that Simon had to help him mount his horse. Three days later the men rode into the camp.[42]

The empresario's arrival, recalled one soldier, "was clamourously and joyously hailed by the whole army." Austin, feeling somewhat better but exhausted from the ride, had Simon spread blankets on the ground so he could rest. Soon the various officers began calling to discuss the army's disorganized situation. Elections for commander-in-chief of the Army of the People, as it was now being styled, were scheduled for the following day. When the time arrived, John A. Wharton, usually such a bitter opponent, placed Austin's name in nomination for the command. "Austin can come nearer uniting the people than any other man, and furthermore," Wharton argued, "it will give us better standing abroad." No one seemed willing to dispute this logic, and Austin was elected general "with little active opposition." Noah Smithwick, soldier, blacksmith, and gunsmith to the army, did not think that Austin "had any personal desire for the position," and Moses Austin Bryan recalled that his uncle agreed to accept the command only after "earnest entreaty." Given the fragile state of his health and his general dislike for things military, Austin probably did not relish the appointment. But for him to turn down the most important position in Texas affairs at this point would have been unthinkable. Neither his ego nor the apparent reality that only he could bring unity to the army would allow him to consider refusing. In his speech to the men at the time of the election, Austin, according to Smithwick, referred to his weak physical condition but declared, "I will wear myself out by inches rather than submit to Santa Anna's arbitrary rule."[43]

The new commander-in-chief moved decisively. Immediately after his election he issued his first order, directing the army to muster at nine o'clock the next morning to begin the march to San Antonio to expel General Cos's army from Texas. Austin's military experience was limited. His foray against the Fredonian rebels in 1827 and most of his expeditions against Indians had been resolved relatively peacefully, showing his preference for diplomatic solutions. Likewise, in his one extended military campaign—the seven-week excursion with the Missouri militia during the War of 1812—he had not seen actual combat. That campaign, however, surely proved invaluable in teaching him the value of organization, military intelligence, adequate supplies, and above all, discipline. Thus Austin included a stern reminder to his troops in his first official order: "The Commander in chief deems it his duty to remind each citizen soldier that patriotism and firmness will avail but little, without discipline and strict obedience to orders. The first duty of a soldier is obedience."[44]

On October 12 the army took up the line of march. Noah Smithwick left a vivid account of the troops' appearance that day. "Buckskin breeches were the nearest approach to uniform," he wrote, "and there was wide diversity even there, some being new and soft and yellow, while others, from long familiarity with rain and grease and dirt, had become hard and black and shiny." A sprinkling of military caps took their place alongside the beaver hats of planters, Mexican sombreros, and the occasional "coonskin cap, with the tail hanging down behind, as all well regulated tails should do." Mounts ranged from the "big American horse" to the "nimble Spanish pony" to the "half-broke mustang" to the "methodical mule." Some men carried the famed Kentucky long rifle, while others sported shotguns or—of great concern to Austin—no firearms whatsoever.[45]

A week later the ragtag army arrived on Salado Creek five miles east of San Antonio. Cos had fortified the town and the old Alamo mission compound across the river. Twelve well-placed cannons made his defensive position a formidable one. Austin sent Cos an offer to negotiate a peaceful settlement, but Cos refused unless Austin disbanded his force, which Austin would not consider. Both armies were receiving reinforcements; Cos's force soon numbered more than six hundred, and new arrivals to the Texan army brought its number to more than four hundred. Two new six-pound cannons bolstered Austin's meager firepower. Among the arrivals was James Bowie, the hard-drinking slave trader, land speculator, and inventor of the knife that bore his name. Six feet tall, stern of demeanor, and a veteran Indian fighter, the forty-year-old Bowie seemed a natural leader of men. Moreover, he had lived in San Antonio since 1828 and had married into the prominent Veramendi family there, giving him an intimate acquaintance with the theater of operations in the present

Col. Juan Nepomuceno Seguín. The son
of Austin's Tejano ally Erasmo Seguín,
Juan Seguín rendered valuable service to
Austin, and later to Sam Houston, in the
Texas revolutionary army. *Courtesy, Texas
State Library and Archives Commission.*

campaign. His wife's death from cholera in 1833, the Santa Anna government's attempted crackdown on Anglo land speculators, and the prospect
of a good fight persuaded him to join the current struggle.[46]

Other latecomers further encouraged Austin. Like Bowie, Erastus
"Deaf" Smith had lived in San Antonio for several years and was married
to a Mexican woman. A native New Yorker, the red-headed, forty-eight-
year-old Smith was tough and fearless, an excellent horseman, and fiercely
independent. He was somewhat hard of hearing—hence the nickname—
which tended to make him a loner. The hearing impairment notwithstanding, he would make an ideal scout. Arriving at the Texan camp, Smith told
Austin that he intended to remain neutral in the conflict, a position that
Austin apparently respected. But on Smith's return home from a hunting
trip, Mexican soldiers had blocked his entry into San Antonio and treated
him roughly. Galloping back to the Texan camp amid a hail of gunfire,

he told Austin, "Sir, I now tender you my services as the Mexicans acted rascally with me."[47]

But perhaps the most important occurrence from Austin's perspective came just after the army arrived outside San Antonio. Juan Seguín, the twenty-eight-year-old son of Austin's oldest Tejano friend, rode into the Texan camp with thirty-seven men who tendered their services to the cause. Seguín had served as alcalde and political chief and, like his father Erasmo, staunchly opposed centralism. Soon other Tejano volunteers began to arrive, bringing the number of Mexican Texans under Austin's command to 135. Like Seguín, many of the Tejano recruits had grown up on the ranches south of San Antonio. After appointing Seguín to the rank of captain, Austin immediately set him and his men about the critical task of foraging for provisions for the hungry army. Besides their strictly military importance, the incorporation of a significant number of Tejanos into the Army of the People would help to reduce the dangerous possibility that the conflict would become defined strictly in ethnic or racial terms, Anglo versus Mexican. Their presence also lent legitimacy to the Texans' official position that the revolt was being fought against centralism, not for independence — important if the Texans wanted aid from other Mexican federalists. For Austin, who for so long had striven to build bridges between the Anglo and Tejano communities, it was an encouraging development.[48]

On October 22, Austin chose Bowie and James Fannin, a young Georgian who had two years of military training at West Point, to reconnoiter closer to San Antonio in search of a site for a better base of operations. Two skirmishes occurred over the next two days, but no major engagement took place. As Bowie and Fannin scouted the area, Austin faced his first serious episode of dissension in the ranks. A number of officers had been elected as delegates to the Consultation, which was to reconvene on November 1. Those men were preparing to leave just as provisions grew short, creating much complaining among the men. Some wanted everyone to stay and fight, some wanted the army to disband and go home, and others favored some middle course. On the 25th, Austin called a council of all his officers. Several representatives from the Consultation rode to San Antonio to participate. One particular visitor, however, caused the greatest stir when he rode into the camp. It was Sam Houston, delegate from Nacogdoches, "mounted on a little yellow Spanish stallion so diminutive that old Sam's long legs, incased in the conventional buckskin, almost touched the ground." [49]

All the Anglo men in Texas knew Sam Houston by reputation. Born in Virginia the same year as Austin, he had grown up in Tennessee and distinguished himself in battle under Andrew Jackson in the War of 1812. With Jackson as his mentor, Houston rose to the position of general of the Tennessee militia, congressman, and governor before resigning in disgrace over a scandalous failed marriage. In 1832, after several years of self-imposed exile among the Cherokee Indians, he came to Texas. Austin granted him a league of land in his colony, but Houston settled in Nacogdoches, where he practiced law, speculated in land and horses, and dabbled in politics. Although a periodic heavy drinker, his military experience, charisma, and imposing physical presence commanded the attention of the assembled officers and dignitaries. [50]

Throughout his long career Houston cultivated a reputation for flamboyance and reckless daring, but as a military commander he believed in caution and preparedness. [51] Like Austin and Zavala, he recognized the critical importance of the upcoming Consultation and spoke strongly in its favor. But he counseled against an assault on Cos's strong position in San Antonio until the army was better trained and had more artillery. Austin listened attentively to the speeches of Houston and others, and soon it was his turn to address the men. Moses Austin Bryan reported that his uncle was so ill that he "was just able to sit on his horse," but Austin's address put an end to any possibility that the army might take Houston's caution as a justification for withdrawing the army from San Antonio. "Uncle in his short speech told them that he would remain as long as 10 men would stick to him," Bryan wrote, "because the salvation of Texas depends on the army being sustained and at the same time the meeting of the Convention." [52]

The following morning Austin felt better than he had for several days, although Bryan described him as still being "slightly salivated." He had won the debate over proceeding with the campaign against Cos, but he had not abandoned all caution. The situation of Bowie and Fannin concerned him the most. With their small force of about a hundred men,

Austin had again sent them out to probe closer to San Antonio, this time in the vicinity of the old Concepción mission just two miles south of town. Concerned that they would be drawn into a fight without the main body of the Texan army to support them, Austin sent Bowie an emphatic order to "make your report with *as little delay as possible,* so as TO GIVE TIME TO THE ARMY TO MARCH AND TAKE UP ITS POSITION BEFORE NIGHT. Should you be attacked by a large force send an express *immediately* with the particulars." [53]

A few hundred yards opposite the mission, the San Antonio River formed a horseshoe bend. The wooded river bottom lay about six feet below the flat, open surface of the prairie leading to the mission. Bowie saw the sunken riverbank as a strong defensive position for his riflemen, and he divided them along the two prongs of the horseshoe. Peering over the rim of the bank, their backs to the river, they settled in for the night. They knew that Cos's scouts had seen them. An attack could come any time. [54]

Six miles south Austin waited anxiously with the main body of his army. Although he had orders to report back to Austin in time for the two parts of the army to be reunited before nightfall, Bowie had taken all day to find the position along the riverbank. Now he sent a messenger explaining that he intended to hold the position. Austin was angry that Bowie had disobeyed orders, but there was little he could do before morning. He told his officers to be prepared to march at dawn, and, with Bowie in mind, drafted an order reminding them that they would be court-martialed for disobedience.

Austin spent a sleepless night worrying about Bowie and his men. Dawn brought new troubles. An entire company from East Texas — the camp guard — had deserted in the night. Austin sent two companies in pursuit but they returned alone after two hours. By the time the army began its march toward the Concepción mission, four hundred of Cos's troops were attacking the hundred men under Bowie and Fannin. It was exactly the sort of numerical mismatch Austin had hoped to avoid. Fortunately for the Texans, the Mexicans were about to receive their first costly lesson in warfare against American frontiersmen. Cos's men charged over open ground, only to be mowed down by deadly accurate fire from the

Texans' long rifles, which had more than double the effective range of the Mexicans' smooth-bore muskets. The Mexican cannon and musket fire whistled harmlessly over the heads of the Texans, so well protected by the riverbank.

Hearing the gunshots, Austin quickened the pace of the march to the battlefield. He and the army arrived in time to see the last of Cos's soldiers fleeing back to San Antonio. More than fifty Mexicans lay dead or wounded on the field; the Texans had lost only one man. Realizing the disarray of the enemy, an excited Austin declared that they should be pursued and San Antonio taken. His officers protested, reminding him of the strong fortifications and numerous cannons that awaited them. Austin continued to argue for an immediate attack, but his officers finally convinced him otherwise. Austin exercised sound military reasoning in wanting to follow up such a resounding victory while the enemy was stunned and disorganized. In this case, however, the voices of caution probably spoke wisely. A frontal assault on San Antonio could have proved disastrous to the Army of the People. Of course, considering the events of the past several days, Austin's decision against an attack may not have been entirely voluntary. Officers and men alike had shown a disturbing tendency toward insubordination. With Bowie, Fannin, and others opposing the attack, Austin probably knew better than to test his shaky authority; he could lose all credibility as a commander in the face of an open mutiny. Democracy is a poor system for running an army, but Austin apparently believed that he had no choice but to defer to his officers when they presented a united front against him.

For the first two weeks of November the two armies played a game of cat and mouse. Austin again divided his forces, leaving Bowie and Fannin south of San Antonio and taking the rest of the army north of town. He regularly sent out cavalry patrols to try and draw the Mexicans into a fight, but Cos had learned his lesson and stayed behind his fortifications. On November 2, Austin called another council of war, in which his officers again voted for siege rather than attack. A few miles to the south, Bowie's officers agreed with this decision and also voted to reunite their unit with Austin's. An insulted Bowie resigned his command and left for San Felipe. The weather turned cold and unpleasant, supplies remained

scarce, and the men became increasingly dissatisfied. Illness and deser-
tion grew worse. Drunken soldiers disrupted camp life. "In the name of
Almighty God," wrote a desperate Austin to the Consultation, "send no
more ardent spirits to this camp—if any is on the road turn it back, or
have the head knocked out."[55]

Austin looked to the Consultation, which finally achieved a quorum
on November 3, to alleviate the worsening conditions. Unfortunately, the
nearly sixty men who gathered in San Felipe, like the army in the field,
were deeply divided into feuding factions and handicapped by ambitious
men vying for position. Austin recommended Zavala to preside over the
convention, but the recommendation went unheeded. Instead, the delegates chose a man with close ties to the War Party, Branch T. Archer, a sign
that the more militant Anglo views would receive a hearing. Nonetheless,
the Consultation was more or less evenly divided between War Party men,
Peace Party men, and a third group of moderates. Only those who were
perceived as having been too long pro-Mexican and those identified with
the Monclova Speculations were underrepresented. This group included
Austin's two closest kinsmen in Texas, James Perry and Henry Austin,
both of whom met with overwhelming defeat in their races for delegate
at the hands of the Wharton faction. Their absence would limit Austin's
influence over the proceedings.[56]

On the first crucial issue to be debated, however, the War Party met
defeat; the delegates voted against a declaration of independence and instead pledged rather ambiguously to create a provisional state government
loyal to the Constitution of 1824 and Mexican federalism. This move
should not conceal the true intentions of Austin, who supported it, or of
most of the delegates who voted for it. Their ultimate aim was clearly the
independence of Texas. Declaring Texas a state of the Mexican federation was a subterfuge made necessary by political and military realities.
Declaring independence now might needlessly antagonize Mexican federalists and unite them with Santa Anna in a patriotic campaign to prevent
Mexico's loss of Texas. "This declaration," wrote Austin, "secures to
Texas *everything,* and without any hazard, for it satisfies the federal party,
and is sufficient to secure their support and cooperation." A declaration
of independence, he explained, "would injure us abroad by giving an idea

that we are unstable in our opinions and it would paralise the efforts of the federal party which are now in our favor, and no doubt turn them against us." In short, Texas needed to buy time—time for Santa Anna to be weakened by federalist revolts in other parts of Mexico and time for the Texans to grow stronger and better able to resist an invasion. Indeed, even as the Consultation deliberated, Gen. José Antonio Mexía was in New Orleans outfitting an expedition to Tampico to oppose Santa Anna's regime there. The Texans could not afford to antagonize Mexican federalists like him, who might distract Santa Anna from Texas.[57]

The vote against immediate independence was about the only thing that went Austin's way during the Consultation's two weeks of deliberations. After that, the delegates blundered repeatedly. Rather than form an effective framework of government as Austin and Zavala had hoped, the representatives provided for a governor and a General Council composed of one delegate from each district. The Council's powers were vaguely defined; it and the governor were supposed to govern jointly. This lack of checks and balances or separation of powers was a near-fatal flaw in the plan and would soon lead to a total breakdown in the government.[58]

Near the end of the meeting the convention addressed the other crucial issue of the day, the organization of the army. The delegates created a regular army modeled after that of the United States—a sound move—but they gave this paper army no control over the volunteers already in the field. With no unified command structure under the control of a civil government, the disorder and insubordination that Austin had battled among the volunteer army would only grow worse. In sum, the Consultation failed miserably on the two most important tasks it faced, forming an effective civilian government and bringing order to the military effort.[59]

Before the Consultation adjourned it chose men to lead the new provisional state government and the regular army. On the civilian side, they again blundered badly, electing Henry Smith provisional governor. Smith, a longtime War Party man with close ties to the Whartons, was an obstinate, narrow-minded Kentuckian whose chief credential for leadership was his intense prejudice against all Mexicans, including the Tejanos who supported the Texan cause. His utter lack of diplomacy and unwill-

Henry Smith. As provisional governor of
Texas during the early phase of the Texas
Revolution, Smith proved contentious
and ineffective. He later opposed Austin
in the presidential election of 1836.

ingness to compromise soon led him into bitter conflict with the Council
and resulted in the paralysis of the provisional government.[60]

To command the nonexistent regular army, the delegates unanimously
elected Sam Houston. That the Tennessean harbored intense ambitions
cannot be doubted. He played a major role in the proceedings of the
Consultation, all the while politicking behind the scenes for the commission he coveted. Houston understood that being named major general of
the regular army would be meaningless at the present, because there was
no regular army. He needed the government to place him at the head of
volunteers as well, or else have Austin's volunteer force disbanded and
reorganized as regulars. Houston's detractors—and there was never a
shortage of them—believed that Houston purposefully worked to undermine Austin's authority, even to the point of trying to plot the defeat of
the troops at San Antonio so that he could take over their command.[61]

Although he certainly used his influence with officers like Bowie and Fannin to help discourage an assault on Cos, proof of a plot to have Austin removed from command or to engineer an actual defeat in the field rests on circumstantial evidence or on the testimony of partisan observers. Delegate Anson Jones, for example, wrote that on the night after his arrival at the Consultation, "I was kept awake nearly all night by a drunken carouse in the room over that in which I 'camped.' Dr. Archer and Gen. Houston appeared to be the principal persons engaged in the orgie, to judge from the noise. What made the whole thing more unpleasant to me, was, that the whole burden of the conversation, so far as it was, at times, intelligible, appeared to be abuse and denunciation of a man for whom I had the highest respect, Gen. Stephen F. Austin, then in command before San Antonio de Béxar, for not breaking up the siege of that place, and retreating to the east of the Colorado." Jim Bowie, following his abrupt resignation from the army in November, rode to San Felipe, where he went on a drinking spree, presumably in company with Houston at least part of the time. When he later returned to San Antonio, he was said to be acting as Houston's spy. Fannin, ambitious for a high command in the regular army, also remained in close contact with Houston while serving under Austin at the front.[62]

Houston's ambitions notwithstanding, no one recognized the need for a better-organized army under an experienced military man more than Austin himself. On November 8, Austin wrote a frank letter to the Consultation: "My own judgement assures me that my proper station is in the convention, and that a man of robust health could do more good as a commander than I could. It is an office that I never sought, and tryed to avoid, and wish to be relieved from if another who is more competent can be appointed. I have no ambition but to serve the country in the station where it is considered I can best serve. I believe that my worn out constitution is not adapted to a military command, neither have I ever pretended to be a military man."[63]

Four days later the Consultation reached a decision that would profoundly affect the remainder of Austin's life. The delegates voted to send him to the United States to solicit support for the Texan cause. To accompany him on the mission they appointed his longtime political enemy, William H. Wharton, and the presiding officer of the Consultation, Dr. Branch T. Archer.

Austin learned of the convention's action on November 18 but kept the information to himself. Despite the overwhelming difficulties he had faced in commanding his rambunctious troops, he remained convinced that San Antonio could be taken. He determined to mount the assault before he left the army. On the twenty-second he told his officers to assemble their men at 3 o'clock the next morning for a dawn attack. The weather had turned bitterly cold and damp. At 1:00 A.M. one of his two divisional commanders, Lt. Col. Philip Sublett, awakened Austin with the news that a majority of the officers and men of that division were "opposed to the measure and unwilling to attempt it." A hasty conference with the other divisional commander, Lt. Col. Edward Burleson, revealed similar sentiments among the men of his division. Austin, according to one of his staff officers, "was greatly astonished & mortified" at this news. Although he still believed that San Antonio could be taken, he could see no alternative but to cancel the attack. With that, Stephen F. Austin's military career came to a frustrating close.[64]

On November 24, Austin paraded the troops for the final time. He informed his men that he had accepted the Consultation's appointment as commissioner to the United States. The siege of San Antonio should continue, he avowed, and he asked how many were willing to remain with the army. About four hundred agreed, and immediately they elected as their new commanding general Edward Burleson, a veteran Indian fighter who had commanded militia companies in Missouri, Tennessee, and in Austin's Colony.[65]

The empresario had compiled a mixed record as general. His worst failure had been his inability to command the unquestioning obedience of his senior officers. Against his own wishes, he had conducted the army as a democracy, with all important decisions put to a vote. The critical element of decisiveness was thus lost. Not once did he actually force a showdown with his officers when they questioned his orders. Austin's warnings that disobedient officers would face court-martial proved to be empty threats.

Still it is an open question whether anyone else could have done better. No one knew the temperament of these men better than Austin. If he believed that overruling his officers would bring a disastrous mutiny, he was probably right. After Austin's departure, the rough-and-ready Burleson faced all the same problems and found no better solutions. Indeed, by the time Austin had been gone a week the army was on the verge of dissolution. Only when Burleson decided to lift the siege and withdraw to winter quarters did a quasi-mutiny led by Ben Milam result in a hastily contrived assault on San Antonio. The attack succeeded with light losses, vindicating Austin's repeated assertion that the town could be taken. At the very least, Austin had held the fractious army together and maintained the pressure on Cos for six critical weeks—accomplishments that perhaps no other commander could have achieved under the conditions he faced. A story in a Kentucky newspaper offered a surprisingly astute assessment of Austin's leadership during the campaign. The item noted that "there is in Col. Austin the courage of the lion: and there is in him, *at all times,* the caution of the fox. With him in command, if we don't hope for a speedy victory, we at least do not for a defeat."[66]

In his farewell address Austin thanked his troops "for their obedience and good conduct as soldiers and men"—this was no time to dwell on their true behavior—and he exhorted them "to be true to Texas and obedient to their commander" after his departure. "The men came up and shook hands with him in tears and silence," recalled Moses Austin Bryan, "for many thought they would never see him more, and knew his devotion to them and Texas; that he had never faltered in the wilderness, council, prison or the battle field." The next morning the empresario, accompanied by his bodyservant Simon and nephew Bryan, rode out of the camp, bound for San Felipe.[67]

The Road to Independence
1835–1836

With his slight build, narrow chin, broad forehead, large brown eyes, and unruly dark hair, William Harris Wharton bore a passing physical resemblance to his political arch-enemy, Stephen F. Austin. Yet it would be difficult to find two men who differed more in personality or politics. Growing up in Nashville, Wharton and his brother John moved in the same political circles as Sterling Robertson and Sam Houston. If association with Nashville's Jacksonian Democrats was not sufficient to place Wharton in opposition to Austin, his life after coming to Texas did. Soon after arriving in Texas in 1827, the twenty-five-year-old Wharton courted and won the hand of Sarah Ann Groce, daughter of the imperious planter Jared Groce, who did not get along with Austin. Legend has it that Austin had once been a suitor of Sarah Ann, and that his troubled relations with the Groces and Whartons resulted from his failed competition with William Wharton. There is no real evidence for this unlikely tale, however. Groce gave his new son-in-law a large plantation named Eagle Island, not far from the Austin-Perry estate at Peach Point. Over the next several years Wharton used his wealth and connections, together with his keen mind and acerbic

William Harris Wharton. The fiery Tennessean led the
pre-war political opposition to Austin, only to become
his staunch friend and supporter after the men served
together as commissioners to the United States.
*Courtesy, Texas State Library
and Archives Commission.*

tongue, to oppose Austin's peaceful policies. After the bitter exchange of
accusations during Austin's imprisonment in Mexico, their political differences turned personal. More recently, as judge advocate of the Army of
the People, Wharton had been among those rumored to have conspired
with Sam Houston to undermine Austin's authority in the field.[1]

In mid-November 1835, having left the army, Wharton received word
that the Consultation had named him commissioner to the United States,

along with Austin and convention president Branch Archer. Wharton respectfully declined. The Consultation's vaguely worded declaration in support of the Constitution of 1824, he explained, "appear[s] to me to be too indefinite to induce foreign governments or capitalists to lend us their aid, either of a pecuniary or other nature." He had originally gone along with the Consultation's decision not to declare independence immediately, for he wanted to "neutralize, or enlist the sympathies and assistance of the federal party of the Interior in our favor." But now he concluded that "both parties of the Interior will unite against us, whatever be our declaration." Anything short of "absolute independence" would fail to attract the necessary aid because Americans would view the Texan revolt as little more than an "internal domestic quarrel."[2]

For once, there was some room for agreement between Austin and Wharton. Austin had also criticized the ambiguity in the Consultation's declaration of causes and the weak, makeshift government it created. Like Wharton, he feared that Santa Anna would succeed in uniting all Mexican parties against the Texans in a patriotic war to preserve the republic's territorial integrity. But Austin was still not entirely certain that a declaration of independence was the only solution; the Texans might still organize a state government that conformed to the Mexican federalist model and, as he put it, make a "clear and positive declaration that it was done as a member of the Mexican confederation under the constitution of 1824." The only other viable option, he insisted, was an unequivocal declaration of independence, the course that Wharton already favored. Both of the would-be commissioners agreed that a new convention must meet to make this determination. Moses Austin Bryan, who had accompanied his uncle from San Antonio back to San Felipe at the end of November, believed that if the commissioners were not given the authority to negotiate the annexation of Texas by the United States, Austin probably would refuse to go. With both Austin and Wharton apparently on the verge of declining their appointments, the government risked losing two of its three commissioners-designate.[3]

By early December both men had changed their minds. Neither gave specific reasons, but perhaps they took encouragement from the fact that the General Council agreed on the need for a new convention. On Decem-

ber 2, Austin personally appeared before the Council and argued that the
convention should be called "as soon as possible." Council member John
Wharton, no doubt echoing the views of his brother, endorsed Austin's
call and suggested that the convention meet on January 15. The Council
ultimately decided on the later date of March 1, an unfortunate delay. But
at least there would be a convention. Austin and Wharton put aside their
misgivings and, along with Archer, accepted their commissions.[4]

Austin spent Christmas Day 1835 at the mouth of the Brazos River
preparing for another long absence from Texas. He once again left his
private business affairs in the care of James Perry. Sam Williams, dogged
by the unpopularity of his land speculation deals at Monclova, would not
be home from the United States for some time. However, Austin owned
some land at the mouth of the river, and when Williams returned, the two
longtime associates, along with Thomas McKinney, planned to develop
the town of Quintana there. "Williams is a good hand at arranging speculations of this kind to the best advantage," the empresario told Perry.[5]

The three commissioners sailed for New Orleans on December 26.
Austin must have known that he risked losing his treasured standing as
leader of the Texans by disappearing just as the real war was beginning.
But under the circumstances, the decision to undertake the mission made
sense. Austin was clearly unsuited to military life and made no secret of
it. Likewise, everyone knew that he excelled at diplomacy. He could take
comfort from the examples of Benjamin Franklin, who similarly served his
country in France during the American Revolution, and Thomas Jefferson, whose diplomatic posting in France was followed by his election to
the presidency. Moreover, Austin had to consider the fact that the government—such as it was—had appointed him, and it was his patriotic duty
to obey the call. The diplomatic mission would give him a chance to visit
the United States, something he had been planning ever since his release
from prison. Serious as the mission was, he might even enjoy it.

Except for the matter of his traveling companions. Wharton, he complained, was "a man that I cannot act with—a man whose conduct proves
that he is destitute of political honesty, and whose attention is much more
devoted to injure me than to serve the country. . . . Dr. Archer, I believe,

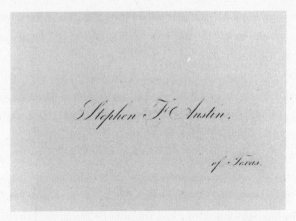

Stephen F. Austin's calling card. Austin probably had
these cards printed for his diplomatic mission to the
United States in 1836. He obviously believed that the
leading citizen of Texas needed no identification
other than the simple announcement
"Stephen F. Austin, of Texas."

is governed by pure intentions, but he is very wild, as I think as to his politics. . . . Associated with such men, what have I to expect? or what has the country to hope?"[6]

He had equally little confidence in the provisional government. "The fact is that Texas is now in the hands of a party, and the whole objects of this party are to retain the power and serve themselves," he charged. "If they are not checked they will saddle the people with an army and a debt, and involve them in a war that will be difficult to bear." The old gloom and self-pity followed him like a shadow. "I find that I have but little to expect . . . and that I can be of but little use to Texas. . . . I have been called to go, and I obey the call; but if party influence and low intrigues and cabals are to govern Texas, I wish to have as little to do with her affairs in [the] future as possible."[7]

Bitterness mixed with his pessimism. "Perhaps I am myself somewhat to blame. My unsuspicious disposition and the great importance I have always attached to union and harmony, may have led me into errors by trusting and countenancing men who were unworthy of my notice or of confidence." Now those War Party men to whom he had reached out in the spirit of nonpartisanship had betrayed him and seemingly controlled the government. "I have never been a party man," he declared, but in the future the lines should be clearly drawn so the people could judge for themselves. "Jackson's rule is a true one," he said, " 'everything for friends and nothing for enemies.' " This uncharacteristic endorsement of partisanship would not last long. Soon he would again be calling for unity and cooperation, calls that his fellow Texans refused to heed.[8]

The weeklong voyage to New Orleans gave the commissioners time to become better acquainted and to discuss their impending mission. Their instructions called for them to negotiate a million-dollar loan, receive donations, buy munitions and supplies for the army, purchase naval vessels, and encourage volunteers. On the matter of annexation, which Austin now advocated, they were empowered only to learn the attitude of the American government; they were to await the governor's authorization before conducting actual negotiations.[9]

On the evening of January 6 they attended "one of the largest and most respectable meetings ever held in the city of New Orleans." Each commissioner took his turn addressing the gathering, and the meeting ended with the passage of resolutions praising the Texan struggle for "truth, light and liberty, against tyranny, priestcraft and military domination." Only two weeks after leaving Texas, Austin changed his mind about the expediency of delaying a declaration of independence. In New Orleans he learned that Santa Anna definitely had begun marching north toward Texas with a large army. Based on public opinion in New Orleans, Austin concluded that only a fight for independence would arouse Americans' sympathy and bring the aid that was so desperately needed. Wharton had been right about the futility of courting Mexican federalists.[10]

The day after the New Orleans meeting the empresario wrote several letters home. To Henry Austin he stated, "*I go for Independence.* . . . I advise you to take an open and bold stand for Independence at once. I hope all my friends will do the same. . . . I am informed that the Federal Party have done nothing for us — and will do nothing. If so it is a folly to maintain our present position any longer." He admitted that caution had caused him to counsel against a declaration while in Texas. Writing to Sam Houston, he explained that he felt a "heavy responsibility" to the families he had brought to Texas. "I have felt it to be my duty to be very cautious in involving the pioneers and actual settlers of that country, by any act of mine, until I was fully and clearly convinced of its necessity, and of the capabilities of our resources to sustain it." But now he had crossed the Rubicon of independence publicly, as he had done privately four months ago.[11]

To cousin Mary in Kentucky he now expressed exuberance over the prospect of an independent Texas. "The War for Liberty goes on prosperously, so far, in Texas," he wrote. "It must, and will, end in Independence — *a full Declaration* will be made in March. . . . A new republic is about to rear its independent banner over a country but lately a wilderness. There is magnificence in the idea — prosperity freedom and glory in the results." Texas would need aid from the United States, but he believed that if the Texans could "weather the storm until June all will end well and prosperously." Before closing his letter to Mary, he voiced the hope that he could visit her in Lexington. But it was clear that the visit was official, not personal. The entire letter had been devoted to the situation in Texas. With more paper, he noted, he could write even more about it. The subject "is a copious one, and I am perhaps rather enthusiastic in the view I take of it. My whole heart and soul is devoted to it. I am well."[12]

The results of the New Orleans stop encouraged him. Besides finding "great enthusiasm in favor of Texas in this city, and all over the U.S. — a thousand fold more than I had any idea of" — the commissioners succeeded in negotiating two loans totaling $250,000. Unfortunately, they received only 20 percent of that amount immediately; the balance was to be paid when the March convention ratified the loans. The lenders stipulated an interest rate of 8 percent, but they retained the option to take land in repayment at the rate of fifty cents an acre, which they fully intended to do. Since the government had no money and would almost certainly be unable to repay in cash, all parties understood that the practical effect of the commissioners' work was to sell massive amounts of Texas lands to wealthy American land speculators. Despite the stiff terms, Austin was pleased with the results.[13] Sensitive to the accusation that they were squandering the public domain, he took pains to point out that the terms of these loans were vastly more favorable to Texas than the Monclova legislature's near-giveaway of eight hundred leagues the previous year.[14]

Wharton left for Nashville on January 16, leaving Austin and Archer in New Orleans to finish the commissioners' business there. Scarcely a day passed without some new rumor from Texas. One such report troubled Austin considerably. Mosely Baker supposedly had gotten up a mob at San Felipe with the aim of destroying the provisional state government and restoring the old state of Coahuila y Texas. As one of the participants in the infamous Monclova Speculations, Baker, like Sam Williams, Thomas McKinney, and others, might plausibly have financial interests in seeing Texas remain attached to Coahuila, whose legislature had sanctioned their speculations.[15]

The rumor apparently proved untrue, but the Monclova Speculations continued to fester in the midst of Texan affairs. If one of the speculators supported military resistance to Santa Anna, the public assumed that it was because Santa Anna had annulled the speculative contracts. If a speculator opposed independence, it was to protect his speculation. For Austin the problem was twofold. First, it created divisions among the Texans at a time when unity was needed. Second, since most of the speculators were friends and associates of the empresario, the public often assumed that Austin had taken part in the deals. "God poured upon Texas his most bitter wrath, when he suffered the last Monclova Legislature (of most infamous memory) to meet at all," Austin bitterly wrote. "*Years* will not relieve Texas from the evils produced by that legislature."[16]

The issue threatened to estrange Austin from the members of his inner circle. The situation of Thomas McKinney illustrates the problem. The enterprising McKinney, business partner with Williams, had taken part in the speculations. In 1835, McKinney devoted his resources to the resistance against Santa Anna (who, it will be remembered, had annulled the Monclova land contracts and dissolved the legislature). But McKinney vehemently opposed independence for Texas, presumably because he knew that the Texas government would also annul the contracts. He watched with anger and dismay as Texas moved closer to a declaration. As Austin was leaving Texas, McKinney lamented that a "wild unthinking faction" (that is, the War Party) was gaining the upper hand. "God forbid" that Austin would join them. "You have the power of saving Texas if you will exert it," he implored the empresario. "What is to become of us?"[17]

Realizing where McKinney stood, Austin wrote from New Orleans urging him to support independence. When McKinney received the letter, he replied that he and Austin must now "sever totaly in any thing of a political character" and that his confidence in Austin was "for ever at an end." Blaming all his troubles on Austin, McKinney declared, "I do not intend to say you are dishonest no Sir but you are from your nature useless in any thing like a public capacity."[18]

Losing McKinney's friendship hurt, but more troubling was the situation with Williams. Ever since learning of Williams's participation in the Monclova Speculations, Austin had consistently given his longtime friend the benefit of the doubt. "Great pains have been taken by my enemies and Williams' to sow suspicion in my mind against him," Austin confided to Perry just before his departure. "All this is intrigue of the basest kind. . . . My confidence in him is in no way affected by such efforts." It is a near certainty that at this point the empresario had never learned all the details of the Speculations or of the precise role of Williams, McKinney, and several more of his close associates in the matter. But Austin knew that it was unlike Williams not to write him more frequently. Letters had been scarce since the news of the Speculations broke. Austin was worried. "No news from W.," he told McKinney. "I fear he is dreaming somewhere. God grant that his dreams may be less injurious to Texas than some which were drempt at Monclova." Over the next seven months, Austin would discover just how injurious Williams's "dreams" had been—injurious to Texas and especially to Stephen F. Austin.[19]

Austin and Archer boarded a steamboat on about January 25 and sailed up the Mississippi River. The weather turned bitterly cold, and their trip was delayed by icebound rivers and roads. Finally arriving in Nashville on about February 8, they found Wharton sick in bed with the flu, which Austin promptly caught. Ill health and bad weather, however, did not prevent the commissioners from attending another enthusiastic meeting publicizing the Texas cause. Although glowing resolutions of support did not translate into hard cash, Austin's confidence continued to rise. "We can get all the aid we need to sustain our independence," he asserted, "and I think it will not be difficult to procure the recognition of the U.S.

Govt. Nothing is wanted but union and concert of action and of purpose at home and an unqualified declaration of independence at once." [20]

As Austin wrote these words, both unity and a declaration seemed far away. Governor Smith, representing War Party views, found himself increasingly isolated from his General Council, whose membership shifted to include a majority of conservative Peace Party men hesitant to push for independence. In January, Smith suspended the entire Council, branding them "scoundrels" in an intemperate letter, and assumed sole authority over the provisional government until the new convention could meet. The Council promptly impeached and deposed Smith, replacing him with Lt. Gov. J. W. Robinson. The Mexican government, whose instability Anglo-Texans so often criticized, seemed almost serene in comparison with the virtual anarchy in Texas. Had the plight of the Texans not been so deadly serious, it would have been comical. But Texas could not afford political paralysis. On February 16, Santa Anna pushed his army across the Rio Grande. [21]

Austin's unwillingness to endorse independence before leaving Texas had contributed to the crisis in the state government. Many of the leaders in the anti-Smith movement had followed the empresario's cautious policy and were still following it even after Austin pronounced for independence. Smith blamed Austin. Writing to Smith after the commissioners' departure from Nashville, William Wharton's wife, Sarah, tried to defend Austin, attributing the change in the empresario's political stance "more to a want of moral courage than baseness of principle. You would be astonished to see how warm he now is for independence," Sarah exclaimed. [22]

The weather slowly improved, as did Austin's health. By the end of February he and Archer could proceed to their next destination, Louisville, although Wharton was still too sick to travel and had to be left in Nashville. The war in Texas and the weather had conspired to prevent much news from reaching the commissioners, and they were growing anxious. It would be "almost useless for us to appear in Washington," wrote Austin and Archer to Smith on March 3. Significant aid from the United States and possible annexation required diplomatic recognition, which could not be obtained without a declaration of independence. In reality, the long-awaited convention had met the day before at Washington-on-the-Brazos and issued the declaration, but there was no way for the commissioners to know this. They pleaded with Smith to send the declaration to them "*by express*, with full powers to act under it," if he had not done so already.[23]

Though hamstrung by the silence from Texas, the commissioners had a mission to fulfill. On the evening of March 7, a "very large audience of Ladies and Gentlemen" assembled at the Second Presbyterian Church of Louisville. Austin spoke for more than an hour. Not surprisingly, he made his appeal for aid in patriotic language that Jacksonian Americans could understand and appreciate. The war in Texas, he began, "is the cause of light and liberty;—the same holy cause for which our forefathers fought and bled:—the same that has an advocate in the bosom of every freeman, no matter in what country, or by what it may be contended for." He gave a detailed history of Texas since 1821, emphasizing, as he always did, the many hardships that the colonists overcame in order to redeem the land from its "wilderness" state. He then outlined the many "guaranties" that the Mexican government had made to the settlers, including their right to separate statehood from Coahuila whenever they could sustain it. He was imprisoned in Mexico without being formally charged with a crime, an incident that not only violated his constitutional rights but was an outrage against the people of Texas, whom he represented. "Our forefathers in '76 flew to arms for much less," he noted, but the Texans "forebore and remained quiet"—a slight exaggeration on Austin's part, but of course this was propaganda, and certain liberties could be taken with the facts. Austin declared that when Santa Anna switched allegiance to the "aristocratic and church party," abrogated the Constitution of 1824, and abolished the federal form of government, the Texans were fully justified in resisting.[24]

Here Austin posed a rhetorical question: "*What are the objects and intentions of the people of Texas?* To this we reply that our object is *freedom*—civil and religious freedom—emancipation from that government and that people who . . . have shown that they were incapable of self government, and that all hopes of anything like stability or rational liberty in their political institutions—at least for many years—are vain and fallacious." What followed was, in part, a subtle defense of his cautious policies since 1833. The Texans sought their deserved freedom first as a state of the Mexican federation, but events had now rendered that prospect impossible. The only remaining options were independence or annexation. He placed a rather artful construction on the current lack of a declaration of independence, saying that the acts of Mexico had rendered Texas independent by default, because the Consultation's declaration of causes in November had stipulated that Texas would remain faithful to Mexico only "so long as that nation is governed by the constitution and laws that were framed for the government of the political association." Austin took great pains to refute the charge that the Texans were ungrateful to Mexico. If anything, he suggested, it was Mexico that had been ungrateful to the Texans who by the sweat of their brows made a worthless wilderness valuable at no cost to the government.

Austin closed his speech with a classic expression of what would someday become known as Manifest Destiny. "The emancipation of Texas," he asserted,

> will extend the principles of self government over a rich and neighboring country, and open a vast field there for enterprise, wealth, and happiness. . . . It will promote and accelerate the march of the present age, for it will open a door through which a bright and constant stream of light and intelligence will flow from this great northern fountain over the benighted region of Mexico.
>
> That nation of our continent will be regenerated; freedom of conscience and rational liberty will take root in that distant and, by nature, much favored land, in which for ages past the upas banner of the inquisition, of intolerance, and of despotism has paralized, and sickened, and deadened every effort of civil and religious liberty.

But speaking as he was before a slave-state audience, his paean to Manifest Destiny was delivered in a distinctly Southern voice. Texas independence was not just a fight for liberty, but it was necessary in order to protect the "southwestern frontier — the weakest and most vulnerable in the nation" from "mistaken philanthropists, and wild fanatics" who "might attempt a system of intervention in the domestic concerns of the South, which might lead to a servile war, or at least jeopardize the tranquility of Louisiana and the neighboring States." Austin clearly felt uneasy bringing up the subject of slavery. "This view of the subject is a very important one," he explained, "so much so that a bare allusion to it is sufficient to direct the mind to the various interests and results, immediate and remote, that are involved."

Seated in the audience that night was one listener who needed no lesson in Texas history. Samuel May Williams was on his way back to Texas after a long trip to the East to sell stock in his bank. After the fighting commenced, he had also done his part to raise funds, buy provisions, outfit ships, and recruit men for the war effort. It was mere happenstance that he and Austin arrived in Louisville at the same time. Happy, and probably relieved, to see his old friend after so many months incommunicado, Austin apparently saw no need to bring up the matter of the Monclova Speculations. That was old history. Instead, the two discussed the war effort, the climate of opinion in the United States, and Williams's bank. Williams showed Austin the bank notes he had had engraved in Philadelphia, and Austin took some of them to show off as proof of economic progress in Texas. It was their last face-to-face meeting.[25]

Austin now faced a difficult decision. Bad weather and illness had put the commissioners behind schedule. Cincinnati was the next planned stop, but Austin badly wanted to visit Lexington, Kentucky, where he could promote the cause among his extensive network of college friends. He would also get to see Mary Austin Holley for the first time since that long-ago Christmas holiday in Texas. He put Archer on the boat to Cincinnati and set out for Lexington. After fifteen grueling hours in a bumpy coach on an icy road, he arrived at Mary's doorstep.[26]

Mary must have been saddened to see the extent to which Stephen had aged in the four years since their last meeting. His long ordeal in Mexico, two months in the field with the army, and his repeated bouts with illness had taken their toll. His hair was thinner, and the long sideburns he had grown seemed to accentuate the lines in his face and the ever-present sadness in his brown eyes.[27]

In the warmth of Mary's parlor on Constitution Street, the cousins caught up on all the news of family, friends, and the Texan struggle. Stephen gave Mary the manuscript of his Louisville address, and she promised to get it published in Kentucky newspapers. She also asked

Stephen F. Austin near the end of his life. This likeness, which shows the effects of illness and hardship, was probably painted for either Henry Austin or Mary Austin Holley. The image later appeared on Republic of Texas fifty-dollar bills. *Courtesy, Texas State Library and Archives Commission.*

permission to include it in her new book on Texas, to which the empresario readily agreed. Together they discussed plans to have the ladies of Lexington sponsor a company of volunteers for Texas, and Austin even showed her his design for a flag for the proposed company—a horrendous amalgam of the Union Jack, the Stars and Stripes, and the Mexican flag, all with a sun in the middle radiating beams of liberty, with the head of George Washington at its center. He had earlier proposed a similar one for Texas itself. Stephen F. Austin was a man of many talents; flag design was not among them.[28]

Austin stayed only one night in Lexington. Before his departure, he and Mary visited several of Austin's old friends, who pledged their support to the Texas cause. At nine o'clock on Sunday evening he boarded the stage for Cincinnati and waved a final goodbye to Mary.[29]

Austin rejoined his fellow commissioners on the Ohio River. More public meetings were held in Cincinnati and Maysville, and by the end of March the Texans had arrived in Washington, D.C. There their efforts to arrange loans and secure recognition from the American government continued to be frustrated by the lack of a declaration of independence from Texas. Word of the March 2 declaration finally came through the newspapers, but without formal notification from the Texas government, and lacking proper diplomatic authority to negotiate either recognition or annexation, the commissioners could accomplish nothing. Their desperate letters to "the Government" of Texas (not knowing who was really in charge there) went unanswered. All three commissioners were confident that both diplomatic recognition and substantial loans would be forthcoming if only they would hear from Texas.[30]

After a week in the capital the Texans split up, Archer going south to Richmond and Austin north to New York by way of Baltimore and Philadelphia. Wharton, because of his personal acquaintance with fellow Tennessean Andrew Jackson, was better connected in Washington and stayed there. In Philadelphia, Austin unsuccessfully approached Nicholas Biddle, president of the Bank of the United States, about a half-million-dollar loan. On April 12 the empresario arrived in New York City and checked into the American Hotel. Over the next three weeks he met with the leading financiers and politicians of the city. The high point was another large public meeting, held in the Masonic Hall on April 26. By this time sketchy reports of the fall of the Alamo and the massacre of three hundred Texan prisoners at Goliad had reached the East Coast. The tone of Austin's public utterances grew more strident. On May 4, Austin wrote a letter to L. F. Linn, U.S. senator from Missouri. The letter was widely published in American newspapers, which Austin probably intended. Its tone demonstrates the extent to which the empresario had been forced to turn his back—at least publicly—on Mexico and its people.[31]

"A war of extermination is raging in Texas," he wrote, "a war of barbarism and of despotic principles, waged by the mongrel Spanish-Indian and Negro race, against civilization and the Anglo-American race." He recounted the fifteen years in which he had labored "like a slave to *Americanize Texas*" so that the southwestern frontier of the United States would be safe. "But the Anglo-American foundation, this nucleus of republicanism, is to be broken up," he declared, "and its place supplied by a population of Indians, Mexicans, and renegadoes, all mixed together, and all the natural enemies of white men and civilization." There was only one "preventive" that could be applied: "Let an army of the United States march into Texas, and say to the pirate Santa Anna, 'Stop:' a great and philanthropic and free people will not stand tamely by and see justice, constitutional right, and humanity, wantonly violated at her door—nor can a paternal government tolerate a state of things on its most vulnerable and important frontier, that will, and *must* bring the bloody tide of savage war and the horrors of negro insurrection within its limits."[32]

Austin's racist diatribe, with its dire pronouncements about miscegenation and slave rebellions, could easily be dismissed as the typical ranting of a southern slaveholder if not for his long history of relative racial and ethnic tolerance. He had no closer personal friends than the Seguíns and Navarros in Texas, and his respect for Mexican leaders like Terán, Alamán, and Zavala was genuine. But his statements now were precisely like his position on slavery in Texas; the interests of Texas required him to talk and act like a Southerner, even if that contradicted his private beliefs. The reality in the spring of 1836 was that support for the Texas cause had to come from Jacksonian Democrats, not from the cautious Whigs who were Austin's natural allies by virtue of his background, education, and elitist worldview. The Democratic Party's base of strength lay in the South, and with southern, slaveholding politicians like Andrew Jackson. As always when Texas was involved, expediency took precedence over principle.

Throughout their tour of the United States the commissioners had been met with coolness from Whig politicians and newspapers, in contrast to the wild enthusiasm of Democrats. The New York City public meeting of April 26 was chaired by Jackson crony Samuel Swartwout, the controversial collector of the Port of New York and a wheeler-dealer of monumental proportions. One conservative New York paper, while sympathizing with the plight of Texas, echoed the Whig complaint that the Texas cause in New York was being directed by unscrupulous Democratic land speculators who were interested only in lining their own pockets. It was unfortunate, the *New York Herald* editorialized, "to have the glorious cause deposited in the hands of stock gamblers in Wall street, who would be sufficient to send to perdition any cause however honest—or any purpose however praiseworthy." With men like Swartwout "coming forward and taking the lead in such a question, it is enough to create a broad laugh throughout the whole city." Privately Austin probably would have agreed with this criticism. Men such as Swartwout, who would later flee the country after embezzling more than a million dollars from the government, were necessary, if unsavory, allies.[33]

The news from Texas grew increasingly grim. "My heart and soul are sick but my spirit is unbroken," Austin wrote on April 24. "I foresaw the evils of War and have (as is well known) tried to keep them out of Texas." Little did he know that three days earlier Sam Houston's army had caught the Mexicans by surprise at San Jacinto, crushing Santa Anna's army and taking *el presidente* prisoner. The weeks in New York produced only a $100,000 loan, of which a mere $10,000 was paid up front. Austin made a quick train trip to Philadelphia at the beginning of May to speak at a public meeting there, then returned to New York for another week. On May 13 he checked out of the American Hotel, paid the $300 bill for himself and Wharton (of which a considerable amount went for liquor and cigars), and took the train back to Washington. On May 24 he boarded the train for Baltimore, spent one night there, then proceeded overland to

Stephen F. Austin, by William H. Brown, 1836.
Brown, a well-known silhouette artist, probably
produced this drawing when Austin was on the East
Coast seeking aid for the Texas cause. *Courtesy, Center
for American History, University of Texas at Austin
(S. F. Austin Papers #CN07585).*

Wheeling, where he caught a steamboat for the long trip down the Ohio
to the Mississippi. Along the way he heard of Houston's great victory.
"The situation of matters requires that I should proceed home as rapidly
as possible," he wrote to Mary Holley from aboard his steamboat on the
Ohio River. "Shall therefore not detain a moment at any place except to
wait for a boat for N. Orleans." [34]

He now realized that the trip to the United States had been a mistake.
The moneylenders of New York and Philadelphia, like the politicians of
Washington, simply would not commit themselves without more defini-
tive news from Texas. "Had I known as much of those kind of people last

winter as I do now, I should not have spent any time upon them," Austin confessed to Mary. Meanwhile, important events were moving forward without him. He burned to be back in Texas. *"I must be at home without delay,"* he wrote, "much more now depends on a correct course, & union at home, than on any thing else. . . . Nothing shall induce me to leave home again until all is settled there."[35]

If the six-month tour of the United States had brought disappointing results officially, one positive development gave Austin some personal satisfaction. That was his relationship with his fellow commissioners. Austin told James Perry of the change: "The most perfect harmony exists between all the commissioners," he declared. "Archer is truly a noble fellow. I have never known him intimately before, and I am very much attached to him. Wharton and myself are on the best of terms and I have no doubt will always continue to be in [the] future—it is not any fault that we ever were otherwise—heretofore we [have] not known each other personally as we might and ought to have." For a man who was prone to see enemies at every turn, this ability to repair relationships and turn those enemies into cordial friends remained one of the most surprising—and admirable—elements of Austin's complex character. Both Wharton and Archer would remain devoted supporters of the empresario to the end.[36]

Austin landed in New Orleans on June 10, where he learned of Santa Anna's capture following the Battle of San Jacinto. With only Sam Houston standing between him and the Texan troops calling for his head, the Mexican president had agreed to order his remaining troops back across the Rio Grande. Texas was independent, at least for the moment. Realizing that food and other necessities would be scarce in the aftermath of the war, Austin lingered in New Orleans long enough to arrange for a shipload of provisions to be sent to Texas. Then he booked passage for home.[37]

Home
1836

ustin arrived at the mouth of the Brazos on June 27, seasick
as usual. With his head literally still swimming from his voyage on the Gulf, he immediately leaped into motion to bring
the disorganized affairs of Texas into some semblance of
order. Not surprisingly, he believed that his countrymen
were blundering in their handling of the current situation. Most Texans
seemed to think that the danger from Mexico was past and that the war
was over for good. Austin wrote to Mirabeau B. Lamar, who was commanding the army while Sam Houston received treatment in Louisiana
for his battle wound. "No treaty made with Santa Anna will be respected"
by the Mexican government, he warned prophetically. Volunteers en route
from the United States would turn back when they heard that the war was
over. "In Gods name no more armistices or treaties with prisoners," he
urged Lamar. "Our course now appears to be a plain one. The country
must rally *en masse* and meet the enemy. . . . I shall try and be with you in
the army as soon as I can, as a private soldier. Every man in Texas must
shoulder his arms."[1]

Austin did not march off to join the army right away, of course. He
spent the next two weeks on the lower Brazos, conferring with his old

friend David G. Burnet, who had been elected provisional president by the March convention, and the other civil and military leaders of the new Republic. Austin was devising a plan to end the war permanently and guarantee the safety of Texas. The scheme required the cooperation of two generals-turned-presidents, Antonio López de Santa Anna and Andrew Jackson. The idea was to get Santa Anna to write to Jackson with a request that Old Hickory mediate a permanent cessation of hostilities between Texas and Mexico, to be backed up by the U.S. military, after which Santa Anna would be returned to Mexico.[2]

The Mexican president was being held twelve miles up the river near the village of Columbia, where the provisional government had established its temporary capital. Col. Juan Almonte, who had often visited Austin in his Mexico City prison cell in 1834, and another of Santa Anna's staff officers, Col. Gabriel Nuñez Ortega, were also housed in the small cabin owned by William Jack. The government had moved them to this isolated location after repeated death threats from revenge-hungry Texans. On the afternoon of July 1, Austin arrived there and was ushered in to meet with Santa Anna. The two-room Texas cabin contrasted sharply with the National Palace in Mexico City, scene of their last meeting. If Austin took any noticeable satisfaction from their reversal of fortunes, there is no record of it. Perhaps he reminded himself that it was Santa Anna who had let him out of prison in Mexico City. In any case, this was no time for reproaches. Austin got down to business and carefully explained the situation to the captive president. After a long discussion, Santa Anna agreed to Austin's plan. Austin returned each of the next three days, finally leaving for Velasco with Santa Anna's letter to Jackson in hand.[3]

Ultimately, Jackson could not agree to Austin's plan, because the United States had already recognized the new regime in Mexico City, which had repudiated Santa Anna. But it was clear from Austin's actions since returning to Texas that he intended to resume the central role in Texas affairs that he believed was rightfully his. He was, in essence, already acting as chief diplomatic strategist for the provisional government. Austin explained his position in a letter to U.S. Army Gen. Edmund P. Gaines, to whom he had written urging American military intervention on Texas's behalf. "I make these suggestions as a citizen of Texas," he stated. "I hold no office, but can go into the Cabinet whenever it may be necessary." Indeed, one observer unfriendly to Austin described him as "being defacto the head or ruler of the present cabinet." The next few weeks, though, revealed that Texas's needs—as Austin perceived them—would not allow him to continue as a mere citizen or even as a cabinet member. The increasingly unpopular Burnet called for the election of a permanent government in September. It was impossible for Austin to stand by and watch others take control of his beloved Texas at such a critical time.[4]

On July 20, Austin traveled back down the Brazos to Velasco to meet with Archer and Wharton, who had just returned from the United States. For two days the reunited commissioners worked to produce a formal report of their mission, along with a detailed account of their receipts and expenditures on the trip. Naturally the talk turned to politics and the upcoming elections. In a brief memorandum of the visit, Austin left a two-sentence account of what transpired: "Archer and Wharton at this time requested that I would be a candidate for the Presidency of Texas. B Hardiman [Bailey Hardeman], S. Rhoads Fisher and many others also requested it."[5]

It is unlikely that Austin needed much persuasion. He had consistently demonstrated his belief that he knew best how to guide the affairs of Texas, and his actions since returning from the United States reinforce the conclusion that he had no intention of returning to private life at this critical time. On August 4 he announced his candidacy:

> I have been nominated by many persons, whose opinions I am bound to respect, as a candidate for the office of President of Texas, at the September elections.
>
> Influenced by the governing principle which has regulated my actions since I came to Texas, fifteen years ago, which is to serve the country in any capacity in which the people might think proper to employ me, I shall not decline the highly responsible and difficult one now proposed, should the majority of my fellow citizens elect me.
>
> My labors and exertions to settle this country and promote its welfare are well known. My object has been the general good,

and the permanent liberty and prosperity of Texas. In the pursuit
of this object I can say with a clear conscience that I have been
honest and sincere in my intentions, and shall continue to be so,
whether I am acting as a private citizen or as a public officer.

He concluded his announcement by stating his position in favor of immediate annexation of Texas by the United States.[6]

Austin retired to Peach Point for a few days of rest. His health had
been poor since his return to Texas. As soon as he announced his candidacy, defamatory rumors about him began to circulate. The most persistent one was that he had been involved with Sam Williams and the others
in the now infamous Monclova Speculations. "This is utterly false," he
wrote to Thomas Rusk on August 9. "I never have been, am not, and
never will be interested in those speculations, directly nor indirectly, and
no one in Texas is more opposed to them than I am." He disclaimed full
knowledge of the Speculations until very recently, "and I do not know that
I understand it all yet," he declared, "for these events all took place in my
absence." By this point he probably understood more than he admitted,
but it was certainly true that he had disapproved of the transactions from
the beginning and that he had no personal interest in them. In their two
brief meetings since 1834, Williams seems to have made a point of not discussing the affair, and Austin, valuing their long friendship, appears not
to have asked.[7]

The other damaging rumor was that Austin had saved Santa Anna.
"That man was saved by Gen. Sam. Houston . . . [and] by the Cabinet of
Texas subsequently," he correctly pointed out. "I think he merited death,
and that the country ought not to have been compromised to save him."
In the latter statement Austin was speaking disingenuously, or from a lack
of full understanding of the events following the Battle of San Jacinto.
Houston's shrewd handling of Santa Anna after the battle had resulted in
the removal of all remaining Mexican troops from Texas. Austin claimed
that this "saved the balance of the Mexican Army" to invade another day,
but Houston, who was in a better position to know the capabilities of his
own army in the chaotic aftermath of the battle, understood that having
those Mexican troops out of Texas was far safer than continuing the cam-

paign in hopes of another improbable victory. As a candidate, Austin simply could not go on record as favoring the sparing of Santa Anna. He rationalized his own subsequent dealings with the Mexican leader on the grounds that "my object was to try to get the intervention of the U.S. and to have Texas annexed to the U.S." Persuading Santa Anna to write Jackson with the mediation proposal did no harm, and might have done much good, he emphasized.[8]

Opposing Austin in the race was Henry Smith, who sought vindication for his controversial — and nearly disastrous — course as governor during the revolution. Smith no doubt believed that he could count on the support of former War Party men like himself, in opposition to the Peace Party candidate, Austin. But Austin had good reason to believe that he himself could be elected. With Wharton and Archer — themselves both old War Party men — endorsing him, and with the support of his own colonists and friends, surely he could defeat Smith, whose ego and tactlessness had almost cost Texas the war.

Austin soon found it difficult to contain the rumors and accusations that his opponents were spreading. The charges that he had been involved in the Monclova Speculations and had saved Santa Anna were at least legitimate political issues — had they been true. But now the opposition stooped even lower, criticizing him for leaving the country during the war "to eat fine dinners, drink wine, etc.," while others bore the brunt of battle.[9]

Part of Austin's problem was the perception of him as the "government" candidate, due to his long standing as a political leader, his friendship with the unpopular Burnet, and his active role in current public affairs. One foe, army officer Henry Millard, succeeded in combining this perception with all the other accusations into one remarkably scurrilous charge — that the "primary object" of the provisional government "is now to Elevate Stephen F. Austin to the presidency and no stone will be left unturned by them to effect their object that they may again come into power under his patronage. Genl. Austin is with them hand and glove and their ostensible object in my opinion is to throw us back under the Mexican Dynasty by the release of santa Anna who will confirm their power in Texas with all their fra[u]dulent claims of 1300 Leagues and powers to perpetuate their authority." [10]

From his position as editor of the pro-Austin *Telegraph*, Gail Borden watched with dismay as the empresario's political capital plummeted. The future milk entrepreneur wrote Austin on August 15, saying that even some of Austin's "*old* devoted friends" would not vote for him unless they could be convinced he had taken no part in the Monclova Speculations. Still resting at Peach Point, the candidate had done little to counter the charges. At Borden's urging he published a letter emphatically denying involvement in the Speculations and defending his actions as commissioner to the United States. He also answered the charge that he had opposed independence, justifying his pragmatic course during the fall of 1835 as a well-intentioned attempt "to keep the seat of war beyond the limits of Texas, until the country was better prepared, and by that means save the families from the devastations of invasions which they have suffered." In doing so, he argued, he was merely adhering to an "idea which was entertained by many" at the time and sustaining the Consultation, which adopted the same policy. [11]

The accusations hurt, but Austin still felt confident enough in his election to offer the secretary of state's office to William S. Archer, provided, as Austin noted, "that the *sovereigns* elect me." Archer, an influential U.S. congressman from Virginia and kinsman of Branch Archer, would help Austin achieve his primary platform promise—securing the annexation of Texas by the United States. [12]

Austin's hopes were shattered on August 20, when, with less than two weeks remaining before the election, Sam Houston entered the race. Like Austin, Houston acted the reluctant candidate, claiming to have been spontaneously nominated by various groups throughout Texas. He explained in his announcement that "the crisis requires it or I would not have yielded." [13]

No record survives of the empresario's reaction to this news. After Austin's death, his relatives claimed betrayal on Houston's part, saying that Houston reneged on an earlier promise never to oppose Austin for any public office in Texas. The only firsthand account of this promise

Sam Houston as he appeared around the
time of the 1836 Texas presidential
election. Houston disagreed with
Austin's strategies as commander of the
army and ran against him for the
presidency, but he appointed Austin
secretary of state and was among the first
to laud Austin as the Father of Texas.
Courtesy, Center for American History,
University of Texas at Austin (Prints and
Photographs Collection #CN03649).

comes from Houston himself years later. Writing to Austin's nephew Guy
Bryan in 1852, Houston told of a "free friendly and confidential interview" that the two men had on the eve of Austin's departure for Mexico
City in 1833. "I assured him if he succeeded in obtaining a State Government, that I would never oppose him, for any Civil office in the state, but
render him my cordial support thereafter," Houston recalled. He claimed
that he made this promise so that Austin would not worry about Houston
engaging in "intrigue against him" in his absence. Austin of course did
not succeed in getting statehood for Texas during his Mexico trip, so if
Houston's version is correct, the promise was moot in 1836. Nevertheless,

in his 1852 account Houston still provided a reasonable justification for his decision to run. With Austin representing the Peace Party and Smith the War Party, he explained, "I was firmly impressed with the belief, that if either of the Gentlemen should be elected, it would be next to an impossibility to organize and sustain a Government. . . . Not being identified with either of the Parties, I believed, I would be enabled to consolidate the influence of both, by harmonizing them so as to form and sustain an administration." He offered a similar explanation to Emily Perry in 1844, who dismissed it as a "lame excuse."[14]

Broken promise or not, Austin now realized that he stood little chance of election. He still knew his fellow Texans better than anyone did, and he accurately predicted what would happen: Houston would carry East Texas, the Red River settlements, and most of the army vote. Most discouraging, though, was his realization that he could not even count on his own colonists. "Many of the old settlers who are too blind to see or understand their interest will vote for him," he told James Perry, suggesting that he clearly considered himself a superior choice for president.[15]

Three days later Austin's predictions proved accurate. The Hero of San Jacinto won in a landslide with 5,119 votes to Austin's 587. Perhaps most humiliating was the fact that Henry Smith polled 743 votes, even though he had withdrawn from the election and thrown his support to Houston. James Morgan, one of Austin's old settlers, echoed the disappointment of the empresario's supporters: "The first general election of Texas is now all over and a majority of the candidates have the sad news by now. Austin knew long ago that he would be turned down by the people he had tried so hard to serve. Republics are proverbial[l]y ungrateful and we feel certain that Austin anticipated just about the kind of political deal that was handed to him." Another friend, Edmund Andrews, sought to console the defeated candidate in a colorful analogy with which Austin undoubtedly would have agreed. "The body Politic is unlike Every other machine that Ever Existed," Andrews theorized, "other machines may be thrown out of order by some accident but this is only right by accident."[16]

The impact of the defeat on Austin can be gauged only indirectly. He certainly tried to take it in stride. In his pre-election letter to Perry predicting the outcome, he seemed to express some relief that he would "have a good prospect of some rest this year, and time to regulate my private affairs, which need regulating very much." To his credit, his correspondence reveals no record of lingering bitterness; apart from a passing remark about the "blindness" of the colonists who voted for Houston, he had no negative words about the victor. Indeed, the week Houston was inaugurated Austin told James Perry, "I think that matters will go on well and smoothly in both the Executive and Legislative departments. There evidently is a disposition to harmonise in all persons." [17]

Despite his apparent indifference to the outcome, the election must have wounded Austin deeply. It could not have been easy to accept such overwhelming rejection by his people in favor of a relative newcomer whose principal contribution to Texas (at least in Austin's estimation) had been one lucky military victory. Yet Austin had virtually predicted his own fate long before the Texans rose in revolt against Mexico. The words he wrote to Mary Holley in 1831 now proved singularly prophetic:

> A successful military chieftain is hailed with admiration and applause, and monuments perpetuate his fame. But the bloodless pioneer of the wilderness, like the corn and cotten he causes to spring where it never grew before, attracts no notice. He is either cried down as a speculator, or his works are too unostentatious to be worthy of attention. No slaughtered thousands or smoking cities attest his devotion to the cause of human happiness, and he is regarded by the mass of the world as a humble instrument to pave the way for others. [18]

The final days of the presidential race coincided with Austin's worst attack of fever since the death of his brother. He had ridden out to the army's headquarters at Victoria, probably to electioneer among the troops. The fever struck while he was there, and he made it back to Peach Point only with great difficulty. For the rest of September he languished in bed at his sister's house. By the first of October he was "just able to sit up," and on the twelfth he reported that he was "now barely able to crawl about a little." His illness interfered with his plans for picking up the pieces of his long-neglected and highly complicated private business affairs. He had no house of his own; San Felipe had been put to the torch during the Revolution. The land office had been closed during the war, and many settlers still awaited titles. He had hundreds of outstanding accounts to collect. Austin asked Perry to build him a two- or three-room cabin at Peach Point to house himself, the clerks he would need to employ in finishing up the land business, and visiting settlers. Furnishings would have to be sent from New Orleans.[19]

By late October he was still weak but recuperating enough to make plans for attending Houston's inaugural ball. "I have been solicited to go into the new cabinet as Secretary of State—or to go to the U.S. as minister," he reported on the twenty-fifth, three days after the inauguration. "I have declined." The "solicitation" appears not to have been a formal invitation from Houston to join the cabinet; probably it was some sort of preliminary inquiry aimed at discovering Austin's current state of mind. In fact, he expressed interest in the diplomatic mission to Washington, but leaving Texas at this point was out of the question. "I have all the land office business to close," he told Perry. "Who can I trust it with in my absence? If S. M. Williams failed me while I was in prison in the city of Mexico, who can I hope will not fail me now? Besides all this my health is gone, and I must have rest to nurse my constitution and try and restore my strength."[20]

The Williams situation tormented him. The more Austin had learned of the Monclova Speculations, the more he held Williams responsible for their baleful consequences. Although the empresario had criticized the Speculations since he first heard of them in Mexico City, the presidential race forced him to condemn his old friend's actions much more publicly than he had done before. The condemnations were not just for political purposes, either; Austin truly resented Williams for jeopardizing Austin's reputation, as well as the security of Texas itself in 1835. The controversial actions of the Monclova legislature, after all, had helped to set in motion the events that propelled Santa Anna and his army into Texas in the first place.

Williams remained in the United States during the presidential campaign. There he learned that Austin was speaking out against him in

Texas. "I am informed that you charge me with a want of regard for your standing and character," he wrote to Austin. The denunciations by Austin "hurt and crushed . . . my spirit," he declared. Convinced that he had done nothing wrong, he prayed Austin to tell him "of what it is you complain in me." Williams could only believe that disloyal friends had turned Austin against him. "And be assured," he told his longtime mentor, "great as is my affliction under your censure—greater is my esteem for you; and no matter what may be the exertions of my enemies; no matter what you may believe necessary as your course toward me—and no matter what I may suffer—I will disappoint their hearts expectation; for long long ago have I sworn eternal friendship—long ago have I sworn, come what will, come *what* may never to forget the confidence which once existed between us, and all the machinations of hell shall not change my purpose nor my determination." As much as Austin's criticism stung him, the proud Williams would not admit wrongdoing. In that regard, as in so many others, the two men were much alike.[21]

It was a month before Austin received the letter and two more weeks before he was well enough to answer. "I read your letter with such feelings as a drowning man would seize a plank," the empresario wrote.

Sam Williams you were wound around and rooted in my affections more than any man ever was or ever can be again. I wished and hoped to see or hear something that would convince me I was wrong or had too seriously viewed your acts etc since I left in 1833. [Y]ou were to have closed the land business pending of the old colonies and attended to the last one. [N]othing was done or next to nothing, and I still have all that cursed trouble on my hands besides the censure and Gabble of discontent. . . . [Y]ou also must have known that all the odium of those things, would be cast on me by the envious and slanderous owing to our long friendship and relations. The fact is Williams that all those Monclova matters, I mean the speculations, and precipitating the country into war, were morally wrong, they have some very criminal and dreadfull features. I am too much debilitated to say more. [Y]ou say your motives were good. In the name of God convince me of that.[22]

Three more weeks passed. Though he still had heard nothing from Williams, Austin could no longer stand the thought of a permanent estrangement between them. It was his forty-third birthday, and he was depressed, lonely, and ill. He urged Williams to return to Texas and "to stop all that kind of wildness both in talking, acts and business—harm enough has been done already by it—do no more. [Y]ou have greatly vexed and worried and distressed me. So much so that my brain has been greatly fevered. . . . [Y]ou have done wrong and have greatly injured, your friends, yourself, and your country—but that is past—let it be a lesson to you for the future." Austin recommended that Williams forget about public affairs and focus his considerable talents on business. As for the Monclova Speculations, Austin stated, "I am trying to banish even the recollection of it from my mind, and when I fully recover my health, hope shall be able to do so. In [the] future I never mean to speak of it or allude to it, if I can avoid it." Austin apparently still believed that Williams had cost him the presidency and—much more important—his standing as the leader of the Texans. But he had "cursed" the Monclova affair "in so many forms and shapes," he added, "that my anger is becoming almost exhausted and will, I sincerely hope, finally wear away." The final words to his letter reveal both the lingering hurt and the continuing bond that the empresario felt for his old protégé: "Williams you have wounded me very deeply, but you are so deeply rooted in my affections, that with all your faults, you are at heart too much like a wild and heedless brother to be entirely banished. Come home." [23]

Sam Houston won the presidency in a landslide, but along the way he had created some bitter opponents, many of them Austin's friends and supporters. They charged him with cowardice during the long retreat across Texas following the fall of the Alamo. They blamed him for the burning of San Felipe. They said his officers forced him against his wishes to turn and fight at San Jacinto. They pointed to his failed marriage and his drinking as evidence of moral depravity. To Austin's credit, he never indulged in any of this mudslinging, even in private correspondence. His intelligence and astuteness as a judge of character somehow enabled him to see that the new president—so different in background, style, and temperament from himself—would not be the loose cannon aboard the ship of state that many supposed. Ultimately Austin probably could see some of the validity in Houston's justification for entering the race; the heroic general *could* be a unifying factor in these critical first days of the new republic.

"I have *full confidence* that all will go right," Austin told James Perry, "and that by next March we shall belong to the U.S." He and the new president agreed on the main issue of the day—the desirability of annexation—and even on lesser matters, such as what to do with the still-captive Santa Anna. As Houston began forming his cabinet, Austin again voiced his approval, saying that "the administration of Genl. Houston has entered upon its duties under the most favorable auspices, and the utmost harmony, and union prevails in all the departments and also in the community at large."[24]

On October 28, 1836, Houston wrote to inform Austin of his confirmation as secretary of state by the Texas senate. Houston either ignored Austin's earlier, informal refusal of the offer or—more likely—he knew not to take it seriously. In any case, Houston presented the appointment to Austin as a fait accompli, putting a certain amount of pressure on him to accept. Austin's relatives subsequently claimed that the empresario agreed to serve reluctantly, but Houston recalled it differently in 1852, saying that Austin "readily accepted" the appointment. Houston's version appears closest to the truth, for Austin accepted the offer on October 31, only three days after Houston offered the already-confirmed position. Allowing time for Houston's letter to travel down the river from Columbia to Peach Point, Austin could not have agonized for long. He did, however, accept the office conditionally. "Your Excellency is fully aware of the debilitated state of my constitution and health, and also of the labors which devolve upon me in the land department," he reminded Houston. "I however accept of the appointment and am ready to enter upon the duties of the office, with the understanding that I be allowed the privilege of retiring should my health and situation require it."[25]

Houston kept his promise to form a government in which all former factions would be represented. To counterbalance Austin, he appointed Henry Smith treasury secretary. Wharton received the important post of minister to the United States. The war department portfolio went to Houston's own trusted lieutenant, Thomas J. Rusk, while Austin's old friend and supporter Samuel Rhoads Fisher became navy secretary. In the September election Texans had voted almost unanimously in favor of seeking immediate annexation by the United States. As Austin remarked a week after assuming office, "public opinion has settled down upon one all absorbing point, which is *annexation to the United States without delay.*"[26]

Austin's task was to set the diplomatic wheels in motion. It was not a particularly burdensome duty. He drafted formal instructions for Wharton to take with him to Washington. Arrangements were completed for Santa Anna's release; in accordance with the wishes of both Austin and Houston, the Mexican leader would be quietly escorted out of Texas and accompanied to Washington, where he would meet with Andrew Jackson before being sent home. Once back in Mexico, his presence would surely prove divisive enough to divert attention from Texas. Other items on the secretary of state's agenda included efforts to arrange an exchange of prisoners from the recent war, and the drafting of a proclamation against the African slave trade.[27]

Attending to his private business affairs probably occupied more of Austin's time and energy during November and December than did his official duties. He described the state of those affairs in a letter to an old family friend from Missouri:

I have no house, not a roof in all Texas, that I can call my own. The only one I had was burnt at San Felipe during the late invasion of the enemy. I make my home where the business of the country calls me. . . . I have no farm, no cotton plantation, no income, no money, no comforts. I have spent the prime of my life and worn out my constitution in trying to colonize this country. Many persons boast of their 300 and 400 leagues acquired by speculation without personal labor or the sacrifice of years or even days. I shall be content to save twenty leagues or about nineteen [ninety] thousand acres, *acquired very hard and very dear indeed.* All my wealth is prospective and contingent upon the events of the future.[28]

The events of the past three years had changed Austin's personal financial outlook, both for the better and the worse. In the short term things were worse. The expenses of his long ordeal in Mexico, the mission to the United States, and the call of public service in Texas had resulted in new debts that could be paid only by selling land at depressed wartime prices. However, he still had massive landholdings, and with Texas now free from Mexico, there would be no limits on the amount of land an individual could own. (Mexican law would have required him to sell all but eleven leagues, or about forty-five thousand acres, after twelve years.) He knew that taxes would be high in the new republic, and he would have to sacrifice much land in order to hold onto the remainder. One thing had not changed since 1821: Stephen F. Austin's financial future was still closely tied to that of Texas itself. The key to that future now lay with annexation. If Texas could enter the Union, the U.S. Army would assume the burden of national defense; all trade barriers between Texas and the United States would be removed; and most important of all, prospective land buyers would pour into the new state, knowing that their property would be secure.

Complicating Austin's business affairs was the situation of his sister's family. He was very concerned about Emily. Her health had not been good for some time, and the war had created much hardship for her and her family. Back in June, just as Austin was returning from the United States, she had made plans to sail for New Orleans to escape the expected reinvasion by Mexico and to make arrangements for placing her younger children in school. But Austin, acutely aware of how it would look if his own family fled at that time, apparently insisted that she "stay at home and abide the fate of Texas." Now he sold enough land to raise $3,000 for her to make the trip. "I would sell all I have at any sacrifice rather than she should continue in the unhappy and fretful state she has been in ever since I returned home," he told Perry. "She must spend next Summer in the U.S. It will restore her health and spirits, and correct the fretful habit which sickness and hardships have produced." Austin would not consider letting Perry sacrifice his own land for the purpose. He also purchased a twenty-seven-year-old slave, a mule, and a pony and sent them to Perry for use at Peach Point until such time as he could retire from public life and begin farming for himself. In spite of all that had happened, he still clung to his old fantasy of a quiet life on the farm.[29]

Columbia, Texas, was a raw little village wholly inadequate to serve as the capital of the new republic. Austin found lodging at the home of George B. McKinstry, an Irishman who had come to Texas in 1829 by way of Georgia. He and Austin had not gotten along particularly well in past years, because McKinstry had been a War Party activist and close ally of the Whartons in prerevolutionary days. McKinstry's house was little more than a shack on the outskirts of town. He rented Austin a "shed room" on the house's north side, which served as both bedroom and office for the secretary of state. The room had no fireplace or stove. Between official visits from congressmen and colonists concerned with land matters, he found few opportunities for quiet or privacy.[30]

In late December a bitter norther blew into Texas. Austin caught a severe cold. It would not have been a cause for concern in a healthy person, but he had not been healthy for months. Moses Austin Bryan was again serving as his uncle's secretary, and he grew concerned. Henry Austin arrived, as did George Hammeken, who had been such a good friend to Austin in Mexico City. Branch Archer, who had a medical degree from the University of Pennsylvania, monitored his condition and administered opium. By Christmas Day Austin's condition had improved. At Henry's suggestion, the men shaved him, changed his linen, and carried him from his bed in the cold north room into the main room of house and made him a pallet in front of the fireplace. The weather had moderated, but later another strong norther blew in. At Austin's request, he was carried back to his bed in the other room.

His conditioned worsened. The cold settled into his lungs and turned into pneumonia. Two more doctors were called in on the twenty-sixth, and after some disagreement they agreed to administer an emetic, or vomiting agent, in hopes of clearing his lungs. The remedy seemed to work, but it left the patient very weak. He returned to the pallet before the fire, where he passed a sleepless night. Several times during the night he managed to leave the pallet and sit down at a small table, with his head resting in his hands, a position which allowed for better breathing. But he was too weak to sit upright long, and soon he had to lie down again.

At daybreak on the twenty-seventh James Perry arrived, and Moses Austin Bryan showed him to Austin's bedside. The empresario was lucid, but the doctors were on the verge of giving up. At nine o'clock one of the doctors applied a blister to Austin's chest, which somehow seemed to offer some relief. "Now, I will go to sleep," Austin whispered. For the next two hours he drifted in and out of consciousness, occasionally waking enough to ask for a little tea. Around eleven-thirty he woke, as if from a dream, and in a faint voice said, "The independence of Texas is recognized! Don't you see it in the papers? Doctor Archer told me so!" He then slipped back into unconsciousness. Thirty minutes later he died.[31]

The Father of Texas
Stephen F. Austin in Retrospect

Sam Houston was among the first to hear the news of Austin's death, and he immediately ordered the secretary of war to issue an official government notice of the melancholy event. "The Father of Texas is no more!" the announcement read. "The first pioneer of the wilderness has departed!" Houston commanded all officers of the government to wear black arm bands for the next thirty days in "respect to his high standing, undeviating moral rectitude, and as a mark of the nation's gratitude for his untiring zeal, and invaluable service." "The president also ordered every military post to fire a twenty-three-gun salute — one volley for each of the republic's counties — and to "have the garrison and regimental colors, hung *black* during the space of mourning for the illustrious deceased."[1]

The following day Gail Borden printed the funeral announcement:

THE PATRIARCH HAS LEFT US.

WE perform a most painful duty in announcing the death of GENERAL STEPHEN F. AUSTIN, who departed this life, yesterday, at half-past 12 o'clock, P.M. at the house of judge McKinstry. His

THE PATRIARCH HAS LEFT US.

WE perform a most painful duty in announcing the death of GENERAL STEPHEN F. AUSTIN, *who departed this life, yesterday, at half-past 12 o'clock, P. M. at the house of judge McKinstry. His friends and relations have sustained an irreparable loss; his country, just merging into existence, the best and tenderest of fathers; the sons and daughters of Texas have now full cause for mourning, with one solitary consolation, that they will meet the just man above.*

His remains will leave for Peach Point, for interment, at twelve o'clock to-day.

Columbia, December 28, 1836.

P. S. The steamboat having arrived, the remains of General Austin will be removed from judge McKinstry's at eight o'clock to-morrow morning, to the steamboat, at Columbia Landing, and not to-day, as above stated.

Austin's funeral notice, printed by Gail Borden. *Courtesy Center for American History, University of Texas (Broadsides Collection #CN07728).*

friends and relations have sustained an irreparable loss; his country, just merging into existence, the best and tenderest of fathers;
the sons and daughters of Texas have now full cause for mourning, with one solitary consolation, that they will meet the just
man above.[2]

On the morning of December 29, Austin's body was carried on board
the steamboat *Yellowstone* at Columbia for the short trip down the Brazos
River to Peach Point. Sam Houston, members of the cabinet, a military
escort, Moses Austin Bryan and assorted friends accompanied the remains. From James Perry's river landing the mourners traveled two miles
to the family burial plot, where the empresario was laid to rest. Houston
threw the first handful of dirt on the coffin.[3]

The funeral marked the beginning of a long and complex process
in which Texans and others sought to understand, explain, and exploit
Austin's legacy. Friends like Gail Borden earnestly believed that Austin
should be universally recognized not only as the Father of Texas but also
as a martyr who had sacrificed his interests, health, and finally his life
for his country. From New Orleans, Father Michael Muldoon eulogized
Austin in a lengthy romantic poem intended for publication. Muldoon,
who had been such a staunch ally and friend of Austin, praised the empresario as "our Great Founder, that most wondrous man," who "rang'd
the Desert as our Pioneer!!":

> He peopled Texas, by a solemn clause
> Of legal Treaty, and Religion's laws.
> He bow'd obedience to the great Command
> "Till up the Desert—Cultivate the Land" . . .
> The Great Republic—source of Liberty
> Has taught chain'd nations that they can be free.
> Thou lov'd Dispenser of the gifts of Mars
> We shall be free—assisted by your stars.
> But . . . STEPHEN AUSTIN to our Texas dear
> The muse thus sings & drops a silent tear.[4]

Austin's relatives particularly felt a keen interest in securing his reputation as the Father of Texas. As his distant cousin in Philadelphia,
Thomas Leaming, explained, "He has left a fame and reputation which
will never die but like that of William Penn his great model and type will
continue to increase with years and his countrymen in after times will
know him as The Good and Just, 'The Father of his Country.'" But at the
time of his death and for many years thereafter, it was by no means certain that Austin's life and works would be viewed in such a positive light.
Austin had gained many bitter enemies over the years, including Sterling
Robertson, Thomas Jefferson Chambers, and Henry Smith. Even though
Austin ultimately had earned the respect and even the friendship of the
Whartons, Archer, and Houston, many former War Party men still nursed
their political grudges against him after his death. The widely held views
of Austin as unscrupulous land speculator and pro-Mexican tory per-
sisted.[5]

In the years immediately following his death, James and Emily Perry
and Mary Austin Holley led the family's crusade to right these wrongs.
"The earliest period of Texas history is what wants clearing up," Emily
wrote to Mary in 1844. "Who could fix the name of Columbus to America
—having been Rifled from him in the beginning?" Clearly the Austin
relatives believed that if something were not done soon to rehabilitate
Austin's name, he might never occupy the place in history that they believed he deserved.[6]

The family concluded that a biography was needed. As it happened,
even before Austin's death, none other than Mirabeau B. Lamar had
begun research on a biography, a task he had begun with the approval and
active assistance of Austin himself. Lamar put out a public call for Texans to contribute information on Austin's life, justifying his undertaking
as follows:

He was not only the founder of our Republic, but there is scarcely
a blessing which has flowed to the country that may not fairly
be attributed to his untiring efforts for its welfare; whilst almost
every calamity and misfortune which have befallen it, might have

been averted by an adherence to his wise and prudent counsels. The world has afforded but few examples of superior intelligence and sagacity; and as for disinterested and extended philanthropy—his long sufferings for the weal of others—his patient endurance under persecution—his generous forgiveness of enemies—and his final sacrifice of health, happiness and life in the service of his country, all conspire to place him without a modern rival amongst the first of patriots and the best of men.[7]

Lamar, however, succeeded Sam Houston in the presidency and never found time to write the book. Austin's relatives continued to bemoan the empresario's low standing in the hearts and minds of their fellow Texans. Emily and Mary finally determined that David Burnet would be the best man to set the historical record straight regarding Austin. "Burnet is a sincear and warm frend of Stephens (and with the exceptions of his relatives) is the only one of his early acquaintinces, now living [who] chereshes, and respects his memory," Emily wrote. If Burnet would undertake a biography of Austin, perhaps in collaboration with Mary Holley, "justice would be done to his memory." But Burnet never wrote the biography.[8]

Finally Austin's family agreed that Holley would write a "neat and concise history of him, that will bring out his name from the rubbish that surrounds it, in bright relief before the country and the world." Emily provided a revealing explanation of why this was not to be a full-length biography: "It would not do to write a full and correct history of my Brother and of Texas, to be published at this time; for you know that their were many persons whose names would appear that took a very desided part in those trying times to defeat Stephen in all his endeavours [and] plans for the prosperity of his adopted country, some are dead many of them are still living; and those that are dead, have relatives who would be mortified to see their names brought before the publick at this time." But the decision to have Holley write the biography went beyond simply a solicitous obligation to avoid "mortifying" Austin's old enemies. Emily was certain that if a family member did not remind the public of the "great difficulties encountered by Stephen," then "those things will be forgotten. . . . Nobody else cares—public men will not risk popularity by contending for the truth. *Expediency* rules all."[9]

Holley soon began work on the biography, assisted by another public call for those who knew Austin to contribute materials. As she worked she reminded Emily Perry that "it is time it was done. There are people in the Country who scarcely know the name of him who was its Father & Founder." Holley eventually wrote seven short chapters on Austin. In the introductory chapter she stated the rationale for the work. Her cousin had not received the credit he deserved because he was an unconventional hero, "who with persevering effort, calm wisdom, & patient industry" reclaimed the wilderness to found a republic. This was essentially the same claim that Austin himself had frequently made and that his supporters would continue to press into the twentieth century. The purpose always was the same—to earn for Austin a permanent place as a Texas icon alongside Sam Houston, whose military exploits at San Jacinto had earned him instant heroic status.[10]

Holley died before completing the Austin biography. Although the Austin family continued its campaign to vindicate the empresario's name, there would be no serious attempt at a biography for half a century. Over time it became apparent that the fate of Austin's reputation was entangled in the politics of nineteenth-century Texas. The Austin relatives were convinced that only someone who had been active in Texas public affairs and had been a political friend of Austin's could be trusted to do the job. In the eyes of the Austins, anyone politically aligned with Sam Houston was not to be trusted.

From the end of the Texas Revolution to the start of the Civil War, Texas politics largely revolved around the personality and policies of Sam Houston, dividing Texas into pro- and anti-Houston factions. Austin's relatives never really forgave Houston for running for president of the Republic in 1836 in violation of his alleged promise never to oppose Austin for public office. Their distrust made them natural allies—or in some cases, tools—of the anti-Houston faction, led by Houston's bitter political enemies, Lamar and Burnet. The family's courtship of Lamar and Burnet as potential biographers makes sense in light of these politics. Lamar also must have taken pleasure in the success of his pet project, moving the seat of government to a new town on the frontier and naming it after Austin. This was a backhanded slap at Sam Houston, who preferred that the capital be located in the new city named after *him*.

Houston's appointment of Austin to the cabinet and his famous "Father of Texas" eulogy indicate that Houston personally never harbored any desire to antagonize Austin or his relatives. In the years after Austin's death Houston continued his efforts to win the confidence of the Austin kin. Emily Perry saw Houston frequently during the republic era, and Houston never failed to speak well of Austin. But referring to Austin's name, Emily was sure that "Houston does not like it *so well as his own*. Though, to me, he is always praising Stephen—says he is *imitating him* and so on. Does'nt [*sic*] quite come up to the pattern, though." Clearly the Austins did not trust Houston.[11]

But if Houston spoke highly of Austin (at least within earshot of Austin's relatives), other political opponents of the late empresario were less tactful. Emily heard that a one-time friend, William H. Jack, was spreading the rumor that the Mexicans had bribed Stephen Austin to oppose the independence movement. *"Stephen Bribed!"* she exclaimed. "If such as [Jack] . . . can propagate such lies, what will the rest do, and where shall we look for truth?" Emily had also heard that Anson Jones, the last president of the republic, had spoken of "the [Joseph] *Hawkins* name as dear to Texas as that of Austin—and so on." Such reports, accurate or not, drove the Austin relatives nearly to despair. "There seems to be a fatality attached to the Austin *name*," Emily protested.[12]

The histories of Texas written in the mid-1800s illustrate the ambiguous place of Stephen F. Austin in the public affections of Texans. The first serious historian of the state was Henderson Yoakum, a Huntsville lawyer and personal friend of Sam Houston. Published in 1855, Yoakum's two-volume history respectfully acknowledges Austin's importance as the first empresario but essentially stops there. In his one-paragraph summation of Austin's services to Texas, Yoakum argued that the empresario laid "the foundation of a great state," but this is a far cry from the hero-worship that would characterize twentieth-century accounts.[13]

Even more indicative of Austin's questionable status in the 1850s

is Jacob De Cordova's *Texas: Her Resources and Her Public Men.* At
the hands of De Cordova, Austin receives no mention at all, although
other dead heroes of the revolution—Ben Milam, Branch Archer, and
Thomas J. Rusk, for example—are featured prominently.[14]

The Austin relatives fought back. Guy Bryan inherited his uncle's
voluminous papers and became a leading authority on the early history of
Anglo Texas. In 1880 he published a short biography of Austin in the *Gal-
veston News,* and in the 1890s he wrote the chapters on Austin and his era
for Dudley Wooten's *A Comprehensive History of Texas.*[15] Moses Austin
Bryan also did his part, writing his "Personal Recollections of Stephen F.
Austin," which his son Beauregard had published in the *Texas Illustrated
Monthly Magazine* in 1897. Both works depicted Austin in a heroic light
as the Father of Texas, although Moses Austin Bryan also tried to give
Sam Houston his due. As Bryan put it, "Two names will always stand
first—Austin and Houston. The last, however, never endured, made sacrifices and suffered for Texas as did Austin." Bryan's memoir closed with
a revealing statement about the continuing dispute between the admirers
of Austin and Houston: "Houston in his heart ever recognized the high
qualities and claims of Austin, and, as far as I know, never denied them.
There is no good reason at this day that his friends should not do justice
to Austin, or that Austin's friends should deny the just claims of Houston,
for both are historical characters, and as such should be judged without
passion or prejudice, in reference to their motives, merits, deeds and the
effect of their imprint upon the country." [16]

The Bryans did not limit their efforts to the written word; they were
also concerned that Austin lacked the proper visual tributes. In 1875 Guy
Bryan donated a portrait of his uncle to the state for placement in the governor's office.[17] At about the same time, Bryan's brother, Moses Austin
Bryan, suggested to painter Henry McArdle that he execute a work on
Austin. The result was one of the best-known and most interesting depic-
tions of Austin, *The Settlement of Austin's Colony,* better known as *The
Log Cabin.* The painting shows Austin issuing land titles in 1824 when a
scout arrives to warn of impending Indian attack. Austin holds the *Laws
of Mexico* in one hand, symbolizing his love of the rule of law and his
fidelity to his adopted country, while reaching for his gun with the other,

an indication that he would fight for the interests of his colonists. This was exactly the sort of image of Austin that the Bryans wanted to present— Austin as the man of peace who would not shy away from war. The public perception that Austin had shirked his fighting responsibilities during the revolution had not disappeared entirely.

Moses Austin Bryan pledged to pay for the painting and donate it to the state, but he was unable to fulfill his financial obligation. The painting hung in the capitol on loan from the artist for several years, and in 1888 McArdle tried lobbying the government to purchase it. The legislature refused to purchase the " 'fancy' painting of Austin" (as the legislative committee termed it), an act that enraged Austin partisans. The state did not acquire the famous painting until 1928, long after Austin had achieved icon status.[18]

That Austin had not yet achieved that status in the 1890s is demonstrated by the publication of Victor M. Rose's *Stephen F. Austin in the Balances* (c. 1890). Born in 1842, Rose served in the Confederate Army and later became a newspaper editor, a poet, and a historian. *Stephen F. Austin in the Balances* is a ten-page poem that viciously castigates Austin as a rapacious, pro-Mexican coward. The poem was dedicated to Henry Smith, whose "fairly-won fame," according to Rose, had "been filched from him" by Austin and his kin. In Rose's poem, other Austins also receive their share of abuse: Moses Austin's mule is said to be "more deserving" of fame than Moses, and Guy Bryan is criticized for his "stupidity and clannishness." Rose appended anonymous letters from "Old Texians" testifying that Texas would have lost the Revolution if Austin had remained in command and that Austin saved all the best lands in Texas for himself. "Austin was a selfish, narrow-minded and jealous-hearted man. He lacked the essential elements of greatness in character," one of these letters reported.[19]

The cause of Rose's spleen cannot be stated with any certainty, and it might be dismissed as simply a personal vendetta if Rose had been alone in criticizing Austin in the 1890s.[20] But criticism of Austin also continued to appear in history books. In his well-known two-volume *History of Texas,* historian John Henry Brown argued that Austin did not deserve to be called the Father of Texas. Portraying Austin as merely a business-

Henry Arthur McArdle, *The Settlement of Austin's Colony*, or *The Log Cabin*, 1875. Although commissioned by Austin's family with the intention of placing it in the state capitol, the state did not purchase the painting until 1928. *Courtesy, Texas State Library and Archives Commission.*

man and one of many empresarios, Brown states that Austin's biographers "have attributed to him merit that he did not possess." For unclear
reasons, Brown vigorously took Sterling Robertson's side in the famous
Robertson Colony controversy. Curiously, however, in a condensed version of his book intended for schoolchildren, Brown reversed himself and
praised Austin as the Father of Texas. Brown's contradictory writings are
symptomatic of the ambiguous public image that the Austin name still
carried as the nineteenth century drew to a close.[21]

But the Bryans were persistent, and as the century drew to a close
they scored a major victory in their long campaign to restore Austin's
reputation. The occasion was the 1893 World's Fair in Chicago. In 1892
the group in charge of the Texas exhibition, the Board of Lady Managers,
approached famed sculptor Elisabet Ney to execute life-sized statues of
Austin and Houston. Ney relied heavily on the advice and assistance of
Guy Bryan, who saw a golden opportunity. Ney failed to complete the
Austin statue in time to be displayed in Chicago, but over the next several
years parallel movements commenced to have the original plaster statues
of both Austin and Houston rendered in marble and have one set placed
in the state capitol and another in the National Statuary Hall of the federal capitol. In 1903 the statues of Austin and Houston were unveiled in
the state capitol, and in 1905 the other pair was presented to the federal
government.

Ney's conception of Austin bore the unmistakable influence of Guy
Bryan. The artist portrayed Austin in buckskin, with a Kentucky long rifle
cradled in the crook of one arm while holding a map of Texas open with
both hands. Austin gazes thoughtfully but somewhat dreamily toward the
horizon, as if contemplating the magnificent future of Texas. The statue
contrasts sharply with that of Houston, which shows the hero of San
Jacinto in a much more aggressive stance, hand on his sword, his eyes
fixed on a much more immediate object, as if surveying his troops. Bryan
had impressed upon Ney the idea that Austin's heroic qualities were of
a different sort than Houston's: Austin the planner, builder, and visionary, a man of peace; Houston the pragmatic commander, a man of war.
Implicit was the idea that both men—indeed, both *types* of men—were
necessary to the birth of Texas. When asked why Austin was as deserv-

Elizabeth Ney, statue of Stephen F. Austin, 1903. This
statue, and a matching one of Sam Houston, were
placed in the state and national capitols. *Courtesy,*
Texas Highways *magazine.*

ing as Houston to be thus immortalized, Ney replied that "though nature
printed upon him less the stamp of an aggressive warrior, his deeds, his
courage, his sufferings, his love for others entitled him to equal recognition with those who became foremost on the battlefields of actual war."
Guy Bryan had performed his task well.[22]

The Daughters of the Republic of Texas had spearheaded the fundraising drive that placed one copy of the Austin statue in the National
Statuary Hall, and their strategy is instructive. The Daughters knew that
they would not be able to raise the $8,000 needed to have both the Austin
and Houston statues cut in marble and sent to Washington. So they decided to devote their fundraising efforts to paying for the Austin statue,

and then to petition the state legislature to pay for the Sam Houston piece. As the DRT forthrightly explained, they did this "knowing the State would respond to the call for the Houston statue." In other words, the patriotic ladies of the DRT knew that if Austin were securely enshrined in the nation's capitol, the legislature would have no choice but to send Houston along to accompany him; but Austin's standing among Texans was still not quite certain enough for the Daughters to be sure that the legislature would respond positively if the situation were reversed. It was a clever and prudent ploy.[23]

With Austin now standing sentinel in Italian marble alongside Houston in both the state and national capitols, the stage was set for the final steps in the rehabilitation of Austin's reputation. The process had only taken seventy-five years. In 1910, the Texas legislature made arrangements for Austin's remains to be exhumed from their resting place at Peach Point plantation in Brazoria County and buried with high honors in the State Cemetery in Austin. On October 18 a group of legislators and Austin relatives opened Austin's grave and found the empresario's bones "in a state of complete preservation." Services were held in Houston, and then the bones were brought by train to Austin, where a military escort accompanied them to the state capitol. From there they were taken to the State Cemetery and reinterred on the highest point on the grounds. Elder statesman Alexander W. Terrell completed this extraordinary two-day ritual with a moving speech in a solemn ceremony in the senate chamber. Sculptor Pompeo Coppini was commissioned to create the large bronze statue that marks the grave site today. In the state's evolving civil religion, Stephen F. Austin was now a sacred icon.[24]

From the perspective of the Austin family, only one thing was missing. There was still no biography of the great man. Throughout the late 1800s, Guy Bryan had sought a biographer who could do full "justice" to his famous uncle. In the final decade of the century, at least three writers laid plans for such a work. James T. DeShields and John G. James both made starts, but neither got very far. Finally Bryan found his man in Lester G. Bugbee, a young historian at the University of Texas. Bugbee's mentor at the University, Professor George P. Garrison, interceded with Bryan to secure access to the Austin Papers. Garrison knew exactly what to say to Stephen Austin's elderly nephew, explaining that "while Mr. Bugbee would never fail to use conscientiously any material that might fall into his hands, and while he would in no case swerve from the substantial truth to save the reputation of any man of whom he had to write, you will find him thoroughly courteous and discreet." Bryan granted Bugbee access to the Austin papers, still housed in Bryan's home at Quintana. In 1898, at Garrison's prodding, Bryan finally brought the papers to Austin and deposited them in a fireproof room in the state capitol. The family later donated them to the university's archives.[25]

In early 1901, Bugbee's poor health forced him to retire to "ranch life" in West Texas. Guy Bryan died a few months later, and Bugbee died the following year, having produced several scholarly articles but nothing on the biography. The stage thus was set for Eugene C. Barker, another University of Texas historian. Barker had begun his career with an interest in Texas-Mexican relations, preferring to leave the work on Austin to his friend and colleague, Bugbee. But Bugbee's death, combined with Austin's growing public reputation, led Barker to reconsider the direction of his own scholarly career. Shortly before Bugbee's death Barker had asked his ailing colleague whether a "collection of Austin's letters" would constitute a good "adjunct to your life of him." "They would certainly make good reading," Barker reasoned, "and I believe the whole would sell well." Barker began the laborious task of editing the papers for publication. Bugbee's death led Barker to realize that if he did not undertake an Austin biography, someone else surely would.[26]

His professorial duties and the magnitude of the editing job on the Austin papers delayed the biography for many years. Barker faced a formidable task. He had to conduct his research comprehensively and write objectively, but at the same time he sought to portray Austin as the modest, determined, self-sacrificing Father of Texas that the public—and Barker himself—believed Austin to be. When *The Life of Stephen F. Austin* appeared in 1925, it was rightly hailed as a masterpiece. The book established Barker as a giant of Texas historiography and fixed the mythic Father of Texas image of Austin in both the public and the scholarly minds. Only in recent times have scholars offered any significant revisionist views of Austin, in some cases echoing the criticisms of Austin that had been made in his own lifetime.[27]

Measured by the goals he set for himself, Stephen F. Austin's life was uncommonly successful. He achieved his early ambition of restoring his family's fortune; after his death, officials of the Brazoria County Court appraised his estate at $527,485. Even though most of this wealth was in land and could not have commanded anywhere near that figure on the open market in 1837, it left his heirs a substantial legacy.

But it was in his pursuit of his larger goals that Austin enjoyed the most success. His great dream of "redeeming" Texas from its "wilderness" state, of peopling the land with enterprising families, was certainly realized. Thanks in large measure to the unceasing efforts of his family, he also became generally regarded as the father of his country, although he died much as he lived, never feeling fully appreciated. Yet Austin lived to see enough of his principal design fulfilled that he could take personal satisfaction from his achievements. As he told Mary Holley in 1831, "The credit of settling this fine country and *laying the foundation for a new Nation which at some future period will arise here can not be taken from me.*"[28]

However, like all great achievements, these were purchased at a cost. Ultimately there would be no place in Austin's Texas for the Indians whom the Anglo settlers displaced from the land. The more-or-less pristine environment that he explored with awe in 1821 was forever altered in his own lifetime. Austin's Tejano friends and their descendants eventually found themselves pushed to the margins of the society that he helped create. Slavery, which Austin described as "that curse of curses" but which he did so much to perpetuate in Texas, brought sorrow to untold thousands of black Texans and a devastating Civil War to Austin's native country. Nor did he realize his oft-stated personal desire to settle down to a quiet life as a gentleman farmer, surround himself with congenial friends and family, and pursue his idealistic educational schemes.

Historians are necessarily wary of speculation about "what might have been" in history; alternative outcomes can never be known. It nonetheless seems appropriate for a biography to ask what difference its subject made in history. How would the history of Texas, Mexico, and Westward Expansion read without Stephen F. Austin? Given Mexico's economic and political weaknesses and the United States' relentless appetite for new lands, it is hard to imagine a scenario in which Mexico could have retained Texas and the rest of the Southwest indefinitely. What Austin made possible was the peaceful, and mostly lawful, occupation of Texas by thousands of American families. Without that occupation, the subsequent chain of events by which Mexico lost its northern provinces would be dramatically different, albeit in ways unknowable.

Austin's legacy, then, like his life, is complex and contradictory. No one understood this better than Austin himself. "Such is life!" he declared to Mary Holley in 1832, " — *a speck between two eternities*. . . . But it is our all." Stephen F. Austin knew that life was short and uncertain. He sought to live it purposefully, and did.[29]

✢ Appendix ✢
Austin's Circle

After making a few special bequests to individual friends and relatives, Austin left half of his estate to Brown Austin's son, eight-year-old Stephen F. Austin, Jr., and the other half to his sister Emily Perry. However, Austin's namesake died in February 1837, so the entire estate reverted to Emily. James Perry was executor of his brother-in-law's will. Emily and James lived at Peach Point plantation until their deaths, hers in 1851 and his two years later. Emily was survived by six children, three by her first husband, James Bryan, and three by James Perry.

The three Bryan brothers all enjoyed long lives and productive careers. The eldest, William Joel Bryan, prospered as a planter, town developer, banker, and railroad promoter. The city of Bryan, Texas, which he helped to found, bears his name. Moses Austin Bryan, who had so many adventures as his uncle's traveling companion, secretary, and military aide, served as secretary of the Texas legation to the United States and in the armies of both the Republic of Texas and the Confederacy. As a founder of the Texas Veterans Association, he did much to preserve the history of early Anglo Texas. The youngest of the brothers, Guy Morrison Bryan, served in the army of the Republic, the U.S. Army during the U.S.-Mexican War, and the Confederate Army. He also spent ten years in the Texas legislature and two in U.S. Congress. He was a founding member of the Texas Veterans Association and the Texas State Historical Association.

Two of Emily's children by James Perry never married. The son who did marry, Stephen Samuel Perry, inherited the family estate at Peach Point. His descendants still own the plantation.

Henry Austin's devotion to his cousin continued after the empresario's death. At James Perry's request, he spent much of 1837 producing a detailed report on all of the empresario's land business, fulfilling a directive from the Texas senate. Henry never succeeded in any of his business ventures. He died in 1852, ending, as he put it in his will, "a long life of incessant enterprise, toil, privation, and suffering."

Samuel May Williams returned to Texas and settled down in Galveston, where he concentrated on his banking business and dabbled in politics. There is no record of his ever again mentioning the name of Stephen F. Austin. He died in 1858.

Erasmo Seguín lived on his ranch near San Antonio until his death in 1857. His son Juan fought with Houston at San Jacinto, buried the remains of the Alamo defenders, served three terms in the Republic of Texas congress and two as mayor of San Antonio. Accused of disloyalty by Anglo Texans, he spent six years in exile in Mexico and fought with Mexican troops against the Americans in the U.S.-Mexican War. After the war he returned to South Texas, where he became active in local Democratic politics. He died in Nuevo Laredo in 1890 and was reburied in 1976 in the Texas town that bears his name.

Arthur Wavell received his own empresario contract after Austin abandoned their partnership, but the project failed. He died in London in 1860.

José Antonio Mexía worked for a New Orleans import-export company for three years following the Texas Revolution. In January 1839 he joined a federalist uprising in Tampico. Four months later he was captured and executed by a firing squad on the orders of Santa Anna.

Lorenzo de Zavala served as David Burnet's vice-president in the interim government that ruled Texas from March until October 1836. He contracted pneumonia and died at his home on Buffalo Bayou in November, five weeks before Austin's death.

Lucas Alamán remained active in Mexican politics. The erstwhile author of the Law of 1830 recommended Mexican recognition of Texas in 1840 on practical grounds and later became an open advocate of monarchy. Before his death in 1853 he wrote a multi-volume history of Mexico and several other scholarly works.

Antonio López de Santa Anna eventually returned to Mexico, where he regained popularity for heroic action against the French in the so-called Pastry War. He alternated between the presidential palace and exile until his death in 1876.

Valentín Gómez Farías returned from exile to serve once more as Santa Anna's vice-president but broke with him when Santa Anna betrayed him yet again. He died in 1858, a dedicated federalist to the end.

Juan Nepomuceno Almonte returned to Mexico with Santa Anna after the Texas Revolution and rose to the rank of general. He later served as Mexico's minister to the United States, Great Britain, and France, where he died in 1869.

George L. Hammeken moved from Mexico City to Texas on the advice of his friend Stephen F. Austin. After the war he participated in railroad and mercantile ventures and married the daughter of José Antonio Mexía. He died sometime after 1845.

Anthony Butler was recalled by the U.S. government from his diplomatic post in Mexico in January 1836. After the Revolution he settled in Washington County, Texas, and served in the Republic's congress. He died in a steamboat fire on the Mississippi River in 1849 or 1850.

William H. Wharton failed in his efforts to secure the annexation of Texas by the United States. Returning to Texas in 1837, he was captured by a Mexican ship and imprisoned in Matamoros. He soon escaped to Texas, where he was elected to the Republic's senate. He was killed in a firearms accident in 1839.

Branch T. Archer served the Republic as speaker of the house and as secretary of war under Mirabeau B. Lamar. He remained active in Texas politics until his death in 1856. A town and a county in North Texas were named in his honor.

Henry Smith served as treasury secretary during Sam Houston's first administration and later in the Republic's congress. He retired from public life in 1841 but in 1849 set out for the California gold fields. He found no gold and died in a mining camp in 1851.

Sterling C. Robertson ignored the Monclova legislature's act returning the Upper Colony to Austin and Williams, and he continued to issue titles to settlers in the grant until the Revolution shut down the land offices. The independence of Texas ended the empresario system, but for years Robertson doggedly pursued a lawsuit against the Republic to have himself recognized as empresario so that he could claim his premium lands. In 1841 the courts ruled in his favor and he received title to some 138,000 acres (cut in half when the state of Texas appealed). He died the following year.

Sam Houston was twice elected president of the Republic, followed by a distinguished thirteen-year career in the U.S. Senate. Elected governor of Texas on a unionist ticket in 1859, he was forced from office in 1861 when he refused to take an oath of allegiance to the Confederacy. He died at his home in Huntsville in 1863.

Michael Muldoon remained a staunch supporter of Texas interests. After writing his poem eulogizing his friend Austin, he next appeared in Matamoros, where he helped William H. Wharton escape from jail. He briefly served as Catholic vicar general of the Republic of Texas before disappearing from the historical record.

Mary Austin Holley made several trips back to Texas after her cousin's death, in part to gather information for the biography of Stephen F. Austin that she planned to write. In 1845 she returned to Louisiana and resumed her duties as governess to the Labranche family. She died there of yellow fever the following year. She never remarried.

✦ Notes ✦

Abbreviations

AGEC	Fondo de Instituto Estatal de Documentación, Archivo General del Estado de Coahuila, Saltillo.
AGN	Archivo General de la Nación, Mexico City.
AP	Eugene C. Barker, ed., *The Austin Papers*, 2 vols. (Washington, D.C.: Government Printing Office, 1924, 1928); 3rd vol. (Austin: University of Texas, 1927).
BA	Béxar Archives
CAH	Center for American History, University of Texas, Austin
FJPB	Fondo Jefatura Político de Béxar
HT	*The New Handbook of Texas*, 6 vols. (Austin: Texas State Historical Association, 1996).
LSFA	Eugene C. Barker, *The Life of Stephen F. Austin, Founder of Texas, 1793–1836: A Chapter in the Westward Movement of the Anglo-American People* (Nashville: Cokesbury, 1925; reprint ed., Austin: University of Texas Press, 1969). Throughout this book I have used the most recent edition of Barker's work. The 1925 work was republished with new pagination in 1949, and all citations found here correspond to the pagination of the post-1949 editions.
PCRCT	Malcolm D. McLean, ed. and comp., *Papers Concerning Robertson's Colony in Texas*, 3 vols. (Fort Worth: Texas Christian University Press, 1974–76); 15 vols. plus intro vol. (Arlington: UTA Press, 1977–93).
PTR	John H. Jenkins, ed., *The Papers of the Texas Revolution, 1835–1836*, 10 vols. (Austin: Presidial Press, 1973).
SFA	Stephen F. Austin
SWHQ	*Southwestern Historical Quarterly*

Introduction

1. *LSFA*, vii. There are several minor biographical works devoted to Austin. Sallie Glasscock's *Dreams of an Empire: The Story of Stephen Fuller Austin and His Colony in*

Texas (San Antonio: Naylor, 1950) is brief, adulatory, and adds little to our understanding of Austin. Two other works, Carleton Beals's *Stephen F. Austin: Father of Texas* (New York: McGraw-Hill, 1953) and Barker's *The Father of Texas* (Indianapolis: Bobbs-Merrill, 1935), are both intended for juvenile audiences.

2. Moses Austin to SFA, December 16, 1804, *AP,* I, 93.

3. Mary Austin to Rebecca Leaming, September 2, 1813, Leaming Papers, CAH (first quotation); SFA to the Colonists, August 6, 1823, *AP,* I, 680 (second quotation).

4. Frederick Jackson Turner, "The Significance of the Frontier in American History," in *The Frontier in American History* (New York: Holt, Rinehart and Winston, 1962), 1–38. This essay, first delivered in 1893, has been reprinted many times in various forms.

5. Paul D. Lack, "In the Long Shadow of Eugene C. Barker: The Revolution and the Republic," in Walter L. Buenger and Robert A. Calvert, eds., *Texas Through Time: Evolving Interpretations* (College Station: Texas A&M University Press, 1991), 134–64. On Barker's life, see William C. Pool, *Eugene C. Barker: Historian* (Austin: Texas State Historical Association, 1971).

6. For a sampling of the some of the more general works of the New Western History, see William Cronon et al., eds., *Under an Open Sky: Rethinking America's Western Past* (New York: W. W. Norton, 1992); Patricia Nelson Limerick, *The Legacy of Conquest: The Unbroken Past of the American West* (New York: W. W. Norton, 1987); Limerick et al., eds., *Trails: Toward a New Western History* (Lawrence: University Press of Kansas, 1991); Richard White, *"It's Your Misfortune and None of My Own": A New History of the American West* (Norman: University of Oklahoma Press, 1991); Donald Worster, *Under Western Skies: Nature and History in the American West* (New York: Oxford University Press, 1992).

7. Lack, "In the Long Shadow," 135.

8. By my count Texas is mentioned in eleven different paragraphs in Limerick's 349-page book. Her treatment of Texas colonization and the Texas Revolution are confined to two paragraphs on pp. 230–31; see Limerick, *Legacy of Conquest,* 36–37, 145, 227, 229–32. Richard White's sweeping survey of western history is more inclusive of Texas, devoting five pages to the Anglo settlement and conquest of Texas and including Texas in many of its thematic chapters; see White, *"It's Your Misfortune,"* 64–69 and passim. For a revealing analysis of how a broad cross-section of western writers and historians define the West, see Walter Nugent, "Where Is the American West? Report on a Survey," *Montana: The Magazine of Western History* 42 (Summer 1992): 2–23.

9. The size and scope of the recent historical literature on the antebellum South precludes citing specific works here; two of the best guides to that literature are Arthur S. Link and Rembert W. Patrick, eds., *Writing Southern History: Essays in Historiography in Honor of Fletcher M. Green* (Baton Rouge: Louisiana State University Press, 1966); and John B. Boles and Evelyn Thomas Nolen, eds., *Interpreting Southern History: Historiographical Essays in Honor of Sanford W. Higginbotham* (Baton Rouge: Louisiana State University Press, 1987).

10. SFA to Mary Austin Holley, December 29, 1831, *AP,* II, 730 (first quotation);

SFA to Wiley Martin, May 30, 1833, ibid., 981 (second quotation); Harold Schoen, "The Free Negro in the Republic of Texas," *SWHQ* 39 (April 1936): 292–301.

11. For example see SFA to Samuel May Williams, April 12, 1832, *AP*, II, 765; SFA to Horatio Chriesman, June 19, 1832, ibid., 783.

12. There is a growing body of scholarly literature devoted to Hispanic Texas and its *Tejano* (native Hispanic Texan) population. Among the more recent of these works are Donald E. Chipman, *Spanish Texas, 1519–1821* (Austin: University of Texas Press, 1992); Arnoldo De León, *The Tejano Community, 1836–1900* (Albuquerque: University of New Mexico Press, 1982); Timothy M. Matovina, *Tejano Religion and Ethnicity: San Antonio, 1821–1860* (Austin: University of Texas Press, 1995); Gerald E. Poyo and Gilberto M. Hinojosa, eds., *Tejano Origins in Eighteenth-Century San Antonio* (Austin: University of Texas Press, for University of Texas Institute of Texan Cultures at San Antonio, 1991); Andrés Reséndez, "Caught Between Profits and Rituals: National Contestation in Texas and New Mexico, 1821–1848," Ph.D. diss., University of Chicago, 1997; Jesús F. de la Teja, *San Antonio de Béxar: A Community on New Spain's Northern Frontier* (Albuquerque: University of New Mexico Press, 1995); Andrés Tijerina, *Tejanos and Texas Under the Mexican Flag, 1821–1836* (College Station: Texas A&M University Press, 1994).

13. Josefina Zoraida Vázquez, "De la difícil constitución de un Estado: México, 1821–1854," in Vázquez, ed., *La fundación del Estado Mexicano* (Mexico City: Nueva Imagen, 1994), 37 (first quotation); Vito Alessio Robles, *Coahuila y Texas desde la Consumación de la Independencia hasta el Tratado de Paz de Guadalupe Hidalgo* (Mexico City, 1945), xi. The two best modern general treatments of Mexican politics in the 1820s and 1830s, one published in Spanish by an Englishman and the other in English by an American, are, respectively, Michael P. Costeloe, *La Primera República Federal de México (1824–1835)* (Mexico City: Fondo de Cultura Económica, 1975), and Stanley C. Green, *The Mexican Republic: The First Decade, 1823–1832* (Pittsburgh: University of Pittsburgh Press, 1987). Much of the most useful recent work on the period has been published in anthologies, some in English and some in Spanish, with essays by both Mexican and foreign authors. Among these are three books edited by Jaime E. Rodríguez O.: *The Evolution of the Mexican Political System* (Wilmington, Del.: Scholarly Resources, 1993), *The Independence of Mexico and the Creation of the New Nation* (Los Angeles: UCLA Latin American Center Publications, 1989), and *Patterns of Contention in Mexican History* (Wilmington, Del.: Scholarly Resources, 1993); Vázquez, *La fundación del Estado Mexicano*, and *De la rebelión de Texas a la Guerra del 47* (Mexico City: Nueva Imagen, 1994). Studies with a local or state focus, such as Peter Guardino's *Peasants, Politics, and the Formation of Mexico's National State: Guerrero, 1800–1857* (Stanford: Stanford University Press, 1996) are shedding important new light on the era, but no such work has thus far appeared for the state of Coahuila y Texas, leaving Robles's book the standard work on the state.

14. David J. Weber, *The Mexican Frontier, 1821–1846: The American Southwest Under Mexico* (Albuquerque: University of New Mexico Press, 1982), and *The Spanish Frontier in North America* (New Haven: Yale University Press, 1992), 11; Gregory H.

Nobles, *American Frontiers: Cultural Encounters and Continental Conquest* (New York: Hill and Wang, 1997), xii. It can be argued that there are actually two schools of New Western History. The best-known school, whose members have been called New Western Regionalists, rejects the concept of the frontier as hopelessly ethnocentric and triumphalist and insists that the West can be understood only as a geographic region defined by aridity. The other school envisions a Greater Western History, rejecting the ethnocentrism of the Turner school but still analyzing frontier experiences in continental or even global contexts. Any approach to Texas history — if it hopes to incorporate the most important and viable tenets of the New Western History — has no choice but to embrace this Greater Western variant on the revisionist theme. In other words, the concept of *frontier* must be shorn of its chauvinist overtones of manifest destiny and Anglo, male, elite triumphalism. For a sophisticated overview of these issues, see Kerwin Lee Klein, "Reclaiming the 'F' Word, or Being and Becoming Postwestern," *Pacific Historical Review* 65 (May 1996): 179–215.

15. Useful overviews of these themes can be found in Marvin Meyers, *The Jacksonian Persuasion: Politics and Beliefs* (Stanford: Stanford University Press, 1957), esp. chap. 3; Edward Pessen, *Jacksonian America: Society, Personality, and Politics* (Homewood, Ill.: Dorsey, 1969), esp. chap. 2; and Glyndon Van Deusen, *The Jacksonian Era, 1828–1848* (New York: Harper and Brothers, 1959), esp. chap. 1; and Harry L. Watson, *Liberty and Power: The Politics of Jacksonian America* (New York: Noonday, 1990), esp. p. 6.

16. SFA to Thomas F. Leaming, June 14, 1830, *AP*, II, 415.

17. Abraham Lincoln, "First Inaugural Address," in Brooks D. Simpson, ed., *Think Anew, Act Anew: Abraham Lincoln on Slavery, Freedom, and Union* (Wheeling, Ill.: Harlan Davidson, 1998), 88; Leo M. Kaiser, ed., "Stephen F. Austin's Oration of July 4, 1818," *SWHQ* 64 (July 1960): 77; SFA to Lucas Alamán, January 20, 1824, *AP*, I, 728.

18. Larry McMurtry, "How the West Was Won or Lost," *The New Republic,* October 22, 1990.

19. Limerick, *The Legacy of Conquest,* 44.

20. SFA to James F. Perry, July 11, 1830, *AP*, II, 447.

ONE

A Foundation for Greatness
1793–1810

1. The scenario offered in this and the following paragraphs is based on Moses Austin to SFA, December 16, 1804, *AP*, I, 93–94. In this letter Moses Austin acknowledged having received SFA's letter of September 26 "in due time." Travel time from Missouri to Connecticut in 1800 was roughly four to five weeks, so SFA's letter must have been greatly delayed. However, if there were no delays Moses's return letter should have arrived in Connecticut in late January; see map in Glyndon G. Van Deusen, *The Jacksonian Era, 1828–1848* (New York: Harper, 1959), 4.

2. Moses Austin to SFA, December 16, 1804, *AP,* I, 93–94. The quotations and information in the next four paragraphs are also from this letter.

3. All of the information on the Austin forebears found in this and the following seven paragraphs is taken from David B. Gracy II, *Moses Austin: His Life* (San Antonio: Trinity University Press, 1987), 5–52, passim.

4. SFA to Mary Austin Holley, December 29, 1831, *AP,* II, 727. See also Moses Austin's remarks about Maria in Gracy, *Moses Austin,* 27.

5. Maria Austin to SFA, January 19, 1822, *AP,* I, 467. For evidence of Maria Austin's piety see Mary (Maria) Austin to Rebecca Leaming, August 28, 1814, Leaming (Thomas F.) Papers, CAH; Maria Austin to SFA, August 25, 1821, *AP,* I, 408–10. The only direct evidence of Maria's religious upbringing is the fact that she and Moses were married in Philadelphia's Christ Church, an Anglican congregation, but she also had numerous Quaker ancestors. For the religious background of both Moses and Maria, see Gracy, *Moses Austin,* 12–13, 23, 24.

6. Emily Margaret Brown Austin was born on June 22, 1795; see Gracy, *Moses Austin,* 52.

7. Gracy, *Moses Austin,* 53–60; the quotations are from Henry Rowe Schoolcraft, *Travels in the Central Portions of the Mississippi Valley* (quoted on p. 59 of Gracy).

8. Gracy, *Moses Austin,* 60–65. The name Mine à Breton was bastardized over the years, and after the Louisiana Purchase it was more often called Mine a Burton (or some variation thereon). I will adhere to the more correct Mine à Breton.

9. George P. Garrison, ed., "A Memorandum of M. Austin's Journey from the Lead Mines in the County of Wythe in the State of Virginia to the Lead Mines in the Province of Louisiana West of the Mississippi, 1796–1797," *American Historical Review* 5 (April 1900): 518–542 (quotation on p. 542); Gracy, *Moses Austin,* 66.

10. Gracy, *Moses Austin,* 66–68.

11. Ibid., 68–69.

12. Ibid.; Record of Moses Austin and Family, n.d., *AP,* I, 2.

13. Gracy, *Moses Austin,* 60–61, 78–79.

14. Nicolas de Finiels, *An Account of Upper Louisiana* [1803], ed. Carl J. Ekberg and William E. Foley (Columbia: University of Missouri Press, 1989), 49–50; H. M. Brackenridge, *Recollections of Persons and Places in the West* (Philadelphia: James Kay, Jun., and Brother, [1834]), 25–29 (quotations on pp. 28–29).

15. Gracy, *Moses Austin,* 72–79.

16. Ibid., chaps. 6–8, esp.p. 128 (estimate of assets); and 71–73, 114 (Mine à Breton descriptions).

17. Gracy, *Moses Austin,* 73, 114–115 (quoting from SFA to the Cherokees, *AP,* I, 1308). On Missouri as a "frontier of inclusion," see John Mack Faragher, " 'More Motley than Mackinaw': From Ethnic Mixing to Ethnic Cleansing on the Frontier of Missouri, 1783–1833," *H-West,* 1997 (internet article: www.h-net.msu.edu/~shear/motley3.htm).

18. Gracy, *Moses Austin,* 91; Garrison, "Memorandum of M. Austin's Journey," 519. In 1819 Moses Austin wrote a short chronology of the family's history, and in the section

where he mentioned the 1802 Indian attack, he tersely noted that "the french gave No assistance"; see Record of Moses Austin and Family, *AP,* I, 2.

19. Gracy, *Moses Austin,* 100–118.

20. Moses Austin to Daniel Phelps, *AP,* I, 92–93.

21. Moses Austin to SFA, December 16, 1804, *AP,* I, 93.

22. Moses Austin to ?, n.d. (c. fall 1804), *AP,* I, 95–96; Gracy, *Moses Austin,* 115–16.

23. Moses Austin to ?, n.d. (c. fall 1804), *AP,* I, 95.

24. Theodore R. Sizer, *The Age of the Academies* (New York: Bureau of Publications, Teachers College, Columbia University, 1964), 1–11.

25. Aram Damarjian, "Bacon Academy History," in Bacon Academy *Alumni Beacon* (1953), pamphlet in Cragin Memorial Library, Colchester, Connecticut, 12–28; Franklin Bowditch Dexter, *Biographical Sketches of the Graduates of Yale College with Annals of the College History,* V (New York: Henry Holt, 1911), 133–35.

26. Damarjian, "Bacon Academy History," 24–25.

27. *Original Miscellany: Being the Exercises Performed at the Exhibition of the Adelphian Society in Bacon Academy, Colchester; May 6, 1806* (New London, Conn.: Cady & Eells, 1806) (all quotations in this and the preceding paragraph except the Webster quotation); Webster quoted in Bernard C. Steiner, *The History of Education in Connecticut* (Washington, D.C.: Government Printing Office, 1893), 49.

28. Certificate of Scholarship and Conduct, January 7, 1808, *AP,* I, 144; Damarjian, "Bacon Academy History," 27–28 (quotations).

29. Dexter, *Biographical Sketches,* 134; Certificate of Scholarship and Conduct, January 7, 1808, *AP,* I, 144.

30. Damarjian, "Bacon Academy History," 25, 28; John C. Pease and John M. Niles, *A Gazetteer of the States of Connecticut and Rhode-Island* (Hartford: William S. Mahan, 1819), 151; Janet W. Pendleton, "Slavery and Colchester's School for Colored Children," *Connecticut League of Historical Societies League Bulletin* 21 (December 1969): 130.

31. Certificate of Scholarship and Conduct, January 7, 1808, *AP,* I, 144 (quotation); Maria Austin to Moses Austin, September 8, 1811, copy in David Gracy Papers, Trinity University, San Antonio, Texas.

32. Austin received his Certificate of Scholarship and Conduct from Bacon Academy in January 1808. No documentation of his life from that time until he completed his studies at Transylvania in 1810 exists, but it is unthinkable that he would not have visited home after such a long absence. The Certificate of Attendance he received from Transylvania in April 1810 states that he had attended "two sessions & a half." As of 1805, the academic year had consisted of two sessions per year, beginning in November and May. If this was still the normal schedule four years later, and if Austin's two and a half sessions were consecutive ones, then he would have first entered the university in late 1808 or the beginning of 1809. However, the length and timing of sessions may have varied over time, and Austin may not have attended back-to-back sessions, so it is possible that he began earlier in 1808. See Certificate of Attendance at Transylvania University, April 4, 1810, *AP,* I, 171; John D. Wright, Jr., *Transylvania: Tutor to the West,* rev. ed. (Lexington: University Press of Kentucky, 1980), 50.

33. Wright, *Transylvania,* 16–19; Richard C. Wade, *The Urban Frontier: Pioneer Life in Early Pittsburgh, Cincinnati, Lexington, Louisville, and St. Louis* (Cambridge: Harvard University Press, 1959; reprint ed., Chicago: University of Chicago Press, 1964), 49–53.

34. Niels Henry Sonne, *Liberal Kentucky, 1780–1828* (New York: Columbia University Press, 1939), chap. 1.

35. Sonne, *Liberal Kentucky,* chaps. 1–2 passim, esp. 10, 23 (quotation), 33–39, 67–68, 73–77.

36. Wright, *Transylvania,* 39–41, 48–50, 52. When Austin left the university in 1810 there were about seventy students in attendance; see Isaac L. Baker to SFA, August 5, 1810, *AP,* I, 179.

37. Certificate of Attendance at Transylvania University, April 4, 1810, *AP,* I, 171; Wright, *Transylvania,* 52.

38. Robert S. Todd to SFA, May 17, 1810, *AP,* I, 172; Isaac Baker to SFA, February 25, 1811, ibid., 183. Also see Isaac L. Baker to SFA, July 1, 1810, ibid., 174–76; Isaac L. Baker to SFA, August 5, 1810, ibid., 178–79; John Bowman to SFA, April 28, 1811, ibid., 189. Mary Todd Lincoln's biographer reports that "by the time she [Eliza Parker] was fifteen gossip linked her name to that of two young students at the university: Stephen Austin and Robert Smith Todd." See Jean H. Baker, *Mary Todd Lincoln: A Biography* (New York: W. W. Norton, 1987), 11. The source of this gossip is not clear. Many years later another of SFA's Transylvania classmates, John M. McCalla, reported to SFA on an Eliza "for whom we both had pretty strong *penchants,*" but it is clear from McCalla's letter that this is a different Eliza; see John M. McCalla to SFA, October 6, 1829, *AP,* II, 261. It seems probable that the "Eliza P." whom Robert Todd mentioned in 1810 was indeed Eliza Parker.

39. Isaac L. Baker to SFA, July 1, 1810, *AP,* I, 175; John Bowman to SFA, April 28, 1811, ibid., ; Isaac L. Baker to SFA, February 25, 1811, ibid., 185.

40. Wade, *Urban Frontier,* 236; Wright, *Transylvania,* 37 (first quotation); Maria von Phule (?) to Anna Gist, April 8, 1808, Henrietta Clay Collection, Transylvania University (second, third, and fourth quotations). For Austin's love of dancing, see SFA to James Bryan, January [?], 1814, Austin Papers, Series II, CAH; SFA to Mary Austin Holley, January 4, 1832, *AP,* II, 733; C. Richard Kind, ed., *Victorian Lady on the Texas Frontier: The Journal of Ann Raney Coleman* (Norman: University of Oklahoma Press, 1971), 33; Moses Austin Bryan, "Recollections of Stephen F. Austin," *Texas Magazine* 3 (September 1897): 102; *LSFA,* 389.

41. Certificate of Attendance at Transylvania University, April 4, 1810, *AP,* I, 171.

42. Mary [Maria] Austin to Moses Austin, August 26, 1811, photocopied typescript in Gracy Papers, Trinity University; Gracy, *Moses Austin,* 127–33.

TWO
Successes and Failures
1810–1818

1. Gracy, *Moses Austin,* 128. Austin left Kentucky in April 1810, and he can be placed at home in Missouri as of June 10; see Isaac L. Baker to SFA, August 5, 1810, *AP,* I, 178–79. The historical record is almost entirely silent on Austin's activities during the last six months of 1810, but based on business records from early 1811 it seems nearly certain that he had spent the previous months learning his father's mercantile business.

2. Gracy, *Moses Austin,* 128–32. Moses's nephew Henry Austin spent most of a year, presumably with Moses paying his expenses, in Washington, D.C., unsuccessfully lobbying Congress to pass a bill incorporating the mine.

3. Herculaneum was the second of three American towns that could claim Moses Austin as their founder. Austinville, Virginia, was the first, and in 1814, Moses Austin laid out the town of Potosi, Missouri, adjacent to the Mine à Breton tract; see Gracy, *Moses Austin,* 124–26, 151–52.

4. *Missouri Gazette* (St. Louis), February 7, 1811 (quotation); Gracy, *Moses Austin,* 129. The attack took place on January 23.

5. Maria Austin to Moses Austin, October 25, 1812, typed copy in David Gracy Papers, Trinity University, San Antonio, Texas (first, second, third, and fourth quotations); Maria Austin to SFA, January 19, 1822, *AP,* I, 468 (fifth quotation).

6. J. E. B. Austin to Emily M. Perry, February 28, 1826, *AP,* I, 1268; SFA to Emily M. Perry, January 26, 1833, *AP,* II, 922.

7. See J. Austin to SFA, January 12, 1811, George English to SFA, February 14, 1811, J. W. Cooper to SFA, February 24, 1811, J. W. Love to SFA, March 8, 1811, *AP,* I, 182, 183, 185, 186; Accounts of John W. and Benjamin Coleman, October 5, 1811, Austin Papers, Series V, CAH; *Missouri Gazette,* August 8, 1811; SFA to James Bryan, October 8, 1811, *AP,* I, 195; Maria Austin to Moses Austin, November 12, 1811, typed copy in Gracy Papers.

8. Gracy, *Moses Austin,* 133–36; Maria Austin to Moses Austin, September 8, 1811, and November 12, 1811, typescripts in Gracy Papers.

9. Maria Austin to Moses Austin, November 12, 1811, typed copy in Gracy Papers (first quotation); SFA to James Bryan, October 8, 1811, *AP,* I, 195 (second quotation). One of the most complete accounts of the New Madrid earthquake is Robert Sidney Douglass, *History of Southeast Missouri* (Chicago: Lewis, 1912), 1: 212–33. Also see David D. March, *The History of Missouri* (New York: Lewis Historical Publishing, 1967), 266–70.

10. Maria Austin to Moses Austin, June 7, 1812, typed copy in Gracy Papers.

11. Gracy, *Moses Austin,* 137.

12. Moses Austin, Memorandum and Instructions for Stephen Fuller Austin respecting the business of Moses Austin and Co in New York and New Orleans, April 28, 1812, Austin Papers, Series III, CAH; Moses Austin to SFA, April 28, 1812, *AP,* I, 202–5 (quotations). There is no record of SFA having companions on the journey, but it seems

unlikely that he could have steered a lead barge single-handedly. Presumably he was accompanied by hired hands or slaves.

13. Moses Austin to SFA, April 28, 1812, *AP*, I, 203–4.

14. Ibid., 203; Douglass, *History of Southeast Missouri*, 1: 214–23; Stephen F. Austin's Diary, [May 17–19, 1812], *AP*, I, 205–8.

15. Gracy, *Moses Austin*, 139–40; *Louisiana Gazette and New-Orleans Daily Advertiser* (New Orleans), July 10, 1812.

16. SFA to Moses Austin, July 12, 1812, *AP*, I, 216; Gracy, *Moses Austin*, 140.

17. Moses Austin to James Bryan, October 19, 1812, *AP*, I, 218–219 (quotation); *Louisiana Gazette*, August 22, 1812.

18. Maria Austin to Moses Austin, August 4, 1812, typed copy in Gracy Papers; Gracy, *Moses Austin*, 142–45.

19. Stephen F. Austin's Diary, February [1813], *AP*, I, 208–209; Maria Austin to Moses Austin, June 23, 1812, ibid., 213; Moses Austin to James Bryan, January 4, 1813, ibid., 223.

20. Militia Appointments, April–September, 1813, Missouri Militia Collection, Missouri Historical Society, St. Louis. As it turns out, the scattered bands of Sacs and Foxes remained divided in their loyalties. Their traditional enemies, the Osages, had enjoyed good relations with the Americans for some time and could not be induced to join the British-Indian alliance. As for the Shawnees and Delawares, some remained neutral and others actively served the American side. See Eugene Morrow Violette, *A History of Missouri* (Boston: D. C. Heath, 1918), 66–68; William Thomas Hagan, *The Sac and Fox Indians* (Norman: University of Oklahoma Press, 1958), 52–59; Williard H. Rollings, *The Osage: An Ethnohistorical Study of Hegemony on the Prairie-Plains* (Columbia: University of Missouri Press, 1992), 232; C. A. Weslager, *The Delaware Indians* (New Brunswick, N.J.: Rutgers University Press, 1972), 346.

21. Kate L. Gregg, "The War of 1812 on the Missouri Frontier," part 2, *Missouri Historical Review* 33 (January 1939): 184–88; Benjamin Howard to the Secretary of War (John Armstrong), September 3, 1813, in Clarence Edwin Carter, ed., *The Territorial Papers of the United States*, vol. 15: Territory of Illinois, 1809–1814 (Washington, D.C.: Government Printing Office, 1948), 394; SFA's Service Record, Compiled Military Service Records, War of 1812, Col. McNair's Mounted Regiment, Illinois and Missouri Mounted Militia, Records of the Adjutant General's Office, Record Group 94, National Archives.

22. Mary [Maria] Austin to Rebecca Leaming, September 2, 1813, Leaming Papers, CAH, University of Texas, Austin (quotations); Emily Austin-James Bryan marriage certificate, August 31, 1813, Texas Memorial Museum Collection, CAH.

23. Benjamin Howard to [Adjutant General?], September 1, 1813, War of 1812 Manuscripts, Box 64, Env. 6261, Office of the Adjutant General, Record Group 94, National Archives; SFA's Service Record.

24. Gregg, "The War of 1812 on the Missouri Frontier," 196–98; Randall Parrish, *Historic Illinois: The Romance of Earlier Days* (Chicago: A. C. McClurg, 1905), 242–44; Alec R. Gilpin, *The War of 1812 in the Old Northwest* (East Lansing: Michigan State Uni-

versity Press, 1958), 245–46; *Missouri Gazette,* November 6, 1813; David Murphy Diary, David Murphy Papers, Missouri Historical Society (quotation).

25. *Missouri Gazette,* November 6, 1813 (first quotation); Murphy Diary (second quotation); Benjamin Howard to the Secretary of War, October 28, 1813, *Territorial Papers,* 16: 372.

26. SFA to James Bryan, January 19, 1814, Austin Papers, Series II, CAH (quotation); S. Hammond to Moses Austin, December 29, 1813, *AP,* I, 232-33; SFA to James Bryan, December 30, 1813, ibid., 234; Gracy, *Moses Austin,* 159-60.

27. The negotiations were off and on for several weeks, probably because Butler was on campaign with Jackson's army in Louisiana. The Austins may have met Butler through a mutual friend, Joseph Ficklin. Butler's wife and Ficklin seem to have had a part in the negotiations, with Butler either participating via correspondence or perhaps during a furlough home. See Moses Austin to James Bryan, September 2, November 25, 1814, January 6, 1815, *AP,* I, 241, 243-44, 247; Moses Austin to John S. Brickey, February 22, 1815, ibid., 247-48; Moses Austin to James Bryan, December 7, 12, 1814, February [?], 1815, Austin Papers, Series II, CAH; Moses Austin to children, January 22, 1815, ibid. (quotation); Gracy, *Moses Austin,* 157-58. *AP* contains an enumeration of slaves, along with their names and weekly allotment of food, but it is unclear whether these are the Butler slaves, or if the list is even complete. See Memorandum of the Negroes Names and Messes, n.d., *AP,* I, 250.

28. Gracy, *Moses Austin,* 158-59.

29. Emily M. Bryan to James Bryan, November 6, 1816, James Franklin and Stephen Samuel Perry Papers, CAH; Gracy, *Moses Austin,* 162.

30. Gracy, *Moses Austin,* 147, 162-63; Moses Austin to James Bryan, January 4, 1813, *AP,* I, 223.

31. Gracy, *Moses Austin,* 162-64; Deed Book A, 107-111, November 18, 1816, Washington County Deeds, Potosi, Missouri, transcript in Gracy Papers; SFA to James Bryan, February 11, 1817, *AP,* I, 300.

32. SFA to James Bryan, February 11, 1817, *AP,* I, 299-300.

33. *Louisiana Gazette,* August 8, 1811.

34. SFA Militia Commission, January 24, 1815, Stephen F. Austin Scrapbook (Box 3L81, unbound), CAH; Gracy, *Moses Austin,* 165.

35. *Missouri Gazette,* August 19, December 9, 1815; Gracy, *Moses Austin,* 165.

36. *Missouri Gazette,* December 23, 30, 1815, January 6, March 23, 1816; SFA, Bill to Establish a Lottery for Construction of Roads, *AP,* I, 285-86.

37. *Missouri Gazette,* December 16 (first quotation), 23, 1815, February 24, 1816; William E. Foley, *A History of Missouri* (Columbia: University of Missouri Press, 1971), 1: 172-74; Hattie M. Anderson, "Frontier Economic Problems in Missouri, 1815-1828," *Missouri Historical Review* 34 (October 1939): 38-40; Address by Austin to Colonists, June 5, 1824, *AP,* I, 818 (second quotation).

38. *Missouri Gazette,* July 27, 1816, January 11, 18, 25, February 1, 1817; Gracy, *Moses Austin,* 165-66.

39. Gracy, *Moses Austin,* 169-70. For a detailed overview of the Missouri banking

situation in these years, see Breckinridge Jones, "One Hundred Years of Banking in Missouri," *Missouri Historical Review* 15 (January 1921): 345–92.

40. Moses Austin, Moses Austin on Plan of Reorganization of the Bank of St. Louis, [December 1816–January, 1817], *AP,* I, 265–71; SFA, Notes for a Speech by Stephen F. Austin Against Charter of the Bank of St. Louis [*sic*], Missouri, [c. December 1816], *AP,* I, 272–81; Gracy, *Moses Austin,* 170–71.

41. Anderson, "Frontier Economic Problems," 60–61; Gracy, *Moses Austin,* 171–72.

42. Robert Simpson to John B. C. Lucas, March 3, 1818 (quotation), Lucas Papers, Missouri Historical Society, St. Louis; *Missouri Gazette,* December 18, 1818; Jones, "One Hundred Years of Banking," 360–64; Gracy, *Moses Austin,* 172–73; President and Directors of the Bank of St. Louis v. Stephen F. Austin, April 1819, Territorial Records of Missouri, Court Cases, Missouri State Archives, Jefferson City.

43. Moses Austin to James Bryan, September 13, 1818, *AP,* I, 333.

44. SFA to James Bryan, December 31, 1818, *AP,* I, 335.

THREE
New Beginnings
1819–1820

1. *Arkansas Gazette* (Arkansas Post, Arkansas), February 2, 1821; Rex W. Strickland, "Miller Country, Arkansas Territory, the Frontier That Men Forgot," *Chronicles of Oklahoma* 18 (1940): 16; SFA to James Bryan, [January] 3, [1819], *AP,* I, 330 (quotation). In *AP* there are three egregious errors that have misled all previous Austin scholars as to the timing of his plunge into Arkansas land speculation. All of these errors involve the dates of letters. In the SFA to William M. O'Hara letter on p. 329 of *AP,* I, the date was mistranscribed as March 4, 1818; the letter was actually written on March 4, *1819.* (The date was hopelessly smudged on the original, but the letter refers to events of 1819, not 1818. See original in the Darby Papers, Missouri Historical Society.) In the SFA to James Bryan letter on p. 327 of *AP,* I, the date is mistakenly given as January 3, 1818; the letter actually was written on January 3, *1819.* (In *AP,* the year of the letter was transcribed correctly, but Austin himself made the common beginning-of-the-new-year error of writing the prior year's date on the letter—i.e., he wrote 1818 when he meant to write 1819. As in the previous case, this can be established as a fact by the content of the letter, which places it definitively in 1819.) In the SFA to James Bryan letter on pp. 330–31 of *AP,* I, the date was mistranscribed as July 3, 1818; it also was actually written on *January 3, 1819.* (This is a case of a double error. First, Austin made the same mistake as in the previous letter: writing 1818 instead of 1819. In addition, the editor of *AP* misread SFA's abbreviation of January ["Jany."] as "July." See the original in the Austin Papers, Series I, CAH.) These letters to James Bryan were obviously written the same day (January 3, 1819), because one refers to the other. Bryan was in Louisiana, but SFA did not know whether he was in Natchitoches or Alexandria, so he wrote him these nearly identical letters at the same time and mailed one to each town. The cumulative effect of these three dating errors in *AP* has been to mislead scholars into thinking that SFA acquired his Red River property and

grew interested in speculation via the New Madrid certificates nearly a year earlier than he actually did; *LSFA,* 22; Gracy, *Moses Austin,* 179–80; Robert L. and Pauline H. Jones, "Stephen F. Austin in Arkansas," *Arkansas Historical Quarterly* 25 (Winter 1966): 337–38. The earliest actual reference to SFA's "business on Red River" in the Austin Papers is SFA to James Bryan, November 2, 1818, *AP,* I, 333–34.

2. Lonnie J. White, *Politics on the Southwestern Frontier: Arkansas Territory, 1819–1836* (Memphis: Memphis State University Press, 1964), 20.

3. The best account of Missouri territorial land policy in general, and of the New Madrid claims in particular, can be found in March, *History of Missouri,* vol. 1, chap. 6, esp. pp. 237–40.

4. SFA to James Bryan, January 3, [1819], *AP,* I, 327.

5. Ibid., 330–31 (first and second quotations); SFA to James Bryan, November 2, 1818, ibid., 333 (other quotations).

6. Memoranda Concerning Land Speculation, January–February, 1819, *AP,* I, 337; SFA to Emily M. Perry, July 24, 1828, *AP,* II, 76–78; Deed from William M. and Susan O'Hara to SFA, February 25, 1819, Knight Collection, Arkansas History Commission, Little Rock; Gracy, *Moses Austin,* 181.

7. Dissolution of Partnership between SFA and James Bryan, November 3, 1818, Austin Papers, Series II; SFA to James Bryan, [January] 3, [1819], *AP,* I, 330 (first quotation); President and Directors of the Bank of St. Louis v. Stephen F. Austin, April 1819, Territorial Records of Missouri, Court Cases, Missouri State Archives, Jefferson City; SFA to William M. O'Hara, April 5, 7 (second quotation), 1819, *AP,* I, 341, 342; Gracy, *Moses Austin,* 177.

8. SFA to William M. O'Hara, March 4, 181[9], *AP,* I, 329; William M. O'Hara to SFA, April 6, 1819, Uncatalogued Austin Family Papers, Beinecke Rare Book and Manuscript Library, Yale University; SFA to William M. O'Hara, April 7, 1819, *AP,* I, 342 (quotation). At one point that spring, for example, SFA borrowed $150 from William M. O'Hara, promising to repay the loan in ten days. The promissory note shows that six years later the debt still had not been paid; see Promissory Note, SFA to William M. O'Hara, March 5, 1819, Chester Ashley Papers, Arkansas History Commission. However, Austin did send O'Hara three shares of bank stock, which he thought could be sold for $85 apiece, more than enough to cover the $150 debt. O'Hara, who was cashier of the Bank of St. Louis, apparently did not consider this a satisfactory discharge of the debt; see SFA to William M. O'Hara, April 7, 1819, *AP,* I, 342.

9. SFA to William M. O'Hara, April 7, June 16, 1819, *AP,* I, 342–45; Memoranda Concerning Land Speculation, ibid., 337; Jones and Jones, "Stephen F. Austin in Arkansas," 338–39; Gracy, *Moses Austin,* 181.

10. Memoranda Concerning Land Speculation, *AP,* I, 337; SFA to William M. O'Hara, June 16, 1819, ibid., 344–45; SFA to James Bryan, April 30, 1820, ibid., 358–59; SFA-Bryan business accounts, November 6, 1820, Austin Papers, Series II, CAH.

11. SFA to William M. O'Hara, June 16, 1819, *AP,* I, 344; Moses Austin to Henry R. Schoolcraft, July 4, 1819, Austin Papers, Series II, CAH; Moses Austin to James E. B. Austin, August 12, 1819, *AP,* I, 346; Bill of Sale, June 19, 1819, *AP,* I, 345.

12. SFA to Jacob Pettit, October 5, 1819, Austin Papers, Natchez Trace Collection, CAH (quotations); Leroy Ferguson to SFA, January 27, 1820, *AP*, I, 353; Memoranda, January 1 [to February 20], 1820, ibid., 351–52; Richard Thurmond to SFA, February 15, 1820, ibid., 356. The available records, admittedly thin, do not support David Gracy's contention that Austin's Long Prairie operation "prospered" during the summer and fall of 1819; see Gracy, *Moses Austin*, 182. A more accurate appraisal can be found in Jones and Jones, "Stephen F. Austin in Arkansas," 341.

13. Anderson, "Frontier Economic Problems in Missouri," 48–57; Court Judgments Against Stephen F. Austin, November 16, 1819, *AP*, I, 349; Gracy, *Moses Austin*, 182–91.

14. Jones and Jones, "Stephen F. Austin in Arkansas," 342–44; Robert W. Trimble, "Manuscript History of Arkansas," n.p., n.d. (quotation), in Robert W. Trimble Collection, Arkansas History Commission, Little Rock. SFA's activities as merchant and land speculator clearly had not affected his popularity with his immediate neighbors; in his new home county of Hempstead, he received 180 votes to his nearest competitor's 102; in neighboring Clark County he finished second by only eight votes.

15. Jones and Jones, "Stephen F. Austin in Arkansas," 341–42. The town site adjacent to Long Prairie was named Fulton.

16. It seems that a decade earlier an itinerant hunter had erected a shack at the spot and squatted there for a few months, thus establishing a shaky preemption claim. The claim changed hands several times over the next few years, ending up in the hands of a group led by St. Louis speculator William Russell.

17. James Bryan (representing the Austins) was in partnership with William O'Hara. In the case of the Little Rock speculation, the largest share of these particular New Madrid claims were held in O'Hara's name. The story of the founding of Little Rock and the battle between rival groups of speculators has been told numerous times. The best concise account is in Charles S. Bolton, *Territorial Ambition: Land and Society in Arkansas, 1800–1840* (Fayetteville: University of Arkansas Press, 1993), 64–66. More exhaustive accounts include: Dallas T. Herndon, *Centennial History of Arkansas* (Chicago: S. J. Clarke, 1922), 1: 819–24; Marie Cash, "Arkansas in Territorial Days," *Arkansas Historical Quarterly* 1 (March 1942): 228–34; Ira Don Richards, *Story of a Rivertown: Little Rock in the Nineteenth Century* (n.p., 1969), 5–10.

18. SFA had learned of the Russell group's attempt to establish a preemption claim during a December trip to Little Rock, during which he had expressed the fear that the conflict would "bring about a personal dispute" between himself and Russell (SFA to William M. Russell, December 31, 1819, Darby Papers, Missouri Historical Society, St. Louis). Arriving at Arkansas Post, SFA also found that the partners' attorney, Amos Wheeler, had not managed affairs well and should be replaced. Furthermore, SFA had lost confidence in the honesty of their principal partner, William O'Hara, and he warned Bryan to handle him with care. SFA to James Bryan, April 30, 1820, *AP*, I, 359 (quotation).

19. Bolton, *Territorial Ambition*, 65.

20. SFA to James Bryan, April 30, 1820, *AP*, I, 359.

21. All the circumstances surrounding Bryan's transfer of his share to Henry Elliott

are not known. However, the transfer had already taken place by December 1821, the time of the compromise settlement; see White, *Territorial Ambition,* 32. Austin himself is the source for the information that Elliott had been granted Bryan's share; see SFA to Emily M. Perry, January 26, 1833, *AP,* II, 921–22. In 1824, Elliott's wife told Austin that "the property was put into [Henry Elliott's] hands confidentially to save it," and Austin held out the hope that the family might still recover something from the proceeds of the land sales; see SFA to Mrs. James F. Perry, December 17, 1824, *AP,* I, 991. Emily Bryan explained in 1825 what happened to the property after Elliott's death; see Emily Bryan to SFA, July 1, 1823, Perry Papers (Emily Austin Bryan Perry Letters), CAH; SFA to Mrs. Emily Perry, May?, 1825, *AP,* I, 1109.

22. SFA to James Bryan, June 2, 1820, *AP,* I, 363–64; Jones and Jones, "Stephen F. Austin in Arkansas," 346–47.

23. SFA's Commission as Judge, July 10, 1820, *AP,* I, 365–66; Jones and Jones, "Stephen F. Austin in Arkansas," 348. Jones and Jones state that Austin "permitted his friends to urge his appointment, but refused to let himself be optimistic," but they offer no proof for this assertion. They also mistakenly write that Austin's appointment was to the Second Circuit Court rather than the First Circuit. Austin's appointment had apparently been in the mill for several months, for the Executive Register of the territory shows the appointment being made in February. Austin's commission is dated July 10, however, and he took the oath of office the following day. How long he had known about the appointment prior to July is unknown; see Gracy, *Moses Austin,* 267 n8.

24. *Arkansas Gazette,* February 12, October 28, 1820; E[lias] A. E[lliott] to James Bryan, July 28, 1820, Austin Papers, Series II; *Louisiana Advertiser,* May 1, 1822, *Arkansas Gazette,* August 6, 1822. In their article "Stephen F. Austin in Arkansas" (p. 349), Jones and Jones erroneously attribute the July 28 letter to Moses Austin. For instances in which SFA was referred to as Judge Austin, see Joseph H. Hawkins to SFA, May 31, 1822, *AP,* I, 521; *Arkansas Gazette,* August 6, 1822; and Robert Leftwich's Mexico Diary, July 25, 1822, *PCRCT,* intro. vol., 269.

25. R. C. Bruffey to Henry R. Schoolcraft, March 14, 1820, Austin Papers, Series II, CAH (quotations); *Arkansas Gazette,* September 30, 1820, April 14, 1821; George Tennille to Pierre Laforge, June 13, 1820, *AP,* I, 365; Anderson, "Frontier Economic Problems," 57–60; SFA to Emily M. Perry, January 26, 1833, *AP,* II, 921–22.

26. SFA to James Bryan, April 30, 1820, *AP,* I, 359.

27. Moses Austin to James Bryan, January 4, 1813, *AP,* I, 223.

28. Frank Lawrence Owsley, Jr., and Gene A. Smith, *Filibusters and Expansionists: Jeffersonian Manifest Destiny, 1800–1821* (Tuscaloosa: University of Alabama Press, 1997), 32–60, 178–80.

29. Leo M. Kaiser, ed., "Stephen F. Austin's Oration of July 4, 1818," *SWHQ* 64 (July 1960): 71–79.

30. Garrison, "Memorandum of M. Austin's Journey," 520. This journal kept by Moses Austin on his first trip to Spanish Louisiana in 1797 includes an introduction, quoted here, written in the late 1820s by SFA.

31. Garrison, "Memorandum of M. Austin's Journey," 521.

32. Moses Austin to Henry R. Schoolcraft, July 4, 1819, September 17, 1819, Austin Papers, Series II, CAH.

33. This interpretation, and the arguments that follow, agree in large part with those put forward in Charles A. Bacarisse, "Why Moses Austin Came to Texas," *Southwestern Social Science Quarterly* 40 (June 1959): 17-19. Even if the Long expedition failed, the unsettled political situation in Spain would have made it difficult for the Austins to lay definite plans before late 1820. In 1819, when Moses began talking about a trip to Texas, a conservative government was back in power in Madrid, meaning that liberalized trade and emigration policies for Texas were not likely. Furthermore, well into 1820 it looked as though the 1819 Transcontinental Treaty would not be ratified, thus casting renewed doubts on whether Texas land titles would have any validity; see Weber, *Mexican Frontier,* 17; William Earl Weeks, *John Quincy Adams and American Global Empire* (Lexington: University Press of Kentucky, 1992), 170-73.

34. Moses Austin to J. E. B. Austin, February 8, 1820, *AP,* I, 355; SFA to James Bryan, June 2, 1820, ibid., 364.

35. Moses left Hugh McGuffin's cabin between Natchitoches and the Sabine River on November 27. It would have been quite possible for him to make the trip from central Arkansas to Natchitoches, and from there to McGuffin's, in ten days, assuming there were no serious delays. See Memorandum and Itinerary, n.d., *AP,* I, 368; Gracy, *Moses Austin,* 200. Illness or no illness, it seems unlikely that ever-impatient Moses would have lingered in Little Rock for five months (thus pushing his travel into midwinter) if his Texas plans were already fully developed. Perhaps, as his biographer suggests, he got caught up in the raging Little Rock dispute and it distracted him from his Texas plans. The timing of his eventual departure is significant, however. The delay allowed for four significant things to happen before his departure: first, the Arkansas legislature abolished SFA's short-lived judicial position, leaving Stephen free to participate in his father's project; second, news of the Long expedition's apparent failure reached Arkansas (*Arkansas Gazette,* June 3), presenting the hope that Texas would be at peace and Spain in control of it; third, word arrived that the king of Spain had been forced to reinstate the liberal constitution of 1812 (*Arkansas Gazette,* November 11); and finally, Moses learned that Spain had at last ratified the Transcontinental Treaty, meaning that the Spanish authorities would be in a position to issue valid land titles (see Examination of Moses Austin, December 23, 1820, *AP,* I, 370-71). With this information, Moses could leave with some confidence that he would not be stumbling into a revolution or petitioning a hostile or powerless government. He might or might not have known before his departure that Long had subsequently reentered Texas. On his arrival in San Antonio, Moses told the authorities "that he had heard it said at Natchitoches that Long has been abandoned by his men" and that Long's would-be accomplice, Jean Lafitte, was also on the run (see ibid.). In short, it is safe to conclude that Moses learned of all four events in close succession and that he set out for Texas only when he knew these things to be true.

36. Record of Moses Austin and Family, n.d., *AP,* I, 3; J. Meigs to Moses Austin, March 9, 1820, ibid., 356; Gracy, *Moses Austin,* 196-98.

37. SFA's arrival in New Orleans can be dated to November 1820 by a letter he re-

ceived from Elias Bates. Bates, writing from Missouri on December 2, addressed his letter to SFA in New Orleans. So SFA must already have been in New Orleans by the beginning of December. Since Moses Austin did not leave Arkansas until sometime in November, and Stephen helped to outfit him for his trip, Stephen most likely could not have left Arkansas before November. Furthermore, the Arkansas legislature did not abolish SFA's judicial position until late October.

38. Garrison, "Memorandum of M. Austin's Journey," 521; SFA to Maria Austin, January 20, 1821, *AP,* I, 373.

39. Maria Austin had become so worried about Moses, whom she had not heard from in months, that she sent his nephew, Elias Bates, to Louisiana in search of news. Stephen would not have withheld such news had he possessed it; see Gracy, *Moses Austin,* 204.

40. SFA to his mother, January 20, 1821, *AP,* I, 373.

41. Ibid.

FOUR
Texas
1820–1821

1. SFA to Maria Austin, January 20, 1821, *AP,* I, 373.

2. Ibid., 373–74.

3. Moses Austin to William Kenner, June 20, 1807, *AP,* I, 128; Moses Austin to SFA, April 28, 1812, ibid., 203; SFA to Maria Austin, January 20, 1821, ibid., 373. Several years later SFA referred to Kenner, saying, "I wish to have nothing to do with him. . . . I shall never ask him for any favor, I may do him injustice but I do not like him." See SFA to J. E. B. Austin, May 4, 1824, ibid., 786.

4. Eight years older than SFA, Hawkins was elected to the Kentucky House in 1810 — SFA's last year in Lexington — and served two terms as speaker. After serving in the Kentucky militia in the War of 1812, he filled the seat in Congress vacated by Henry Clay, who had been sent to Europe to negotiate the peace treaty. See Gregg Cantrell, "The Partnership of Stephen F. Austin and Joseph H. Hawkins," *SWHQ* 99 (July 1995): 3.

5. SFA to Maria Austin, January 20, 1821, *AP,* I, 373–74; Cantrell, "Partnership of Stephen F. Austin," 4, fn9.

6. Fayette County (Kentucky) Tax List, 1815; *Kentucky Gazette* (Lexington), January 1, January 15, February 12, 1816; SFA to Maria Austin, January 20, 1821, *AP,* I, 374 (first quotation); SFA to J. E. B. Austin, June 13, 1823, ibid., 672 (second quotation); Cantrell, "Partnership of Stephen F. Austin," 5. The same hard times that had ruined the Austins had forced Hawkins's own move to New Orleans several years earlier.

7. Moses Austin Bryan, "Personal Recollections of Stephen F. Austin," I, *Texas Magazine* 3 (September 1897): 102; [W. S.] Lewis, "The Adventures of the 'Lively' Immigrants," part 1, *Quarterly of the Texas State Historical Association* 3 (July 1899): 8.

8. Bryan, "Personal Recollections," 102; Henry R. Schoolcraft, *Personal Memoirs*

of a Residence of Thirty Years with the Indian Tribes on the American Frontiers (Philadelphia: Lippincott, Grambo, 1851), 36; SFA to W. H. Wharton, April 24, 1829, *AP,* II, 209. For other self-descriptions of his temper and temperament, see SFA to Josiah H. Bell, January 8, 1824, *AP,* I, 722; SFA to B. W. Edwards, September 15, 1825, ibid., 1204; SFA to Josiah H. Bell, March 17, 1829, ibid., 189.

9. José María Sánchez, "A Trip to Texas in 1828," trans. Carlos E. Cantañeda, *SWHQ* 29 (April 1926): 271 (first and second quotations); Jean Louis Berlandier, *Journey to Mexico During the Years 1826 to 1834* (Austin: TSHA, 1990), 321 (third, fourth, and fifth quotations); José María Balmaceda to José Francisco Madero, June 3, 1833, in *Gaceta del Goierno Supremo del Estado de Coahuila y Tejas* (Saltillo), May 27, 1833 (sixth quotation) (Balmaceda used the plural of the word *manejo* in describing SFA, a word that also carries connotations of "management," "scheming," and "intrigue.")

10. John Adams Paxton, *The New-Orleans Directory and Register* (New Orleans: Benjamin Levy, 1822), entry for Joseph H. Hawkins (n.p.); Family Meeting of the heirs and friends of the late Joseph Hawkins, December 16, 1823, Court of Probates, New Orleans Public Library; Inventory of the Estate of Joseph H. Hawkins, G. R. Stringer, Notary, in Old Inventories, Court of Probates, New Orleans Public Library. Hawkins's library included some three hundred volumes.

11. *Louisiana Courier* (New Orleans), November 3, 10, 1820, January 21, 1821; James Trager, *The People's Chronology: A Year-by-Year Record of Human Events from Prehistory to the Present,* rev. ed. (New York: Henry Holt, 1992), 391.

12. Scholars have questioned the veracity of the Austin-Bastrop encounter, but Moses Austin's biographer argues convincingly for its plausibility; see Gracy, *Moses Austin,* 201–2.

13. Charles A. Bacarrisse, "Baron de Bastrop," *SWHQ* 58 (January 1955): 319–30; R. Woods Moore, "The Role of the Baron de Bastrop in the Anglo-American Settlement of the Spanish Southeast," M. A. thesis, University of Texas, 1932, chaps. 2–4; Land Grant, June 20, 1796, Baron de Bastrop Papers, 1795–1823, Natchez Trace Collection, CAH. Bastrop's popularity in San Antonio can be gauged by the fact that at one point he was elected *alcalde,* a position roughly analagous to a mayor in the United States.

14. Gracy, *Moses Austin,* 201–3; Antonio Martínez to Joaquín de Arredondo, December 26, 1820, *PCRCT,* I, 301.

15. Gracy, *Moses Austin,* 203–5; Hardships of Travel (note by Guy M. Bryan), n.d., *AP,* I, 377; Record of Moses Austin and Family, n.d., ibid., 3.

16. Hardships of Travel (note by Guy M. Bryan), n.d., *AP,* I, 377 (first quotation); Record of Moses Austin and Family, n.d., ibid., 3 (second quotation); Moses Austin to Governor Martínez, January 26, 1821, ibid., 377–78; Moses Austin to Baron de Bastrop, January 26, 1821, ibid., 379–80 (third quotation); Moses Austin to Felix Trudeau, February 3, 1821, ibid., 381–82; Gracy, *Moses Austin,* 205–7. Erasmo Seguín, a respected citizen of San Antonio, had traveled to Natchitoches on behalf of Governor Martínez to inform Moses of the decision. From there Seguín mailed the news to Moses in Missouri. This marked the beginning of a long and fruitful relationship between the Seguín and Austin families. See Ambrosio María de Aldasoro to Antonio Martínez, January 17, 1821, *AP,* I,

371–73; Moses Austin to SFA, May 22, 1821, *AP*, I, 393; Gracy, *Moses Austin,* 207; Antonio Martínez to Moses Austin, February 8, 1821, in SFA, *Establishing Austin's Colony* (San Felipe de Austin: Godwin B. Cotten, 1829; reprint ed., Austin: Pemberton, 1970, edited by David B. Gracy II), 33–34. The original title of SFA's 1829 pamphlet was *Translation of the Laws, Orders, And Contracts of Colonization, From January, 1821, Up To This Time, In Virtue Of Which Col. Stephen F. Austin Has Introduced And Settled Foreign Emigrants In Texas, With An Explanatory Introduction.*

17. Gracy, *Moses Austin,* 208–9.

18. Moses Austin to J. E. B. Austin, April 8, 1821, *AP*, I, 385.

19. Moses Austin to SFA, May 22, 1821, *AP*, I, 393.

20. Maria Austin to SFA, June 8, 1821, *AP*, I, 395; Gracy, *Moses Austin,* 214–15.

21. SFA, "Journal of Stephen F. Austin on His First Trip to Texas, 1821," *Quarterly of the Texas State Historical Association* 7 (April 1904): 286; Joseph H. Hawkins to Mrs. Maria Austin, June 27, 1821, *AP*, I, 397–98.

22. José Erasmo Seguín to the Governor of Texas, June 23, 1821, Nacogdoches Archives, typescript in CAH; SFA to Dear Sir, July 1, 1821, published in the *Frankfort* (Kentucky) *Argus,* and reprinted in the *Arkansas Gazette,* September 29, 1821. Word of Moses's grant had already spread through the Red River Valley. A number of Missourians and others had actually already crossed into East Texas and had thrown up cabins illegally, a development that Seguín characterized as a "scandalous proceeding." The appearance of Stephen Austin in Natchitoches offered Seguín, as well as the American squatters, a way out of a potentially troublesome situation. These itinerant Americans would also help form an advance guard of settlers for Austin's colony, for they were closer to the future colony than those who learned of the Texas opportunity through the newspapers. See José Erasmo Seguín to the Governor of Texas, June 23, 1821, Nacogdoches Archives, typescripts in CAH.

23. SFA to Jacob Pettit, July 1, 1821, Austin Papers, Natchez Trace Collection, CAH.

24. "Journal of Stephen F. Austin," 286–88; SFA to Maria Austin, July 13, 1821, *AP*, I, 401–2.

25. SFA to Maria Austin, July 13, 1821, *AP*, I, 401.

26. Maria Austin to SFA, January 19, 1822, *AP*, I, 468. My account of Moses Austin's enthusiasm and SFA's reluctance agrees in most respects with that found in Andreas V. Reichstein, *Rise of the Lone Star: The Making of Texas* (College Station: Texas A&M University Press, 1989), 25–29.

27. "Journal of Stephen F. Austin," 288.

28. Chipman, *Spanish Texas,* 206; Ibid., 288–89; W. B. Dewees to ?, June 10, 1821, in W. B. Dewees, *Letters from an Early American Settler of Texas* (Louisville: Morton & Griswold, 1852; reprint ed., Waco: Texian Press, 1968), 22–23.

29. The account of the journey from Nacogdoches to San Antonio given in this and the preceding three paragraphs is from the "Journal of Stephen F. Austin," 289–96. Additional information on the landscape, flora, and fauna can be found in Robin W. Doughty, *Wildlife and Man in Texas: Environmental Change and Conservation* (College Station: Texas A&M University Press, 1983), 13–15. Also see Félix D. Almaráz, "Gov-

ernor Antonio Martínez and Mexican Independence in Texas: An Orderly Transition," *Permian Historical Annual* 15 (December 1975; reprint ed., San Antonio: Béxar County Historical Commission, 1979).

30. Austin had obviously studied some French, perhaps at Transylvania University and most recently in New Orleans. He may also have picked up a smattering of the language as a child in Missouri, where many of the locals still spoke French. See Baron de Bastrop to SFA, September 12, 1821, *AP,* I, 413–14 (letter in French).

31. Antonio Martínez to Moses Austin, February 8, 1821, in Dudley G. Wooten, ed., *A Comprehensive History of Texas, 1685–1897* (Dallas: William G. Scarff, 1898), 1: 470–71; Antonio Martínez to SFA, August 14, 1821, ibid., 471–72; Antonio Martínez to SFA, August 19, 1821, ibid., 472; Antonio Martínez to SFA, August 24, 1821, ibid., 472 (quotation); SFA to Antonio Martínez, August 18, 1821, *AP,* I, 407.

32. "Journal of Stephen F. Austin," 296–98 (quotation on p. 297). There was a settlement in Laredo, far to the southwest on the Rio Grande River, but the Rio Grande Valley was not considered part of Texas until the Anglo Texans claimed it after the Texas Revolution. Nacogdoches in East Texas was at this point all but abandoned. I will generally use the more familiar "Goliad" rather than "La Bahía," even though the new name was not actually adopted until 1829.

33. "Journal of Stephen F. Austin," 298–99 (first quotation); John Sibley to Josiah Stoddard Johnston, October 5, 1821, quoting letter from SFA to Sibley, Josiah Stoddard Johnston Papers, microfilm in Tulane University Library (originals in Historical Society of Pennsylvania).

34. "Journal of Stephen F. Austin," 299–302; Tomás Buentello to Antonio Martínez, August 26, 1821, Béxar Archives; Itinerary and Report of Manuel Becerra, September 11, 1821, Béxar Land Papers, Box 126, Folder 6, Spanish Collection, Archives and Records Division, Texas General Land Office; SFA to Antonio Martínez, October 13, 1821, *AP,* I, 417. Whenever possible I have used the spelling of Indian tribes employed in W. W. Newcomb, Jr., *The Indians of Texas: From Prehistoric to Modern Times* (Austin: University of Texas Press, 1961). There is no standardized spelling of Texas Indian tribes, and early-day Texans used a bewildering array of names to identify them. Presidio La Bahía and its companion mission, Espiritu Santo, were actually moved twice, first to a site on the Guadalupe River in 1726, and then to its final location at Goliad in 1749. For a map of the area and a discussion of the history of the presidio and mission, see Craig H. Roell, *Remember Goliad!: A History of La Bahía* (Austin: Texas State Historical Association, 1994), chap. 1. SFA's knowledge of the geography was so poor and his description of the landmarks so inconclusive that his route on this entire trip cannot be stated with certainty.

35. Itinerary and Report of Manuel Becerra, September 11, 1821 (first quotation); Tomás Buentello to Antonio Martínez, September 15, 1821 (second and third quotations), both in Béxar Land Papers, Box 126, Folder 6, Spanish Collection, Archives and Records Division, Texas General Land Office.

36. "Journal of Stephen F. Austin," 304. On the Karankawas, see Newcomb, *Indians of Texas,* 59–81, and "Karankawa," in Alfonso Ortiz, ed., *Handbook of North American Indians,* vol. 10: Southwest (Washington, D.C.: Smithsonian Institution, 1983),

359–67; James Curtis Hasdorff, "Four Indian Tribes in Texas 1758–1858: A Reevaluation of Historical Sources," Ph.D. diss., University of New Mexico, 1971, chap. 1; Robert A. Ricklis, *The Karankawa Indians of Texas: An Ecological Study of Cultural Tradition and Change* (Austin: University of Texas Press, 1996).

37. Juan Antonio Padilla, Report on the Barbarous Indians of the Province of Texas, December 27, 1819, in Mattie Austin Hatcher, trans., "Texas in 1820," *SWHQ* 23 (July 1919): 51; "Journal of Stephen F. Austin," 304–5 (quotations). The Karankawas' alleged penchant for cannibalism is questioned by scholars. At most, it appears that the practice was performed as a ritual and not as a means of sustenance, and even this is founded on unreliable evidence; see Newcomb, *Indians of Texas,* 77–78; Chipman, *Spanish Texas,* 11; Hasdorff, "Four Indian Tribes," 38; Ricklis, *Karankawa Indians,* 147.

38. "Journal of Stephen F. Austin," 305–6.

39. Ibid. When he edited the Austin Papers for the published edition, Barker apparently mistook the number "10" for the number "1," thus erroneously indicating that SFA arrived in Natchitoches on October 1, an error which he then incorporated into his 1925 biography; see SFA to Antonio Martínez, October 12, 1821, *AP,* I, 417; *LSFA,* 33. This can be independently verified by the fact that on October 5 John Sibley in Natchitoches quoted extensively from SFA's August 30 La Bahía letter but made no mention of his having arrived in Natchitoches. Furthermore, Austin wrote a permission for Josiah H. Bell to settle in his colony from Nacogdoches on October 6, a reasonable four-day ride from Natchitoches. See John Sibley to Josiah Stoddard Johnston, October 5, 1821, Johnston Papers; SFA to J. H. Bell, October 6, 1821, *AP,* I, 415.

40. SFA to Antonio Martínez, October 12, 1821, *AP,* I, 417–18. In this letter SFA also made changes in his recommendation about the quantities of land to be distributed to the colonists. He now proposed that each colonist receive a square mile of land (640 acres), plus 320 acres for each woman, 160 acres for each child, and 80 for each slave, divided equally between grazing and farm land. He explained, accurately enough, that these quantities were almost the same that he proposed in San Antonio in August; the formula was merely somewhat different. Granting land in units of 80, 160, 320, and 640 acres conformed to the system to which the settlers were accustomed in the United States, a system in which the basic unit was the section (640 acres). He also now recommended that town lots not be granted to the farmers; they would have to live on their land anyway in order to work it. In time all of this proved moot, because the final formula under which settlers received land was determined by national (and later state) colonization laws, which granted much larger amounts of land to colonists.

41. SFA to Antonio Martínez, October 13, 1821, *AP,* I, 419–21. The news of the fifty emigrants who were prepared to leave almost immediately was contained in the October 12 letter.

42. Moses Austin to J. E. B. Austin, March 28, 1821, April 8, 1821, *AP,* I, 384–87.

43. SFA to Antonio Martínez, October 13, 1821, *AP,* I, 419–21 (quotation on p. 420). The earliest indication of the twelve-and-a-half-cent per acre fee is in SFA to J. H. Bell, October 6, 1821, ibid., 415; also see SFA to William Kincheloe: Permit to Settle, October 16, 1821, ibid., 422. SFA never received explicit written permission from the Mexican

government to charge this particular amount, but he made no secret of it and clearly received the tacit approval of the authorities in Texas. It was publicly stated to all prospective colonists in the "Permit and Conditions for Colonization" that SFA issued on November 23, 1821; see ibid., 435–36. For a full and accurate account of this matter, which later became a source of great public debate, see Address by Austin to Colonists, June 5, 1824, ibid., 811–24, esp. 812–13.

44. Interview with Angelina Eberly, in Mary Austin Holley, "Interviews with Prominent Texans of Early Days," Mary Austin Holley Papers, CAH (quotation); Stephen F. Austin to [Joseph H. Hawkins], July 20, 1821, *AP,* I, 402–404. This letter soliciting immigrants appeared first in the *Louisiana Advertiser* on September 3, 1821, and later in the *Arkansas Gazette* of October 6. It probably appeared in other major western newspapers at about the same time. For the Baltimore notice, see James T. Dunbar and Others to SFA, December 13, 1821, *AP,* I, 447.

45. For a debt example, see Appearance Bond: Stephen F. Austin, June 4, 1821, *AP,* I, 393–94; Robert C. Bruffey to SFA, December 12, 1821, ibid., 446–47. For an eyewitness account of some of Austin's activities during the month he spent in New Orleans (including his stay at the Kelso & Richardson's Hotel), see Lewis, "Adventures of the 'Lively' Immigrants," part 1, 10–14.

46. Agreement Between Austin and Joseph H. Hawkins, *AP,* I, 428–429. In the *AP* the legal term "copartnery" was mistranscribed as "copartnecy." SFA later claimed that the true amount he received from Hawkins was only $1,600; see Stephen F. Austin to [Edmund H.] Martin, September 14, 1832, *AP,* II, 864. For an overview, see Cantrell, "Partnership of Stephen F. Austin."

47. Lewis, "Adventures of the 'Lively' Immigrants," part 1, 11–12; Lester G. Bugbee, "What Became of the Lively?" *Quarterly of the Texas State Historical Association* 3 (October 1899): 141–48. On the purchase and outfitting of the *Lively,* see Stephen F. Austin to [Edmund H.] Martin, September 14, 1832, *AP,* II, 860–61; Price List: Supplies of Schooner Lively, October 29, 1821, *AP,* I, 422–23 (Hawkins paid $50 and SFA $40 on this account). Edward Lovelace sailed on the *Lively* but died in 1824. The debt remained unpaid until 1847, when it was settled by James and Emily Perry; see Edward Lovelace to SFA: Loan, November 20, 1821, ibid., 431; SFA's Account with Edward Lovelace, March [30], 1822, with note dated May 3, 1847, ibid., 490; "Edward Lovelace," *HT,* I, 306.

48. Agreement with Emigrants, November 22, 1821, *AP,* I, 432–33.

49. Maria Austin to SFA, August 25, December 15, 1821, *AP,* I, 408–10, 450–52.

50. Record of Moses Austin and Family, *AP,* I, 3; Moses Austin to J. E. B. Austin, February 2, February 8, February 23, 1820, ibid., 353, 354–55; Henry Clay to Hon. Secretary of the Navy, March 16, 1820, Henry Clay Papers, Filson Club, Louisville, Kentucky; Moses Austin to J. E. B. Austin, March 28, April 8, 1821, *AP,* I, 384–86; Maria Austin to J. E. B. Austin, August 3, 1821, ibid., 404–5 (quotation on p. 404); Maria Austin to SFA, August 25, 1821, ibid., 410. It has often been mistakenly assumed that Brown Austin attended Transylvania; see Gracy, *Moses Austin,* 213; *HT,* I, 291. It seems odd that Brown did not enroll in Transylvania, especially since Horace Holley (Mary Austin Holley's husband) had become president of the institution. Brown probably was not academi-

cally prepared to enter the university, for with Holley's arrival academic standards had risen. Instead, Brown went to Nicholasville, where he studied under a man named Wilson, presumably in preparation for matriculating at Transylvania. Mary Austin Holley's biographer states that Brown boarded with the Holleys in Lexington for a season after spending the previous year in Nicholasville. This may be accurate, but sources for this information are not given; see Rebecca Smith Lee, *Mary Austin Holley: A Biography* (Austin: University of Texas Press, 1962), 130–31, 145.

51. Maria Austin to J. E. B. Austin, August 3, 1821, *AP,* I, 405; Maria Austin to SFA, August 25, 1821, ibid., 410.

52. SFA to James Bryan, November 10, 1821, *AP,* I, 426–27.

53. James Bryan to SFA, December 15, 1821, *AP,* I, 450; J. E. B. Austin to SFA, January 29, 1822, ibid., 471; Maria Austin to SFA, August 25, 1821, ibid., 410. Correspondence indicates that SFA was in Nacogdoches on December 17. Since he undoubtedly was in a hurry to reach his grant, he would not have lingered there for long. Since the trip from the border to Nacogdoches is about a three-day ride, in all likelihood he entered Texas between the seventh and fourteenth of December; see James Gaines to SFA, January 5, 1822, ibid., 460.

FIVE
Mexico
1821–1823

1. Green, *Mexican Republic,* 52–57; Ruth R. Olivera and Liliane Crété, *Life in Mexico under Santa Anna, 1822–1855* (Norman: University of Oklahoma Press, 1991), chap. 1; Timothy Anna, *The Fall of the Royal Government in Mexico City* (Lincoln: University of Nebraska Press, 1978), 8–24; Michael C. Meyer and William L. Sherman, *The Course of Mexican History,* 5th ed. (New York: Oxford University Press, 1987), 203–19, 273–77. For convenience, these statistics include in the mestizo category most of the Mexicans of African descent, few of whom were of unmixed African ancestry by the time of independence.

2. Green, *Mexican Republic,* chap. 5; Meyer and Sherman, *Course of Mexican History,* 264–72, 304–5.

3. Green, *Mexican Republic,* 72–82; Donald Fithian Stevens, *Origins of Instability in Early Republican Mexico* (Durham: Duke University Press, 1991), 32; Michael P. Costeloe, *Church and State in Independent Mexico, 1821–1857* (London: Royal Historical Society, 1978), passim, esp. chap. 2; SFA to J. E. B. Austin, June 13, 1823, *AP,* I, 671 (quotations).

4. Green, *Mexican Republic,* 82–86.

5. For overviews of the independence movement, see Meyer and Sherman, *Course of Mexican History,* 285–97; Victor Alba, "Mexico's Several Independences," in W. Dirk Raat, ed., *Mexico: From Independence to Revolution, 1810–1910* (Lincoln: University of Nebraska Press, 1982), 6–16; Timothy E. Anna, *The Mexican Empire of Iturbide*

(Lincoln: University of Nebraska Press, 1990), 1–26; Anna, *Fall of the Royal Government;* Brian R. Hamnett, *Roots of Insurgency: Mexican Regions, 1750–1824* (Cambridge: Cambridge University Press, 1986).

6. Anna, *Mexican Empire of Iturbide,* 4–11; Agustín de Iturbide, "Plan de Iguala," in Raat, *Mexico,* 46–48.

7. At times the Eastern and Western Interior Provinces were ruled by one commandant general, and at other times the two groups of provinces had separate commanders. See Meyer and Sherman, *Course of Mexican History,* 257–59; Green, *Mexican Republic;* 21; Weber, *Spanish Frontier,* 224; John Francis Bannon, *The Spanish Borderlands Frontier, 1513–1821* (Albuquerque: University of New Mexico Press, 1974), 181–82. For the origins of the principal Tejano community, see de la Teja, *San Antonio de Béxar.*

8. Alessio Robles, *Coahuila y Texas,* 50; Tijerina, *Tejanos and Texas* 12–15; Chipman, *Spanish Texas,* 236–37; Félix D. Almaráz, Jr., *Tragic Cavalier: Governor Manuel Salcedo of Texas, 1808–1813* (Austin: University of Texas Press, 1971), 178–80; de la Teja, "Rebellion on the Frontier," in Poyo, *Tejano Journey,* 15–30; Weber, *Mexican Frontier,* 4; Robert A. Calvert and Arnoldo de León, *The History of Texas,* 2nd ed. (Wheeling, Ill.: Harlan Davidson, 1996), 33–46. The village of Nacogdoches was almost abandoned in 1820, but a mixed population of Tejanos, Indians, Anglo-Americans, and other ethnic Europeans, many of them squatters, still inhabited farms in the countryside around Nacogdoches.

9. Jesús F. de la Teja and John Wheat, "Béxar: Profile of a Tejano Community, 1820–1832," in Poyo and Hinojosa, *Tejano Origins,* 1–24; de León, *Tejano Community,* 2–9; James Whiteside to George D. Foster, April 2, 1822, Whiteside Letters, CAH (quotation). For a succinct summation of Spain's lasting impact on Texas, see Chipman, *Spanish Texas,* chap. 12.

10. Weber, *Mexican Frontier,* 44, 53; Chipman, *Spanish Texas,* 201–202; Odie B. Faulk, *The Last Years of Spanish Texas, 1778–1821* (The Hague: Mouton & Co., 1964), esp. chap. 10; Antonio Martínez to Gaspar López, February 6, 1822, *AP,* I, 472–75 (quotation); also see Joseph Carl McElhannon, "Imperial Mexico and Texas, 1821–1823," *SWHQ* 53 (October 1949): 117–50, esp. 119–22.

11. Lewis, "Adventures of the 'Lively' Immigrants," part 1, 16–22; Bugbee, "What Became of the Lively?" 143; *LSFA,* 38.

12. John Sibley to Josiah S. Johnston, November 1, 1821, Johnston Papers (first quotation); John Sibley to George C. Sibley, October 29, 1821, Sibley Manuscript Book, Vol. I, Missouri Historical Society, St. Louis (second quotation); Daniel Dunklin to SFA, December 25, 1821, *AP,* I, 455; James Bryan to SFA, January 15, 1822, ibid., 463; James Bryan to SFA, January 15, 1822, ibid., 465; J. H. Bell to SFA, January 17, 1822, ibid., 466; John Sibley to Josiah S. Johnston, March 11, 1822, Johnston Papers. Also see the numerous letters from prospective colonists in *AP,* I, 451–62.

13. From 1804 to 1820, the minimum amount of land that could be bought was 180 acres, at two dollars an acre, payable in four annual installments. The 1820 law reduced the minimum to eighty acres and the price to $1.25 an acre, but with the credit feature

eliminated, the actual amount of up-front cash required to buy eighty acres was now greater than the initial amount previously required to obtain 180 acres; see John B. Boles, *The South Through Time: A History of an American Region* (Englewood Cliffs, N.J.: Prentice Hall, 1995), 171; Barker, *LSFA,* 80–81.

14. Austin's Memorial to Congress, May 13, 1822, *AP,* I, 511; *LSFA,* 38; J. E. B. Austin to SFA, January 29, 1822, *AP,* I, 471.

15. Austin's Memorial to Congress, May 13, 1822, *AP,* I, 511; Antonio Martínez to Gaspar López, November 18, 1821, ibid., 429–30; Contestación de la superioridad [López to Martínez], December 15, 1821, ibid., 430–31; Address by Austin to Colonists, June 5, 1824, ibid., 814 (quotations).

16. SFA to J. E. B. Austin, March 23, July 8, 1822, *AP,* I, 487, 530–31; SFA to Antonio Martínez, October 12, 1821, ibid., 419; Jesús F. de la Teja, ed., *A Revolution Remembered: The Memoirs and Selected Correspondence of Juan N. Seguín* (Austin: State House Press, 1991), 7–8.

17. SFA to J. E. B. Austin, March 23, 1822, *AP,* I, 487.

18. Ibid. (first quotation); Austin's Passport to Mexico, March 13, 1822, ibid., 483; SFA, *Establishing Austin's Colony,* 7; SFA to J. H. Hawkins, [about May 1, 1822], *AP,* I, 504.

19. SFA to J. E. B. Austin, July 8, 1822, *AP,* I, 531; Green, *Mexican Republic,* 29; Anna, *Fall of the Royal Government,* 5–6, 22.

20. Andrew Erwin and Robert Leftwich to Messrs. Ripley and Hawkins, May 8, 1822, *PCRCT,* intro. vol., 128–29; Robert Leftwich to John P. Erwin, July 28, 1822, ibid., 275.

21. Austin's Memorial to Congress, May 13, 1822, *AP,* I, 510–16 (quotation on p. 514). The Memorial is in Spanish, with a note at the beginning saying that it is a literal translation from the French. SFA may have been unable to find someone who could translate English into Spanish, and his own Spanish skills were still meager at this point. However, while he had studied French (and could certainly read it), it seems unlikely that he was much more proficient in writing that language than Spanish. A plausible explanation is that he found someone who could help him translate his English into French, having already secured someone else to translate the French into Spanish. This would also help to explain the two-week delay in presenting the Memorial to congress. For a more detailed discussion of the Memorial's specifics, see *LSFA,* 47–48.

22. Antonio López de Santa Anna to Agustín de Iturbide, April 15, 1822, quoted in Anna, *Mexican Empire,* 59 (quotation), and 57–75 passim. Also see Green, *Mexican Republic,* 9.

23. SFA to J. H. Hawkins, [about May 1, 1822], *AP,* I, 505; SFA to J. E. B. Austin, May 22, 1822, ibid., 518–19; Anna, *Mexican Empire,* 61–69.

24. SFA to Emperor Iturbide, May 25, 1822, *AP,* I, 518–19.

25. The provisional junta that had ruled Mexico until February 1822 (when the congress was installed) had also considered a colonization bill; see *LSFA,* 44–45.

26. SFA to J. E. B. Austin, July 8, 1822, *AP,* I, 531 (quotation). For contemporary

descriptions of the city and similar observations on its population by other American visitors, see Joel Roberts Poinsett, *Notes on Mexico Made in the Autumn of 1822* (reprint ed., New York: Frederick A. Praeger, 1969), 45–52; Edward Thornton Tayloe, *Mexico, 1825–1828: The Journal and Correspondence of Edward Thornton Tayloe,* ed. C. Harvey Gardiner (Chapel Hill: University of North Carolina Press, 1959), 50–73.

27. SFA to J. E. B. Austin, June 13, 1823, *AP,* I, 671 (first, third, fourth and fifth quotations); SFA to J. E. B. Austin, May 20, 1823, ibid., 645 (second quotation). Compare Austin's statement with the remarks of Joaquín Fernández de Lizardi (known as *El Pensador Mexicano,* the Mexican Thinker), arguably the most influential political intellectual of the period: "There is still much fanaticism in my country which should be gradually eliminated. The people must be made to understand that being fanatics and ignorant is not the same as being a Catholic nor that the superstitious are the devout" (quoted in Costeloe, *Church and State,* 37). Also see James Ernest Crisp, "Anglo-Texas Attitudes Toward the Mexican, 1821–1845," Ph.D. diss., Yale University, 1976, esp. 34–35.

28. SFA to James Bryan, November 23, 1821, *AP,* I, 434; SFA to J. E. B. Austin, March 23, 1822, ibid., 487 (first and second quotations); SFA to J. E. B. Austin, May 22, 1822, ibid., 518; SFA to J. E. B. Austin, July 8, 1822, ibid., 530 (third and fourth quotations); SFA to J. E. B. Austin, December 25, 1822, ibid., 561; SFA to J. E. B. Austin, January 1, 1823, *AP,* I, 566; SFA to J. E. B. Austin, June 13, 1823, ibid., 671.

29. Robert Leftwich to John P. Erwin, February 19, 1823, *PCRCT,* intro. vol., 425. The earliest document that I have been able to find that is definitely written in Spanish in SFA's own hand is a draft of the November 6, 1822, petition to congress; see original in the Austin Papers, Series I, CAH. It is, of course, possible that SFA hired scribes to help him put his earliest documents into proper Spanish, although he left no record of having done so.

30. Mattie Austin Hatcher and Edith Louise Kelly, eds., "Tadeo Ortiz de Ayala and the Colonization of Texas, 1822–1833," part 1, *SWHQ* 32 (July 1928): 74–83; Robert Leftwich's Mexico Diary and Letterbook, 1822–1824, entries of June 5, July 9, 1822, *PCRCT,* intro. vol., 202–3, 243–44; SFA to J. H. Hawkins, [about May 1, 1822], *AP,* I, 505. Leftwich and Irwin were accompanied to Mexico City by the only Mexican investor in the Texas Association, Félix de Armas, but he departed the city in July, leaving the two Americans much more dependent on Austin, who was speaking decent Spanish by that time. For Edwards, see *HT,* II, 798. For the petitions of Woodbury, Parrott, and Wolfe (all dated January 13, 1823), see AGN Transcripts, Fomento, vol. 310, Colonización, CAH.

31. Robert Leftwich's Mexico Diary, April 30, June 5, July 9, July 25, 1822, *PCRCT,* intro. vol., 107 (first quotation), 202–3 (second and third quotations), 243–44; 268 (fourth quotation).

32. SFA to J. H. Hawkins, [about May 1, 1822], *AP,* I, 505; General James Wilkinson: Introducing Austin, May 15, 1822, ibid., 517; James Wilkinson to SFA, March 6, 1823, ibid., 583–84. Leftwich actually cut Wilkinson in on a share of the Texas Association's stock in return for his influence in Mexico; see Robert Leftwich's Mexico Diary, June 7,

July 5, 1822, *PCRCT,* intro. vol., 204–10, 222–23. Wilkinson also knew the group of New Orleans lawyers and businessmen who supported various Texan and Mexican causes in the 1810s and 1820s, a group that included Joseph Hawkins, Nathaniel Cox, Abner L. Duncan, and William Christy. Austin, through his connection with Hawkins, seems to have been a sort of junior member of this group during his time in New Orleans. Among other things, Wilkinson supposedly loaned Hawkins money in exchange for a mortgage on his house and slaves, money that Hawkins may have used in part to finance Austin's venture; see Cantrell, "Partnership of Stephen F. Austin," 20, fn47. On Wilkinson, see James Ripley Jacobs, *Tarnished Warrior: Major-General James Wilkinson* (New York: Macmillan, 1938), esp. 332–39.

33. Statement by A. G. Wavell relative to his lands in Texas, 1855, Wavell Papers, Texas State Library, quoted in Robert W. Amsler, "General Arthur G. Wavell: A Soldier of Fortune in Texas," *SWHQ* 69, part 1 (July 1965): 5. Amsler's article, which is concluded in the October 1965 *SWHQ* (pp. 186–209) draws conclusions similar to my own regarding the Wavell-SFA relationship.

34. SFA, Power of Attorney to Arthur G. Wavell, June 27, 1822; SFA and Arthur G. Wavell: Agreement, July 4, 1822 (quotation); Arthur G. Wavell's Application for a Grant, July 4, 1822, all in *AP,* I, 527–29.

35. Wavell, quoted in Amsler, "General Arthur G. Wavell," pt. I, 11.

36. Arthur G. Wavell to SFA, May 22, 1823, *AP,* I, 646.

37. Arthur G. Wavell to SFA, November 21, 1822, *AP,* I, 553; SFA to Arthur G. Wavell, [about July —, 1824?], ibid., 869.

38. The evidence for a cordial relationship between Herrera and SFA is admittedly incomplete. Most of the evidence of their dealings comes from Leftwich; see Robert Leftwich's Mexico Diary, June 15, July 5, 1822, February 2, 1823, *PCRCT,* intro. vol., 215, 221–22, 413–14. Although colored by a strong negative bias, the best contemporaneous sketch of Herrera's life is in Lorenzo de Zavala, *Ensayo histórico de las revoluciones de México* (Paris, 1831; reprint ed., Mexico City: Editorial Porrúa, 1969), I: 130–31. Also see Wilbert H. Timmons, *Morelos: Priest, Soldier, Statesman of Mexico* (El Paso: Texas Western Press, 1963), 148–50; Alejandro Villaseñor y Villaseñor, *Biografías de los héroes y caudillos de la Independencia* (Mexico City: Editorial Jus, 1962), 2: 236–42; also see Wilbert H. Guzmán, "La misión de José Manuel de Herrera en Estados Unidos," *Boletín del Archivo General de la Nación,* vol. 10 (January-March, April-June 1969), 255–88. Documents that accompany the Guzmán article (see pp. 278–80, 287) reveal that in 1815 Herrera became acquainted with Abner L. Duncan, a New Orleans businessman who had longstanding interests in Mexican affairs and who later was an associate of Joseph Hawkins and SFA.

39. See SFA to [Anastacio Bustamante?], May 10, 1822, *AP,* I, 507–10; Anastacio Bustamante to Gaspar López, March 3, 1823. Bustamante, a personal favorite of Iturbide, did not immediately take command of the Interior Provinces (he was named to command the interior provinces of both the west and the east), because his loyalty to Iturbide led to his detention by Nicolás Bravo until December 1824. Gaspar López continued in command of the Eastern Interior Provinces and was replaced by Felipe de la Garza in

the spring of 1823. After being released in December 1824, Bustamante did finally take command of the Provinces; see Green, *Mexican Republic,* 190; Alessio Robles, *Coahuila y Texas,* I: 150–51.

40. *LSFA,* 53; J. B. de Arizpe to SFA, May 24, 1823, *AP,* I, 646–48; SFA to Robert Leftwich, April 23, 1823, *PCRCT,* intro. vol., 482–83. Also see Robert Leftwich to SFA, April 30, May 20, 1823, ibid., 634, 646. On Arizpe, see Israel Cavazos Garza, *Diccionario biográfico de Nuevo León,* (Monterrey, Mexico: Universidad Autónoma de Nuevo León, 1984), 1: 26. Barker (p. 75) mistakenly asserts that Juan Bautista Arizpe and Miguel Ramos Arizpe were brothers.

41. Robert Leftwich's Mexico Diary, July 5, 1822, *PCRCT,* intro. vol., 221–22; *LSFA,* 58, 63; Margaret Swett Henson, *Lorenzo de Zavala: The Pragmatic Idealist* (Forth Worth: Texas Christian University Press, 1996), 4; Zavala, *Ensayo histórico,* 2: 432 (quotation); SFA to James F. Perry, September 30, 1835, *AP,* III, 141. Leftwich does not specifically say that SFA was present at the meeting with Zavala cited in this note, but it is reasonable to assume that he was, since Leftwich uses the pronoun "we," and he and Austin often paid their calls to Mexican officials together. Upon returning to Texas, SFA sent his regards to his "friend" Zavala; see SFA to Erasmo Seguín, [about January 1, 1824?], *AP,* I, 719.

42. *LSFA,* 57, 63; Lillian Briseño Senosiáin, Laura Solares Robles, and Laura Suárez de la Torre, *Valentín Gómez Farías y su lucha por el federalismo, 1822–1858* (San Juan Mixcoac, Mexico: Instituto de Investigaciones Dr. José María Mora, 1991), 34, 293–98; SFA to Erasmo Seguín, [about January 1, 1824?], *AP,* I, 719 (quotation).

43. In the context of Mexico in the 1820s and 1830s it is difficult to use the terms "liberal" or "conservative" without oversimplifying or misidentifying individuals; in the political environment of 1822–23 it is virtually impossible; see Vázquez, *La fundación del Estado Mexicano,* 9–12; and Guardino, *Peasants, Politics,* 112. Mier is a good example of the difficulty. He has been portrayed as liberal, conservative, or moderate, depending on one's perspective. Although more supportive of a strong central government than the aforementioned leaders, Mier was still an ardent republican and opponent of Iturbide's regime in 1822. SFA mentions his friendship with Mier in the same letter that he refers to his "amigos" Zavala and Gómez Farías; see SFA to Erasmo Seguín, [about January 1, 1824?], *AP,* I, 719. See Nettie Lee Benson, "Servando Teresa de Mier, Federalist," *Hispanic American Historical Review* 28 (November 1948): 514–25; Green, *Mexican Republic,* 33–34; Tocurato S. Di Tella, *National Popular Politics in Early Independent Mexico, 1820–1847* (Albuquerque: University of New Mexico Press, 1996), 65, 118–19; Charles A. Hale, *Mexican Liberalism in the Age of Mora, 1821–1853* (New Haven: Yale University Press, 1968), 83, 196–97. For SFA's visit to Mier, see SFA to James F. Perry, *AP,* II, 1051.

44. Although normal Spanish practice would properly render his last name as "Mier y Terán" (and most modern scholars have opted for that rendering), Terán himself and most of his contemporaries commonly identified him simply as "Terán," a practice which I have chosen to follow; see, for example, the listing of members of the Colonization Committee in the *Noticioso General,* August 5, 1822, a Mexico City newspaper.

45. Robert Leftwich's Mexico Diary, July 9, 1822, *PCRCT,* intro. vol., 243, mentions

his visit with Terán. This is another instance in which Leftwich does not specifically say that SFA was present, but it is likely that he was. If not, it is inconceivable that SFA would not have met Terán, given the general's prominent position as a member of the colonization committee. SFA's later good relations with Terán would be difficult to explain if not for a favorable first impression made during the 1822–23 Mexico City trip. The one important statesman whom SFA did not meet on this trip was Lucas Alamán. Alamán had arrived in Mexico from Europe only in March 1823, and he was appointed minister of relations by the post-Iturbide interim government on April 15, just three days before SFA left for Texas; see Green, *Mexican Republic,* 14. On Terán, see Ohland Morton, *Terán and Texas: A Chapter in Texas Mexican Relations* (Austin: Texas State Historical Association, 1948); *HT,* IV, 716–17.

46. James David Carter, *Masonry in Texas: Background, History, and Influence to 1846* (Waco, Texas: Committee on Masonic Education and Service for the Grand Lodge of Texas, A. F. and A. M., 1955), 190, 193–94, 219–22; Luis J. Zalce y Rodríguez, *Apuntes para la historia de la Masonería en México* (2 vols., Mexico City, n.p., 1950), I: 58–60; Henson, *Lorenzo de Zavala,* 15–16; Costeloe, *La Primera República,* 20–21, 49–52; Green, *Mexican Republic,* 89–91.

47. *Nashville Whig,* September 25, 1822, reproduced in *PCRCT,* intro. vol., 455–57; SFA to Josiah H. Bell et al., July 26, 1822, *AP,* I, 535.

48. Except where otherwise noted, this paragraph and the eight that follow rely primarily on chap. 3 of *LSFA* for the factual account of the politics surrounding Austin's effort to have his grant confirmed. Readers interested in the details of the Mexican government's deliberations should consult Barker's account, which was thoroughly researched and meticulously presented using the proceedings of the Mexican congress, documents from the Archivo General de la Nación, and other sources. More general summaries of the government's actions on colonization, which are also used in the following account, can be found in two important essays by Nettie Lee Benson: "Texas as Viewed from Mexico, 1820–1834," *SWHQ* 90 (January 1987): 224–43, and "Territorial Integrity in Mexican Politics, 1821–1833," in Rodríguez O., *Independence of Mexico,* 276–85. Under the plan agreed on by SFA and Antonio Martínez in 1821, a married colonist with two children would have received 1,280 acres, or two square miles of land. Under the proposed colonization law (and eventually under SFA's personal agreement with the government), families received a league and a labor, the equivalent of about seven square miles.

49. Robert Leftwich's Mexico Diary, August 27, 1822, *PCRCT,* intro. vol., 336–41 (quotations on p. 338).

50. SFA to [Edward Lovelace?], November 22, 1822, *AP,* I, 555. Traditional historiography has portrayed Iturbide's dissolution of congress as an act of despotism, but a more recent interpretation emphasizes the incompetence of the congress and the balanced makeup of the Junta, and suggests that Iturbide remained committed to a system of constitutional monarchy; see Anna, *Mexican Empire,* 112–23.

51. SFA to [Edward Lovelace?], November 22, 1822, *AP,* I, 555.

52. SFA to J. E. B. Austin, December 25, 1822, *AP,* I, 561. On the uprisings against Iturbide, see Anna, *Mexican Empire,* chap. 6.

53. Robert Leftwich's Mexico Diary, February 2, 19, 1823, *PCRCT,* intro. vol., 414 (quotation), 418.

54. Anna, *Mexican Empire,* 184, states that Herrera "suddenly resigned" on February 26, but Carlos María de Bustamante, who kept a contemporaneous diary of political events, recorded on February 22 the rumor that the resignation of Herrera and the other cabinet ministers had already been received, and in his entry of February 23 he noted (accurately) that José de Valle was his replacement; see Bustamante, *Diario histórico de México, diciembre 1822–junio 1823* (Mexico City: Instituto Nacional de Antropología e Historia), 158. The actual resignation date was no later than the 24th, because Leftwich recorded in his diary entry of the 25th the appointment of José de Valle as his replacement; see Robert Leftwich's Mexico Diary, March 25, *PCRCT,* intro. vol., 449.

55. In his diary Robert Leftwich noted that he and SFA rode together out to Bustamante's headquarters, where Leftwich asked for and received an introductory letter to the new minister of relations. Leftwich does not specifically say that Austin requested such a letter, but it is reasonable to assume he did; see Robert Leftwich's Mexico Diary, February 25, 1823, *PCRCT,* intro. vol., 449 (quotation). SFA did receive a letter of recommendation from Bustamante addressed to Gaspar López, the lame-duck commandant general of the Interior Provinces, as well as his passport; see Anastacio Bustamante to Gaspar López, March 3, 1823, *AP,* I, 581; Anastacio Bustamante to Austin: Passport, March 3, 1823, ibid., 581–82.

56. Benson, "Texas as Viewed from Mexico," 235–36; and various applications for empresario grants in AGN Transcripts, Fomento, vols. 307–10, CAH. For the full text of the documents that made up SFA's grant confirmation in its final form, see Confirmation of Austin's Grant, [cover letter dated March 20, 1823, but composed of documents bearing various dates], *AP,* I, 590–601. For his final request to the restored congress, see SFA to Congress, April 5, 1823, ibid., 629–30.

57. SFA to J. E. B. Austin, April 23, 1823, *AP,* I, 631; SFA to J. E. B. Austin, May 10, 1823, ibid., 638; SFA to [Baron de Bastrop], [May 17, 1823], ibid., 643.

58. There is no full-length biography of Ramos Arizpe; for a brief outline of his life, see Pablo C. Moreno, *Galería de Coahuilenses distinguidos* (Torreón, Coahuila: Imprenta Mayagoitia, 1966), 13–17. For Ramos Arizpe's deposition of López, see Nettie Lee Benson, *The Provincial Deputation in Mexico: Harbinger of Provincial Autonomy, Independence, and Federalism* (Austin: University of Texas Press, 1992), 68–70. The best sources for information on his overall political career are (in English and Spanish, respectively) Benson, *Provincial Deputation,* and Alessio Robles, *Coahuila y Texas.* Two months before SFA's visit, following the abdication of Iturbide, Ramos Arizpe had led the successful movement to depose Gaspar López, the pro-Iturbide commandant general and political chief of the Eastern Interior Provinces.

59. SFA to J. E. B. Austin, May 10, 1823, *AP,* I, 638 (first quotation); SFA to [Baron de Bastrop], [May 17, 1823], ibid., 643 (second quotation); *LSFA,* 77. For a sketch of

Garza, see L. Randall Rogers, *Two Particular Friends of Stephen F. Austin* (Waco: Texian Press, 1990), 37–66; also see Anna, *Mexican Empire,* 107. It appears that Ramos Arizpe had been initiated into the Masonic order while serving in the Spanish Cortes, and Masonic historians have concluded that Masonic ties helped SFA form his friendship with Garza, who in turn provided SFA with his introduction to Ramos Arizpe. Much of this is based on inference; as Rogers and Carter, both Masonic historians, suggest, the term "particular friend" was a code word for a fellow Mason. For Ramos Arizpe's Masonic membership, see Zalce y Rodríguez, 58–60; Carter, *Masonry in Texas,* 189–90, 220–22. The role of Masonic connections is also is a major theme of Reichstein, *Rise of the Lone Star,* esp. 31–35, 191–92, although Reichstein may have overstated their overall significance in Texas affairs.

60. SFA to J. E. B. Austin, May 20, 1823, *AP,* I, 644–45; SFA to Felipe de la Garza, May 27, 1823, ibid., 651–52; SFA to ?, May 28, 1823, ibid., 654; *LSFA,* 77. For an overview of political affairs in the Eastern Interior Provinces and Garza's activities during this time, see Benson, *Provincial Deputation,* 107–11.

61. Austin's Plan for Organization of Congress, August 1822, *AP,* I, 538–41; Reflections Addressed to the Junta Instituyente, January 16, 1823, ibid., 568–72; Project of a Constitution for the Republic of Mexico, March 29, 1823, ibid., 601–27. For an extended analysis of these three documents, see *LSFA,* 70–74.

62. Moreno, *Galería de Coahuilenses,* 14 (first quotation); SFA, "A Plan of Federal Government," May 1823, *AP,* I, 656–69 (second and third quotations on pp. 668–69); William Archibald Whatley, "The Formation of the Mexican Constitution of 1824," M.A. thesis, University of Texas, 1921, 70–72; *LSFA,* 75–76.

63. Benson, *Provincial Deputation,* 123–24; Jaime E. Rodríguez O., "The Constitution of 1824 and the Formation of the Mexican State," in Rodríguez O., *Evolution of the Mexican Political System,* 71–90, esp. 89.

64. SFA to J. E. B. Austin, May 10, 1823, *AP,* I, 638.

65. SFA to Mary Austin Holley, August 21, 1835, *AP,* III, 103.

66. Weber, *Mexican Frontier,* 282; Benson, "Territorial Integrity," 282–83, 307 (Alamán quotation on p. 282).

67. SFA to J. E. B. Austin, June 13, 1823, *AP,* I, 670–71.

SIX

Empresario Estevan F. Austin

1823–1825

1. *Arkansas Gazette,* August 6, 1822, reprinting story from the *Nashville Clarion* (quotation); *Arkansas Gazette,* August 13, 1822; Hugh McGuffin to SFA, September 22, 1822, *AP,* I, 545–46; J. H. Kuykendall, "Recollections of Capt. Horatio Chriesman," in "Reminiscences of Early Texans," *Quarterly of the Texas State Historical Association* 6 (January 1903): 237.

2. *Arkansas Gazette,* August 6, 1822 (first, second, and sixth quotations); Septem-

ber 12, 1822 (third and fourth quotations); *Missouri Republican* (St. Louis), October 16, 1822, reprinting story from the *Arkansas Gazette* (fifth quotation); J. E. B. Austin to SFA, May 4, 1823, *AP,* I, 636.

3. Hugh McGuffin to SFA, September 13, 1822, *AP,* I, 546; J. E. B. Austin to SFA, May 4, 1823, ibid., 635–36.

4. *LSFA,* 88–89. García replaced José Felix Trespalacios, who had replaced Antonio Martínez.

5. Bastrop to the Colonists: Proclamation, August 4, 1823, *AP,* I, 677.

6. SFA to the Colonists, August 6, 1823, *AP,* I, 679–81.

7. Ibid.

8. Ibid.

9. Ibid.

10. Luciano García, "Descripcíon englobo de la provincia de Texas," Eberstadt Collection, CAH; *LSFA,* 87–88.

11. In rendering the names of Indian tribes, I have arbitrarily chosen to follow the spellings in Newcomb's *History of Texas Indians.* Most of the tribes had anglicized as well as hispanicized names—for example, *Wacos* versus *Huecos*—and of course there were multiple spellings and pronunciations by speakers of both languages.

12. J. H. Kuykendall, "Extracts from a Biographical Sketch of Capt. John Ingram," in Kuykendall, "Reminiscences," part 2, 328; W. B. Dewees to ?, August 29, 1823, in Dewees, *Letters,* 40–41; 324; Newcomb, *Indians of Texas,* chap. 3, esp. pp. 63–65, 69, 71, 77–78; and 341–43; also see chap. 4, nn37 and 38.

13. Kuykendall, "Recollections of Capt. Horatio Chriesman," 236–40. In Kuykendall's reminiscence of Judge Thomas M. Duke, the same story is told, except that the settlers involved are identified as the survivors of the shipwrecked schooner *Lively;* see J. H. Kuykendall, "Recollections of Judge Thomas M. Duke," in "Reminiscences," 1: 247–48. This is an error, because the *Lively* had arrived earlier and its passengers had no encounters with Indians; see Bugbee, "What Became of the Lively?" and Lewis, "Adventures of the 'Lively' Immigrants," parts 1 and 2.

14. Militia Organization, December 5, 1823, *AP,* I, 715; SFA to Military Commandant, April 20, 1824, ibid., 768 (quotations); J. H. Kuykendall, "Reminiscences of Capt. Gibson Kuykendall," in Kuykendall, "Reminiscences," 2: 35.

15. Austin's Diary of Campaign Against Karankaways, August 30–September 7, 1824, *AP,* I, 885–87 (first and second quotations on p. 886); SFA to Authorities of La Bahia, about November 1, 1824, ibid., 931 (third quotation); Kuykendall, "Reminiscences of Gibson Kuykendall," 35–37; Newcomb, *Indians of Texas,* 341. SFA's diary covers only the first phase of this expedition. The same week that Austin was looking for the Karankawas, a separate company of colonists had a "severe engagement" near the mouth of the Colorado with a combined force of Cocos and Karankawas, in which both sides suffered casualties; see Randal Jones to SFA, September 7, 1824, Austin Papers, Series III, CAH.

16. For an overview of the Tonkawas, see Newcomb, *Indians of Texas,* chap. 6.

17. SFA to Luciano García, August 28, 1823, *AP,* I, 688; SFA to Luciano García,

October 20, 1823, ibid., 701–702; Kuykendall, "Recollections of Capt. Gibson Kuykendall," 31–32.

18. W. B. Dewees to ?, December 1, 1823, in Dewees, *Letters,* 44–45 (first quotation); Kuykendall, "Recollections of Judge Thomas M. Duke," 252 (second quotation). For subsequent trouble with the Tonkawas under Chief Sandia, see SFA to Amos Rawls, [June 22, 1824?], *AP,* I, 840; and SFA to Saucedo, May 19, 1826, ibid., 1341–42. In the latter letter we learn that Carita had died and that his band had resumed its old ways.

19. Kuykendall, "Recollections of Judge Thomas M. Duke," 252.

20. SFA to J. M. Guerra, [about July 18, 1823?], *AP,* I, 675; SFA to Josiah H. Bell, August 6, 1823, ibid., 682 (quotations).

21. Thomas M. Duke to SFA, June—, 1824, *AP,* I, 842–43; Powers of Commissioners to Waco Indians, [June—, 1824], ibid., 843–44; SFA to Waco Indians: A Talk, June—, 1824, ibid., 844–45; Kuykendall, "Recollections of Judge Thomas M. Duke," 249 (quotation).

22. Referendum on Indian Relations, September 28, 1825, *AP,* I, 1208–11.

23. John P. Coles to SFA, January 7, 1826, *AP,* I, 1246. Later that year, when word arrived that the Wacos and Tawakonis were about to join with the Comanches in a major war against the colony, SFA prepared for a serious fight. Again, however, the proposed war did not develop, and the Mexican government managed to negotiate a peace treaty with all the hostile tribes, no doubt to SFA's relief. See Mateo Ahumada to SFA, May 4, 1826, ibid., 1321; SFA to Mateo Ahumada, May 8, 1826, ibid., 1323–25; SFA to James J. Ross and Aylett C. Buckner, May 13, [1826], ibid., 1332–33; Francisco Ruiz to SFA, June 2, 1827, ibid., 1653; Peter Ellis Bean to SFA, June 3, 1827, ibid., 1656; Anastacio Bustamante to SFA, June 19, 1827, ibid., 1660.

24. For an overview of this topic that agrees in the main with the interpretation presented here, see Valentine J. Belfiglio, "The Indian Policy of Stephen F. Austin," *East Texas Historical Journal* 32 (Fall 1993): 15–22.

25. For a more extended treatment of these elections, see *LSFA,* 88–89.

26. SFA sent the Civil and Criminal Regulations to his alcaldes soon after they were promulgated in January 1823, and they went into effect immediately. SFA eventually published them, along with a short history of his colony and other documents, as *Translation of the Laws, Orders and Contracts, on Colonization, from January 1821, up to 1829; in Virtue of Which, Col. Stephen F. Austin Introduced and Settled Foreign Emigrants in Texas, with an Explanatory Introduction* (San Felipe de Austin: Godwin B. Cotten, 1829). This publication is regarded as the first book published in Texas. It was reprinted in 1837 by Borden & Moore in Columbia, Texas; in Wooten, *Comprehensive History,* I, 481–92; and in David B. Gracy II, ed., *Establishing Austin's Colony* (San Felipe de Austin: Godwin B. Cotten, 1829; reprint ed., Austin: Pemberton Press, 1970), 75–89. My citations are from the Gracy reprint.

27. Gracy, *Establishing Austin's Colony,* 77 (quotation). The history of SFA's early efforts to establish a system of government for the colony, and particularly the drafting of his Civil and Criminal Regulations, is ably told in Eugene C. Barker, "The Govern-

ment of Austin's Colony, 1821–1831," *SWHQ* 21 (January 1918): 223–52, esp. 226–30; and Joseph W. McKnight, "Stephen F. Austin's Legalistic Concerns," *SWHQ* 89 (January 1986): 248–56; also see Barker, *LSFA,* 109–11. In 1826, Austin appointed an appellate court, consisting of any three alcaldes, to relieve him from his duty as appellate judge.

28. Gracy, *Establishing Austin's Colony,* 85 (quotations); McKnight, "Stephen F. Austin's Legalistic Concerns," 251.

29. Gracy, *Establishing Austin's Colony,* 86–88; McKnight, "Stephen F. Austin's Legalistic Concerns," 251; Barker, "Government of Austin's Colony," 229–30; Petition of SFA to the General Commanding the Eastern Interior Provinces, May 27, 1823, Translation of the Record of Documents and Titles in Austin's First Colony, 1840, Archives and Records Division, Texas General Land Office; Report of the Committee of the Provincial Deputation, June 2, 1823, ibid.; Resolution of the Most Excellent Deputation in Assembly, June 11, 1823, ibid.; Decree of Felipe de la Garza, June 16, 1823, ibid.; SFA to Lucas Alamán, January 20, 1824, *AP,* I, 727–28.

30. Gracy, *Establishing Austin's Colony,* 86–87. Political Chief José Antonio Saucedo gave his official stamp of approval to both the civil and criminal regulations when he visited the colony in May 1824; see Gracy, *Establishing Austin's Colony,* 82, 89.

31. Decree of the Emperor, February 18, 1823, in Gracy, *Establishing Austin's Colony,* 39 (first quotation); Littleberry Hawkins to SFA, April 24, 1823, *AP,* I, 631; J. E. B. Austin to SFA, May 25, 1823, ibid., I, 650; W. B. Dewees to ?, August 29, 1823, in Dewees, *Letters,* 42. Dewees's "letters," which were published in the 1850s, must be used with caution because it is clear that they were written, or at least embellished, after the fact. However, Dewees *was* in Texas during these years, and his letters generally can be considered as reliable as the memoirs or reminiscences of other settlers; see the introduction to Dewees, *Letters.*

32. Lester G. Bugbee, "The Old Three Hundred," *Quarterly of the Texas State Historical Association* 1 (October 1897): 108–9; Edwin P. Arneson, "The Early Art of Terrestrial Measurement and Its Practice in Texas," *SWHQ* 29 (October 1925): 91–92; Joseph H. Hawkins to SFA, May 30, 1822, *AP,* I, 520; SFA to Baron de Bastrop, August 12, 1823, ibid., 686; SFA to Captain Dickson, November 10, 1823, ibid., 707; Contract for Surveying, October 1, 1824, ibid., 911–12; W. B. Dewees to ?, August 29, 1823, in Dewees, *Letters,* 42.

33. W. B. Dewees to ?, December 1, 1823, in Dewees, *Letters,* 43.

34. SFA to Miguel Ramos Arizpe, about July 31, 1824, *AP,* I, 863; also see SFA to José Antonio Saucedo, June 20, 1824, ibid., 836. The 272 figure comes from Bugbee, "Old Three Hundred," 108. Bugbee enumerated a total of 297 families who received titles in the colony. The editor of the *PCRCT* uses the 297-family figure to assert that SFA never fulfilled his first empresario contract; see *PCRCT,* V, 48. However, it is ahistorical to take a list compiled from complex, often-ambiguous records, count only 297 "families," and conclude flatly that SFA failed to fulfill his 300-family contract. For example, some of the titles were issued jointly to two single men, who were arbitrarily paired together to form a "family." If, therefore, one counts adult males (many of whom married and started

families after coming to Texas) who obtained land in Austin's first colony, the number is actually higher than 300. And of course, a handful died, failed to cultivate their land, or returned to the United States, thus forfeiting their titles. Given the highly complex and ambiguous nature of counting families, it would have been difficult for SFA or anyone else to give a precise count of the families who had legally met the settlement terms as stipulated in his contract. But nobody in Texas, Coahuila, or Mexico City ever questioned the fact that Austin had materially fulfilled the terms of his contract in good faith, and the evidence, taken as a whole, bears that out. For a more detailed analysis of the makeup of the Old Three Hundred, see note 40 below.

35. W. B. Dewees to ?, August 29, 1823, in Dewees, *Letters,* 42; SFA to Josiah H. Bell, September 28, 1823, *AP,* I, 695; SFA to ?, October 20, 1823, ibid., 703. The October 23 letter is the earliest surviving letter written by SFA and carrying the San Felipe de Austin place name. The September letter to Bell merely says "At the home of McFarland." Dewees uses the San Felipe name in his August "letter," but this should not be used as evidence that the town had already been named by then, because many of Dewees's "letters" were edited, or perhaps even composed, years later. The best source on the history and physical layout of San Felipe is Margaret Swett Henson, "San Felipe de Austin: Capital of the Austin Colony," unpublished paper read at Stephen F. Austin State University, October 28, 1993, at ceremonies commemorating SFA's two hundredth birthday. A copy of this paper is in my possession. Henson argues that the name San Felipe de Austin must have originated with Commandant Gen. Felipe de la Garza in Monterrey, for Governor García would not have had authority to name a town and St. Philip was Garza's patron saint. However, García's official order naming the town survives; see Luciano García to Baron de Bastrop, July 26, 1823, in Gracy, *Establishing Austin's Colony,* 43. It is possible, of course, that García was simply passing along Garza's name for the town, but the records do not survive to verify this theory.

36. SFA to Josiah H. Bell, September 28, 1823, *AP,* I, 695.

37. Bill for Surveying, September 30, 1824, *AP,* I, 908; Henson, "San Felipe," 5. The early history of San Felipe is poorly documented; Henson's unpublished paper is the best source. Streets in San Felipe carried the names of such national figures as Guadalupe Victoria, Vicente Guerrero, Nicolas Bravo, Lucas Alamán, and Manuel de Mier y Terán. Streets named for Texas officials included Antonio Martínez, José Felix Trespalacios, Luciano García, Antonio Saucedo, and the all-important land commissioner, the Baron de Bastrop.

38. Henson, "San Felipe," 5. No good description of SFA's first residence in San Felipe survives. We know, however, that in 1828 he had the cabin rebuilt, much larger and nicer, on the outskirts of the village. See M. M. Battle to SFA, September 12, 1827, *AP,* I, 1682–83; and SFA in Account with Mills M. Battle, 1826–28, ibid., II, 121. In 1828, SFA had his first log cabin enlarged and converted into a hotel, which he leased to James Whitesides. The new house was on the northern edge of the village, away from the bustle and noise; see Henson, *Samuel May Williams,* 16–17. In the spring of 1828, a new immigrant named J. C. Clopper visited San Felipe and described SFA's residence as "quite

a commodious and respectable dwelling." Since Clopper's visit and the precise date
of SFA's move from his first home to his second is unknown, we cannot know for sure
which version of the house Clopper was describing. He is probably describing the first
structure, though, for it appears that the new house was not finished until the fall of 1828;
see J. C. Clopper, "J. C. Clopper's Journal and Book of Memoranda for 1828," *Quarterly
of the Texas State Historical Association* 13 (July 1909): 58; and the above-cited Account
with Mills M. Battle. Another description, definitely of the second house, can be found
in Noah Smithwick, *The Evolution of a State, or Recollections of Old Texas Days* (1900;
reprint ed., Austin: University of Texas Press, 1983), 40. The log structure on Commerce
Street that SFA used as the first land office became San Felipe's Council Hall after SFA
moved. It was the site of the Texan conventions of 1832 and 1833 and the Consultation of
1835. All of the preceding information is confirmed by Joy Klein, tour guide at Stephen F.
Austin State Park in San Felipe and an expert on the early history of the town (author's
tour and interview with Joy Klein, San Felipe, July 22, 1995).

39. SFA to Josiah H. Bell, September 28, 1823, *AP*, I, 695; Henson, *Samuel May
Williams*, 1–13.

40. The government's decrees provided that colonists who intended to farm would
receive one labor (177 acres) of land. Those who intended to raise livestock qualified for
a league. Colonists could profess their intention to engage in both activities and receive a
league and a labor. Furthermore, at his discretion Austin could grant additional amounts
if he thought a settler merited it. Since virtually all "farmers" also raised some livestock,
they all could qualify for the full league. Using the list of the Old Three Hundred compiled in Bugbee ("The Old Three Hundred," 108–17), I have calculated that 180, or 63
percent, of the 287 actual "families" of the Old Three Hundred received a single league of
land. Forty-two families, or 15 percent of the total, received a league and a labor. Eighteen
families received only one or two labors (these were probably mechanics or merchants),
and 48 received more than a league and a labor. Trying to enumerate the Old Three
Hundred with precision is difficult, if not impossible. Some families received more than
one land title, while others were able to get two or more geographically distinct tracts
encapsulated in one title. Single men were placed in groups of two or three and counted
as a family. This is further complicated by the fact that some of these single men later married and then received an additional tract. In some cases names are duplicated, and it is
unclear whether this was because two men had the same name or one person simply got
listed twice because he gained title to separate tracts of land (probably at different times).
A handful of colonists forfeited their titles because they returned to the United States
or failed to cultivate their land within the required period of time. Some died or were
killed and their titles issued to an heir. My count of 287 actual "families" (excluding SFA
himself, and including each partnership of single men as a family) differs slightly from
Bugbee's; he counted 297. Bugbee was unclear on how he conducted his count, but the
discrepancy is probably explained by my excluding duplicate names. Any two counters
would probably come up with a different final tally, and my own count has no claims to
definitiveness. The only conclusion that can be stated with certainty is this: more than

three hundred individuals got title to land in Austin's Colony, even though the official number of families was less than three hundred.

41. For SFA's three-year, any-goods-acceptable payment plan, see SFA to the Colonists, August 6, 1823, *AP*, I, 680. The stricter two-year payment plan was published in American newspapers after SFA's return to Texas from Mexico City; see St. Louis *Missouri Republican*, November 12, 1823, reprinting letter from SFA to a Citizen of the State [of Tennessee], July 19, 1823, originally published in the *Nashville Whig*. For SFA's willingness to accept only livestock or slaves in lieu of money, see SFA to ?, October 20, 1823, *AP*, I, 704; and SFA to Josiah H. Bell, December 6, 1823, ibid., 716.

42. Anthony R. Clarke to SFA, February 3, 1824, *AP*, I, 739 (first quotation); P. T. Dimmitt to SFA, June [about 15], 1824, ibid., 832 (second quotation). For a lengthier treatment of these complaints and of the entire land-fee controversy, see Barker, "Government of Austin's Colony," 231–39; and *LSFA*, 87, 97–106. Barker is factually accurate, but he uncritically accepts SFA's own justifications of the fees. While those justifications were on the whole reasonable, they fail to take into account the huge disparity between the total outlay that colonists had planned for under the original plan, and the much larger outlay required by the large grants.

43. José Antonio Saucedo to Colonists, [May 18], 1824, *AP*, I, 754; Proclamation of Political Chief, May 21, 1824, ibid., 796; *LSFA*, 100–101. Saucedo's actions are hard to understand, but he must have concluded that the premium lands that SFA was to receive were compensation enough. He would later change his mind, for in SFA's second colonization contract Saucedo would build into the official fee schedule a reasonable reward for the empresario.

44. Address by SFA to Colonists, June 5, 1824, *AP*, I, 823; *LSFA*, 105; SFA to [Edmund H.] Martin, September 14, 1832, *AP*, II, 860.

45. Address by SFA to Colonists, June 5, 1824, *AP*, I, 811–24 (quotation on p. 821); *LSFA*, 101–6.

46. Address by SFA to Colonists, June 5, 1824, *AP*, I, 822 (quotation). In 1827, Governor José María Viesca took SFA's side in the land fee dispute, saying that the settlers really did not have to pay the government the fee that Saucedo had imposed, but of course by this time it was a moot point; see José María Viesca to Congress, October 24, 1827, Primer Congreso Constitucional, Primer Congreso Ordinario, 1827, Comisión de Gobernación, Leg. 1, Exp. 61, Archivo del Congreso del Estado de Coahuila, Saltillo, Coahuila, Mexico.

47. Amounts of land are all from Bugbee's list of the Old Three Hundred. Information on Coles is from *HT*, II, 204; and *LSFA*, 87. On Groce, see Rosa Groce Bertleth, "Jared Ellison Groce," *SWHQ* 22 (April 1917): 358–68.

48. SFA to Josiah H. Bell, December 4, 1823, *AP*, I, 715. A few months later SFA gave Bell an extra league in back of the one he already had, with instructions that Bell should "keep the above arrangement to yourself"; see SFA to Josiah H. Bell, July 12, 1824, Austin Papers, Series II, CAH.

49. James Gaines to SFA, November 10, 1824, *AP*, I, 939.

50. One such policy was a requirement that squatters in East Texas relocate to Austin's Colony or leave Texas.

51. Seth Ingram to SFA, January 16, 1825, *AP,* I, 1019-20; A. C. Buckner to SFA, April 20, 1825, ibid., 1076-77.

52. SFA to José Antonio Saucedo, June 6, 1825, *AP,* I, 1123-24; SFA to Colonists, June 7, 1824, ibid., 1124-28 (quotations).

53. Aylett C. Buckner to SFA, June 10, 1825, *AP,* I, 1132 (quotation); Subpoena for Witness, June 7, 1825, ibid., 1131.

54. William and Andrew Rabb to SFA, June 10, 1825, Andrew Rabb to SFA, June 11, 1825, Jared E. Groce to SFA, June 11, 1825, all in *AP,* I, 1133.

55. SFA to James Cummins, June 13, 1824, *AP,* I, 1134-35 (first, second, third, and fourth quotations); Aylett C. Buckner to SFA, August 10, 1825, ibid., 1162; SFA to Ross and Buckner, May 13, [1826], ibid., 1332-33; SFA to Mateo Ahumada, June 16, 1826, ibid., 1359-60; Mateo Ahumada to SFA, June 27, 1826, ibid., 1369; Thomas M. Duke to SFA, January 4, 1827, ibid., 1569. Also see "Recollections of Judge Thomas M. Duke," in Kuykendall, "Reminiscences of Early Texans," 248-49, 251; *HT,* II, 805-6; William Ransom Hogan, "Rampant Individualism in the Republic of Texas," *SWHQ* 44 (April 1941): 457-58.

56. Tijerina, *Tejanos and Texas,* 95-96, 104; Baron de Bastrop to SFA, March 18, 1824, *AP,* I, 752.

57. de la Teja, *Revolution Remembered,* 8-9; Tijerina, *Tejanos and Texas,* 97; SFA to Luciano García, October 20, 1823, *AP,* I, 703 (quotation). On SFA's draft constitution and the role of Ramos Arizpe, see chap. 5.

58. SFA to Erasmo Seguín, about January 1, 1824, *AP,* I, 718-19.

59. When Texas was joined with Coahuila, the Texas provincial deputation was abolished. In San Antonio, Saucedo and the other members of the deputation briefly staged a miniature rebellion and declared the law null and void. Cooler heads eventually prevailed, and the Tejano leaders resigned themselves to the union with Coahuila. See Tijerina, *Tejanos and Texas,* 97-101; Weber, *Mexican Frontier,* 24; de la Teja, *A Revolution Remembered,* 8-9; Charles A. Bacarisse, "The Union of Coahuila and Texas," *SWHQ* 61 (January 1958): 341-49. The May 7, 1824, decree of congress giving Texas the right to apply for statehood left the wording vague. It read: "As soon as [Texas] is in a position to figure as a State by itself, it can notify the general congress for its resolution"; see Manuel Dublán and Jose María Lozano, eds., *Legislación Mexicana,* 3 vols. (Mexico City: Imprenta de comercio á cargo de Dublan y Lozano, hijos, 1876), I, 706.

60. Erasmo Seguín to Baron de Bastrop, March 24, 1824, *AP,* I, 758. Neither the Constitution of 1824 nor the Colonization Laws of 1823 or 1824 mentioned slavery. The Decree of July 13, 1824, provided that "commerce and traffic in slaves proceeding from any country and under any flag whatsoever, is forever prohibited in the territory of the United Mexican States." See Randolph B. Campbell, *An Empire for Slavery: The Peculiar Institution in Texas, 1821-1865* (Baton Rouge: Louisiana State University Press, 1989), 16-17.

61. Proclamation, May 1, 1824, *AP,* I, 781; SFA to Gaspar Flores, October 27, 1824, ibid., 929; SFA to Rafael Gonzales, March 16, 1825, ibid., 1056 (second and third quotations).

62. SFA to Supreme Power of the Republic, October 1, 1824, *AP,* I, 912–13; SFA to Supreme Executive Power of the Republic, November 6, 1824, ibid., 935–36; SFA to State Congress, November 6, 1824, ibid., 936; Baron de Bastrop to SFA, May 6, 1825, ibid., 1087; Colonization Law of the State of Coahuila and Texas, in Gracy, *Establishing Austin's Colony,* 50–57; Contract with the Government of the State for the Colonization of Five Hundred Families, April 27, 1825, ibid., 58–61; Official Letter of the Governor Extending the Foregoing Contract, to Five Hundred Families, May 20, 1825, ibid., 61; Barker, *LSFA,* 120–21.

63. Rafael Gonzales to SFA, April 27, May 20, 1825, in Gracy, *Establishing Austin's Colony,* 58–61; Colonization Law of the State of Coahuila and Texas, ibid., 52; Regulations for Immigrants, [May—, 1825], *AP,* I, 1106–7; SFA to Mrs. Emily Perry, May—, 1825, ibid., 1109 (quotation). Also see SFA to Mrs. Emily M. Perry, December 12, 1825, ibid., 1238–39.

64. SFA to Mrs. James F. Perry, December 17, 1824, *AP,* I, 991.

65. James Bryan to SFA, January 15, 1822, *AP,* I, 465–66; Gracy, *Moses Austin,* 218; Maria Austin to SFA, July 24, [1823], Austin Papers, Series II, CAH; Emily Bryan to SFA, July 1, 1823, Perry Papers (Emily Austin Bryan Perry Letters), CAH.

66. SFA to Mrs. James F. Perry, December 17, 1824 *AP,* I, 992 (first quotation); SFA to Josiah H. Bell, December 4, 1823, ibid., I, 714; SFA to J. E. B. Austin, [May 4, 1824], ibid., I, 787–90 (second quotation on p. 789); SFA to Mother and Sister, May 4, 1824, ibid., I, 784–87 (subsequent quotations on p. 785).

67. J. E. B. Austin to SFA, May 23, 1824, *AP,* I, 799–800; Gracy, *Moses Austin,* 220; J. E. B. Austin to SFA, July 18, 1824, *AP,* I, 854 (quotation).

68. J. E. B. Austin to SFA (with note by Emily at bottom), September 6, 1824, *AP,* I, 891; SFA to Mrs. James F. Perry, December 17, 1824, ibid, 991.

69. SFA to Mrs. James F. Perry, December 17, 1824, *AP,* I, 991–93.

70. SFA to J. E. B. Austin, June 13, 1823, *AP,* I, 672; Joseph H. Hawkins to SFA, February 6, 1822, ibid, I, 476 (second, third, and fourth quotations); Joseph H. Hawkins to SFA, May 31, 1822, ibid., I, 521 (fifth and sixth quotations).

71. SFA to Josiah H. Bell, January 8, 1824, *AP,* I, 722; SFA to Mother and Sister, May 4, 1824, ibid., 786; SFA to Mrs. Joseph H. Hawkins, April 20, 1824, ibid., 773.

72. SFA to Mrs. Joseph H. Hawkins, April 20, 1824, *AP,* I, 774; Cantrell, "Partnership of Stephen F. Austin and Joseph H. Hawkins," 12–24.

73. J. E. B. Austin to Emily M. Perry, February 28, 1826, *AP,* I, 1268–69.

74. SFA to B. W. Edwards, September 15, 1825, *AP,* I, 1205.

SEVEN
Staying the Course
1825–1827

1. Green, *Mexican Republic,* 50–51.

2. Two works that emphasize regional autonomy prior to independence are Benson, *Provincial Deputation;* and Hamnett, *Roots of Insurgency.*

3. Blaming Mexico's post-independence instability on any single factor — self-serving *caudillos,* the economic devastation of the Wars for Independence, or ideological divisions, to name a few traditional interpretations — has given way to deeper historiographical explanations. What most recent scholars seem to emphasize, however, is a combination of economic problems, clashing regional interests, and class divisions along socioeconomic lines. See, for example, Green, *Mexican Republic,* 233; Stevens, *Origins of Instability,* 107–18; and Michael P. Costeloe, *The Central Republic in Mexico, 1835–1846: Hombres de Bien in the Age of Santa Anna* (Cambridge: Cambridge University Press, 1993), 1–30.

4. Weber, *Mexican Frontier,* 276, 282.

5. Members of the Legislature of Coahuila and Texas, [November 16, 1824?], *AP,* I, 942; Bastrop in the Legislature of Coahuila and Texas [various documents from the fall of 1824], ibid., 942–69; Moore, "Role of the Baron de Bastrop," 92–101; *LSFA,* 120–23; Ricki S. Janicek, "The Development of Early Mexican Land Policy: Coahuila and Texas, 1810–1825," Ph.D. diss., Tulane University, 1985, 204–14. For the national and state colonization laws, see Gracy, *Establishing Austin's Colony,* 48–58.

6. Gaspar Flores to SFA, December 6, 1824, *AP,* I, 983–84; SFA to Gaspar Flores, [Answering letter of December 6, 1824], ibid., 984–86. SFA's letter is translated in *PCRCT,* II, 240–45 (quotations on pp. 241–42). Flores, the alcalde of San Antonio, was acting as a go-between for SFA and Seguín.

7. Information Derived from Hayden Edwards, 183 ?, in *The Papers of Mirabeau Buonaparte Lamar,* ed. Charles Adams Gulick, Jr., and Katherine Elliott (6 vols. in 7; Austin: Von Boeckmann-Jones, 1921–1927), III, 260 (quotation). This document is also excerpted in McLean, *PCRCT,* II, 289–93.

8. Malcolm D. McLean argues that SFA was attempting to betray not only the other aspiring empresarios but also Bastrop. McLean refers to this as the "Most Dramatic Moment in the Colonization of Texas" (*PCRCT,* II, 53), citing the "Information Derived from Hayden Edwards" document in support of this hypothesis, but he erroneously states that Austin never intended for Bastrop to know about SFA's plan. The Edwards document states that when Edwards, Leftwich, and Thorn read the letter, "they were all shocked at this and could not reconcile it with his past professions; Bastrop himself affected much surprise, and was unable to account for it" (see *PCRCT,* II, 292). Bastrop may indeed have been surprised by SFA's proposal (or it may have been "affected" surprise, as the document suggests). But it does not stand to reason that Bastrop would have felt betrayed by SFA's plans to exclude him from his future colonizing plans in favor of Seguín, or that Austin sought to keep Bastrop in the dark about it. The Baron would *have*

to know about the plan, for it would be up to him to secure its approval by the state. SFA obviously must have thought that Bastrop would see the merits of the scheme and promote its passage, and SFA certainly knew Bastrop well enough to know whether he would consider the plan a betrayal. The reality is that the Baron was sixty years old and probably in poor health (he died before he could return to Texas), and the role that SFA proposed for Seguín would be arduous and of long duration. Moreover, Bastrop was himself a foreigner, and SFA's argument that one of the co-empresarios be a native Mexican made perfect sense. Bastrop already stood to reap rewards from SFA for his many services, without having to become SFA's co-empresario. And most significant of all, it would be much easier for Bastrop to sell the idea of a SFA-Seguín colonizing monopoly to the state government than to sell them on the notion of such a monopoly that would involve himself as a major beneficiary. Even by Saltillo standards, this would constitute a fairly blatant conflict of interest. This interpretation is further bolstered by the fact that Bastrop, who was not shy about complaining when he thought SFA had ignored him, never said a word about SFA's plan in any of his correspondence, and he continued to express friendship and trust in SFA, even naming him first executor of his will (see Baron de Bastrop's Will, January 16, 1827, *AP,* I, 1582–83). Therefore, while McLean is correct in suggesting that SFA was willing to sabotage the plans of Edwards and the other aspiring empresarios, the evidence does not support his claim that SFA intended to betray Bastrop, or that Bastrop felt any such betrayal.

9. For examples of cooperation and good relations between SFA and other empresarios, see SFA to B. W. Edwards, September 15, 1825, *AP,* I, 1201–5; Benjamin W. Edwards to SFA, October 1, 1825, ibid., 1218–19; SFA to [Saucedo?], about May 31, 1826, ibid., 1349–50; Green De Witt to SFA, September 3, 1826 (two letters), ibid., 1444–45; Green De Witt to SFA, about December 1, 1826, ibid., 1526–27; Green De Witt to SFA, April 3, 1827, ibid., 1624–25; H. H. League to SFA, August 28, 1827, ibid., 1677–78; H. H. League to SFA, September 10, 1827 (two letters), ibid., 1679–82; SFA to Joel Poinsett, November 3, 1827, ibid., 1703–5; Frost Thorn to SFA, July 22, 1828, ibid., II, 74–75; SFA to David Porter, February 16, 1829, ibid., 166–68; SFA to David Porter, June 8, 1829, ibid., 220–21.

10. Mary Virginia Henderson, "Minor Empresario Contracts for the Colonization of Texas, 1825–1834," *SWHQ* 31 (April 1928): 298–99. Tamaulipas rancher Martín de León had already been granted a contract by the provincial deputation of Texas in April 1824, making him the first native Mexican empresario. De León's colony would be located to the south of Austin's Colony, with its capital at Victoria.

11. *LSFA,* 88; Jodella D. Kite, "A Social History of the Anglo-American Colonies in Mexican Texas, 1821–1835" Ph.D. diss., Texas Tech University, 1990, 31–33, 43, 44, 85, 109, 111.

12. Smithwick, *Evolution of a State,* 55–56.

13. *Missouri Intelligencer* (Franklin), October 14, 1822, typescript in Austin Papers, Series III, CAH (first quotation); SFA to Luciano Garcia, October 20, 1823, *AP,* I, 702 (second quotation). Also see Regulations for Immigrants, [May , 1825, ibid., 1106.

14. J. E. B. Austin to SFA, September 14, 1824, Austin Papers, Series II, CAH; SFA

to Emily M. Perry, June 26, 1833, *AP,* II, 922; Maria Austin to SFA, April 4, 1822 [1823], Austin Papers, Series II, CAH (first quotation); [Emily M. Bryan] to SFA, September 28, 1823, ibid. (second quotation); Henson, *Samuel May Williams,* 7; Henry Smith, "Reminiscences of Henry Smith," *Quarterly of the Texas State Historical Association* 14 (July 1910): 26 (third quotation); J. Thomas to SFA, April 15, 1824, *AP,* I, 765–66 (fourth quotation).

15. Rosa Groce Bertleth, "Jared Ellison Groce," *SWHQ* 20 (April 1917): 358–68; SFA to B. W. Edwards, September 15, 1825, *AP,* I, 1204; Deposition, July 18, 1825, ibid., 1149; Judicial Procedure: Maritime Insurance, July [19?], 1825, ibid., 1150–51; Jared E. Groce to Hyde and Merit, July 19, 1825, ibid., 1151–52; Sheriff's Sale, [about May 8, 1826], ibid., 1328–29; Court Costs, May 10, 1826, ibid., 1329; SFA to José Antonio Saucedo, May 19, 1826, ibid., 1343; Andrew Erwin to SFA, September 11, 1824, ibid., 894 (quotation).

16. J. E. B. Austin to SFA, August 22, 1826, *AP,* I, 1433; John P. Coles to SFA, November 1, 1824, ibid., 931; Andrew Erwin to SFA, September 11, 1824, ibid., 893–94; Andrew Erwin to SFA, August 29, 1825, ibid., 1185–87; James Erwin to SFA, September 30, 1825, ibid., 1213–16; Col. Morgan's Affidavit, n.d., *PCRCT,* I, 505–14; Kuykendall, "Reminiscences of Gibson Kuykendall," 35; Price List: SFA to Jared E. Groce, October 18, 1823, *AP,* I, 700–701; SFA to Jared E. Groce, October 19, 1823, ibid., 701; Thomas Westall to Jared E. Groce, March 5, 1825, ibid., 1055; Jared E. Groce to SFA, June 11, 1825, ibid., 1133; SFA's Expense Account in the Fredonian Rebellion, January 30, 1827, ibid., 1596.

17. Barker's chapter on the Fredonian Rebellion provides a comprehensive and accurate account of this important episode; see *LSFA,* chap. 7. For a more exhaustive treatment relying heavily on the Béxar and Nacogdoches Archives, see Edmund Morris Parsons, "The Fredonian Rebellion," *Texana* 5 (Spring 1967): 11–52. Barker's account is strongest for the background and early phases of the revolt, while Parsons more thoroughly recounts the actual rebellion and its aftermath. Except where otherwise noted, the factual chronology for the following account is drawn from these two sources.

18. Baron de Bastrop to SFA, March 19, April 9, April 27, May 6, 1825, *AP,* I, 1057, 1072, 1082, 1087 (all containing "amigo" quotation); Haden Edwards to SFA, January 9, 1826, ibid., 1246–47.

19. SFA to B. W. Edwards, September 15, 1825, *AP,* I, 1201–5 (quotations on pp. 1203–4).

20. Benjamin W. Edwards to SFA, October 1, 1825, *AP,* I, 1218–19.

21. Haden Edwards to SFA, January 9, 1826, *AP,* I, 1246. A copy of Edwards's proclamation to the East Texas settlers, dated October 25, 1825, is in AGEC: FJPB, Caja 1, Exp. 29. An original in Edwards's hand, dated November 12, 1825, is in Caja 2, Exp. 2.

22. SFA to Haden Edwards, about March 15, 1826, quoted in *LSFA,* 156. This letter is not included in the published *AP,* nor has it been located in the unpublished Austin Papers. Barker quotes it at length in the text of his SFA biography, but we must take his word for its authenticity.

23. In their accounts, neither Barker nor Parsons suggest that Haden Edwards

had foreknowledge of the November coup, although Parsons takes Edwards's professed innocence more seriously than does Barker. Parsons writes, "That the dissident settlers were inspired by local problems and were not initially directed by the Edwards brothers is demonstrated by their early arrest of Haden Edwards, and by Edwards' own denial of complicity in the first stages of the uprising." It is possible that Parmer did act unilaterally, but the arrest and subsequent release of Edwards by his ally Parmer does not conclusively "demonstrate" Edwards's lack of "complicity" in the uprising. The fact that a month later Haden Edwards would be "major general" of the rebels and Parmer only a "colonel" certainly leaves the question open to debate. See *LSFA,* 166; and Parsons, "Fredonian Rebellion," 14–19.

24. SFA to José Antonio Saucedo, December 4, 1826, *AP,* I, 1528.

25. SFA to John A. Williams and B. J. Thompson, December 14, 1826, *AP,* I, 1532–34.

26. SFA to B. J. Thompson, December 24, 1826, *AP,* I, 1539, 1541. Austin had known Thompson for eight years, dating back to Missouri days, and SFA had defended him in a letter to vice-governor Victor Blanco as recently as late October; see SFA to Victor Blanco, October 24, 1826, Wagner Texas and Middle West Collection, Beinecke Rare Book and Manuscript Library, Yale University.

27. The recruitment of the Cherokees marked a potentially serious development. Back in 1825, SFA had harbored suspicions that the Cherokees, dissatisfied with the Mexican government's failure to guarantee the tribe's lands, were conspiring to unite Texas Indians in a general war against the Mexicans and Anglo-Americans. SFA at that time had suggested that such an alliance might be prevented if the government would grant the Cherokees' land, but the government failed to act. The feared alliance did not materialize, and in the spring of 1826, SFA succeeded in enlisting the Cherokees' prom- ise to participate in a joint campaign against the troublesome Wacos and Tawakonis. The Mexican military officials canceled the campaign at the last minute, afraid that it might ignite a wider war that would spread to the Anglo and Mexican settlements. Thus the alliance between Austin's Colony and the Cherokees was never put to the test. The Cherokees, having lost the chance to curry favor with the Mexican government and parlay that favor into secure land titles, turned to the Fredonian rebels. See Dianna Everett, *The Texas Cherokees: A People Between Two Fires* (Norman: University of Oklahoma Press, 1990), chap. 2, esp. pp. 26, 36–42.

28. B. W. Edwards to Jesse Thompson, December 26, 1826, *AP,* I, 1548 (quota- tions); also see letters from Edwards to Inhabitants of Pecan Point, to James Ross, and to Aylett C. Buckner, December 25 and 26, 1826, ibid., 1542–48.

29. SFA to Citizens of Victoria, January 1, 1827, *AP,* I, 1558 (first, second, and third quotations) [Victoria was one of the political districts of Austin's Colony]; SFA to the inhabitants of the Colony, January 22, 1827, in Henry Stuart Foote, *Texas and the Texans* (2 vols.; Philadelphia: Thomas, Cowperthwait, 1841), I, 266 (fourth quotation); also see SFA to His Colonists, [about January 5, 1827], *AP,* I, 1570–71.

30. SFA to Citizens of Victoria, January 1, 1827, *AP,* I, 1558.

31. Also participating in the making of these plans was Peter Ellis Bean, an Ameri-

can expatriate who had fought in the Mexican Wars for Independence and who now held the position of Indian agent for the Mexican government in East Texas. Bean was returning from a business trip to Mexico City when he learned of the rebellion in East Texas. Intimately acquainted with the region and its inhabitants, he remained in San Felipe with Austin and the recently deposed Nacogdoches military commander Sepúlveda during the time that the Mexican troops were en route from San Antonio and played an important role in shaping the policies that led to the suppression of the revolt. On Bean's fascinating life, see Bennett Lay, *The Lives of Ellis P. Bean* (Austin: University of Texas Press, 1960).

32. Everett, *Texas Cherokees,* 47.

33. SFA to Samuel May Williams, March 4, [1827], *AP,* I, 1610.

34. J. E. B. Austin to Mrs. E. M. Perry, February 23, 1827, *AP,* I, 1605.

35. War Department to SFA, April 19, 1827, *AP,* I, 1633; Anastacio Bustamante to SFA, March 26, 1827, ibid., 1620. SFA received a similar commendation from the governor of Coahuila y Texas; see Governor [Acting Governor Victor Blanco?] to SFA, March 7, 1827, Wagner Texas and Middle West Collection, Beinecke Rare Book and Manuscript Library, Yale University; also see Governor Ignacio de Arispe's Certificate, November 21, 1827, Perry (James Franklin and Stephen Samuel) Papers, CAH.

36. SFA to John A. Williams and B. J. Thompson, December 14, 1826, *AP,* I, 1533.

37. SFA to Mary Austin Holley, December 29, 1831, ibid., II, 730 (quotation). The best overview of slavery in Austin's Colony and SFA's attitudes toward it can be found in Campbell, *Empire for Slavery,* 3, 15–16, 18–33.

38. SFA to Samuel M. Williams, April 16, 1831, *AP,* II, 645 (first quotation); SFA to Thomas F. Leaming, June 14, 1830, ibid., 415 (second and third quotations).

39. Most of these antislavery expressions came in the period following the passage of the Law of April 6, 1830, which banned the further introduction of slaves into Texas. SFA seemed relieved that slavery had been outlawed, and several times he wrote that he hoped it would be excluded forever. By that time, however, Texans had already resorted to the subterfuge of making their slaves indentured servants for life, and the law did not truly threaten to emancipate them. Moreover, he continued to lobby the government to have Texas excluded from the ban at the same time he was voicing support for emancipation. For expressions of pleasure at the exclusion of slavery from Texas, see SFA to Thomas F. Leaming, June 14, 1830, *AP,* II, 415; SFA to Richard Ellis et al., June 16, 1830, ibid., 421; SFA to S. Rhoads Fisher, June 17, 1830, ibid., 795; SFA to [Edward Livingston?], June 24, 1832, ibid., 797. For SFA's efforts to preserve slavery during this same period, see SFA to Samuel M. Williams, February 19, 1831, ibid., 603; SFA to Samuel M. Williams, April 16, 1831, ibid, 645; SFA to Wiley Martin, May 30, 1833, ibid., 981.

40. For one of SFA's typical expressions of this logic, see SFA to Governor Rafael Gonzales, April 4, 1825, *AP,* I, 1067.

41. SFA to Mary Austin Holley, July 19, 1831, *AP,* II, 676.

42. Bill and Argument Concerning Slavery, August 18, 1825, *AP,* I, 1170–80.

43. SFA to State Congress, August 11, 1826, *AP,* I, 1406–9; Eugene C. Barker, "The Influence of Slavery in the Colonization of Texas," *SWHQ* 27 (July 1924): 12–13. This article was also published in the *Mississippi Valley Historical Review* 11 (June 1924): 3–36.

44. SFA to Mrs. Emily Perry, October 22, 1825, *AP,* I, 1228; SFA to Mrs. Emily M. Perry, December 12, 1825, ibid., 1238; SFA to George Orr, March 10, 1826, ibid., 1272; J. E. B. Austin to SFA, September 3, 1826, ibid., 1445; J. E. B. Austin to SFA, October 31, 1826, ibid., 1482–83; Articles of Partnership, November 22, 1825, ibid., 1234 (quotation).

45. J. E. B. Austin to SFA, September 23, 1826, *AP,* I, 1461–62; J. E. B. Austin to SFA, October 9, 1826, ibid., 1474; Bastrop to SFA, November 18, 1826, ibid., 1505; Barker, "Influence of Slavery," 14–15.

46. SFA on the State Constitution, May 29, 1827, *AP,* I, 1648–49. The exact date of SFA's return to the colony is uncertain. A letter he wrote to José Antonio Navarro in late February gave San Felipe as the place of origin, but this must have been done only for return-address purposes, for on March 4 he was just preparing to leave Nacogdoches on his inspection tour of the Sabine region with Ahumada, a tour that took several weeks. The earliest actual evidence of his return to San Felipe is a notice to the colonists published on April 16. See SFA to José Antonio Navarro, February 27, 1827, ibid., 1608; SFA to Samuel M. Williams, March 4, [1827], ibid., 1610; SFA to Colonists, April 16, 1827, ibid., 1631.

47. Moore, "Role of the Baron de Bastrop," chap. 5, esp. p. 113; J. E. B. Austin to SFA, August 22, 1826, *AP,* I, 1431; Baron de Bastrop, Apuntes sobre Tejas parte del Estado de Coahuila y Tejas, March 6, 1825, Segundo Congreso Constitucional, Primer Periodo Ordinario, Comición de Gobernación, 1825–29, Leg. 1, Exp. 18, Folio 13, Archivo del Congreso del Estado de Coahuila, Saltillo, Coahuila, Mexico. A measure of Bastrop's standing with his fellow legislators is his election in January 1825 as vice-president of the legislature. While leadership posts in the body seem to have rotated among the members, it is still significant that Bastrop, himself an immigrant to Mexico, would have been chosen for this position at such an early date in the legislature's history. See Gov. Rafael Gonzales to 1st Constitutional Alcalde of Saltillo, January 15, 1825, Caja 70, Expediente 37, Archivo Municipal de Saltillo, Presidencia Municipal, Saltillo.

48. Tijerina, *Tejanos and Texas,* 111–15; Janicek, "Development of Early Mexican Land Policy," 192–98.

49. Tijerina, *Tejanos and Texas,* 111–17.

50. Robert Lewis to SFA, May 12, 1826, *AP,* I, 1330 (first quotation); Baron de Bastrop to SFA, April 27, 1825, ibid., 1083, trans. in *PCRCT,* II, 295 (second, third, and fourth quotations); Baron de Bastrop to SFA, May 6, 1825, *AP,* I, 1088–89, trans. in *PCRCT,* II, 311–314 (fifth and sixth quotations on p. 313). In *PCRCT,* II, 314, fn2, editor Malcolm McLean leaves the impression that SFA left Bastrop totally without financial support in Saltillo, citing only the letters to SFA in which Bastrop asked for funds. SFA's accounts, however, show the following payments: $250 to reimburse Frost Thorn for money he had lent to Bastrop and $100 cash sent to Bastrop (November 1825); $260 to reimburse Fernando Rodríguez for money he had lent to Bastrop (June or July 1826); $60 credited by SFA to Joseph Duty for money he had lent to Bastrop (July 1826?); $126.54 to reimburse "Mr. Lewis" for money he had lent to Bastrop (September 1826); and another $100 entry dated September 1826 which is partially illegible but seems to indicate another payment to Bastrop. The preceding dates indicate the approximate times when SFA

recorded his payments in his account book, not the actual dates when Bastrop received the funds; see Austin Account Book, 1825–43, CAH, pp. 29, 55, 56, 59, 60, 61. Records of some of these payments can also be found in an account sheet dated about June 1827, from Austin Papers, Series IV (Box 2Q416), CAH.

51. Baron de Bastrop to Robert Leftwich, May 30, 1826, *PCRCT,* II, 597.

52. Moore, "Role of Baron de Bastrop," 121, 126. Also see J. Antonio Padilla to Congress, March 15, 1827, Congreso Constituyente, 1827, Comisión de Hacienda, Leg. 7, Exp. 12, Archivo del Congreso del Estado de Coahuila, Saltillo, Coahuila, Mexico. In his account of Bastrop's death (*PCRCT,* II, 314) Malcolm McLean fails to mention SFA's reimbursement to Padilla, but see account sheet dated about June 1827, Austin Papers, Series IV (Box 2Q416), CAH. If SFA had mistreated Bastrop to the extent that McLean suggests, it seems unlikely that Bastrop would have named SFA first administrator of his estate.

53. For the legislative rivalry between the liberal Monclova/Parras-based Viesca group (which the Anglos and Tejanos supported), and the conservative Saltillo-based faction, see Bastrop to SFA, March 19, 1825, *AP,* I, 1057–60; Baron de Bastrop to SFA, July 26, 1825, ibid., 1147; Tijerina, *Tejanos and Texas,* 112–16.

54. Treaty with the Karankawa Indians, May 13, 1827, *AP,* I, 1639–41; Anastacio Bustamante to SFA, June 19, 1827, ibid., 1660; SFA to Colonists, April 16, 1827, ibid., 1631; SFA to James F. Perry, May 26, 1826, ibid., 1646 (quotations).

55. Smithwick, *Evolution of a State,* 40–41; Samuel C. Hirams to SFA, October 23, 1826, *AP,* I, 1480; M. M. Battle to SFA, September 12, 1827, ibid., 1682–83; SFA to the Governor, October 11, 1827, ibid., 1687; SFA to Mrs. James F. Perry, December 17, 1824, ibid., 992 (quotation); Henson, *Samuel May Williams,* 16–17. A boys' school, the Austin Academy, was founded in early 1829 by Thomas J. Pilgrim; see *HT,* IV, 202.

56. Henson, *Samuel May Williams,* 8, 19, 25; J. E. B. Austin to SFA, August 22, 1826, *AP,* I, 1434.

57. Henson, *Samuel May Williams,* 16–17.

58. Ibid., 16–17; H. H. League to SFA, September 10, 1827, *AP,* I, 1680.

59. SFA to Samuel M. Williams, May 8, 1831, *AP,* II, 661 (quotation); M. B. Lamar, Biographical Notes upon M. B. Buckner and Doctor Deaton, *Lamar Papers,* IV, 254–55.

60. This story appeared in a clipping in part 2 of the Austin Scrapbook, CAH. It is from the *Galveston News,* apparently from the year 1877, although the exact date of the item cannot be determined. In the margin of the clipping is written, "One of the Three Hundred — A. Underwood." This notation was apparently written by Guy Bryan or Moses Austin Bryan, and the "A. Underwood" is almost certainly Ammon Underwood. However, Bryan is mistaken about Underwood being one of the Old Three Hundred, for he did not arrive in Texas until 1834; see *HT,* VI, 621.

61. SFA's precise travel dates are impossible to ascertain. A document in the Béxar Archives fixes his presence in San Antonio on August 9, and his first letter written from Saltillo is dated October 11. See SFA affidavit, August 9, 1827, Béxar Archives; H. H. League to SFA, August 28, *AP,* I, 1677; SFA to the Governor, ibid., 1687–88.

62. Regulations for Immigrants, [May ?, 1825], *AP,* I, 1106–7; J. E. B. Austin to

SFA, August 22, 1826, ibid., 1431–32; SFA to Bastrop, November 3, 1826, ibid, 1488; SFA to Colonists, April 16, 1827, ibid., 1631; SFA to the Governor, October 11, 1827, ibid., 1687–88; SFA to State Congress, October 11, 1827, ibid., 1689–92; SFA's Draft for Report of Committee on Colonization, [about October 11, 1827], ibid., 1692–96. Settlers who received less than a league paid only $30.

63. SFA to Governor, October 11, 1827, *AP,* I, 1697–98; Galen Greaser et al., "Austin's Colony: The Cradle of Modern Texas," map published by the Texas General Land Office, Austin, 1993.

64. The early history of the Texas Association's colonization efforts are traced in great detail in the intro. vol. and vols. 1–3 of *PCRCT.* See especially Memorial of the Texas Association to the Congress of Coahuila and Texas, [March 7, 1827], *PCRCT,* III, 230–36.

65. H. H. League to SFA, August 28, 1827, *AP,* I, 1677–78; H. H. League to SFA, September 10, 1827, ibid., 1679–80; H. H. League to SFA, September 10, 1827, ibid., 1680–82 (the preceding documents are also reproduced in *PCRCT,* III; Austin's Petition as Agent of the "Nashville Company," [October 11, 1827], *PCRCT,* III, 294–98; Contract Between the Nashville Company and the State of Coahuila and Texas, [October 15, 1827], ibid., 299–303; SFA to H. H. League, October 20, 1827, ibid., 304–5. In the introduction and footnotes that accompany this volume of the *PCRCT,* editor Malcolm McLean strongly criticizes SFA's actions regarding the boundaries for the new Texas Association colony and his own Little Colony. The facts are as follows: the original limits of Leftwich's grant stopped short of the Colorado River on the west and were bounded by a line through modern-day Comanche, Hamilton, Coryell, McLennan, and Limestone counties on the north. In its official memorial to the legislature (dated March 7, 1827), the company requested only that the government "extend the limits of the Colony," without specifying the directions in which those limits should be extended. However, in his accompanying letter to SFA, League explained that the company wanted the western boundary to be extended *to the Colorado* and in any other directions possible. It is important to note that SFA had seen neither the company's petition nor League's letter until they arrived in Saltillo at the beginning of October. At this point SFA was only a week away from presenting his own October 11 petition for the Little Colony; by then he almost certainly had already formulated his request for that contract, which included the same Colorado River frontage that League was now requesting for the Texas Association. SFA, then, was faced with a choice. He could cancel his own well-developed plans for the Little Colony in favor of this last-minute, surprise request of League's, or he could move forward with his own petition for the Little Colony and request in the name of the Texas Association everything League had mentioned except for the area encompassed by the Little Colony. In doing the latter, he would still be entirely faithful to the company's official March 1827 petition, which had requested only in general that the boundaries be extended. In the end, of course, SFA chose to move forward with his own plans for the Little Colony and to petition for the Texas Association everything that the association and League had requested except for the area of the Little Colony. SFA did, in fact, request a considerable extension of the boundaries of the colony as the March petition specified;

the company's new contract nearly doubled the size of the original Leftwich grant to the north. Yet McLean characterizes SFA's actions as "duplicity" (*PCRCT,* III, 289, n4). It it true that SFA was less than candid about what he had done, telling League that "the land bordering on the Colorado is all disposed of to other Empresarios except a small corner which is not of much importance" (*PCRCT,* III, 288). This "small corner," of course, was the Little Colony, which SFA was requesting for himself. SFA would have been more honest simply to tell League the truth — that he had decided to apply for this land before he ever learned of the company's desire for it. McLean's charges of "duplicity," however, apply only to SFA's after-the-fact explanation of what happened, not in the actual action that the empresario took in securing his own contract for the Little Colony. In reality, SFA had at least as much right to apply for the area as League; his plans to apply for the contract probably predated League's, and he — not League — was the one who had actually made the difficult journey to Saltillo to make a presentation to the government. SFA still had faithfully done everything in his power to secure all the terms of the company's March 1827 petition, and he had been highly successful. He had saved the company the expense of having to send League to Saltillo and, through his considerable influence, had probably saved the Texas Association from oblivion.

66. SFA to ?, November 8, 1827, *AP,* I, 1710–16; SFA's Argument Against Law Regulating Slavery, [November 8, 1827], ibid., 1716–20; José Francisco Madero, Primera lectura á la Comisión de Legislación, July 7, 1827, Primer Congreso Constitucional, Primer Periodo Ordinario, 1827, Comisión de Gobernación, Leg. 1, Exp. 43, Archivo del Congreso del Estado de Coahuila, Saltillo, Coahuila, Mexico (quotations); Barker, "Influence of Slavery," 14–16.

67. SFA to Governor J. M. Viesca, November 6, 1827, *AP,* I, 1705–1706; J. M. Viesca to Agustín Viesca, November 20, 1827, ibid., 1723; Ignacio de Arispe to ?, December 21, 1827, ibid., 1731.

68. SFA to J. H. Bell, January 1, 1828, *AP,* II, 1.

EIGHT
Crises, Personal and Political
1828–1830

1. SFA to James F. Perry, March 31, 1828, *AP,* II, 29; SFA to E. M. Perry, October 25, 1828, ibid., 136.

2. The fourth contract, commonly called the Coast Colony, encompassed part of the land included in SFA's first contract. The National Colonization Law of 1825 prohibited the further settlement of foreigners within ten leagues of the coast or twenty leagues of the Louisiana border without federal approval, so settlers who immigrated under SFA's second and third contracts could not settle within the coastal reserve. This left ample vacant land along the coast, even after all of the Old Three Hundred had received their titles. Austin first requested permission to reopen the reserve to colonists in 1826, but it was mid-1828 before he secured the necessary federal approval. The state then issued the

contract. See *LSFA,* 119–20, 126; SFA to [Governor of Coahuila and Texas], June 5, 1826, *AP,* I, 1353; J. Antonio Padilla to SFA, July 12, 1828, ibid., II, 70.

3. Censo y Estadística, Estado de Coahuila y Tejas, Año de 1828, June 1, 1828, AGEC, FJPB, Caja 8, Exp. 1, Saltillo, Coahuila. The figure for Béxar was 1,375, and that for La Bahía was 570. The census report noted that figures had not been received for Nacogdoches, and that the totals also did not include those "foreigners established illegally" (*extrangeros establesidos malamente*) in Nacogdoches, Pecan Point, and Atascosito.

4. One change stipulated that slaves would not gain their freedom if a master died in an unknown or unnatural way, a measure designed to discourage the murder of masters by their slaves. The other allowed a slave to "change his master," provided the new master compensated the old. This subterfuge would allow the continuation of the domestic slave trade.

5. These acts are well summarized in *LSFA,* 207–9 (quotation on p. 209, quoting H. P. N. Gammel, ed. and comp., *Laws of Texas* [Austin: Gammel Book Co., 1898] 1: 202). Also see Campbell, *Empire for Slavery,* 21–25.

6. On the establishment and functioning of the ayuntamiento, see Barker, "Government of Austin's Colony," 242–52; Tijerina, *Tejanos and Texas,* chap. 2.

7. Barker, "Minutes of the Ayuntamiento of San Felipe de Austin, 1828–1832," *SWHQ,* XXI, 311 (quotation); John Gibson to SFA—Bill of Sale, February 6, 1828, *AP,* II, 13; *LSFA,* 209–11; Campbell, *Empire for Slavery,* 23–24.

8. Barker discusses this law in considerable detail; see *LSFA,* 194–99. Viesca's August 8 letter to SFA (*AP,* II, 88–89) provides evidence of the close working relationship between the two men.

9. Bastrop issued the deeds to SFA's twenty-two and a half leagues on September 1, 1824. In all, Bastrop accounted for 272 titles. Flores was appointed commissioner after Bastrop's death, but various delays, including the Fredonian Rebellion, prevented him from issuing all the remaining deeds until the spring of 1828; see Bugbee, ed., "Old Three Hundred," 108–17; SFA to His Colonists, March 16, 1828, *AP,* II, 26–27. For an English transcription of Austin's original titles plus the certification by Flores, see *Translations of the Spanish Records in the Archives of the County of Brazoria,* pp. 177–88, Brazoria County Clerk's Office, Angleton, Texas.

10. Austin Account Book, 1825–1843, CAH, entry of April 16, 1833; SFA to E. M. Perry, October 25, 1828, *AP,* II, 136; SFA to E. M. Carr, March 4, 1829, ibid., 177 (quotation); SFA to Emily M. Perry, January 26, 1833, ibid., 922; SFA to Nathaniel Cox, March 10, 1829, ibid., 181; Cantrell, "Partnership of Stephen F. Austin and Joseph H. Hawkins," 15–16.

11. SFA to E. M. Perry, October 25, 1828, *AP,* II, 135–36; SFA to E. M. Carr, March 4, 1829, ibid., II, 179 (quotations); *HT,* I, 291–92.

12. The best modern monographic treatments of party politics in the early republic are Costeloe, *La Primera República;* and Green, *Mexican Republic.* Valuable anthologies include Vázquez, *La Fundación del Estado Mexicano;* and Rodríguez O., *Independence of Mexico.*

13. According to the Constitution of 1824, state legislatures elected Mexican presidents; the candidate winning a majority of the states was the winner. Gómez Pedraza won ten of the nineteen states; federalists of course charged fraud.

14. Costeloe, *La Primera República,* chaps. 5–8; Green, *Mexican Republic,* chaps. 6–7; Barbara A. Tenebaum, " 'They Went Thataway': The Evolution of the *Pronunciamiento, 1821–1856,"* in Rodríguez O., ed., *Patterns of Contention,* 187–205, esp. 192–93.

15. SFA's friends Juan Antonio Padilla and José Antonio Navarro expressed far more concern over the situation than did SFA; see J. Antonio Padilla to SFA, October 18, December 13, December 27, 1828, *AP,* II, 132–34, 151–52, 154–55, José Antonio Navarro to SFA, January 8, 1829, ibid., 156–57. Austin merely made the questionable observation that "this great question is now finally settled in a legal and constitutional manner and tranquility is fully restored." He could take this rosy view in part because he believed that a Guerrero-led government would sanction religious toleration. He already thought that it would be safe for colonists to hold informal Protestant worship services "provided it is not done in a way to make a noise about public preaching"; see SFA to Josiah H. Bell, ibid., 173. Moreover, the prominence of the powerful Viesca brothers in the Guerrero administration guaranteed that Coahuila y Texas would have the ear of the new administration. The point would soon prove moot, for the Guerrero regime would last only a year before being overthrown itself.

16. See Chapter 5.

17. Morton, *Terán and Texas,* 49, n10; Green, *Mexican Republic,* 88.

18. Morton, *Terán and Texas,* 48 (quotation); Barker, *Mexico and Texas,* 38–39.

19. Morton, *Terán and Texas,* 49–54. In addition to Morton's study, the best secondary accounts of the expedition are Alessio Robles, *Coahuila y Texas,* 1: chap. 17; and Alleine Howren, "Causes and Origin of the Decree of April 6, 1830," *SWHQ* 16 (April 1913): 378–422, esp. 391–98. Diaries and memoirs of participants give the most thorough primary accounts of the journey; see Berlandier, *Journey to Mexico;* Sánchez, "Trip to Texas"; and Manuel de Mier y Terán, "Comisión de Límites: Diario de General Terán," Wagner Texas and Middle West Collection, Beinecke Rare Book and Manuscript Library, Yale University (microfilm copy at CAH). References to the various Spanish-language editions of Berlandier and Sánchez can be found in the notes of the English translations; there is no published or translated version of Terán's diary.

20. For a concise sketch of Terán's life, see *HT,* IV, 716–17; for a fuller treatment, including much information on his family background and early life, see Morton, *Terán and Texas,* esp. chap. 1.

21. Manuel de Mier y Terán to Guadalupe Victoria, March 28, 1828, in Terán's Letterbook, Wagner Texas and Middle West Collection, Beinecke Rare Book and Manuscript Library, Yale University.

22. Manuel de Mier y Terán to Guadalupe Victoria, March 28, 1828, in Terán's Letterbook. This figure almost certainly exaggerates the number of slaves Groce owned.

23. Manuel de Mier y Terán to Guadalupe Victoria, March 28, 1828, in Terán's Letterbook.

24. Sánchez, "Trip to Texas," 271; Manuel de Mier y Terán to Guadalupe Victoria, March 28, 1828, in Terán's Letterbook.

25. Manuel de Mier y Terán to Guadalupe Victoria, March 28, 1828, in Terán's Letterbook.

26. For example, see Manuel de Mier y Terán to Guadalupe Victoria, June 30, 1828, AGN Transcripts, Guerra, CAH (translated in part in Howren, "Causes and Origin," 395–98); and Manuel de Mier y Terán, "Comisión de Límites: Diario de General Terán," Wagner Texas and Middle West Collection, Beinecke Rare Book and Manuscript Library, Yale University (microfilm copy at CAH).

27. Sánchez, "Trip to Texas," 271; Berlandier, *Journey to Mexico,* 2: 321. Berlandier had the advantage of hindsight in his evaluation of SFA's motives, but Sánchez's diary appears to have been a true contemporary account.

28. Berlandier, *Journey to Mexico,* 322; Morton, *Terán and Texas,* 76–77.

29. SFA to Manuel de Mier y Terán, May [about 24], 1828, *AP,* II, 42–45.

30. Manuel de Mier y Terán to SFA, June 24, 1828, *AP,* II, 52.

31. "Apuntes relativos a la Colonia de Austin en Texas," enclosure in SFA to Manuel de Mier y Terán, June 30, 1828, *AP,* II, 60–66; for the original in Samuel May Williams's hand, see Terán's Letter Book.

32. Following a similar account in 1829, SFA wrote, "You must pardon my egotism in speaking so much of myself, but the history of this settlement is so closely connected with *me* individually, that one cannot be clearly explained without allusion to the other." See SFA to James Breedlove, October 12, 1829, *AP,* II, 269.

33. Manuel de Mier y Terán to SFA, July 8, 1828, *AP,* II, 70.

34. For example, see José Antonio Facio to Secretary of Relations [Lucas Alamán], January 23, 1830, quoting Terán letter of December 14, 1829, AGN Transcripts, Fomento, vol. 312, CAH; Constantino de Tarnova [*sic*] to Minister of War and Navy [José Antonio Facio], [January 6, 1830], *PCRCT,* III, 467–79.

35. Brown died on August 14. For an account of the epidemic see *New Orleans Courier,* August 12, 1829. For details of his death see H. D. Thompson to SFA, August 19, 1829, *AP,* II, 247–48.

36. SFA to Thomas F. Leaming, October 6, 1829, Stephen F. Austin Collection, Special Collections, University of Houston (first quotation); SFA to Henry Austin, September 22, 1829, *AP,* II, 258 (second quotation); Thomas Davis to Ramón Músquiz, September 14, 1829, ibid., 257 (third and fourth quotations); SFA to James W. Breedlove, October 12, 1829, ibid., 271 (fifth quotation); Eliza W. Austin to Emily Perry, January 6, 1830, ibid., 318.

37. SFA to José Antonio Navarro, October 19, 1829, *AP,* II, 272.

38. SFA to José Antonio Navarro, December 24, [1829], ibid., 302 (quotation); SFA to John Durst, November 17, 1829, ibid., 288–89. The support of Terán also was important. In any event, the state law allowing settlers to introduce slaves under the pretext of indentured servitude had already been passed, so Texan slaveholders likely could have carried on in spite of the Guerrero decree. See *LSFA,* 213–18; Campbell, *Empire for Slavery,* 25–26. The decree was issued in September 1829.

39. J. E. B. Austin to Mrs. E. M. Perry, May 26, 1829, *AP*, II, 218; Eliza W. Austin to Mrs. Emily Perry, January 6, 1830, ibid., 319; SFA to James F. Perry, December 31, 1829, ibid., 307; SFA to James F. Perry, January 3, 1830, ibid., 317.

40. Eliza W. Austin to Emily Perry, January 6, 1830, *AP*, II, 319; SFA to James F. Perry, December 31, 1829, ibid., 307–9; SFA to James F. Perry, January 1, 1830, ibid., 311–12; SFA to James F. Perry, January 3, 1830, ibid., 317–18 (second quotation); SFA to James F. Perry, January 16, 1830, ibid., 321–22; SFA to James F. Perry, March 28, 1830, ibid., 351–53.

41. Green, *Mexican Republic*, 189–93; Costeloe, *La Primera República*, 249–53; Morton, *Terán and Texas*, 87, 94; Benson, "Territorial Integrity," 288–300.

42. Anastacio Bustamante to SFA, March 20, 1830, *AP*, II, 347.

43. SFA to Thomas F. Leaming, June 29, 1830, "The Austin-Leaming Correspondence, 1828–1836," *SWHQ* 88 (January 1985): 263.

44. See Chapter 5.

45. José Antonio Facio to Secretary of Relations [Lucas Alamán], January 23, 1830, quoting Terán's letter of December 14, 1829, AGN Transcripts, Fomento, vol. 312. Also see Morton, *Terán and Texas*, 105.

46. Constantino de Tarnova [*sic*] to Minister of War and Navy [José Antonio Facio], [January 6, 1830], *PCRCT*, III, 467–79.

47. Alamán's iniciativa is available only in Spanish; see Lucas Alamán, "Iniciativa de ley proponiendo del gobierno las medidas que se debian tomar para la seguridad del Estado de Tejas . . . ," in Vicente Filisola, *Memorias para la Historia de la Guerra de Tejas* (Mexico City: R. Rafael, 1849), 2: 590–612. The Law of April 6, 1830, can be found in its original Spanish in Dublán and Lozano, *Legislación Mexicana*, 2: 238–40. English translations are in *PCRCT*, III, 494–98; and Howren, "Causes and Origins," 415–17. Also see Benson, "Territorial Integrity," 300–301.

48. SFA to Anastacio Bustamante, May 17, 1830, *AP*, II, 377–78.

49. SFA to General Gaines, July 27, 1836, *AP*, III, 403.

NINE
We Will Be Happy
1830–1831

1. SFA to Anastacio Bustamante, May 17, 1830, *AP*, II, 377–79; SFA to Manuel Mier y Terán, May 18, 1830, ibid., 380–81. SFA apparently composed a third letter to Lucas Alamán, who had been the bill's principal proponent within the Bustamante administration, but not knowing Alamán personally, he decided not to send it; see SFA to [Lucas Alamán?], [May 18, 1830], ibid., 382–85.

2. The Law of April 6, 1830, in Dublán and Lozano, *Legislación Mexicana*, 2: 238–40; *LSFA*, 266–69. Subsequent references in this chapter to specific articles of the Law of April 6 will not be cited individually; readers should refer to the text of the law as cited above in Dublán and Lozano, or to the English translations in Howren or McLean.

3. *LSFA,* 269–71; SFA to Benjamin Milam, June 29, 1830, John Peace Collection, Special Collections, University of Texas at San Antonio; SFA to Anastacio Bustamante, May 17, 1830, *AP,* II, 378 (second quotation). SFA used almost identical language in his letter to Terán, but he prudently omitted the word "all" (*todas*) in referring to the families who were under contract and in the process of emigrating; see SFA to Terán, May 18, 1830, ibid., 380. An examination of the register that Austin kept of immigrants between 1825 and the passage of the 1830 law indicates that the vast majority of settlers received permission to colonize only after arriving in person in the colony. See Villamae Williams, ed., *Stephen F. Austin's Register of Families,* typescript from the originals in the Texas General Land Office, 1984.

4. *LSFA,* 271, 275–76.

5. Margaret Swett Henson, *Juan Davis Bradburn: A Reappraisal of the Mexican Commander of Anahuac* (College Station: Texas A&M University Press, 1982), 47–56.

6. Tariff Exemption for Texas, September 29, 1823, *AP,* I, 696; SFA to Ayuntamiento of Béxar, November 7, 1826, ibid., 1495–98.

7. Marilyn McAdams Sibley, *Lone Stars and State Gazettes: Texas Newspapers Before the Civil War* (College Station: Texas A&M University Press, 1983), 47–52; *Texas Gazette* (San Felipe), January 30, 1830.

8. Sibley, *Lone Stars,* 52; *Texas Gazette* (San Felipe), June 28, July 3, September 25, 1830; SFA to Thomas F. Leaming, June 14, 1830, *AP,* II, 418.

9. SFA to Samuel May Williams, February 19, 1831, *AP,* II, 601.

10. James F. Perry's Diary, c. March 21–May 8, 1831, *AP,* II, 347–50.

11. SFA to Mrs. James F. Perry, May 16, 1830, *AP,* II, 375.

12. SFA to James F. Perry, March 28, 1830, *AP,* II, 352; James F. Perry to SFA, July 18, 1830, ibid., 458.

13. James F. Perry to SFA, July 18, 1830, *AP,* II, 458.

14. SFA explained to Perry that in order to convince the officials in Saltillo to make a grant of this size, he had to put half the grants in Perry's name and the other half in Emily's to make it look as if there were two families involved. Although he did not mention it, he probably also wanted to make certain that Emily could independently provide for her children from her first marriage. See SFA to James F. Perry, September 22, 1830, *AP,* II, 494.

15. SFA to James F. Perry, September 22 and 26, 1830, *AP,* II, 493–97 (quotations); SFA to James F. Perry, December 27, 1831, ibid., 726; SFA to Mary Austin Holley, November 17, December 29, 1831, ibid., 706, 728.

16. SFA to James F. Perry, September 22, 1830, *AP,* II, 495.

17. Henson, *Samuel May Williams,* 30–31.

18. SFA to James F. Perry, July 14, 1830, *AP,* II, 452; SFA to Samuel M. Williams, March 22, 1831, ibid., 611.

19. SFA to James F. Perry, December 19, 1830, *AP,* II, 564 (first quotation); SFA to Samuel May Williams, December 28, 1830, ibid., 568 (subsequent quotations).

20. SFA to Samuel M. Williams, December 28, 1830, *AP,* II, 567; SFA to Samuel M.

Williams, January 3, 1831, ibid., 571; SFA to Samuel M. Williams, January 9, 1831, ibid., 581–83; SFA to Samuel M. Williams, January 13, 1831, ibid., 584–85 (quotations).

21. SFA to Samuel M. Williams, December 28, 1830, *AP,* II 567 (first quotation); SFA to Samuel M. Williams, February 5, 1831, ibid., 594; SFA to Samuel M. Williams, March 12, 1831, ibid., 611–12; SFA to Samuel M. Williams, April 16, 1831, ibid., 645; SFA to Samuel M. Williams, April 30, 1831, ibid., 658 (second and third quotations). For a concise discussion of the shortcomings of the judicial system, see Eugene C. Barker, *Mexico and Texas, 1821–1835* (1928; reprint ed., New York: Russell & Russell, 1965), 91–99. All the laws passed during the session can be found in Spanish and English in John P. Kimball, comp., *Laws and Decrees of the State of Coahuila and Texas* (Houston: Secretary of State, 1839), 169–83.

22. Eugene C. Barker, "Land Speculation as a Cause of the Texas Revolution," *SWHQ* 10 (July 1906): 77; Henson, *Samuel May Williams,* 45–46; Amelia Williams, "A Critical Study of the Siege of the Alamo and of the Personnel of Its Defenders," chap. 3, *SWHQ* 37 (October 1933): 98–99.

23. The history of SFA's attempts to secure title to the site of the present-day city of Austin is long and complicated. He had identified the site and begun his plans for it as early as 1830, when he petitioned the state government for one eleven-league grant and sought permission from then-empresario Benjamin Milam to locate the grant on the right bank (south shore) of the Colorado River; see SFA to Benjamin R. Milam, June 18, 1830, Box 23, Folder 26, Spanish Collection, Archives and Records Division, Texas General Land Office. The portion on the left bank would fall within the limits of SFA's own Little Colony. The Law of April 6 suspended Milam's contract, and Austin decided to seek to buy the left-bank acreage, along with the other two eleven-league parcels. Several documents in Box 23, Folder 26, of the General Land Office records (cited above) trace these attempts. Also see SFA to Samuel M. Williams, May 8, 1832, *AP,* II, 770, SFA to Samuel M. Williams, ibid, 775–80; SFA to James F. and Emily Perry, April 19, 1833, ibid., 951; SFA to James F. Perry, April 20, 1833, ibid., 956–57 (quotations); SFA to Samuel M. Williams, May 31, 1833, ibid., 983; SFA to Samuel M. Williams, August 14, 1833, ibid., 999; SFA to Samuel M. Williams, August 21, 1833, ibid., 1000; SFA to Samuel M. Williams, November 5, 1833, ibid., 1015; Henson, *Samuel May Williams,* 46–47; Sam A. Suhler, "Stephen F. Austin and the City of Austin: An Anomaly," *SWHQ* 69 (January 1966): 266–86. For various reasons SFA never secured clear title to these grants. When he returned to Saltillo in 1832, however, he did make an additional payment of $700 or $800 on the land; see Moses Austin Bryan to Wharton Branch, May 20, 1885, John Henry Brown Papers, CAH.

24. SFA's plan for an academy at the future site of Austin, Texas, was but one in a series of stillborn educational schemes. Twice he drew up plans for a state-supported school in his colony, but nothing came of them. In 1829, with the arrival of schoolteacher Thomas J. Pilgrim at San Felipe, he sought to get a school founded by the ayuntamiento, but it failed for lack of public support. Pilgrim did operate a private boys' school in San Felipe for a while. See *LSFA,* 228–29; *HT,* II, 788–89, V, 202.

25. See Chapter 5.

26. *PCRCT,* III, 40–43, 48–50, 52–54, and IV, 60–65; *LSFA,* 191–93, 288–92.

27. Robertson had formed a partnership with one Alexander Thomson in May 1830 to bring families to the Nashville grant. Robertson rode ahead of Thomson and the nine families to prepare the way, arriving in San Felipe on October 10, where he secured the power of attorney from League. Thomson and the nine families reached Nacogdoches on October 28. Colonel José de las Piedras had just received the order from Terán requiring that all immigrants present a valid passport or a certificate showing they were bound for Austin's Colony. These families, of course, had neither, and thus were refused passage into the interior of Texas. The authorities allowed Thomson and four others to proceed on to San Felipe with the understanding that if SFA would give them permits to settle in his colony, the families would be allowed to stay in Texas. Otherwise they would have to leave. The families were allowed to camp east of town, but soon they grew weary of the wait and clandestinely cut a trail around Nacogdoches and continued to the Brazos. This defiance of a military order was the beginning of a long ordeal for the families, some of whom eventually settled in Austin's Colony. See *PCRCT,* IV, 62–63, and V, 42–45.

28. Hosea H. League to Sterling C. Robertson, Power of Attorney, October 10, 1830, *PCRCT,* IV, 594; Sterling C. Robertson to the Congress of Coahuila and Texas, April 2, 1834, *PCRCT,* VIII, 356 (quotation).

29. It is important to note that the account of SFA giving Robertson his "word of honor" to help save the contract comes from Robertson himself in 1834, by which time he had long been engaged in a vitriolic campaign to prove to the government that SFA had deprived him of the empresario contract by fraudulent means. There is no documentation from 1830, when the meeting allegedly took place, to establish what sort of assurances, if any, SFA gave Robertson. The particulars of Robertson's account must be doubted.

30. Apart from Robertson's testimony three years later, when with bitter resentment he was petitioning the state to return the contract to him, the only evidence that we have of any conversation between the two men prior to SFA's departure for Saltillo is a letter that Robertson wrote to SFA in June 1831, as soon as SFA had returned. At that point Robertson was still waiting to find out what SFA had accomplished in Saltillo. "I am anxious to know our fate," he wrote in the letter, adding that he cared not about his own fate but was concerned about the "unfortune settlers" he had brought to Texas. See Sterling C. Robertson to SFA, June 7, 1831, *AP,* II, 664.

31. Robertson's crime, trial, and conviction can be followed in *PCRCT,* III, 62–65, and VII, 42–43. He was not found guilty on the charge of murder; the records use the phrase "felonious slaying," which the editor of the *PCRCT* reasonably interprets as manslaughter. The appeals court later upheld Robertson's conviction, although the governor rescinded the branding portion of the punishment. In 1832, Robertson returned to Nashville, where he was made to serve 148 days of the nine-month jail sentence; see *PCRCT,* VII, 27–28.

32. SFA's account of the inquiry he made on Robertson's behalf is certainly believable. In 1834, in a letter to Thomas F. McKinney, he related what had happened on his arrival in Saltillo:

Secretary Santiago de Valle I presume will recollect that he was much hurt at me for requesting that the time should be extended to the Nashville Co. for he said I knew it was impossible as they were all citizens of the U.S. and the April law was then in force. It could not be granted to R. or extended to the Nashville Co. This was impossible. I enquired if it could be done and gave offense by making the enquiry. It was applied for by a french Co. and others and would have been granted to some one, had I not procured it just as I did. I thought it was my duty to Texas to try to keep it out of the hands of those foreign companies, for they have only done harm or at least as yet have not contributed *much* to settle the country. . . . My intentions were good and had the gen[l] good in view.

See SFA to Thomas F. McKinney, October 18, 1834, *AP*, III, 13. He later repeated this version of events to Williams; see SFA to Samuel M. Williams, March 21, 1835, ibid., 51.

33. Stephen F. Austin's Application for a Colonization Contract for Himself and Samuel M. Williams, February 4, 1831, *PCRCT*, V, 487–91; the Austin & Williams Contract, February 25, 1831, ibid., 563–72; SFA to Samuel M. Williams, March 5, 1831, *AP*, II, 607 (quotation). Ambiguity in the surviving documents has created confusion over whether SFA originally intended to seek the contract exclusively for Williams or whether he intended all along for them to become co-empresarios, as they ultimately did. The confusion stems from a February 5, 1831, letter from SFA to Williams, written shortly after SFA's arrival in Saltillo. In it Austin tells Williams that the government record office "has been searched for your petition in vain, it cannot be found. This morning I told the secretary that I would present another petition as your agent, he said that he would look once more, and if the other could not be found that I could present a new one, and the Gov[r] has promised that it shall be *immediately* dispatched" (see SFA to Samuel M. Williams, February 5, 1831, *AP*, II, 594). This led Williams's biographer to conclude that the "petition" referred to in the letter was a petition from Williams for the empresario contract (see Henson, *Samuel May Williams,* 52–53). However, a careful reading of the letter indicates that SFA was referring to petitions for *land grants,* not empresario contracts. And in fact, Williams was also in the process of applying for several leagues of land as compensation for his long service to the colony, and this is almost certainly what SFA was referring to. There is no mention in the February 5 letter of any empresario contract. On March 5, SFA wrote Williams again, this time telling him that "your petition was granted. . . . The power of attorney is effected in union with myself." This time SFA is clearly talking about the application for the new empresario contract, for he goes on to describe its boundaries (see SFA to Samuel May Williams, March 5, 1831, *AP*, II, 607).

Malcolm McLean, the editor of the *PCRCT,* muddies the waters greatly in his discussion of these documents. On p. 51 of vol. 5, he reaches the correct conclusion regarding what "petition" SFA's February 5 letter is referring to: the letter was referring to Williams's petition for *land.* But then, on p. 53, McLean quotes the same February 5 letter as if SFA was referring to Williams's "petition" for the Nashville Company's *colonization contract.* Throughout this section of McLean's text, he is leading the reader to the conclusion that SFA alone made the decision to apply for the contract without telling

Williams, and that he made the decision after arriving in Saltillo. As the centerpiece for this hypothesis, McLean presents a spurious theory concerning the power of attorney from Williams that SFA presented in Saltillo, by which he was able to apply for the colony in both his and Williams's name.

When SFA applied for the contract on February 5, he presented a power of attorney, printed on official stamped paper, signed by Williams and witnessed and signed by all the proper authorities at San Felipe. The instrument was dated December 17, 1830, just before SFA left for Saltillo. McLean suggests that the power of attorney was actually con-cocted illegally by SFA after his arrival in Saltillo, using a pre-signed blank form. In the past SFA had prepared blank, pre-signed forms to be used for land titles and immigrant passports when he knew he would not be present to sign for them, and McLean suggests that SFA could have had one of these blanks with him in Saltillo. He then reproduces a facsimile of the December power of attorney to prove his theory. A power of attorney was a shorter document than a land title. This one, according to McLean, was written with ab-normally large margins on the sides, top, and bottom, and with curlicues added to fill up some of the extra space so that the text would extend down to the pre-existing signatures. Upon examining the facsimile, however, there is nothing unusual about the margins, and the ornamentation that McLean describes as "curlicues" is also not unusual in Mexi-can documents of this period. The spacing and overall appearance of the document is quite conventional. Moreover, in his haste to present the power of attorney as fraudu-lent, McLean overlooked one fact fatal to his argument: the entire document is written entirely in Williams's unmistakable and unduplicable hand. SFA could not have forged it in Saltillo. See Power of Attorney from Samuel M. Williams to SFA, December 17, 1830, 338–40, and the facsimile, 336–37.

It is unclear what point McLean is trying to make with all this, unless it is to suggest that the Austin and Williams contract was illegal because it was based on a fraudulent power of attorney. However, McLean never makes this argument explicitly. McLean's presentation, however, has confused subsequent scholars; see Reichstein, *Rise of the Lone Star,* 48 (including nn55–56).

34. Because of the raging controversy that later erupted between SFA and Robert-son (and their respective partisans), SFA's motives are very important. Beyond what has already been said and what has been written by Barker, McLean, and others, one key point bears emphasizing: the 1831 grant to SFA and Williams geographically encompassed not merely the area of the Nashville grant, but also the whole of SFA's other colonies, excluding the ten-league-wide coastal reserve. Austin's first empresario contract was long since complete; his second one was about to expire, leaving two others that would both expire within three years. There was still unoccupied land in the areas covered by those old contracts, and without a new contract it would revert back to the government. Austin's interest, therefore, in celebrating this newest contract was not merely to obtain the Nashville Company's grant but also to allow for the continued settlement of Austin's Colony once his earlier contracts began expiring.

35. SFA to Samuel M. Williams, March 5, 1831, *AP,* II, 607 (first and second quota-tions); SFA to Samuel M. Williams, April 2, 1831, ibid., 639 (third and fourth quotations);

SFA to Samuel M. Williams, February 19, 1831, ibid., 602 (fifth and sixth quotations); Manuel de Mier y Terán to SFA, March 21, 1831, ibid., 622.

36. SFA to Samuel M. Williams, May 8, 1831, *AP*, II, 661; Sterling C. Robertson to SFA, June 7, 1831, ibid., 664.

37. *LSFA*, 138; José María Viesca to Ramón Músquiz, December 20, 1828, Box 126, Folder 3, p. 30, Spanish Collection, Archives and Records Division, Texas General Land Office; Miguel Arciniega to Ramón Músquiz, November 26, 1830, Box 126, Folder 4, p. 40, ibid. The numbers of titles issued under SFA's various contracts can be derived by means of a tabulation from the General Land Office's General Index.

38. An October 1831 census counted a total population in the Villa de Austin of 5,665; see "Estadistica del Departamento de Texas," 1831, Wagner Texas and Middle West Collection, Beinecke Rare Book and Manuscript Library, Yale University. The best concise summary of religion in Austin's Colony is in Kite, "Social History," 161–71. Also see Mary Angela Fitzmorris, *Four Decades of Catholicism in Texas, 1820–1860* (Washington, D.C.: Catholic University of America, 1926), chap. 2.

39. SFA to Samuel M. Williams, January 13, 1831, *AP*, II, 585 (first and second quotations); SFA to Samuel M. Williams, February 5, 1831, ibid., 594 (third and fifth quotations); SFA to Samuel M. Williams, February 19, 1831, ibid., 603 (fourth quotation); *HT*, IV, 880; Kite, "Social History," 163–65.

40. *Mexican Citizen* (San Felipe), May 26, 1831 (first and second quotations); J[ohnathan] H[ampton] K[uykendall], "Father Michael Muldoon," part of a typescript entitled "Sketches of Early Texians," 44–47, c. 1857, Kuykendall Family Papers, CAH (second quotation); Clipping from the *Galveston News*, c. 1877, in Austin Scrapbook, part 2, CAH. This scrapbook appears to have been kept by SFA's nephew, Moses Austin Bryan, and the item above is a reminiscence apparently written by settler Ammon Underwood.

41. Aylett C. Buckner to SFA, July 2, 1831, *AP*, II, 672; Kuykendall, "Father Michael Muldoon," (quotations). For a sample of Muldoon's political activism, see Miguel Muldoon to SFA, November 10, 1832, Austin (Stephen F.) Collection, CAH; José Antonio Mexía to SFA, March 27, 1833, *AP*, II, 933. Interestingly, Muldoon publicly announced that he would "Baptize and Marry the black race of both sexes, without receiving from them, or their masters any gratification. He feels it his incumbent duty, and very cordial pleasure to succor and patronize distress in whatever colour or condition it may appear." See *Mexican Citizen* (San Felipe), May 26, 1831.

42. Moses Austin Bryan to William Joel Bryan, February 5, 1831, Perry Papers, CAH.

43. James F. Perry to Israel McGready, October 1, 1831, *AP*, II, 694–95; SFA to James F. Perry, November 17, 1831, ibid., 706; SFA to James F. Perry, November 15, 1831, ibid., 704 (quotation); *HT*, V, 157.

44. Austin's House Plans, November 30, 1831, *AP*, II, 715–20. The house was never built at Chocolate Bayou, for Perry soon came around to SFA's position and decided that Peach Point was the better location after all. The house that Perry built there was similar to the one SFA had designed for Chocolate Bayou.

45. SFA specified that Guy Bryan should become a lawyer, William Joel Bryan a planter, and Moses Austin Bryan a merchant. All were to learn Spanish and attend dancing school. See SFA to James F. Perry, April 20, 1833, *AP,* II, 957–58.

46. See, for example, SFA to James F. Perry, November 15, 17, 21, December 23, 27, 1831, February 10, March 6, 1832, *AP,* II, 704, 707, 710, 725, 726, 748, 756–57.

47. See, for example, James F. Perry to SFA, July 18, 1830, *AP,* II, 457–58; SFA to James F. Perry, November 15, 1831, ibid., 704; SFA to Emily M. Perry, November 5, 1832, ibid., 884; SFA to Emily M. Perry, January 26, 1833, Austin Papers, Series II, CAH.

48. James F. Perry to Israel McGready, October 1, 1831, *AP,* II, 695; Emily M. Perry to James F. Perry, December 1, 1831, *AP,* I, 720.

49. William Ransom Hogan, "Henry Austin," *SWHQ* 37 (January 1934): 185–214; *HT,* I, 291; SFA to Mary Austin Holley, December 29, 1831, *AP,* II, 728.

50. Lee, *Mary Austin Holley,* passim; *HT,* III, 667–68; Mary Austin Holley to SFA, January 2, 1831, *AP,* II, 570–71.

51. SFA to Samuel May Williams, April 2, 1831, *AP,* II, 638 (first quotation); SFA to Mary Austin Holley, July 19, 1831, ibid., 674.

52. Lee, *Mary Austin Holley,* 223–26; Henson, *Juan Davis Bradburn,* 58–84; SFA to Mary Austin Holley, November 14, 1831, *AP,* II, 701–2; SFA to Father Muldoon, November 15, 1831, ibid., 703; SFA to James F. Perry, November 15, 1831, ibid., 704; SFA to James F. Perry, November 21, 1831, ibid., 710 (quotations); SFA to Emily M. Perry, December 23, 1831, ibid., 725.

53. Lee, *Mary Austin Holley,* 229–34.

54. SFA to Mary Austin Holley, December 25, 29, 1831, January 4, 14, 30, February 19, 1832, *AP,* II, 725–26, 727–30, 732–33, 736–38, 745, 753–54. For SFA's description of himself as "taciturn," see SFA to Samuel M. Williams, March 5, 1831, ibid., 607; SFA to Mary Austin Holley, February 19, 1832, ibid., 754.

55. SFA to Mary Austin Holley, December 29, 1831, *AP,* II, 728–29.

56. SFA to Mary Austin Holley, December 29, 1831, *AP,* II, 729 (first and second quotations); SFA to Mary Austin Holley, January 4, 1832, ibid., 733 (third quotation); SFA to Mary Austin Holley, February 19, 1832, ibid., 754 (fourth quotation); SFA to James F. Perry, [December] 27, 1831, ibid., 726 (fifth quotation).

57. Green, *Mexican Republic,* 228; SFA to Mary Austin Holley, December 29, 1831, *AP,* II, 729 (first quotation), 730 (second quotation).

58. SFA to Mary Austin Holley, January 4, 1832, *AP,* II, 733.

TEN
The Call of Duty
1832–1833

1. The most thorough telling of these events is in Henson, *Juan Davis Bradburn,* 81–83. Also see Morton, *Terán and Texas,* 150–52.

2. Fisher, a Hungarian-born Serb, had immigrated to the United States in 1814. He went to Mexico in 1825, where he helped to establish the first York Rite Masonic lodge

there. After becoming a naturalized Mexican citizen in 1829, he was named customs collector at Galveston. After Terán ordered the port suspended, Fisher served as secretary of the San Felipe Ayuntamiento, but the colonists removed him from that position when they suspected him of acting as a secret agent of the national government. He was reinstated as customs collector at Anahuac in 1831, whereupon he issued the unpopular order leading to the so-called Anahuac Disturbances. See *HT*, II, 1010; Bessie Lucille Letts, "George Fisher," M.A. thesis, University of Texas, 1928.

3. SFA to John Davis Bradburn, December 30, 1831, *AP,* II, 731–32.

4. SFA to Manuel de Mier y Terán, January 8, 1832, *AP,* II, 733–35.

5. Manuel de Mier y Terán to SFA, January 27, 1832, *AP,* II, 742–44.

6. Morton, *Terán and Texas,* 152.

7. SFA to William H. Wharton, April 24, 1829, *AP,* II, 211. Also see SFA to General William H. Ashley, October 10, 1832, ibid., 873–74.

8. SFA to Thomas F. Leaming, June 14, 1830, *AP,* II, 416.

9. SFA to S. Rhoads Fisher, June 17, 1830, *AP,* II, 427 (quotation). For similar sentiments, see SFA to Henry Austin, [June 1, 1830], ibid., 405; SFA to Thomas F. Leaming, June 14, 1830, ibid., 415; SFA to Mary Austin Holley, December 29, 1831, ibid., 730.

10. SFA to Mary Austin Holley, December 29, 1831, *AP,* II, 730. Surprisingly, SFA even explained these options to Terán; see SFA to Manuel de Mier y Terán, September 17, 1830, ibid., 486.

11. As SFA recovered at the end of November he obtained a doctor's certification explaining that the fever and the mercury he was given as medicine rendered him too sick to make the journey for at least another month. Then he procrastinated even further. He hated the grueling trip to Saltillo and the tedium of legislative duty. He was certainly well enough by mid-December to make the ride to Brazoria in bitterly cold weather for the visit with Mary, although the trip was painful. He rode back to San Felipe in January, made another long trip to the coast in February, and returned to San Felipe once more, all while the legislature was meeting. See SFA to Ramón Músquiz, November 29, 1831, *AP,* II, 715; Certificate of Robert Peebles, November 29, 1831, ibid.; José María Letona to SFA, January 9, 1832, Austin (Stephen F.) Collection, CAH; Santiago del Valle to Congressional Deputies, January 19, 1832, Western Americana Collection, Beinecke Rare Book and Manuscript Library, Yale University; José Maria Letona to SFA, January 21, 1832, *AP,* II, 738–39; SFA to Manuel de Mier y Terán, March 21, 1832, Streeter Collection of Texas Manuscripts, Beinecke Rare Book and Manuscript Library, Yale University; SFA to Samuel M. Williams, April 9, 1832, *AP,* II, 762.

12. Moses Austin Bryan, "Reminiscences of M. A. Bryan," Moses Austin Bryan Papers, CAH.

13. SFA to Samuel M. Williams, April 28, 1832, *AP,* II, 767 (quotation); SFA to Horatio Chriesman, June 19, 1832, ibid., 787; Ayuntamiento of San Felipe to Supreme Government, February 18, 1832, *AP,* II, 749–52. The ayuntamiento of San Antonio endorsed the contents of the San Felipe petition, but the members resented not being first consulted by the colonists. The San Antonio council therefore agreed to endorse the petition only if the members were allowed to antedate their version so that it appeared

that they had acted before receiving the petition. SFA readily agreed to this requirement. See SFA to Samuel M. Williams, ibid., 758; *LSFA*, 331. For the laws passed in the session, see Kimball, *Laws and Decrees*, 183–98, esp. the retail law (p. 185), the colonization law (pp. 189–93), and the creation of the municipality of Brazoria (p. 197).

14. SFA to Samuel M. Williams, May 22, 1832, in Maria Grace Ramirez, ed., "Stephen F. Austin Letters," *East Texas Historical Journal* 6 (October 1968): 147–48.

15. Moses Austin Bryan to Wharton Branch, May 20, 1885, John Henry Brown Papers, CAH.

16. SFA to Samuel M. Williams, May 8, 1832, *AP*, II, 772 (quotations). That same confidence extended to SFA's relationship with Minister of Relations Lucas Alamán, the key policy maker in the embattled Bustamante administration in Mexico City. For SFA's attempts to influence Alamán in favor of Texas, see Lucas Alamán to SFA, April 21, 1832, Streeter Collection of Texas Manuscripts, Beinecke Rare Book and Manuscript Library, Yale University. SFA's letter to Alamán has not been located.

17. Bryan, "Reminiscences," 4; SFA to Samuel M. Williams, April 28, 1832, *AP*, II, 769 (second quotation); SFA to Samuel M. Williams, May 22, 1832, in Ramirez, "Stephen F. Austin Letters," 147–48 (third quotation); Morton, *Terán and Texas*, 166–69.

18. Morton, *Terán and Texas*, 170–72.

19. SFA to Samuel M. Williams, June 15, 1832, *AP*, II, 781.

20. SFA to James F. Perry, June 29, 1832, *AP*, II, 803; SFA to Samuel M. Williams, July 1, 1832, ibid., 807–8.

21. Manuel de Mier y Terán to SFA, June 25, 1832, *AP*, II, 799.

22. SFA to Samuel M. Williams, July 1, 1832, *AP*, II, 808; SFA to Manuel de Mier y Terán, June 27, 1832, ibid., 802–3 (quotations).

23. Manuel de Mier y Terán to Lucas Alamán, July 2, 1832, quoted in Morton, *Terán and Texas*, 182–83.

24. Morton, *Terán and Texas*, 178.

25. Terán committed suicide on July 3. By July 9 the news had reached SFA in Matamoros, for he referred to the *"finado"* (deceased) Terán in a letter of that date to Governor Letona, in which SFA notified Letona that he would be sailing with colonels Mexía and Guerra to Texas. That same day he accepted Mexía's invitation to accompany him on the expedition. See SFA to Governor Letona, July 9, 1832, *AP*, II, 813–15; SFA to José Antonio Mexía, July 9, 1832, ibid., 813.

26. Except where otherwise noted, the following account of the Anahuac Disturbances and their aftermath is derived from Henson, *Juan Davis Bradburn*, 58–113; *LSFA*, chap. 12; Henson, *Samuel May Williams*, 34–41; and *HT*, I, 159–60.

27. For the resolutions, see Ernest Wallace and David M. Vigness, eds., *Documents of Texas History* (Austin: Steck, 1963), 73.

28. Despite his conciliatory actions at Anahuac, Piedras remained steadfastly loyal to the Bustamante regime. He removed Bradburn and effected the release of the Anglo prisoners at Anahuac only because he feared losing an armed confrontation with the settlers. The subsequent actions of the Mexican rank-and-file soldiers at Anahuac and Velasco in pronouncing for Santa Anna confirmed his fears. Piedras returned to Nacog-

doches only to find that the ayuntamiento there had formed a militia demanding that Piedras and his garrison declare for Santa Anna. Piedras refused, and in the battle that followed forty-seven of his troops were killed and forty others wounded. Piedras's men finally turned against him, and, like the garrisons at Anahuac and Velasco, declared for Santa Anna. Piedras was taken to San Felipe and turned over to Austin, who paroled him and sent him back to Mexico. James Bowie marched the three hundred men who had constituted Piedras's command back to San Antonio, where they were discharged, thus clearing deep East Texas of Mexican troops. Piedras's misadventures can be followed in Henson, *Juan David Bradburn*, 105–112; *HT*, IV, 923.

29. SFA to Samuel M. Williams, April 12, 1832, *AP*, II, 765 (first quotation); SFA to Samuel M. Williams, July 2, 1832, ibid., 810 (second and third quotations).

30. As already noted, Travis, Jack, Buckner, and John Austin were among the instigators of the disturbances at Anahuac and Velasco. Several of Austin's closest associates in San Felipe—Frank W. Johnson, Luke Lesassier, and Robert M. Williamson—also disagreed with Austin's conciliatory policy.

31. SFA to James F. Perry, July 11, 1830, *AP*, II, 445–47; John P. Austin to SFA, October 10, 1831, ibid., 696; Archibald Austin to SFA, October 24, 1830, Austin Papers, Series II, CAH; James F. Perry to Messrs. Gill Ferguson & Co., May 13, 1831, Perry Papers, Series A, CAH.

32. SFA to Samuel M. Williams, July 19, 1832, *AP*, II, 822 (first quotation); José Antonio Mexía to John Austin, July 23, 1832, Brazoria, Austin (Stephen F.) Collection, CAH (second quotation).

33. SFA to Samuel M. Williams, July 19, 1832, *AP*, II, 821 (first quotation); P.S. written on July 20, pp. 822–23 (second and third quotations); Henson, *Samuel May Williams*, 41.

34. *Constitutional Advocate and Texas Public Advertiser* (Brazoria), September 5, 1832.

35. Ibid.

36. SFA to Thomas F. Leaming, July 23, 1831, *AP*, II, 678 (first quotation); SFA to Samuel M. Williams, April 9, 1832, ibid., 762 (second quotation); SFA to Ramón Músquiz, July 28, 1832, *AP*, II, 826 (third quotation).

37. SFA to Ramón Músquiz, August 15, 1832, *AP*, II, 839.

38. Cantrell, "Partnership of Stephen F. Austin and Joseph H. Hawkins," 6–16.

39. Ibid., 16–17.

40. SFA to W. C. Carr, March 4, 1829, *AP*, II, 177; SFA to James F. and Emily Perry, April 19, 1833, ibid., 951–52; SFA to James F. Perry, September 27, 1832, ibid., 867 (first and second quotations); SFA to Public, October 9, 1832, ibid., 870–71 (third quotation); Ramón Músquiz to SFA, October 11, 1832, ibid., 874–75.

41. The story of the 1832 convention and its aftermath, and SFA's role in these events, it is ably told in *LSFA*, 348–59, and forms the basis of the information in this and the following two paragraphs.

42. SFA to James F. Perry, January 20, 1833, *AP*, II, 917. For the San Antonio petition, see David J. Weber, ed., *Troubles in Texas, 1832: A Tejano Viewpoint from San*

Antonio with a Translation and Facsimile (Dallas: Wind River Press for the DeGolyer
Library of Southern Methodist University, 1983).

43. On the convention, see *LSFA,* 359–62. SFA's address to the convention, the
memorial to congress requesting separate statehood, and the 1833 constitution all can be
found in Wallace and Vigness, *Documents of Texas History,* 74–85.

44. John P. Coles to Anthony Butler, July 15, 1833, John P. Coles Papers, CAH.

45. SFA to James F. and Emily Perry, April 19, 1833, *AP,* II, 951; SFA to Henry
Austin, April 19, 1833, ibid., 953 (quotations).

46. SFA to Henry Austin, April 19, 1833, *AP,* II, 953 (first and third quotations),
954 (second quotation).

47. SFA to Henry Austin, April 19, 1833, *AP,* II, 953; SFA to Mary Austin Holley,
[April 20, 1833], ibid., 954–55.

48. SFA to Emily M. Perry, August 21, 1826, *AP,* I, 1427 (first quotation); SFA to
Mary Austin Holley, [April 20, 1833], *AP,* II, 955 (second quotation); SFA to William H.
Wharton, April 24, 1829, ibid., 208–9 (third quotation). Despite his statement to Mary,
on the very same day SFA was still telling James Perry that when he returned from Mexico
he intended to "close all my affairs and settle myself and get a wife and be a farmer." See
SFA to James F. Perry, April 20, 1833, ibid., 957.

49. SFA to Mary Austin Holley, [April 20, 1833], *AP,* II, 956.

ELEVEN
Prison
1833–1834

1. SFA to James F. Perry, April 22, 1833, *AP,* II, 960; SFA to Luke Lesassier, May 6,
1833, ibid., 961.

2. SFA to Henry Austin, April 19, 1833, *AP,* II, 954.

3. SFA to Luke Lesassier, May 6, 1833, *AP,* II, 961–63 (quotation on p. 961). For
the Tejano perspective on SFA's unsuccessful efforts, see José María Balmaceda to José
Francisco Madero, June 3, 1833, in *Gaceta del Gobierno Supremo del Estado de Coahuila y
Tejas* (Saltillo), May 27, 1833.

4. SFA to Vicente Filisola, [May 30, 1833], *AP,* II, 973–75; SFA to Ayuntamiento of
Nacogdoches, May 30, 1833, ibid., 975–77; SFA to Wily Martin, May 30, 1831, ibid., 977
(quotations); SFA to Samuel M. Williams, May 31, 1833, ibid., 983.

5. SFA to Samuel M. Williams, May 31, 1833, *AP,* II, 983; SFA to James F. Perry,
July 30, 1833, ibid., II, 992 (quotation).

6. SFA to Central Committee, July 24, 1833, *AP,* II, 988–89.

7. SFA to James F. Perry, July 30, 1833, *AP,* II, 991. The particulars of Austin's
diplomatic efforts of July and August are ably summarized in Barker, *LSFA,* 370–72; the
pertinent documentation can be found in *AP,* II, 988–98.

8. SFA to Samuel M. Williams, August 21, 1833, *AP,* II, 999 (quotations); SFA in
Account with Washington Hotel, July 16–August 22, 1833, ibid., 1002; SFA in Account

with Washington Hotel, September 30–October 31, ibid., 1011–12; SFA in Account with Washington Hotel, November 1–December 10, ibid., 1018. This tally of SFA's liquor and cigar bills does not include the account from the period of August 23–September 29, which does not survive.

9. SFA to Samuel M. Williams, September 5, 1833, *AP*, II, 1003–1004; SFA to Samuel M. Williams, September 11, 1833, ibid., 1005; SFA to James F. Perry, September 11, 1833, ibid., 1005.

10. SFA to Samuel M. Williams, September 11, 1833, *AP*, II, 1005 (first quotation); SFA to James F. Perry, September 11, 1833, ibid., 1006; SFA to James F. Perry, October 2, 1833, ibid., 1006–7 (second, third, and fourth quotations); SFA to Samuel M. Williams, November 5, 1833, ibid., 1013.

11. SFA to Ayuntamiento of Béxar, October 2, 1833, *AP*, II, 1007–8.

12. SFA to Rafael Llanos, January 14, 1834, *AP*, II, 1028.

13. SFA to Ayuntamiento of San Antonio, October 16, 1833, *AP*, II, 1016.

14. SFA to Samuel M. Williams (telling of the Coles letter), November 5, 1833, *AP*, II, 1014; SFA to Juan N. Seguín, January 17, 1834, ibid, 1042 (quotation).

15. Ramón Músquiz to Samuel M. Williams, April 17, 1834, *PCRCT*, VIII, 381.

16. SFA to Samuel M. Williams, November 5, 1833, *AP*, II, 1014; SFA to Erasmo Seguín, [about January 1, 1824?], ibid., I, 719 (quotation).

17. SFA to Minister of Relations, August 1, 1833, *AP*, II, 994 (first and second quotations); SFA to James F. Perry, October 23, 1833, *AP*, II, 1008 (third quotation). Barker leaves the mistaken impression that SFA's interview with Gómez Farías took place the same day (October 2) that he wrote the letter to the San Antonio ayuntamiento. According to Barker, SFA returned "to his quarters" after the meeting and wrote the letter "under the spell of his disappointment" with the vice-president's response to his demands. However, SFA's account of the meeting with Gómez Farías came in a letter dated October 23—three full weeks after the October 2 letter—at which time he referred to the meeting as having taken place only "the other day." Unless one interprets "the other day" as having been precisely three weeks to the day earlier, it is impossible to sustain Barker's contention; see *LSFA*, 373.

18. SFA to Samuel M. Williams, November 5, 1833, *AP*, II, 1014; Victor Blanco to Governor, November 6, 1833, Stephen F. Austin Collection, Special Collections, University of Houston. According to Vito Alessio Robles, the four cabinet ministers were Carlos García (Relations), Andrés Quintana Roo (Justice), Miguel Barragán (War), and José María Bocanegra (Treasury); see Alessio Robles, *Coahuila y Texas,* 1: 474. SFA recalled the meeting, which he dated November 5, in his "Explanation to the Public Concerning the Affairs of Texas," trans. Ethel Zivley Rather, *Quarterly of the Texas State Historical Association* 8 (January 1905): 250.

19. SFA to Samuel M. Williams, November 5, 1833, *AP*, II, 1014 (quotations); SFA to Samuel M. Williams, November 26, 1833, ibid., 1016; Austin, "Explanation to the Public," 250.

20. SFA to Samuel M. Williams, November 26, 1833, *AP*, II, 1016 (quotations). In

this letter SFA also mentioned that he thought it "doubtfull whether my letters reach Texas," giving him even less cause for concern over the possible response to his letters to San Antonio.

21. SFA, "The 'Prison Journal' of Stephen F. Austin," ed. W. P. Zuber, *Quarterly of the Texas State Historical Association* 2 (January 1899): 184.

22. SFA, "Prison Journal," 184–207 (quotations). For a perceptive analysis of SFA's views on religion and on Mexico's Catholic Church, see Howard Miller, "Stephen F. Austin and the Anglo-Texan Response to the Religious Establishment in Mexico, 1821–1836," *SWHQ* 91 (January 1988): 283–316.

23. SFA, "Prison Journal," 203.

24. Ibid., 193–94; SFA to Samuel M. Williams, January 12, 1834, *AP*, II, 1024. SFA had first thought he would travel in company with General Lemus from Mexico City to Coahuila, but apparently Lemus left before SFA; see SFA to Samuel M. Williams, November 26, 1833, ibid., 1016.

25. Ayuntamiento of Béxar to SFA, October 31, 1833, *AP*, II, 1012.

26. Benjamin Lundy, *The Life, Travels and Opinions of Benjamin Lundy* (Philadelphia: William D. Parrish, 1847), 77–79. Vidaurri had become acting governor when Juan Martín Veramendi of San Antonio died in the cholera epidemic. Veramendi himself had been an acting governor, elevated to the post when the elected governor, José María Letona, died; see *HT*, IV, 172; VI, 722.

27. J. Miguel Falcón to the Political Chief of Béxar, December 11, 1833, *PCRCT*, VIII, 153 (Falcón was the governor's secretary); Francisco Vidaurri y Villaseñor to Most Excellent Sir [Secretary of War?], December 11, 1833, AGN Transcripts, Fomento, vol. 304, CAH. The sequence of events immediately before and after SFA's arrest has confused scholars. Barker states that Gómez Farías ordered the arrest after Governor Vidaurri forwarded SFA's October 2 letter to Mexico City. This is not incorrect, but it leaves the misleading impression that Governor Vidaurri played only a middleman's role in bringing about the arrest. To the contrary, Vidaurri clearly was the first to order SFA's arrest, and his inflammatory letter of December 11 to the central government surely played the leading role in convincing Gómez Farías to issue his own arrest order. Gómez Farías may indeed have been "gravely outraged," as Barker put it (there is no direct documentation of his immediate response to SFA's letter), but Vidaurri's outrage was unmistakable. Moreover, SFA himself understood that "the governor of the state is my accuser." This was further confirmed by Ramón Músquiz, who was in Monclova at the time and later stated, "The fact is that first orders were issued for the arrest of Don Stephen by the Government of the State, and afterwards he was arrested and conducted to Mexico City by order of the General Government." See Barker, *LSFA*, 375; SFA to Rafael Llanos, January 14, 1834, *AP*, II, 1029; SFA to James F. Perry, January 14, 1834, ibid., 1033; Ramón Músquiz to Samuel M. Williams, April 17, 1834, *PCRCT*, VIII, 381.

28. Pedro Lemus to Secretary of War and Marine, January 3, 1834, AGN Transcripts, Fomento, vol. 330, CAH.

29. SFA, "Prison Journal," 194; Order of the Most Excellent Vice President, Janu-

ary 22, 1834, AGN Transcripts, Fomento, vol. 330, CAH (fourth and fifth quotations). Gómez Farías's precise wording in describing SFA was *"un Reo de Estado de la m[ay]or grabedad."*

30. SFA to Samuel M. Williams, January 12, 1834, *AP,* II, 1024–26.

31. SFA to Ayuntamiento of San Felipe, January 17, 1834, *AP,* II, 1039 (first and second quotations); *Advocate of the People's Rights* (Brazoria), February 22 (third quotation), March 27, 1834 (fourth quotation).

32. Pedro Lemus to Minister of War and Marine, January 19, 1834, Gabriel Valencia to Secretary of War, February 13, 1834, AGN Transcripts, Fomento, vol. 330, CAH.

33. SFA to James F. Perry, *AP,* II, 1049–51 (first quotation on p. 1050); SFA, "Prison Journal," 199 (second quotation).

34. SFA to James F. Perry, *AP,* II, 1049–51; SFA, "Prison Journal," 196–98 (second quotation on p. 197); Bryan, "Personal Recollections," 106.

35. Michael Muldoon to Oliver Jones, May 14, 1834, quoted in Oliver Jones to James F. Perry, June 10, 1834, *AP,* II, 1063 (first and second quotations); SFA, "Prison Journal," 198 (third quotation), 209; SFA to James F. Perry, May 10, 1834, *AP,* II, 1053.

36. SFA, "Prison Journal," 201 (quotations), 202–203.

37. SFA to James F. Perry, May 10, 1834, *AP,* II, 1053 (quotation); SFA, "Prison Journal," 204.

38. Sterling C. Robertson to the Congress of Coahuila and Texas, [April 2, 1834], *PCRCT,* VIII, 353–63. In his zeal to support Robertson's claims, Malcolm McLean, the editor of the *PCRCT,* spares no effort to cast SFA in the worst light possible, even publishing the Robertson "family tradition," which holds that SFA (then under arrest in Mexico) had somehow hired an assassin to murder Robertson on the road to Monclova (see *PCRCT,* VIII, 42–45). Yet in his treatment of the central document in the entire Robertson saga—Robertson's April 2, 1834, petition to the state government for return of the colony—McLean makes no mention of the lie on which Robertson built his case. Instead, McLean simply discreetly places "1830" in brackets after Robertson's own "1829" at both locations in the petition where the fabricated date appeared, and then allows the correction to pass without comment, as if it had been a mere careless error. It is, of course, impossible that this could have been an error on Robertson's part; the date is all-important. Unless Robertson could place the start of his colonization efforts in late 1829 instead of the actual late 1830, he had no case. Barker recognized this misdating, but in his typical understated fashion he simply suggested that "Robertson's memory played him strangely false." Barker knew that the events Robertson related in the petition had happened a year earlier than Robertson claimed, but knowing nothing about Robertson's whereabouts in 1829, Barker had to admit that it was at least possible that Robertson had been in Texas (see Barker, *LSFA,* 309). We now know that Robertson was in Nashville that entire year, and that in the closing months of the year he was preoccupied with his murder trial. While documents that have come to light since Barker's time help to fill in some of the blank spots in the Robertson-Austin dispute, Barker's meticulous account remains the most reliable and (although charitable to SFA) most balanced treatment of

this long and bitter controversy, notwithstanding the nineteen volumes of the *PCRCT*. For a shorter but accurate account of the controversy from the viewpoint of Samuel May Williams, see Henson, *Samuel May Williams,* 51–60.

39. The depositions, seven in all, were sworn before the San Felipe ayuntamiento in December 1831 and January 1832. They remain something of a mystery. Barker convincingly suggests that they were carefully coached, though this cannot be proved. Certainly the evidence was hearsay. Motives for the witnesses are even harder to ascertain, but at least one them, William Pettus, was known to harbor bitter personal animosity toward SFA. The editor of the *PCRCT* reproduces the depositions and provides a master list of all the names of Robertson's alleged 146 settlers. Only in a handful of cases can arrival dates in Texas be determined with any accuracy, and all of these were after April 6, 1830. Further research in the records of the GLO and other sources might reveal arrival dates for many of the remaining colonists, but it seems probable that the bulk of them arrived in late 1830 or early 1831. See Introduction, *PCRCT,* VIII, 24–26; and various depositions, ibid., 55–64, 68–71, 91–103.

40. In mid-1833, as he was lobbying the government in Mexico City, SFA had learned that Robertson had secured the affidavits: "How he could get men to state such falsehoods or agents to advocate and arrange them I am at a loss to imagine—it has really surprised me." In April 1833, Robertson actually had petitioned the state for return of the colony, but the legislature failed to act on his request. The 1834 petition was his second try. See SFA to Samuel M. Williams, August 21, 1833, *AP,* II, 1000; *PCRCT,* VII, 34–35.

41. Introduction, *PCRCT,* VIII, 33–53; Decree of the Congress of Coahuila and Texas Awarding the Colony to Robertson, [April 29, 1834], ibid., 401–403. The governor ruled in favor of Robertson on May 22, 1834.

42. Oliver Jones to James F. Perry, June 10, 1834, *AP,* II, 1063; John T. Mason to Gentlemen [of the Galveston Bay and Texas Land Company?], July 28, 1834, U.S. Boards of Commissioners, 1849, Case Files for Claimants (1848–51), November Terms, Claim #184, National Archives, copy in possession of Galen Greaser, GLO; Jack, quoted in Henson, *Samuel May Williams,* 60; Barker, *LSFA,* 315. Margaret Henson agrees that the charge of bribery "had substance"; see Henson, *Samuel May Williams,* 58.

43. SFA to Samuel M. Williams, September 7, 1834, *AP,* II, 1088. A computerized tally furnished by the GLO listing the acreage awarded to SFA as premium lands places the total at 219,700 acres. SFA had undoubtedly sold or otherwise disposed of portions of this by 1834 (as in the settlement with the Hawkins heirs, for example), but he had also acquired significant acreage from other grantees over the years.

44. Notice to the Public, [Entered under December 30, 1832], *PCRCT,* VII, 384–86 (first and second quotations on p. 385); To the Public, [Entered under December 2, 1833], ibid., VIII, 149–52 (third and fourth quotations on p. 149; fifth quotation on p. 152). The dates of these documents, and whether they were published as broadsides or in newspapers, are uncertain. Robertson also went to great lengths in the first of these documents to repeat the decade-old scandal concerning Williams's shady past.

45. F. W. Johnson to R. M. Williamson, March 10, 1834, *AP,* II, 1047; "Land in the

Colony of the Nashville Company," broadside, July 2, 1834, *PCRCT*, IX, 143. The broad-side was published in July and then reproduced in the Brazoria *Texas Republican* on November 29. A facsimile of the broadside is on p. 141 of the *PCRCT* volume.

46. SFA to Oliver Jones, May 30, 1834, *AP*, II, 1058; SFA to James F. Perry, August 25, 1834, *AP*, II, 1078 (quotation).

47. SFA to James F. Perry, August 25, 1834, *AP*, II, 1075–85.

48. George L. Hammeken, "Recollections of Stephen F. Austin," *SWHQ* 20 (April 1917): 373. This memoir was written in 1844, in the form of a lengthy letter to Guy Bryan.

49. SFA to James F. Perry, August 25, 1834, *AP*, II, 1075–84 (first and second quotations on p. 1077; third quotation on p. 1083); William H. Wharton to the Public, November 9, 1834, *AP*, III, 25–26.

50. Alexander Calvit to José Antonio Mexía, August 29, 1833, AGN Transcripts, Fomento, vol. 304, CAH.

51. SFA to Oliver Jones, June 2, 1834, *AP*, II, 1059 (quotations); SFA to Samuel M. Williams, June 3, 1834, ibid., 1060–61. On the reforms of 1834, see Barker, *Texas and Mexico*, 130; Tijerina, *Tejanos and Texas*, 134–35; Eugene C. Barker, "Land Speculation as a Cause of the Texas Revolution," *SWHQ* 10 (July 1906): 78–79.

52. Barker, *LSFA*, 384–85.

53. Private instructions of Almonte, quoted in Helen Willits Harris, "Almonte's Inspection of Texas in 1834," *SWHQ* 41 (January 1938): 195–211.

54. Anonymous letter in New Orleans *Commercial Bulletin,* written from Matagorda and dated February 17, 1834, quoted in AGN Transcripts, Fomento, vol. 304, CAH; Barker, *LSFA*, 395. SFA later learned that the government had this letter. Calling it a "silly letter from Matagorda written I suppose by some one who only wants ears to be a jack-ass," he believed it had "done great harm very great indeed." See SFA to James F. Perry, November 6, 1834, *AP*, III, 22–23.

55. "O. P. Q." to ?, February 8, 1834, in J. M. Winterbotham, ed., "Some Texas Correspondence," *Mississippi Valley Historical Review* 11 (June 1924–March 1925): 116 (first quotation); SFA to Samuel M. Williams, May 6, 1835, *AP*, III, 73 (second and third quotations); Harris, "Almonte's Inspection," 206–207; Barker, *LSFA*, 395. Scholars have uniformly agreed with this negative assessment of Butler's conduct while in Mexico. One historian describes him as "arrogant, vulgar, and calculating, a man completely lacking the qualities of a diplomat"; see Gene Brack, "Mexican Opinion and the Texas Revolution," *SWHQ* 72 (October 1968): 175.

56. SFA to James F. Perry, May 10, 1834, *AP*, II, 1053; Juan Nepomuceno Almonte to Secretary of Relations, May 20, July 22, August 7, 1834, AGN Transcripts, Fomento, vol. 318, CAH; Harris, "Almonte's Inspection," 206; Barker, *LSFA*, 398.

57. P. W. Grayson to James F. Perry, July 25, 1834, *AP*, II, 1066; M. A. Bryan to James F. Perry, August 7, 1834, ibid., 1072; Peter W. Grayson to Mirabeau B. Lamar, February 17, 1837, in "The Release of Stephen F. Austin from Prison," *SWHQ* 14 (October 1910): 158–59; Alessio Robles, *Coahuila y Texas,* 1: 478; Thomas W. Streeter, *Bibliography of Texas, 1795–1845,* 2nd ed. (Woodbridge, Conn.: Research Publications, 1983), 262.

Barker states that Grayson and Jack picked up a pro-SFA petition from the San Antonio ayuntamiento on their way through that town, but he cites only letters stating that the two men *expected* to obtain such a petition. Records of such a petition would certainly appear in the Béxar Archives, but none exist. Moreover, after the arrival of Grayson and Jack, SFA expressed disappointment that the "representations" they brought were "in the English language." He never makes any mention of one from San Antonio, although such a petition alone would have done more to secure his release than all those of the Anglo ayuntamientos combined. See SFA to Thomas F. McKinney, October 18, 1834, *AP,* III, 10–11.

58. Hammeken, "Recollections," 373–74.

59. SFA to Samuel M. Williams, October 6, 1834, *AP,* III, 7. He made similar comments in a letter to James F. Perry on the same date.

60. SFA to Thomas F. McKinney, October 18, 1834, *AP,* III, 10–13.

61. Ibid., 11 (first, second, and third quotations); SFA to James F. Perry, November 6, 1834, *AP,* III, 19 (fourth, fifth, and sixth quotations).

62. SFA to James F. Perry, November 6, 1834, *AP,* III, 18 (first quotation); SFA to Samuel M. Williams, December 31, 1834, ibid., 37 (second quotation).

63. SFA to Samuel M. Williams, December 31, 1834, *AP,* III, 36 (first quotation); Peter W. Grayson to Mirabeau B. Lamar, February 14, 1837, in "Release of Stephen F. Austin," 160 (second and third quotations).

64. W. S. Parrott to James F. Perry, December 24, 1834, *AP,* III, 35; SFA to Samuel M. Williams, December 31, 1834, ibid., 36; Peter W. Grayson to Mirabeau B. Lamar, February 14, 1837, in "Release of Stephen F. Austin," 161.

TWELVE
War Is Our Only Resource
1835

1. SFA in Account with Washington Hotel, December 27, 1834–April 2, 1835, *AP,* III, 89–90; Hammeken, "Recollections," 374–75 (first, second, and third quotations); SFA to James F. Perry, March 10, 1835, *AP,* III, 48 (fourth quotation).

2. SFA to James F. Perry, March 4, 1835, *AP,* III, 46.

3. Jodella D. Kite, "The War and Peace Parties of Pre-Revolutionary Texas, 1832–1835," *East Texas Historical Journal* 29 (1991): 11–24.

4. Samuel M. Williams to SFA, March 31, 1835, *AP,* III, 57; Asa Brigham to His Brother and Sister, March 8, 1835, Asa Brigham Papers, CAH (first quotation); George W. Smyth to B. W. Isbell, c. May 1835, Smyth Papers, CAH (second quotation). For a detailed discussion of the various population estimates as of 1835, see Kite, "Social History," 37–40.

5. Paul D. Lack, *The Texas Revolutionary Experience: A Political and Social History, 1835–1836* (College Station: Texas A&M University Press, 1992), 14–15.

6. Weber, *Mexican Frontier,* 247–48.

7. The replacement of liberal federalists at all levels of the national government continued through August; see Costeloe, *Central Republic,* 35–37.

8. Williams's coparticipants in the initial land purchase were John Durst, the representative from Nacogdoches, and James Grant, a Scotsman who represented the Coahuilan town of Parras in the legislature. The land was in northeast Texas, in an area that had once been part of the empresario grant of Gen. Arthur Wavell. The men involved in the second four-hundred-league transaction, which took place on May 11, were Williams and his fellow Texans, Frank Johnson and Robert Peebles. For a succinct but thorough account of the so-called Monclova Speculations and Williams's other activities in Monclova, see Henson, *Samuel May Williams,* 67–68.

9. SFA to Samuel M. Williams, April 15, 1835, *AP,* III, 62–63.

10. Ibid., 62 (first quotation); J. G. McNeel to James F. Perry, c. June 22, 1835, ibid., 77 (second quotation).

11. SFA, "Explanation to the Public," 232–58 (first quotation on p. 233; second quotation on p. 254; third quotation on p. 255); SFA to James F. Perry, February 6, 1835, *AP,* III, 42 (fourth quotation). The original version of the *Esposición,* in Spanish, was published in Mexico City in January 1835 by the publishing house of Cornelio C. Sebring. It was reprinted in facsimile along with Pablo Herrera Carrillo's *Las siete guerras por Texas* (Mexico: Editorial Academia Literaria, 1959).

12. SFA to James F. Perry, March 4, 1835, *AP,* III, 45.

13. On Santa Anna and his political maneuvers in 1834 and 1835, see Costeloe, *Central Reublic,* chaps. 2–3, esp. pp. 48–52.

14. SFA to James F. Perry, March 10, 1835, *AP,* III, 47.

15. SFA to Samuel M. Williams, April 15, 1835, *AP,* III, 63 (first, second, third, fourth, and fifth quotations); SFA to Samuel M. Williams, April 29, 1835, ibid., 68 (sixth and seventh quotations).

16. SFA to Samuel M. Williams, May 6, 1834, *AP,* III, 74.

17. SFA to James F. Perry, July 13, 1835, *AP,* III, 90–91.

18. SFA's Passport, *AP,* III, 88–89; Hammeken, "Recollections," 376.

19. The exact date of SFA's arrival in New Orleans is not known, but the *New Orleans Bee* of August 12, 1835, reported his presence in the city. Unless the voyage across the Gulf of Mexico took an unusual length of time, he would have been in New Orleans for at least a week by then.

20. The only Texans to answer Viesca's call were a group of one hundred Tejano militia from San Antonio under the command of Juan Seguín; see Tijerina, *Tejanos and Texas,* 135–36; Lack, *Texas Revolutionary Experience,* 21–22; Henson, *Samuel May Williams,* 73–74.

21. Lack, *Texas Revolutionary Experience,* 25–27.

22. SFA to Mary Austin Holley, August 21, 1835, *AP,* III, 101–3.

23. Ibid., 102–3.

24. SFA in Account with Hotchkiss & Co., August 19, 1835, *AP,* III, 101.

25. Williams's biographer Margaret Henson paints a very different picture of the meeting, stating specifically that Williams did not "keep secret his activities at Monclova"

and that in September 1835, SFA "defended both the individuals and the legislature."
However, the letters she cites do not support these claims. The three letters cited in
footnote 41, p. 78, are SFA to Williams, August 22, 1835, Williams Papers; SFA to D. C.
Barrret, n.d. [*sic*], quoted in Foote, *Texas and the Texans,* II, 155–57; and SFA to Gail
Borden, Jr., August [18], 1836, *AP,* III, 418–20. In none of these is there any evidence that
Williams told SFA of his central role in the Monclova Speculations; indeed, the absence
of any mention of the affair in SFA's August 22 letter to Williams suggests the opposite. (It
is worth remembering that Williams had already neglected to mention the speculations
to SFA in the one letter he wrote to SFA after the deal was done.) Nor did SFA really
"defend" the speculators and the legislators in the letter to Barrett (which, incidentally,
was dated December 3 in Foote's reprint). In that letter Austin *does* state that it was "not
my intention to cast any censure on the legislators of Coahuila, or on the individuals who
purchased" (p. 155), but later in the letter he does condemn the Speculations, describing
them as "ruinous" and deploring the fact that a "large portion of this country has thus
been thrown into the hands of speculators, and entangled by conflicting claims" (p. 157).
See Henson, *Samuel May Williams,* 77–78.

26. *New Orleans Bee,* September 16, 1835; *HT,* V, 839; VI, 475; Bryan, "Personal
Recollections," 1: 107–8 (quotations). There are some minor discrepancies in these four
accounts of the engagement, but they agree on most points.

27. Bryan, "Personal Recollections," 1: 108.

28. Campbell, *Sam Houston,* 48.

29. Bryan, "Personal Recollections," 1: 108.

30. Ibid.

31. Welcome to SFA, [September 8, 1835], *AP,* III, 115–16.

32. SFA to the People of Texas, September 8, 1835, *AP,* III, 116–19.

33. Henry Austin to Mary Austin Holley, September 10, 1835, *AP,* III, 120.

34. Bryan, "Personal Recollections," 1: 108; Henry Austin to Mary Austin Holley,
September 10, 1835, *AP,* III, 119–20.

35. F. W. Johnson to SFA, September 5, 1835, *AP,* III, 114; W. B. Travis to SFA,
September 22, 1835, ibid., 133.

36. SFA to James F. Perry, September 9, 1835, *AP,* 121; SFA to Columbia Committee, September 19, 1835, ibid., 128–29.

37. SFA to James F. Perry, September 30, 1835, *AP,* III, 140–41.

38. Ibid., 141.

39. Lorenzo de Zavala to SFA, September 17, 1835, *PTR,* I, 453–54 (quotations);
Lack, *Texas Revolutionary Experience,* 39–40 and passim; Margaret Swett Henson, "Tory
Sentiment in Anglo-Texan Public Opinion, 1832–1836," 1–34, esp. 19–20.

40. Stephen L. Hardin, *Texian Iliad: A Military History of the Texas Revolution,
1835–1836* (Austin: University of Texas Press, 1994), 7–14; Colonel Ugartechea to SFA,
October 4, 1835, *AP,* III, 155 (quotations).

41. P. W. Grayson et al. to SFA, October 6, 1835, *AP,* III, 161.

42. Bryan, "Personal Recollections," 1: 109.

43. Alwyn Barr, *Texans in Revolt: The Battle for San Antonio, 1835* (Austin: University of Texas Press, 1990), 5–6; *LSFA,* 415–16; William T. Austin, "Account of the Campaign of 1835 by William T. Austin, Aide to Gen. Stephen F. Austin and Gen. Edward Burleson," *Texana* 4 (Winter 1966): 294 (first quotation); Smithwick, *Evolution of a State,* 74 (second, third, fourth, fifth, and seventh quotations); Bryan, "Personal Recollections," 1: 109 (sixth quotation).

44. General Order No. 1, October 11, 1835, "General Austin's Order Book for the Campaign of 1835," *SWHQ* 11 (July 1907): 1–2.

45. Smithwick, *Evolution of a State,* 75 (quotations); Barr, *Texans in Revolt,* 7–8; Hardin, *Texian Iliad,* 26–27.

46. Barr, *Texans in Revolt,* 16–17; Hardin, *Texian Iliad,* 29.

47. Quoted in Barr, *Texans in Revolt,* 17.

48. Ibid., 18; de la Teja, *Revolution Remembered,* 24–25; Lack, *Texas Revolutionary Experience,* 184–85.

49. Barr, *Texans in Revolt,* 18–20; Hardin, *Texian Iliad,* 28–29; Smithwick, *Evolution of a State,* 76 (quotation).

50. The major biographies of Houston are Marquis James, *The Raven: A Biography of Sam Houston* (New York: Blue Ribbon Books, 1928); Llerena B. Friend, *Sam Houston: The Great Designer* (Austin: University of Texas, 1954); M. K. Wisehart, *Sam Houston, American Giant* (Washington: Robert B. Luce, 1962); Donald Braider, *Solitary Star: A Biography of Sam Houston* (New York: G. P. Putnam's Sons, 1974); Clifford Hopewell, *Sam Houston: Man of Destiny* (Austin: Eakin Press, 1987); Madge Thornall Roberts, *Star of Destiny: The Private Lives of Sam and Margaret Houston* (Denton: University of North Texas Press, 1992); Campbell, *Sam Houston;* Marshall De Bruhl, *Sword of San Jacinto: A Life of Sam Houston* (New York: Random House, 1993); John Hoyt Williams, *Sam Houston: A Biography of the Father of Texas* (New York: Simon and Schuster, 1993).

51. See esp. Campbell, *Sam Houston.*

52. Barr, *Texans in Revolt,* 20–21; Moses Austin Bryan to James F. Perry, October 26, 1835, *PTR,* II, 222.

53. Moses Austin Bryan to James F. Perry, October 26, 1835, *PTR,* II, 223; SFA to James Bowie, October 27, 1835, "General Austin's Order Book," 32.

54. The account of the Battle of Concepción presented in this and the following three paragraphs is compiled from Hardin, *Texian Iliad,* 29–35; and Barr, *Texans in Revolt,* 22–26.

55. SFA to President of Consultation, November 5, 1835, *PTR,* II, 322.

56. Election returns in the Brazoria *Texas Republican,* September 26, 1835, indicate that William H. Wharton, Henry Smith, and Branch T. Archer, all War Party men, received 58, 63, and 63 votes, respectively, while James F. Perry received only 4 votes. Also see Lack, *Texas Revolutionary Experience,* 43–47.

57. SFA to Provisional Government, December 14, 1835, *AP,* III, 282–83. In a December 2 letter to the provisional government, SFA had expressed concern that the November declaration was not "clear and positive" enough in declaring Texas's loyalty to

the Mexican federation, but this was a criticism more of its wording than of the "political position" it established for Texas; see SFA to Provisional Government, December 2, 1835, ibid., 274.

58. Lack, *Texas Revolutionary Experience,* 50–51.

59. Ibid., 51–52.

60. *HT,* V, 1099. Paul Lack writes that Smith had "spendid credentials for bigotry"; see Lack, *Texas Revolutionary Experience,* xxiv.

61. Hardin, *Texian Iliad,* 57–58, 62–63.

62. Anson Jones, *Memoranda and Official Correspondence Relating to the Republic of Texas, Its History and Annexation* (New York: D. Appleton, 1859), 13; Hardin, *Texian Iliad,* 62–63; Barr, *Texans in Revolt,* 36.

63. SFA to the President of the Consultation, November 8, 1835, *AP,* III, 247.

64. William T. Austin, "Account of the Campaign of 1835," 317.

65. M. A. Bryan to James F. Perry, November 30, 1835, *AP,* III, 268; Bryan, "Personal Recollections," 2: 166; Barr, *Texans in Revolt,* 36–37; Hardin, *Texian Iliad,* 62.

66. Hardin, *Texian Iliad,* chap. 5; clipping from unidentified Kentucky newspaper dated October 22, 1835, in SFA Scrapbook, part 1, CAH (quotations). For a similar assessment of SFA's overall record as commander, see Barr, *Texans in Revolt,* 61–62.

67. Bryan, "Personal Recollections," 2: 166.

THIRTEEN
The Road to Independence
1835–1836

1. *HT,* VI, 908–9; Reichstein, *Rise of the Lone Star,* 63–64; Barr, *Texans in Revolt,* 36. The story of the Wharton-Austin competition for the affections of Sarah Ann Groce can be found in a typescript entitled "The Whartons of Old Brazoria," p. 24, in the James Perry Bryan Papers, CAH. No author is listed, but the writer says the following: "Beauregard Bryan, related to Austin and splendidly informed in the lore of those days, once told me that Stephen F. Austin had been a suitor for the hand of beautiful Sarah Ann Groce and that Wharton's successful rivalry had helped estrange them." Bryan was a grandnephew of SFA and never knew the empresario personally, so the story can be credited only as family lore, and obscure lore at that.

2. William H. Wharton to Branch T. Archer, *AP,* III, 266.

3. SFA to Provisional Government, December 2, 1835, *AP,* III, 273 (quotations); M. A. Bryan to James F. Perry, ibid., November 30, 1835.

4. SFA to D. C. Barrett, December 3, 1835, *AP,* III, 279 (quotation); Ralph W. Steen, "Analysis of the Work of the General Council of Texas, 1835–1836," *SWHQ* 15 (April 1937): 323–24.

5. SFA to James F. Perry, December 25, 1835, *AP,* III, 294–95.

6. Ibid., 293.

7. Ibid.

8. Ibid., 293–94.

9. Steen, "Analysis of the Work of the General Council," 322; Commission of SFA, Archer, and Wharton, December 7, 1835, in George P. Garrison, ed., *Diplomatic Correspondence of the Republic of Texas,* 3 vols., published as *Annual Report of the American Historical Association* (Washington, D.C.: Government Printing Office, 1908, 1911), 1: 51–52; Henry Smith to SFA, Archer, and Wharton, December 8, 1835, ibid., 52–54.

10. *New Orleans Bee,* January 7, 1836.

11. SFA to Henry Austin, January 8, 1836, *AP,* III, 297–98; SFA to Sam Houston, January 8, 1836, ibid., 298.

12. SFA to Mary Austin Holley, January 7, 1836, *AP,* III, 300–301.

13. SFA to Henry Austin, January 8, 1836, *AP,* III, 297.

14. His point was valid. The Monclova legislature sold Texas lands at about a penny an acre compared with the fifty cents obtained by the commissioners in the United States. SFA made this point in his January 21 letter to McKinney, seemingly unaware that McKinney had been involved, via Williams, in the Monclova Speculations. This further supports the theory that SFA had not been told the full story of the Speculations before his trip to the United States; see SFA to Thomas F. McKinney, January 21, 1836, *AP,* III, 309.

15. SFA to Thomas F. McKinney, January 16, 21, 1836, *AP,* III, 305, 308.

16. SFA to Thomas F. McKinney, January 16, 1836, *AP,* III, 305.

17. Thomas F. McKinney to SFA, December 17, 1835, *AP,* III, 286.

18. Thomas F. McKinney to SFA, February 22, 1836, *AP,* III, 317.

19. SFA to James F. Perry, December 25, 1835, *AP,* III, 294–95; SFA to Thomas F. McKinney, January 21, 1836, ibid., 309.

20. SFA to Henry Austin, February 14, 1836, *AP,* III, 314.

21. Lack, *Texas Revolutionary Experience,* 58–60; Henry Smith to Council, January 9, 1836, *PTR,* III, 459.

22. Sarah A. Wharton to Henry Smith, March 26, 1836, John Henry Brown Papers, CAH.

23. SFA to James F. Perry, March 4, 1836, *AP,* III, 317; SFA and Archer to the Governor of Texas, March 3, 1836, in Garrison, *Diplomatic Correspondence,* 1: 72–73 (quotations).

24. The full text of the Louisville address can be found in Mary Austin Holley, *Texas* (1836; reprint ed., Austin: Texas State Historical Association, 1990), 253–80. All quotations in this and the following two paragraphs are from Holley's edition. Also see Rebecca Smith Lee, "The Publication of Austin's Louisville Address," *SWHQ* 70 (January 1967): 424–42.

25. Henson, *Samuel May Williams,* 83–84.

26. Lee, *Mary Austin Holley,* 269.

27. This description is based on the portrait of SFA painted late in his life — probably in New Orleans during one of his three visits there in 1835 and 1836 — and passed down through the Henry Austin family. See p. 342.

28. Lee, *Mary Austin Holley,* 269–70; Mary Austin Holley to SFA, June 1, 1836, *AP,* III, 362; SFA to David G. Burnet, March 4, 1836, in Jacqueline Beretta Tomerlin,

comp., *Fugitive Letters, 1829–1836: Stephen F. Austin to David G. Burnet* (San Antonio: Trinity University Press, 1981), 39–41. Also see George P. Garrison, "Another Texas Flag," *Quarterly of the Texas State Historical Association* 3 (January 1900): 170–76.

29. Lee, *Mary Austin Holley,* 270–71.

30. See SFA to [David G. Burnet?], April [actually May] 3, 1836, *AP,* III, 341–42. Also see SFA, Archer, and Wharton to the Government of Texas, April 6, 1836, in Garrison, *Diplomatic Correspondence,* I, 79–80; Wharton to the Governor of Texas, April 9, 1836, ibid., 81–82.

31. *LSFA,* 428; Barker, "Finances of the Texas Revolution," 633; SFA to Nicholas Biddle, April 9, 1836; *AP,* III, 328–30; *New York Evening Star,* April 27, 1836; *New York Herald,* April 28, 1836; *New York American,* April 10, 1836; SFA to Senator L. F. Linn, May 4, 1836, *AP,* III, 344–48. The letter to Linn was also published in the *St. Louis Commercial Bulletin,* June 3, 1836, and the *Baltimore Republican and Commercial Advertiser,* May 10, 1836, and probably in many other major U.S. papers.

32. SFA to Senator L. F. Linn, May 4, 1836, *AP,* III, 344–48.

33. *HT,* VI, 165–66; *New York Herald,* April 30, 1836 (quotations). For more of the partisan debate over Texas, see *New York Herald,* April 28, 1836; *New York American,* April 28, 1836. For a good account of the April 26 public meeting, see *New York Evening Star,* April 27, 1836.

34. SFA to William Bryan, April 24, 1836, *AP,* III, 340 (first and second quotations); SFA to Mary Austin Holley, May 29, 1836, Collections of the Dallas Historical Society; *Baltimore Republican,* May 26, 1836.

35. SFA to Mary Austin Holley, May 29, 1836, Collections of the Dallas Historical Society.

36. SFA to James F. Perry, March 4, 1836, *AP,* III, 318.

37. SFA to David G. Burnet, June 10, 1836, in Garrison, *Diplomatic Correspondence,* I, 98–99; SFA to George C. Childress, William H. Wharton, and Robert Hamilton, June 11, 1836, Austin (Stephen F.) Collection, CAH.

FOURTEEN
Home
1836

1. SFA to M. B. Lamar, June 27, 1836, *AP,* III, 372–73.

2. For SFA's plan, see SFA to President Jackson, July 4, 1836, *AP,* III, 380–83; SFA to General Gaines, July 4, 1836, ibid., 384–85; SFA to M. B. Lamar, July 8, 1836, ibid., 389–90.

3. Margaret Swett Henson, "Politics and the Treatment of the Mexican Prisoners after the Battle of San Jacinto," *SWHQ* 94 (October 1990): 202; Gabriel Nuñez Ortega, "Diario de un prisonero de la guerra de Texas," *Boletín del Archivo General de la Nación* 4 (November–December 1933): 855–57; Antonio López de Santa Anna to Andrew Jackson, July 4, 1836, in Garrson, *Diplomatic Correspondence,* 1: 106–7. Moses Austin Bryan

gives a rather romanticized version of the meeting between SFA and Santa Anna; see Bryan, "Personal Recollections," 2: 169.

4. SFA to General Gaines, July 4, 1836, *AP,* III, 385; Henry Millard to Thomas B. Huling, August 21, 1836, *PTR,* VIII, 282; Henson, "Politics and the Treatment of Mexican Prisoners," 204.

5. Memorandum by SFA, July 20, 1836, *AP,* III, 399 (quotation); SFA, Archer, and Wharton to Burnet, July 21, 1836, ibid., 399–401; SFA, Archer, and Wharton to Burnet, July 21, in Garrison, *Diplomatic Correspondence,* I, 111–12. Hardeman had served as secretary of the treasury and secretary of state in the provisional government, and Fisher would serve as secretary of the navy in Sam Houston's first administration; see *HT,* III, 448–49, and II, 1012.

6. SFA to the Editor of the Telegraph, August 4, 1836, *AP,* III, 411–12. The letter appeared in the the August 9 issue of Gail Borden's *Telegraph and Texas Register,* published at Columbia. That issue also listed Henry Smith and Branch T. Archer as presidential candidates. The August 16 issue listed only Austin and Smith as candidates and carried a letter from Archer saying that his name had been put forward without his knowledge or consent. "My name is withdrawn under the full conviction that General S. F. Austin has higher, and indeed much better claims to that station than myself," Archer wrote. "Fifteen years of the prime of his life have been devoted to this country. He has nursed and raised it from infancy to nearly mature age, and I will not claim his offspring in its maturity."

7. SFA to Thomas J. Rusk, August 9, 1836, *AP,* III, 413.

8. Ibid., 413–14.

9. SFA to W. S. Archer, August 15, 1836, *AP,* III, 416.

10. Henry Millard to Thomas B. Huling, August 2, 1836, *PTR,* VIII, 104–5 (quotations). Also see Millard to Huling, August 21, 1836, ibid., 282, in which Millard refers to "the cabinet and Austin faction," and the similar letter from Millard to Huling, August 23, 1836, ibid., 300–301.

11. SFA to Gail Borden, Jr., August 15, 1836, *AP,* III, 418–21. The letter was printed both as a handbill and in the August 23 issue of the *Telegraph and Texas Register.*

12. SFA to W. S. Archer, August 15, 1836, *AP,* III, 416.

13. *Telegraph and Texas Register,* August 23, August 30 (quotation), 1836.

14. Sam Houston to Guy M. Bryan, November 15, 1852, in Amelia W. Williams and Eugene C. Barker, eds., *Writings of Sam Houston* (Austin: University of Texas Press, 1941), 5: 368; Emily M. Perry to Mary Austin Holley, April 25, 1844, Austin Papers, Series II, CAH; Lee, *Mary Austin Holley,* 335. In his letter to Bryan, Houston referred to the two "parties" as the "Austin Party" and the "Wharton Party," which were not uncommon designations for the two pre-Revolutionary factions, but of course William H. Wharton himself was supporting SFA in the election. Nonetheless, Houston's description of the two factions is basically accurate. The Houston-SFA relationship receives a thorough examination in Ann H. Froelich, "The Relationship of Stephen F. Austin and Sam Houston," M.A. thesis, Sam Houston State University, 1971.

15. SFA to James F. Perry, September 2, 1836, *AP,* III, 428.

16. James Morgan to Samuel Swartwout, September 5, 1836, quoted in Stanley

Siegel, *The Political History of the Texas Republic, 1836-1845* (Austin: University of Texas Press, 1956), 55; Edmund Andrews to SFA, September 8, 1836, *AP,* III, 430.

17. SFA to James F. Perry, September 2, 1836, *AP,* III, 428; SFA to James F. Perry, [October] 25, 1836, ibid., 438.

18. SFA to Mary Austin Holley, December 29, 1831, *AP,* II, 729.

19. Gail Borden, Jr., to SFA, September 19, 1836, *AP,* III, 431; SFA to Samuel M. Williams, October 12, 1836, ibid., 435 (quotations); SFA to S. H. Everett, October 22, 1836, ibid., 437; SFA to Joseph Ficklin, October 30, 1836, ibid., 441; SFA to James F. Perry, September 2, 1836, ibid., 428. The inventory of SFA's estate made after his death listed 709 claims against others, totaling $54,263.96. Most of these are for $30, $40, and $50, almost certainly surveying fees and other land fees owed by settlers; see Brazoria County Wills, Book A, Brazoria County Courthouse, Angleton, Texas.

20. SFA to James F. Perry, [October] 25, 1836, *AP,* III, 438.

21. Samuel M. Williams to SFA, August 29, 1836, *AP,* III, 424-25.

22. SFA to Samuel M. Williams, October 12, 1836, *AP,* III, 435-36.

23. SFA to Samuel M. Williams, November 3, 1836, *AP,* III, 446-47.

24. SFA to James F. Perry, [October] 25, 1836, *AP,* III, 439 (first and second quotations); SFA to Joseph Ficklin, October 30, 1836, ibid., 442 (third quotation).

25. Sam Houston to Guy Bryan, November 15, 1852, in Williams and Barker, *Writings of Sam Houston,* 5: 368 (first quotation); Sam Houston to Guy Bryan, November 1, 1853, ibid., 461; SFA to Sam Houston, October 31, 1836, *AP,* III, 444 (second quotation).

26. SFA to Henry Meigs, November 7, 1836, *AP,* III, 449.

27. SFA to William H. Wharton, November 18, 1836, in Garrison, ed., *Diplomatic Correspondence,* 1: 127-35 (general instructions) and 135-40 (private and special instructions); *LSFA,* 443-45; Henson, "Politics and the Treatment of the Mexico Prisoners," 215-16.

28. SFA to Joseph Ficklin, October 30, 1836, *AP,* III, 443.

29. SFA to Henry Austin, June 27, 1836, *AP,* III, 371 (first quotation); SFA to James F. Perry, December 2, ibid., 465 (second and third quotations); SFA to James F. Perry, November 11, ibid., 453.

30. *HT,* IV, 422; Bryan, "Personal Recollections," 2: 171 (quotation).

31. The preceding account of SFA's death is compiled from two sources: Bryan, "Personal Recollections," 2: 171-72; and Hammeken, "Recollections," 378-80. Both men were present during SFA's final days and at his bedside at the moment of his death. The quotation of SFA's last words is from Bryan (p. 172). Hammeken's version of the last words was: "Texas recognized. Archer told me so. Did you see in in the Papers?" I have used Bryan's version because Hammeken admitted that his version might not have been "exactly in these words yet the import most certainly was."

EPILOGUE
The Father of Texas: Stephen F. Austin in Retrospect

1. General Orders Concerning Austin's Death, December 27, 1836, Williams and Barker, *Writings of Sam Houston,* II, 28–29.

2. Funeral Announcement, Stephen F. Austin Collection, Special Collections, University of Houston.

3. Bryan, "Personal Recollections," 2: 172.

4. Michael Muldoon, "Texas: *Arma Virumque Cano*" [I sing of arms and men], Streeter Collection of Texas Manuscripts, Beinecke Rare Book and Manuscript Library, Yale University.

5. Thomas F. Leaming to James F. Perry, March 18, 1837, Leaming Papers, CAH.

6. Emily M. Perry to Mary Austin Holley, April 25, 1844, Austin Papers, Series II, CAH.

7. Mirabeau B. Lamar to Gail Borden, January 20, 1837, *AP,* III, 483.

8. Emily M. Perry to Mary Austin Holley, undated [probably 1844], Austin Papers, Series II, CAH.

9. Mary Austin Holley to Emily Perry, March 23, 1844, Austin Papers, Series II, CAH; Emily M. Perry to Mary Austin Holley, undated [probably 1844], ibid.; Emily M. Perry to Mary Austin Holley, April 25, 1844, ibid.

10. Mary Austin Holley to Emily Perry, March 23, 1844, Austin Papers, Series II, CAH; Mary Austin Holley, "Life of Stephen F. Austin," chap. 1, pp. 1–2, mss. in Mary Austin Holley Papers, CAH; Lee, *Mary Austin Holley,* 335.

11. Emily M. Perry to Mary Austin Holley, April 25, 1844, Austin Papers, Series II, CAH; Lee, *Mary Austin Holley,* 335. In 1852 Guy Bryan wrote Houston in Washington, D.C., to ask if the rumors of Houston's animosity toward Austin were true. Houston replied in a long, cordial letter that the rumors were untrue. Houston's answer failed to satisfy Bryan, who responded with a rather accusatory letter. Houston, somewhat irritated, replied with another long letter that closed by calling for an end to their correspondence. See Guy M. Bryan to Sam Houston, March 11 and April 21, 1852, Sam Houston Hearne Papers, CAH; Sam Houston to Guy M. Bryan, November 15, 1852, and November 1, 1853, in Williams and Barker, *Writings of Sam Houston,* 5: 364–69, 459–63.

12. Emily M. Perry to Mary Austin Holley, April 25, 1844, Austin Papers, Series II, CAH.

13. Henderson Yoakum, *History of Texas, From Its First Settlement in 1685 to Its Annexation to the United States in 1846,* 2 vols. (New York: Redfield, 1855), 2: 202–3.

14. Jacob De Cordova, *Texas: Her Resources and Her Public Men* (Philadelphia: E. Crozet, 1858), 127–87.

15. Wooten, *Comprehensive History,* vol. 1, chaps. 2–7. Bryan's sketch can be found in the Austin Scrapbook, part 2, CAH. He also contributed a similar piece to the *Encyclopedia of the New West* the following year.

16. Bryan, "Personal Recollections," 2: 172–73.

17. Richard Coke to Guy M. Bryan, July 22, 1875, Guy M. Bryan Papers, CAH. This

portrait later burned, and when the new capitol was built in the 1880s the Bryans donated a new portrait of Austin based on the 1833 William Howard minature; see "Extract from the Journal of the House of Representatives, Relating to the Presentation to the State of Texas of the Portrait of Stephen F. Austin," Twenty-first Legislature [1889], CAH.

18. Sam DeShong Ratcliffe, *Painting Texas History to 1900* (Austin: University of Texas Press, 1992), xx, 14–15, 103. Also see "The Settlement of Austin's Colony" and accompanying correspondence, typescripts in Guy M. Bryan Papers, CAH.

19. Victor M. Rose, *Stephen F. Austin in the Balances* (n.p., c. 1890).

20. Rose's father, John Washington Rose, served in the state legislature and the secession convention with Guy Bryan, and it is possible that the men were political enemies, although they both were pro-secession Democrats. It seems unlikely that either Victor or John Rose could have had a personal grudge against Stephen F. Austin himself, because the Rose family did not move to Texas until after Austin's death. No connection between the Roses and Henry Smith can be verified. Further research may still discover the cause of Victor Rose's extraordinary hatred of the Austins. See *HT*, V, 677, 678–79.

21. John Henry Brown, *History of Texas, 1820–1895*, 2 vols. (St. Louis: L. E. Daniell, 1892), 114–17; and *A Condensed History of Texas for Schools* (Dallas, 1895), 170. Eugene C. Barker provided a biting commentary on Brown's handling of the Robertson Colony controversy in chap. 11, footnote 66, of *LSFA*. "It would be a pleasure to abbreviate this controversy," Barker wrote, "but Brown [*History of Texas*, 1: 312–40] has published Robertson's side of it so fully, with gratuitous interpolations and distortions, that a detailed analysis of the case is unavoidable." Barker must have felt very strongly about Brown's work to depart from his usual dispassionate tone.

22. Emily Fourmy Cutrer, *The Art of the Woman: The Life and Work of Elisabet Ney* (Lincoln: University of Nebraska Press, 1988), 123–27, 132–42, 192–96. The quotation is from a letter to Rebecca Fisher, July 18, 1900 (p. 139).

23. "The Stephen F. Austin Statue Fund," *Quarterly of the Texas State Historical Association* 5 (July 1901): 68–69.

24. Alexander W. Terrell, "Stephen F. Austin: A Memorial Address," *Quarterly of the Texas State Historical Association* 14 (January 1911): 182–97.

25. George P. Garrison to Guy M. Bryan, December 22, 1896, Guy M. Bryan Papers, CAH.

26. Herbert L. Osgood to Lester G. Bugbee, March 5, 1901, Lester G. Bugbee Papers, CAH (first quotation); Eugene C. Barker to Lester G. Bugbee, February 2, 1902, ibid.

27. For example, see Henson, *Samuel May Williams;* Reichstein, *Rise of the Lone Star;* McLean, *PCRCT.*

28. SFA to Mary Austin Holley, July 19, 1831, *AP*, II, 676.

29. SFA to Mary Austin Holley, January 4, 1832, *AP*, II, 733.

+ An Essay on Sources +

Listed here are the most important sources used in the writing of this book. For a list of all sources consulted, see the notes.

Primary Sources

A significant proportion of the relevant primary source documents concerning Stephen F. Austin's life are available in printed form. The indispensable source is Eugene C. Barker, ed., *The Austin Papers* (see p. 385 for full citation). In the early 1920s, Barker persuaded the American Historical Association to publish the papers as its *Annual Report*. Compiled by Barker from the papers of Moses and Stephen Austin and from numerous other sources, the first volume was published in two parts and ran 1,824 pages. When the second volume required 1,185 pages but brought the story up to only 1834, the AHA pulled the plug on Barker's project. He then took his case to his employer, the University of Texas. The university agreed to publish a slimmed-down third volume, which brought the project to a conclusion. Barker not only published the papers donated to the University of Texas by Austin's family, but he also brought together a range of letters and documents from such collections as the Samuel May Williams Papers at the Rosenberg Library in Galveston, the Archivo General de la Nación (AGN) in Mexico City, the Saltillo Archives, the Béxar Archives, the Nacogdoches Archives, and the General Land Office in Austin.

Other published correspondence pertaining to Austin includes the following:

Clarence Edwin Carter, ed., *The Territorial Papers of the United States,* 17 vols. (Washington, D.C.: Government Printing Office, 1934-).

George P. Garrison, ed., *Diplomatic Correspondence of the Republic of Texas,* 2 vols. (Washington: Government Printing Office, 1908, 1911).

Charles Adams Gulick, Jr., and Katherine Elliott, eds., *The Papers of Mirabeau Buonaparte Lamar,* 6 vols. (Austin: Von Boeckmann-Jones, 1921-27).

John H. Jenkins, ed., *The Papers of the Texas Revolution, 1835-1836,* 10 vols. (Austin: Presidial Press, 1973).

Anson Jones, *Memoranda and Official Correspondence Relating to the Republic of Texas, Its History and Annexation* (New York: D. Appleton, 1859).

Malcolm D. McLean, comp. and ed., *Papers Concerning Robertson's Colony in Texas,* 3 vols. (Fort Worth: Texas Christian University, 1974-76); 15 vols. plus intro. vol. (Arlington: UTA Press, 1977-93).

Maria Grace Ramirez, ed., "Stephen F. Austin Letters," *East Texas Historical Journal* 6 (October 1968): 147-48.

Andreas Reichstein, ed., "The Austin-Leaming Correspondence, 1828-1836," *SWHQ* 88 (January 1985): 247-82.

Jacqueline Beretta Tomerlin, comp., *Fugitive Letters, 1829-1836: Stephen F. Austin to David G. Burnet* (San Antonio: Trinity University Press, 1981).

Amelia W. Williams and Eugene C. Barker, eds., *Writings of Sam Houston,* 8 vols. (Austin: University of Texas Press, 1941).

J. M. Winterbotham, ed., "Some Texas Correspondence," *Mississippi Valley Historical Review* 11 (June 1924-March 1925): 99-127.

Several important documents written by Moses and Stephen Austin themselves have appeared in print, including the following:

"Explanation to the Public Concerning the Affairs of Texas," trans. Ethel Zivley Rather, *Quarterly of the Texas State Historical Association* 8 (January 1905): 232-58.

"General Austin's Order Book for the Campaign of 1835," *SWHQ* 11 (July 1907): 1-55.

"Journal of Stephen F. Austin on His First Trip to Texas, 1821," *Quarterly of the Texas State Historical Association* 7 (April 1904): 286–307.

Translation of the Laws, Orders, And Contracts of Colonization, From January, 1821, Up To This Time, In Virtue Of Which Col. Stephen F. Austin Has Introduced And Settled Foreign Emigrants In Texas, With An Explanatory Introduction., published as David B. Gracy II, ed., *Establishing Austin's Colony* (San Felipe de Austin: Godwin B. Cotten, 1829; reprint ed., Austin: Pemberton Press, 1970).

George P. Garrison, ed., "A Memorandum of M. Austin's Journey from the Lead Mines in the County of Wythe in the State of Virginia to the Lead Mines in the Province of Louisiana West of the Mississippi, 1796–1797," *American Historical Review* 5 (April 1900): 518–42.

Leo M. Kaiser, ed., "Stephen F. Austin's Oration of July 4, 1818," *SWHQ* 64 (July 1960): 71–79.

Villamae Williams, ed., *Stephen F. Austin's Register of Families,* typescript from the originals in the Texas General Land Office, 1984.

W. B. Zuber, ed., "The 'Prison Journal' of Stephen F. Austin," *Quarterly of the Texas State Historical Association* 2 (January 1899): 183–210.

Published diaries, memoirs and other contemporary accounts include the following:

William T. Austin, "Account of the Campaign of 1835 by William T. Austin, Aide to Gen. Stephen F. Austin and Gen. Edward Burleson," *Texana* 4 (Winter 1966): 287–322.

Jean Louis Berlandier, *Journey to Mexico During the Years 1826 to 1834,* 2 vols. (Austin: Texas State Historical Association, 1990).

H. M. Brackenridge, *Recollections of Persons and Places in the West* (Philadelphia: James Kay, Jun. and Brother, [1834]).

Moses Austin Bryan, "Personal Recollections of Stephen F. Austin," *Texas Magazine* 3 (September and November 1897): 101–9, 161–73.

Carlos María Bustamante, *Diario histórico de México, diciembre 1822–junio 1823* (Mexico City: Instituto Nacional de Antropología e Historia, 1980).

J. C. Clopper, "J. C. Clopper's Journal and Book of Memoranda for 1828,"

Quarterly of the Texas State Historical Association 13 (July 1909): 44–80.

W. B. Dewees, *Letters from an Early American Settler of Texas* (Louisville: Morton & Griswold, 1852; reprint ed., Waco: Texian Press, 1968).

Vicente Filisola, *Memorias para la Historia de la Guerra de Tejas,* 2 vols. (Mexico City: R. Rafael, 1849).

Nicolas de Finiels, *An Account of Upper Louisiana,* ed. Carl J. Ekberg and William E. Foley (Columbia: University of Missouri Press, 1989).

Henry Stuart Foote, *Texas and the Texans,* 2 vols. (Philadelphia: Thomas, Cowperthwait, 1841).

George L. Hammeken, "Recollections of Stephen F. Austin," *SWHQ* 20 (April 1917): 369–80.

C. Richard King, ed., *Victorian Lady on the Texas Frontier: The Journal of Ann Raney Coleman* (Norman: University of Oklahoma Press, 1971).

J. H. Kuykendall, "Reminiscences of Early Texans," *Quarterly of the Texas State Historical Association* 6 (part 1, January 1903; part 2, April 1903): 236–53, 311–30; vol. 7, part 3, July 1903: 29–64.

[W. S.] Lewis, "The Adventures of the 'Lively' Immigrants," *Quarterly of the Texas State Historical Association* 3 (part 1: July 1899; part 2: October 1899): 1–32, 81–107.

Benjamin Lundy, *The Life, Travels and Opinions of Benjamin Lundy* (Philadelphia: William D. Parrish, 1847).

Gabriel Nuñez Ortega, "Diario de un prisonero de la guerra de Texas," *Boletín del Archivo General de la Nación* 4 (November–December 1933): 833–81.

Joel Roberts Poinsett, *Notes on Mexico Made in the Autumn of 1822* (reprint ed., New York: Frederick A. Praeger, 1969).

José María Sánchez, "A Trip to Texas in 1828," trans. Carlos E. Cantañeda, *SWHQ* 29 (April 1926): 249–88.

Henry R. Schoolcraft, *Personal Memoirs of a Residence of Thirty Years with the Indian Tribes on the American Frontiers* (Philadelphia: Lippincott, Grambo, 1851).

Henry Smith, "Reminiscences of Henry Smith," *Quarterly of the Texas State Historical Association* 14 (July 1910): 24–73.

Noah Smithwick, *The Evolution of a State, or Recollections of Old Texas Days* (1900; reprint ed., Austin: University of Texas Press, 1983).

Edward Thornton Tayloe, *Mexico, 1825–1828: The Journal and Correspondence of Edward Thornton Tayloe,* ed. C. Harvey Gardiner (Chapel Hill: University of North Carolina Press, 1959).

Lorenzo de Zavala, *Ensayo histórico de las revoluciones de México* (Paris, 1831; reprint ed., Mexico City: Editorial Porrúa, 1969).

Laws and other miscellaneous published documents can be found in the following:

Eugene C. Barker, "Minutes of the Ayuntamiento of San Felipe de Austin, 1828–1832," *SWQH* 21–24 (published in 11 parts, January 1918–July 1920).

Manuel Dublán and José María Lozano, eds., *Legislación Mexicana,* 3 vols. (Mexico City: Imprenta de comercio á cargo de Dublán y Lozano, hijos, 1876).

H. P. N. Gammel, ed. and comp., *The Laws of Texas,* vol. 1 (Austin: Gammel Book Co., 1898).

John P. Kimball, comp., *Laws and Decrees of the State of Coahuila and Texas* (Houston: Secretary of State, 1839).

Ernest Wallace and David M. Vigness, eds., *Documents of Texas History* (Austin: Steck, 1963).

David J. Weber, ed., *Troubles in Texas, 1832: A Tejano Viewpoint from San Antonio with a Translation and Facsimile* (Dallas: Wind River Press for the DeGolyer Library of Southern Methodist University, 1983).

The size of the Austin Papers, the limitations imposed by publishers, and the acquisition of new papers from various sources left roughly a thousand Austin letters and documents that did not make it into Barker's published volumes. These additional letters can be found in manuscript or typescript form in the unpublished Austin Papers, CAH, arranged in several series.

The Center for American History at the University of Texas houses a number of other important manuscript collections, including the Austin Account Book, 1825–1843; the Stephen F. Austin Collection; the Asa Brigham Papers; the John Henry Brown Papers; the Guy M. Bryan Papers; the James Perry Bryan Papers; the Moses Austin Bryan Papers; the John P. Coles Papers; the Mary Austin Holley Papers; the Natchez Trace Collection; the Eberstadt Collection; the Sam Houston Hearne Papers; the Kuykendall Family Papers; the Thomas F. Leaming Papers; the James Franklin and Stephen Samuel Perry Papers; the George W. Smyth Papers; and the James Whiteside Letters. The Austin Scrapbooks, also at the CAH, contain a large collection of rare newspaper clippings and other materials compiled by the Bryan brothers and other Austin family members.

The Beinecke Rare Book and Manuscript Library at Yale University houses several valuable collections, including the Uncatalogued Austin Family Papers, the Streeter Collection of Texas Manuscripts, the Wagner Texas and Middle West Collection, and the Western Americana Collection. In the course of writing his biography of Moses Austin, David Gracy assembled many useful documents, which can be found in the Gracy Papers, Special Collections, Trinity University, San Antonio. Smaller numbers of manuscripts were found at the following archives (see the notes for citations to specific collections): Collections of the Dallas Historical Society; Special Collections, University of Houston; Special Collections, University of Texas at San Antonio; the Missouri Historical Society, St. Louis; the Missouri State Archives, Jefferson City; the Filson Club, Louisville; the Arkansas History Commission, Little Rock; and the Tulane University Library, New Orleans.

Many records of Austin's landholdings and estate are still housed in the Brazoria County Courthouse in Angleton, Texas. Others can be found in the Spanish Collection at the Texas General Land Office's Archives and Records Division.

Mexican archival records are vital to the study of Stephen F. Austin. Although years of research in the vast AGN in Mexico City and in other governmental archives of the Mexican capital would probably reveal additional documents, the great majority of AGN documents pertaining to Austin were transcribed by a number of scholars and are now housed in the Center for American History. The same is true for the legislative journals in the Archivo del Congreso del Estado de Coahuila (the state congressional library) and the Fondo de Instituto Estatal de Documentación, Archivo General del Estado de Coahuila (popularly known as the Saltillo Archives) in Saltillo, although firsthand research in these two repositories did yield some additional sources. Transcripts or microfilm of the Béxar and Nacogoches archives were available at the CAH. Barker, of course, included many of these documents in the published *Austin Papers.*

Austin's career is documented in a handful of Texas newspapers. The *Texas Gazette,* later renamed the *Mexican Citizen,* was published at San Felipe and served as Austin's mouthpiece, as did Gail Borden's *Telegraph and Texas Register,* published first at Columbia and then at Houston. In Brazoria the *Advocate of the People's Rights* and later the *Texas Republican* spoke for the Wharton brothers and their War Party allies. The *Gaceta del Goierno Supremo del Estado de Coahuila y Tejas* was the state government organ in Saltillo. Austin's movements can be followed in these U.S. newspapers: the *Kentucky Gazette* (Lexington); the *Louisiana Courier* (New Orleans); the *Louisiana Gazette and New-Orleans Daily Advertiser* (New Orleans); the *Nashville Whig;* the *Missouri Gazette* (St. Louis); the *New Orleans Bee;* the *New Orleans Courier;* the *New York American;* the *New York Evening Star;* the *New York Herald;* and the *St. Louis Commercial Bulletin.*

<hr>

Secondary Sources

Until the present work, Eugene C. Barker's *Life of Stephen F. Austin* (1925) was the only full-length, scholarly biography of the empresario. Barker's book remains a valuable resource, especially for political matters.

Moses Austin's career, and much of SFA's early life, is presented in the thoroughly researched *Moses Austin: His Life* (San Antonio: Trinity University Press, 1987), by David B. Gracy II. For background on Stephen F. Austin's years in Missouri, Connecticut, Kentucky, and Arkansas, see the following:

Hattie M. Anderson, "Frontier Economic Problems in Missouri, 1815–1828," *Missouri Historical Review* 34 (October 1939): 38–70.

Jean H. Baker, *Mary Todd Lincoln: A Biography* (New York: W. W. Norton, 1987).

Charles S. Bolton, *Territorial Ambition: Land and Society in Arkansas, 1800–1840* (Fayetteville: University of Arkansas Press, 1993).

Marie Cash, "Arkansas in Territorial Days," *Arkansas Historical Quarterly* 1 (March 1942): 228–34.

Aram Damarjian, "Bacon Academy History," in Bacon Academy *Alumni Beacon* (1953), pamphlet in Cragin Memorial Library, Colchester, Connecticut, 12–27.

Robert Sidney Douglass, *History of Southeast Missouri*, vol. 1 (Chicago: Lewis, 1912).

William E. Foley, *A History of Missouri*, vol. 1 (Columbia: University of Missouri Press, 1971).

Alec R. Gilpin, *The War of 1812 in the Old Northwest* (East Lansing: Michigan State University Press, 1958).

Kate L. Gregg, "The War of 1812 on the Missouri Frontier," part 2, *Missouri Historical Review* 33 (January 1939): 184–202.

William Thomas Hagan, *The Sac and Fox Indians* (Norman: University of Oklahoma Press, 1958).

Dallas T. Herndon, *Centennial History of Arkansas*, vol. 1 (Chicago: S. J. Clarke, 1922).

James Ripley Jacobs, *Tarnished Warrior: Major-General James Wilkinson* (New York: Macmillan, 1938).

Breckinridge Jones, "One Hundred Years of Banking in Missouri," *Missouri Historical Review* 15 (January 1921): 345–92.

Robert L. and Pauline H. Jones, "Stephen F. Austin in Arkansas," *Arkansas Historical Quarterly* 25 (Winter 1966): 336–53.

David D. March, *The History of Missouri*, vol. 1 (New York: Lewis, 1967).

Randall Parrish, *Historic Illinois: The Romance of Earlier Days* (Chicago: A. C. McClurg, 1905).

Ira Don Richards, *Story of a Rivertown: Little Rock in the Nineteenth Century* (n.p., 1969).

Willard H. Rollings, *The Osage: An Ethnohistorical Study of Hegemony on the Prairie-Plains* (Columbia: University of Missouri Press, 1992).

Niels Henry Sonne, *Liberal Kentucky, 1780–1828* (New York: Columbia University Press, 1939).

Rex W. Strickland, "Miller County, Arkansas Territory, the Frontier That Men Forgot," *Chronicles of Oklahoma* 18 (1940): 12–34.

Eugene Morrow Violette, *A History of Missouri* (Boston: D. C. Heath, 1918).

Richard C. Wade, *The Urban Frontier: Pioneer Life in Early Pittsburgh, Cincinnati, Lexington, Louisville, and St. Louis* (Cambridge: Harvard University Press, 1959; reprint ed., Chicago: University of Chicago Press, 1964).

C. A. Weslager, *The Delaware Indians* (New Brunswick, N.J.: Rutgers University Press, 1972).

Lonnie J. White, *Politics on the Southwestern Frontier: Arkansas Territory, 1819–1836* (Memphis: Memphis State University Press, 1964).

John D. Wright, Jr., *Transylvania: Tutor to the West,* rev. ed. (Lexington: University Press of Kentucky, 1980).

The secondary literature on Austin and the era of Anglo colonization in Texas is sizable. The most valuable reference tool is *The New Handbook of Texas,* 6 vols. (Austin: Texas State Historical Association, 1996). More specialized works include the following:

Robert W. Amsler, "General Arthur G. Wavell: A Soldier of Fortune in Texas," *SWHQ* 69 (part 1, July 1965; part 2, October 1965), 1–21, 186–209.

Edwin P. Arneson, "The Early Art of Terrestrial Measurement and Its Practice in Texas," *SWHQ* 29 (October 1925): 79–97.

Charles A. Bacarrisse, "Baron de Bastrop," *SWHQ* 58 (January 1955): 319–30.

Charles A. Bacarisse, "The Union of Coahuila and Texas," *SWHQ* 61 (January 1958): 341–49.

Charles A. Bacarisse, "Why Moses Austin Came to Texas," *Southwestern Social Science Quarterly* 40 (June 1959): 16–27.

Eugene C. Barker, "The Government of Austin's Colony, 1821–1831," *SWHQ* 21 (January 1918): 223–52.

Eugene C. Barker, "The Influence of Slavery in the Colonization of Texas," *SWHQ* 27 (July 1924): 1–33.

Rosa Groce Bertleth, "Jared Ellison Groce," *SWHQ* 20 (April 1917): 358–68.

Lester G. Bugbee, "What Became of the Lively?" *Quarterly of the Texas State Historical Association* 3 (October 1899): 141–48.

Lester G. Bugbee, "The Old Three Hundred," *Quarterly of the Texas State Historical Association* 1 (October 1897): 108–17.

Randolph B. Campbell, *An Empire for Slavery: The Peculiar Institution in Texas, 1821–1865* (Baton Rouge: Louisiana State University Press, 1989).

Gregg Cantrell, "The Partnership of Stephen F. Austin and Joseph H. Hawkins," *SWHQ* 99 (July 1995): 1–24.

James David Carter, *Masonry in Texas: Background, History, and Influence to 1846* (Waco, Texas: Committee on Masonic Education and Service for the Grand Lodge of Texas, A. F. and A. M., 1955).

Robin W. Doughty, *Wildlife and Man in Texas: Environmental Change and Conservation* (College Station: Texas A&M University Press, 1983).

Dianna Everett, *The Texas Cherokees: A People Between Two Fires* (Norman: University of Oklahoma Press, 1990).

Mary Angela Fitzmorris, *Four Decades of Catholicism in Texas, 1820–1860* (Washington, D.C.: Catholic University of America, 1926).

James Curtis Hasdorff, "Four Indian Tribes in Texas, 1758–1858: A Re-evaluation of Historical Sources," Ph.D. diss., University of New Mexico, 1971.

Mary Virginia Henderson, "Minor Empresario Contracts for the Colonization of Texas, 1825–1834," *SWHQ* 31 (April 1928).

Margaret Swett Henson, *Samuel May Williams: Early Texas Entrepreneur* (College Station: Texas A&M University Press, 1976).

William Ransom Hogan, "Henry Austin," *SWHQ* 37 (January 1934): 185–214.

William Ransom Hogan, "Rampant Individualism in the Republic of Texas," *SWHQ* 64 (April 1941): 454–80.

Alleine Howren, "Causes and Origin of the Decree of April 6, 1830," *SWHQ* 16 (April 1913): 378–422.

Ricki S. Janicek, "The Development of Early Mexican Land Policy: Coahuila and Texas, 1810–1825," Ph.D. diss., Tulane University, 1985.

Jodella D. Kite, "A Social History of the Anglo-American Colonies in Mexican Texas, 1821–1835," Ph.D. diss., Texas Tech University, 1990.

Bennett Lay, *The Lives of Ellis P. Bean* (Austin: University of Texas Press, 1960).

Rebecca Smith Lee, *Mary Austin Holley: A Biography* (Austin: University of Texas Press, 1962).

Bessie Lucille Letts, "George Fisher," M.A. thesis, University of Texas, 1928.

Joseph W. McKnight, "Stephen F. Austin's Legalistic Concerns," *SWHQ* 89 (January 1986): 239–68.

R. Woods Moore, "The Role of the Baron de Bastrop in the Anglo-American Settlement of the Spanish Southeast," M.A. thesis, University of Texas, 1932.

W. W. Newcomb, Jr., *The Indians of Texas: From Prehistoric to Modern Times* (Austin: University of Texas Press, 1961).

Alfonso Ortiz, ed., *Handbook of North American Indians.* vol. 10: *Southwest* (Washington, D.C.: Smithsonian Institution Press, 1983).

Edmund Morris Parsons, "The Fredonian Rebellion," *Texana* 5 (Spring 1967): 11–52.

Andreas V. Reichstein, *Rise of the Lone Star: The Making of Texas* (College Station: Texas A&M University Press, 1989).

Robert A. Ricklis, *The Karankawa Indians of Texas: An Ecological Study of Cultural Tradition and Change* (Austin: University of Texas Press, 1996).

Craig H. Roell, *Remember Goliad!: A History of La Bahía* (Austin: Texas State Historical Association, 1994).

L. Randall Rogers, *Two Particular Friends of Stephen F. Austin* (Waco: Texian Press, 1990).

Harold Schoen, "The Free Negro in the Republic of Texas," *SWHQ* 39 (April 1936): 292–301.

Marilyn McAdams Sibley, *Lone Stars and State Gazettes: Texas Newspapers Before the Civil War* (College Station: Texas A&M University Press, 1983).

Sam A. Suhler, "Stephen F. Austin and the City of Austin: An Anomaly," *SWHQ* 69 (January 1966): 266–86.

A number of works in English and Spanish help to provide the Mexican context to Austin's life and times. The most useful of these follow:

Timothy E. Anna, *The Mexican Empire of Iturbide* (Lincoln: University of Nebraska Press, 1990).

Michael P. Costeloe, *The Central Republic in Mexico, 1835–1846: Hombres de Bien in the Age of Santa Anna* (Cambridge: Cambridge University Press, 1993).

Michael P. Costeloe, *La Primera República Federal de México (1824–1835)* (Mexico City: Fondo de Cultura Económica, 1975).

Stanley C. Green, *The Mexican Republic: The First Decade, 1823–1832* (Pittsburgh: University of Pittsburgh Press, 1987).

Michael C. Meyer and William L. Sherman, *The Course of Mexican History,* 5th ed. (New York: Oxford University Press, 1987).

Jaime E. Rodríguez O., ed., *The Evolution of the Mexican Political System* (Wilmington, Del.: Scholarly Resources, 1993).

Jaime E. Rodríguez O., ed., *The Independence of Mexico and the Creation of the New Nation* (Los Angeles: UCLA Latin American Center Publications, 1989).

Jaime E. Rodríguez O., ed., *Patterns of Contention in Mexican History* (Wilmington, Del.: Scholarly Resources, 1993).

Josefina Zoraida Vázquez, *De la rebelión de Texas a la Guerra del 47* (Mexico City: Nueva Imagen, 1994).

More specialized, but also useful, are the following:

Timothy Anna, *The Fall of the Royal Government in Mexico City* (Lincoln: University of Nebraska Press, 1978).

Nettie Lee Benson, *The Provincial Deputation in Mexico: Harbinger of*

Provincial Autonomy, Independence, and Federalism (Austin: University of Texas Press, 1992).

Nettie Lee Benson, "Servando Teresa de Mier, Federalist," *Hispanic American Historical Review* 28 (November 1948): 514–25.

Michael P. Costeloe, *Church and State in Independent Mexico, 1821–1857* (London: Royal Historical Society, 1978).

Peter Guardino, *Peasants, Politics, and the Formation of Mexico's National State: Guerrero, 1800–1857* (Stanford: Stanford University Press, 1996).

Wilbert H. Guzmán, "La misión de José Manuel de Herrera en Estados Unidos," *Boletín del Archivo General de la Nación* 10 (January–February–March and April–May–June 1969), 255–88.

Charles A. Hale, *Mexican Liberalism in the Age of Mora, 1821–1853* (New Haven: Yale University Press, 1968).

Brian R. Hamnett, *Roots of Insurgency: Mexican Regions, 1750–1824* (Cambridge: Cambridge University Press, 1986).

Ruth R. Olivera and Liliane Crété, *Life in Mexico Under Santa Anna, 1822–1855* (Norman: University of Oklahoma Press, 1991).

W. Dirk Raat, ed., *Mexico: From Independence to Revolution, 1810–1910* (Lincoln: University of Nebraska Press, 1982).

Donald Fithian Stevens, *Origins of Instability in Early Republican Mexico* (Durham, N.C.: Duke University Press, 1991).

William Archibald Whatley, "The Formation of the Mexican Constitution of 1824," M.A. thesis, University of Texas, 1921.

Luis J. Zalce y Rodríguez, *Apuntes para la historia de la Masonería en México*, 2 vols. (Mexico City, n.p., 1950).

A growing body of literature places Texas in the context of the Hispanic Borderlands, Texas-Mexican relations, the politics of Coahuila y Texas, or the Tejano population. The most important of these works for purposes of this book are the following:

Eugene C. Barker, *Mexico and Texas, 1821–1835* (1928; reprint ed., New York: Russell & Russell, 1965).

Nettie Lee Benson, "Texas as Viewed from Mexico, 1820-1834," *SWHQ* 90 (January 1987).

James Ernest Crisp, "Anglo-Texas Attitudes Toward the Mexican, 1821-1845," Ph.D. diss., Yale University, 1976.

Jesús F. de la Teja, ed., *A Revolution Remembered: The Memoirs and Selected Correspondence of Juan N. Seguín* (Austin: State House Press, 1991).

Margaret Swett Henson, *Juan Davis Bradburn: A Reappraisal of the Mexican Commander of Anahuac* (College Station: Texas A&M University Press, 1982).

Margaret Swett Henson, *Lorenzo de Zavala: The Pragmatic Idealist* (Forth Worth: Texas Christian University Press, 1996).

Ohland Morton, *Terán and Texas: A Chapter in Texas-Mexican Relations* (Austin: Texas State Historical Association, 1948).

Andrés Resésendez, "Caught Between Profits and Rituals: National Contestation in Texas and New Mexico, 1821-1848," Ph.D. diss., University of Chicago, 1997.

Vito Alessio Robles, *Coahuila y Texas desde la Consumación de la Independencia hasta el Tratado de Paz de Guadalupe Hidalgo* 2 vols. (Mexico City, 1945).

Andrés Tijerina, *Tejanos and Texas Under the Mexican Flag, 1821-1836* (College Station: Texas A&M University Press, 1994).

David J. Weber, *The Mexican Frontier, 1821-1846: The American Southwest Under Mexico* (Albuquerque: University of New Mexico Press, 1982).

Of less direct importance to Stephen F. Austin, but still helpful in establishing the Hispanic context, are the following:

Félix D. Almaráz, "Governor Antonio Martínez and Mexican Independence in Texas: An Orderly Transition," *Permian Historical Annual* 15 (December 1975; reprint ed., San Antonio: Béxar County Historical Commission, 1979).

John Francis Bannon, *The Spanish Borderlands Frontier, 1513-1821* (Albuquerque: University of New Mexico Press, 1974).

Donald E. Chipman, *Spanish Texas, 1519–1821* (Austin: University of Texas Press, 1992).

Jesús F. de la Teja, *San Antonio de Béxar: A Community on New Spain's Northern Frontier* (Albuquerque: University of New Mexico Press, 1995).

De León, Arnoldo, *The Tejano Community, 1836–1900* (Albuquerque: University of New Mexico Press, 1982).

Odie B. Faulk, *The Last Years of Spanish Texas, 1778–1821* (The Hague: Mouton, 1964).

Helen Willits Harris, "Almonte's Inspection of Texas in 1834," *SWHQ* 41 (January 1938): 195–211.

Joseph Carl McElhannon, "Imperial Mexico and Texas, 1821–1823," *SWHQ* 53 (October 1949): 123–50.

Timothy M. Matovina, *Tejano Religion and Ethnicity: San Antonio, 1821–1860* (Austin: University of Texas Press, 1995).

Pablo C. Moreno, *Galería de Coahuilenses distinguidos* (Torreón, Coahuila: Imprenta Mayagoitia, 1966).

Frank Lawrence Owsley, Jr., and Gene A. Smith, *Filibusters and Expansionists: Jeffersonian Manifest Destiny, 1800–1821* (Tuscaloosa: University of Alabama Press, 1997).

Gerald E. Poyo and Gilberto M. Hinojosa, eds., *Tejano Origins in Eighteenth-Century San Antonio* (Austin: University of Texas Press, for University of Texas Institute of Texan Cultures at San Antonio, 1991).

David J. Weber, *The Spanish Frontier in North America* (New Haven: Yale University Press, 1992).

Austin's role immediately before, during, and after the Texas Revolution itself, and the events immediately preceding and following it, are well documented the following:

Eugene C. Barker, "The Finances of the Texas Revolution," *Political Science Quarterly* 19 (December 1904): 612–35.

Eugene C. Barker, "Land Speculation as a Cause of the Texas Revolution," *SWHQ* 10 (July 1906): 76–95.

Alwyn Barr, *Texans in Revolt: The Battle for San Antonio, 1835* (Austin: University of Texas Press, 1990).

Gene Brack, "Mexican Opinion and the Texas Revolution," *SWHQ* 72 (October 1968): 170–82.

Stephen L. Hardin, *Texian Iliad: A Military History of the Texas Revolution, 1835–1836* (Austin: University of Texas Press, 1994).

Margaret Swett Henson, "Politics and the Treatment of the Mexican Prisoners After the Battle of San Jacinto," *SWHQ* 94 (October 1990): 189–230.

Margaret Swett Henson, "Tory Sentiment in Anglo-Texan Public Opinion, 1832–1836," *SWHQ* 90 (1986): 1–34.

Jodella D. Kite, "The War and Peace Parties of Pre-Revolutionary Texas, 1832–1835," *East Texas Historical Journal* 29 (1991): 11–24.

Paul D. Lack, *The Texas Revolutionary Experience: A Political and Social History, 1835–1836* (College Station: Texas A&M University Press, 1992).

Rebecca Smith Lee, "The Publication of Austin's Louisville Address," *SWHQ* 70 (January 1967): 424–42.

Stanley Siegel, *The Political History of the Texas Republic, 1836–1845* (Austin: University of Texas Press, 1956).

Ralph W. Steen, "Analysis of the Work of the General Council of Texas, 1835-1836," *SWHQ* 40 (April 1937): 323–24.

✛ Index ✛

Saltillo (continued)
lature in, 230–38 passim, 240; SFA attends 1832 legislature in, 251–53; SFA arrested in, 277; state capital moved from, 300; mentioned, 145, 225, 260, 263, 306. *See also* Coahuila y Texas

San Antonio: Moses Austin plans to visit, 76; Moses Austin visits, 85–86; SFA visits, 93–94, 110, 131, 133–34, 198; troops proposed for, 120–21; ayuntamiento of, 193, 251, 262, 263, 271–73, 277; Terán in, 208–9; citizens debate statehood, 268; mentioned, 267, 292; in Texas Revolution, 315, 316–22 passim, 327, 328; Juan Seguín serves as mayor of, 382; mentioned, 92, 107, 145, 159, 174, 182, 184, 185, 191. *See also* Tejanos

San Antonio River, 95, 138, 321
San Antonio Road, 92, 97, 147
San Augustine, municipality of, 291
Sánchez, José María, 210, 212
Sandia, 139
San Felipe (schooner), 308–9
San Felipe de Austin: SFA explores site of, 97; founding of, 146–49; *1824* constitution celebrated in, 161–62; during Fredonian Rebellion, 184, 186; *1827* constitution read in, 192; description of, 195–96; as scene of Dayton incident, 196–97; ayuntamiento of, 203, 233, 251, 262, 279, 291; boundary commission visits, 211–12; press established in, 225; gives SFA hero's welcome (*1832*), 258–59; as site of 1832 convention, 262; as site of 1833 convention, 263; SFA's return to (*1835*), 312; Committee of Correspondence and Vigilance of, 312; as site of 1835 Consultation, 323, 326, 328; burned, 357; mentioned, 176, 187, 194, 201, 202, 223, 237, 243, 246, 265, 267, 278, 336

San Jacinto, Battle of, 345, 351, 370
San Jacinto River, 118, 203

San Luis Potosí, 112, 275, 277
San Patricio, municipality of, 291
Santa Anna, Antonio López de: endorses constitutional monarchy, 113; rebels against Iturbide, 125; rebels against Gómez Pedraza, 206; rebels against Bustamante, 246, 253, 263; SFA supports, 254–55, 257, 259; colonists support, 256–59, 261; elected president, 263, 264; Gómez Farías acting president in absence of, 269; 273, 300; resumes presidency, 274, 289, 300; meets with SFA, 274, 275; relationship with SFA, 289–90, 294, 304; proposes amnesty for political prisoners, 297; becomes centralist, 300, 303, 309, 311, 339; suppresses Zacatecas federalists, 304, 305, 309; plans to visit Texas, 307; leads campaign against Texas, 334, 338, 344; captured at San Jacinto, 345, 347; as captive, 348, 349, 351–52, 361; post-1836 career, 383; mentioned, 269, 298, 316, 323, 324, 331, 336, 357, 382

Santo Domingo, 189
Santo Domingo Plaza (Mexico City), 281
Saucedo, José Antonio: instructs colonists to heed SFA, 153–54; overturns SFA's land fees, 154, 221; authorizes new land fee schedules, 154, 163; requested by SFA to intervene in Buckner case, 157; named political chief, 159; friendship for SFA, 159; during Fredonian Rebellion, 182, 183, 185, 186; supports SFA on slavery issue, 191; as key member of liberal faction, 193; replaced by Músquiz, 193

Schoolcraft, Henry R., 82
Scottish Rite Lodge. *See* Freemasonry
Seguín, Erasmo: travels to meet Moses Austin in Natchitoches, 88; meets SFA in Natchitoches, 89; accompanies SFA to Texas, 92–93; plays host to Brown Austin, 110, 133; represents Texas in